THE
RELUCTANT
BILLIONAIRE

THE RELUCTANT BILLIONAIRE

How **Dilip Shanghvi** Became
the Richest Self-Made Indian

SOMA DAS

PENGUIN
BUSINESS

An imprint of Penguin Random House

PENGUIN BUSINESS

USA | Canada | UK | Ireland | Australia
New Zealand | India | South Africa | China | Singapore

Portfolio is part of the Penguin Random House group of companies
whose addresses can be found at global.penguinrandomhouse.com

Published by Penguin Random House India Pvt. Ltd
4th Floor, Capital Tower 1, MG Road,
Gurugram 122 002, Haryana, India

First published in Portfolio by Penguin Random House India 2019
This edition published in Penguin Business by Penguin Random House India 2024

Copyright © Soma Das 2019

ISBN 9780670088577

Typeset in Minion Pro by Manipal Digital Systems, Manipal
Printed at Replika Press Pvt. Ltd, India

www.penguin.co.in

This is a legitimate digitally printed version of the book and therefore might not
have certain extra finishing on the cover.

For Bapu dhana,
Shanti-kaka,
and fathers who let their children be

CONTENTS

PART II

PART III

INTRODUCTION

Should a story be told when the subject is unwilling? Maybe 'not' if it's an ordinary story of a private person, or maybe 'yes' if it's in the guise of fiction where it is easy to speak the truth. But what if the story happens to be of a man who arose from the anonymity of a small wholesaler to become the richest man in a country of a billion-plus people and as many dreams? And he did so, not by creating a conglomerate, which depends on cronyish connections and government concessions, but by building a global firm focused only on making medicines. Isn't his story more than just his, a story that belongs to a generation, a nation?

And when he became the richest man of the country in 2015 and was asked how he felt, he replied, 'Uncomfortable, very uncomfortable.' Despite living what could be argued as one of the most remarkable life of his generations, his mind feels like a black box.

Dilip Shanghvi is one of the most interesting and least understood business minds of India today. For someone, unschooled in degrees of sciences and management, who worked his way up from a tiny shop in the bylanes of Dawa Bazaar in Calcutta of the 1970s to create one of the country's most valuable enterprises, he is also one of the least documented and least studied capitalists.

One reason behind this is his own unwillingness to share his story. He doesn't care about being celebrated, and stubbornly disapproves, even casts off attempts to document him. Another part is because with no drama, no modulation in pitch, few words and fewer expressions, he neither fits the bill of a conventional inspiring pin-up business leader nor does he make for a great colourful flamboyant story. It is easy to miss the intensity of someone who is more presence than personality.

What compounds this conspicuous absence from mainstream is a past yet unsearched but which, on the surface, doesn't show up juicy controversies to merit an investigation, and a lifestyle that could appear normal enough to be boring. No wonder the media was ready to spare him the limelight he so avoided. From time to time, when the need arose, he was profiled with a few recycled facts thrown in—that he borrowed 10,000 rupees from his father to start his firm Sun Pharma with two medicines for psychiatry and that in his sixties now, he is a fan of Harry Potter books. What happened in the interim was left to the imagination.

This un-deliberate arrangement of mutual disinterest worked fine till one day—the maths of life changed it all. That day in March 2015 his net worth crossed that of Mukesh Ambani and he was pronounced India's richest man. The country was curious to know who this guy was, how he had done it.

If the search and discovery had been so easy, answers to these questions wouldn't have remained so elusive.

Shanghvi, known to shun press conferences, interviews and parties expressed his unwillingness for this book when approached initially. 'You will probably put my face on the cover and I would be recognized by many more people on the streets and that's always a problem. It takes away from my freedom.'

'Your life has become such that there's no more a question of whether a book would be written on it. The only question is who would and how,' I replied, not knowing whether he knew at the time that three other books on him were at various stages of being commissioned. Once he knew that we (the publisher and I), were going ahead with the research on the subject, he agreed to give access to friends and company colleagues to the extent that he had never before done. And in hindsight, without these people he allowed access to, the book couldn't even have scratched the surface of his life.

But we are not hardwired to see such acts of out-of-character generosities, particularly coming from top-league wealth creators, without feelings of scepticism and obligation—all at once. Battling this contrast of emotions, I tried to explain to him the fundamentals of the project, to clear expectations—that the narrative would try to recreate the human story of his enterprise, which would mean, at times, getting into the messy and sensitive zones of his life, such as the first set of founders among his friends who formed the company, and what happened to them. To my relief, he responded, 'You must know that everyone is a sum-total of their positives and negatives. And I don't think hiding the negatives and only highlighting the positives would be valuable for your readers.'

Did it roll from here on, the project? Or was it just the beginning of true challenges?

In July 2016, one year into my research, Shanghvi sat across the table, his polite and firm self but still wearing his inhibitions, claiming he didn't remember many of these anecdotes I had gathered from family, friends and associates, and co-passengers of his life. There were moments when I felt he tried to lower that guard and wasn't able to or chose not to as an afterthought. A silent third one, cold and correct, and unemotional, witnessed the conversation in the conference room: the tape recorder. But did it record the moments of my wordless disappointments, did it record where Shanghvi's silences spoke louder than words? Unfortunately, you cannot quote silence.

In my flight back to Delhi that night, a little upset, my inner voice was chattering, 'The idea is not to change the person, the idea is to understand him. If being private is his nature, the subject cannot change himself just because a book on him is being written. I had seen fleeting glimpses of that struggle in him—his wish to not disappoint me, but his inability to open up any more in front of a stranger than what was required. If the only approach today is to understand his journey from his co-passengers, so be it. We wouldn't achieve what we set out to, but we may still achieve what is best possible as of today, and that is more than what we knew yesterday.' Later I was to qualify that inner banter as an insight. Did it roll on from there?

Not once did I feel that Shanghvi tried to block my creative freedom as I interviewed over 150 of his friends, extended family members, rivals, present and former aides and business associates. As for Shanghvi himself, did he live up to the reputation of being Mr Consistent through the project? Was there a breakthrough and did he open up? Or did he remain what he promised at the outset—Unwilling and Cooperating? Read on.

DRAMATIS PERSONAE*

1. Aalok Shanghvi: Dilip Shanghvi's son
2. A.B. Patra: Well-known psychiatrist of West Bengal
3. Abhay Gandhi: He rose through the ranks of Sun to become the CEO of the India market and then CEO, North America.
4. Anjan Boral: Kolkata-based senior psychiatrist
5. Arun Sawhney: Former CEO, Ranbaxy Labs
6. Arvind Valia: Shanghvi's first cousin on the maternal side and the first auditor of Sun Pharma, and partner at Valia & Timbadia
7. Ashok Butta: Friend and a business associate
8. Ashwin Dani: Non-executive chairman, Asian Paints, and former independent director, on the board of Sun Pharma
9. Babu-bhai: Business partner of Shanghvi's father
10. Barrie Levitt: Former co-owner and chairman of Taro, an Israeli target company Sun acquired after a bitter legal battle
11. Benny Klener: Former global head of manufacturing, Sun Pharma, and former senior executive at Teva
12. Bhagwat Yagnik: First head of human resources at Sun, who later headed the human resources department of Ranbaxy Ltd
13. Bharati Nadkarni: Head of Intellectual Property at Sun Pharma
14. Carlos Hardenberg: Served as Global Portfolio Manager, Franklin Templeton Investments, during which time Sun acquired Taro, a company in which Templeton was a stakeholder
15. Chintan Gandhi: Son of H.I. Gandhi
16. Daniel Movens: CEO, Caraco Pharma, between 2005 and 2009
17. Debasis Bhattacharya: Senior psychiatrist based in Kolkata
18. D.G. Shah: Business associate

* Only main characters have been included in this list

19. Dhanji Narang Shanghvi: Shanghvi's great grandfather
20. Dinesh Thakur: Whistle-blower of Ranbaxy Labs that led the company to shell out the largest fine to the US government paid by any generic drugs firm
21. Dipti Modi: Shanghvi's sister
22. D.N. Nandi: Prominent Kolkata-based psychiatrist
23. D.S. Brar: Former CEO of Ranbaxy Labs
24. Dwarkadas Morarji Shah: A well-known business founder in Zanzibar of the 1910s
25. Gajendra Holkar*: Name changed, a senior professional Sun hired from a top multinational in the late 1990s
26. Gaurang Bhatt: Shanghvi's friend
27. Girindrasekhar Bose: A twentieth-century maverick psychoanalyst, who was the founder of Indian Psychoanalytic Society and carried on an intellectual exchange through mails with Sigmund Freud for years
28. Girish Desai: Friend and founder of Milmet, a target company specializing in opthalmology drugs that Sun Pharma acquired
29. G.P. Singh: He rose through the ranks of Sun Pharma in sales and marketing to become CEO of Caraco Pharma in 2010, the first company Sun acquired in the USA.
30. Harkuvar-ben: Shanghvi's maternal grandmother
31. Hasmukh Shah: Former director on the board of Sun Pharma
32. H.I. Gandhi: Former owner of Gujarat Lyka which Sun Pharma acquired
33. Hiren Desai: One of the first executives at Sun Pharma's Mumbai office, who started as an office assistant and rose to the ranks of vice-president in the company
34. Hitendra Kansal: An early medical representatives of Sun in north India
35. Hitesh Sheth: Childhood friend of Shanghvi
36. H.K. Pahwa: One of the early sales and marketing professionals at Sun
37. Indrajit Banerjee: Former CFO, Ranbaxy Labs
38. Israel Leshem alias Reli: A reputed lawyer in Tel Aviv, who represented Sun in the winning case of Taro against Levitt and Moros, former owners of the company

39. Israel Makov: Chairman of Sun Pharma, former CEO of Teva
40. Jai Shah: Shanghvi's former neighbour at his Calcutta home
41. Jayant Sanghvi: Younger brother of Shanghvi
42. Jayanta Basu: Senior psychiatrist based in Kolkata
43. Jayesh Shanghvi (Upen-bhai): First cousin of Shanghvi from the paternal side and a former partner in Sun Pharma
44. Jeyram-bhai Aghara: Owner of Rivex, maker of clocks and watch cases
45. Jim Kedrowski: Former interim chief executive officer of Taro Pharmaceutical Industries. He served as an executive vice-president and in charge of Chattem Chemicals, a company Sun acquired in the US.
46. Jitendra Doshi: Interim CEO, Caraco Pharma, between 2009 and 2010. He stepped down in 2010 due to health reasons.
47. Joji Nakayama: Chairman, Daiichi Sankyo
48. Karishma: Shanghvi's daughter-in law
49. Karl Sundaram: Pharma industry veteran. At present, CEO, India and Emerging Markets, at Sun Pharma, and executive non-independent director on board of Sun. Sundaram was the managing director of GlaxoSmithKline Pharmaceuticals India and, later, in a regional role, he spearheaded the firm's emerging market strategy, when he joined Sun in 2010.
50. Keki Mistry: Former director on the board of Sun Pharma
51. Kirti Bavishi: Shanghvi's childhood friend, who is a doctor
52. Kirti Ganorkar: Joined as Shanghvi's executive assistant in 1996 and rose to become Head of Global Business Development at Sun Pharma.
53. Kumud Shanghvi: Mother of Dilip Shanghvi
54. Madhav Bhatkuly: One of the earliest investors at Sun Pharma after listing
55. Madhu-bhai Jhani: Business partner of Shanghvi's father
56. Mahesh Mehta: First distributor of Sun Pharma based in Calcutta
57. Manesh Shrikant: Educationist, former dean of S.P. Jain Institute of Management and Research, mentor to Shanghvi while he was professionalizing the company
58. Manjula Masi: Sister of Shanghvi's mother

59. Mark Mobius: An emerging markets fund manager and founder of Mobius Capital Partners LLP. He was the executive chairman of Templeton Emerging Markets Group, having joined Templeton in 1987, and his story crossed Shanghvi's during Sun's acquisition of Taro, a company in which Templeton was a stakeholder.

60. Milan Sinha: A pharmaceuticals industry veteran, who joined Sun as sales head of north India in 1997 and subsequently launched their oncology therapy division

61. Mira Desai: Started as Shanghvi's first executive assistant and headed communications at Sun Pharma

62. Mohan Chand Dadha: Former co-owner of Tamil Nadu Dadha Pharmaceuticals Ltd, which Sun acquired. Also, TDPL was the company for which Shanghvi's father was a distributor in West Bengal.

63. Mohanlal Karsandas Doshi: Shanghvi's maternal grandfather, who is said to have great business acumen that remained mostly unrealized

64. Mukul Pipalia: Childhood friend of Dilip Shanghvi

65. Nagardas Dhanji Shanghvi: Shanghvi's grandfather

66. Nandkumar: Started as one of the first MRs of Sun in Mumbai and went on to head a therapy division

67. Natwar Lal Bavishi/Natu-kaka: Business partner of Shanghvi's father

68. Nitin Mehta: Childhood friend and former business partner

69. Other psychiatrists who wish to be anonymous

70. Pankaj Patel: Chairman, Cadila Healthcare

71. Parvinder Singh: Former owner of Ranbaxy Labs

72. Piyush Doshi: Friend and a former business associate

73. Pradip Ghosh: First medical representative of Sun Pharma who Shanghvi hired in Calcutta

74. Pravin or Praveen Bavishi: An initial investor in Sun Pharma

75. Rajesh Kikani: A top executive at Sun Pharma, who joined from Alembic in Baroda in the early '90s

76. Rajesh Kumar: A senior sales and marketing executive who did two stints in Sun Pharma, once between 1990 and 1996, when he joined from Sarabhai Chemicals in Baroda in 1990 and, again,

between 1998 and 2002, when he came to the company when it acquired Milmet.

77. Rajiv Gulati: Former top executive at Ranbaxy Labs Ltd

78. Ranabir Ghosh Roy: Senior psychiatrist based in Kolkata

79. Rasika Masi: sister of Shanghvi's mother

80. S. Bhowmick: One of the senior-most resource person in the R&D ecosystem of Sun Pharma; senior vice president, Sun Pharma Advanced Research Company

81. Sailesh Desai: Childhood friend turned business partner and now, an executive director on the board of Sun Pharma

82. Shantilal Shanghvi: Father of Shanghvi

83. Shashi-bhai/Shashikant Shanghvi: Business associate and mentor of Shanghvi, and owner of Onyx Labs

84. Shyamal Ghosh: Joined Sun as senior manager, marketing planning in 1991 from Sarabhai, and rose to become general manager by 1995. He entered Sun for the second time from Milmet in 1998 and rose to become the senior vice-president, a top executive in the firm, in command of the largest number of therapeutic divisions in his time.

85. S.K. Jani Miya: One of the first medical representatives of Sun in Andhra Pradesh who today owns his own company Crescent Formulations

86. Srinivas Lanka: Executive director in Sun Pharma in later 1990s

87. Subba Rao Changati: An author writing on specialized topics of pharmaceuticals, who worked as director of marketing in Sun Pharma in the 1990s

88. Sudhir Mehta: Chairman Emeritus and co-owner of Torrent Group—a conglomerate with diverse interests including pharmaceuticals

89. Sudhir Valia: Brother-in-law of Shanghvi, former CFO at Sun Pharma, co-promoter Sun Pharma, executive director in the board of Sun Pharma

90. Sundaresh Raju: First head of sales and marketing at Sun Pharma, and a former business associate of Shanghvi's father as a senior executive at TDPL (Tamil Nadu Dadha Pharmaceuticals Ltd)

91. Suresh Shanghvi (Nana-bhai): First cousin of Shanghvi from the paternal side

92. T. Rajamannar: A top resource in the R&D ecosystem of Sun Pharma. Head of R&D at Sun Pharmaceutical Industries Limited, and non-executive director on the board of Sun Pharma Advanced Research Company (SPARC)

93. T.K. Roy: One of the first-line managers at Sun Pharma Mumbai who rose to the level of senior vice-president, marketing and sales, and headed four strategic business units—that includes different therapies at different times—drugs for the central nervous systems, respiratory conditions, ophthalmology, gynecological and infertility issues.

94. Tsutomu Une: Former chairman, Ranbaxy Labs

95. Uday Baldota: Started as executive assistant of Shanghvi in the 1990s, headed Investor Relations at Sun and went on to become the CFO of the company; is now CEO of Taro

96. U.N. Mehta: Founder of Torrent Pharmaceuticals

97. Varsha Doshi: Sister of Shanghvi

98. Vibha Shanghvi: Wife of Dilip Shanhgvi

99. Vinod Mody: Friend

100. Vivek Hattangadi: One of the first product managers at Sun

101. Yakob*: Name changed, head of marketing at Sun in the early 1990s

102. Yashwant Shanghvi (Baba-bhai): First cousin of Shanghvi from the paternal side

103. Many characters, though unnamed are no less important

PART I

CHAPTER ONE

BOY BEFORE THE BILLIONAIRE

And before the hindsight, a view from the back. There were three of them in their underpants, on the brink of breaking into their teens—facing a large pool of water, feeling every bit the thrill that the splash of the first dive in life brings. Little did it matter that the pool was a pond, a brilliant mossy green stagnant mass of water, described by its swimmers as a habitat of every deadly microbe the humankind has ever known.

Of the clique, one was a skinny hyperactive boy, the colour of caramel, on whom a tan camouflaged itself well. The second one was an angelic innocent face, easily mistaken for an Italian. The third was a plump soft-faced quiet kid, whose countenance did not betray any emotion until he smiled to flash a twinkle in his eyes.

A swimming instructor from what was called PYMA—Paddapukur Young Men's Association—modelled after YMCA, was releasing them into the water, helping them learn pedalling and swimming for a small fee. To everyone's shock, the lean boy, who aced all adventure antics among the trio froze and didn't jump. The handsome one gasped for breath once under the water managing somehow to do a lap. But 'motu', as the third one was affectionately called by the other two, quickly mastered the technique, took to water like a fish, and went on to complete nine laps of the 50-metre stretch. The skinny one's jaws dropped, and he shouted from the platform clapping his hands 'Ah motu, I know what's keeping you afloat, it's the buoyancy factor, it's the buoyancy factor.'

Two of them finally emerged from under the water, giggling and exchanging glances, and then pushed the screaming unsuspecting one into the water, and the actor that he was, given to theatrics,

---

* Names that appear with this asterisk the first time indicate that they have been changed in order to conceal the identity of the individual.

3

didn't disappoint. He did a drowning gig and made his friends laugh some more. This unstirred pool of water, in their neighbourhood Bhowanipore, became a regular after-school 'go-to' place. It helped them beat the insane sultry heat of the Calcutta summer in 1967.

Adventures of Mind, Fallacy of Age

This is not the starting point, but some point closer to the start in the story of Mukulia, Hitya and Dilpa. They were the tight threesome who didn't expect to add a fourth. There had been a fourth though, Chandu— Chandravadan Patel. But he had ditched the friends to move with his parents to Gujarat and would grow up there with no contact with the rest.

Of the remaining; Hitya, Hitesh Sheth, had drop-dead gorgeous looks that made everyone fall in love with him instantly, and elicited a cuddle and a pet from didis, aunties and grannies around. Mukulia, Mukul Pipalia, the ultimate attitude dude, lavish with his words and exuberant with his exploratory drive, could befriend any type—boys and girls in an age they mattered—in a snap. And Dilpa, Dilip Shanghvi, who seemed nothing much on the surface, except for a strange and amusing ability to talk to an adult like an adult. No one could truly tell what's inside of him, but he had his ways to surprise people. It was difficult to predict that this overweight boy, allergic to sports and unremarkable in athletic performance, would suddenly swim effortlessly to complete countless laps in Paddapukur, that literally translated into 'a pond of lotus', with hardly a lotus in sight! Or was there one?

The only time Mukul and Hitesh saw him run his fastest sprints, was on Sunday dawns. It didn't have much to do with physical fitness but the sambhar-idli served at Ram Krishna Lunch Home which ran out of 'tiffin' by 7 a.m. 'Dilip would come knocking to rouse us from deep sleep at 5.30 a.m. on Sundays. I would be mad but Hitesh would be absolutely furious rubbing his eyes, stretching his arms and mumbling—'you don't Motu, have any other business in life? You are waking people at this ungodly hours to drag them to what—sambhar-idli,' Mukul recalled. Not that Dilip cared much, he continued to rush them up, and then sprint again till the sambhar aroma hit his nostrils and he knew for certain that they wouldn't miss the south Indian fare this week.

Otherwise, in matters of physical adventures, Dilip preferred clapping from a distance, rather than shaking an arm or a leg, which is so usual of boys in growing-up years. Mukul recounted his own daredevil stunts, at Alipore Bridge, the 30-foot normal curve that arches over Tolly's nullah, a marshy tributary of the Hooghly that they crossed often. 'I was this skinny little kid, wanting to try out acrobatic stuff. It was an easy curve by my standards. I would never walk the road, always climbing up the arch of the bridge and then sliding down the other way. A stupid show-off, now that I think of it, but back then it seemed such a cool balancing manoeuvre,' Mukul reminisced.

Dilip, he said, wasn't the stuff of adventure, reluctant to try the stunt for the longest time, till one day they goaded him into it. He scampered up in quick little steps, for about 10–12 feet on the arch, then froze and freaked out. 'He was stuck there, neither able to climb up nor descend. Standing there, he let out the choicest of Gujarati expletives, of which he possessed a rich vocabulary back then. We were rolling with laughter. Hitesh and I have played a lot of these pranks on him, and he was such a sport, when it came to taking it from his closest friends,' Mukul laughed, reliving the moment.

In school, he didn't figure in the list of merit and medals, not at least till he reached class IX, the grade in which he chose commerce as a stream and started to be recognized by his masters for what his friends dubbed a streak of 'unorthodox intelligence'.

With a bit of a shaky start, he sailed through, passing junior classes— unexceptional, undistinguished and without attracting the attention of the good or bad kind. At the start of school years in Balmandir, the Gujarati 'bourgeois' version of kindergarten, a friend recalled him struggling with some subjects. Mukul has this incident imprinted mainly for two reasons: it was his first practical lesson in letter writing and brought him a realization of how much his buddy meant to him.

That year for summer vacation, Dilip had gone to Amreli with his parents. 'It was, in most likelihood, the English class. The teacher announced that all those who hadn't passed, would have to take a re-examination or would be detained in the same class for a year. It was a big deal. Dilip had left the station, and if he didn't get to know of the re-examination thing, he would have to repeat the class. I ran to my dad, who suggested, 'Why don't you write him a letter?' That was the first time I wrote a post card, 'Buddy, you need to cut short your vacation and come back. There's big trouble brewing here. If you don't clear this re-examination and slip a grade, we wouldn't be together again.'

Shanghvi couldn't recall being with Mukul in Balmandir, his distinct memories of their friendship dated to their days in 'Bhagushala' (probably a derivative from Bhowanipore Gujarati Pathshala), later renamed JJ Ajmera, and now rechristened BGES (Bhowanipore Gujarati Education Society) School. Mukul changed his school a year or two before Dilip, and it was here that Hitesh joined them from Hartley's and the three formed their tight threesome.

The school textbooks might have failed to excite him, but early on, Dilip was becoming a reader of all books outside of curriculum, which he sourced from varied quarters—an uppity friend of Mukul's who studied at Saint Lawrence, striking deals at second-hand book shops in New Market, where they borrowed a book for 50 paise and returned them after a week of marathon read. Later they borrowed from libraries and Dilip's cousin Upen (Jayesh Shanghvi). 'He had this annoying habit of becoming absolutely unresponsive when his head was drowned in a book. Then you could scream into his ears, call him names or try any distracting trick, but he wouldn't budge, as if the world around didn't exist,' Hitesh recalled.

This is a fact alluded to by his cousins as well. 'The one thing that wouldn't ditch you in Calcutta was load-shedding inflicting hours of darkness. If Dilip was reading and the lights went out, you would see a torch flash beaming on a book. His father, who all of us including Dilip called kaka, would be scolding him, 'What is this Dilip! Why don't you go and check the electric box whether the outage can be fixed. But the reader hardly ever obliged,' Upen recalled.

Dilip devoured racy edge-of-the-seat detective thrillers—Erle Stanley Gardner's Perry Mason series, James Hadley Chase, Alistair Maclean, Robert Ludlum and Ian Fleming. However, Hitesh recalled that it was Ayn Rand's *Fountainhead* that Dilip was visibly impacted by. Ayn Rand and her books will have to wait for a few years till Dilip reaches his mid-teens.

School wasn't the place that could hook Dilip in the initial years and it appears as if he was waiting for his release into life. 'I wasn't exactly bored in school but what the teachers were teaching in school was all very easy. I never felt the need to study at home or make any fair notes. But I was curious about everything else around food, technology, human behaviour,' recalled Shanghvi. And for him, life in his pre-teens already meant business, with its shops, factories, buyers and sellers—a world where success was measured not by the subjective assessment of marks but an objective and definite currency, money.

'The moment he came home from school, he threw his bags, gobbled something and went running to kaka's shop. There he would be checking the medicine boxes, turning them upside down. He flooded us with questions, how are these drugs made, what are they prescribed for, these ingredients—how much do they cost, where do people buy these, how do they make tablets out of them, how much money do they make when they sell it to us, how much do we make when we sell it . . . For most of those questions at that time, neither kaka nor I had answers. In our family, we were largely happy and content people, who didn't bother much beyond our own work boundaries,' an elder cousin of Dilip, Nana-bhai (Suresh Shanghvi) said.

'I couldn't wait for the holidays to go to my father's shop. It was there that I sat from the time I was seven or eight years of age. I could effortlessly commit to memory the names of all drugs and what diseases they were meant for. I was not only enjoying looking at the activities, but actively participating in them including handling customers,' said Shanghvi.

Through his mid-teens, Dilip's quest to understand life and business was no longer restricted to the shop of his father. Mukul, for instance was fascinated by Dilip's ability to behave like a perfectly seasoned businessman, having an adult-to-adult conversation with his father who had an office-cum-shop of scientific instruments. This shop was three floors above Medcom Enterprises, the medicine distribution agency shop of Dilip's father Shantilal Shanghvi, in Mehta Building.

'He called my father 'bhai' just like I did. I called his father kaka, just like he did,' Mukul said.

'If you hadn't yet entered my shop, and heard him talking from outside—in a formal restrained tone he reserved for elders, starting his sentences with—Bhai, the thing is that . . ., you would imagine he was a contemporary of my dad in a serious conversation. And then you entered and found the back of this cute adorable child, perched on a seat across my father's table, asking him about his supply chain, import policy, handling of customers, and you watch the scene with amazement,' Mukul recalled.

And the very next moment, out of that setting, back with Mukul, Dilip was his animated and argumentative self again, just the way his original teen-vibe with his friend was. This cultivation of father figures, particularly people who might have appeared reasonably successful businessmen from where he was looking, seemed to be a trait that emerges from the experience of many other close friends.

Hitesh related similar instances with his father. 'My father would reach home at about 6.30 p.m. and settle there in the living room, on the single seater of the sofa with Dilip, usually to his side. He spoke in a measured tone but would take in details of the jute business—end to end,' Hitesh recalled. As a child interested in games and fun, Hitesh found this exceptional curiosity in Dilip about business of various types puzzling, but what baffled him even more was a quality that he doesn't seem to be able to describe even today.

'When he spoke, people listened. I don't know why. He would speak softly, using few words, as he does today, so it was not the tone or modulation. His language skills were basic, so it wasn't the beauty of words or literary embellishments. But he must have made sense or said something valuable, for people listened to him with rapt attention,' said Hitesh. He added, when kids from his neighbourhood came in, and he made introductions, he found it perplexing that while everyone talked over each other, creating a cacophony, they usually went quiet when Dilip spoke, which he did less often than others.

While connecting to their fathers, Dilip could make his friends feel that he was twenty years older than they. On the contrary, their experience with Dilip's father had been extraordinarily friendly. Kaka, as Shantilal Shanghvi was known to them, could effortlessly become one of them, unlike their own fathers, whom they treated with a respectful distance that was so typical of their generation in Indian families. With kaka, they could totally act their age, crack jokes, play cards and carom without bothering to be watched or judged by a 'distant fatherlike figure'.

'He didn't come across as dead serious about life; he was playful, happy-go-lucky and took life as it came. They didn't have a lot but kaka was content with what they had,' Mukul recalled. Hitesh recalled how in one of those fun moments, kaka taught him to tie the lungi.

Every single morning in that house of Paddapukur, Jai Shah, their neighbour from the floor below, recalled knocking at their door and asking kaka to knot his tie, compulsory at his school at Hartley's. 'Our father had walked out on us in our childhood and kaka brought us vegetables every single day,' he recalled. Hitesh remembered him as this kind person, wishing well for others. 'We played a lot of carom together at Dilip's place.'

Dilip's cousin Nana-bhai who called him G-kaka, following a family tradition of not addressing elders by their names, said, 'Kaka was unlike other uncles. You could share with him things that you shared with your friends but not parents. He was more a friend than uncle, and we went for movies together in Bombay. In his approach to work, he was like most of us, not very ambitious, content with whatever we had.'

At the same time, Dilip, even when he was just fifteen years of age, could come across within his immediate family and in his own eyes as a mature fifteen year old. 'I think Dilip-bhai was born grown-up and responsible. I was a dud of a student till my eighth and ninth class, and though he was never home, he figured out that I was screwing up my maths. It was he who arranged for my tuition. Later in life, I saw this ability in him to infer things about places where he is not even physically present, helping a lot in his professional journey,' Jayant Sanghvi, who is younger to Dilip by ten years, said.

Jayant was pampered by their mother Kumud who was described by her neighbour Mrs Shah and Dilip's friend as a quiet, beautiful lady of few words, well read and well versed with current affairs, and a devout Hindu who went to the temple every day. Jayant was letting life happen to him till the day when lightning struck his blithe adolescence.

That was the day Dilip told him to crack the IIT (Indian Institute of Technology).

'I roamed dazed for a few days. I mean what was he thinking, expecting something out of the world from someone who was so happy being one of the bottom-rank-holders in his class. But for us if Dilip-bhai had said it, it had to be done, somehow, anyhow.'

In subsequent days, neighbours described a plump Jayant, known in the neighbourhood as Munna-bhai, as a permanent fixture on a rocking jhula at his home, eating and studying, studying and eating, till he cracked the IIT. With time, Dilip would master this art of making people—family, friends, colleagues and employee—achieve things that they thought impossible.

'Our parents were never the anxiety-spilling, make-something-out-of-life, warning-us-off-this-and-that, imposing-their-dream types. They were the most non-interfering sorts who let their children be as long as they were passing their exams and life was passing trouble-free. Despite being able to afford way more comforts and luxury today, I would rate that phase of my life psychologically better,' Jayant wistfully narrated. The only time his father really lost his temper was during Diwali when Dilip let him buy as much crackers as he wanted. Upon his return from the market, they got a good scolding for blowing so much money on what would turn into ash the next day.

Shanghvi shared that his father never treated him like a kid. 'I don't remember being treated as a child ever by my father. My father always treated me like an adult. When I was just fourteen, he sent me off to Bombay on my own to bring my mother back in a train after she had a major surgery. I always felt responsible for my sisters and brothers more as a parent than an elder sibling. My mother didn't have help from any extended family in raising us, so when she went out shopping for grocery, I would babysit my younger siblings. It could sound strange given I wasn't much older to my sisters, but that was how it was,' Dilip recalled. Conclusions can be reversible enough to sound inconclusive. Kaka's non-interfering friendly daddy-ing ways let Dilip grow up and assume responsibilities beyond his age. Or maybe the realization of having a grown-up son prompted kaka to go easy and let Dilip take on responsibilities beyond his age.

The Argumentative Indians—Yin and Yang

Dilip's 'no-holds-barred argumentative side of persona' was usually reserved for friends in his intimate circle. In front of extended group and rank outsiders, he mostly kept his mind and counsel to himself, unless he deemed the opposite necessary. But two people, subject most to his intellectual muscles, in pre- to mid-teens were Hitesh and, even more acutely, Mukul.

'Historically, we never spared each other. We were best friends and arch rivals. We cared deeply for each other, but as kids, we were always at verbal duels, not so much because there was a reason to argue, but kids like a bit of show-off. Hitesh, who actually looked a baby version of his surname "Sheth"—posh and handsome would often stand as a patient witness while we were blasting each other off on the most banal topics and stayed at it until the cows came home.'

But, these clamorous puerile face-offs assumed philosophical and ideological slants, once adolescence kicked in, shaping their sensibilities. As Dilip and Mukul grew up, their interests diverged, turning them into personalities that were wonderful opposites, reflected later in their life choices. Mukul fell in love with classical music, started his training with V.G. Jog, famously credited for introducing violin in Hindustani classical music. He immersed himself in the world of music and literature.

Mukul's love for music had begun at home with the collection of his father's records. He soaked in Ravi Shankar and Nikhil Banerjee's sitar plays, often breaking into a game with Hitesh's father, another connoisseur of music, that they called 'Raag ki pehchaan'. They revelled in the thrill of guessing and discovering the 'Raag' behind old Hindi film songs by Lata Mangeshkar, Mohammad Rafi and Talat Mehmood. Dilip often contributed to these discussions by saying 'Beta Mukul, kuchh kaam ki baat karo, (Let's get over this nonsense and talk business) earning him the sobriquet of 'Aurangzeb' from his friends.

'Dilip had a sharp sense of money to begin with and I was in a bit of a dreamy world. He was dismayed that I was wasting my life away without understanding the mechanics of money operations. I was spending too much time dabbling in art and music, which he regarded with an amused lack of interest. Being so focused on business, Dilip often quizzed me out with genuine and innocent curiosity about how I profited out of this,' Mukul said.

When his love affair with music was at its peak, Mukul would sneak out for *juba* melas (fairs where youth would congregate to meet, greet and have fun), where musicians like Ali Akbar Khan played all night. The next day Dilip would try one of his Birbal-ic witticisms to dampen his spirits. 'Beta Mukul, there was this super-rich man, whose super-spoilt brat was desperate to earn fame overnight as a sitarist. He was put under the tutelage of the finest maestros in the most established gharanas, but within a month, the influential father decided it was time to launch his son as a musician in the grandest of public concerts ever organized. On the big day, on the big stage, the son got stuck on one note and kept playing that over and over. An expert seated in the audience right next to the rich man, murmured in his ears gently, 'We have seen so many sitarists playing. They keep moving their hands up and down the strings. But your son, he seems to be stuck on one note.' The rich man, spit his betel nut to declare, '*Dekho* bhai, those grand masters never found their *sur*, so they kept searching for it. My son has found it in the first instance. So, beta Mukul, would you like to be that son?'

'I was never a singer, but I don't remember hating music. Mukul was too much into it. I considered spending nights over music a waste,' Shanghvi said.

'Knowing Dilip, even as Hitesh and I chatted about music, he kept thinking how one makes good commerce out of arts. Can one turn sitar playing into a profitable business? How can Ravi Shankar market himself better? If the organizers change the venue and spruce up the presentation, can they jack up the ticket prices and turn it viable as an enterprise? At the same time, he was trying to make sense of this part of me, which he didn't understand, and thought that I was engaged in what he saw as an unproductive pursuit,' Mukul said.

This auto-processing of business occurred in his mind almost reflexively in his growing-up years, and Shanghvi mentioned it in another context: 'Whatever I saw, my mind automatically worked on the creative processes that made that business happen. Even when I saw a roadside tea stall, my mind would be calculating how many cups would this boy be selling, what would be the quantity of the ingredients—milk, sugar, tea leaves—that he would need, how much money would he be making, and can he do it any better if he changed anything about his business. It was happening in auto-mode in my mind, and I don't think I am done with it yet. Even today, if I meet someone in a business I don't know the ins and outs about, I flood them with questions about their business. My wife sometimes gets upset about it because I come out looking a little probing at times, but my interest area is truly in his business—not his life.'

At school, as soon as Dilip chose commerce as his stream, he improved dramatically in academics. According to school records, he finished second in his batch. Hitesh, who remained Dilip's best chum in this phase, recalled masters allowing Dilip special status, and welcoming, even indulging his provocations, while dismissing others. 'He was far from studious. But he had questions and arguments that earned him extra allowances in his teachers' eyes,' Hitesh said.

During higher secondary, accountancy professor Saha and Dilip were often seen bickering affectionately about the ways to arrive at a solution. Saha, Hitesh said, wrote the problem on the blackboard, and Dilip would solve it the fastest, but not employing the usual method prescribed in the textbook. Saha would then fake a fume, 'Dilip, how many times have I asked you to follow the method given in the syllabus? 'Sir, you stated a problem, I have found a solution through a method shorter than yours. You should now see that I have solved the problem by an alternative route which was so far missed by others.'

But when Saha left the last-period-induced-reasonless-hysteric class in a huff, it was Dilip who went after him to do the tricky job of cajoling him back to class, a classmate Dayal Rajani recalled. It was again Dilip doing the job when Saha left the class, annoyed, after classmates were found copying in an exam, echoed classmate Gaurang Bhatt.

Dilip also struck a special rapport with other economics and business management teachers—Mr Roy, Mr Chakraborty—and his English teacher Mrs Mahadevan. All of them saw a spark in him, mainly because of his deep questions. Polite though he was, his persistent questioning once reduced a new teacher, a soft Gujarati lady, to tears, Hitesh recalled. 'I harassed a lot of teachers by posing difficult questions,' Shanghvi admitted.

This was the time, when Dilip was coming into his own. 'In my life, I have only studied for three years from class IX to XI, neither before nor after. I don't know what happened, I became serious or mature,' said Shanghvi. About the same time he explicitly opened up to experiments, new friends and newer experiences. One such adventure was lighting his first cigarette, aided and abetted by Mukul. That evening was pregnant with possibilities when after school they made a first deviation, by walking into the Chinese restaurant Golden Dragon on Park Street. It was located close to the confectionary shop Flurys, where Dilip used to relish the pastries. It was a break from their tradition of having south Indian or Punjabi-dhaba vegetarian food. Mukul lit the first cigarette, a Wills Filter and passed it to Hitesh, who passed it to Dilip, and the first puff was taken. Hitesh recalled Dilip holding the ciggie, puffing on it, looking at the menu and ordering vegetable fried rice, vegetable manchurian, American chop suey and sweet corn soup. Another look at the menu, then up again, 'Make it two by three,' he said. This was to become their staple order at Golden Dragon for many years, for which Dilip was to turn a chain-smoker.

'We smoked Wills Filter, and Dilip would often say that he would graduate to India Kings when he earned well. Ironically, by the time he started doing well, he was no longer smoking,' Hitesh reflected. Mukul said that introducing his friends to smoking was one of his biggest regrets in life. 'As a child, you do not realize how cruel and damaging some of your acts can get. The realization came to me after losing my Polish partner of eleven years to cancer. I take full responsibility for this smoking initiation, and I wrote them mails expressing how much I repent it,' he said with a tinge of guilt and then in a visible effort to lighten up matters he added, 'But hey, hang on, hang on. I admit being the black sheep, the rebel of the group, trendsetting about adolescence. But I came from a family where no one smoked. Kaka smoked at Dilip's, Kishore-bhai, his brother, at Hitesh's. I wish they had been original and adventurous enough to have taught me to smoke so that I didn't live with this regret all my life.'

Dilip was blossoming to allow new experiences and people into his life but most of these remained Gujarati while Mukul had turned into what he calls a *paati* (ordinary) *bangali* having befriended hordes of Bengalis. I bet Dilip's adolescent fantasies were about business, not girls, guessed a friend. 'Dilip had started thinking out of the box, some of his professional ideas were sounding outrageous then, but make sense now. But when it came to culture, I think he had clear, demarcated boundaries, he was totally into inculturation, and I was enjoying acculturation dissolving into Bangla literature, movies and art,' Mukul said.

For instance, once Mukul recalled dating a beautiful Bengali girl who invited him over for lunch at her place in Dover Lane. When he came back excited to rave to Dilip and Hitesh about it, Dilip's eyebrow rose, eyes popped above the frame of his glasses as, for him, the news was sensational. 'Beta Mukul, will you marry a Bengali *chhori*?' Mukul recalled him exclaiming, scandalized. 'He thought I had lost it. Bengali girls were on his forbidden list as well, and he had no doubt that that was the end of my dharma,' Mukul laughed.

Some of these differences in inclinations between friends started finding shape and form in their arguments about the interactions and coexistence of the migrant Gujarati population settled in Calcutta and native Bengalis. Mukul, who got lost in old musty *Rabindra Rachanabali* in his Bangla friends' places, most of whom shared his passions in art and music, literally dissolved himself in that *paribesh* (environment). He would argue about how sonorous the language and refined its literature was. 'I was even romanticized by the idea that they were ready to starve to pursue music and literature. How beautiful such a thing sounds when you are young.'

Dilip, though mostly reserved his comments on the matter, argued that they are refusing to shed the inertia of past culture, and that's partly what is stopping them from becoming industrious as a community. It was blocking their movement forward, marring growth prospects of the region. Mukul once recalled dragging him to watch Satyajit Ray's masterpiece *Charulata,* and found the slow-mo idleness of the movie getting on Dilip's nerves. 'He was utterly bored with a "spare me" look on his face. The subject matter (extramarital affair of a bored industrialist's wife) was highly unappetizing to him. He questioned the point of making such movies,' Mukul said.

Even if Bhowanipore was not, Calcutta was a big enough city for Dilip to dodge Mukul's art movie stuff. He would tag Hitesh along to watch a lot of English thrillers, like *Guns of Navarone, Mackenna's Gold, The Magnificent Seven* and even Hindi action thrillers starring wrestler Dara Singh. 'I am willing to bet all my money—that's not a whole lot when Dilip is worth billions—that he would go to watch Dara Singh's movies over *Charulata*. It took a lot of hard work to pull him to that avant-garde stuff, but at last he won by not coming for most of those,' Mukul said.

In his fascination for Dara Singh movies, Shanghvi shares the illustrious company of celebrated actor Naseeruddin Shah, who was a big fan of the wrestler actor, because his screen persona was capable of doing things Shah dreamt of attempting but couldn't. 'I think the whole point of watching movies and reading books was the debate that followed, as if they had been created for that very purpose. We took a tram to Victoria Memorial on Sundays, bought *chana zor garam* and then dissected the movies from every angle,' Hitesh pointed out.

One such morning distinctly etched in Hitesh's memory was when Dilip had come running to him with bloodshot eyes brimming with excitement. 'He hadn't batted an eyelid the night before. After picking up Ayn Rand's *Fountainhead*, he hadn't been able to put it down till he had finished reading 690 pages of the book overnight. He was blown away by the strength of Rand's ideas. He had been struck by tenets of capitalism, yes, but what had left more profound grooves on the terrain of his mind was objectivism as a philosophy,' Hitesh felt.

By that his friend meant not only Rand's 'concept of man as a heroic being, with productive achievement as his noblest activity, and reason as his only absolute', but also the other ideas contained in the book such as discarding conventional routes to create a better life or choosing rational decision making over emotional decision making. More fundamentally, this was a throb of vindication within him, that there ought to be a singular objective in life like in case of Rand's protagonists and all your pursuits and activities must be pursued in preparation of making that happen.

Dilip's lack of interest in music, other sports, fashion and even girls, in a way, was a validation of the approach he had found purposeful and useful in life: focusing on just one thing at all times.

Shanghvi admitted to having been smitten by *Fountainhead*. 'Yes, it had left a lasting impression on my mind and helped me firm up some of my initial principles and thought processes.'

Mukul gravitated more towards Maxim Gorky and other Russian authors at the time, which was shaping his 'left of centre' political ideology, from where capitalism appeared as a model based on greed. Shanghvi recalled that their arguments were based on their differences around political and economic philosophies. 'I had a stronger leaning towards open markets, he was more communist,' he said. Mukul remembered having an argument with Dilip on Rand and *Fountainhead*, but couldn't recall the contours of the debate sharply enough to confidently swear to it in a court of law. 'Faintly I remember, he was focusing on how, without any support and despite odds and early setbacks, the protagonist Roark single-handedly created a success of himself drawing on his substance and merit, finally leading to his material success. And I was more interested in how he was changing the face of the earth, by redefining the rules of architecture, mainly because he was heeding the call of his heart, and being original in art.'

The day Mukul had imprinted this more clearly came a few months or after probably a year or two later in the chronology of life. As near-adults, he and a few more friends were half-stretched on a bed strewn with a deck of cards with which they had just finished playing a game of bridge in what was Dilip's bachelor den. This was a room that stood last to the right, when you walked through the narrow corridor that faced the entrance door of his home. Among the kids in the family, it was known as 'Dilip-bhai na room', and privacy of young men was always respected in that small space.

There was no interference when friends were chatting except the few times kaki would send tea and snacks of *muri* (puffed rice) or *khandvi* (rolled bite-sized pieces made of gram flour and yoghurt), through sisters Dipti or Varsha. It was one of those moments of twilight, when the daylight had gone dim but the home lights had yet to be switched on when Dilip asked Mukul to draw a logo for a company he would have one day. 'From the idea and brief that Dilip gave out, the artist in me had an awakening. I pulled a scratch paper from the table, and sketched what looked vaguely like a Sun, but more like a Yin and Yang symbol.' This symbol powerfully packed the duality of existence and was to emerge as one of the most ragingly popular tattoo symbols in future decades of body-art fashion. However, it did not become the first logo of Dilip's company. It was probably a little too bohemian for the owner's taste. But in a sense it had used the pictographic script potently to code the story of two friends. Mukul had accidentally narrated their story—his and Dilip's—in a circle split into half.

Some friends reported finding him scouring Calcutta libraries for a name. But Shanghvi couldn't put his finger on the first source of his inspiration for the name of his company—Sun, saying 'it has always been there with me, since I remember thinking about forming my own company, Sun being the perennial source of all energies.'

Maybe the cover design of Rand's *Fountainhead* and *Atlas Shrugged* had something to do with it. The *Fountainhead* cover shows an angular masculine protagonist holding a radiating Sun in his fist throwing its shine on to the face of the earth, and the *Atlas Shrugged* cover shows a muscular protagonist taking his face between arms, while the Sun rises in the backdrop, its rays lighting up the world. When asked if that was his inspiration, Shanghvi answered, 'I do not clearly remember the cover designs of those books I read. Given how many second-hand books we read, it was perfectly possible that the books I read didn't even have a cover.'

To Bombay and Back

Adolescence to late youth is the time that life shuffles its deck of cards most vigorously for most. Before you realize, the game has been reset in a way as if it has never before existed and might never exist again.

Against the grain of his first few years of non-gregarious ways, Dilip was beginning to open up to a wider circle of friends. This was around the time when he passed his higher secondary and decided to leave for Bombay. He enrolled himself in graduation course in commerce in Lala Lajpat Rai College there. 'I will be back in one to one-and-a-half-years,' Hitesh recalled Dilip telling him, knowing fully well that a BCom degree takes three years to complete.

Among those he said goodbye to in Calcutta was a fawn-eyed, shy, sentimental boy, Nitin Mehta, who had turned his friend after the two had first hit it off acting together in a play for the annual community function of Vaishnav Kapols that happened before Diwali, in which Dilip had been goaded to play the blink-and-you-miss part of an electrician on stage. What helped their friendship more was that Nitin flunked in sciences and joined his batch in commerce. He had introduced Dilip to his friends from the sciences. Sailesh Desai, a strong outspoken but sensitive chap, who appeared taller than he was, played the man among the boys, and could be counted upon to be 'the protector' if a verbal or physical threat presented itself in the process of manning up from boyhood. Like every protector he could appear 'assertive' to the protected but borderline 'aggressive' to the bully.

Sailesh was a batch senior to Dilip. But his friendship with Dilip got sealed with a glue of strength, when he by chance got a glimpse of the inviolable inner core of this soft-spoken introvert of a boy. The day Sailesh's friend Pradip died in a freak bus accident, Dilip did not chicken out seeing the blood and gore, instead volunteering to accompany Sailesh for 2–3 days, getting the post-mortem done. Sailesh noticed that while everyone around the event had been overwhelmed with emotions of the tragedy, amidst all the primal screams, tears and sobs, his new friend had quietly, on the side, studied the fine print of insurance papers, suggesting a way to handle the case and conduct official formalities that could help his friend's financially strapped family get the maximum claim.

Besides Sailesh, others whom Dilip bid adieu to while hopping on to the train to Bombay included Vinod Mody—the lanky nerd sporting thick black-framed specs, who topped the science stream; Piyush Doshi, the sharp-nosed, fashion-conscious, enterprising hunk who had arrived from Rangoon, as a challenger to the unbeatable topper Vinod. He often descended from an egg-shaped vintage car in front of the school in an era where having a car was the primary cut-off criteria to be declared rich.

For Piyush, who had been a late addition to the group, Dilip came across as a boy to watch out for, after he had totally surprised him in an extempore competition at the All India Leo Convention—the youth wing of international community service grouping Lions Club—held at Ranchi. This was in contrast to the impression Dilip's early childhood friends had carried. 'I don't recall the topic, but the impression I took home was that wherever you make this boy stand, he could speak. His words and construction of sentences were very simple, but the content so bold. He started his debate with a line—we have a defence minister, who cannot even hold a gun. How do you expect him to defend the whole country? This is the tragedy of Indian politics. Mind you, he was speaking at Ranchi and Babu Jagjivan Ram, who was from Bihar was then the defence minister. He got a standing ovation for that opening which was a call for technocrats to take over the leadership at the Centre, an issue the country is still debating over forty years after a teenager made that statement.' And there was Kirti Bavishi to say bye to, who by virtue of having taken admission in a medical school, prescribing pills liberally to his friends on his way to doctorhood, was the only one whose career looked secure and settled from where they looked.

But none of those boys, not even Mukul, bolted the door from the inside and shed tears like Hitesh, who—having spent every single day with Dilip since his memory began—didn't know what to do with the vacuum in his heart and void in his time. And he knew at that very moment what he had felt for long—that histories and literature celebrated romance way too much and underrated friendship.

As Dilip was looking out of the train window into flashes of his future criss-crossing from the east coast to the west coast of the country, Hitesh, shut in his room, was picturing past from what was already a point in future—from the time Dilip only had two friends, to have allowed a world of people to different degrees of closeness, someone at arm's length, some at elbow's length and only a handful up close. He laughed at how often they made pucca promises to study together, which turned into an impossible proposition given that Dilip studied through the night and Hitesh, an early-to-rise-early-to-bed boy, crammed throughout the day.

The day their higher secondary exams got over, Hitesh saw Dilip take over his father's duties at the shop, without a day's break, without waiting for the result, without waiting for life to begin. On some days, if a familiar old Hindi film song played in the backdrop, the same that some of his Leo Club friends sang on the train on their way to their trip to Delhi, Ludhiana and Agra, Hitesh remembered how Dilip, despite not yet being a member of Leo Club then, had tagged along with the band of boys from Calcutta to Delhi.

The part he loved to replay in his mind was the surge of pride he had felt at Delhi, opposite Pragati Maidan, in the dining hall of the National

Sports Club of India. The programme head had shocked them with a rude comment on how expensive a proposition it had been to host the eastern delegation of Leo Cubs, following which there had been nervous whispering and embarrassed elbowing among Cubs from Bengal borne out of unpreparedness of public speaking. Within seconds he saw Dilip disappearing from his side and appearing in front of the microphone on the dais saying something along the lines, 'It has been an absolutely enriching experience for our young minds to absorb the processes followed in the factories of Ludhiana and architectural wonders like the Taj Mahal. It is sad that you feel that you spent too much money in making this happen for us, but I am sure one day you will realize their worth and consider them an investment in future.' There had been sporadic claps rising only from one corner of the hall, the eastern delegation, but Hitesh sat there agape. He knew at that moment that a friend was now breaking his shell. It was just a matter of time before Dilip would breach his comfort zone by miles.

~

In Bombay, Dilip first stayed with his father's eldest brother.

'My eldest uncle had been the anchor who held the extended Shanghvi family together. When hard times befell us and my father and uncles migrated to different cities, my eldest uncle who had moved to Bombay continued to write three postcards every Sunday to all his brothers who lived in Indore, Calcutta and Cuttack,' Upen said.

Dilip's eldest uncle's house in Crawford Market was a small flat, already tightly packed, but as Nana-bhai, one of his three sons said, 'There was hardly any space with a big family like ours occupying every inch of that one-bedroom flat. But Dilip was my uncle's son and it had never even occurred to us that he would live elsewhere.' Dilip met his other relatives in Bombay, and when his maternal aunt Manjula Maasi congratulated him on higher secondary marks and asked whether he would do as well as his cousin Baba-bhai who was already making a few lakhs a year, he stunned her by his matter-of-fact reply. 'I am not satisfied with that. I will make a business empire like the Tatas and Birlas.' Shanghvi, however, couldn't recall this incident.

Those days, Nana-bhai recalled Dilip spending a good part of his day in Dawa Bazaar. He surveyed the prices of medicines and jotted down points that he summed up as briefly as he could in a call that he made to Calcutta almost every night. 'Trunk calls were expensive then. And one of us would walk with Dilip till the phone booth at the GPO (General Post Office), about 5 kilometres from our home. The operator would ask—normal, urgent or lightning—and we would go with normal, others were too expensive. In three minutes, Dilip would rattle off to his father G-kaka, the details of Bombay's wholesale rates and take instructions for what needed to be bought. Back home, he would bring empty cartons, pack the stuff he had bought from Dawa Bazaar into them, insert the whole thing into gunny bags and stitch it with a needle and thick string,' Nana-bhai recalled.

'My father was undergoing a separation with his business partner at the time I came to Bombay, so I was trying out some business here,' Shanghvi recalled. He hardly recalled ever attending college in Bombay, but on an average, he was completing one book every day during his stay at his cousin's. Nana-bhai recalled, when his father acted strict, which was often and switched off lights at night so that boys could catch some sleep, Dilip would say nothing but slip under a sheet and switched on a torch inside to read all night.

One day something prompted Dilip to break his graduation midway and return to Calcutta in one-and-a-half years. One close friend was under the impression that some of the medicines were sold to Dilip cheap because the dealer sourced it directly from the factory without the knowledge of its owner. Dilip became uncomfortable as he did not want to associate with somebody, or do something, which he felt was akin to being a link in an 'unclean business'. It is not clear if that was the case, but the final trigger seems to be something else. While Dilip was visiting Calcutta on a vacation, his father's new partner Natwar Lal Bavishi (in a second partnership firm, Medcom Enterprises, he had formed for the drug wholesale business) was arrested. As days rolled by, Dilip started helping in his father's business, never to return to Bombay to complete his graduation. A few days before he was to leave Bombay for Calcutta, he had stopped a cousin's breath by saying, 'We can become a Tata or Birla, if we apply ourselves to it.'

After his return to Calcutta, a few close ones sensed a change in him. 'I think his drive had intensified after he returned from Bombay. Also, about that time he made up his mind that he wouldn't continue in trading, the traditional mainstay of our family,' younger brother Jayant recalled. 'Philosophically, I felt trading is an opportunistic one-time relationship, where you don't create any long-term value. And I realized that I wouldn't be able to do trading. It didn't excite me essentially because your customer doesn't see any value in what you are doing. I knew it when I was handling the shop at the age of 12–13 years but as a realization, it came on strongly as I was working in Bombay,' Shanghvi said.

Bombay was the maximum city that packed maximum action, and it was possible that he found this reset of the clock more in sync with his inner calling than what he had felt in Calcutta. 'Bombay being a dynamic city did him good. In Calcutta, if someone came asking for a balm to a shop at 2 p.m., the shopkeeper would ask him to return after 4 p.m., even if the balm was lying at an arm's distance. And here he had landed in a city that doesn't sleep even at night. Also, he was very clear that in trading, the margins were wafer-thin even if your turnover was high. But if you could dare to venture into manufacturing, margins were far better,' Nana-bhai recalled. 'The whole thought process of having my own company started around that time, and I put a lot of thought into how I wanted to do it,' Shanghvi said.

Clues in Walka-thinkathons

By the time Dilip came back to Calcutta and enrolled himself into the bachelor's programme in commerce at BGES (Bhowanipore Gujarati Education Society) college, a paradox was waiting for him. The one friend of his who had already turned an entrepreneur was at heart a musician. And Mukul's business had nothing to do with musical instruments.

'Despite our polarized orientations in life choices, it was funny that I took the first plunge into entrepreneurship. My dad gifted me seed capital in 1972 to start a firm named 'Electro-scientific', Mukul said, adding, 'and the first thing we set out to make was a disposable thermocouple, a sensor to measure temperature almost up to 1600 degree C—in our case, molten steel. Amongst us was a soon-to-be doctor, Kirti, who would come along with me to libraries and helped me crack the "thermodynamics" part. Dilip was probably thinking, finally this guy has fallen in line, and I was guessing why he is being so nice to me all of a sudden. Jokes apart, that entrepreneurial adventure was always throwing up challenges, and Dilip was always ready with an ear and rapt attention, his forte.'

Their college, BGES, being run by a Gujarati trust, was sensitive to the needs of the migrant community and allowed its students to have a working life through the day. Hitesh had joined his father's flourishing jute brokerage business. Nitin was settling into his father's wall-clock distribution agency of the company Rivex. Sailesh had lost his father young and had started going to their family-owned aluminium stationeries factory managed by his elder brother.

Dilip's residential building has always had a water supply issue. A neighbour from one floor down, Mrs Shah, recalled Dilip fetching bucketfuls of water for his morning bath from the tube well dug in the common veranda before leaving for the shop. In a matter of just days, Dilip figured out that he was much smarter than kaka and his partner Natu-bhai put together. He knew he could manage the wholesale drug business by only as much as flexing his little finger, but remained immensely respectful to both of them. Friends close to him echoed this sentiment.

'Kaka and Dilip were poles apart in their approach to business; kaka was happy-go-lucky, in business, as well as in life, Dilip absolutely driven and focused,' Sailesh said. '"Like father, like son" is not an adage you could use for Dilip and kaka,' Hitesh felt. 'I joked at times with my jovial maasa (Shantilal Shanghvi)"Are you sure he is your and maasi's son, maasa?"' his maternal cousin Arvind quipped.

'Dilip loved his dad beyond anything, but I don't think he would call his dad his hero. Kaka was self-content and took each day as it came. His approach to handling the shop reflected his personality—casual and nowhere as serious as Dilip was programmed to be to begin with. In time, Dilip became protective of kaka. They were frank about it, and kaka was too good-humoured to mind,' Mukul recalled.

There were days when Dilip climbed up to Mukul's shop on the third floor and shared his disbelief at the way things were conducted at his own shop, including kaka's goof-ups. 'Can you believe what just happened,' he exclaimed, adding, 'kaka and his friends have left the shop to that assistant boy, for a tour of the new restaurant at the turn, and when the boy asked them what should he say if buyers turned up, kaka joked, 'Customer *aane se bol dena ki* circus *mein gaya hai babulog.*' Shanghvi said this possibly couldn't be an accurate memory given that his father and his partner ensured that at least one of them was always at the cash counter and they did not give the responsibility of managing cash to the boys.

Interestingly, despite the perceived contrast in personalities, Shanghvi said he had learned two most crucial lessons of business management from his father. One of frugality and cost-consciousness, which led Dilip to internalize a belief, 'Luxuries of lifestyle shouldn't dictate work choices. Once luxuries become personal habits, they force their way into professional decisions. Keeping your needs simple is a good way to keep your life simple.' And the second was what kaka had repeated to him, 'Turnover is important, but profit is more important. How much you count at the shop doesn't matter so much as how much you take home. It's like this: the cashier at the bank you see deals with lakhs but doesn't take home more than a few hundred at the end of the month.' Asked how kaka who was himself content about his business impart such a message, Shanghvi reckoned, 'Maybe he was not driven. But that doesn't mean his wasn't a thinking mind.'

In the evenings, after he had finished his day at the shop, Dilip would come searching for Mukul upstairs coaxing, forcing and even dragging him, if need be, to give him company on a walk back home. The moment the clock struck 6.30 p.m., Mukul tried to dodge him by hiding somewhere. 'Bhowanipore from Canning Street then was a good forty-minute walk. He had a purpose—to lose weight. And I shot back, "You are the one who wants to lose weight, why don't you take a walk and I take a bus,"' Mukul said. Piyush guessed he walked those long distances home to save bits of money. It could be both, money-saving weight-loss scheme for Dilip, but Mukul, despite plotting escapes then, is today nostalgic about those walks in the twilight, when 'the intimacy was so deep, and mood so reflective'. Walks, train travels and car rides—journeys using various modes of transport—were to later turn into Shanghvi's favourite mode of brainstorming sessions with friends and colleagues.

But those days were still far, and at the time of those walks, Mukul often shared with Dilip challenges of his new venture. His brother had managed a big order from Bokaro Steel Plant, and to ensure delivery on due date, they had piled up a large inventory. Dilip was aghast. Pat he calculated—at this interest rate, you would be losing so much money; instead if you spend the same as working capital, your output could go up by multiples.

During those days, Dilip found enough time to venture out every alternate day to Nitin's shop for an afternoon snack, where Sailesh appeared as well. Other days, he and Hitesh would walk up to the idli-vada restaurant near the market. It was around this time, the four of them—Dilip, Nitin, Sailesh and Hitesh—started getting closer than the rest, meeting every night at Mathur Tea Stall, at the crossing of four lanes of Paddapukur, better known as chaurasta for their nightly chat sessions.

They were from time to time joined by Vinod, Piyush (Piyush Doshi) and other friends, Piyush Kampani, Ashok Butta and Kirti. 'It may sound a little odd, contradictory even, that he spoke few words, but still was the life force of the group. That was maybe because his sense of humour was spontaneous, out of the blue, and his comedy was situational, a bit like Birbal. He would crack his joke, it would take a second for people to fathom, and then there would be roaring laughter,' Vinod recalled. He recalled once listening to a cricket commentary on radio, hushing up everyone around, and Dilip pretending to support him kept asking the score from time to time, tempering with—wow, bravo; and at the end of it all, with an innocent face asked, 'But who was playing whom?' He was also known to regale the group with a rich treasure trove of jokes and, apparently, was a master at off-colour jokes.

The larger group, most of them Jains, and a few Vaishnavs like Dilip and Nitin made trips to Shikharji, the Jain pilgrimage in Bihar twice a year. Holy shrine though it was, for the boys of that age, it was more fun than devotion. Once aboard Black Diamond or Coalfield Express, Dilip and Mukul could argue for hours over topics like what's ailing Bokaro Steel Plant, whether it should severe Russian collaboration and try for German partnership, creating ready entertainment for fellow passengers. 'I craned my neck to look from right to left, left to right from Dilip to Mukul Pipalia for five hours, our destination arrived but their argument didn't conclude,' Nitin recalled. 'We deboarded, hired a taxi for the dharamshala where we were to put up and restarted the argument,' Mukul reminisced.

But he also remembered the time when he got a heat stroke on the way to the dharamshala, and Kirti, the doctor of the gang, prescribed pills and cold compress. It was Dilip who offered to stay back and look after Mukul. It was a different matter that by the time friends had been to hills and got back, they found Dilip in a state of shock. 'Beta, this guy scared the wits out of me. Delirious, he started mumbling something like that this is his last day on earth and he is dying.' Dilip was muttering even as Mukul was laughing uncontrollably.

While Mukul suspected Dilip's long trips on foot to Shikharji an extension of his weight-losing programmes, Nitin felt that over time he had become a staunch believer of Bhomiya Baba, the protector and wish-fulfilling deity of the mountains.

Once at Shikharji, the boys spent countless hours late into the nights sitting and chatting in the courtyard of a temple in Madhuvan. Other times, the gang packed up Gujarati snacks and sailed in a boat in the Hooghly River to the Botanical Gardens for winter picnics, but even after spending so much time together, most of the boys in the extended group were left feeling that they didn't know enough of Dilip to know him enough.

Hot debates between friends scorched the lawns of Victoria Memorial on Sundays from where a fashion-keen Hitesh would drag Dilip along to Bentinck Street for clothes shopping, where if he had to—which was rare given he made do with few sets of bush shirts and boot-cut pants flared at the bottom (after all it was the 1970s)—he would pick sober plain-looking shirt material and order to get stitched at a tailor at Dharmatala. Trendier-dressed friends like Piyush occasionally took fun potshots at Dilip, on his terrible lack of fashion sense and boring uniform dressing, to which Piyush recalled being told by Dilip, 'What do you think of the fashion sense of the Father of the Nation then? Two unstitched pieces of clothing were enough for him to do what he set out to do.'

Hitesh, who hailed from the wealthiest family amongst friends thought Dilip was clearly attracted by the energy of strong successful personalities who were seen as ethical in the community and created conditions to engage with them on various topics, but mostly business and ethics. Hitesh's father had a flourishing jute brokerage business and was well known in Calcutta's Gujarati community. Most evenings, Dilip would settle on the settee as Hitesh's father reclined on the single-seater sofa, after a hard day's work.

Hitesh recalled getting utterly bored, as Dilip spouted endless questions on sourcing of jutes, processing, selling. Specifically when his father proceeded to explain how the banking sector worked to fund the business through something called the bill-purchase system, Hitesh watched his friend's attention assuming a sharp keenness.

On days Dilip would also try to understand the unethical practices in jute business. How a substantial chunk of players promise superior quality but end up supplying products of inferior quality. Hitesh recalled his father telling him, 'You make money quick indulging in such short cuts but these don't serve you well if you take long-term view of life because business is all about reputation, and sooner than later, your wrongs catch up with you, the word spreads. And in business, if you lose your reputation, you lose trust, no one is willing to do business with you, the game is over.'

Another regular sight alive in Hitesh's mind is Dilip sitting next to Nitin's father at their Radha Bazaar shop, discussing the rights and wrongs of their business. 'My father used to do a lot of community charity work and Dilip-bhai had questions on the rationale of why we do what we do. He would listen intently when my father narrated stories of Jeyram-bhai Aghara, owner of Rivex, whose distribution agency my father ran. Jeyram-bhai was unschooled but ended up building the second largest wall clock empire of the country between 1966 and 1980. At his peak, he employed 7000 people and was India's largest manufacturer of watch cases, commanding a 75 per cent market share. My father would espouse his example to underline how being ethical has actually contributed to the exceptional loyalty he commanded and made him more successful.'

Nitin's father often told how Morbi, a hub of wall clocks in Gujarat, had been ravaged by floods, but Aghara, who was based in Rajkot, instead of inflating prices to milk profits out of the short supply, persuaded his distributors to not misuse the natural disaster to fill the coffers, and helped his rivals recoup. The extraordinary loyalty that Nitin's father had towards his owner had something to do with how he had acted when his northern counterpart, the Kanpur distributor, died untimely. Instead of handing over the agency to so many vying for it, Aghara made sure that his children's education was paid for and waited for them to grow up and decide whether they wished to take the agency forward.

'In his prime youth, Dilip may not have totally agreed to everything the elders were saying, but the plinth of Dilip Shanghvi's philosophical edifice was being laid by a bunch of straightforward ethical businessmen, who had spent their lives believing that ethics make a good business case, when the horizon you are mapping is a lifetime. Fundamentally, I believe Dilip even today cannot commit wrongs in business intentionally, and this belief is shared by financial markets as well,' Hitesh, who now works with a stock brokerage firm, said.

Hitesh thought Dilip was like a suction machine, eager to absorb the knowledge around him. 'He would engage intensively with people and in two to three months straight, he would have totally grasped everything, say, my business, Nitin's and Sailesh's, his uncle's, his uncle's neighbour's. It is not an exaggeration to say that Dilip concerned himself with his own business and the business of the whole village,' Hitesh recalled.

Mukul seconded that. 'Irrespective of whose business was being discussed, Dilip would start thinking on how they could do it differently by either improving the product or brand to make it bigger and valuable. Of course, he did not stop at Sailesh's and Nitin's business. Sitting at that tea stall at Paddapukur chaurasta, sipping the cutting chai, he was suggesting how the Tatas and Birlas should run their business differently. You can't fault us for cutting him as outlandish then, when he was thinking out of the box.'

But while doing all that he did, Dilip was so low-key in his exteriority that it was easy to miss his high-pressure inside. Mukul's 12×12 shop on the third floor of Mehta Building labelled 'Scientific Appliances' was one refuge where Dilip climbed up frequently for a break. There were cabinets full of dial thermometers, hydrometers and microphones covering the walls. The peon would be sent to fetch some muri, and Dilip would busy himself with their Bengali secretary for a while till Mukul's father dealt with clients.

On occasions such as this, he sat as an onlooker to transactions from the fence, but not as passively as it seemed. A customer whined offhandedly to Mukul's father, 'You forgot to send the manual when you sent the stuff last time.' Immediately ordering another one for him, Mukul's father replied, 'Never mind, here is another one for you.'

After the man left, Dilip remarked, 'That's ₹35 gone, deducted from your net sale. Bhai, I think he was surely taking you for a ride on this manual. I have seen how your stuff is packed, there is very little chance that you missed inserting it.'

'I know that. The manual has tables to look up readings for hydrometers. He will probably sell it somewhere for ₹50–60. But the gesture would probably bring him back here. That's more important. Second, what's gone off the cake is a bit of icing, the cake is still with us. We have 100 per cent mark-up on every piece we stock. We can do that because we stock imported stuff on licence and are the only ones in the market to stock it, that makes it more of a seller's market when your offering is exclusive, rare or different,' Mukul's dad explained.

Dilip's father's wholesale business in generic medicine was a volumes game and depended on how much you can sell. Their shop counter often had queues, from medicine retailers hailing from the remote corners of Bengal, Orissa and Bihar. 'Theirs was a buyers' market, with a lot of nickel and diming; that was the nature of the business and I guess he was learning the difference between buyers' and sellers' markets,' Mukul recalled.

Eventually however, Dilip's father had two lines of business, one that of generic medicine wholesale and second of stocking and distributing branded drugs of pharma companies like Torrent and TDPL. From here Dilip picked up the value a brand commanded in the market vis-à-vis, selling cheap, low-margin, pure generics. Behind creating a brand, he grasped an art called 'marketing'.

Unlike Mukul's shop, Medcom's merchandise was all sourced locally, but what took Mukul by surprise was the zeal with which Dilip would jump to his place to listen to conversations between his father and brother on how the import policy known as red books would impact their business when it was announced every year. He would then attend all those import policy debugging sessions that happened in the building where businessmen got together to whine about murderous levies and duties of the non-transparent government, and then, over the next few hours, brainstorm to find ways to outsmart the new rules and system. Sometimes Dilip inquired about the banking system from Mukul's father, displayed a fascination for price points of different merchandise and other obscure business issues. These dry topics were miles away from Mukul's interest zone, and he vacated his seat for Dilip, not only to spare himself from the tedium of exchanges but out of respect to the sincerity of those conversations.

'My father was a high-school dropout but you couldn't tell. He spoke a bunch of languages, was well read, had a refined taste in Gujarati literature and spoke Bangla fluently. He had succeeded in a technical business where very few thought he would without his science background. The one thing I heard him discussing with Dilip often was the subtle cultural aspects of customer care. He explained to Dilip how his fluency in Bangla and our Bengali secretary consolidated our customer base,' Mukul recalled.

Mukul's father would explain to Dilip why the customer has to like you, and if you are not able to sell yourself well, don't expect the product to sell itself. 'Dilip probably realized that my Dad's Bangla, and our Bengali secretary make our customers comfortable here vis-à-vis other orthodox Gujarati set-ups, and that is what made them return; and these repeat customers were the key to our success.' Mukul's father also taught Dilip that the cookie-cutter approach of one size fits all doesn't work with sophisticated customers in value businesses. 'You must learn to invest in the customer to retain his loyalty, and if the customer is from Punjab or Bihar, the presentation of the seller should adapt,' he said.

Talks seamlessly turned into arguments, when Mukul and Dilip started their walks back home. These walks were only pleasant in parts, as the city had been dug up for metro construction. They strolled through Brabourne Road, Writers' Building and Raj Bhavan hitting the Maidan where Dilip lit a cigarette, making a small concession to his weight-loss programme by stopping over for a phuchka or jhal-muri at the row of street vendors.

One of those evenings Mukul recalled fretting about a missing deadline on an order, and how the Marxist government had left them powerless, and the labourers they had hired were threatening to march in protest. It was an autumn night in 1977, and the two hung around the chaurasta at the flagpole, whitewashed every Independence Day for hoisting the tricolour, reflecting on their future and the future of the country.

Dilip confided, 'I want to start my own business too. But it can't be a medicine tableting unit straightaway. I need to test the waters. But I am scared looking at your condition, the power shortages, labour issues, government apathy, so much is out of hand in this city. Despite that one day . . .'

'Dilip, when my dad gave me that sum, I didn't know where it would go, how this would work out. Remember how you and Hitesh taught me swimming, by pushing me into the water from the platform. Just jump,' Mukul recalled telling him in response, remembering how at times Dilip trailed off, left things half-said, not completing his sentences, as if the supporting mental images and structures were still not fully formed.

Those half-sentences would complete themselves in time as the deck of life's cards reshuffled once more. It is Dilip who would dive headlong into the adventure of business and factories, about the same time when Mukul, finding himself incapable of ignoring his inner calling, would head for the US and continue to pursue music.

Forty years later, this is how Mukul, settled in the US, felt, 'Going by the jungle principle, accumulation of wealth was never my thing. My core belief had shaped in a way that convinced me that if you commit too much to the cause of capital, you incur a debt on the soul. What gave me pure bliss was if for a moment, I played sitar like Nikhil Banerjee. However, by the same token Dilip excelled at what he did, by focusing as Arjuna centred his attention on the fish's eye in the Mahabharata, and that is what makes me so proud as a friend today. I google him at times, and I don't know how to go about telling people that my friend has made $20 billion, starting from nowhere. I don't see him as a multi-billionaire, I don't know how I would behave or how he would expect me to behave in his current setting. I don't let that pressurize me too much. My warmth for him comes from the old friend that I had in him, and that is what makes me feel so protective about him, even if I am 10,000 miles and decades away from that experience.'

Forty years back, however, Mukul hadn't proved to be a reliable co-walker, for Dilip's walkathons-cum-thinkathons. So he had roped in more willing partners like Ashok Butta, who had recently joined a firm in the neighbourhood of his shop. Ashok, the lone Punjabi among Gujaratis was Hitesh's friend from the neighbourhood who had joined them at times while studying for BCom exams. On their walks, Ashok charmed Dilip at times by stories of his earlier jobs.

The first of it he had landed up while 'loafing around' his famous dentist dad's office one early morning, when B.K. Birla, a client had walked in and his father had made an introduction of his fresh commerce graduate son. He was called to Birla's office next morning—for which he had dressed up in his brightest tie—when he was assigned his job. A man thumped a big khata (ledger) on his desk, that would open when you rolled the key. There were innumerable rows, which he counted to be ninety, along which he had to total the sum of the figures and write in pencil, pages after pages. That is all he did, total, total, total and landed up with dark circles and red eyes in two months.

After he completed his law course, Ashok landed up with another job at Himmatsinka's, the famous solicitors. His responsibility there added up to numbering the pages of the petition, making a hole through reams of pages, inserting a string and tying the knot. This knot was the crux of his job—it had to be tied to perfection. It was here that he met a friend who offered him a way out of knots.

This friend was working in his elder brother's firm that dealt in a host of liasioning work on import licences between government and private players. In this job, Ashok's responsibilities included convincing government authorities to give licence for imports in the 1970s. The location of the office facilitated his walks with Dilip.

'We were a generation of starvation, Emergency, Naxalism, no jobs, no power, no cars. We spent half our days queuing up for everything—bread, milk, sugar, phones. This is what Dilip and I debated during those walks. We boiled at the injustice of buses and trams getting burnt, and people being left helpless and were always racking our brains on what can be done about it,' Ashok recalled.

That day, they had started off from Brabourne Road–Canning Street crossing, the point where Ashok waited for Dilip to arrive every evening. It was probably Ashok again who had broached his recent experience of a few days back, when he was gheraoed by a bunch of hooligans while walking towards Jayashree Textiles Mills. The hooligans caught hold of the loose end of his tie, and pulled it like a leash, fiddling around, mocking him. In the background, an Amra Bangali (literally, We are Bengali, the name of an organization) march was on with radical slogans, shouts and threats of setting Bengal on fire if their demands were not met. Ashok was left physically unharmed but humiliated and hadn't been able to shake off the chill that ran down his spine that day.

They stopped midway for their regular break of salted peanuts and half a cigarette—they bought one, broke it from the middle and then smoked one half each—lamenting how things have gone wrong in this beautiful city, how this city presumed that 'being rich is criminal, earning profits a sin', how the common expression of youth has become to destroy—arson, burning trams, setting buses and factories on fire.

By the time they reached Alexandra Court, where Dilip saw Ashok off, he was suggesting, 'AB, I think we should write a letter to the chief minister. We are also young people, and he needs to know how we feel about the state of the city we have grown up in. Also we have just had a new chief minister; maybe he would like to wipe the slate clean.'

Over the next few days, Dilip dictated the letter to Ashok addressing West Bengal chief minister Jyoti Basu, who had assumed office just a few months back. 'I was the kind of person who wanted to change the world,' smiles Shanghvi, at the mention of the letter. Neither has preserved the letter, but Ashok recalled it had been a plea to the leader to engage millions of the young and unemployed minds productively by creating employment opportunities in the state. About this being the only way to stop them from being destructive; about the only way to do this was by allowing jobs to be created. More than the body and substance of the letter, this was what had stuck to Ashok strongly. After completing the letter, Dilip had returned it to Ashok and asked him to edit some words in it, 'AB, instead of working class, write proletariat, instead of middle class, just write bourgeois.

'Of course we received no reply from the CM. As for Dilip, he understood the human mind. He knew that however subtle it may be, a Marxist leader responds viscerally to certain terms. I think that is what helped him grasp so much so soon and expand limitlessly. He intuitively and effortlessly understood the individual and collective mindset of patients, medical specialists and communities. When he sits across ten people, it appears that he would just be listening, but actually he probably would have figured out their mindsets without letting them know,' Ashok felt.

Dilip didn't go extreme like some of his friends but he wasn't the type to sit idle when the city was reeling under so much unrest. Mukul recalled them going to Shahid Nagar, to hear out Raj Narain who was giving a fiery speech against Indira Gandhi. Shanghvi remembered walking up to listen to Jayaprakash Narayan and other leaders of the Janata Party.

'The atmosphere was politically charged. If you excuse the accuracy of our information, we can even claim that we were politically informed at a very young age. The lawns of the Victoria Memorial were set on fire with our debates, where both Dilip and I supported Atal Bihari Vajpayee and Janata Party, and railed heavily against friends who supported the Congress party and the communists,' Hitesh said.

One of those days, Hitesh and Dilip were sitting at Golden Dragon arguing about which of the newspapers was doing a better job at covering the turmoil in the city. Hitesh said he loved the *Amrita Bazar Patrika*, because it covered sports so well. Dilip was routing for the *Statesman*, mainly because he saw the paper as objective, its opinion pieces rich in in-depth analysis, building in all sides of the story, while he thought that the *Amrita Bazar Patrika* could be blatantly partisan, and some pieces in it bordered on being sensational.

After wiping their American chop sueys clean, they left for Binay Badal Dinesh or BBD Bagh on an errand, and it was on their way back, the discussion veered around the doldrums of adolescence and life goals. What is it that they wished to accomplish?

'If I make ₹1 crore, I will retire and enjoy life,' Hitesh said. Dilip cut Hitesh in the middle, and there was something in his voice that made Hitesh's head turn. 'Never set a financial limit for your growth, Hitesh.

You set out to achieve something. Money will follow. What you need to do is just focus on what you want to do.' Though he had turned around to face Dilip, what caught Hitesh's attention was a brilliant sunset against the Raj Bhavan radiating through the taxi window.

Three years later, on a lazy afternoon in 1978, Dilip's parents had been out for a wedding, and a bunch of young men—who, Ashok recalled, included Sailesh, Piyush and Mukul were luxuriating, half-stretched in his bachelor den. They had generously treated themselves to home-made khandvi and tea supplied by Dilip's sister Dipti. Hitesh strolled in late, finding Jayant rocking in the jhula, he started a game, calling him Johnson Jayant. Another friend shouted back—Hitachi Hitesh, yet another yelled—Dunlop Dilip, to roaring laughter.

When they had exhausted their freshly coined branded nickname game, and all of them had fallen silent, Dilip said, 'I want to set up a pharmaceuticals company. And I am deciding a name for it.'

One of those present came back with, 'What name?'

Dilip asked, 'Sun, how's Sun?'

One wisecracked, 'Very Chinese, Sun-Soon-Siin, Sun Yat-sen, no, no—no one will buy your meds with such a Chinese name.'

Ashok recalled butting in with, 'If you are forming your company, why shouldn't I?'

Another one chipped in, 'Wow Ashok, what will you call your company?'

'Why, after my adorable cartoon—Bambi and Thumper?'

One of them got a little serious, questioning the audacity of these entrepreneurial fantasizing. 'It's no child's play. Dilip, you say you will have a pharmaceuticals company. It sounds like big talk. What do you even know about making a company? What do you have to start a company?'

Piyush remembered turning around to hear Dilip say what he said, 'It doesn't matter what I have, what matters is what I do with what I have.'

And what did he have—a medicine shop, a bunch of friends and a dream. Beyond that, maybe a few words left unsaid and things that he wanted done.

CHAPTER TWO

FIRST DAYS OF KNOWING
THE LAST MILE

Windmills, steam-powered boats and solar systems—even a pumping heart—crammed the tables in the hall. But what caught the school secretary's attention was an ambitious-looking 'Iron and steel plant' model, detailing conveyor belts fitted with a furnace that smelted iron and made steel. When the secretary sought an explanation of the exhibit, the boys behind the table turned to the one who had made it.

That one, that plump one sandwiched between the tall fair one and the fawn-eyed shy one, started with the raw ingredients—iron ore, coking coal, limestone—and went on to detail the burning of blended coal in ovens to make coke, mixing of iron ore with coke and limestone, blasting of hot air in the furnace, to producing a lava of molten iron. He did it with as much ease as his mother reeled off the recipe of cooking khandvi in their kitchen.

Impressed, the school secretary asked the boy, 'It's a piece of art in a science exhibition. You know your subject. Which one is your favourite? Physics or chemistry?'

'Economics and business management studies.'

'You mean outside of your stream, those subjects fascinate you?'

'I am from the commerce stream, sir.'

The boy who rarely spoke out of turn and almost never explained himself didn't tell the secretary that factories fascinated him. It was the business behind that steered him to grasp the science of it, end to end. The secretary, surprised to discover a commerce student at the science exhibition, couldn't have guessed at the moment that the boy would go on to make and buy dozens of factories, the real ones.

'Dilip had modelled it after an exhibit he had seen at the Birla Museum,' said Hitesh, who stood on one side, while Nitin flanked Dilip on the other. One can't blame the school secretary for failing to detect the drive in Dilip, for he was part of a majority, which included mentors who missed the 'point of him', when they met him on his climb up the life.

'Dilip-bhai's drive is like that fever that doesn't show up on the skin. The skin doesn't feel hot, but poke a thermometer in the mouth and you know there is a fever, that's how his drive has been since very early days,' his friend Ashok asserted.

That teenage dream of a private enterprise was being showcased by Dilip in 1972. This was the very year the government took over the management of the country's first steel plant Indian Iron and Steel Company Limited (IISCO) at Burnpur, just 200 kilometres from where the science exhibition was being held in Calcutta.

'These were also the years when the government nationalized coking coal mines, predominantly owned by Gujaratis. The migrant community consisted mainly of merchants from Gujarat, historically seafarers, who had arrived in vessels to the shores of Calcutta, which offered business opportunities during the British era. They settled in and around the city in coal-mining areas such as Asansol, Jharia, Dhanbad,' narrated Pradip Sheth, a second-generation Gujarati from Calcutta, also a schoolfellow of Dilip. The loss of coal mines jolted the Gujaratis settled over generations in Calcutta by rendering the 'Sheths' (mine owners) helpless and their numerous small Gujarati suppliers and thousands of employees jobless overnight, he added.

The push turned to shove for the 'peace-loving but enterprising' community in Calcutta, when Naxalism—a violent insurgency movement inspired by a Mao Zedong ideology—gained ground in Calcutta in 1971–72. One of its leaders, Charu Majumdar gave a call to its armed revolutionaries to annihilate lines of businessmen along with landlords, police officers and others, whom he labelled 'class enemies'.

But since when has turmoil—political or economic—been able to stop dreamers from finding their corner and a moment to give birth to their imagination. And if the dreamers were doers, and the corner wasn't warm enough to nourish their dreams, they let them grow wings and fly to a safer land, where their winged dreams could metamorphose into reality.

Do I Belong Where I Stand?

One such dream found its address at that small shop in the ground floor of Mehta Building, Canning Street, in Calcutta. It sat in the narrow criss-crossing lanes of Dawa Bazaar under a lethal mess of tangled electrical wires, where Dilip was helping his father sell wholesale medicines at the counter. Sitting at that shop, Medcom Enterprises, he had mastered the answers to questions he had asked as a child to his cousin and father. He found out ingredients of medicines, how much they cost, the cost of turning them into tablets, why a brand commanded creamier profits than a pure generic drug, and all the links that there were to complete the business supply chain of medicines. Once he figured the business, he found it silly to continue at the address and links chosen by his father, where little value had to be added and the least money was to be made in the entire chain.

'In our community, which mainly comprises traders, the tradition was fairly uncomplicated. Once you are through with your studies, you join your father's shop or business and carry it forward. Dilip was different, and had a deeply inquiring mind,' Upen said.

'Whichever link of the chain Dilip stood on, he didn't keep standing there but looked forward and backward. In no time, he ended up demystifying the entire chain. What are the margins of those who are supplying to me and of those whom I am supplying to, what exactly are they doing to command that price? Can there be a cheaper way to make, a better way and more alluring market to sell?' Upen added.

He was exceptional in *'padtar'* (Gujarati for 'costing' and in an expanded sense price fixation), classmate Gaurang Bhatt reckoned. It would take him a few seconds to do the numbers and give you a fair estimate of the price of 'anything' that market was ready to absorb for a specific product, Bhatt claimed.

No one knew that better than Hitesh, who would often catch up with him over idli-sambhar breaks in the afternoons and witness that costing record play out. 'It was one of his favourite pastimes, cracking those calculations and then wondering: 'Look, Hitesh, the margins are 2x on this drug, on that one it's 4x, Dilip wondered.' Hitesh, whose mental adventures were clearly more in music, fashion and the stock market, would pay scant attention to such dry topics but he distinctly recalled that it was during one of those idli conversations that Dilip had broached lithium carbonate, the medicine that would become Sun's first.

Between the two companies, Tamil Nadu Dadha Pharmaceuticals Ltd (TDPL) and the Ahmedabad-based Torrent Pharmaceuticals Ltd, for which Shanti-kaka served as a stockist, Dilip had a fit sampling of the pharma universe with the former representing the drug business for acute diseases, mainly antibiotic and pain management, and the latter representing the drug business for chronic diseases, with a specialization in psychiatry. In pharma industry parlance, acute drugs are medicines concerned with the immediate and early specialist management, while chronic drugs are medicines that specialists prescribe for longer durations, lasting for months or years. Given Dilip's penchant and the nature of his father's business, he wouldn't have taken long to figure out that neuropsychiatry as a segment had far fewer players and steeper margins than general acute drugs.

Flipping through the spectrum of business was sufficient for Dilip to conclude that the space of general medicines for acute diseases marketed by TDPL may have more sales but also had more players crowding the market, and thus clocked slimmer margins. Those drugs were also dearer to market involving reaching out to tens of thousands of general practitioners, which required so many more feet to be hired. Psychiatry, on the other hand, had a market which was small, defined and restricted to a group of a few hundred psychiatrists in West Bengal and a few thousand in the entire country.

Shanghvi maintained that entry into psychiatry for him was the path of least resistance—more out of a dearth of resources to hire medical representatives, and a conscious choice to not clash with major pharma companies on their home turf. But he couldn't have missed the fact that this niche segment offered loftier margins, partly because psychiatric disorders, at that time, were perceived as obscure and the ailment of the affluent.

This was still the decade of the 1970s when India was grappling with a monstrous burden of infectious diseases, antibiotics were hot, making up over 75 per cent of domestic medicine sales and very few pharma firms had heard about a man named Abdel Omran. Omran was a professor of epidemiology at the School of Public Health at the University of North Carolina, at Chapel Hill. He propounded a jargon-laden theory of 'epidemiological transition' in 1971 to predict that 'chronic diseases'—such as arthritis, cardiovascular diseases like heart attacks, strokes, diabetes, cancer, etc.—will replace 'infectious diseases' as a country develops and its sanitation and public health improves.

Through the 1970s, Shanti-kaka was the sole Calcutta stockist in Bengal to Torrent, the only Indian company to focus on psychiatry. Torrent's decision to zoom in on this rarified segment had been more personal than commercial. This was indicated in the Kumarpal Desai–authored Gujarati biography of its founder Uttam Nathalal Mehta, known in industry circles as Uttam-bhai or U.N. Mehta.

Mehta was a medical representative of the American multinational Sandoz in the 1950s. But he developed a mental illness after getting addicted to medicine for the cold—Amphetamine (used as a decongestant till the 1950s). Popping too many of those cold-curing pills which, apparently, made him feel all charged and energetic, allegedly wrecked havoc on his mind. It caused him to slip into bouts of depression, turn anxious and suspicious of relatives and, at times, become violent enough to tear off important papers. He suffered 'physical ruin, financial pressure and social disregard' and was shown the door at Sandoz, before embarking on a long-determined journey of personal recovery. This led to awe-inspiring commercial success for an entrepreneurial venture that he kick-started well past the prime of his life and after losing almost everything to a psychiatric condition.

He would be the first among a classroom full of teachers whom the eternal student in Dilip picked out to learn some of his initial pharmaceuticals business lessons from, even without ever having a personal one-on-one meeting with him, if you excluded the fleeting pleasantries and wave of hands at crowded conferences. Unwittingly, U.N. Mehta would play a quintessential Dronacharya recognizing, early on, the sharp student who would adapt some of his innovative but crude strategies and better them to beat his company at its own game.

By the 1980s, when Torrent's next generation—Sudhir Mehta and Samir Mehta—started mulling diversification into sectors like power and finance, senior Mehta pushed back and warned them to focus on pharma or risk losing their dominance in the market.

'My father was very clear of Dilip-bhai's potential. He told us to expand in neuropsychiatry but cautioned that if we are not vigilant and dilute our pharma focus, we will lose market share because he is smarter, agile and much more focused,' Sudhir Mehta, the eldest son of U.N. Mehta, recalled. But at the time, tabooed and neglected psychiatry segment had so much room for both companies to grow (at least for a decade) that their race only helped bring to the fore their fierce competitive edges.

Since discovering Mehta, a part of Dilip only turned more and more of an ace learner like Eklavya, as he chose his teachers, irrespective of their consent. But Dilip was never the type to chop off his thumb like the archer in the Mahabharata, if the teacher so commanded. One always found more constructive non-zero-sum ways to repay one's debts.

Over and above the illustration of Torrent, Dilip's dogged pursuit of 'costing', 'price fixation' and 'value addition', the one thing that convinced him to move to manufacturing from 'trading' was his first experience with the start-up that he co-founded with his cousin Upen-bhai. So, in a purely technical sense, Sun Pharma may not go down as Dilip's debut venture in history, if you take into consideration 'B.N. Enterprises', a 'water for injection' trading firm.

In that sense, Dilip, who shares his year of birth with two of the most celebrated tech-entrepreneurs-turned-empire-builders—Bill Gates and Steve Jobs—beat them on time when it came to making an experimental entrepreneurial debut. Sure, it didn't start in a garage, as Apple or Microsoft did, but it did start in a godown. One didn't have to go down but go up two storeys above his father's shop in Mehta Building to find a small warehouse that bore the sign *'B.N. Enterprises'*. The abbreviation stood for Bhushan Nanalal Enterprises', named after Upen's youngest brother.

Upen made no big deal of it and Shanghvi insisted 'it was primarily Upen-bhai's venture' that he was supporting. 'In Gujarati families like ours, it wasn't unusual for teenagers to try out something like that. Once we finished schools, jobs and higher studies were never our aspirations, as we didn't want to work under somebody. The whole mindset was to join a family business or start something of your own,' Upen asserted.

Just out of Stewart School, Cuttack, in 1971–72, Upen headed to Calcutta's St Xavier's College for his graduation. Just out of his high school in Calcutta, Dilip had moved to Bombay for his graduation and helped with his father's wholesale business from there. That is where the synchronization for the venture began.

'Dilip would procure orders in Bombay for "water for injection" from traders who dealt with generic drug companies, and I would get the stuff made from Calcutta, which was then the national hub for "water for injection", Upen recounted. Ampules, tubings were all made by hand and not machine, mainly in and around Calcutta during those times. Collecting these was Upen's responsibility; to get it bundled with the dry sachet of medicines that generic drug players made in Bombay was Dilip's.

The venture wrapped up quickly within a year and a half, as Dilip returned to Calcutta, dropping out of his college in Bombay. Soon after, Upen packed off for Cuttack to help his maternal uncle's business.

But this experience, along with his accumulated insights from sourcing of medicines for his father's business, gave him a deep and wide view into the transactions of Dawa Bazaar. This probably turned into a conviction, what had been a feeling that he didn't belong where he stood in the chain.

'I realized I don't like to do transactional business. Where I have to compete with people and the only judgement to evaluate relationships is price. That is not something that excites me,' Shanghvi summed up his lessons from B.N Enterprises.

'One insight was that I would make a lousy businessman,' Shanghvi further shared.

He went on to add, 'By businessman, here, I mean trader. I like to do a business that has continuity.' This meant he wasn't ready to compromise his tomorrow and day after to win a game today. This meant he was always ready to let go of 'instant gratification' for the distant goal in the horizon, that he was in for the marathon, not the 100-metre dash. This meant Dilip was priming for the big leap and was set to challenge the status quo.

A Lithium-flavoured Dream to Sell

One look at Shanti-kaka's portfolio that included Torrent can serve as a fair proxy indicator of how Dilip could have hit upon psychiatry as a segment of choice. But what still remains a bit of mystery is how he precisely zeroed down on lithium carbonate as his first choice, particularly when this was not amongst the psychiatric medicines Torrent sold at the time? In fact, in a queer-seeming incident, Torrent— his soon-to-become arch rival—would become one of his first confidants with whom he shared his future business plan. But why?

A fellow Gujarati schoolfellow, Girish Desai, who had aspirations of creating his own pharma company, similar to Dilip's, had a shop Milan Metals near Shanti-kaka's shop in Mehta Building. They were stockists to pharmaceuticals multinationals like E-Merck, who had a version of this product by the brand 'Lithocarb' and there was a time when Girish and Dilip, two young men, were seriously exploring whether they could pursue their dreams of building a pharma enterprise in a partnership. Since Dilip frequented Girish's shop and often had detailed conversations with managers of multinational companies—it seemed a distinct possibility that he chanced upon the potential of this neglected drug here.

However, Dilip disagreed and said, 'Lithocarb was never our focus. It wasn't even the focus of its parent E-Merck, which had easier products to sell like Neurobion and Polybion. Psychiatric products were too small a part of its business, and its medical reps wouldn't spend hours waiting to meet a psychiatrist.' Shanghvi recalled that he had walked into a polyclinic opened by friend Ashok Butta's father, K.K. Butta, a famous dentist then in Calcutta, and met a psychiatrist there who had indicated the potential of lithium carbonate.

'Lithium', the chosen first one for Dilip, being touted as the 'hottest commodity', 'most precious metal' and 'magical element' due to its multiple essential uses and acute scarcity, today, would in an uncanny way come to not only symbolize Dilip's business philosophy of spotting rarified business opportunities but also mirror his future business interests—by turning into 'the holy grail of renewable energy'. But those business fireworks for Sun (interestingly it is lithium again which gives fireworks their intense red colour) were still decades away in the late 1970s, and the immediate work at hand was to make and sell a lithium carbonate drug with resources that amounted to almost nothing.

An idea was now in place but Dilip was probably not even sure how Shanti-kaka would react to his plans of starting an independent business.

The Calcutta grapevine has it that Shanti-kaka wasn't very pleased to hear of Dilip's plans, and some rumours picked up at Dawa Bazaar even suggested that he refused to financially support his business venture at some stage. It sounds plausible that Shanti-kaka who had seen through his struggle years and observed the toll that rash ambition had taken on lives didn't share his son's sense of entrepreneurial adventure and yearned for a life of peace and stability, after leading a near-nomadic life in his early youth. That his own business was too modest to offer any substantial financial backing for Dilip's grand plans is evident beyond doubt. What could have added to his apprehension was 'what if we take on debt and the business sinks?'

Nana-bhai also related instances where kaka had brought up concerns on Dilip's manufacturing ambitions and his foray into the risky zone.

However, Dilip's younger brother Jayant clarified, 'My father was sceptical about his decision to leave trading and enter manufacturing. But it never reached an "I wouldn't let you do this" point. And Dilip-bhai had absolute clarity from the time he returned from Bombay, that he doesn't want to do trading.'

Jayant didn't recall the nitty-gritty of those conversations much of which would have anyway happened in the shop. 'And we bring very little shop to home, we would go mad, if we did that,' Jayant laughed. The Dawa Bazaar rumours of such initial reservations were also dismissed by Shanghvi who recalled kaka procuring a loan of ₹10,000–20,000 to help his entrepreneurial venture'.

And thus started his story of 'what he did with what he had'.

In 1978, Sudhir Mehta of Torrent had been to Calcutta where he got a dinner invitation from his stockist. At night, at his stockist's Bhowanipore home, he met his son Dilip for the first time, who was a year younger to him. Over dinner, he asked Dilip about his future plans.

Mehta recalled Dilip replying, 'I want to start a pharma company. I want to enter niche areas rather than antibiotics or other crowded segments. I want to start with the neuropsychiatry segment. If I am successful, then I will expand to other areas.' That must have sounded a little familiar, considering Mehta's own company was doing almost that, focusing on neuropsychiatry. Dilip went on to reveal the two drugs he had in mind to start with, none of which were being marketed by Torrent then.

'He believed in his idea, but he said he had very little access to funds to start any business,' Mehta recalled. If it was on Dilip's mind to gauge Torrent's investment interest, he didn't seem to have mentioned it. If Mehta understood it to be so, he probably didn't take the cue. Years later, remembering the details, it didn't strike Mehta as unusual that a person who is known to keep his cards so close to his chest, unravelled his business plan in front of a person whose business model he wanted to emulate. 'My father's stockist agency was one among the many Torrent had spread across the country. So they were too large for me to see them as competition, and we were too small to matter to them,' Shanghvi recollected. So it remained a casual chat between the two young contemporaries who would turn fierce competitors in the near future and then graduate to become great friends in the far future.

Among the 'resources' that he really could count on in 1978 were the same bunch of friends who met every night at the tea stall and a few more who met him in his shop every other day. One of them was Ashok Butta, who hailed from a family of famous dentists. But with no interest in the architecture of teeth, he was on to his third job, but his first if you counted those which actually paid a salary. Being right in the middle of the era of 'licence raj', helping companies obtain licences and sort out their issues with the government had helped Ashok do well in his job and make useful connections in the corporate world of Calcutta—that included multinational pharma firms.

But Ashok secretly harboured entrepreneurial ambitions and had compelling incentives (other than just the proximity of his office) to be at Dilip's shop around noon. Ashok said he loitered around Dilip's shop to learn a few tricks of the trade, or 'understand business'. No less important for him was Shanti-kaka's daily call, 'Ashok, have you had your lunch? Come join us.'

'One day over lunch at his shop, Dilip casually asked me whether I could source this stuff—lithium carbonate, an imported product with which he wanted to manufacture drugs,' Ashok recalled. He made a mental note, discussed it with his friends back in office, pored over documents to find out who could be selling this bulk drug and zeroed in on a company.

The very next day, he was sitting at an export house, Macneill & Magor, with a senior executive of its import division, trying to strike a deal for his friend. Trying his level best to feign 'serious business', Ashok asked, 'Do you have stocks of lithium carbonate bulk drugs? It's for a friend who manufactures and markets drugs.'

'Yes, we have some stocks. Not much, though we can spare around 5–10 tonnes.'

'That will be good. That will be good,' Ashok said, trying to contain the excitement of having discovered the rare bulk drug. He stepped out of the building at the Red Cross Place, crossed the red heritage building of the Central Telegraph Office and rushed to a public telephone booth.

'Dilip, I got it, I got your lithium carbonate stuff. It's going to be a deal here. Just tell me how many tonnes you want?'

'Tonnes, what are you saying, AB? I want a few kgs, man,' he heard Dilip say on the phone.

'Kilograms! I was doing a deal for 5–10 tonnes, man. It will be too embarrassing to go back and ask for a few kilos. We will at least have to buy one or two bags that weigh 25 kilos each.'

'But AB, that would cost a lot. What about the payment?'

'Don't worry. I will work out a credit arrangement, where you can pay the amount in instalments.'

Above all he was ecstatic about having found the stuff of his business dream. So, when Ashok insisted on buying a little more, he relented. 'OK, go ahead, we will place an order for 100 kg then, but, AB, how on earth did you find this?'

'You leave that to me, Dilip,' Ashok grinned.

After hanging up, Dilip made a call to old chum Hitesh and called him to the closest idli joint. There they ordered idlis, sambhar and asked the waiter for five rough papers from a notepad. 'It was a different frenzy. He kept on popping idlis and doing calculations, figuring out the conversion cost of that drug and showing me, 'See, Hitesh, this one is 4x, and so on. I, for some reason, ended up preserving those five slips of paper, which were to start his dream run,' Hitesh recalled, of that evening.

Ashok zoomed in on his green Rajdoot the very next day, in front of Medcom Enterprises with a demi-official letter, and the bag of raw material. 'I still remember he cut two cheques, one for the company and, to my utter surprise, one for me, of ₹345. I told him not to bother, and he could have just got away saying 'thank you very much'. After all he was my friend, but he didn't take it as a friendly favour and insisted that I kept the money, and I think that was the mark of a good businessman, you pay what's due and you pay on time,' Ashok said.

Afterwards, when Mukul was trying to quietly slip out from the side lane so that he could dodge one of Dilip's long evening-walk invitations, he recalled being witness to a rare sight. He remembered Dilip taking a moment off to smell the stuff of his dream, the silvery white powder. Unable to resist the taste of future success, he gathered a pinch of that powder between his fingers and put a little bit of it on his tongue. He didn't know he was being watched, and was startled to hear Shanti-kaka scream in rage from behind, 'What do you think you are doing?'

That threw Mukul off balance as well. 'Kaka was the most mild-mannered man I knew, and I had never seen him lose temper like that. Dilip, obviously, was monkeying with the idea of a drug business but you don't start a tableting unit by tasting a chemical like that,' laughed Mukul, remembering the sight. Shanghvi frowned at the piece of memory and said this possibly couldn't have happened, after all 'raw material for drugs came all sealed and packed'. The spirit of childhood argumentative tradition using forceful logic between the two continues, only the realm of the clash has shifted to memories.

Don't Miss the Shadow

Piyush Doshi, the group's style icon, the same one with backcombed hair, dense moustache and a 1959-make egg-shaped vintage car, had, over time, grown a special spot for Dilip in his heart. In 1972, when

Piyush was taking the oath for the presidency of Leo Clubs, of which he was a founder of sorts in Calcutta, it was Dilip who had dug out a gem that he would treasure for life. 'Dilip was the one who established that my family had set a world record in the year 1972. My father was the president of Lion's Club, my mother became the president of Lioness and I was leading Leo, and all of us were taking oath at the same time. Dilip made the special moment unforgettable by gifting me that information nugget of a family memorabilia.'

A few years later, Piyush had floated his creative boutique advertising agency, with one artist and a peon. He was about one client old when Dilip called him to discuss business. At the time Piyush qualified as more experienced than his friend was in manufacturing. Only he didn't know what awaited—fierce training sessions into every little aspect of his own work. The two met at Raj, their favourite south Indian joint, and Dilip made him the offer to design the literature of his first product—an anti-depressant. Together, the two friends brainstormed on depression, the creative graphic that can support it, paid their own bills, which was always the case when friends of that group met, and left.

Within the next few days, Piyush came up with an idea, which Dilip found brilliant. 'I suggested we go with a man facing a wall. That's what depression is all about, a feeling as if you have hit a wall, with no windows, no door, no paths leading to anywhere, no?' Piyush recalled as saying then.

'Too good, bullseye,' Dilip exclaimed, discussed the positioning of the wall and the human form and told him he couldn't wait to see the design layout.

Two days later, Piyush spread before him the page layout of the creative design for his final approval.

'He kept looking at it for a few seconds and then pop he went— Piyush, there should be a shadow on the wall, don't you think? And I agreed, he had spotted something which felt like an obvious missing link but was profound in its own way, yes, there should have been a shadow on that wall. So we created that effect,' Piyush Doshi recalled.

How could Dilip skip the Sun in his first ever design, and what was depression if not blocking out a little Sun from your life to slip into a patch of darkness—the shadow!

Piyush, who primarily thought of himself as a designer, relished creative stimulation but didn't share the same passion for other mundane tasks—like the offset printer, the thickness of paper, the ink that goes on it, etc. He put up with those aspects of business, because they had to be put up with. The same rules he discovered didn't apply to Dilip, who would delve into the smallest of details.

After they were through with graphics, Dilip inquired about the paper he would use.

'The standard,' Piyush replied.

Dilip felt that convention may have become the standard, but it ought not to be so.

'It is technical stuff, not your domain, why do you care?' Piyush retorted.

'I have to, now it's part of my business, and whatever is, I must understand the entirety of it.'

'I guess we will use 160 gsm [grams per square metre], which the industry uses as a standard for "non-see-through" fliers of these types.'

'What about 130 gsm? Have we tried the look and feel of that?'

'Dilip, that's not the way things work. Even if you think a little scientifically, one is 20–23 per cent thinner than the other, it is bound to show up in look and feel.'

'I will agree with your observation, if we get both papers and touch it.'

Piyush at that time indulged in the exercise, not to prove or disprove any point but simply knowing that there was no escape. But when they did bring the samples and touched the two varieties, he was shocked to find no perceptible difference between the two and that 130 gsm would work for them.

And Dilip explained, 'Piyush, each paisa counts. Even if I save like 2 paise on each of this, we will save so much when we print millions of these. And we will print millions of these, because we will grow.'

This would go on—if Piyush quoted a price for paper, Dilip pushed him to visit the wholesale market and bargain for the best price. When he introduced a man who managed all his printing, Dilip softly advised, 'Do not give my work to your usual middleman, go straight to the offset printer.'

'He didn't honour the supply chain just because it existed for so long. He disrupted it and changed the rules of the game for aspects of my business which even I considered peripheral. Usually my clients don't bother with these things—paper, printing, ink—but the details that Dilip wanted to be made aware of made me wonder that this guy will go somewhere one day,' Doshi said, remembering his first days of work with Dilip, which he admitted could be exhausting to a different level for average people.

One of those days, Piyush got a call from Dilip to help fix the packaging. 'It was a fairly straight matter. There were a few people in Calcutta who specialized in that foil-strip packing, whom everyone went to. Those days it was a crude method where tablets were packed into a strip and printing was done with the help of a machine run by feet. But Dilip started navigating the route to the outskirts to explore all other options in remote interior parts I had never been to,' Piyush recalled. It fatigued Piyush beyond endurance, and he didn't remember much of the day except the fact that he sneaked into his home way past midnight after the 'packaging project'.

I had never seen anyone getting into such minute details, so I asked him a few times, 'Dilip, these are established practices, why are we going over these and trying to reinvent the wheel?' To this he replied, 'Piyush, only if we feel the roots, can we touch the sky,' Doshi added, admitting that many times, those seemingly meaningless and tiring exercises did make some difference, however small it was.

Countdown to the Flight of a Dream

Despite spending almost his entire youth in Calcutta, Dilip hardly had a Bengali friend to count in his tight circle of buddies. In fact, so thick was the Gujarati fervour in his gang that his very few non-Gujarati friends, like Ashok Butta, admitted they felt out of place at times in what felt like an 'extended family' bursting into jokes in Gujarati over a card game of bridge and pure vegetarian food.

The closest he came to having a bosom Bengali buddy in pre-Sun days, was in Mukul, a Gujarati by birth but Bengali by spirit. Dilip would sit with Mukul for hours and at times with his Bengali friends to get a grip on the psycho-sociology of Bengali psychiatrists.

Mukul's first-ever attempt at sketching the 'yin and yang' logo for Sun Pharma had felt a little too gypsy for Dilip's minimalist taste, so he tried another hand, not very far. During one of their usual chilling-out sessions at 'Dilip-bhai na room' he enlisted Ashok's younger brother, Kishore, to design the logo. Kishore, a mechanical engineering student at BIT Mesra then, who had just won an All India Logo Championship at college, came up with a blue and angular one. It was closer, Ashok remembered, in visual sense to the logo of Sun Microsystems, another Silicon Valley computer giant. Only that Kishore's logo pre-dated Sun Microsystem's by a few years and had come and gone before its Silicon Valley lookalike took shape.

Someone like Dilip, who fretted so much about creating a story through packaging, was keen to make that 'gem' inside the packet in his own facility. But setting up factories cost big money, and what Dilip thought of as his company was an assemblage of ragtag resources. So at the time the only viable option in front of him was 'loan licensing', which basically meant procuring a government licence to make his drugs by renting a small part of a factory that already had a licence to make such drugs.

He must have seen such arrangements working out for years. Mukul's father had a similar tie-up for dial thermometers with one Usman Khan's factory at Park Circus since the time he remembered.

The company Dilip was closely watching, Torrent, was also manufacturing drugs on loan licence till the early 1970s at a few factories including one that was called after a gemstone, 'Ruby Company'. In a freak coincidence, the company where Dilip began his 'loan-licensed' journey was called Onyx Labs, named after another gemstone, with a striking red variant. This model allowed Dilip to test his business case and his potential.

It is too simplistic to fancy that all Dilip found around him was support. 'Of course there were a few friends who would throw jibes at him for dreaming so big. In that impressionable age, everyone is a bit critical of each other, so a few friends goaded him to focus on the shop and not chase the "impossible",' Ashok said, adding that their motivation ranged from concern to envy. He also pointed out that Dilip was nurturing his dreams at a time in a city when the prevailing socio-political environment was hostile for business.

Dilip had been great at warding off emotional noise. The first such test in his business presented before him through a Bengali factory owner where the two mutually decided to make the drug under the terms of loan licensing.

But Dilip soon realized that after starting the business with him, the owner was often found missing in action. During repeated follow-up attempts, he was elusive. Finally, Dilip—not yet willing to accept that he had been so harassed—landed up at the doorsteps of his first mentor, seeking a way out.

Just days before that the night-time tea-mates got a sneak peek into how Dilip's resolve could stiffen up when put under test. They used to catch up with each other thrice a week in cheap south Indian joints and, once, in a slick upmarket Park Street cafe, and when the bills arrived, all of them reached for their pockets—they always went Dutch.

In fact, schoolfellow Girish recalled how Dilip had the mildly embarrassing habit of sniffing the food to guess what had gone into making the dish. 'If he is having dosa, he would not only reel off the ingredients, but the fundamentals of the fermentation process, where else is fermentation used, and how it determines the extent of sourness of the dosa we were having on our plates,' he recalled. On one of their good-restaurant days, they had just ordered two cups of masala tea for the non-drinkers and a beer for Dilip at Hotel Oasis.

While they were scanning the menu for the main course, Sailesh whispered into Dilip's ears, 'Piyush's dad is here.' In their circle, mainly comprising of 'Jains' and 'Vaishnavs', unless you have been dubbed outcaste, boys would rather be caught dead than drinking. There was a strong social taboo on it and it was seen as a sign of disrespect to elders. Almost as a reflex, Dilip grabbed the beer mug and gulped it down in one go, leaving his friends gaping. But then things blurred, and what followed was the rush to the toilet, the puke, the mess. They had planned a stag party at a friend's place that night and Dilip didn't cancel it but couldn't help puking twice more through the night. The next day, the hangover was over, forever. Nitin recalled him taking a vow that day to quit drinking and never touching any form of alcohol again. At times, it was important to lose a battle to win a war.

There is more than one version of the story of how Dilip landed at his first mentor's doorstep. According to Shanghvi's first mentor, an official at the state drug regulatory office suggested to Dilip an alternative for loan licensing, which must have sounded almost too personal when it hit his ears at first. 'Go to S. Sanghvi, on the ground floor of Mehta Building. He hails from Amreli in Gujarat and earlier had a shop at Bagri Market.'

This would have matched a 'ready-to-fit' description of Dilip's father, S. Sanghvi from Amreli who first had his shop in Bagri Market and then at Mehta Building. Only it was not the official address of his father but soon to become a father figure. It was the address of not Shantilal Shanghvi, but Shashikant Sanghvi, the owner of Onyx Labs.

'By the time Dilip came to me, or rather was sent to me by the drug controller, he had already faced a blow at another manufacturer's hands who had even digested his raw materials and had returned nothing. He was a total fresher straight out of his BCom course but the boy had a lot of desire to learn,' Shashikant Sanghvi, known in Calcutta Dawa Bazaar as Shashi-bhai, recalled.

Dilip recalled a different version of choosing Shashi-bhai, not because the drug regulator asked him to, but because he had immense respect for this self-made man. He had seen Shashi-bhai trust his assistants in his shop as if they were his own boys. 'Shashi-bhai trusted his boys enough to let them independently handle cash, something that didn't happen in our shop. From him, I learnt that if you trusted people, they responded by keeping that trust and trusting you back,' Dilip said.

'Dilip would spend 2–3 days every week at my factory at Panihati learning from my technicians and chemists and return with me in my car,' Shashi-bhai recounted. Those who rented out their premises, usually didn't allow the loanees such free passes into their factories (under law only the loanee's chemists had the rights to enter the factory). But Dilip had touched a chord in Shashi-bhai, and the fulfilment he derived from this experience was to turn him into a serial mentor.

Nurturing newbies and helping them take off, Shashi-bhai realized, filled him with an incredible satisfaction that he had not known in manufacturing and selling medicines. 'Guidance' was something his own abandoned mentor-less youth of struggle had missed sorely. Born into the family that owned M. Dharsi-bhai, one of the oldest medicine shops in Dawa Bazaar, Shashi-bhai was studying to be a doctor at the National Medical College, and Mehta Building is where his shop, home and life were.

Then one night changed everything for him, quashed his dream of becoming a doctor and turned him homeless. He entered home at 10 p.m., humming a song. His eldest uncle—the patriarch of the family, screamed, 'This is not an hour to come home.' Shashi retorted, 'You hush past the door at 1 a.m. at night. I have just come at 10 p.m., is it such a big sin?'

He was thrown out of the house in the middle of the night, disowned by the family that very moment. It was not only because he had challenged the head of the family, but in doing so, he had also indicated a vice of his uncle which had remained hitherto unacknowledged. In one set of clothes, he shared the tin shed of the guard on the roof of Mehta Building for the next six months with no bathroom, no electricity and no fees to pay for his medical school any more.

'I survived on muri [puffed rice] those six months bought by money earned from running errands for anyone who needed anything in Mehta Building. I knocked every door—my uncles, acquaintances for—my medical fees, but no one paid heed,' Shashi-bhai, who went on to found Onyx Labs in Kanpur, recalled. He later came back to buy his '100-year-old' shop at Mehta Building once his uncle passed away.

'So many people ask me today that if Dilip Shanghvi got his learnings at your place, and reached where he has, why couldn't you do what he could? I tell them that over the years there hasn't been one but many mini Dilip Shanghvis that this factory has spawned,' he said, referring to owners of smaller companies such as DD Pharma and A.N. PharmaCia with a neuropsychiatry focus, who started their journey at his Panihati factory as loan licensees after Dilip Shanghvi.

It is difficult to say whether Dilip-bhai brought out the teacher in Shashi-bhai or Shashi-bhai brought out the brilliance of the student in him. 'However, what happened afterwards was that Shashi-bhai's factory turned into a school of sorts for entrepreneurs. We have seen so many boys striking out on their own from his facility,' Swapna Patidar, a family friend of his, asserted.

However, Shashi-bhai paused and reflected, 'To tell the truth, so many have come and gone, there have been none like the first one—Dilip.' Shashi-bhai harboured a special soft corner for that 'well-mannered' boy he saw as 'striving hard' and 'self-taught', but admitted that he would have failed the test miserably had he been asked four decades back what was to become of Dilip. 'He came across as a straight and honest boy you could trust with money matters but it was impossible to imagine the potential he had inside. He was so low-key, that I don't think anyone then could have guessed the peaks he would scale,' Shashi-bhai said.

Unlike others, Dilip never understood what a half-hearted or a quarter-hearted effort could feel like. So he started in earnest learning even the technical bits of his business, including that of a chemist while at Shashi-bhai's Panihati factory. But the law required him to hire a chemist, or at the very least someone with a chemistry degree. He knew one such guy, who had tea with him every night and at whose factory he had been spending his weekends lately.

'Sailesh, would you join the company as a chemist? All you have to do is sign the register at the Panihati factory twice a month,' Sailesh Desai recalled being offered by Dilip, one of those days. Of course, he knew that the offer had a tone of request and was a call for help from a friend who was struggling about carving a dream out of an under-resourced existence. Sailesh, friends believed, was an 'OCH' or 'Obsessive Compulsive Helper' and helped whosoever was in need. He just asked one question before popping a yes to the proposal, 'Are there any risks in this, Dilip?' And thus this friend of Dilip, presently a director on the board of Sun, signed off as its first chemist for one-and-a-half years at the Panihati factory, without charging a penny.

By the time Dilip popped this offer, the two had already begun to bond beyond their group, and would hold Saturday sessions at Sailesh's aluminium stationeries factory where they brainstormed business solutions to problems.

On occasions, these 'issues' could run into touchy emotional realms as well. Sailesh had just joined the factory that was run by his elder brother who was the main decision maker. Dilip would suggest certain measures which meant more profits but disrupting a traditional way of life at the factory, which could backfire if it didn't work or hurt his brother's sentiments, something that Sailesh, who valued his relationships more than success, was reluctant to risk.

When he confessed his dilemma to Dilip, this is what he recalled his friend advising him to do, 'Just act on the decision we believe in. Stop trying to convince anyone or seeking approval from them before implementing it. Ultimately, our objective is doubling the profit, and once it happens it benefits everyone including your brother.'

He has absolute clarity of thought on core issues in life, and on those issues, he doesn't let anyone influence him even if these people are close to his heart—his family, parents, brothers or friends, Sailesh reckoned.

As the bond between the two deepened, it would see the tangling and untangling of intangible knots that mark the progression of deepening of any bond and in fact is an inevitable by-product of it. But that was later. For now they were still discovering how formidable a team the two of them made.

Listening to Dilip's advice at least on this occasion helped Sailesh not only earn the profit targets but his brother's confidence to try out more such experiments in their family business. Emboldened, he took up another challenge to triple his profits in a fortnight by delivering on a disproportionately large order for the size of their factory to meet a sudden spurt in demand. 'Dilip and I would sit and flesh out a crude-looking but deeply yielding business plan, something small factories are not used to having. During those meetings, it occurred to me how far we were from extracting maximum juice out of what we had,' Sailesh contemplated.

Besides shifting with his bedroll into the factory premises, the 'fortnight plan' Dilip and Sailesh had drawn up was not much beyond clever temporary fixes. It included steps like small-time tweaking 'per man' cost, outsourcing metal-cutting work, dynamic pricing of labour by paying some of them double their salary to work overtime. But pieced together and executed flawlessly, the strategy worked.

It was nearing success and Sailesh had already begun planning celebrations for a 'fortnight challenge' when one weekend Dilip confided that he had run into a challenge. He said his own product, lithium carbonate, had seen an unexpected demand spike as the competing company had hit supply issues, but the labour at Shashi-bhai's factory just wouldn't cooperate. Sailesh, who had been literally living with his workers on the shop floor, suggested, 'Why don't you take my workers and work Sundays at his factory?'

The plan stuck, and Sun started operating on Sundays from the Panihati factory to meet the excess demand. But Dilip was never one to be content with short-term fixes. Besides labour issues, he was beginning to realize that the scientists at the factory were not up for solving the sophisticated challenges that the complex chemistry of psychotropic drugs threw up. And this was not the corner where his dream could be hatched beyond.

They were driving back from Panihati to the Mehta Building. Shashi-bhai was at the wheel, Dilip on the passenger seat.

'Shashi-bhai, I want to set up my own factory,' Dilip said.

'In that case don't build it here in Calcutta. You will regret for life if you ever finish building it. Leave Bengal if you want to make anything out of it,' Shashi-bhai said after a pause.

'Will you help me set it up, Shashi-bhai?'

And so Shashi-bhai would go on to become one of the first of Dilip's own to take a train from Calcutta to Bombay, hop into a second train from there to reach Vapi, and see the land where Dilip would build his first machine temple.

'I knew he wouldn't stay. I knew all along why he was learning what he was learning at my factory. He wanted to start his own. Loan licensing was the launching pad, a test case of whether his drugs were selling all right in the market, whether he was getting the process of manufacturing right, the equipment and finance that you needed to set up a factory,' Shashi-bhai reminisced.

'Only I didn't want him to repeat the mistake I had made, by not leaving Calcutta when I could and grappling all my life with this "*hochchhe hochchhe*", "*hobe hobe*", "*ki kore hobe*" culture. "Work is constantly, "would happen, how would it happen" mode here, it never is "let's make it happen" or "we have made it happen",' he exclaimed.

Shashi-bhai said he earned his guru-dakshina a few years back when Dilip was being felicitated by the Gujaratis of Calcutta in a ceremony at

Bhowanipore Gujarati Education Society. 'I was sitting in the audience, and Dilip went up the dais when his name was called out. And suddenly he was pointing towards me from the podium, saying, "I am standing before you as what I am because of this person." I had earned the wealth of a lifetime,' an emotional Shashi-bhai said.

The dawn broke, and Dilip picked three of his friends—Hitesh, Sailesh and Nitin to head towards Panihati. It was the day when the first of his tablets were to gain form and shape, and packed into foils that bore a bold print: Manufactured by: **Sun Pharma, 57/2A, Paddapukur Road, Calcutta–700025.**

The three of them went about quietly packing their friend's first consignment into cartons, loading it atop a yellow taxi, proud to be a worker one moment and a porter another, proud to play their parts in the making of a dream. It would have been great had any of them peeped out of the window at the Bhowanipore turn to notice if a lotus was actually blooming that day in the eponymous Paddapukur and if the sun was shining upon this resilient flower, which blooms regardless of its surrounding. But that was not to be, they were fanning themselves with newspapers inside the cab. People making history do not always know it while making it. Life would be unbearably ceremonious that way.

Later that evening, Mukul, the one with a historical record of delirium albeit fever-induced, was put up to the challenge of testing the drug for safety. 'I was the guinea pig, an experiment for him, the "beta-guy". It was a joke for me, so I said, "bring it on"—grabbed it and, pop, swallowed it. For a few seconds my friends were aghast, had I done it,' Mukul recalled of that evening. After the moment sank into consciousness, Dilip said 'Beta, don't worry, don't worry, nothing will happen. You will wake up fully alive tomorrow.' Shanghvi couldn't remember this but Mukul recalled sleeping well and waking up hale and hearty the next morning, which he said was a testimony to the fact that the drug was safe.

But had Mukul succumbed to the hallucinatory powers of psychotropic drugs and woke up dreamy, hazarding a guess as to where this drug was going to take his friend, that his friend would one day grow richer than 'the Tatas and Birlas', would the rest of his friends have bought the prophecy then?

'Had I uttered such a thing after waking up, friends would have thrown cold water on me to bring me back to my senses and labelled Dilip's new drug dangerously hallucinatory,' laughed Mukul.

CHAPTER THREE

A GROWING PRESCRIPTION
OF TRANQUILITY

The round cherubic face wearing a chirpy smile peeped inside the half-open door of the clinic, which was nothing more than a room and half a corridor in the backyard of the doctor's ancestral two-storey house in Calcutta. The doctor, who had just finished explaining to the patient's daughter what a bipolar disorder is, looked up towards the door and flashed a smile.

'Oh Lithosun, how are you doing? Come, have a seat, let me finish with the prescription.' His head was one among the three others sticking in from the door. All were trying their luck to be spotted at the end of the day. But the psychiatrist had grown fond of this boy in the last few months and found him and his partner fascinating to chat with. Besides, there had been other strange small comforts, albeit useful ones.

This boy 'Lithosun' had brought a plumber to fix the leaking tap in the garden when he had found the doctor's wife struggling with it one day, on his way out of the clinic. The incident had never been explicitly mentioned between them, but the doctor's wife had identified him as a 'nice boy' and offered him tea. A few days later, he brought and quietly placed a pen stand on the doctor's table, no big feat for a medicine company. But after he left, when the doctor picked up to check for the company's logo, there was none. Lithosun had noticed the doctor's aversion to use slip pads and pens promoting drugs.

'So Lithosun, where are you making your medicines?' the doctor asked for the ninth time in the last eight months.

'Sir, right now our company is making its drugs at a factory in Panihati, owned by Onyx Labs. But we are soon going to have our own factory,' said Lithosun, as if he had been posed the question for the very first time. He also observed that today, even at this unexpected evening hour, the patient flow had not tapered off, and one could hear muffled voices complaining from the corridor along with the smell of tea wafting from upstairs, which meant the doctor could be planning to wind up for the day. Sensing the plan, he said, 'Sir, today looks like a busy day, I will come tomorrow evening.'

'That will be better, Lithosun,' the doctor said, now pushing the button signalling the attendant to send in the next patient. As he reached out for the door knob, the doctor called out again, 'What's the name of your company, Lithosun?'

'It is Sun Pharma, sir,' he said.

'And what is yours, Lithosun?' the doctor smiled.

'Pradip, sir, Pradip Ghosh, but Lithosun is also fine,' he smiled back.

After stepping out of the clinic on that February evening of 1979, Ghosh did what had become his ritual for the last eight months. He checked at the neighbourhood chemists for any prescriptions that the doctor may have written for the only drug of their newborn company. No miracle had happened. The doctor hadn't.

Ghosh hopped on to the closest tram, which was numbered 14 and asked for a ticket for Canning Street. On his way back, he smiled at a co-passenger as a gesture of shared understanding of travel discomfort, squeezed himself into an edge of the seat and started writing a minute-by-minute account of the day for his boss, the only other employee in their company sitting at his shop at Medcom Enterprises, in Mehta Building—the place where his journey had begun on a hot sunny holiday.

Pradip was working as a steno for a private company at the time, when he spotted a medical representative job advertisement in the *Statesman*. He didn't even know the name of the company he was applying for. 'It was a bit of a mystery, and exciting, as the little block seeking job application only had a post box number, with no name or address,' Ghosh recalled. It was only when Ghosh's brother read out the interview letter, that he realized that he was going to appear for a job in Sun Pharma, 57/2A, Paddapukur Road, Calcutta.

He had been asked to appear for an interview in a building in Bagri Market, in Dawa Bazaar on 22 June 1978, which was a Sunday.

In Calcutta, a city with a laid-back attitude where people love their daily afternoon siesta under whirring fans, this was a fair warning for candidates for the demands of the job. When Ghosh criss-crossed the narrow winding lanes of Dawa Bazaar to reach the spot at 2 p.m., the man standing at the foot of the building stared at him and guessed it right.

'Oh, interview, it's already on, since morning. Get in, get in.' Ghosh walked up the stairs to find some young men discussing the questions they had been quizzed on, with someone cracking a joke, 'Not sun, it's the moon waiting inside the room, good luck.' When his turn came, Ghosh said he found two men—a middle-aged one with a shiny bald pate and a young, plump, bespectacled guy with a dense crop.

The old man was the one grilling job hopefuls, asking them to read aloud and make sense of a bunch of drug literature scattered on the table. The younger guy was more keenly watching the old man, as if training himself in the art of taking interview. 'For a second I was confused as to who was who and thought the old guy must be the proprietor,' Ghosh quipped. The old guy was, in fact, one Mr Banerjee, a regional manager at Bihar Remedies who had been enlisted for hiring the first medical representative of Sun Pharma.

Sitting next to him was Dilip who emerged from the room to tell Pradip after a while, 'Not to be told to others. Please meet us at Mehta Building in the next lane tomorrow morning at 10 a.m.' For Pradip the mystery was fully solved when Dilip added softly, 'And do bring a leather detailing bag to carry the medicine samples.' Ghosh believed that what helped him bag that job was his ability to pronounce the word 'asthma' as 'azzma', just the way Bengali doctors preferred to hear it. 'It was at that precise moment when I uttered "azzma" that I saw the two of them changing approving glances across the table, and felt my chance of getting the job brightening up,' Ghosh said.

On his way back, Ghosh disembarked at Sealdah station and bought a bag for ₹55. 'That was all the money I had at the time,' he said.

The next morning Dilip first introduced Ghosh to his father Shanti-kaka, standing right in front of Medcom Enterprises. He brought out his own bag, a tan-coloured leather Echolac, and pulled out samples to hand over to Pradip.

When Ghosh retrieved his new bag from the packet and thrust some samples inside it, Dilip remarked, 'But Pradip, this is not leather.' But no faux leather had the nerve to diminish the vigour of the moment for Dilip and Pradip who stood facing each other in the dusty, crowded streets taking in the promise, action and dream of the future as the scorching June sun of Calcutta shone its blessings on them. A dribble of sweat flowed across his face as Dilip said, almost to himself, 'First representative of my organization, Sun.'

Dine and Distribute with Thy Neighbour

Marketing is not all that a company needs. There were many other things, such as distribution. Mahesh Mehta was not Dilip Shanghvi's date. Yet Dilip spent a good number of hours in his youth sitting across him, looking at his face, passing smiles at him throughout the day and exchanging sweet nothings. Like your blood relatives, you didn't have much choice in picking your neighbours in the cramped Mehta Building. Mahesh sat right across the narrow lane that separated Medcom Enterprises from Vinod Medico. Mahesh's wholesale medicine shop, Vinod Medico, was smaller than Dilip's small shop and was managed by the joint family headed by the patriarch uncle—Mahesh's father's elder brother—whom he called Bhai-ji.

Both young hearts of twenty-something years filled their empty hours with each other by sharing their dreams. On one of those afternoons Dilip told Mahesh, 'I am planning to make my own drugs. What do you think?' Mehta, who said he couldn't tell how making a drug was any different from making the bhujia he was munching right then, indulged him. 'I think it's a great idea, Dilip. Go ahead, we are with you.' And then Dilip popped another question, 'If I go ahead, will you become my distributor?'

'I knew Dilip-bhai was bold. And some of his boldness rubs off on you when you are spending so much time with him. And somewhere by making that offer, he was tapping into a deep desire within me. I had wanted to move up the value chain from wholesaling to distribution. Wholesaling meant daily business and distribution meant forging long-term relations and that's what I wanted, long-term relations in business,' Mehta reminisced, sitting at his Gandhi Building shop even as his charming son Jai Mehta with two more employees punched in the day's orders into the computers.

'I am not sure whether I told Dilip-bhai about my wish to enter distribution or he just read my mind,' Mehta strained to remember and added, 'But when he made the offer, I dived right in. It felt as if I was diving into a dream. It was a dream because it held hope and promise but it was also a dream because at that time there was very little reality in the name of a company that one could hang on to.'

But Mahesh's longing for long-term relations in business extracted a hefty price in his life, his long-term relations with his family. When he told Bhai-ji that he wanted to turn stockist, he was first quizzed about the company. When he revealed it was Dilip's company, Bhai-ji laughed it off as a fun game that kids were playing. But when products actually started arriving one day in a yellow Ambassador taxi which Dilip and three of his friends, Hitesh, Nitin and Sailesh, unloaded at the doorstep of Vinod Medico's, Bhai-ji frowned.

It was an amusing sight. The lane where the first freshly made drugs of Sun Pharma were being unloaded was flanked on one side by the distribution shop owned by Dilip's father and his partner, which was already stocking psychiatry products for Torrent. But instead of turning that side, here Dilip was turning the other side, unloading his first-ever consignment and adjusting it in the cramped shelf space of a neighbour's shop who was turning stockist that very day on a bit of borrowed boldness from Dilip to shape his destiny.

What could be the exact reason that pushed Dilip to not use kaka's agency to stock his drugs, which would have easily translated into lower costs for him? One old-timer from the market suggested that kaka's partner Natu-kaka was apprehensive about Torrent's reaction to Dilip's plan. 'He didn't think it was prudent to lose what he had in the name of business to what could become business some day in future,' the stockist at Canning Street said.

Another contemporary of Dilip, who is also a stockist at Dawa Bazaar said, 'Dilip-bhai wanted a different speed and energy in his new venture, and he was too respectful to order around kaka or Natu-kaka to pick up the speed of their distribution. So he wanted everything new and young. With Mahesh, he was much more comfortable and could ask him to do the running around.' It could very well be that Dilip-bhai knew that if his venture succeeded, he would have to take Torrent head-on sooner than later. This would have been perceived as a direct conflict of interest and hurt his father's business. Shanghvi cited a reason close to the third hypothesis. 'I was to operate in psychiatry and my father was the stockist of Torrent and at no cost would I have wanted my father to lose his business because I was starting my own that had the potential to clash with Torrent.'

After the stuff had been unloaded that evening, Mahesh pulled out some of the other cartons from the top centre of the overstuffed shelf and positioned one of the cartons right there in the middle, high up on the shelf allowing a visibility at 65, Canning Street. If someone thought of his shop's centre wall as a sky, he would have placed the sun right at that spot. But the next day, by the time Mahesh reached his shop in the morning, the carton had been tucked away somewhere else. He found it again and replaced it exactly at the same spot. That carton, which carried the dreams of a few young boys, was to become a permanent fixture at Vinod Medico and adorned that place for six long months, during which demand for its products would remain exactly zero.

Once the demand trickled in, Mahesh would have to take his scooter at any odd hour and zip to the outskirts. He would zoom back and forth from north to south Calcutta to fill in emergency supplies. He would earn ₹2 per strip and end up burning petrol worth much more. The tension that was building up between him and Bhai-ji since he stocked Dilip-bhai's medicine exploded one day.

'Just what do you think you are doing Mahesh, whiling away your time after nothing?' confronted Bhai-ji. 'You are spending all your time after a silly illusion while our family business is suffering. You take one box to Dumdum, and earn ₹20 while you burn ₹30 from your own pocket. This is not business, boy. You are running after your Dilip-bhai, who cannot give you any guarantee of his own future, leave alone yours. Don't give up your bread for a butter that might turn sour tomorrow.'

In a conservative Gujarati joint family, when patriarchs like Bhai-ji spoke, you were supposed to lower your head and listen. But Mahesh had the colour of bold splashed all over him those days.

'Bhai-ji, we have just sown the seeds, it cannot become tree today and bear fruits tomorrow. But when it grows into a tree, it will bear fruits and many of them,' he replied firmly.

A stunned Bhai-ji, not in a habit to be challenged, said, 'Then look for your patch of soil to plant the tree.' This became the primary cause of the family breaking up and Vinod Medico, named after Mahesh's cousin, got divided into two shops.

Asked why he stuck to the name Vinod Medico, if he was anyway striking out on his own, Mehta said, 'If I had gone for another name, we would have to obtain another licence. But more importantly, the name Vinod Medico has goodwill accumulated over generations and it stands for integrity in the market.' A boy when he takes 'maal' from Vinod Medico doesn't have to stand in queue to get payment because the client trusts us not to send lesser goods or jack prices unfairly. The same boy if he changes jobs is not meted the same treatment, because he is not wearing the Vinod Medico jersey any more.'

Trust is all that we have earned, said Mehta, as he showed how he has preserved every single challan of Sun Pharma for the last thirty-eight years starting with the first one signed off by Dilip Shanghvi. He continued to remain the stockist of Sun, and one of the rare occasions when he took offence in that relationship was when, a few years back, the company, now India's largest in the pharmaceuticals sector, sent a paper agreement to be signed.

'I refused to sign it and turned them away. Till we believe each other's word, we will carry the relationship. The day we cannot take each other's word and have to depend on a piece of paper, perhaps it is not worth it any more,' Mehta felt. His wish of a long-term business relation has been fulfilled on a currency of trust, where a near-four-decade professional marriage has thrived without a proof of a contract signed on any paper.

Oliver Hardy on a Green Rajdoot

On day two, Pradip showed up for work with a cheery yellow tie, borrowed from his friend to be taken seriously on the job. After all that was the norm in the business—that little neck-piece made things look so tight and professional. But Dilip's turned-up nose made him quietly loosen the knot at the throat. Dilip, it seems, had a congenital allergy to the family of frills and all things oozing 'show off'. Not tie but trust would be used to woo doctors, he explained to Pradip as he psychoanalysed the Calcutta psychiatrists—his first set of customers.

More than one psychiatrist in Calcutta indicated that their lot, particularly the initial practitioners who paved the way for the discipline in the decade of the 1960s, were perceived as 'eccentric' in their own way. One of them narrated a joke about two psychiatrists walking on the Digha beach, with one asking the other, 'You look fine. How am I?'

Debashish Bhattacharya, a psychiatrist who has practised in the state for over three decades, says that till the late 1970s, 'psychiatry in India was on the fringes of medicine, in its infantile phase and the number of companies catering to this therapy could be counted on fingers— just a few multinationals like Smith and Kline, E Merck—that's it.' In a nutshell, psychiatrists were not a pampered lot.

Recounting memories of a decade earlier than that, of the 1960s when 'insulin injection was still being used on severe psychiatric cases to induce hypoglycaemic coma, as a substitute to electric shock therapy', he said, 'Those days, at times, we saw our professors of other departments in medical colleges stomping into newly formed psychiatry departments with a student who seemed eccentric or a little off-balance and saying—keep this one, he will fit here.' Bhattacharya also shared an oft-used Bengali pedestrian proverb of yesteryears that loosely translates into 'Crazies treat crazies'.

Regardless of the self-deprecating humour of Bengali psychiatrists and the truism that psychic patients were stigmatized and psychiatrists viewed through a veil of mystery, it was Calcutta that served as one of the cradles for evolution of psychiatry in India.

In 1921, a thirty-five-year-old man from Calcutta, Girindrasekhar Bose, started a series of exchange of ideas and notes with none other than Sigmund Freud. He also sent Freud a copy of his thesis, 'The Concept of Repression'. Bose, who wore Gandhi-style round-rimmed glasses, just as Freud could be seen wearing in his vintage pictures, started off as an amateur magician and hypnotist while studying medicine and floated an 'Eccentric Club'. He energized the practice of the discipline in India by founding the Indian Psychoanalytical Society in 1922, which was immediately made a member of International Psychoanalytical Association (formed by Freud in 1910).

Many luminaries of the discipline who shaped the Indian psychiatry space and subsequently ruled it from the 1950s to the 1980s, such as Ajita Chakraborty and Dhirendra Nath Nandi, were a product of their first-hand experience with psychoanalysis practised by Bose, dubbed the first non-Western psychoanalyst. It was Bose who shifted the (perceived) role of a psychiatrist from 'doctors of the insane to those who understand the mysteries of conscious and unconscious', according to N.N. Wig, another Chandigarh-based eminent Indian psychiatrist, inspired by Bose.

Dr Chakraborty told Wig that she had undergone personal psychoanalysis in Calcutta before taking up psychiatry as a career, and Dr Nandi was closely associated with the Psychoanalysis Association in Calcutta. That Dr Nandi was inspired by Bose is also clear from the fact that the first private outreach centre for psychiatry that was formed under his leadership was named after Girindrasekhar Institute of Psychological Education & Research and set up at 14, Parsibagan Lane, an address that was home to Bose .

'These were passionate, strong-willed individuals who went against the flow of prevailing mainstream in search of something elusive, and ended up shaping psychiatry in India,' Bhattacharya said about his mentor Dr Chakraborty, her rival Dr Nandi and their ilk.

It was this 'passionate ilk' and their first-generation students that Dilip had set out to win and the first message he gave Pradip was, 'Never commit anything you cannot do, and once you commit, do it anyhow.'

'We knew that we would be psychoanalysed by our customers. Given their profession, could they help it? We knew how fragile their trust could be, companies which couldn't live up to their own word were labelled fraud instantly and once you lost the customers' trust there was nothing more to lose in our business. We saw so many companies getting born and dying because of a trust deficit,' Ghosh said.

What also worked for the duo, technically the full strength of the company then, was Dilip-bhai's clarity that trust couldn't be bought by throwing money or earned overnight. 'Initially many doctors had apprehensions about lithium carbonate, mainly because of its toxicity. But I only had this one drug for two years, so I had to promote and make them prescribe. After a year of promoting one drug, the product had become me and I had become the product. But Dilip-bhai had tremendous patience. Launching a drug without scientific background and financial backing was no joke,' said Ghosh.

In fact, Dilip had done a good deal of homework much before Pradip joined.

Ambika Charan Dutta, an octogenarian psychiatrist, once the superintendent of Girindrasekhar clinic, remembered Dilip coming to see him twice a week, with a bag slung across his shoulders, wearing a bush shirt, bell-bottoms and leather chappals, riding a Lambretta scooter or a motorbike.

The scooter had been his father's and the motorbike was a green Rajdoot, borrowed from his friend Ashok Butta. 'Those were carefree days and among friends anyone could take anyone's things without asking. But unlike many others Dilip would always refill the tank before returning the bike,' Butta recalled. Besides the bike, he had also borrowed the expertise of Mukul and his Bengali friends to dissect how the minds of Bengali doctors work and understand their typical tastes and queer needs. Dilip worked on polishing his Bengali and understood the doctors' need to be engaged intellectually in a pre-Google age. At times doctors themselves could be witterers, but most of them were suckers for a meaningful conversation. What helped was that lithium, known chemically as 'Li' has had a thrilling history and Dilip-bhai had an unquenchable thirst for knowledge.

In the 1920s, lithium was to a popular lemon-flavoured fizz drink (marketed by St Louis-based The Howdy Corporation) what caffeine was to Coca-Cola. This soda drink, launched weeks before the Wall Street Crash of 1929 was '7 Up', in which according to one rumoured theory, '7' was a secret code referring to the atomic mass of lithium (6.941 amu). By 1948, '7 Up' had become the third-bestselling soft drink in the world, when lacing soda drinks with tranquilizer lithium citrate was banned in the US. Also, its use as a substitute of dietary table salts in cases of hypertension and heart disease was stopped after reports of death due to its overdosing surfaced.

A year later John Cade, an Australian psychiatrist, while injecting rodents with urine extracts of schizophrenic patients in an experiment, discovered that lithium salts are causing the animals to become tranquil. He quickly followed up with hospitalized chronic patients with mania, and lithium worked as a tranquilizer.

Ronald Fieve, a psychiatrist who passed out from the Harvard Medical School, picked up Cade's research thread in America and conducted the first controlled clinical trial for depression, setting up the first lithium clinic in 1966. He continues to have a thriving private practice in New York at 'Fieve Depression Centre' which is said to be 'crammed with Wall Street tycoons and Hollywood producers'. Fieve was part of a lithium task force that convinced the US Food and Drug Administration (USFDA) to approve the drug for the management of manic illness in 1970, making it, in his words, the 'first medication that specifically treated a specific psychiatric disorder'. He also brought lithium mainstream by authoring a bestseller *Moodswing* in 1975, which introduced 'bipolar disorder to the American public', and then following it with *Bipolar II* and *Bipolar Breakthrough*.

Dilip-bhai started the search for his first drug in the years when *Moodswing* was making waves in America. He seems to have followed Fieve's research closely as at least one psychiatrist, who was then a postgraduate student in R.G. Kar Medical College, faintly recalled him having mentioned the American psychiatrist's research in a conversation. Shanghvi recalled gifting that book to a few psychiatrists. One of these was the second-hand book he had read himself. 'I have had limited conversations with Shanghvi, but whatever little I have seen of him he didn't speak like a salesman. He would talk like a scientist or a social scientist, at times explaining the working of the drug in the body and at times justifying its need in our socio-economic milieu,' Bhattacharya echoed.

A major nub of chats with doctors, Shanghvi recalled, was around this. 'At that point in time there was large amount of literature saying that maniac depressive psychosis or MDP is significantly under-diagnosed globally and in many cases such patients are treated as schizophrenics. So schizophrenia is over-diagnosed and MDP is under-diagnosed.' He also realized that doctors around the world, particularly in India, would wake up to this fact eventually. And as they start to diagnose their patients better, the usage of lithium carbonate was bound to shoot up.

Distributor Mehta said Dilip-bhai's telephonic chats with some top psychiatrists could go on for really long. 'Those days intercity trunk calls were very expensive and we kept it brief, restricting it to 2–3 minutes at the most. But once Dilip-bhai called Dr Nandi from Bombay and went on chatting for over forty-five minutes,' Mehta said, laughing about how jumpy he felt about the bill.

Some students of Dr Nandi also mentioned about these long telephonic chats, even though they said their professor kept referring to him as 'Shinghvi' instead of 'Shanghvi'. Interestingly, for every four doctors who saw a spark in Dilip, six others in Calcutta admitted that they had missed it altogether. They confessed they had known him, but not in their wildest imagination could they have guessed what was to become of him.

When Dilip was doing his rounds alone, he took buses and trams to the private clinics of doctors, some of whom saw medical reps only after 10 p.m. That meant he would have to walk back home late at night having missed all the buses of the day. 'Once Pradip was hired, I often saw the two of them together,' Dutta said. Mostly they still took trams or buses to meet doctors, but if it got late in the evening, Dilip at times hired a private car.

Dilip was plump but not as heavily built as Oliver Hardy, and Pradip was slim but not as skinny as Stan Laurel. Yet among the students of R.G. Kar Medical College, the duo came to be called 'Laurel and Hardy'. 'I don't know how it started but the impression was that these two young lads—Laurel and Hardy—landed from nowhere, smiling at you, would strike a conversation asking you to prescribe their medicines,' this psychiatrist who was doing his internship in the late 1970s from R.G. Kar Medical College said. 'We smiled back, chatted along but medicine was serious business and we never prescribed their medicine for a very long time,' he added.

Another batchmate of his, Jayanta Basu, laughed and confirmed the Laurel and Hardy story as one they inherited from seniors at the medical college. He said that although Dilip and Pradip's medicine was never prescribed, they didn't fail to turn up and smile; people often smiled in return. And this went on for months at a stretch, before a day in 1979 when the tables might have started turning for 'Laurel and Hardy'.

That day Dilip and Pradip waited outside Dr Nandi's outdoor clinic at R.G. Kar Medical College, amidst patients swarming the hallways, some leaning on the walls, many perched on floors, others queuing up in front of the door next to Dr Nandi's cabin, waiting for their turn of shock therapy. It was the usual humdrum in the hospital, but when their turn came, that day Dr Nandi didn't politely shoo them off saying, 'I will see'.

Despite his star status, he made them sit and took some time to explain why he wasn't comfortable prescribing a drug like lithium carbonate. 'This drug has a history of becoming toxic. Beyond a threshold level, this chemical turns dangerous in the blood. This therapeutic window, the difference between the level at which the drug works best and the level at which it turns toxic needs to be monitored carefully in patients. For that they need to do the blood serum estimation test periodically, say every month. But it costs a lot of money, almost ₹40 per test, and my patients are often too poor to afford that much. At government set-ups, we don't have the means to do that test and so it's not safe, you see . . .'

There was a brief but unmistakable pause that followed, which was to emerge as a signature response style of Dilip-bhai in the years to come. But what followed made the senior resident, who was helping out Dr Nandi, turn around and take notice of this 'Oliver Hardy'.

'Sir, we can sort that issue. I will work with a private lab to pay half of that cost for as many patients you think need it. We can give you cards and whenever you feel that the patient can't afford that test, you can hand him over that card, which he can show to the lab to get a 50 per cent discount,' Dilip suggested.

'I think many of us took notice of him that day. It was a master stroke; in one precise moment he had dramatically changed the equation,' Jayanta Basu exclaimed. 'Since childhood, a story of how George Bernard Shaw made his books sell had fascinated me. When his books despite being great were not selling, he would repeatedly send his friends with inquiries to bookshops, which prompted the vendors to start stocking his books giving them the best display; Shanghvi did a

Shaw that day,' he added. Sitting at his Salt Lake clinic forty years later, Basu smiled and said, 'Isn't it Bernard Shaw who once said that some men see things as they are and ask why. Others dream things that never were and ask why not.'

Basu felt that day Dr Nandi would have ended his discussion on a polite but regretful note having explained why lithium carbonate was a troublesome drug to prescribe and bid goodbye. But that didn't happen, and Bernard Shaw perhaps had a better quote to qualify what had just happened. 'The people who get on in this world are the people who get up and look for the circumstances they want and if they can't find them, make them.'

Pradip recalled them heading straight to Saxena Labs at Girish Park, from Dr Nandi's clinic and Dilip talking to the proprietor. 'Within the next few days, Dilip-bhai arranged for a flame photometer (a device to determine the concentration of lithium ions in blood) to be set up at Saxena Labs. Using that they could start with the tests right away and then he supplied Dr Nandi with the cards, using which his patients could get that test done at ₹20 instead of ₹40,' Ghosh recalled.

In fact, the response to Dr Nandi which had seemed spontaneous had been prepared, and Shanghvi had previously made similar arrangements for smaller clinics in Calcutta and remote towns in Bengal and Orissa. 'Where the usage was high, we got in touch with path labs and if they couldn't afford setting up the equipment, I loaned them money and took it back over time. Other labs did potassium and sodium tests. We helped them buy a lithium filter so that they could do this test as well. Lithium was a great drug with very few side effects, and unlike its alternatives, which clearly made the patient look drugged and drowsy, you couldn't tell if a patient is on lithium,' Shanghvi said.

'There was no explicit quid pro quo, and I don't remember them coming after us when we wrote prescriptions of other established companies which made the same molecule,' Basu said. 'But after about two weeks of writing brands of other so-called established companies, I felt a twitch in my conscience. These are two young boys helping our patients, doing something no big company had ever done and we cannot even write a prescription for them. So I began by writing every eleventh prescription for them, not all. I cannot speak for others with certainty but believe that many of my contemporaries must have felt the same way,' Basu added.

Basu's gut was bang on. Mahesh Mehta's phone buzzed, and a voice from the other side inquired, 'Do you stock Sun Pharma's Lithosun? There are prescriptions pouring in from Dr Nandi's clinic.' Mehta, who was in an 'I will prove it to you' mode to his uncle, but hadn't managed to sell a single prescription in the last many months, almost stammered with excitement, 'Yes, yes. You have called the right address. And where are you calling from?'

'From Dey's Medical Store,' the voice said.

Mehta couldn't believe his ears. 'Dey's was the retail store of Calcutta, the only one which remained open 24/7 in those days. It was a shop that commanded respect among doctors and patients alike. And if our drug was stocked at Dey's, we had arrived in business,' Mehta said, calling his first order in Calcutta a turning point.

Warm Efficiency Does It!

The first prescription in Calcutta wasn't worth more than ₹100, and it wasn't essentially the first for Sun Pharma. It might have been for the stockist in Calcutta, but the real first order for the company had already come in weeks before that, at Bardhaman.

Pradip's day usually began with a phone call which he ran to receive at a neighbour's house at Raja Bazaar. 'I didn't have a landline at home then. First thing in the morning used to be a call from Dilip-bhai at my friend's place where we would go over the plan for the day,' Ghosh said.

Many psychiatrists would wake up to prescribing lithium with Sun Pharma. But to begin with, there were just twenty out of the hundred-odd psychiatrists in Calcutta then, who, according to their list, were prescribing lithium brands of other companies such as Delhi-based La Medica or E Merck, a German multinational. They were targeted first, then those post-graduating in psychiatry.

At the time, engaging with young medical students helped them prepare better to deal with senior specialists, who couldn't be expected to spare their precious time on such newbies from nowhere. A decent share of prescription at well-known doctors' clinics was written by their senior students, so there were chances of a breakthrough too.

Also those who are students of psychiatry today would be star psychiatrists tomorrow; just like struggling pharma entrepreneurs would create pharma empires of tomorrow. There was much to be gained by growing together, a thought that would eventually turn into a full-blown 'catch them young' strategy at Sun.

And of course, those initial days, these young students were mines of indispensable information about psychiatry and psychiatrists that could be employed back in marketing strategies. These customized strategies could help to convert lithium-prescribing doctors over to lithosun from other brands and non-prescribers to neo-prescribers. Each potential doctor was discussed thoroughly between Dilip and Pradip as they filled their evenings with 'who had been converted, who needs to be converted, and how'.

Outside of Calcutta, one such doctor was Dr Asit Baran Patra, who was proving to be a lot of hard work but was too important to ignore. He saw over 100 patients every day at his Bardhaman clinic. On Wednesdays when he went to Asansol, there would be endless queues snaking outside his small clinic, where the number of patients easily crossed 200. Among lithium options, his staple was Lithanate, a brand promoted by La Medica, effectively the only serious competition Sun's brand had.

By the time Pradip joined, Dilip had already made over 35–40 visits to Dr Patra's clinic, before he finally managed to meet him in person. Once Pradip was in, the two of them started making those weekly trips together. 'Before getting on the train to Bardhman, Dilip-bhai would buy heaps of magazines to read during the journey. He would often joke that he was spending too much on books,' Pradip said.

When Dilip wasn't reading, the two of them went on devising strategies to corner at least a third of Patra's prescriptions. This brainstorming session lasted over puri bhaji outside the station and beyond till they reached the clinic. This became a ritual for the next six months, before the doctor decided to give them a chance and write a prescription. 'You can't pin down the exact circumstances that prompted the doctor to write our prescription. It could have been our sincerity and consistency or it could have been some of Dilip-bhai's conversations on the science of the drug. He had that art of striking meaningful conversation at different frequencies. Whosoever spoke to him once, wanted a repeat experience and doctors were no exception,' Pradip said.

That six-month-long wait, for one prescription, didn't strike Pradip as too long. 'We were a new company, a new face. The doctors were judging our credibility and integrity. It's like if today, after thirty-eight years at Sun, I go to a doctor representing another company, can they believe it?' Pradip asked, almost disbelieving himself.

During one of those stimulating conversations, Patra had mentioned his patients complaining about their lithium drug getting powdered in no time, making it inconvenient for them to swallow the tablet.

But this problem was not exclusive to Sun's competitors. Shortly after Sun's medicine started getting prescribed, this problem hit this new start-up as well. 'The moment reports of the drug getting floured reached Dilip-bhai, he took it as a "make or break" emergency, even though he realized that to some extent it was in the nature of the molecule which was hygroscopic,' Pradip said. A hygroscopic substance absorbs moisture from the atmosphere. Hence the tablets had a tendency to turn into powder.

Dilip told Pradip that Sun cannot afford this, and sat through two days and nights with the scientists at his rented facility at Panihati to sort this problem of binding.

Till it got sorted, he bought special packaging material along with catch cover hoping that it could temporarily resolve the problem. 'I still remember it was a Wednesday and it was 5.30 in the morning, and I was aboard the Black Diamond Express for Dr Patra's Asansol clinic. That's when I spotted Dilip-bhai. He was looking for me, he had come straight from the plant with a packet of freshly made drugs,' Pradip said.

'We have tamed lithium, Pradip, it will behave this time,' Dilip smiled at Ghosh. For Ghosh, what followed was like jumping from the cliff of victory into the valley of opportunity.

Their aim was to wrestle out a third of the rival's market share at Patra's clinic within the next few months, but over a few weeks, Ghosh realized that the opponent wrestler had fallen under his own weight.

When he reached Patra's Asansol clinic one day, he realized there was commotion in the pharmacy counter next door because Lithanate supply had not arrived, which meant they had to supply the rest of the lithium. 'Due to La Medica's organizational problems and financial difficulties, they couldn't supply the products on time and then discontinued it altogether. That product sold like hot cakes, counterparts from multinationals were pricey and the Sun upped its game at the right moment,' distributor Mehta said.

An interesting but bizarre story was cited by a few psychiatrists in Calcutta who seemed to believe that Sun Pharma's take-off was a direct consequence of Congress politician Sanjay Gandhi's death in a plane crash in 1980. They believed La Medica, a Delhi-based company commanded a clout in the market in the era of licence raj because of their great relations with late Sanjay Gandhi and once that advantage was gone, the company got mired in a tangle of issues, creating a supply gap, which Sun Pharma, a struggling newbie, was primed to fill in. While the story couldn't be independently verified, Shanghvi saw a semblance of truth in it.

For Dilip-bhai dealing with doctors was never a matter of anaesthetized efficiency of the cold corporate types. He never believed that standardized corporate gifts, a fad those days, could fetch him prescriptions, of the size and time length he was gunning at. He would exhort Pradip to search for small opportunities, where they could help the doctor with the 'warmth of a close one'. It was not about snooping or spying but keeping your eyes open to an opportunity to help. And never ask for anything in return, as that fails the purpose. 'Doctors could take care of their big academic and medical decisions, we took care of small things, where they felt inefficient and helpless,' Ghosh said.

When Dilip chanced upon a senior psychiatrist frustrated with his patients for crumpling the prescription to an extent that he couldn't read his own handwriting, which was an insect crawl to begin with, he ordered special, small-sized, handy plastic folders. When he found one Dr Dutta yelling at his compounder for not attending to termite-ridden cabinets in the clinic, he offered to help. Before he finished offering, Pradip went out to catch hold of a carpenter in the locality to work up the wooden racks. Pradip, naturally gregarious, took this to the next level.

When he heard Dr Nandi talking about power cuts during small-scale CME (continuing medical education)-like programmes that he held in his clinics, he learnt a trick from an electrician friend. He switched from alternating to direct current (AC to DC) to avert electricity disruption during programmes, which earned him an epithet of 'a friend in need, a friend indeed' from Dr Nandi.

It worked often, but could backfire at times. On one occasion, Pradip thoughtfully packed some snacks for doctors taking a train to Darjeeling for Eastern Zonal Conference. A few of them turned it into 'doctors taking service from pharma companies' issue at their annual general meeting. Pradip was called to be present, but in general, doctors in Calcutta cutting across their rivalries loved him, and such issues fizzled out. That remained the case thirty-eight years later. 'For some reason, Sun's product felt like home-made, handcrafted and made with care. Gradually, Lithosun became to lithium carbonate, what Xerox had become to photocopying, a synonym,' Bhattacharya said.

Besides doctors, the list Dilip-bhai had readied was of existing and potential places where he could get orders to supply Lithosun in bulk. And that meant spending a good amount of time not only with doctors but striking friendships with a range of people—from purchase managers to storekeepers. 'With the storekeeper of Gobra Mental Hospital, a diehard communist supporter, Dilip-bhai would profess unstinting support for the Communist Party of India (Marxist),' Ghosh said. 'It was perfectly possible that he stepped into another doctor's clinic next and supported the Congress party, and in the very next swore by Jana Sangh. He always taught me not to argue with the customer and that too much talking is not wise marketing,' Ghosh continued. Besides mental hospitals, he also cracked places like Dumdum Jail, which emerged as a ready marketplace for antidepressants, given the state of mind of prison inmates.

As Sun grew, this 'warm efficiency' culture with customers turned into its single most effective marketing strategy. The 'professional' had always been dealt with a personal touch, never in a 'strip off emotion' or 'dry formality' mode. And every one responds to warm care and respect, even doctors. Many doctors in Kolkata cite recent instances of 'Sun Company' helping senior doctors receive treatment in Mumbai.

'In one case of a very senior doctor here, Dilip visited the hospital in Mumbai so many times while Pradip arranged for everything else. It is so reassuring, they are there for you when you need them the most,' a psychiatrist said.

In 2015, Dr Patra, who had given Sun its first prescription, turned ninety-three. 'He had some trouble, and I got a call first from Pradip and then from Dilip-bhai to sort it out. When I did sort it out and was leaving his Bardhaman residence, he suddenly hugged me tight for five long minutes. I was speechless, but then he said, "The first two minutes of the embrace was for you and the last three for Dilip. Tell him, I may not meet him in this life, but wherever I am in my next, I will catch up with him again,' Butta said and paused. After a few seconds, he resumed, 'This is the emotional capital Dilip-bhai has invested and earned here in Calcutta.'

Lithosun to Prodep

Finally, Ghosh had an answer to a question of psychiatrists that had started haunting him by the second year, 'Lithosun, when is your second Sun coming?'

There were times then, when Ghosh felt impatient flogging only one drug, especially during initial errands at chemist shops where he struggled for months to get orders for two boxes of Lithosun, and saw chemists placing orders of twenty boxes of Phenergan over phone.

'But I knew we were preparing to launch more drugs. Molecules, especially that of Torrent Pharm, were dissected by Dilip-bhai for their potential. Interestingly he focused more on the smaller ones (those with a smaller market size) than the bigger ones,' Ghosh reckoned.

Just as the sale of Lithosun picked up, which it did starting about the ninth month, Sun launched Promasun (Promethazine hydrochloride), positioning it as a drug that tackled the side effects of other psychotropic drugs and followed it up with Nitrosun (a treatment for insomnia). By the end of the first or second year, Sun had earned ₹25,000, and by the next year-end it was adding over ₹50,000 every month to its revenue, distributor Mehta estimated. By 1982, it had already clocked a yearly revenue of ₹10 lakh.

Dilip and Pradip took interviews together and hired mostly a bunch of freshers—Satya, Shubhashish, Shambhu, Sudeep, at times debating over how much does appearance matter. Pradip insisted it surely does for a marketing job while Dilip argued—none at all. 'It's only what's inside that matters, rest can always be donned to the need, was Dilip-bhai's thought,' Pradip said.

And some of those sessions were fun riots. 'Dilip-bhai had such a talent to mimic doctors; he could make us roll with laughter. One serious candidate walked in with large spectacles covering half his face, who didn't smile at all, not even at an intended joke. The moment he walked out, Dilip-bhai said, "Oh my god, this one is an incarnate of Dr A.B. Dutta," and both of us had a good laugh.' At times, he picked guys from Dawa Bazaar he judged as sharp. One of them was Pulak Mukherjee, who was working at friend Girish's medicine shop. Of the employees who wore badges of—001 to 010, eight are still working with Sun. One has passed away working for Sun and one was asked to leave.

Starting 1980, they started growing their market outside of West Bengal—in Bihar, Orissa and the north-east. On one occasion, Dilip and Pradip travelled to Ranchi on unreserved tickets, by striking a friendship with the TTE (travelling ticket examiner) to crack the psychiatry institute. They started supplying to institutes like Davis Institute, but when it came to exploring individual doctors in Bihar, Pradip was at a loss when some of them asked, 'Have you brought positive gift?' It was later while exchanging notes with other medical representatives that he realized that 'positive gift' is the local code for liquor. Dilip was often seen riding pillion on distributor Pappu's bike in Patna, waiting at the reception counters at doctors' clinics along with other medical reps to generate business.

In Orissa, they checked into Bombay Hotel near Cuttack station owned by a Gujarati. 'Orissa, we entered in 1981 to a great response. Dr Arjuna Reddy* started prescribing Lithosun from day one. But on the third visit, he screamed at me, "What happened! I am the only one writing your drug, no one else is. If your plane doesn't take off on time, it will crash. Make others write, or I stop,"' Pradip said. But others started soon after, and prescriptions for Promasun and Nitrosun came in plenty. The north-east proved to be almost a virgin territory for psychiatry, when Pradip penetrated it with colleague Sudeep. Their

Assam stockist Laurel placed an unthinkable record first order of 800 boxes of Trazine S, their latest launch in 1982.

By 1983, Dilip had started testing the Bombay market and felt they were ready to spread their wings. 'Armed with five drugs, Dilip-bhai declared it was time for us to participate in national conferences, and the conference of the Indian Psychiatrist Society to be held at KEM (King Edward Memorial) Hospital on 4 January was the first such conference we attended,' Ghosh said. Dilip adopted his Calcutta-tested 'catch them young' model to befriend Michael Pareira* and Narendra Gaske* and other postgraduate students of psychiatry at Nair Hospital, who were organizing the conference. This helped him access the list of participating doctors and chalk out names they wanted to go after.

Pradip, along with his wife and the new Sun recruit Satya, packed 100 kilos of Lithosun promotional literature into cartons along with *luchi* and *aloor dom* (deep-fried flatbread somewhat similar to puri and a potato-based dish like dum aloo) for their journey to Bombay. 'One early winter morning, I spotted Dilip-bhai pacing across a platform at Dadar station, peeping into train windows looking for us. He was there to receive us with a trolley and a coolie,' Pradip said. But the train authorities had them put the stuff in cargo, dubbing it too heavy for passenger cabin and it had to be retrieved at Victoria Terminus (now Chhatrapati Shivaji Maharaj Terminus) station.

Cartons rocking atop their cab, they left for Dilip-bhai's uncle's place at Mahim, where all of them put up for the next two days. But that amounted to just a few hours of stay at the uncle's residence, considering the number of doctors they had to chase. 'The doctors from Calcutta were much more accessible in Bombay, and we made the most of it, meeting as many we could, looking after their needs, pitching our drug,' Pradip said.

Dr Bhattacharya, who was putting up at YMCA for that conference, remembered Sun coming into its element in that conference. So did Ranabir Ghosh Roy, another practising psychiatrist who was a chain-smoker. During the conference, Roy, stepped out for a smoke and chat every now and then with other young psychiatrist friends of his. On one such occasion, out of habit he reached out to his pocket to draw out a cigarette pack, and found it empty. From behind him, he saw a stretched palm offering him a cigarette of just the brand he smoked. He turned around expecting a familiar face, but found a stranger, and these moments of smoke-filled camaraderie were not unusual in such buzzing conferences.

It was a three-day conference, and the first two days the food was oily junk, Ghosh Roy remembered. 'The last day when we had to rush for Goa, I remember Sun hosting the lunch and the food felt so home-made, just the kind you like to have while travelling. That is where I spotted the cigarette-offering stranger, running around,' Ghosh Roy added.

Since he knew Pradip from Calcutta, he took him to a side and casually asked, 'Pradip, is this fellow who's running around your Bombay medical representative?'

Pradip erupted into full-throated laughter 'I am sorry, sir, I forgot to introduce you. This is my boss, Dilip Shanghvi, the owner of Sun Pharma.'

That left Ghosh Roy gaping for a moment. 'I had seen many company owners, but none like Dilip. The usual owner likes to order around—"Hey, Pradip, can you bring a cigarette for the doctor?" But this man was so different, I couldn't resist embracing him,' Ghosh Roy said. The incident continues to move him even after three decades.

Ghosh Roy hugged him right there without caring about the crowd of the conference and prophesied, 'You really own the Sun, Dilip, and sky is the limit for you. Remember my words when you reach there.' After a decade, he would again remind these words to Dilip Shanghvi, when Sun Pharma went public.

Dilip and his team celebrated the success of their first conference with a song and movie. Back home, Pradip picked up a harmonium and sang a Bengali bhajan, which Dilip translated to Gujarati for his mother. But when his mother said, 'Let's make it a ritual, Pradip, we can do this more often,' Dilip laughed and said, 'No, no, this much song and dance is enough.' Late that night, all of them went out for the last movie show of the day running at the nearest theatre.

As Dilip started focusing on engineering growth elsewhere, Pradip consolidated their gains in the eastern region. That meant having, among a range of other qualities, a back that could take nights of bus travels on bumpy roads, a heart that could digest with a smile unprovoked anger of some big egos who had a rightful claim to treat egos of others, and a wife who didn't mind cooking *ghugni* (dried yellow peas cooked with gravy) and turning her home into an office for an ever-growing army, that called themselves the Sun boys.

The back-breaking trips for Pradip to expand and deepen Sun's footprints could be tiring in most parts but also dangerous in some. One such experience happened just two days before Dilip's wedding in Bombay in 1982. An excited Pradip along with his wife had bought tickets and gifts for the occasion. Three days to the marriage, Pradip was travelling from Assam to Calcutta via Siliguri to screen marketing representatives and also to appoint the company's stockist there. He wanted to reach home quickly as they were to leave for Bombay the next day, but unfortunately the North Bengal tour of the then prime minister Indira Gandhi coincided with his own and all day buses were cancelled due to security reasons. So he went to book himself on what were known as 'rocket buses' for their speed despite their creaking bodies.

The only seat available was one in the last row, and because Pradip was fatigued travelling for the last few days, he booked himself into another private bus, where the ticket-counter man promised him the prized seat next to the driver. 'The driver drove like mad, with passengers swaying wildly, only to run into a head-on collision at Malda. The driver died on the spot and his blood spilled all over,' Pradip recalled.

When he picked up his belongings including the blood-soaked Lithosun samples from the gruesome site, trying to make sense of what had just happened, he was told by another passenger that he was bleeding profusely. They saw the rocket bus speeding by and the passengers screamed, jumped and waved, pleading the bus to stop, but it sped past.

When they finally managed to catch a vehicle to Calcutta, they found the 'cruel rocket bus' parked ahead of them. Passengers led by Pradip went to scold the driver for his lack of empathy, only to find him frozen on his seat in what looked like an empty bus. 'When you were waving at me to stop, I was driving the vehicle at gun point. Some robbers had hijacked and looted the bus, the passengers having fled for their life,' the trembling driver mumbled. Pradip thanked his stars for the 'double life line' he had been blessed with that day.

Home with thirteen stitches and a severe elbow fracture, Pradip's biggest regret was that he had missed Dilip's marriage. Almost a week after that, a black sedan stopped at his doorstep. Dilip had returned to Calcutta the same day and taken Hitesh's car to look him up. He sat on the head of his bed, asking after his health, as Pradip's wife brought him tea and ghugni, complimenting him for the beautiful wedding ring on his finger. Two days later, Pradip picked himself up against all medical advice, wrapped a shawl around himself to cover the plaster, and took off for a medical conference with Lithosun samples in his bag. He even narrated his 'miraculous escape' to all those who asked him, amidst all the clinical chatter and cutlery clink.

Pradip who has been by the side of Calcutta doctors, when someone's wife was having a difficult childbirth, compiling the residential addresses of all doctors to distribute wedding invitation cards for someone's son, picking a colour for someone's newly built home, and helping with funerals of senior doctors and their fathers, is not seen in Calcutta as any other usual pharma salesperson. 'We invite very few pharma marketing men to our social functions. But Pradip babu has been to my son's wedding, and I have been to his daughter's. He is different,' Bhattacharya said. He defied the image of just another professional and had woven himself into the social milieu of doctors' lives in the city. Peers saw him as someone who could dig out 'access routes to doctors' kitchens'.

Doctors, who started practising in Calcutta since the early 1990s, including those whose fathers had served as well-known psychiatrists in the city, see 'Pradip-da' as the lifeblood of the company. 'Pradip-da is special. I remember when my father's driver fell ill, he would send his driver for weeks on end, no questions asked, while he himself took the tram to work,' Anjan Boral, a psychiatrist whose father G.C. Boral was an eminent psychiatrist, said.

The day Boral junior passed his MBBS, Pradip happened to visit Boral senior. 'Those were monsoon days, and it was pouring in Calcutta, and Pradip-da had brought an umbrella as a gift for my father. The moment my father told him about my clearing MBBS, he fished out another umbrella and gifted me, saying, "You have earned your own now,"' Boral junior said. And, of course, Pradip was right there when Boral senior's last rites were being performed.

About Pradip's equation with Dilip, a famous psychiatrist said, 'Dilip treated Pradip just like his Lakshman, and Pradip treated himself like Hanuman to his Dilip-bhai.' Almost one decade after Pradip had been rechristened 'Lithosun', Dilip, famously stingy with compliments, launched another antidepressant drug and called it 'Prodep'.

The medical community in Calcutta suspected that it was his own unsaid way of honouring an indispensable lieutenant. 'If it was named Anti-dep, it was understandable but why would an antidepressant be named Prodep if not after Pradip,' Basu said, disregarding the fact that the original corresponding brand promoted globally by Eli Lilly was called 'Prozac'. For a very long time, all of us called 'Pradip babu' lovingly 'Prodep', Bhattacharya recalled.

Long after that, when music maestro A.R. Rahman's debut song of the super-hit romantic thriller *Roja* that went:

I have a little heart, a little hope,
an innocent hope of a fun-filled heart,
All I want is to touch the moon and the stars,
all I want to do is fly in the sky,

played out of psychiatrist Basu's television set, the image that flashed across his mind was not of the movie's fresh-faced starlet Madhu but that of a young Dilip. He was at that time still two years away from taking his company public.

CHAPTER FOUR

DIY KIT FOR MAKING A MILLION

Nitin owed Dilip one, Dilip owed Nitin big time and Nitin owed Vinod big time too. Since Sailesh never smoked, he didn't owe to either of them, when it came to bets and cigarettes. In the late 1970s, theirs was a 'missed call' gang, which met up between 8.30 and 10.30 p.m., at Mathur Tea Stall. The tea stall was ironically located at a crossroads, a chowrasta, where four lanes of Bhowanipore converged.

Betting at a crossroads

'Either of us—Dilip, Sailesh or I would first give a missed call on the others' landline, which essentially was a coded invitation to the tea stall. If the others were ready, each of them would return a missed call, which meant that the plan was on and we would see each other in a few minutes,' Mehta smiled. When they gathered, it would be general chatter over repeats of cutting chai, and about 10–12 cigarettes for Dilip, which he smoked in quick succession over two hours. 'He wouldn't smoke his cigarette till the end, but light up a fresh one with his half-burnt one,' Sailesh recalled.

Interestingly, a psychiatrist who is a smoker himself identified this quirk with ambitious and driven individuals, who are in a hurry to achieve things, and are not necessarily enjoying the act of smoking.

Nitin was almost a tea addict, and would easily order 4–5 repeats of cutting chai. One of those days, Dilip placed a bet with Nitin.

'Nitin, it's not great to slurp so much tea in one go. You will become dependent on that stuff,' Dilip advised.

'It's not so healthy to smoke cigarettes as well. I can quit tea, what can you quit?'

'I can quit cigarettes, if you quit tea. Here it goes', Dilip said, dropping his lighted cigarette butt right there, crushing it under his slippers.

'It's a bet then, but mind you, it's not so easy to quit smoking in a blink. If you really manage to quit, I would pay you 100 bucks on top of quitting tea,' Nitin said. He was speaking from experience, having known the struggle of quitting cigarettes at the age of eighteen, after facing a threat of being ostracized. Nitin was heading for a movie, when class topper Vinod Mody announced that he couldn't be friends with anyone who was a 'smoker'.

'Nitin thought no one knew that he smoked too. But I knew all along. He wouldn't do so in the open knowing all too well how much I detested smoking, but the way Dilip quit smoking that day in an instant was remarkable,' Sailesh recalled.

'For many years after that bet I didn't touch tea and Dilip-bhai quit smoking altogether, I guess. I owe Vinod for the nudge to give up smoking and now that you have reminded me, I owe Dilip-bhai ₹100 for that bet plus interest, of course,' Nitin chuckled, after almost four decades. It was a bet where no one lost, and it was one of the first glimpses into an art Dilip would master, to create such non-zero-sum deals.

Friends had begun to notice another talent in Dilip. Just like he changed opinions in debates with a few potent words, he could create causalities to have the effect he desired, like quitting cigarettes or setting up a factory, getting the people he wanted to be with him. He could softly bend people's will and direct them to achieve what he wanted, and that included his own, foremost.

A Shuffle and the Shift

'I had promised that I would help him, but the boy had tremendous guts to have taken the plunge to build a factory, when all he had was three products in his kitty and a precarious financial backing,' Shashi-kant said.

'For the first few years, it would have been much more viable to have continued with that loan-licensing model, given the size of operations and the total sales at the time. In the initial years, running the factory for 7–8 days a month was enough to meet the demand. Anyone else in his place would have perhaps continued with loan licensing for a few years more. But Dilip was very clear that he wanted his own place to make the drug,' Upen added.

To many around him, the decision to shift to Bombay and build a factory at Vapi appeared super bold and instant, almost impulsive, but was it? On a Saturday get-together, friend Vinod Mody recalled Dilip informing their group that he planned to visit the Grand Hotel the next day where the chief minister of Gujarat, Madhav Singh Solanki, was to speak.

'Our forefathers had left Gujarat in search of opportunities. Solanki was trying to reset the clock and exhort Gujaratis to return to their roots and explore business opportunities back in the state. Gujarat was not the top business story then. It became one after the Narmada dam was built and later during Narendra Modi's time,' Vinod said. But to his utter surprise, by the next evening, when the group met again, Dilip had not only been to the Grand, but had also booked a shed of 4000-odd square feet in Vapi to start his factory.

'This twenty-five-year-old goes to hear out a chief minister. There on the spot he makes a decision to build a factory at a place where he has no base. It came as a thud to us, like a romantic tale. Our first reaction was that of being overwhelmed, none of us could imagine one among us taking such a leap. Where was the experience, the knowledge, the resources to buy such pricey machines that go into making a factory? His talent was all too latent, and most of us were living too sheltered a life in our joint families to start dreaming of a future independent of it,' Vinod wondered. He had a point—most of them had joint families or business set-ups, some sort of a safety net to bank on, but not Dilip, not matching his burning drive and talent.

And Dilip's plunge that appeared so impulsive to his friends like Vinod actually wasn't so. It would be among the first of his business decisions that struck bystanders as 'too sudden to be premeditated', but was not. There had been an advice and assurance from his father figure Shashi-bhai to leave Calcutta. And before he had booked the shed, he had been looking for a piece of land in Gujarat for some time. In those uncertain moments an impatient Dilip had started mulling a factory in Calcutta, one of the rare occasions when Shanti-kaka blasted him.

Also, about the same time Mukul's elder brother was considering a similar move and studying Gujarat as his option to start a manufacturing unit. 'That day when he came upstairs to our shop, my brother was leafing through reams of papers to understand the tax regime of Gujarat which was then inviting industries. I remember Dilip keen on those papers, borrowing them. And probably, he would act upon it after I left for the US. My brother couldn't make that attempt unfortunately, as he got stuck with our Calcutta factory,' Mukul recalled.

Dilip wanted Bombay to be his karmabhoomi, not because it was a city he found himself in greater sync with his energy, but because products made in the western part of India enjoyed higher credibility. He knew if they were to grow bigger and sell nationally, it would become a struggle to supply from Calcutta. Vapi, located on the southern border of Gujarat, the one it shares with Maharashtra, is around 180 kilometres away from Bombay. It was a backward area that Gujarat Industrial Development Corporation or GIDC was promoting. So land there was cheap. 'Business apart, he also felt responsible for his younger siblings and their future. And a base in Bombay would have made it much easier to find eligible suitors for his sisters—Varsha and Dipti,' Sailesh felt.

Friends in Calcutta would start seeing less and less of Dilip from this moment on. His missed calls grew infrequent as he shuffled between Bombay, Vapi and Calcutta. But what they saw through the little glimpses and heard from each other surprised them no end. He had zilch interest in sports during school, so his physical endurance had remained untested. Friends didn't see him indulging in exercise of any sort and his body type was hardly athletic enough for them to imagine the kind of stamina they saw him drawing out of some hidden reservoir.

'His physicality tells you a deceptive story about his fitness. Apart from endless gruelling journeys in second class, he spent nights living out of that factory, sleeping on a wooden table and cycling 5 kilometres to catch a meal of vada-pao in between work. The factory site was in the wilderness and work went on through the nights,' Nitin said. He also shared that when friends visited the spot, all of them including Dilip and Upen stayed at cheap budget hotels where you could cram in as many beds for ₹30 each. His cousin Nana-bhai, a structural engineer, who designed the layout, recalled sitting with Dilip on heaps of sands, supervising work through the nights. What Dilip had learnt at Shashi-bhai's factory came handy while constructing his own.

And before friends, Shashikant was the first to have hopped on to a train and visit Vapi. 'He showed me the site and we discussed the structure and equipment, a bit about the placements of machines and such things,' Shashikant recalled.

In Bombay, one of the first people Dilip contacted was his cousin, Arvind Valia, the son of his eldest maternal aunt. He was a chartered accountant, and Dilip offered him the tax and accounting work of his new company. 'We were the statutory auditors of Sun Pharma until after the listing. During Dilip's Vapi days, he lived at Krishna Kunj, our ancestral home from his mother's side. I remember visiting him in 1981–82 and finding his head buried in those scary-looking thick books on pharma machinery and equipment,' Arvind recalled.

He especially dreaded Dilip's invitation to join him for the new computer courses that he was attending in the town. 'Computers were almost like extraterrestrial gizmos back then in India, and computer courses were not my idea of fun. So every time he coaxed me, I asked Dilip to save me the computer torture,' Arvind quipped. 'Apparently, most of those pharma equipment he was reading about were imported. But later he would improvise on some of them and get many made right here at just a third of the cost,' Arvind added.

'Some of those equipment we procured on credit and instalments, since the vendors like Solace Engineering were known to us,' Upen said. He had started getting drawn into Dilip's venture, helping him bit by bit until one point when he realized that he was totally in. 'When Dilip started building this factory, I was working with a relative in Bombay who was exporting garments. Then I started helping him with work at Vapi. My involvement suddenly intensified when Dilip contracted jaundice and had to leave for Calcutta to rest for about two months.'

Ashok Butta was packing to leave for Delhi to set up his own company—which he would name Bambi and Thumper when he heard on radio about the floods in Vapi. He wondered how his friend Dilip was doing for himself. But Dilip, when he came back to rest in Calcutta, seemed to be on a different 'mission'. 'He had hardly recouped from jaundice, and he insisted he wanted to come along with us to Shikharji, the Jain pilgrimage in Bihar. We kept urging him not to strain himself and climb the 18-kilometre stretch on foot. But Dilip, who seemed to be on some mission of sorts, reassured us, 'No, I feel like it, my heart says I can do it; I will climb it on foot.' And he did it, without as much as a whine and spent a fairly long time at Bhomiya Baba temple. The rest was between him and God, conversations we were not privy to,' Piyush Doshi said.

Broken Promises

The factory would be in the making for fourteen long years as money trickled in through promises made, promises broken over cold feet, commitment honoured and investment withdrawn. Two close friends confirmed that Dilip was originally meant to start a business in partnership with his schoolmate Girish Desai, who harboured similar dreams of creating a pharmaceutical enterprise. The two had even gone to Gujarat's drug controller together to explore the prospects. The friends and relatives, who knew of this incident, were under the impression that in the nick of time when things were almost getting finalized, the budding partnership fell through as elders in Girish's family objected to a partnership with Dilip on a 'small issue', or perhaps his inexperience, and decided against investing in the venture. Girish would, at about the same time as Dilip left Calcutta, form a company in Baroda by the name Milmet that specialized in ophthalmological products.

Girish Desai, forthcoming on most other issues, said he didn't wish to touch upon this matter and Shanghvi said he didn't recall the specifics, but added, 'Essentially he wanted to be in ophthalmology and since we had a business in psychiatry which we understood better, there was no harmony in the paths we had chosen. So it's possible that it was a mutual decision or I might have communicated that the partnership was not feasible in the context of different interests.' And yet their interests would converge at a critical turn in future.

It was around this time that Natu-kaka, Shanti-kaka's partner helped rope in his cousin Pravin Bavishi to invest in Dilip's nascent venture. Combining that with loans and savings from his business, Dilip built his first factory.

The first tablets from that factory started getting manufactured in 1983, the time in clock and calendar that Sun believes it was truly born. This happened even as the facility was still being built, 'Upgrading the factory year on year was a challenge. We were short of money, not because we were not making enough, but because we had begun to expand markets outside of the eastern states and were introducing new products. For some, we needed to import raw material—the bulk drugs. Demand wasn't huge to start with. But you had to import a basic minimum, if you had to import at all. So those bulk drugs worth lakhs would be preserved like museum artefacts for a whole year. Funds would get locked in, but you couldn't do without that,' Upen, who had joined Dilip as a partner, explained.

'We were growing 100 per cent year on year and we would apply for a 100 per cent increase in facility but banks were always gingerly about parting with money. By the time they released funds, the year for which we had made the application would have passed, and our appetite grown,' he said while describing the company's race against time. At the time, the factory's capacity reached about twelve million tablets but Sun was still selling less than even half a million. Shanghvi started getting offers to rent out the unused capacity to churn out tablets for others, which had the potential to earn him about ₹60,000 every month. But he decided against it, saying that such measures would dilute their focus from creating brands, which is what he had set out to do.

Shashikant shared that Dilip would often show up at his door from time to time. He would ask for a tip on this or that or a few thousand rupees he owed someone—an equipment guy, a raw material guy. 'I always gave him the money, no questions asked. He was someone whom you could trust with money matters,' Shashikant said. Shanghvi said he had an informal trust-based arrangement with Shashi-bhai since the time he used his facility. Whenever Dilip could spare money, he would let Shashi-bhai keep it in his safe with an understanding that it would be given back as and when he needed it. While building his factory he needed all that money plus more, which Shashi-bhai kept lending him from time to time. 'He kept his promise despite losing about ₹40,000 worth of monthly business from Sun,' Shanghvi recalled.

'All that chaotic frenzy that such speedy growth entailed didn't deter Dilip,' Upen said. His mind was focused on solving a problem that had bothered psychiatrists—toxicity levels of lithium carbonate. If he could develop a version of Lithosun that released itself gradually into the human body, rather than in one burst, he could possibly offer a solution and have an edge over his competitors. Thus began work on Lithosun's sustained release, with the two chemists Sun had recruited in Vapi.

Torn between too many things, it was time for Dilip to ring up old friends, and offer not just an unwinding stories-filled evening over tea at the chowrasta. Maybe the wait at the crossroads was over, may be it was time to choose a path.

Dial-up Friends

In January 1983, when Nitin's phone started ringing, he wasn't expecting a call from Dilip. He knew Dilip was yet to return from his honeymoon in Darjeeling. Marriage had marked the end of the 'missed calls' era for friends. Dilip got married in November 1982 to Vibha. A year before, Nitin and Sailesh had also got hitched.

The call for Nitin turned out to be an offer, the path he was so looking for, to leave Calcutta and try out something else in life. But it arrived in an anticlimactic style. When they met, Dilip offered Nitin something but the latter had no clue how to handle it.

'But Dilip, I am zero when it comes to manufacturing and pharma industry. I know nothing about sales tax and excise either,' a puzzled Nitin answered.

'I know that too, but I would still want you to take charge of Vapi operations. I have seen how you have learnt the charity work from your father and the honesty with which you perform it. Also, I will be there every third day to back you, but the only condition is you would have to settle in Vapi,' Dilip was extremely straightforward with him. Nitin knew Dilip was architecting a non-zero-sum deal like the cigarette-tea one, but the offer had bounced at him out of the blue. He sought a week's time to rearrange his thoughts, consult his father and respond.

Both Dilip and Nitin knew that time was running out for the winding wall clock business his father owned, as they stood on the cusp of a technological revolution in watchmaking, where a quartz-crystal-powered science had already taken Switzerland, the Mecca of the watch industry, by storm. This revolution was also shaking up the Indian clockmakers, most of whom were still stuck in the mechanical clock period. Nitin didn't take the whole week he had asked for to say yes to Dilip.

The same month Dilip took Nitin and his father around Vapi. But Nitin's yes was not going to be complete without a nod from Jeyram-bhai Aghara, the owner of Rivex, whose clocks they distributed in the eastern region. 'From Vapi, we went to Rajkot to seek Jeyram-bhai's blessing. My father respected him way too much to take major decisions without his advice. And Jeyram-bhai was very practical, always wishing well for us. He told us "Go ahead; that way you have a chance to beat recession in the clock industry. Who knows how deep this slump will be and how dark the coming days can get!" He didn't tell us, but we knew that family disputes had also crept into his business which made the impending threat sound more real,' Nitin recalled.

Nitin was misty-eyed when he parted with family in February. But his father tore out a page of lesson from his life book that Nitin adopted as the philosophy of his own life. 'Son, you will work with your friend. But remember money is transient; it's here today, there tomorrow. The two things that can be earned forever are trust and integrity. Work in a way that no one can ever point a finger at you,' Nitin recalled his father telling him as a parting shot, with a hint of mist in his own eyes.

'It is true that if one had to score on integrity and trustworthiness in the group, I would have marked Nitin right on the top,' friend Vinod Mody said. It is also true that for a long time to come Dilip would rate trust and integrity over competence when it came to recruiting people for his entrepreneurial venture.

By February, Nitin had reached Vapi to join a production chemist, a quality-control chemist, an administrative executive and two other staff to begin his new journey in Sun. He was the second partner outside of family, after Upen, who was Dilip's first cousin.

'When Nitin joined the factory, according to his own admission, he could have gone looking for a horse at the mention of horsepower.

It wasn't easy for a small wall clock trader to start running a factory the next day. But when I went to Vapi for auditing and had lunch at his house, he confided in me, that Dilip trusted him completely and that made it easy for him to learn. Also, Nitin earned tremendous goodwill locally,' Arvind said.

'For the first three months, Dilip would visit Vapi every third day and Upen would turn up twice a week, so that, every other day, someone was there. In three months, this reduced to once a fortnight, and in six months the trips became monthly as I eased into the role,' recalled Nitin. 'It was here and in the years that followed, it struck me how calm Dilip could be under crisis. The first such realization hit me after I committed two blunders in the initial years. He treated them so casually passing them as mistakes one needs to make to learn,' Nitin said.

Those were still early days, and the company was clocking a few lakh rupees in sales when Nitin stared in disbelief at what he had done. A computation error in excise had ended up in a loss of ₹60,000. 'I was shocked and offered to pay up the amount from my salary,' Nitin recalled. '"A mistake is a mistake, you didn't do it on purpose, Nitin, or anyone could have made it, even me," Dilip-bhai said, moving on to crack a joke next.'

But it was his first oversight, and Nitin spent a few sleepless nights mulling over it, meaning to offer Dilip the money once more the next Thursday, when he was to meet him in the Bombay office. Dilip had started off by working from his maternal uncle's Nariman Point office, and then went on to buy 80-sq.ft basement office space in Vile Parle (East) from this uncle, who owned a real-estate firm, Dosti Builders. On Thursday, they were having lunch that had arrived from Upen's place, and Nitin was about to broach the matter when someone told him his father was on the line.

'Thank you. Yes, I am fine. Things are fine,' Nitin murmured to his father over the phone and returned to the lunch table.

'Why did you start with a thank you?' Dilip asked.

'It's my birthday today,' a shy Nitin said.

'I hope you are not going back to Vapi tonight, we must celebrate. I am booking the hotel for dinner, if you have tickets cancel them now,' Dilip said.

'He had completely forgotten what had happened a few days back while I was burning inside. That's how fast he gets over mistakes, how he doesn't allow mishaps to break the tempo of his journey—the reason why he moves on in life,' Nitin said.

Nitin was yet to recover from the first when another thunderbolt struck him. One day he walked into the factory to discover a bulk drug, worth about one lakh rupees, lying waste, probably due to a worker's slippage. Dilip passed that off as a mistake as well, but Nitin hung on to the few words his friend had uttered when he was distraught after the computation error, to learn and forgive himself for mistakes.

'Nitin, we have come empty-handed from Calcutta. We can go back the same any time, no one can stop us from doing that, right!' Dilip had told Nitin.

Making and owning up to mistakes meant that you were still trying, a lesson that would be crystallized into Sun's work philosophy in times to come. Dilip believed that if one person made a mistake and owned up to it, it gave thousands of others in the company a chance to learn from; and if people were not allowed to make mistakes, they froze at work. So product review meetings a decade later would institutionalize these sessions dedicated to 'our failures and what we learnt from them'. And Shanghvi claimed that at Sun people are assessed on the basis of their contribution, not their mistakes.

'If there is something called a "graduation in the discipline of experience", I have earned that degree in Sun Pharma. The one institution that served as an alma mater to me was Sun,' Nitin Mehta felt.

The other friend who had been getting persistent invitations to join Sun was Sailesh. Dilip and his tall, ruddy, warm-hearted friend were meant to be together. They had always been a team and tasted how little victories felt to be relished. This was an opportunity to make something far bigger happen. Besides, his experience of having run a factory made him an asset for Sun.

'After Dilip and Nitin left, life was not the same in Calcutta. Our factory was doing fine, life had settled into the usual humdrum after marriage, but there were no more lively sessions in the evening. Life without friends was a vacuum. I knew Dilip's business was doing well, at least much better than ours. During his Calcutta visits, he kept cajoling me to join him,' Sailesh recalled.

But Sailesh had a situation at home. The moment he tried to bring up the subject to join Dilip, his brother experienced a sharp pang of separation and broke down. Sometime in 1985, when Dilip was in Calcutta, and heard from Sailesh what had been brewing for months, he had a chat with Sailesh's brother. 'What Sailesh would earn and learn there would be so much more. Wouldn't that help the family more? This arrangement would turn out for the better for everyone. And if it doesn't I promise Sailesh can return in a year's time,' Sailesh recalled Dilip convincing his brother. So in 1986, Sailesh dismounted the train at Vapi, to enter the Sun family as the third partner outside of Dilip's family. 'I was living with Nitin for the first three months in Vapi and saw the kind of hard work he had put into running the factory,' Sailesh said. They frequented Bombay often and put up with Dilip at Krishna Kunj with Vibha serving them hot chapattis, amidst roaring laughter and detail-oriented planning that went into the shaping of the company.

The partnership structure that was worked out was interesting. Almost all partners agreed that it was more legalese than reflection of the real roles one held then. There was Sun Industries, the manufacturing and marketing company, in which Dilip Shanghvi, Shantilal Shanghvi and Jayant Sanghvi were partners and then a distribution company, Aditya Medisales in which Dilip's mother Kumud Shanghvi, Jayesh Shanghvi (Upen), Nitin Mehta and Sailesh Desai were partners.

At an earlier date, Pravin Bavishi, Natu-kaka's cousin had invested and been a partner in Sun, but after he had withdrawn his funds in a short span of time, Sun Industries remained strictly owned by the family members. Everyone did a bit of everything when the need arose, but roughly Upen took care of finance, accounts and procurement, Nitin took care of manufacturing and operations. Sailesh had just joined and took over streamlining of the Vapi factory, marketing as well as setting up another factory and keeping regulatory relations going. Dilip was in charge of products and marketing and all things else. He was the managing partner.

Whatever profits the company made, and it made substantial for a start-up, was almost fully ploughed back into four areas—new equipment and machinery, new products, new territories and recruiting people. 'From day one he would use all profits to buy machines that increased production, and lab-testing equipment that helped us cut the number of days for our tests. The rest Dilip-bhai spent on hiring medical representatives and introducing new products,' Nitin said.

In 1984, when Ashok Butta flew in from Delhi, and called Dilip to catch up, he invited him over to his 80-sq.ft office in Ville Parle. 'My business Bambi and Thumper had started doing well. I had been soaking in the flashy show-sha of Delhi culture. So when I landed up in his cubicle-sized office and saw him behind his table, I was like: 'Poor thing, all this way he came from Calcutta with a dream to make it big. But *dhanda* (work) seems to be *manda* (not too great),' Ashok said with a full-throated laughter. 'He recalled feeling sorry for his friend on the basis of a misleading impression based on the size of Dilip-bhai's office. By that time Sun sales had begun to double itself year on year. In the initial years I had never seen him spending money on himself,' Nitin said.

When the three friends joined hands in business, they took an oath. 'We had promised ourselves that we will never ever fight over money. We have united to grow together and enjoy,' Sailesh said. Nitin said in agreement, 'When we started, an internal oath was taken. We were friends and now we were turning partners. I decided if a day comes when I have to choose between friendship and partnership, I will choose friendship over partnership. Friendship is the most precious thing I have earned in my life, and I should be ready to give up business for its sake.' It is an oath they will remember and return to in future.

But before that came the celebrations. They had been to trips earlier to Shikharji, with families, and prayed together for a great future. Now that the future was upon them in 1986, they made a small departure, and booked their first five-star hotel holiday together in Goa. 'It was my first-ever five-star hotel stay, also our first luxury vacation together— the three of us and our families. A three-night package at hotel Fort Aguada and we had a blast,' Nitin reminisced.

The journey from the shores of the Bay of Bengal to the Arabian Sea for the friends had been much more than just a travel of 2000 kilometres. The three friends lazed around on the Sinquerim Beach, with waves lapping at their feet, watching the Sun rise in the distant horizon but it didn't seem so distant from where they sat. And in the waters ahead, the ship sailed.

It would turn out that many among Dilip's family and friends— his sister Dipti, Upen's brother Tripti, friends Vinod Mody and Kirti Bavishi would have either done a stint in Sun in those initial days or remember having been associated with his business in some way or the other. This could be as wide-ranging as importing raw material or being instrumental in the selection of a medicine.

Dilip may have lacked a safety cocoon of business relationships to begin with but he nurtured his friendships and relationships in business, and nourished his business with social capital around him to the maximum. He picked up a number of other friends from his Calcutta group for different sort of business associations in his early days. His classmate Gaurang Bhatt, who still resides in Calcutta, joked, 'You can say, he picked all the assets and left for Bombay and left the liabilities back here in Calcutta.' In that he was probably crafting non-zero-sum deals.

Pradip Sheth, Dilip's senior in school and now a trustee in the board of his school, attributed part of this skill to the 'Gujarati brotherhood' instilled in his school. He cited numerous such instances of smaller business set-ups, where such networks flourished. 'Unlike individualistic one-upmanship culture in today's cut-throat competitive era, our school environment was very focused on imparting a team spirit among Gujaratis. It said, "You are here irrespective of your disadvantages in life because you are a Gujarati. In life, to do well you don't have to defeat your Gujarati brother. If you can stand by him, all of you would prosper."' Sheth's observation has merit, as 99 per cent of the population till the 1970s were Gujaratis in Bhagushala.

But one cannot discount Upen's straight and simple point. 'Where would you go if you are starting a business? The people you have relations with and you trust. Which professional worth his salt will give you his time of the day when you are a nobody? You end up counting on and involving people you know out of necessity, not choice.' Years later Shanghvi seconded that, 'A businessman goes through an entire process of evolution. Right at the beginning, you have anxieties and insecurities about trusting people. Over time you realize that all the functions can be managed by unknown people through establishing processes and systems. Trust is the key driver behind getting people to work with you when you are just about starting. With my friends, they will never short-change, or take undue advantage of a situation. I could trust them totally.'

CHAPTER FIVE

THE SATSANG SALE

Sundaresh S. Raju wasn't a kindred spirit in a strictly technical sense, but it will be difficult to argue otherwise. Being the manager of a company for which Shanti-kaka was a stockist made Raju part of the social capital Dilip inherited. But not everybody working with him in the Bombay basement office at Ville Parle in 1987 knew of that connection. At least, Hiren Desai, his office assistant-cum-accountant-cum-petty cash manager of three years, didn't.

It was Independence Day, 15 August, the sky was overcast, and a patriotic song played at a distance somewhere. Since it was a holiday, Desai didn't rush to keep the register at Dilip-bhai's table. This register had details of how many orders stockists had placed and how much payment they had made the day before. He didn't expect Dilip-bhai to enter the office today with a usual, 'How many orders, how much payment, Hiren?' and then flash a smile if the numbers were good. He loved his boss for this candour.

He had asked Dilip-bhai on the day of his recruitment if he could be considered for a better job, given his degree in commerce. To this he was told that his performance on the current job would decide that later. 'I cannot promise you anything today, because all I have right now is an opening of an office assistant,' Dilip had told him. Desai loved his boss, also because he stood for the possibility what a commerce graduate like him could achieve.

Since the day of the recruitment, Desai had given it his all, working through a fractured hand, working without taking a single holiday for the first five years, knowing all too well that his performance was being monitored. Also he cared for the company he had seen grow from seven employees in 1984 to 150-strong in 1987.

Days were generally long at Sun but this holiday Sundaresh S. Raju had been called for a job interview, and Hiren thought he would be done in a few hours. But Raju's 'interview' started at 10.30 a.m. and lasted well past 6.30 p.m.

The candidate seeking the job had the audacity to chain-smoke in the little air-conditioned cabin of Dilip in the new office they had moved the year before, and instead of being shown the door, he was offered lunch.

To Hiren, it must have seemed odd, because he didn't know that the job-seeker had often shared drinks with the boss's father in Calcutta. Months before the 'interview', Dilip had been catching up with Raju in Delhi where he was setting up a business for his Chennai-headquartered company, Tamil Nadu Dadha Pharmaceuticals Limited (TDPL).

The two usually met at a hotel in Connaught Place (CP), where Dilip sought his advice on various aspects of business. In July, when Dilip called him, Raju said he had fever and was resting in his Janakpuri home. Dilip offered to come and see him there. When he arrived upstairs, keeping his taxi waiting, Raju recalled asking him, 'Why have you come all the way from CP just to say hi?'

'It's a little more than that. I want you to join us,' Dilip told a stunned Raju.

'Dilip-bhai, I am forty-five years old and you have a lot to get done. I have so many responsibilities, my children are studying here, and my parents are retired. This is not an age where you should take me. You should take someone young, who can do a lot of running around,' Raju, while trying to dissuade him, said.

'I understand your point, but I wish you to join us,' Dilip repeated.

And thus the Independence Day day-long 'interview', which Upen qualified more as a 'sales pitch of the company' ended with Raju expressing a desire to see the factory at Vapi. 'In October, his friend Sailesh Desai showed me around the factory. Not that I understood any technical nitty-gritty, but you get a sense of how it is being run. By evening I told him that I would join.'

The same evening, Dilip made an offer to Sun's first all-India sales manager, which included his own car, probably a third-hand Fiat

Premier Padmini, which a former employee said he had bought from a doctor, not because he wanted a car at the time but because the doctor wanted to get rid of the vehicle.

But why did Dilip hire Raju? Raju said he had not thought much about Dilip till that point other than knowing him as the son of a business associate, who had started his own business and sought advice from time to time.

Raju couldn't possibly comment on how keenly he was being watched and since how long. He couldn't gauge whether a pair of adolescent eyes was quietly recording in his mind that he had upped the per month productivity of medical representative in his team from ₹5000 to ₹35,000 at TDPL, which led his company to make a deviation and spruce up the strength of the sales force reporting to him from three to thirteen. All of these turned out to be the top performers in the company. That Raju had been part of a team that was transforming TDPL from merely a medicine supplier to the government to a retail market player, and from one focused on south India to diversify into northern states.

'Why Dilip-bhai chose me is a question he will have to answer. One factor could be his ability to trust. He knew me from my journey at TDPL. Unlike other professionals, I was not so ambitious to go opportunity-shopping to embellish my biodata. Neither did I have an MBA degree nor an agenda,' he reckoned, adding, 'it could be that he was watching me recruiting, training people for TDPL in north India. Or it could be that he could afford me while he couldn't afford high-cost assets from multinationals. All said and done, it was a risk for me to be in an entrepreneurial venture at that stage of my career. But I liked the man, his clarity on the path ahead and the way he treated his people.'

Shanghvi said it was Raju's integrity that emerged as the most critical trait in all those years when he had observed him. 'Mr Raju was the first person I knew who travelled first-class in train at a time when the usual practice was for managers to travel second-class and bill the company on first-class to make personal savings. I respected him for that.' From this observation Dilip designed a travel policy for Sun that was different from its peers, and set a fixed amount of rupees per kilometre, instead of allotting first-or second-class ticket entitlements for his employees. 'I don't want policies that make you lie to me. The relationship between a person and the company needs to be based on trust. I don't want small reasons to distrust people,' Shanghvi stated.

Scoop the Stuff in Interview

Day-long interviews like that of Raju's may not have been commonplace, but those stretching for hours were quite the norm in the basement of Sun's Ville Parle office in the late 1980s, and that was probably the case because Shanghvi never ceased to be a student, not even while taking an interview. An interview at Sun those days was never limited to being a recruitment test of a candidate; it was a whole lot more. It was a lesson in new drugs, sales pitch of Sun and an exercise for gathering market intelligence. And it could very well be that many of those who joined Sun in its toddler days walked in with a clear strategy in their head but walked out having flushed out their own plans. That's what seems to have happened with Vivek Hattangadi.

Sure he was not in Sun's office to join any job but to understand the mind of the guy who had 'dared' to introduce an antidepressant Primox rivalling his employer firm Carter Wallace's star brand Sensival (nortriptyline). For two of the four hours he spent in Shanghvi's cabin, what remains with Hattangadi today is a 'richly gratifying discussion' around a bestselling ulcer drug—Salazopyrin (sulphasalazine). This drug was an exclusive from the stable of Carter Wallace. Hattangadi shared with Shanghvi how this drug treats the disease and what its side effects are.

'The way he could converse about the mechanics of that ulcerative colitis drug in the body made me feel he was more a scientist than a businessman. Since the interview was for a product manager, I started weighing in my mind how interesting it would be to work with an owner so well attuned to the science of medicine, a really rare type in India,' Hattangadi said.

By the end of the interview, Shanghvi had not only pronounced that he would end the exclusivity of the Carter Wallace's ulcer drug in India, but had also enlisted Hattangadi's support in his mission. Soon after, Sun made its foray into the gastro market by launching a hit product

Mesacol (mesalazine) to treat distal ulcerative colitis that became the leading product in its category by 1992.

Not strikingly different was the experience of H.K. Pahwa, who, while working at TDPL, received a call from his just-defected boss Raju, who tried to entice him into joining Sun. Having not heard much about this company, he made a call to his friend at Torrent, a company which he knew to be the ace player in psychotropic drugs.

'It's a tiny company but is rising very fast and giving a tough fight to Torrent in eastern India. If they offer you a tempting salary hike and a plum role, there's no harm considering the job,' Pahwa's friend at Torrent advised. So when he boarded a train for Bombay, he decided that he would take up the assignment only if it paid well.

Raju was waiting to pick him up at the station in a familial hospitality that was to become the hallmark of the company. Pahwa stayed the night over at Raju's place where he shared with him the kind of salary he was expecting if he was to join such a small firm.

At 11 a.m. the next morning, Pahwa was sitting across from this chap, whom he judged to be a few years younger and many kilos heavier than him, 'with a sharp glitter in his eyes that seemed to be taking in details, not so obvious.' He noticed—as any pharma salesperson would—that Dilip wasn't wearing a tie. The discussion that ensued about the chemical composition and working of a cardio drug 'isosorbide mononitrate' shattered all images Pahwa had conjured up of Shanghvi based on the little he had seen of pharmaceuticals business owners.

Pahwa confessed in the interview that he knew little of psychotropic drugs, and asked Shanghvi about the sort of training they would receive to grasp the speciality deeper. It was 1987, and Shanghvi smiled in response and said after a pause of reflection, 'The organization is still shaping up, we are getting there and it would take a year or two to put a formal training practice in place but as you interact with psychiatrists you would understand that they are different from other specialists. It is not so much the details of chemical work that they are interested in.'

And after that came the trump card, an emotional reasoning that stirred something in Pahwa to do a U-turn. 'Mr Raju told me about your salary expectations. What you are expecting is the salary of the second highest paid employee in Sun,' Shanghvi said. 'These are people who have been with me since the beginning and I owe them more than just gratitude. The challenge before me as we start hiring professionals is to strike a balance between their salaries and those of newcomers so that they don't feel left out,' he reasoned.

'What he said touched my heart. I felt if this person cares so much about the people who have stood by him, he would do the same for me tomorrow,' Pahwa recalled. What had also surprised Pahwa a bit was his 'straight, simple, specific' style of communication. 'Which owner wants to talk money and salary? My experience had been that they always made someone else do that, especially if the talk is uncomfortable.'

After saying 'No' to Dilip's question on whether he had any more questions for him, Pahwa recalled walking over to Raju in the basement in a trance and saying 'Yes' to the job at a much lower salary than he had expected. He was made in-charge of the northern region—the states of Delhi, Haryana and Punjab but was given a strange-sounding instruction to steer clear of Uttar Pradesh. When a perplexed Pahwa made further queries on why should a state as large and populous as UP be left out of the territory in the north, he was told in confidence that, 'Lucknow is handled by an old-timer, a Bengali gentleman Pulak Mukherjee, employee number 003. And Dilip doesn't want to send any signal that disturbs his first set of employees.' Pahwa smiled to himself and relished the accuracy of the assessment he had made of his tie-less owner.

Months after discussing cardio-molecule isosorbide mononitrate with Pahwa in his interview, Shanghvi brought it up with his new product manager Hattangadi. 'I have this beautiful cardiac product in mind but the problem is it wouldn't sell here because the lowest price at which we can launch it is still twelve times the existing product it will compete with.' Hattangadi studied the molecule and felt that Sun should go ahead and bet on it, pitching it as a product of the future.

But Shanghvi, the way he was, wouldn't just buy someone else's gut, that had to be his own, unless he was convinced that someone else's first-rate logic was a cut above his own. His team of medical advisers was swinging like a pendulum, first yes—it feels promising, but no— it's too expensive, yes—it feels useful, but no—not at the price he was considering.

Hattangadi recalled how heated and winding those meetings with medical advisers, whom he was trying to persuade, could get at times. True, Sorbitrate, the competing product for angina pain (heart-related chest pain) was selling at just 10 paise per tablet, but the medicine itself was short-acting, which means that once placed under the tongue it would have an effect reduced to half in an hour. That meant the heart patient had to take it thrice or four times a day and still be left with some windows when the drug was not active in the body. Monotrate, the Sun products was by contrast, effective for seven hours, which meant popping it only twice daily would have been enough.

Launching a sustained-release version of Monotrate could bring this to a once-daily regime, which gave the product an edge because that would mean more patients were likely to follow the regimen diligently. But still the most economical price that Shanghvi could work out for the drug was ₹4 per tablet.

'Dilip-bhai had told us that he loved to be confronted for his ideas. That he was always ready to surrender his decision if the other person's logic was superior. Also, I had full conviction about the marketability of this drug, all I had to do was create a basis for it,' Hattangadi said.

He lined up meetings with the country's leading cardiologists—particularly in Delhi and Mumbai—Dr Naresh Trehan, Dr Ashwin Mehta, Dr Dev Pehlajani, Dr M. Khalilullah and others to gauge their response to such a product. That clicked, the feedback was overwhelmingly encouraging. It is these luminaries, who were prescription trendsetters in the cardiac world, and a nod from them couldn't have meant less than a warranty card for the product's success.

Shanghvi, after perusing the thumping pat for Monotrate from leading cardiologists—a set of opinion that can be dubbed as close as one can get to gleaning evidence from the future—gave his green signal to the launch of Monotrate.

Shanghvi must have so wanted to be proved wrong on his apprehension on Monotrate given that he was working all along on a sustained-release version. He knew this would place Sun's once-a-day tablet a notch above imminent competition that was expected to be twice a day.

'Boss has a way of leading you to the solution by asking the right questions. He would just give a lead, and leave us in a maze to figure a way out and come back to him. This happened invariably when we were brainstorming around launching a new brand,' T.K. Roy, another Sun veteran who joined in 1987, said. Sun's first HR head, Bhagwat Yagnik, said in agreement, 'Dilip-bhai has an art of nudging you in the direction of a solution that he wants and then allowing you to believe that you did it.'

Pahwa was settling down in Delhi, when he received a call from Raju that went thus, 'Dilip-bhai is reaching Delhi tomorrow morning by the Air India flight to meet the Drug Controller General of India, Dasgupta. Please receive him.'

'Now when I think, I must have been plain stupid to have reached the airport to receive him on my scooter,' Pahwa recalled.

Shanghvi spotted Pahwa at the airport, looked about him for a taxi and asked him whether he had arranged for one. On knowing he hadn't, he booked one for himself and headed for Taj Mansingh. Not knowing what better to do, Pahwa kick-started his scooter and followed after the taxi, wondering whether his foolishness had annoyed his super-boss.

On reaching the hotel, Shanghvi told him softly, 'Why are you escorting me? Your time would have been more prudently invested had you met two doctors in that hour.' And Pahwa turned, about to leave, wondering for the second time if his assessment of his boss was turning out to be true, whether his slip had offended his chief when he heard Dilip's voice calling for him. When he looked back he realized how you perceive people is not necessarily how they are. 'Can you help me with the tie knot?' Shanghvi said.

In a mild trance again, Pahwa recalled turning around to knot the tie, a shade of steel grey. Pahwa adjusted the tie knot to the right size, and thought that there was no trace of miff on his face, no iota of huff in his voice. 'He didn't want any ego massage,' I realized, 'all he wanted was to get the work done.'

Knitting a Warm Sweater

T.K. Roy had enriched his English vocabulary by a word during his interview with Shanghvi that would stay with him for the rest of his life. 'Boss said I would have to operate in the niche market. Niche was a new word for me. I thought I will check up in the dictionary once home, but then he shared the chronic drugs strategy, and I got a sense of what it meant,' Roy recalled.

'Sir, if I join, I have a very high package at Raptakos, Brett & Co,' Roy told Shanghvi.

'You join. I believe in giving to those people who contribute,' Shanghvi said.

'Contribute, it appealed to me. He was clear, if you produce results, you can command a price. I was sure I would, so I joined.'

Roy was given the charge to launch Sun in Maharashtra, Gujarat and Madhya Pradesh, and later Karnataka and Andhra Pradesh were added to his portfolio. But even before he started, he recalled Shanghvi telling him to keep a few things in mind: 'Operate with a set of values. We are a prescription-driven company. Business must be brought through prescriptions and no other means. That is the starting point. Every other step flows from there. So who can give us prescription? Doctors. They are the most important drivers of our business. So learn to work for and with them. You have to anticipate and fulfil their needs. Second, people are the most important resource. So you must extend all care and concern for them to feel that the company belongs to them and they belong here. That is how you can make them perform their best.'

The company was yet to formulate a decent glossary of designations, so Roy was called something like 'marketing executive'. But in two or three years he was himself going about defining roles and responsibilities, evolving reporting structures for still entrepreneurial but fast-growing Sun. 'Dilip-bhai said, "Since you are from Raptakos, you create standards for travel fares and tools the marketing force uses." In evolving a reporting structure, he asked me to ensure that everyone wrote their own report in a way that before anyone else tells them, they get a mirror view of their performance,' Roy recalled. This was a bit like Shanghvi had made his first employee Pradip Ghosh write daily reports.

'Giving form to this unstructured company, defining what had remained hitherto undefined wasn't as onerous as it may sound. We were not even a few hundred then, and Dilip-bhai was not your typical boss. He would push us to discuss our failures, particularly his own,' Roy said.

Hattangadi recalled Shanghvi emerging out of his cabin one evening in 1989 to have a chat with everyone. He did that on occasion after munching on a snack of *khara sev* (peanut salties) or vegetable sandwich that Desai arranged for him every evening. Like other times, he sat atop a table and asked all executives to appraise him on a Likert scale, spell out his weaknesses and strength. There was a murmur amongst those sitting. 'It was still the 1980s and we had not a whiff of a smart HR concept called 360-degree review. A boss calling upon his subordinates to assess his work was unheard of. We were astonished,' Hattangadi reminisced. 'I want to use this appraisal, every six months, to assess my performance that can help us pave the right path for your company. Would you also prefer to be assessed this way?' Shanghvi asked his executives.

What amused Hattangadi even more than the idea of telling a boss where he was going wrong was his frequent use of the expression 'your company'. 'Sun felt like our company, in fact more like a home you woke up and walked into every morning. So there were times in the Bombay office, when people walked in wearing kurta-pyjamas and chappals,' Hattangadi recalled. And yes, that included Shanghvi as well.

A few minutes later, Shanghvi glanced at the clock that hung on the side wall. It was almost seven, tuition time. A young chemistry lecturer would be waiting in his cabin every alternate day to teach the basics of chemistry. On his way back to the cabin, he stopped by to invite Raju to the class, probably the second time, 'Would you like to join?'

'No, thanks, I am preparing a list of new boys we have hired. I need to start their training in the next few days,' Raju replied.

Raju said he had always been more a physics—maths guy than chemistry. In fact, in his four years of college at Bombay, the first year he had dropped biology, and in the second year, chemistry. He conceded, however, that not learning enough chemistry and grasping the science of drugs may have diverted his course within Sun, once the company started getting bigger.

The first set of boys Dilip and Raju hired were not exactly the best in class and competence. They were far from the slick marketing executives with immaculate mannerisms (not that Sun could really afford them) but those who could learn fast. 'You could be good, but if you are too conscious of that fact, that could be the end of you. We were looking for people not great to start with but with a hunger to learn and the ability to pick up what we wanted to teach. We had confidence in our training,' Raju said. A cursory glance at the class X certificate was enough for Raju to figure out his basic intelligence.

That sounded plausible, given the experiences of the marketing representatives (MRs) who got quick promotions in Sun, like S.K. Jani Miya in the south and Hitendra Kansal in the north. Miya, a commerce graduate who turned up in a Vijayawada interview in slippers because he couldn't afford shoes, got selected out of forty candidates including some from a science background. Shanghvi had asked him a question that neither tested his science nor his sales acumen. 'What do you think of India hosting the Asian Games?' To which Miya replied, 'In India, where for so many like me, food, shelter and jobs are the priority, spending so much on sports is a waste of money.'

Kansal, who started as a Sun MR, and got elevated to regional manager reckoned, 'Usually, when companies are headhunting for a regional manager for cardiology of, say, a region, they would look for candidates of the same profile in another company. Not so in Sun; that company focuses on how well a manager has performed in whatever role he was performing in whichever therapy.' Shanghvi said he hired people not for their knowledge but for their capability, because once the knowledge is transferred, the person has little value.

The other quality Raju said he looked for in the boys was a sort of charm, among other intangible traits. 'We were looking for likeable boys who could talk freely without bringing much complexity in their interpersonal relations.' Boys who were good but too full of themselves were a 'No', the egoless the better.

'Each boy cost us, and if he turned out to be a mistake, that would mean spending again on advertisement, interviews. Dilip-bhai was very cost-conscious and wanted every penny well spent. He was also very conscious of not acquiring a "hire today and fire tomorrow" reputation,' Raju summed up.

The market was full of pharma companies which had institutionalized firing on non-performance. The sector had a high attrition rate, which had become a way of life. Some companies even flaunted this as a filtering process to get rid of incompetents. Sun consciously moulded itself as an antithesis of that. 'After firing so many so fast, some companies got branded as "*kal ka nahin bharosa*". So managers refrained from joining there. No one has ever hesitated to join Sun wondering how long he would last,' Raju claimed.

After all, Pahwa didn't have to wait for two long years for the training and development programme in Sun to get up and running. And he was soon made a trainer himself. Roy, Pahwa, Hattangadi, Raju—all of them trained Sun boys for fifteen to twenty-five days in a non-jazzy, no-frills hotel. 'Each and every aspect was well thought of to save resources and add convenience. But we never compromised on the number of days required to train them.' Dilip-bhai could drop by for a chai-pakora session anytime. Pahwa recalled him meeting the boys mostly on the last day of the session.

Kansal was one of the Sun boys in the batch of 1989, when Shanghvi arrived to chat with them on the last day. The first words he uttered to introduce himself were, 'I am the first employee of Sun Pharma'. That was the day, when while giving a brief glimpse into his ambition, in an eerily accurate piece of crystal-gazing, he had said that in the next ten years, Sun would make it into the top ten pharma companies. 'If I remember correctly, he had also said in the 1989 address that by 2015, Sun would become the market leader in India. Also probably something like its becoming by then amongst the best paymasters. That's the only bit of prediction that we are still waiting for to come true,' Kansal reckoned.

Pahwa replayed Shanghvi's conversations with new recruits. They were almost never about what they learnt on training or the new drugs they were about to promote. If he found a boy from a real-estate background, his discussion could be about how one could play with the strength of concrete by changing the proportion of cement, crushed limestone, granite and sand. If a boy had served in the aviation industry, he could expect an interaction around the make and mechanics of Boeing 737, or what led to a recent crash. 'While I would wonder how he could be sounding so prepared to discuss a topic that deep, his philosophy was simple—if the boy cared to do his last job with involvement, he will do the same here,' Pahwa said.

On an occasion Pahwa remembered Shanghvi making an off-the-cuff remark about a particular boy who stood out as exceptionally bright out of the lot. 'Do you think he will last long in the company?' Shanghvi had asked.

What flashed across Pahwa's eyes was an image of that boy who had promised, the day before, an unstinting commitment to serve the company that had given him a break.

'He is too sharp and smart, will be poached in no time.' Shanghvi had said matter-of-factly, just as he was leaving the training venue. 'The guy left us in months. He could spot unfits on a few occasions applying some fuzzy logic that totally missed us,' Pahwa said.

Those days, when Shanghvi couldn't make it, Shanti-kaka, the chairman of the company, spent the last day with the boys. Most of the trainings ended on a highly intense and emotional note, with Pahwa and the boys holding each other in their arms in total abandon, something that was unusual in professional settings and tears—not wine—flowing freely.

'Raju sir was very humble and was there for us. You could forget during those sessions that he was second in command of the company. And Pahwa sir was an excellent trainer. He gave his heart and soul into it. He could move you and instil a sense of purpose, and then when we were parting, you could share a cathartic cry together,' Kansal recalled. Pahwa admitted he was quick to tears, and hardly remembered any training session where he didn't reach out to his pocket to pull out a handkerchief to wipe his eyes at the closing dinner.

Once, a day after one such highly emotional closing dinner, Pahwa was called by Dilip-bhai to his cabin, 'My father saw how emotional you and the boys got yesterday evening. He reasoned with me that someone who could move grown-up boys enough to cry like babies in twenty days, building such an emotional bond, do you know how many boys he can retain in the company by that power? You need to reward him for creating this attachment. This is what you want your company to stand for,' Shanghvi said, while extending an envelope that contained a ₹5,000 cheque.

Pahwa's eyes misted all over again. He averted his gaze to maintain what he deemed a professional propriety in front of his super-boss. 'It was probably my most gratifying and emotional moment in Sun,' Pahwa reminisced after a quarter-century, and then stopped, half remembering something else. He continued ' . . .or the second most emotional.' The most moving moment of his journey in Sun was yet to come.

This emotional connect was woven as a thread across the hierarchy in Sun, and later almost institutionalized as a strategy. Miya recalled Shanghvi joining him on field for the first few days. 'He prepared by asking a bit about the doctors he was to meet. And even though he didn't speak much, in three days straight I knew he was a relationship-oriented person. And he told me so, that nothing would have as much impact as forging a relationship with the doctor,' Miya said. Shanghvi carried his roti-sabzi in a tiffin box while on the field, and shared it with Miya and other MRs at lunchtime.

Kansal understood the power of emotional connect when, upon turning first-line manager (area manager), his seniors in Lucknow, Pulak Mukherjee and Rajesh Kumar, told him to lead by demonstration, not dictation.

'The moment I turned supervisor, I was explained that my job is not to supervise but to take care of the boys in my team,' Kansal recalled. Raju shared that Sun had a very clear culture around how one should deal with people. 'If an MR is demoralized, his boss will be held responsible. If he is not performing, his boss will be questioned. What is preventing him from performing? Is there a problem at home or in the personal front? Have you been the right role model? If he is not performing, what are you doing about it? If you don't know what the problem is, you are not on your job. If you know and are doing nothing about it, that won't work for you. If you know and don't know what to do, there is a problem as well,' Raju said.

'After my promotion, Pulak-da, my boss in Lucknow, told me that henceforth I had been appointed as the guardian and guide of the five boys in my team. It was now my duty to make each one of them comfortable so that they give their best, and suddenly my own experience as an MR in Sun made sense,' Kansal added. At times, it had struck Kansal as unusual, the level of support and humbleness his bosses at Sun displayed, particularly when elsewhere his counterparts got roughed up and pushed to the edge when targets were not met. That is what made the Sun experience different and the organization worth sticking to for him even when the salaries were not great.

Kansal's contemporary Vinay Sharma* agreed. 'Anyone could pick up the phone and talk to the higher-ups and no one felt bypassed. That openness of communication helped. Also, most of us who stuck around for a decade were constantly growing, with three or more promotions as the company was growing.'

Both Sharma and Kansal warn that they couldn't speak for the Sun of today, and wouldn't be surprised if the size has cost the company its brotherhood and intimacy of entrepreneurial days. Back then, Kansal and Mohit Aggarwal*, an area manager in Sun for six years—from 1989 to 1995—recounted how they were taught to treat medical representative reporting to them as their first customer. 'Just like I had been taught to be humble in front of my doctor—who was my second but original customer—I was to be the same before the MR. After all I had to sell a plan to him. That was the only way they believed and internalized the promotional campaign.'

Before the start of the financial year, the head office designed a common plan of product-detailing activities at an all-India-level meeting attended by all regional managers, sales managers and higher-ups. 'In the months of January–February, there used to be complete detailing across the hierarchy, which, I believe, was unique to Sun then,' Kansal guessed.

This was to ensure that each link in the chain of hierarchy was thorough with the plan. So if Kansal was a regional manager, he would prepare a complete presentation for the higher-ups in the head office. They would shoot a volley of questions, and he would have to pass that test, before making the presentation to his subordinate area managers. Area managers would then have to draw up a similar presentation for a team of regional managers, fielding their questions. If they passed the test, they were allowed to brief the foot soldiers, assuming they were doctors. This exercise was repeated every quarter when the head-office upgraded visual aids, and new product plans. Aggarwal asserted that the philosophy was simple: 'If we are not sure of something, we couldn't expect our MRs to do it. Moreover, if he is not sold on an idea, he can't sell it, not with conviction.'

Varun Sood* (who spent fourteen years at Sun, and now works with a rival company) described how bosses nestled their underlings, till they learnt to fly and became bosses themselves. 'At Sun, everyone, had to do fieldwork. Even a vice-president needed to work half-month in the field, unlike many other companies where the higher-ups have not spoken to a doctor in years,' Sood explained. 'It helps to have first-hand experience of how realities are shifting; then you are aware, and act promptly on it. What other companies are doing, you know. When your MR is facing a genuine issue, your expectations from him wouldn't be unrealistic; you can help him resolve the issue. If your MR is playing you, you know faster,' Kansal described.

Sood felt it built an unsaid bond where the MR felt, 'If my boss is doing it with such sincerity, how can I not.' Kansal explained, 'As an area manager, I had five boys. Unlike other companies where fieldwork meant touch and go for bosses, and ticking off the task, I had to follow a 3+2 schedule for each boy, every month. In my first fortnight, I would spend three days with the boy. The first day I observed him and told him where to improvise. On the second day I observed him work on correcting what I had asked him to and on the third day I gave feedback on his implementation. In the second fortnight, I spent two days again with him.' Area managers and regional managers got about a week to complete their administrative duties, while for the rest of the days, they were expected to be in the field.

'Meetings with medical representatives were mostly focused on activities, not targets. The sense one got from head office was that if you focus on the activity, targets will materialize,' Kansal recalled.

Roy, who was part of the team that drew up the joint fieldwork policy, said that the beauty of joint fieldwork was that in times of crisis no one knew who was shielding whom and how, but the prolonged practice somehow made things fall into place like a synchronized orchestra.

Election season for doctors' associations meant phones at Sun kept buzzing non-stop, the company flooded with requests for sponsorship. The straight short policy of it was that the company couldn't endorse any doctor in elections. But it didn't mind so much if employees created a platform for the contesting doctors, when it suited them, agnostic to what happened on the dais. But when you allowed so much emotion to flow in a profession, could it be dropped at just a beck and call?

It was a hotly fought contest in Madras for the president's post of a psychiatric association between the top psychiatrist of Tamil Nadu, Dr Raghavan* and a leading psychiatrist of Kerala, G. Krishna Gopalan*. Gopalan, after having lost the election, spotted Sun's zonal manager of Tamil Nadu distributing sweets, most likely celebrating his defeat.

By the time, the frightened manager called Roy to admit his folly, Gopalan had already fired him on phone, 'Starting tomorrow, Sun Pharma will be boycotted in Kerala, I will see to that, Roy.' When Roy rushed to tell Dilip-bhai, he already had all the details and a little more from a Benares-based neuropsychiatrist.

'So why are you still here, Roy? Shouldn't you be in Kerala?' Roy recalled Dilip-bhai instructing him when he stomped into the boss's cabin.

Next day, Roy spent hours in Kerala, obviously not reclining on a boat in the backwaters, but cajoling Gopalan in his chamber, soothing his hurt, anger, half-succeeding in calming him down. Then, when he emerged with a sense of achievement, about to make a call to boss to update, he got a call from a rival.

'Mr Roy, Dilip Shanghvi is here in Kerala, what could bring him here?'

Roy instantly knew what might have brought him there but he had no words for what he felt at that moment.

'I managed to mutter something like I would call him back. But this is how a boss is. His wordless action tells you that he stands rock-solid behind you. If you fall, there will be a pair of strong arms to buffer you,' Roy said. And he felt all of this oblivious of the fact that Shanghvi had not even gone to Kerala on this particular occasion (as per Shanghvi's recollection). Based on several past experiences where Shanghvi had rescued people silently from challenging situations, Roy was left in no doubt that he had done so here as well.

This central meridian of emotional connect that began from the foot soldier at Sun ran right across the spine of the company stopping only at Dilip Shanghvi.

'Sun is a warm sweater Dilip-bhai has knitted like a mother,' Yagnik, its first HR head, described. He compared the structure of peer organizations to a stack of cards delicately balanced. You cannot crumble the intertwined bonds at Sun by blowing force. To do that, you will have to pick up a scissor and go snip, snip, snip.

Loyalty Test

So what could possibly happen when someone—forget the scissor—tried wittingly or unwittingly to pull a string of wool out of that sweater.

Somewhere around the summer of the mid-1980s, a now-senior psychiatrist in Calcutta witnessed such a sight. He was sitting in a senior colleague's cabin at a medical college. The colleague was lecturing him on how much money there was to be made in the medicine business, particularly the psychiatry segment. At that time, Sun's Pradip Ghosh walked in for his regular round. By then, psychiatrists in Calcutta had begun to register the roaring success of Sun in their city.

The witness psychiatrist's jaw dropped when his senior said to Ghosh, 'Let's set up our own company. I am serious. You join me as the second in command. And all that you have to do is to replicate what you have done at Sun.'

Ghosh, according to the witness's memory, smiled politely and started retrieving a new drug sample that Sun had launched and walked off. Ghosh recalled getting a tempting offer very early in his career when Sun was stuck with just two drugs.

'The moment I got the offer, I rushed to Dilip-bhai to tell him about it. And he laughed it off saying, "Really, Pradip, you want to go! Okay then, tell me when you are leaving." I went into a fit, did he just ask me to leave, how could he? Forget it; Sun is my company as well.'

Raju admitted that he was being perceived as too loyal to Shanghvi, a label 'not too fashionable'. 'When I joined, it's true I was more Dilip-bhai's father's friend than his employee and he held me in high regard. But after I joined, he was my boss. He was paying me and I had to deliver. There might be some situations where I may not agree with him, but still I had to go ahead and do it with some amount of caution thrown in: "Dilip-bhai, I am doing this only because you want me to."'

He was conscious that it was not too cool to be tagged so loyal, but said that he didn't mind being a little uncool. 'Some of my friends disapproved of the sort of image they thought I was acquiring, that I could do anything for Dilip-bhai. They advised me to check myself. Other well-wishers felt that I was entitled to much more than what I was receiving at Sun. But my understanding with respect to loyalty was very individualistic. And one forceful reason I had chosen to join here was the sync between the company's credo (as spelt out by Dilip-bhai) and my ethos on how people should be treated.'

And that credo may have made Sun a warmer corner in the 1980s and the early '90s. 'You earned a few rupees less at Sun but were never in the mortal fear of losing your job, if you failed to meet your targets. We saw a lot of our friends from multinationals missing targets and living in a perpetual fear of being sacked. I think Sun compensated the money by the peace of mind and motivation it offered,' Kansal felt. Minus the incentives, a medical representative at Sun in Delhi region was making about a third of his Pfizer and Ranbaxy counterpart in 1990.

'People don't leave companies, people leave people—more accurately people leave their bosses,' Raju asserted. By consciously building a brotherhood across hierarchy, creating managers who lead by action, not instruction, aligning goals of everyone, one tried to build a transparent system with as little possibility for friction as possible, Raju explained.

Incentives, an important component of salary, was doled out quarterly and could be as high as 30–45 per cent of the total package. So one couldn't be a lazy bum at Sun. Besides, Sun's products were in such niche categories, at times niche within the niche. 'Doctors continued to give a feedback that we were bringing the right products at the right time. It made us feel like a heavyweight when in hindsight our company, with a few crore worth of sales, was a minnow in front of giants like Ranbaxy or Pfizer,' Sood claimed. Kansal felt that the edge that compounding effect of chronic therapies prescriptions offered was an added charm, which meant once generated, your prescription was yours to keep.

'In Ranbaxy my counterpart would have to wrestle out so many muscular peer firms in a tight-finish game for a prescription that would last him—how long—seven days maximum, because that is as much a dose of antibiotic prescription can last, unless overfed. Mine would be a neuropsychiatry or cardiology prescription, which wasn't crowded at least when I was chasing it. Also, once the specialist starts writing it, it would be a recurring prescription which means it grows the base of incentives I am creating,' Kansal explained.

And on top of the Sun MR's wishlist was the internal promotion, the ultimate reward. Even for that, one had to have shown loyalty in a visible way. The employee had to complete a minimum number of years, and shown at least two years of consistent performance in his existing role.

Almost a decade and half since Ghosh walked out on a psychiatrist's offer to lead his venture, T.K. Roy was deboarding at Ahmedabad airport, when an owner of an Ahmedabad-headquartered pharma major, at that time bigger than Sun met him. 'He literally caught me by my arm and took me to his office,' Roy said. 'Roy, if you join my company, I will double your salary. I am planning to expand my neuropsychiatry drug division,' Roy recalled being told.

After Roy was through with discussing his offer, he quietly slipped out and tiptoed into Sun's office, then in Bombay. The moment he reclined on his chair, the phone on his desk buzzed. It was Dilip-bhai.

'Roy, will you come to my cabin, please?'

When Roy entered his cabin, he asked, 'What's the matter, Roy?'

A few R&D folks who had hopped jobs from Sun to the rival pharma major had spotted their chief sneaking Roy into his office and the first number they dialled was of their former boss.

'Sir, they literally forced me to sign the package.'

'What's the package?'

When Roy informed that he was being offered double of what he was getting at Sun, Shanghvi called his then chief finance officer, Sudhir Valia, also his brother-in-law, and asked Roy, 'Do you have any other issue here?'

'No, sir.'

'We will give you not that much, but nearly the same.'

Upon which Roy—in a spot not many would want to be in despite what he was being offered—placed a proposal, which could have easily been mistaken to be a union demand, if you discounted the context, tone and the fact that it was Roy who was making it.

'Sir, please don't do it. My point is that if they have approached me, they could be targeting our other managers, because by industry standards, we are the lowest paymasters. If you really want to offer, please make a revision across the board.' According to Roy, 'the boss listened'.

Roy recalled the same year, that was 2003, Shanghvi held an all-department meeting discussing ways to cut and pre-empt attrition. 'For the first time at Sun, we saw a great salary revision across the board. We may not have yet become the best paymasters, but are one of the highest incentives paymasters—which brought me back to the day of the interview with boss—giving those who contribute,' Roy said.

'Most people can be happy with their own accomplishments but we were looking for people who can find happiness in someone else's success. We never hired flamboyant people. I, especially, never hired people who couldn't say they didn't know an answer when they didn't know it. When you don't know and still attempt to answer, that shows that you are not truthful. Finally, I looked for people who don't give up easily—those who don't give up just because they have failed in one or two attempts,' Shanghvi said

Loyalty, felt Yagnik, was the cement that bound people of each lower layer with the upper layer at Sun. 'At the grass-roots level, people pulled people. Dilip-bhai would go to Hyderabad and tell the medical representative, "Jani Miya, you have done a great job. Be the first-line manager and bring me five more Jani Miyas." Jani Miya would look for more guys like himself, not the most competent but those who turn dedicated workers, because you trusted them when no one else did. They would be loyal to Jani Miya, who would be loyal to his boss, who would be loyal to Raju, who would be loyal to Dilip-bhai,' Yagnik explained the chain of loyalty within Sun.

They were made to realize that if they stayed loyal to the organization, they would grow with it, a strategy that separated Sun from the rest of its peers, and paid rich dividends. Even today, Shanghvi's ability to create and retain a cadre of loyal senior managers remains a key to Sun's success. Almost half of Sun's employees have had tenures of over five years and close to 500 senior managers have an average tenure of more than a decade, a rarity in the industry.

Selling the Satsang Way

When Sun boys multiplied in the late 1980s and the early '90s, lessons its first medical representatives—Dilip and Pradip—had stumbled on to, evolved into strategies. It was partly the compulsion of not being entertained by therapy leaders, partly the reluctance stemming out of inexperience in their early days that had forced them to befriend young medical students so that they could ready themselves before seeking engagement with star consultants.

Catch Them Young

By 1987–88, when Sun was launching itself in Bombay, it wasn't Dilip and Pradip, but Roy and Raju, who were running the circumference of the city's medical colleges and hostels, chatting with their brightest students long enough to navigate a route into their minds. 'We had figured out that many top specialists were too busy. They would just dictate 'antidepressant' and move on to the next patient. That left the decision on which brand to prescribe in the hands of PG students,' Raju explained, on why cracking PG students helped Sun.

This helped Sun even more because it focused on specialties unlike its peers. 'Dilip-bhai's focus was like Arjuna's. Within chronic therapies, he only focused on low-competition, high-margin products, within those only on prescription by specialists,' Raju pointed out.

Thus, the PG medical students who had decided on their specialities, but were not yet inaccessible stars were a great starting point. 'These PG hostels were an easy, critical access point for making a first mark in the mind space of tomorrow's leaders,' Raju summed it all up.

This strategy became polished to a different level through the 1990s. The hostel and medical colleges turned into a talent-hunting ground for Sun, which started consciously identifying and grooming bright young minds. The idea was to grow together—the company and the budding specialist.

So one way it could work was: if you were on the radar of Sun, its folks would chat about your aspiration and the cities you planned to set up your practice in. The Sun boys would prepare a list of general physicians in the catchment area of that doctor, were he to start his practice. Then

Sun would create a discussion forum and invite the PG guy, to address the general physicians on a medical topic of mutual interest, on a new disorder being identified, or a new drug being launched. In one shot, the budding specialist got a platform to access all physicians in his catchment, who were potential senders of referral cases.

Sun also began the practice of bridging gaps between established leaders and upcoming ones by holding PG educational programmes. The company started inviting authors of the medical textbooks and professors to interact with students in the hostels.

'We also invited examiners and conducted two-day programmes for students complete with mock exams. This built a distinct Sun brand in the minds of rising therapists,' Roy explained. So they already had a relationship going with this company much before they made something out of themselves. The company, also in a subconscious way, got associated with their wild youth days, for which everyone has a special place in their heart.

Catch Them Elsewhere

Dilip had observed that doctors inside their clinics were too busy seeing patients to spare time for them. If you had to access the person inside the doctor you must catch them outside their clinic where they were more chilled out. This Pradip and Dilip had learnt in their first conference at Bombay, where they had managed to break the ice with many psychiatrists of Calcutta who wouldn't as much turn their gaze to say hello to them back home.

'Doctors who are usually pampered in their hometowns, when out for a conference in unfamiliar spaces, struggle to cope for their most basic needs. 'And it became a strategy of Sun to grab their attention when they were outside their zone of geographic influence by attending to their most pressing needs,' a former Sun senior executive said.

'In a mobile-less remotely connected India of the 1980s, even the most celebrated star medical specialist of Madras was worse than the worst salesman when he was in Jaipur,' the executive continued.

At 5 a.m. sharp on a December Sunday in 1989, the phone of a Sun's salesperson rang. In the days of landlines, a call at that odd hour almost always spelt alarm. He jumped out of the quilt and ran to pick up the receiver, wondering whether the bell portended news of one of his sick relatives. It was urgent matter on phone indeed, but not urgent enough to call out for God's help.

After keeping the phone down, however, he didn't hesitate one second before startling another of his Calcutta colleague by calling him at the same ungodly hour. 'Hello, is that Anirban*? Dr Bhatnagar*, a top cardiologist from Bombay, is staying at the the Park Hotel in Calcutta, in Room No. 203, and needs a Gillette double-edged razor. Please rush to deliver. If shops are not open, locate a friend who uses the same. He has to leave for his meeting at 7 a.m.' By 6 a.m. apparently, Dr Bhatnagar was having a good shave with his favourite razor brand.

There must have been several occasions, when the doctors' trip—implying airfare and hotel bookings—were sponsored by a rival company. But that didn't mean that Sun lost out on that opportunity. 'My boys and I would take care of his needs in my city to the best of our abilities, take his wife out to a temple visit, make her shop for local wares when he was attending a conference and change their tickets if they wanted an extended stay,' Mihir Das*, who served as a regional manager at Sun during the 1990s, explained. Das said he saw his seniors do that in the company and his juniors picked it up from him.

Viplav Rao*, another former regional manager at Sun recalled, 'Raju sir told us in a clinic setting that you medical representatives are a distraction for the doctor. Show up somewhere where he wants to see you, do something he wants to get done and that doesn't necessarily have to cost money.'

What could a doctor possibly want to get done that doesn't cost money? One sample cited multiple times by Sun boys was this: In a conference, all large companies put up smart stalls. But come lunch hour, most went unattended as everyone rushed to grab a bite. In a few stalls sleepy MRs who stayed on to guard went into hibernation mode—aware that this was not the hour any doctor would come visiting. 'Our guy manning Sun stall turned into the caretaker for all goodie-bags that doctors had collected from all other companies in the conference. It was the Sun guy who understood, that when doctors went chattering with colleagues in a conference, carrying these fancy bags of varied shapes and sizes could be a real pain.' On occasion, surely the Sun-sent, if not God-sent, gift-keeper could earn more brownies than gift-givers.

Be in the Mind, You Want to Win

'"Sales begin when the customer says no, the journey from point of no to yes is truly the salesman's art," Raju Sir told us,' Vinod Malik*, a former Sun MR said. 'Money can't buy you happiness; money can't even buy you lasting business, what can is how you make your customer feel,' Sanjeev Shekhar*, another MR recalled Raju telling.

Pay attention, and an opportunity would present itself to render a service that could generate a sense of obligation in the customer, the desire in him to do something back for you. This seemed to be at the heart of on-the-job training lessons that hundreds of Sun boys imbibed in the 1980s and the '90s. A warm personal touch and customized attention to select psychiatrists in Calcutta had proved to be an effective formula for Dilip and Pradip. But to impart this 'sense of service' as a part of training to so many men from such diverse backgrounds couldn't be an easy task even if they were pre-screened for specific qualities during recruitment.

'An inevitable by-product of such deeply embedded loyalty is reproduction of alter egos. When you emulate someone you admire, and that brings you success, you end up becoming like him. Just like people who trained under Dilip-bhai couldn't remain untouched by his personality, those on ground became alter egos of Ghosh, Raju, Nand-Kumar, Pulak Mukherjee, Jani Miya. So directly or indirectly everyone was mirroring Dilip-bhai. And that is one way so many boys could internalize that sense of service,' Yagnik explained.

Citing an instance of what he implied, Yagnik added, 'If you wish to see what I mean, try visiting any Sun Pharma programme, where Dilip-bhai is not present. You would feel his presence instantly, people behaving exactly as he would like them to. And the people picked to instil this in boys—such as Raju had a natural sense of humility about them and bonded emotionally with the boys, Yagnik felt. He recalled Raju, who seemed deeply spiritual, didn't mind showing respect to doctors even when they disrespected him.

'There is no point in being right or wrong in an argument with a customer, you may win the argument but lose the customer; the loss is ultimately yours,' Kansal recalled Raju training them.

'Yes, I taught them if the doctor calls you a damn fool, the smartest thing you could do was to smile in return and say—that's a good omen, sir. All my biggest customers started by calling me a fool. That's because the egoless state is the most empowered state, be it sales or spirituality,' Raju said.

And asked if he was spiritual while at Sun, Raju smiled, 'I was an atheist who argued that Man created God, God didn't create Man. I was deeply interested in people and psychology. If I was spiritual, I didn't know it then.'

At one time he was exploring whether he could bring motivational speakers like Shiv Khera, Deepak Chopra to pep-talk boys at Sun, but after calculating the expense, he decided against even taking the proposal to Dilip-bhai and chose to photocopy the relevant pages of their books, and circulate it.

The Sun MR was taught that selling was not a mechanical job. When he was engaging with the doctor, he was engaging a very important mind that he wanted to influence. For that he was competing with numerous others. If the MR did exactly what others did, his chances of succeeding also became as good as others. Hence, it was important for him to stand a little apart from the rest of the crowd.

So selling experience was broken into two parts—objective: where the seller mastered the product details and competing brands; reasoned why his products were better; what the side-effects or contraindications were and other technical jargon. And subjective: where the seller examines the feeling he has generated in the doctor. a liking: good, happiness: better, trust: even better, an obligation: bingo, bull's eye!

Many companies tried to address the latter by splashing gifts and sponsoring leisure travels. It would be incorrect to conclude that Sun didn't do any of that, but it seems Sun didn't stop at that, and definitely didn't depend on that, attempting to do the subjective part a little differently.

'We introduced the human element through the structure by conscious design. MRs could succeed only if they got disproportionate support from the doctors. We do not give opportunities to bribe doctors. You have to do things which mean more to the doctors,' Shanghvi explained.

'My trainer at Sun once likened dropping trendy corporate gifts at doctor's doorsteps to serving an ice cream when someone was thirsty. Many companies splurged much more, their gifts luxurious, trips lavish; but they would give the key to the hotel and air fares, while the doctor would be struggling for local pick and drop and for the little things that matter in a foreign land,' Malik said.

'We would do those small things that usually fall through the cracks but were as important—receiving him, dropping him, changing his tickets, what he needed to get done. We learnt to serve water when the doctor is thirsty.'

'Those corporate gifts, however swanky, didn't have a personal touch about them, the doctor knew that your company has given it. We were encouraged to strike an emotional connect at an individual level. So if you worked around the gift, make sure the doctor has seen you waiting long enough to give it or make a second trip to hand it over,' Shekhar said. When an army forged an emotional connect, and the common thread was Sun Pharma, the positive vibe would be reinforced with the company.

Sun medical representatives were encouraged to make rounds on festival days, to show up on a bad-weather day, when the patients preferred the company of their bad health at their home than a visit to a doctor's clinic. 'When asked by the doctor, "Is it not a holiday for you today?" they could always come up with: "But sir, you are working harder than us,"' Shekhar quipped.

Creating personal connect almost always took a little more than a festival or bad weather, and could get downright hilarious at times. Mohan Gupta* recalled cracking a top cardiologist by importing a pinch of sacred ash powder from his colleague in the south. 'I had seen a little photo of Satya Sai Baba on his table. I enlisted a devotee friend who visited Puttaparthi every year to bring me a pouch of vibhuti. The day I gifted the consultant that pouch was the first time he held me in a long gaze and then confessed how he was planning a Puttaparthi visit for long, but how the divine had sent his blessings through me. It was a breakthrough,' Gupta narrated.

His friend Sailesh Bhandari* made a canine connect as a personal touch with a leading cardiologist in Delhi. 'I spent ₹75 to take this book *How to Train Your Dog* for him as a gift, since he reared half a dozen rare breeds,' Bhandari recreated.

Sood had a particularly difficult doctor who refused to entertain him. His boss suggested, 'Stop being a salesman. Be a caregiver, if you can't be a patient. Take an uncle who had a heart attack. He is bound to ask after your uncle's health when you visit him next.' Pay attention, and the opportunity to serve would present itself.

When a doctor, during a random conversation, mentioned that his wife had been coughing since the day before, Rao returned to him with the best brand, not his own but a competitor's, to tell him that this was the medicine that had worked best, when he was suffering from cold a month back.

You would be grossly mistaken to assume that every doctor under Sun was privileged enough to receive this level of service. Who did, who didn't, was part of a pre-screening strategy that involved meticulous back-room teamwork. This involved intense market research and data crunching.

'Our boys conducted a detailed chemist survey to figure out the list of doctors we need to win over. The godfathers, the prescription trendsetters in our chosen specialities—far and few—in every city were obviously at the top of the heap. But beyond them, we prepared a specific list we needed to chase. Identifying those doctors had to be scientific, based on variables such as the number of patients they see, the molecules they were writing,' Shekhar said.

Follow-up information was collated from chemists and analysed on whether our strategies were working and doctors were getting converted, he claimed. It was doable as about 80 per cent of specialists' prescriptions stayed within a 3-kilometre radius and 50 per cent remained with his neighbourhood chemists.

This internal business calculation on how much could be spent on which doctor had to be prepared on grounds by first-line managers in consultation with their foot soldiers but vetted by headquarters. 'Dilip-bhai insisted that such an exercise was crucial. It helped us identify the doctors where time and energy of the MRs should be prioritized. Otherwise, left to him, an MR, without the vantage point of the big picture, would obviously want to please all doctors across his territory. It also helped the company optimize the marketing spend,' a former Sun executive said.

But just because a detailed strategy was being worked out behind and a set of doctors pursued more vigorously than others, it didn't make the feelings of service for doctors any fake. That experience of devotion, as many former Sun boys insisted and many doctors testified, was very real.

Despite the entire business plan and strategy, Raju insisted that the Sun boys in his times were taught never to indulge in quid pro quo deals with doctors. 'That would have quashed the very thing we stood for. The moment a relationship got purely transactional, all mutual respect was lost. This was the most important relationship in our business and we wanted unsullied, deep, long-term bonds like one develops with family and friends; you cannot quantify give and take in those bonds. That would render it cheap,' Raju said.

At one time Raju codified a detailed list of what one could do or not do with doctors, but that was pulled back. It was on Shanghvi's instruction as he didn't want these intangibles written into an official code and be found pinned on a rival's notice board.

Asked how this sense of service and devotion was made part of the personality of thousands of salespeople, Raju made it sound akin to a cult. 'It was like a Satsang. Have you felt the exhilarating energy of one? It becomes immaterial whether you are a believer or non-believer, spiritual or non-spiritual, people just immerse in that sense of déjà vu, flow in that spirit. Sun was a dizzying growth story, and when people tasted success in it, saw the fundamentals were strong, ethics better than rivals, where bosses not only understood but partook in solving a problem, people adopted the methods they were taught. In short, it worked.'

In 1988–89, the victories came quickly for Sun but celebrations were never loud. It was for the first time Sun's name had figured in an ORG-Marg Retail Audit report, which published sales of top 200 drug firms. It meant Sun was now officially on the map of Indian pharma sector. The year after it clocked one crore rupees monthly sales. Hattangadi distinctly recalled the chilly winter evening when Shanghvi called a quick meeting of senior executives to break the good news.

To mark the occasion, there was no champagne or cake. There was a computer and a computer instructor who would teach the basics of it.

Hattangadi recalled hesitating first, lest something happened to the delicate machine. It sat like a new guest on a new table on this one-crore day. Hattangadi fumbled a bit on the keyboard before pressing S on the left middle row, searching for U in the bottom but finding it somewhere on the top right, instead spotting N in the bottom row to punch in his first few letters.

Raju recalled going into Shanghvi's cabin to suggest that the company give out silver coins embossed '1' to all employees to commemorate the occasion. The idea didn't seem to excite him particularly, but he didn't refuse. And so silver coins were given to employees to mark the occasion.

'Dilip-bhai said, "No short cuts, we are not in a hurry to show results to anyone,"' Raju recalled. For us, to do in three years what others did in ten, we must be ready to work more. Sun was ready to launch more products, and cover more customers, more areas. For someone not in a hurry, there was always too much work lined up for everyone in Sun, including Shanghvi. But this feat didn't happen in Bombay.

Even before Sun had hit the one-crore mark, one Friday he made a call to friend Sailesh, who was staying at Vapi then. 'Hello Sailesh, you came from east coast to west coast, and we are still not together. Shouldn't we be staying together?'

Between them, they were always kidding about this or that. So Sailesh started guessing the joke he thought was being tried on him. 'So what's this about?' he asked.

'Sailesh, if we have to grow fast, we can't be spending so much on real estate. Bombay is becoming too expensive to plan our expansion from. I am serious; let's look for a place in Baroda or Ahmedabad where we can build our headquarters.'

'So when do we start?'

'On Monday, in Ahmedabad.'

Sailesh Desai, then, had a whole weekend to prepare for a visit to consider shifting the headquarters of Sun. In a hurry or not, but there were miles to go before one could even rest at Sun, and the first milestone was still a decade away—too far in time to be visible to all—the one with a signage 'Toppled Torrent'.

CHAPTER SIX

BEATING THE TURRANT EXPRESS

Pradip Ghosh was standing outside Rabindra Sadan, Calcutta late one dark evening in 1987. Head held high, he was peering at the elegant hand-painted fiery orange banner, seriously wondering whether talents like Soumitra and Tapas were better off trying their hand at landscapes instead of working as medical representatives. All of them, the Sun boys, over twenty-eight of them in Calcutta now, wanted this occasion to be red-lettered. It marked, in a way, the formal announcement of Sun's diversification into cardiology, to doctors in the city of its roots.

The customers—neurologists, psychiatrists and now cardiologists—were all expected to be present at the conference of the Association of Physicians of India next day. As they walked in to notice that Monotrate (the drug Sun's stall was highlighting) was not a neuropsychiatric offering, they would realize that the company they saw being born was growing. But just as the thought crossed his mind, he heard thunder strike behind.

'It was all smudged with the ink bleeding through that canvas as the untimely rain lashed out,' Ghosh recalled. Just as he was thinking up an alternative that could be put in place in a few hours before the programme began, Ghosh recalled Tapas and Soumitra coming back to paint it all over again, through the night. 'They sat with their brushes and colours, while other boys arranged for a ladder again, mounting that banner way beyond midnight,' Ghosh reminisced, trying to capture the spirit of Sun.

By the time Raju joined Sun in 1987, Shanghvi had already made a decision: it was time to stretch the boundary of playground beyond neuropsychiatry, and step into other niche therapies, starting with cardiology. The drug he chose to make its debut in cardiology was diltiazem hydrochloride, a calcium channel blocker used for patients with hypertension and angina. 'Angizem' was the brand name he picked for Sun's product. The undisputed market leader in the category was a Torrent drug—Dilzem, followed by JB Chemicals' brand Dilcardia.

Weeks to the launch, every little detail was being planned with the 150-odd people that Sun comprised, when one day, Shanghvi asked Raju to come along to Pune for a national conference hosted by the Association of Physicians of India. Shanghvi drove his pistachio Premier Padmini with Raju by his side. As they reached the medical soiree, Raju feeling a little lost on the spot as to which of these countless anonymous heads belonged to those who specialized in heart, Shanghvi said softly, 'Mr Raju, we have to find a way to identify the cardiologists in the crowd, walk up to them and introduce ourselves.' And so they parted to do the exercise. Interestingly, when Raju went about looking for cardiologists in the mass, one way he recognized a few of them was by seeing whom a Torrent manager promoting cardiology drug Dilzem was speaking to.

After the programme was over, the crowd dispersed. Amid cacophony they headed in small groups of four, five or six, laughing, chatting and arguing among themselves, to an enormous red and yellow shamiana, where dinner was being served. Raju waved at Dilip-bhai standing at the hallway entrance. As soon as they stepped into the tent shelter, Raju, one of a habit developed from childhood, first made his way to the basin on the left to wash his hands before touching his food. As he rubbed his hands under the open tap, he heard Dilip-bhai's voice from behind his shoulders, 'Mr Raju, we are not here to have dinner.'

Raju turned around, absorbing the message instantly, and went looking for more cardiologists.

There they met a top cardiologist of Bombay, who was contesting for the post of secretary of a national-level cardiologists' association. On knowing that theirs was a new company entering the segment, she came up with an idea, 'If you really want to know top cardiologists of the country, why don't you host a dinner tomorrow in a decent hotel? Most of them are around, I can invite them over. Such a platform can help me do a bit of campaigning in the fraternity on how I intend to improve conditions for them, if they vote for me.'

It was opportunity knocking at the door, to target marketing at the corners where it was most intended, the opinion makers in the cardiologist community. In the company's experience, whenever it had cracked a top consultant, there had been 30–40 converts amongst his or her followers to its product without any effort. And here was a tempting window to showcase the company to the leaders—senior cardiologists from across the country—in an uncharted therapy, which it was now looking to conquer. So they readily agreed, and booked hotel Blue Diamond, close to the railway station and not very far from the airport, just in case some doctors were planning to leave the city the same day.

At Blue Diamond the next evening, as one after other celebrated cardiologists stepped into the hall, Shanghvi handed over his own camera to Raju, instructing, 'Make them feel special, Mr Raju. Everyone likes a bit of attention, the feeling of being clicked and a good picture of self, a happy memory to treasure.'

As Shanghvi himself continued to discuss the features of his soon-to-debut products on the sidelines, Raju went about requesting cardiologists to pose, say cheese, in solo, in groups, arresting frame after frame—reigning names of cardiology-waving hands, discussing serious matters of the heart. He started wondering to himself, 'This is it. This is marketing. We have managed to know top forty consultants of the country over a simple dinner. Now they have to be pursued and a trust in our products has to be built. All of this happened almost by destiny, or was it design?'

Dinner was still on, when Raju caught a top endocrinologist, a guest of another cardiologist in the lobby, pacing up and down, checking his watch. Like a true Sun boy, he went after him, 'Sir, do you need a vehicle to be dropped somewhere? I am Sundaresh Raju from Sun Pharma and have a car waiting here at the porch, just in case.'

'Thank you, I have a flight to catch. I need to reach the airport in just half an hour.'

As Raju escorted him out and ushered him into the car, he recognized the executive from their leading rival firm closing in, huffing and puffing, 'Hello sir, I am in charge of dropping you back to the hotel.'

The doctor stared at him for a second and replied before shutting the door on his face, 'Thank you, I am comfortable. I have to be dropped to the airport, not the hotel. And now, I am in a hurry, excuse me.'

Months before pulling off this cardio marketing coup, Shanghvi had begun thrashing out with his product manager Vivek Hattangadi and medical team, a strategy to beat Torrent's Dilzem in the market. Sun had launched a plain Anzigem to cold response in the market and Shanghvi was preparing the ground for a remake and relaunch of the product. 'Dilip-bhai would think around how we could innovate that would differentiate our brand and give us an edge over competing products like that of Torrent,' Hattangadi said. His research on sustained-release version of Lithosun came handy.

'He spent hours with the head of the pharmacology department at KEM hospital to figure out and prove the scientific advantages of a slow-acting version of diltiazem hydrochloride over the plain version sold by Torrent and other companies. It was Dilip-bhai's idea to work on clinical trials with the doctor at KEM and publish the findings in international journals,' Hattangadi recalled.

Those findings which proved the effectiveness of a slow-release version of the drug over the plain version went into an aesthetically designed promotional booklet—which gave the illusion of being a book titled, *The Untold Story*.

'Doctors thought they were being handed over a suspense-thriller novel, a corporate gift item, but when they opened it, it turned out to be, well, a suspense-thriller booklet of a different sort. It was an extraordinarily bold move from a company the size of Sun, which had launched a direct attack on the plain version of the drug, by naming Torrent's brand Dilzem in it,' Hattangadi said.

It was not a typo or an oversight, but a deliberate marketing strategy to straight-talk the message of innovation to win customers. It caused mayhem in the market because till then, it was unheard of that companies could be so aggressive in their marketing, Hattangadi recalled. But it must have worked in the right quarters, as Sun's Angizem started quickly grabbing a sizeable share of the prescription over the next few months.

Shanghvi couldn't recall whether they had mentioned Torrent's brand in what was Sun's first promotional campaign, *The Untold Story*, but he said, 'It was basically to bring out the fact that other similar products in the market were instant-release products. Our promotional campaign was basically saying that the innovator brand on the market, Cardizem, is a sustained-release product and hence other brands in the market are not a therapeutic equivalent to the innovator's product while ours was.'

Tracking the growth of the Angizem prescription closely had made it a foregone conclusion for the company that their brand was on the brink of replacing the second largest, Dilcardia. It was now inching forward to breathe down the neck of market leader Dilzem from Torrent. That was the topic of discussion in the product-review meeting on the day, when the letter arrived. Shanghvi picked up the document, smiled and kept it aside to tend to his next task. It was a legal notice from Torrent. The 'big boy' of niche drugs was feeling the threat and had accepted the challenge, Hattangadi recalled. When asked, Shanghvi couldn't remember whether they had received a legal notice from Torrent.

It had only been a few days since Shanghvi had projected casually before Sun boys in a meeting that it was a matter of time before the company would move ahead of Torrent and enter the top ten. Torrent, with its strong sales force of 600 people, was way bigger than Sun's 140-odd boys in the field when he had predicted the topple.

New drug launches became the race where the heat of competition was felt the most. Hiren Desai recreated the hysteria that preceded a new drug launch. There was a frenzy to beat Torrent to launch. 'Initially we would track their launches carefully, even launch the same drugs. Later, it became a competition to hit the market first on the same drug,' Desai said. At times, the approval for a specific drug was expected to arrive the very same day for both companies from the central drug regulator. In 1987, he recalled getting five approvals on the same day as Torrent that included Anjizem and Trazalon (trazadone).

'As soon as approvals came, the Vapi factory started churning out tablets. The Angadiyas (a set of courier boys whose families are trusted with valuable parcels like diamond and important letters) would have booked an entire bogey in Flying Ranee Express and they would reach us in a few hours. On that particular day in 1987, by the time the Angadiyas booked taxis to get to our office, it was past sunset; to add to that, the lights went out suddenly,' Desai said.

'We had plans to finish writing the names and address of stockists, to launch the drugs the next morning but the electricity fuse had upset the plan,' he added. Just then, he recalled Dilip-bhai emerging from his cabin of the 'Ram Mandir' office and asking, 'What's the matter? You guys haven't started yet.'

'Dilip-bhai, it's dark and so many parcels have to be labelled with stockists' addresses,' Desai said.

'There are candles,' Desai remembered Dilip-bhai replying and lighting one himself before anyone else could. He sat down to begin writing the addresses of stockists on the parcels one after another. Desai remembered everyone in the office picked up the special pens and began inking the names and addresses on the parcels late into the night.

Early next day, medical representatives, office-boys-turned-part-distributors, carried those parcels to hand-deliver to stockists by road or rail, whatever was quicker, to whichever destination to make the launch happen. They had to be super quick to do it faster than Torrent, which had earned the sobriquet 'Turrant' amongst doctors for its lightning speed in launching new medicines. Whosoever launched the drug first ended up garnering a mammoth market share and doctors were mighty stubborn when it came to switching brands once they got used to writing one.

There was also an intensely zealous energy in Sun to topple Torrent. 'Even so, when once an internal perception audit conducted amongst doctors in the 1990s showed up Sun's image as a "younger brother of Torrent", the core team was upset,' Shyamal Ghosh, a Sun veteran, said. They didn't want to be Torrent, they wanted to beat it. This counterpoise surely helped Sun managers erect a tangible goalpost its team wanted to cross.

Shanghvi, however, said, 'This [beating Torrent] was never a message I have used to mobilize MRs. Sales managers in the field may have done it differently, because they have to galvanize a sales force. To channelize energies of so many you sometimes need to erect a milestone that they would resonate with and focus on. [Personally] I haven't competed with Torrent or cared much about beating Torrent.'

Ghosh would have us believe that every Indian cricket team needs a Team Pakistan to fuel itself with a passion and score a victory that means something more than just a game win. Torrent was that Team Pakistan for Sun boys. In a way, that's plain enough. Torrent was a bigger company with the same business model to learn from and race past. But was that all it was for Sun—a must-have stronger necessary opposite in a competition to make your own triumph meaningful?

Searching for clues in lanes of history may yield nuggets strewn here and there that suggest the possibility of it being something more. But people who love Shanghvi, and are the only ones to have seen him close enough to grasp the entirety of his constitution, dismissed these events as too non-material to have a directional bearing in his journey.

The business relations between Torrent and Shanti-kaka's Medcom Enterprises didn't seem to have started without a hiccup or two. Kumar Pal Desai, who authored the biography of U.N. Mehta, depicts Calcutta as a stronghold of 'foreign multinationals' and 'Bengali companies'. Here the owner of Torrent struggled to jump-start his business despite having appointed a sole stockist. It talks of a Calcutta stockist, 'who had given the order' but 'failed to release the goods' in the market, as a roadblock to introduce the company's drugs in the city. It took a trip of senior Mehta himself to Calcutta, a successful meeting with top psychiatrist D.N. Nandi—who immediately started prescribing the company's medicines—for Torrent to enter the eastern market and succeed eventually. There is also unverified gossip that two of Sun's former employees in Calcutta had heard that indicated that a higher-up at Torrent had done some rough talk with Shanti-kaka and his friend Natu-kaka. But the details and origins, the whys and when of these events remain vague. There was nothing irreconcilable, however, considering Shanti-kaka attended the wedding of Mehta's eldest son Sudhir Mehta.

The story is relatively clear from 1982 onwards, when Shanghvi, after tasting success with three psychotropic drugs—Lithosun, Promasun and Nitrosun—did what could have been perceived by Torrent then as 'stepping on its big toe'. He launched 'Trazine S', with the same constitution as Trinicalm Plus, the drug that had been the closest to a blockbuster for Torrent, and for the controversial ingenuity of which Mehta took credit and responsibility.

Mehta had a handful of drugs behind him—Trinipyrin, Trinihemin, Trinibion, Trinichem in 1965, all prefixed with a derivative from the first name of his venture, Trinity. Then he launched Trinicalm, (trifluoperazine), a drug indicated for schizophrenia. Priced at 18 paise per tablet, it steeply undercut the price of multinational Smithkline and French Pharma's (SKF) 'Eskazine', which was selling at 54 paise per tablet, and gave it a run for its money.

Practising in the field himself, Mehta noticed that the drug in many cases induced a tremble in the patient's body and doctors invariably ended up prescribing another Parkinson medicine Pacitane (trihexyphenidyl) to manage that side effect. From that observation, he came up with an idea of a combo drug Trinicalm Plus, (trifluoperazine and trihexyphenidyl), which turned out to be a runaway success and changed the fortune of Torrent. By 1967–68, Torrent had earned ₹66,000 from that single brand and by 1974, sales from this drug had crossed ₹780,000, far exceeding what all its other drugs earned.

The move was ingenuous as it cut the cost and number of medicines a patient had to take. It was controversial because SKF claimed such a combination doesn't necessarily have stability, and has no rational basis. It bred controversy also as it spawned an entire legacy of untested combo drugs in India running into thousands today—dubbed as 'irrational' by experts. They are called irrational, because most chemical combinations have not been clinically tried on human population in a trial set-up to scientifically establish the results and side effects.

To bring this particular drug to the market, Mehta had to sell his ancestral property, shortly after which he found himself wrestling a trademark legal suit in Chennai. To wriggle out of this legal suit, he had to change his company's name from Trinity to Torrent.

Struggle had become the second nature of Mehta's life when, in 1982, his stockist's son launched a direct challenge by introducing a competing product, Trazine S, in the lucrative Calcutta market. It is unfair to impute an emotion to Mehta but it would take a superhuman to not have been affected in such a situation. More so, when the competing product didn't just fizzle out but started making a space for itself in the doctors' minds and chemists shelves.

Son Sudhir Mehta believed his father didn't take competition badly in general because having started as a medical representative himself, he knew it to be the law of the market. And by then, a large part of Torrent's business was being handled by Mehta's son-in-law Dushyant Shah.

Interestingly, just before Shanghvi launched Trazine S, Torrent had started appointing more stockists outside of Shanti-kaka's agency for Calcutta market—shrinking his business.

'Trazine S of Sun was suddenly sucking the lifeblood out of Trinicalm Plus in the Calcutta market. That launch from Sun came right after Torrent started fixing more stockists, a move that almost snuffed out Shanti-kaka's business. First Torrent appointed Bipin Company, then Bhogilal, in the same market. The pie was not so big to be shared between so many distributors,' a veteran at Dawa Bazaar, who was witness to these events, said.

'I made sure for the initial few years that I wouldn't introduce products that Torrent was selling. I didn't want my venture in any way to harm my father's business. And you will realize that my father remained Torrent's stockist for a reasonably long time after I started business,' Shanghvi said. When asked about him launching a direct competition to Torrent's Trinicalm Plus, he said, 'Yes, we did. By then they had appointed stockists other than my father's and one felt no longer an obligation to steer clear of competition. You must also realize that I was young then, and when you are young your decisions of what is right are way different from how one would respond to a similar situation today.'

A tripartite relationship, where a stockist's son turns a competitor and starts 'growing too fast to ignore' for the company by taking its recipe, serving a yummier dish and driving away its customers like a Pied Piper of Psychiatrists, must not have been anything less than awkwardly complex while it lasted; predictably, it didn't last too long.

'The dust settled just before Diwali. Shanti-kaka drafted a few letters on a telegram, framing the message as economically as he could and posted it to Torrent headquarters in Ahmedabad ending the relationship,' another Dawa Bazaar acquaintance of Shanti-kaka recalled. Shanghvi himself couldn't recall how the relationship had ended. It was a short end of one long chapter, and, as always, the beginning of another.

Seen in plain chronology, the Sun–Torrent rivalry grew fiercer in the late 1980s, spilling over to the '90s, after the snap in ties between Shanti-kaka and Torrent. But that could also be in part because Sun had started growing bigger enough, for its challenge to not matter to Torrent. With no familial conflict of interest to fret about any more, this hacking of business association between his father and chosen teacher might have seemed like freedom to Dilip Shanghvi. Or could it have been done on his insistence in the first place?

Shanghvi was not the unconditionally obedient type—definitely not the type to slice his thumb if his chosen distant teacher Dronacharya commanded him to. But he was also not the type to stop learning from him, just because their respective ambitions had pushed them into an uneasy corner, where each found the other standing in the wrestling ring.

So, a combination drug was what he launched, one Amixide H, by combining amitriptyline, an antidepressant and chlordiazepoxide, anti-anxiety. The idea to mix the two had also come from carefully discerning thousands of prescriptions which usually carried the two together. Torrent had done the same for Trinicalm Plus, but was caught napping in this case where it continued to sell the two drugs separately while Sun's combo-brand surpassed its sales in the eastern region swiftly.

'Thousands of prescriptions started pouring in. One doctor in Malda immediately placed an order for 800 boxes of the drug,' Pradip said. Since one of these drugs was prescribed for alcohol withdrawal, the uptake was very high in the hinterland as well and not limited to the affluent strata, as was the case with some psychiatric medicines those days. Shanghvi also learnt from Mehta's model that launching many drug brands in a year was an effective way to occupy the mind space of specialists.

There is no explaining why when one thing starts to go wrong for an entity, others follow suit. That is what seemed to have happened for Torrent in the eastern state post-1986. One of its trusted manager in Calcutta, M. Chaudhury (a former newspaper editor), who had helped Mehta in establishing Torrent in Bengal, passed away. The new set of employees it hired formed a union and gave it a tough time, while Sun was consolidating in Calcutta. And the nail in the coffin was in the works.

Barely weeks before, Ghosh had got his first car, even before Shanghvi bought himself one. He had requested for one over phone to Dilip-bhai, who had, in turn, rung up Hitesh, who in turn called his mechanic, who brought the first second-hand car in the Sun ecosystem for Pradip Ghosh. Months back, for the first time, they also had an office—a brick-and-mortar one, which once upon a time had been the warehouse bearing a signboard B.N. Enterprises, where Shanghvi had a start-up in his student days right over the head of now wound-up Medcom Enterprises. Thus Peter Cat restaurant at Park Street and his home at Raja Bazaar were no longer the places where the Sun boys caught up. It must have been a year since Shanghvi had shifted with his family to Bombay. And they had been asked to keep their eyes and ears open for the opportunity to present itself.

The day it did, Ghosh had reached a top psychiatrist Dr Andin's* home clinic late in the evening and had immediately sensed that something had unnerved the star psychiatrist of Calcutta. 'Sir, is something bothering you?' Ghosh asked him.

Andin poured his heart out, telling him about an academic conference on industrial psychiatry that he was keen on organizing. Since he had great relations with Torrent's U.N. Mehta, and the company had been known to be hosting such academic soirees in the past, he had sent a proposal. To his utter disbelief, the proposal had been turned down. Andin had taken the rejection as a personal affront.

'Sir, we do not have as much resources as Torrent, but on a small scale we can try to do it,' Ghosh offered.

Andin peered at Ghosh from the thick glasses of his big black rectangular frames and said, 'Size and scale don't matter, academics do. Industrial psychiatry may not be glamorous yet, but it is important. Just arrange for the basic logistics. Now, even if Torrent returns, I will not allow them to host this.'

Before this point, whenever Ghosh broached the topic of hosting conferences as a marketing strategy in front of Dilip-bhai, he heard him respond with 'We are not that big, Pradip,' which he decoded to mean, 'We cannot afford flights and hotels, and I wouldn't spread my wings beyond my means.' But he knew that this day would be different, and he wasn't quite off the mark.

'There is a value, there is a perceived value and there is a cost. We always focus on things that cost less than its perceived value,' Shanghvi had said of the ways Sun shaped its marketing.

Ghosh recalled standing at 4.30 a.m. at Howrah station with his Sun boys and an industrial psychiatry banner to receive one guest after the other. The guests were zoomed back and forth in Sun's new second-hand car. They were dropped at the venue—Ramakrishna Mission Institute of Culture near Gol Park. It was a small event, but the same couldn't be said of its impact, not academic but business.

'It was a moment of misjudgement by Torrent that turned into an opportunity for us,' Ghosh recalled. Neither Ghosh nor Andin probably knew at the time that U.N. Mehta had been battling one of the rarest forms of cancer, and its debilitating after-effects were taking a toll on his health and extended to his company.

Eventually, a belief of pharma salesmen in Calcutta—'Once a drug brand made its home in Dr Andin's pen, it was impossible for another to chase that address'—got shattered. Torrent continued to have a great run in the rest of the country but the bastion of the east started falling into Sun's dominance, a process that began after 1986 and gained momentum after 1989. The years it picked up pace were the years when Torrent started diversifying—into power, cable and finance. It was also the same year when Shanghvi had told his flock that Sun was primed to overtake Torrent.

'Dilip-bhai was focused not only in terms of sector but also consistent with the practices he adopted. Our focus was scattered in too many areas. About ten to fifteen years we were lost in that maze of straddling many sectors (power and finance), juggling too many diverse forces,' Sudhir Mehta, of Torrent, reckoned. Mehta happened to tell a friend, Mohan Chand Dadha, in an airport: 'It so happens when you have five children, the one crying most loudly grabs the maximum attention, the one who is doing well independent of you gets neglected—a realization that comes later. Pharma became that child in the Torrent group, which wasn't crying loud enough.'

Exactly, a decade later, Sun toppled Torrent and entered the list of top ten pharmaceutical companies in India by market share. 'What was also culminating at the end of that decade was that those postgraduates we had caught young, and whose journey we had bolstered, were replacing the old opinion makers to become the new star specialists in the therapy. And they now supported Sun. The plants we had watered for a decade had now grown into full-fledged trees,' T. K. Roy said.

That was 1999, the year after the founder of Torrent Group, U.N. Mehta, passed away. He was a fighter who conquered poverty, schizophrenia, cancer, coma and other adversities topping the taxonomy of struggles after leading a dramatically eventful life, but never having a personal one-on-one meeting with the most brilliant student he probably ever inspired—Dilip Shantilal Shanghvi.

Over a decade and a half later, a pharma veteran was taking a class of new recruits in a Bengaluru hotel. He presented a case study of one Vinod Shah who joins Norway Pharma, *not Novartis Sandoz*, as a medical representative. In the 1960s and '70s, when Indian pharma biggies were selling antibiotics, this man spotted the gap in cardiology, *not psychiatry*, and created a basket of products exclusively for cardiologists through his company Quadrant Pharma, *not Trinity*.

By the mid-1990s, Quadrant had become the fifth largest company. But the next generation was keener on information technology, *not power*, and spent 90 per cent of their time there. Shah had a massive heart attack and passed away, while a new firm Venus, *not Sun*, picked up the skeletons of strategy from Quadrant, adapted them to its own philosophies and executed each to the last detail.

This new firm blew the life force into them by adding dimensions such as brand-building, emotional intelligence and an energized field force. Venus unseated Quadrant and went on to reach where Quadrant couldn't. 'Can an adaptation be more original than the original?' a fresh recruit asked this question.

'Innovation spans generations in idea and execution. Can't a student be more talented than his teacher?'

'Whose story is this, sir?'

CHAPTER SEVEN

SUN OF BARODA—A COMPANY ON TRAIN

The man who embarked on Baroda Express that night swiftly arranged his stuff and himself on the allotted lower berth. He thanked God it was already winter, and pulled the sheet over his head after lying down. The decision on whether he would take a nap next or mentally revise the details of his next day's work in Bombay could always be made beneath the veil of the sheet. But no sooner had he done that, the TTE appeared. 'Ticket please,' he commanded. The seconds that followed saw an amateurish and unsuccessful effort on the part of the man pretending to sleep to furnish the ticket without letting the sheet over his face slip.

The TTE peered into the ticket and then into his face 'What's your name?'

'Dilip Shanghvi, it's on the ticket,' he replied, pretending confidence now that feigning sleep hadn't worked.

'Really?'

'What else?'

'I know Dilip Shanghvi well, he is on this train every third day.'

Was this a case of misidentification? If it was, there seemed to be too many cases of misidentifications for Sun officials in the largely 'identity card-less' world of 1989 to 1996, and almost all these run-ins happened on Baroda Express. That particular day, however, it ended up as a joke, as Kirti Ganorkar, who would go on to head business development at Sun later, could no longer keep the laughter inside. He confessed that his own ticket hadn't got confirmed, and so he had to travel on his boss's ticket to complete some urgent task in Bombay.

This, however, had no punch to pass as an amusing tale for Sun old-timers, given the arrangement that lasted seven years. Every day

Hiren Desai booked two tickets on dummy names, with an average age of 40–45 years, from Baroda to Bombay, on Baroda Express just in case someone from the new headquarters had to travel without any prior plan. And whosoever was travelling would be told, 'Your name is Mahesh Patel today, age forty-two years.' And so the adventure was repeated several times for so many Sun executives, that it felt like a mundane chore. The ticket cost ₹150. If it became clear by 9 p.m. that no one was coming on that day, the peon would quickly rush to the station to reclaim the refund of ₹50, which he took home and brought back to deposit in office the next morning. Every penny counted, and was accounted for, in Sun.

Many times it was Shanghvi himself, who was travelling and had to board the train at the last minute, in sleeper class mostly. This when the company had grown large enough to allow its managers a second AC travel allowance, Pahwa recalled. Since travel plans were erratic and two out of six tickets needed to be cancelled, he preferred to start the 'less wastage' principle right at the top.

'There have been times when Dilip and I have even travelled in the guard's cabin. He has had no qualms about the mode of travel when work beckoned.' Other times, he would be in such deep slumber inside the train, that younger brother Jayant, who occasionally turned up at Borivali station to pick him up, recalled having to board the train, search for him and shake him out of his sleep. 'He slept so peacefully that at times he almost missed getting off at Bombay station,' Jayant, who had just joined Sun after completing his graduation at IIT, Powai, said.

Once Sun started becoming familiar in Baroda and its nearby locations, people who knew Shanghvi remotely found it amusing that an owner of a company, however small, was travelling sleeper-class so often. Pahwa recalled once Sailesh Desai's neighbour passing a stray remark, 'I saw your MD boarding second class.' When Desai let this out in office, Shanghvi said, 'Big deal!' Why do you guys make so much fuss about the MD?' Not only that, he went further and at times made the company book all berths—lower, upper, side (upper and lower) in a railway compartment to hold office meetings in the train amidst the cacophony of hawkers selling tea and salted peanuts. Money was clearly not the only resource; when the 'less-wastage principle' was being applied in Sun, it applied equally to time as well. Kirti and his colleagues recalled chalking out promotional details of a new drug, scripting a promising launch with Dilip-bhai. What played out as a background score was the engine music of the chugging train, hissing brakes, clanking metals and a shrill whistle as if it were nodding approval to the plan.

A Touch of Professionalism

Till 1989, the year Sun shifted its headquarters to Baroda, mainly to save some money to grow bigger, given the skyrocketing real-estate prices of Bombay in the years preceding the Harshad Mehta scam it had lived like a big entrepreneurial family. The shift itself was planned with considerations such as the best time for children to get school admissions. So June 1989 it was, when many Sun executives were given the option to shift to the new headquarters in Baroda, yet to be named Synergy House. The building was Jayant's first labour of love in real estate, a project assigned to him by Shanghvi, at a time when he didn't know a plinth from a column, according to his own admission.

Armed with a single-line instruction, an architect and a cousin for an interior decorator, Jayant tried to build a home for the Sun family. But the first project ran into long delays. When Jayant went back to Shanghvi brooding, saying, 'I think I have bitten off more than I can chew. There are so many responsibilities scattered here and there,' big brother reduced his single-line instruction to two words, '*Chew faster.*'

'It wasn't unusual for Dilip-bhai to give us tasks that we were absolutely unfamiliar with, hoping that we would learn quickly. There was never scope for any benefit of doubt that I may not be up to it. A reason for this could be that he was himself so quick to grasp, had learnt everything on his own, and felt it comes as easily to all those whose intelligence and ability he trusted,' Jayant said. The day Jayant was asked to take over manufacturing, he said, 'I have no idea whatsoever of manufacturing.' There was a brief but unmistakable pause from Shanghvi followed by, '*Then, learn it.*'

'It was like someone telling you, if you come from a family of athletes, why don't you just climb the Mount Everest,' Jayant joked. Friend Sailesh had been scaling similar uncharted personal 'Everests' ever since he joined Sun in 1986. In 1987, when operations at the Vapi manufacturing site, which was forever under expansion, had been streamlined to some extent, he was asked by Shanghvi to delve deeper into marketing. 'I was not comfortable, that was neither my zone of expertise nor experience. But when I expressed my reservation, he said, *'Train yourself.'*

Between 1988 and '91, he travelled like Shanghvi across India, setting up, streamlining teams across Tamil Nadu, Maharashtra, Gujarat and Delhi. Somewhere in between, he was forging relations in the government. He also looked at the undirectorial work of haggling for lower rent for Sun employees, fresh immigrants who had come to inhabit the new headquarters at Baroda. It was Sailesh who shifted to Baroda first. Then he and Shanghvi roamed about the whole of Ahmedabad and Baroda. They had settled for a spot in Subhanpura area that fell right at the median of Alembic and Sarabhai, two of India's largest pharmaceutical companies. It was almost as if the force of gravity was working upon the little company by aligning its geographic position, declaring the league it was to soon enter.

'One almost forgot that Sailesh-bhai and Upen-bhai were actually directors of the company. They were like guardians in a new place, arranging for admissions of our children in good CBSE schools and helping us find rented accommodations at good prices and convenient locations. At times they opened their homes for food and stay for us till we were settled,' Pahwa recalled.

The gravitational pull started working its charms right away. Rajesh Kikani, who had served more than a decade in Alembic, of which the last five years as executive assistant of Chirayu Amin, the CMD, started getting feelers from Sun in 1989. His friend from IIM Ahmedabad, with whom he often caught up at alumni meets, told him during one of his casual conversations, 'Why don't you come and meet Dilip?'

'Who is Dilip?'

'He is the MD of Sun Pharma.'

'What is Sun Pharma?' Kikani recalled asking his friend, not able to remember seeing any such company in the ORG Retail Audit that monitored the performance of top 200 companies.

'He is my office neighbour and his is amongst the most outstanding of firms. You must meet him on my request.'

Kikani was not exactly the kill-to-network type and didn't pursue the matter, but his friend persisted for two months and so he relented. Shanghvi asked him whether he would prefer to meet in office or outside. 'I thought there was no crime in meeting someone, and Synergy House was at a stone's throw from the Alembic office,' Kikani recalled. He thought Shanghvi was a super salesman, who could create such an experience that you just couldn't say 'No'.

Kikani said, 'When not an employee, you reserve the right to ask rude and nasty questions. I wasn't rude exactly but I recall asking him, according to me, a very arrogant question for an interviewee, "Where would your company be ten years from now?"'

'In top ten by 2000,' Shanghvi replied calmly.

'How is that even possible?' wondered a jolted Kikani, conjuring up all possible maths and models that he had learnt at the premier management institution.

'What is the value of an Alembic prescription?' Shanghvi asked in Gujarati.

'If it's one product, it could be as less as ₹1.50, if it is three expensive products, it could be a maximum of ₹200.'

'What do you think is the value of my prescription?'

'A few thousand, may be,' Kikani shot out a guess, thinking he had already aimed for the roof.

'Our one prescription would be at the very least 300 times of an acute drug prescription which usually does not exceed ₹50, and we are not aiming for a one-time prescription.' Looking at a dumbstruck Kikani, who had frozen on his seat, Shanghvi continued to explain, 'Your antibiotics, when given for its fullest cycle, can yield business for two weeks. My products are lifetime drugs. Once a specialist like a cardiologist starts writing this, no one can tamper with it unless another cardiologist decides to change it or a competitor manages to influence him. And that shouldn't happen if our robust marketing model works as good as it has on ground. We are fine-tuning it to the next level,' Shanghvi explained, throwing a question, 'OK, Rajesh-bhai, how do you monitor growth?'

'Through annual balance sheets, and you?'

'We grow month on month. Every month we must add at least a lakh worth of sales. And we can only grow from there, as every prescription we add goes to consolidate our base. We cannot slow down, unless people stop taking these medicines, and that is not possible.'

The two went on to compare Sun's 40–50 per cent CAGR (compounded annual growth rate) with single-digit growth of biggies like Alembic and the philosophy underpinning such growth. Shanghvi extrapolated the growth of a few top companies, along with his own to show a projection of the future in his mind. Kikani said he felt like a large frog in a large well. 'Something that seems so obvious now had totally missed the big companies. I was, at that time, in a space that was the conservative amongst the conservatives and I felt that outside this space, the axis of pharma universe was shifting quietly.'

Kikani sought time and did his homework on Shanghvi's model at home. His own arithmetic showed that Shanghvi's assessment of his company sitting on a gold mine of a model may be correct but he knew that if he as much as shared such a prophecy (that Sun would be in top ten in ten years) with anyone in Alembic, he would be dubbed crazy.

After that dizzying first meeting, Kikani met Shanghvi twice. In one of those, he asked Shanghvi about the ownership structure of Sun Pharma.

Shanghvi said, 'It's a partnership firm.'

'How many partners?'

'Outside of family—three.'

'Are they sleeping partners?'

'No, they are in business.'

'Then I am walking into a bloody mess. If one partner doesn't agree to something, the business plan gets stuck right there,' a concerned Kikani shared with Shanghvi. This apprehension was echoed by many senior professionals who joined Sun later, at times verbalized, other times implied. What was also to become a dilemma every time Sun brought a heavyweight like Kikani was where in hierarchy do you place them, relative to other partners, who were not professionally as qualified or had a comparable standing in the industry, but had brought Sun as far as it had come?

At that moment, however, Shanghvi cleared the air effortlessly. 'Even though, we are partners it is clear that when it comes to operational matters, the decision is only mine. They cannot veto what I decide. It is our internal understanding. If you wish to verify, you can walk over to two of them, sitting right here in this office or talk to the one who is stationed in Vapi.' He then picked up the receiver himself without waiting and spoke into the phone, 'Sailesh, Rajesh-bhai is here. Why don't you speak to him?'

Not everyone can claim in a partnership setting with such crystal clarity that he is the boss and others are not. And then exhort you to ask the rest whether he is or not. It is this transparency that stunned Kikani and erased whatever doubts he had had about joining Sun. He walked over to Sailesh's cabin, who struck a friendship with him almost instantly.

The meeting lasted well beyond an hour and they freely chatted about the structure and decision making at Sun, with Sailesh marvelling at Dilip's talents. 'Oh, you should see the kind of domain knowledge Dilip has. None of us can match him. And his business sense is something all of us respect so immensely. It is in our interest and we have agreed that he would run the business.'

After meeting Sailesh Desai, Kikani didn't feel the need to knock on the doors of other partners, but even twenty-five years later he felt it is this clarity and transparency that has taken Sun to the heights it has reached. 'There never was any confusion in the minds of the super-boss and down the line. What was said was what was meant. They knew what they could do, what they could not.' This clarity came especially handy when one dealt with the ambiguities of marketing drugs to doctors.

Once convinced that his joining such a small company was not a suicidal move in terms of his career, Kikani went over to Shanghvi's office to convey a final 'Yes'.

Over tea, Shanghvi asked, 'Rajesh-bhai, what are you doing about the house? Where are you planning to stay?'

'What I can afford, I do not like and what I like I cannot afford,' Kikani joked.

'Is there anything you have seen in particular?'

Kikani was living in a company-allotted house and had to vacate it if he was going to move to Sun. He had been house-hunting and had found a decent house, which overshot his budget by a lakh. He told Shanghvi about the new house he was considering, and how he was planning to bridge the difference.

The next day morning he received a phone call. It was Upen. 'Can I see you for a while? Dilip-bhai has asked me to give you one lakh rupees. When and how would you like to receive it—by cheque or cash?'

'I have not even finalized the house yet,' Kikani replied. But deep down he was floored by the warm friendship, entrepreneurial spark, care and promise of growth—how it looked when all of these were rolled into one package.

What Kikani hadn't realized then but did, eventually, was—'Dilip-bhai was talking to me for the first time and it felt as if everything was happening spontaneously but he had done a thorough background check on me, much more detailed than I had done on him or his company.' This was a small instance of how Shanghvi evaluated cost, value and perceived value.

'Kikani was an IITian and an IIM Ahmedabad alumnus. He was a star of sorts then with a lot of clout. No one in the industry believed till the last minute that he would actually join us. But he did, we pulled off that feat,' Sailesh recounted. Serious reasons aside, Kikani was also looking forward to Sun as one of his friends from Alembic would soon be his new colleague there. This was a friend that Kikani discussed philosophy, psychology and management theories with. In fact, this friend had promised him, 'I will join Sun one day before you so that I remain senior to you there and I can be there to welcome you. This friend was Bhagwat Yagnik, tall, ruggedly handsome and well read, from a well-to-do family.

It was on his way to office, when he had noticed a small board—Sun Pharma—before noticing the logo in the morning newspaper one day. The company had advertised the post of a GM, HR. Feeling curious, Yagnik stopped by to ask a wiry Malayali gentleman with his bush shirt out, smoking a cigarette outside the building. 'What does this company do exactly?'

The man, Anujan, who turned out to be the personal assistant to Shanghvi, replied, 'Sun Pharma, mainly into psychotropic drugs.'

'Are you looking for a GM, HR? I am in HR at Alembic.'

'Yes, we are.'

'Do you have proper a HR department?' he asked tentatively, wondering whether a company so small understood what HR meant.

'No, but we are looking. Why don't you come and meet our MD?'

And so he asked Yagnik to formally apply, so that he could invite him for an interview.

When Yagnik walked in, he recalled meeting a man his own age, dressed in a cream-coloured Terelyne shirt, who instead of interviewing him, shared what he wanted to create. 'I was deeply into psychology then, too analytical. I realized that here is a person, who has a dream beyond this room, even beyond himself. He also has a blueprint to achieve it. And he has a sincerity that makes you feel he means every word he says. When someone is faking it, you can tell. He came across as honest and excited, transparent and trusting.'

'I know you are leaving a company of ₹100 crore to join me, but I can promise you a job you are dying for,' Shanghvi said. It was a line that so beguiled Yagnik that he would use it countless times to attract professional talent at Sun. This was also partly because he didn't have much luxury to promise them other goodies such as tempting packages and perks.

And then the clincher—Shanghvi promised Yagnik that even though he was looking for a GM to head the HR function, he wouldn't hire one unless he was compelled to by his new recruit. 'That is his beauty. He understands you and your need, and places a conviction in you almost by gut. And then he trusts you, almost in advance, before you have proved that you are trustworthy. It was his vulnerability which appealed to me most about him. 'And you know you cannot let him down, ever,' Yagnik reflected.

Dilip understood Yagnik's ambition to experiment in a boutique organization, try out new things and kept his word. Till Yagnik continued in Sun, he remained the head of HR. And thanks to his friendship with Anujan, he even got to choose his own cabin. Never mind that when he joined the Baroda office, most rooms were vacant to start with. He walked out of the cabin on the mezzanine floor, where all cabins were arranged in an arc, and stood at a spot from where one could see the entire open office plan on the ground floor. He counted twenty-six heads working on their desks, this is where he started at Sun.

Beautiful boutique organizations sans brand names come with their own set of hiccups. When Yagnik reached out to professionals to schedule an interview, he would be asked, 'What company did you say? Sunflower Oil Mill,' and, 'Sorry, come again. Where are you calling from? Sunlight detergent?'

Some would simply hang up. And when it came to medical representatives, Raju and Yagnik travelled to places to recruit and, at times, no one turned up. 'Some who did were those who clearly hadn't got a job anywhere else. But you had to recruit. We would sift from those and find the ones who had a hunger to learn,' Yagnik said.

In a way, hiring freshers was a boon in disguise for Sun. Those MRs who had worked in a few multinationals and few large traditional companies were indoctrinated to believe in marketing practices that preached clinical detachment from doctors. They would have been unsuitable to adapt to the new wave of marketing methods the new company was proposing. 'We trusted and trained them, when no one else did, and they outperformed themselves,' Yagnik recalled. What seemed to have worked so spectacularly for Sun and the Sun boys was trust as an investment and success as an aphrodisiac. The new recruits got their promotions quickly in a growing firm, becoming first-line managers in a year or two, second-line managers in four or five. And a field force that felt it owned the company collectively remained the singularly most potent source of market intelligence on what other companies were up to. An emotionally charged army on a mission would be the first to pick up what Torrent, Cadila and Intas were doing on ground, how many people they were recruiting, how many doctors they were covering and how? All this information would move up across the ladder in a telegraphic speed to reach the headquarters.

Professionals Sun went on to woo from this moment on were not a choice-less lot, however, and didn't respond to just emotional mollycoddling. Yagnik pitched, they refused. He pursued, they shrugged politely or arrogantly. He persisted, they considered; and suddenly at one point, even without realizing when that point arrived, many of them found themselves haggling for a salary they thought they deserved. More so, Yagnik did this even when these professionals were leaving an established bigger brand to join a little-known company.

However, in course of time, many came around either through, 'I will give you a job you are dying for' punchline delivered powerfully by an eloquent Yagnik or after a meeting with Shanghvi.

One steady source of professionals was found right around the corner—Sarabhai Chemicals. The company was perceived a little complacent and a tad uppity by its smaller non-VIP neighbour, sandwiched by choice between it and Alembic. What appeared as smugness to Sun executives was pride to Sarabhaians. When Sun's star was on the ascendant, fortunately for it and unfortunately for its much grander and elite neighbour, Sarabhai's fortunes had started waning.

The rot had started setting in in the early 1980s. But it deepened beyond repair in the latter part of the '80s, when the company struggled to repay loans taken on high interest, and stood on the brink of a default. Many Sarabhaians stuck around deep into the decline in reverence of the institution. The company once professionally managed and built on the cornerstone of ethics, was waiting for a miracle to happen. 'I recall when Sarabhai ruled at numero uno position, it would be raining offers for us and even from multinationals like Pfizer, who paid four times more salary but was ranked at number three. And we would shun those overtures, our nose in the air, and tell them, "Aren't you still at number three?"' Rajesh Kumar, then a second-line manager at Sarabhai recounted.

But by 1990–91, symptoms had started manifesting in forms that affect everyday lives—salaries were not coming on time, word had spread around in the industry and panic had begun to creep in. On a winter morning of 1990, Kumar recalled riding his scooter to meet a few doctors, when in his rear-view mirror he saw his secretary chasing him in another scooter, waving at him frantically. 'Telegram has just arrived, we have to suspend all fieldwork,' he panted, making his boss shudder and wonder how far this will tumble downhill before it's all over.

Kumar hadn't reciprocated to feelers from Sun yet, but like a host of other colleagues, he started mulling over the offer seriously. Many of Kumar's peers like Udayan Dasgupta had jumped the ship by then. And others like Shyamal Ghosh and Lokesh Sibal were considering Sun actively. Ghosh had offers from Torrent and Mercury Pharma, a firm led by his batchmate friend.

When Dasgupta urged him to join Sun, extolling the greatness of Dilip Shanghvi and a passionate work atmosphere, Ghosh recalled initially rebuffing him: 'I can see it's not a typical nine to five job like in Sarabhai. You have been coming home at 9.30 in the night. I can't slog so much. I want a life beyond work.'

Undeterred, Dasgupta convinced him to meet Shanghvi once before deciding. Ghosh liked Shanghvi, who he said spoke so softly that he had to strain to hear him. By conventional parameters he knew it made more sense for him to join the larger company Torrent. Also after so much hard-selling and pampering, which made him feel warm and wanted, Ghosh, like so many other professionals, recalled entering a haggling match over salary with Yagnik. 'I felt I deserved more. I was not only coming from Sarabhai but was forgoing an offer at Torrent. And finally I told them, "Forget it, I don't want your job."'

But they wouldn't let him go as well. Yagnik convinced him to meet Shanghvi a second time, who told Ghosh, 'The company will grow and you will grow with it. I can assure one thing—you will not regret this decision ever in your life.' Ghosh went back home all confused, spread three offer letters on his dining table, stared at them for a while and then booked a ticket for Bombay. Next, he was sitting across Subhash Majumdar, a Harvard-educated former CEO of Sarabhai at his Khar home.

'Shyamal, put aside all these offer letters. And tell me about the feelings that crossed your mind while you were being interviewed,' Majumdar said. After Ghosh finished narrating, Majumdar advised him, 'I don't know much about this small company into psychotropic drugs, but if I were you, I would gamble on that.' Ghosh joined, wary of the workload awaiting him at Sun. So did Kumar, after a meeting with Shanghvi where he was ensnared by the story of his rise from a stockist, and his statement—don't think you are joining the 114th rank company on the ORG-Marg list. Whatever you are seeing is an effort of just the last few years and the intention is not to slow down but accelerate. So Ghosh, Kumar, Dasgupta, Kikani, Yagnik among others, drawn from the left-hand neighbourhood and right-hand neighbourhood, became part of the first trickle of professionals who walked into Synergy House to surprise and be surprised by what felt like an unstructured mission in motion in a direction they dared not disturb.

Shocks of Grass-root Culture

Ghosh was used to prim and proper people preparing for pre-scheduled meetings with an air of formality and importance at Sarabhai. At Sun, such meetings could happen at the clap of a hand or a shout of the boss. 'At 2 p.m., we would be told about the meeting at 4 p.m. called by Raju or Dilip-bhai. And then it would linger on till five before we started, while everyone worked as they waited. The meeting would start at 5.30 p.m. and went on till 9 or 10 p.m. over cups of chai and samosa being served,' Ghosh recounted.

Every second they felt was packed with so much action of a diverse nature simultaneously, but the air in Synergy House didn't feel heavy and fatigued with overworked staff. 'In Sun, the air was young and vibrant. If in the morning something was said, by evening they wanted results. At times, you had half an hour to work something out. But somehow everyone was together in it, and you didn't feel any pressure. You just did the best you could in that stipulated time,' Kikani said. Yagnik added that at Sun there were no deadlines, only an expectation that the work at hand gets done at the earliest it could.

And all work didn't mean no fun. Ghosh recalled looking up in surprise to a thumping sound of urgent footsteps to find Dilip-bhai and Sailesh-bhai racing past each other across the corridor like teenage boys. He later found out that both had wagered on who is fatter, and they were running towards the weighing machine to stand on it first. The idea of being weighed came to them just after they had wiped clean plates of pastries ordered from Express Hotel, a regular indulgence, and had accused each other of not resisting sweets.

Back in Sarabhai, quite like in multinational companies, there would be one or two new product meetings every year. In Sun, there was one every month and several follow-up meetings that could happen multiple times a week.

In one such meeting, the first for Rajesh Kumar, salespeople were fixing their own targets for the quarters. When it was Kumar's turn to set a target for himself, he uttered '100 per cent'. 'I was numb. My 100 per cent target was the lowest in the whole group of sales managers, which I set up under tremendous peer pressure. But what do you do, when everybody else around you is chillingly, comfortably, blurting out 150 per cent, 170 per cent, 200 per cent as if it was an auction. Here I was setting a growth target of 100 per cent and still bang at the bottom. It was my true culture-shock moment,' Kumar laughed. Back at Sarabhai, where Kumar worked as a divisional manager, with seventeen people reporting to him, a lower double-digit target would have sufficed to earn laurels from bosses.

Culture shocks confronted 'professionals' in other ways. Shortly after joining Sun, Kikani visited Calcutta, and was scheduled to meet Pradip Ghosh in the morning. After waiting for the whole day, when he had switched off the lights for the day, he heard knocks at 11 p.m. in his hotel room. It was Ghosh, who had gone to attend a doctor after receiving a call from him and he had no doubts about which of the calls was more urgent to attend, never mind that one had travelled from the west coast and another lived in the same city. 'This was Dilip-bhai's teaching. When I asked him, "Dada, let's meet tomorrow," he said, "I cannot promise if another doctor calls the next day. It's better we finish today's work in the night,"' Kikani recalled.

The tremendous grass-roots knowledge that Shanghvi and Desai displayed impressed Kikani no end. When a corporate gift-seller from his Alembic times showed off a fancy spiral-bound notebook everyone liked, and quoted a price of ₹30 per piece, Sailesh Desai asked him to supply the gift at ₹10. The gift-seller looked visibly shocked. 'That's not even my cost!' Desai continued unfazed, 'If you are challenging me on cost, I can deliver this to you for ₹7 and still make a profit. My family had a printing press. I know the price of paper and processing.'

'I would have never known this way of doing purchases—this value engineering. I kept learning something different from them every day but when it came to sharing what I had learnt I was acutely conscious that applying conventional management to Sun's growth engine could be controversial. It was growing on a different fuel and conventional wisdom was absolutely obsolete for them.'

Yagnik, the new HR head, often watched the new lot of professionals intently during meetings and took it upon himself to instil in them what he deemed as a 'Sun Persona' that he had distilled from Shanghvi. He would often go to their cabins to have long chats and explain that at

Sun sincere efforts mattered more than the final outcome. 'Dilip-bhai values inward-looking individuals, who reflect on their responsibilities rather than commanding and controlling their subordinates. Faffing and bossing around is not for this place, nor is flamboyance,' Yagnik would explain.

Resetting the body clock, acclimatizing minds and keeping fingertips up to date with knowledge of their verticals, or getting accustomed to Himalayan growth targets were less bothersome to many Sarabhaians and other professionals from multinationals. What did bother them was architecting a fundamental shift in the marketing model—the doctor engagement practices—which quite a few of them perceived as a moral dilemma, given their puritan approach in their parent companies.

SAS: The Middle Path of Marketing

No single form of growth-driving pharma marketing in India's generic drug space of the 1990s could be totally free from controversy. Marketing strategies including that of Sun which promoted a long-term relationship with doctors polarized professionals on the side of the wave they belonged. But was there a choice? Most large companies and multinationals, which stuck to just what they perceived as 'ethical marketing' built on the premise that only scientific and knowledge inputs would be shared with doctors, were fast slipping into a slow-growth zone, missing out riding a growth curve.

'Sarabhai and some multinationals were fastidious in maintaining hygiene in marketing practices, and a sanitized distance between the doctor and the MR was built into the relationship they cultivated. Some of these companies considered giving anything more than a pen as a gift, a sacrilege. So many of us did go through the initial ethical dilemma of whether what we were doing was the right thing,' a professional who had joined Sun said. He admitted to having been a victim of that complexity in his initial days. Many professionals armed with years of training were conditioned strongly against building close ties with doctors, and battled with their idea of ethical marketing.

Ghosh, when he had just stepped into Sun, couldn't be dubbed an exception. He ran into frequent arguments with Shanghvi on the matter.

He would argue about the righteousness of sponsoring a doctor for a conference, or lavishing them with gifts that seemed expensive. He was so dogged in his pursuit to question Shanghvi that colleagues started warning him to back off. Raju once remarked as he was leaving the meeting room with a sheaf of papers, tucked in his arm, 'You are too much, Shyamal.'

'But I had to be convinced about what I was doing and the only guy who was most patient about my questions was Dilip-bhai. He wouldn't rebuff me. After a while he called me into his cabin and explained the rationale of the model,' Ghosh recounted. His explanation appealed to Ghosh's sense of logic and emotion, making him feel that working seventeen years in companies which sold acute therapies had skewed his perspective.

Shanghvi's point was that till now large companies have mostly done marketing exercises for acute drugs and vitamins, which meant chasing GPs for a prescription of a week or two at the most. More importantly, these older firms sold old-generation drugs that had been in the market for years, which means they had nothing new to share with the doctors on a regular basis.

Since Sun was changing the game, and bringing new drugs to India it couldn't afford to play by the old rules and hope to be effective. They had a duty to inform the doctor about how a new drug behaves inside the body. Also, the model of Sun was meant to shape the market of the chronic drugs. This by its very definition was generating business through lifelong prescriptions of specialists, and in that business landscape, long-term sustainable relationship with doctors were the only framework they had to operate in.

Shanghvi also went into the arduous grind an MR goes through in his daily schedule, competing with countless others in sweat and dust, turned away from the doctor's door after an endless wait. If he got to offer something that had value for the doctor, he would have an advantage over his peers. And then he passed across the table an article from *Time* magazine which narrated, in juicy detail, how big pharmas in the US were flying battalions of doctors to exotic islands in the Bahamas on luxurious junkets.

'We are sponsoring select top doctors, who can jolly well afford their tickets, for medical conferences. Are we doing such leisure trips?'

Shanghvi asked. Ghosh went back to his seat and read the piece many times over. Some of the companies named in the piece were the same which preached ethical practices in India. The maze of marketing ethics could send one into a dizzying spiral, an insoluble puzzle with no base, no bottom.

Before Sun, Torrent had started forging closer ties with medical bodies like Neurological Society of India, Cardiological Society of India and Indian Psychiatric Society. Its founder, U.N. Mehta, having served as a medical representative for years, understood the kind of struggle foot soldiers go through to just find those few minutes to tell a drug's story to the doctor. He therefore started sponsoring conferences, promoting them as platforms MRs could use to mingle with their demigods. This strategy succeeded for Torrent in oiling its customer relations, and was adopted in its various avatars by Sun, Intas, USV and others.

At Sun, Raju christened the strategy 'Scientific and Academic Services' (SAS) as they fine-tuned it. In its basic unrefined form, it meant sponsoring top prescribers to attend medical conferences. 'Through SAS, I wanted to give a clear message that it was not a way of spending money on doctors. That spend has to be with a purpose, that being it should ultimately help doctors treat their patients better,' Shanghvi said. When Ghosh's friends from MNCs derided such practices as inducements to doctors, he tried explaining to them as he had been explained.

'The guys we sponsor for conferences are most celebrated specialists in their therapies and have practices that earn them lakhs every month. They are not at our material mercy to attend a conference, buy an air ticket or stay in a decent hotel. Offering them these things for an academic pursuit is like offering them not inducement but loose change. One must keep in mind that unlike us marketing and sales guys, they are not frequent travellers and could feel awkward and inadequate when they land in a different city. We wish to take away that headache and attend to them so that they feel like guests, not foreigners in an alien land,' he clarified.

This was to also underline the fact that there was a reason why, if a conference was being hosted in Bangalore, the Calcutta regional manager would travel all the way to the southern city to attend to doctors from his own city. Seeing a familiar face in a different city used to lighten up the doctors' faces.

It helped that the Calcutta regional manager who couldn't as much get the high-nosed doctor to look at him back home, could hobnob with him, even swigging a whiskey in the cocktail dinner next to him. Ghosh, Roy and other Sun insiders emphasized that unlike other companies which sponsored a lot of foreign junkets, Sun kept it domestic and restricted it to medical conference venues, a move that must have suited the company's values and pockets alike.

'Marketing spend couldn't be on picnic and fun trips as many other firms were practising then. This devalued the relationship, made it transactional. It eroded respect for the company and was not sustainable in nature,' Raju said.

Reflecting on the practices which he named a quarter-century back, Raju said 'services' in SAS was an integral component in the whole framework of SAS and literally meant devotion. 'That sincerity in emotion that our boys showed towards customers was recognized and paid back handsomely,' he added.

Raju laughed off any reference to the company's marketing strategies as a 'grey zone'. 'There is no grey here because we knew our lines and didn't cross them. Those who referred to it as grey either misunderstood or misinterpreted it,' he asserted.

This sincerity of belief in the company's marketing strategies was all-pervasive among boys who were born and grew up at Sun. They were unapologetic, unabashed and, at times, bordered on boastful, when describing their deep emotional connections with thousands of doctors.

In their scheme, the medical representative scored a point when the doctor called him by first name, he earned five stars when called to the doctor's residence, and obviously, since the relationship was to last a lifetime corresponding with the graph of lifestyle diseases, the boys had to do much better than just this to earn bragging rights. When the doctor reciprocated, he usually did so to the individual and his perseverance, not to a company's call to be closer than the rest.

Rivals and detractors however, for reasons—business and ideological—did not get a hang of the philosophy and claimed that Sun smartly wrapped its commercial motive in a feel-good, emotionally appealing package.

'The shrewd ways Sun developed customer relations under various heads can never be caught. Connect it to academics by a long stretch of imagination, and suddenly every form of marketing, even when they were spending so much, becomes palatable to doctors. Highlight the emotional connect, and suddenly the very motive of that relation, which is business, doesn't sound vulgar. Retrospectively, they out-bade all competitors by practising a strategy which people in the industry took a long time to grasp,' a top executive of a rival firm admitted with grudging admiration of the model.

With a tinge of sarcasm, he pointed out that behind all unbridled emotions—there was cautious arithmetic justifying the business. His contention was not entirely baseless.

Sun picked the doctors it wanted to invest in very carefully, classified them into high-return, medium-return and low-return, depending on their potential calculated on factors like patient flows, number of prescriptions generated and retail sales audit. This marketing spend to sales, according to several former insiders, was roughly 1:10. They however explained that it wasn't designed to be the quid pro quo that it is now being made out to be by some rivals. In fact, the rationale of such a classification was to make best use of the time and energy of the limited number of MRs Sun had at the time.

Once the company chose the specialists it wanted to 'support', the words 'support', 'continuity', 'loyalty' were no more vague values to be made quotes out of and framed on the walls. The chosen set of doctors were sponsored for medical conferences year after year. Sun devised various ways to help their patient flows, expand their market, and in turn its own, by bringing new drugs in their therapies and quench academic thirst of doctors in ways that the medical industry in India had not witnessed till then.

One way Sun started spending its marketing budget on doctors was by gifting them assorted books on interesting topics in their subject, which they wanted to possess but were not inclined enough to buy on their own. Doctors in Calcutta credited Sun for building their library over the years. Ranabir Ghosh Roy, Debashish Roy and other psychiatrists in

Calcutta recalled Sun being the pioneer in distributing pricey textbooks of specialized niche publications. This was a practice which was later emulated by most other firms flogging psychiatric drugs.

'It's not just the books; it's their selection of books. My son was a practising psychiatrist in London at the time. I asked him to buy some books, like the third edition of *The Maudsley Prescribing Guidelines in Psychiatry* (Wiley-Blackwell) and some others, which were not available here; and then it would land up on my table as a gift from Sun,' Debashish Bhattacharya recalled. Sun started giving out expensive international books—the cost of which could run into thousands of rupees—as corporate gifts when La Opala dinner sets were more in vogue. Originally, the trigger for this strategy came from a new marketing director who had joined Sun in 1992 from Glaxo and had earlier worked in the prescription audit market research firm C-Marc. Academically oriented, he was famously known in industry circles as 'more master than marketer who writes a book wherever he goes'.

People who shared corridors and partitioned walls in office at Sun often found Subbarao Chaganti in total love with research and scribbling away. His first of the few published books was *Handbook of Pharmaceutical Marketing in India: Concepts, Cases, Strategy* (Pharma Book Syndicate). One of these was authored at Sun.

'Once we had started doing well, boss exhorted us to do things differently and introduce some new practices. Subbarao had just authored a book on pharma marketing and that became the first book we distributed,' T.K Roy recounted. Subsequently, Subbarao introduced Shyamal Ghosh and T.K Roy to P.T. Rajasekaran, who ran Panther Publishers in Bangalore.

They met Rajasekaran in Bangalore and thrashed out a deal. Rajasekaran reached out to major medical publishers globally, striking exclusive deals on behalf of Sun. He could bring to the table a commitment to buy books in a bulk deal, at discounted prices of course, print the copies in India so that their costs could be contained. On their part the international publishers would have to promise to make it a limited exclusive edition for the company and not bring those titles to India for at least six months to one year till after Sun had distributed them.

It made sense for most international publishers—because their books priced upwards of $20 were niche and not very popular with bookshops either. Even today, with bookshops migrating online, most of these books such as Bhattacharya's favourite copies of *The Maudsley Prescribing Guidelines in Psychiatry* are available for pocket-burning prices of over ₹5000, offered on equal monthly instalments.

'Doctors loved the feel of nicely bound hardbacks on their table. Often doctors were excited about forthcoming titles or journals they were to receive, in those days,' Yagnik recalled.

And which titles Sun would be buying rights for was selected through a rigorous process, in consultation with top opinion-leaders on their relevance in Indian context. 'Over the decade Sun distributed over 150 such titles but the idea itself proved to be a low hanging fruit for other companies to emulate,' Shyamal Ghosh explained.

However, over time, Sun had started enjoying this 'catch me if you can' game with peers and kept adding new marketing strategies. Its SAS had got more refined and by 2003–04, it had come a long way from what it used to be and included more pure academic marketing activities such as offering short courses by inviting international specialists who were known as father figures in their own therapies.

At times, some of these ideas actually popped in the minds of the doctors that there were targeted at, and marketing executives would catch a whiff of these brainwaves and discuss it with Shanghvi. T.K. Roy, for instance, recalled how Dr Uday Muthane, a top neurologist, considered a super-expert in Parkinson's, suggested that they should invite Stanley Fahn, an international star neurologist who treated the greatest American boxer Muhammad Ali to offer short courses on movement disorders in India. Fahn was the sort of guy whose name figured in a rating scale which measure complex nervous disorders such as Parkinson's disease, dystonia, tremor, Huntington's disease. Shanghvi, who was not so free with his compliments, opened his compliments coffers for once on the idea.

By the late 1990s, medical soirees had not only been adopted by many more companies but were also getting grander, hosted in foreign locales and plush five-star hotels. As for the marketing strategies of multinationals in India, a top psychiatrist equated them to 'draping men in sarees'. 'Their understanding of cultural eccentricities and needs of India remain superficial,' he claimed. 'Some Indian companies could go one step further by taking you to a foreign locale promising education and then make a picnic out of it.'

A doctor recalled going to two such foreign trips in the late 1990s, before he stopped accepting more such invitations. 'It was so weird. Those were initial days of such trips and I went with an expectation to learn something and there on the spot they were asking for registration fee I couldn't afford. The manager from the pharma company told us, "Forget it, sir, we have a bus to ourselves and we can go sightseeing together."' He couldn't fathom whether bunking at the age of fifty-two felt more humiliating or juvenile, but something didn't feel right about the ways these programmes were conducted. That was in the year 2000, way before these foreign junkets had become much of a rage for anyone to frown, and countries like the US had enforced the Sunshine Act to bring transparency in financial relationships between doctors and pharmaceutical companies. But when it came to pure academic seminars, there clearly was an appetite, even hunger, among doctors. 'We decided to keep conferences strictly academic and reduce our spend of money and time. We would fly the experts into the country instead of flying Indian doctors abroad unlike others who were flying armies of doctors under the guise of academics, but once at the destination, it was frolic time,' T.K. Roy said.

Sun consciously opted for a venue away from the city, away from the shopping malls and other tempting distractions where there wasn't much to do even if you got away from the conference hall.

Still in every group, there would be a few such aberrations: doctors who requested for a car just as the first hour or so slipped by, and the first few yawns—the most infectious of all involuntary human reflexes—appeared on the horizon. But that's the reason the company decided not to keep too many cars parked near such events. This was just so that they could politely turn down requests of respected customers seeking non-medical, non-academic amusements. Such gestures set the tone for the event and over time, doctors not keen on academic elements opted out on their own, a former manager at Sun said.

These courses spanning typically 3–4 days started at 7.30 a.m., broke for breakfast at 10.a.m., and were over by 1.30 p.m. Post-lunch, these world-renowned experts were made available in the lobby for a one-on-one interaction. Those conferences proved to be smash hits, with Roy realizing that, given the right environment, too many specialists were truly keen to 'learn', not just 'holiday'. 'I saw doctors practising in small towns arriving with videos of their patients to understand about their condition,' Roy said.

When specialists grasped that it was all about real academics, they responded with the help of contacts, feedback, inputs and recommendations, and Sun rolled out conferences, hosting them one after the other. A course on movement disorder was established as an annual affair, courses in epilepsy were shortlisted, and neuro-otology and neuro-ophthalmology became sought-after crash courses. Sun kept on identifying need gaps and extending support in those areas. For instance, when doctors started getting sued for medical liabilities across countries, Sun responded by bringing legal experts to lecture them on defence strategies for their protections.

Some industry veterans, however, hurl accusations at Sun's practices, claiming it was one of the firsts to get cosy with the medical fraternity. It pampered them too much, stoking their greed and some of those gestures reverberated in the industry as murkier practices—with most smaller and a few large pharma companies willing to cross all lines, fix targets and cuts for doctors, even bidding and buying them out.

'As a pure business strategy, SAS was a stroke of absolute brilliance. I have to admit, that many companies which made a noise about Sun polluting the market initially, ended up blatantly aping its marketing moves. Even then, they couldn't copy the execution, which has set Sun apart. But when it comes to ethics, I couldn't keep Sun above others. In the pharma marketing practices of the Indian market, if doctors and pharma companies went to bed together, you could not absolve Sun from that responsibility any more than you could absolve other makers of drugs for chronic diseases,' a top executive of a rival firm felt.

Asked about such accusation, Shanghvi said, 'Even before we started Sun, people were paying doctors for prescriptions. Since I have always consciously focused on the long term, my belief from day one is that the doctor will support the company only if he respects it.

If I do anything by which the respect of a doctor is reduced, I will attain suboptimal results. It is my interpretation of their behaviour and their interpretation of my behaviour that will ultimately decide our success. And above that I have a resource constraint and I have to operate within that resource constraint to earn their respect. So we focused on training our MRs on scientific awareness. My advantage was that I was an outsider in the industry; so I was not viewing things from a coloured perspective; I had no preconceived notions or prejudices. I saw the problems just as they were and sought solutions that would work.'

A large chunk of cardiologists and psychiatrists were in agreement about the emotional connect part. A senior cardiologist from Mumbai was on a Delhi trip to attend a medical conference in the winter of 1999. His trip was being sponsored by one of Sun's rival firm. Early in the morning, after his breakfast and before the conference started, he broke into a cold sweat, panting for breath, and felt his heart sinking. Being a cardiologist, he was the first to diagnose himself and the first call he made was to a manager of Sun named Kunal, managing to utter, 'Kunal, I am having a heart attack.' One came across several such cases of Sun boys rushing to help when doctors turned patients.

This reputation of being 'bankable boys' for some reason also helped Sun shore up a few brownie points in ethics amongst its customers. 'There are always things which are worth much more to you than they are to somebody else, so you give them something which is worth much more to them than it is to you,' Shanghvi said about designing a win-win customer–company relationship.

Ethics in the pharma industry itself continues to be a sticky judgemental concoction of a subject. While responding to the word 'ethical', a large number of doctors, particularly among psychiatrists, perceived Sun as more ethical than its competitors. Factors that helped the perception strangely included continuity of the same people over long years, which made specialists familiar and comfortable with Sun boys, prompting most to conclude that there must be something really good and right about the company.

The second much-repeated factor was that Sun boys usually wouldn't commit to something that they couldn't do. They felt Sun operated under broadly set guidelines, which empowered the first-line managers to take decisions and stick to it.

One Kolkata psychiatrist cited instances where desperation drove medical representatives in other companies to beg for prescriptions. 'The MR would say that he would lose his job if you didn't prescribe his brand, and you were not sure whether you were being emotionally blackmailed or taken for a ride, or being told the plain ugly truth. At least with Sun people, you were not put in that awkward position.'

Some even drew a strangely abstract connection between ethics and Sun's academic orientation in marketing. Somehow Sun's gifts of books and journal, its promptness in helping consultants build their name by publishing and presenting their papers, the academic events it hosts, make it appear more credible and even 'ethical' in the eyes of its customers.

The historical seed for the credibility Sun enjoyed in the eyes of specialists—psychiatrists, cardiologists, endocrinologists—it dealt with was probably sown in 1992–93. Shanghvi, very early on in his career, when he was still working in the field, was once sitting with a senior specialist who casually told him, 'A senior bureaucrat's wife was here and I prescribed her an MNC's product.' It was a product that Sun was also selling.

Shanghvi recalled, 'For me, what was important in that conversation was this: he has not only prescribed a med of an MNC, but he is telling this to me on my face, which means he is taking pride in his action, and trusts the quality of an MNC product more. With no amount of convincing, I will get him to prescribe my medicine unless I earn this respect and trust. With a realization like this, our focus to earn the customer's respect just got stronger. The doctor will never risk the health of a patient because I convinced him that my product is of the best quality. He will do it only when he intrinsically respects my company and trusts the quality of my product. It is this in-depth understanding of the doctor's behaviour that helped us design our policies. And every moment, we were clear that it is through our actions that we have to earn his respect, because I have no parents sitting in the US and Europe who have created a legacy of credibility from whom I can draw that reputation. Either I create it through my actions or I don't get it.'

At a time when few large multinationals and Indian giants like Sarabhai remained puritans by sticking to hygiene and distance practised between medical representatives and doctors, and a clutch of fast-growing lifestyle drug companies and several small up-starts jumped to do anything—bid for the doctors, offered them cash, entered hard bargain and bought them outright—Sun chose the middle path. It spent heavily on marketing and doctors but made the core incentives it offered academic.

This somehow made the favours appear way more legitimate and acceptable to the community, which was struggling to comprehend and cope with the rapid transition in the pharma industry. At the time it was stuck in a moral dilemma between what medical professionals feel—the unprecedented and irresistible temptations dangled by the corporate sector and a conscience call of not allowing a blot on a profession they had grown up believing to be 'noble'.

One elderly psychiatrist called it a pull between 'Lakshmi' (the goddess of wealth) and 'Saraswati' (the goddess of knowledge and wisdom) for the profession. In that confusion which many describe as a vortex of identity crisis for the medical community, accepting academic favours and growing knowledge, which most doctors saw as 'beneficial to patients', felt less burdensome. 'Sun's Lakshmi (marketing spend on doctors) came as Saraswati (academic focus of marketing), resolving a deep-seated conflict in the doctors' minds and making it acceptable to our community,' the psychiatrist concluded.

A former Sun top executive reflected, 'All these years, many pharma companies have been kissing the doctors all over. The equation between Sun and its doctors is unique, they have never kissed, they haven't even stood face-to-face. But they have stood back to back, holding each other's hands tightly clasped, not spelling out in words their relationship, believing that treating it as a transaction will render it vulgar.' There seems to be one common thread between these words and the relationship it is attempting to express in words—both are abstruse and intimate.

CHAPTER EIGHT

DOCTORS, NOT THE ONLY SPECIALISTS

It was just the kind of weather in the winter of 1993, when steaming hot Indian chow mein could beat its Chinese cousin hands down, with generous servings of tomato ketchup and soya sauce, deceiving the senses to think it tasted yummier than it really was. Shyamal Ghosh was outside a Mumbai studio slurping precisely such noodles, experiencing a moment that had the potential to turn into a subject of historical envy down the generations of Sun boys, not for the noodles but the company he shared.

Sun was shooting for a calendar with fresh-faced models striving to create a mark in the industry. Sunil Mahadik, the art designer thought of the theme as one intersecting feminine forces and nature. The photographer David D'souza hadn't come cheap, charging about ₹2 lakh for the assignment. But the company lived up to its reputation of striking the best bargains in town, when it queued up a set of beautiful but little-known models for about ₹10,000 to 12,000 each. Little did they know that the handful of girls were to change the face of the fashion industry, just as Sun was to scorch a trail of its own.

Posing for Sun—as river, twilight, night and other forces of nature—were Malaika Arora Khan, Madhu Sapre, Sonali Bendre, Colleen Khan and Namrata Shirodkar. This was the company that Ghosh kept over chow mein. Posing for Sun as Aruna, the dawn, was none other than, untouched by stardom yet, a stunningly beautiful girl wrapped in yards of burnt-orange-and-fiery-red muslin. That girl, Aishwarya Rai, was yet to wear the crowns of Miss India and Miss World at beauty pageants and create history.

The calendar which may have eventually become a collector's item for spotting India's next top models was struck down at Sun by some who saw it as too 'liquorish' in taste and way too full of oomph for a

171

pharmaceutical company as conservative as Sun. It had the potential to misrepresent its brand amongst customers—another conservative lot.

It was unfair to compare it with the 'Kingfisher calendar', which paraded models in bikinis, when all the skin show in 'the could-have-been-Sun calendar' didn't amount to more than an off-shoulder costume. 'I was all for it and probably Dilip-bhai liked it too, but in matters of popular taste, he mostly stuck to democratic decision making,' Ghosh said.

Fortunately for Sun, another brilliant idea conceived by Shanghvi early that year didn't meet the same end, even though Ghosh and many more under him didn't fancy it at first. It started when Ghosh and Raju were clinking glasses in a Connaught Place hotel after a hard day's work in New Delhi, perusing the starters' menu to order snacks. It was in this convivial setting, with Ghosh pouring Raju a drink, discussing the next day's meetings, when the hotel phone buzzed. From Raju's kinesics and tone, Ghosh figured out it was Shanghvi he was talking to.

'We will have to start a division, exclusively for psychiatry,' Raju said, after keeping the receiver down. Ghosh took a few moments to grasp the concept. Having spent decades in the industry, he knew of the concept of divisions. Zydus had two of these—Cadila and Alida. Ranbaxy had them too, but none that he had heard dedicated to single therapy. These divisions had been floated when the number of products grew too unwieldy. Splitting them basically helped them buy more time at the doctors' clinics. Then, there had been sporadic experiments in the late 1980s of creating divisions by multinationals like Glaxo, to carve out one division dedicated to one product (Pulsar for promoting Zinetac or Ranitidine), that had met with success.

But what Shanghvi was suggesting was that a cadre of his medical reps would engage with only one set of specialists, in this case the 2000-odd psychiatrists across the country. 'Once we had introduced gastro-medicines, and a few anti-infectives, we realized at some juncture that our focus was getting diluted, and our ability to sustain relationships with doctors is getting diffused. It was this connect that had made us what we were, and we were losing it. So we thought of rearranging the field force. And started with what we called the speciality division dedicated to psychiatry, later renamed Synergy,' Shanghvi said.

Ghosh nearly scratched his head on hearing this plan. It was as if not enough that Sun—a tiny speck of a company—had spelt out its larger-than-life plans to make a grand entry into the elite club of top ten pharma companies in India, which Ghosh had laughed off. He was well aware of how companies which went down that path looked and felt from up close. He remembered how he had shared a smoke with Rajesh Kumar and Lokesh Sibal, in his early days at Sarabhai, dreaming of a day when they would run the company. Even before they had reached their middle age, the company was on the brink of being wrapped up.

Now this new order of the day, of a speciality division, was presented to him. While it was an exciting experiment, it was not clear to Ghosh how this would pan out. He was of a mind to list out his apprehensions, but Raju had already begun chalking out the dry run of this new arrangement they had to roll out by the end of that year. 'Shyamal, we need to create a small core team. As the division will deal with neuropsychiatry, we need our old-timers with solid experience in the therapy to join it. Please go to Calcutta and convince the veterans to become a part of this experiment.'

This was important for two reasons: first, Sun had by far built robust connections with the psychiatrist community—and this had been achieved by the old-timers, and second, Shanghvi had designed to start this division with the first set of products he had launched—Lithosun, Promasun and Nitrosun. Most of these old products of Sun had built a steady cash flow, which would ensure that the division wouldn't collapse. Also, given that the sales of these old products had peaked and plateaued at one level, they would probably offer a fair test case to assess whether the idea of specialized attention to medical specialists was effective.

Ghosh, whom most Bengalis called 'dada' or 'Shyamal-da' in the company started his internal recruitment drive in Calcutta. The first medical representative he tried to enlist with a charming smile responded with a flat 'No'. The second and third were more polite but refused nonetheless 'Na dada, hobena' (Sorry, dada, not interested). There were practical and logistical bumps, how would a total strength of seventeen reps and managers cover 2000 psychiatrists across the country. This was an untested formula on ground and meant breathless travelling and dramatic change in the job profile. But these were not the only concerns. An old-timer confessed, between 1980 and 1993, a lot had changed for psychiatrists. From being not so pampered, the lot was now becoming increasingly spoilt for choice, because the success of Torrent and Sun was now getting emulated by many smaller companies.

Many times, psychiatrists could place unreasonable demands on MRs. There was an instance of a Sun MR who got dragged out of politeness from a Benares medical conference to a vegetable *mandi* by a senior doctor, who was hunting for large juicy '*kashi begun*' (brinjal). He bought 10 kilograms of these, with a request (though coming from a doctor to MR it sounded more like an instruction) that the vegetable be delivered at his home in Calcutta. The doctor left, leaving the medical rep, struggling to balance two 5-kg bags on both sides, feeling stupid, stranded in the middle of the vegetable market.

Now that Sun had forayed into cardiology and gastro-drugs, MRs theoretically exercised more choice in the doctors and drugs they wished to focus on while earning targets. They didn't want to surrender that freedom and go for an untested formula. Many believed this experiment could, in the short term, cost these MRs their incentives and, in the long term, their job.

If so much and so many were against this idea, what made Shanghvi so sure that it would click? Was it his childhood conviction that 'focus yields'—drawn from his student life—when subjects went from mainstream to focused stream of commerce, his own performance improved dramatically? Was it, what his friend Ashok Butta observed as the moot mantra of his success: 'Dilip understands the minds of individuals, groups—patients, doctors, psychiatrists, cardiologists, and humanity' playing out in action? Or was it what T.K. Roy believed, 'Once Sun felt its feet on ground, it wanted to do something new and different'? Or was it all the above and a bit more?

What MRs saw as freedom to choose and flit between psychiatrists, cardiologists and gastroenterologists to fill in their quota of sales, could seem 'adultery' to someone who valued relationship with each one of them as central to Sun's success. Shanghvi said one strong trigger for trying out the different divisions was to build meaningful relationships with each community by paying attention to their needs, just as they had done with psychiatrists in their early days.

'I had seen that our ability to succeed was linked with our ability to build relations with doctors. That had been our core business philosophy and approach. But I realized that as an individual you cannot build meaningful relationships with psychiatrists, cardiologists and gastroenterologists, and all the different doctors at the same time,' Shanghvi said.

He was also conscious of preserving the sanctity of relationships, which Sun had developed with each community.

'My approach to business was also that you have to build a relationship of trust and integrity with the customer. That doesn't necessarily happen when you are straddling multiple therapists. When a cardiologist stops prescribing, you switch to a gastroenterologist. So you have no need for being honest in your relationship. But if you only have a psychiatric product, you have to have an honest relation with that community to continue. All psychiatrists in a city know each other, you lie to one and the word spreads and a reputation is built. That was the time I said, "Let's try this."'

Also, it was just around the time Sun had expanded into cardiology and gastroenterology drugs. Shanghvi felt that for an MR to remember so many therapies and so many different pharmacological aspects of drugs was a big challenge. On the contrary, if the MR had already mastered the knowledge of a first-line schizophrenia drug, he would learn about the second line in that therapy much faster; compared to learning about a new therapy area. This saved time could be put to better use in meeting doctors. These MRs would also have an edge over a peer from a corresponding company who was mugging up several drugs from different therapies.

'My learning has always been two ways—from personalities or companies, what I learn to do, what I learn not to do,' Shanghvi had said. So it was possible that Shanghvi was using his second mover's advantage in chronic therapy to the fullest. When Torrent, a company that Shanghvi watched keenly, was expanding into multiple therapies— one reason its hold in psychiatry had started shaking was precisely that. Assume you are an MR with a large basket of products in psychiatry, cardiovascular and 'gastro' segments. The 'cardio' drugs are costlier and the 'gastro' drugs have more uptake and are easier to sell. The reason for the latter is that there are more number of doctors prescribing these medicines including general physicians. You have a target of generating ₹10 lakh per month, of which you easily get ₹7 lakh from 'gastro' and 'cardio' drugs. Would you care to visit the psychiatrist and try hard?

Now that Sun had reached that juncture of entering three or four therapies, it faced the risk of seeing history repeat, with smaller rivals. In small stray pockets, minnows like Talent Healthcare and larger companies like Intas, which had learnt its lessons from Torrent and Sun, were pulling up their socks to challenge the challenger, and Shanghvi had his ears close to the ground.

'How special do you feel when someone does something especially meant for you? Creating a special cadre evoked that sort of feeling in neuropsychiatrists, cardiologists, gastroenterologists and, later, endocrinologists and oncologists. Specialists collectively felt that here is a company which was trying to understand us, our specific traits and customize its approach to our needs,' Milan Sinha, a pharma veteran who worked well over a decade in Sun till 2011 as head of its oncology division, said.

This crystal-clear assessment was brilliant in hindsight, which wasn't so clear to the old-timers. Shyamal Ghosh's excitement for the idea got the better of his apprehension. He was trying very hard to enlist MRs for the new experiment. 'Managers we could pull in, but among MRs, only one or two showed the courage to join. So we had no choice but to recruit afresh and the division was floated with 17–18 people,' Ghosh said.

The success of the therapy-division approach was felt just weeks after the launch, at the Baroda headquarters. Shanghvi monitored sales everyday from the report of orders generated at the Vapi facility. By the end of 1993, the sales growth of old drugs clubbed under the speciality division had shot up from 15–30 per cent to 50–70 per cent. The plateau had begun to peak again and it was clear to all that paying attention to specialists by creating a special cadre of MRs for them was headed for a roaring success.

Somewhere around that time, Shanghvi formalized the first neuropsychiatry division (which went by the name Speciality Division) by christening it 'Synergy', probably to indicate the power-packed growth born out of fusing energies of Sun and its customers. He asked

Ghosh to take charge of the new division as the GM. Ghosh sought a day's time to think, to weigh a final time his apprehension against his excitement. He returned next day to utter a near-confident 'Yes'.

The Unborns: Helios, Apollo and Ra

Shanghvi had set his mind on replicating the model for other therapies. Soon a division of cardiology drugs was set up, and executives were asked to brainstorm on the names. It's very likely that Shyamal Ghosh came up with the name 'Aztec' which Shanghvi liked. The term had its connection to a Sun-worshipping ethnic group of indigenous people who inhabited central Mexico in the sixteenth century.

The possibility of having other subsequent division names after Sun-worshipping communities was also discussed. These included Greek gods Helios and Apollo and the Egyptian deity Ra. Ghosh started buying books for the company's library on Sun-worshipping people, and even planned a calendar to celebrate the idea. However, to his dismay, the plan had to be abandoned as the brand name Aztec got stuck in a trademark litigation. A third division was thus named simply after the company—and called Sun Division which promoted gastroenterological and all other products except neuropsychiatry and cardiology.

Every time new divisions were formed, two things were specially kept in mind. They almost always were started with a set of existing established products and at least a part of the initial team, be it managers or MRs, were Sun veterans, who could provide continuity in the relationship hitherto cultivated with the specialists.

Much later, once divisions were in place and had taken fuller shapes by the late 1990s and the early noughties, Shanghvi's maxim—God and Devil both are in details—would surface during quarterly reviews and monthly meetings held on new products. Every division and each function would fill in a format of fifty-six pages detailing 28–30 heads, and would spend half a day with Shanghvi. At times, these meetings stretched up to 9–10 hours. Roy said people at Sun stopped sleeping at least four or five days before Shanghvi's quarterly reviews were to start.

He would scan every page, and then laser-beam into details that no MD could be bothered to concern himself with. Why has the call average—number of calls made to the doctor per day—of this MR in Tezpur dipped to five? Why was the promotional cost of a new drug so high? Had there been a delay in transporting the material, and instead of usual land transport, air mode had to be employed? So where had the root of this delay begun in the supply chain and how did it compound? He is especially reputed to do a deep dive if he spots unexpected and unexplained departures. And no manager could afford to excuse themselves of being ignorant.

Managers who said, 'I will get back to you on this one, sir,' would invite flinty stares from Shanghvi. A former sales manager at Sun recalled, 'Once Dilip-bhai asked me for some granular number in a quarterly meeting. I had them in the papers, but blanked out there. The moment I shuffled the papers to retrieve it, Dilip-bhai said, "If one has to refer to papers to furnish figures, I can do it instead of you."'

This is how a deep grilling session looked like.

Milan Sinha mentioned one such quarterly meeting with Shanghvi. He had proposed to sack a boy in Raipur, after his manager reported him to be cracking a smart one on the company. 'The manager told me that this boy has managed some settings by striking a deal in a large hospital of the Bhilai Steel Plant for an infusion drug which was not a targeted product (not on the company's priority selling list). So he easily attains his sales target, all at one destination quite comfortably and earns the incentives. He doesn't bother to work the rest of the days.'

'Milan, when did you last go to Raipur? Three to four years back at least?' Shanghvi asked

'Sir, I have never been to Raipur.'

'When did your ZSM [zonal sales manager] go to Raipur the last time?'

'Sir, he goes once a year.'

'You haven't been to that place. Your ZSM goes there once a year, the RSM [regional sales manager] must be going thrice a year at the most and you are writing that boy off! What is your validation for the decision? Do you see his intelligence? He has found value that can be easily created with the least effort without necessarily flouting any rules,' Shanghvi said. He did not point out that part of what the boy was doing at an individual level in his micro-setting—finding a need gap, leveraging his resources to meet it without breaking any rule—which was also what the company did at a macro level.

Sinha was still trying to make sense of the situation and how best to handle it, when Shanghvi spoke again, 'Shift base to Raipur for three months, or at least spend a fortnight there for the next three months.'

On this sudden throw-up of a challenge, Sinha, a national sales manager then protested mildly, 'What shall I do in a small centre like Raipur, sir?'

'Learn to validate before jumping to a conclusion.'

This was not just a great line to Sinha. Bhagwat Yagnik, the highly perceptive HR head of Sun, said he had witnessed numerous cases where he saw people instigating Shanghvi against others in situations where it was easy to believe, but he, despite being a great listener, had a highly sensitive trust meter which worked on his perception of real-life experiences, not on anybody's opinion of somebody else. He was "complain-deaf", another former employee quipped. 'He would give you the impression that he believed you while he was listening, but that's not the case. He would listen to denunciations, rarely, in fact almost never joining in. He was unprovokable,' he added.

Sinha concluded that besides gaining important insights on the Madhya Pradesh and Chhattisgarh market in his three-month stint in central India, he paid attention to that skiver of a boy, who had been skirting organizational goals to achieve some of his own. This boy slowly returned to perform in alignment with the organization. The strands Shanghvi mostly picked in his company relaxed the tension points which were stiffening in the company.

He would ask a division for the launch date of a new drug, and then go back in the chain to review each link where the different preparations converged. For instance, while checking whether promotional material would reach field offices on time for the launch to happen, if he found that it was still in print, he would go back to ask. 'Mahesh, when was the print order given?'

Mahesh Kadam, who looked after the commercial department, was known in the Sun ecosystem as one of the most efficient organizers and archivists. To answer Shanghvi's question, he would immediately retrieve his diary to spell out the date in a blink. Shanghvi would then analyse what had gone wrong, what had caused the delay and how it could be fixed. Actions would be taken right away, calls and arrangements made on the spot. Shanghvi practised this for many years and it reduced the slip of coordination between various functions, a major culprit behind delays, resulting in blame games and bad blood within companies.

These meetings were the points where all the joints of Sun were oiled, with every division, every function—Active Pharmaceuticals Ingredients or (APIs), raw materials used in making medicines production, commercial, purchase, etc. These divisions got together to create what the business development head Kirti Ganorkar called a 'perfectly synchronized relay race'. Someone else referred to these quarterly meetings as a garage where Sun, the giant automobile, used to go for servicing and from where it returned, every part lubricated and nuts and bolts tightened.

Going forward, Sun launched many drugs. Every division lined up five to six drugs in a year, and acquired companies which had their own set of new drugs to be launched or marketed.

Sun also multiplied divisions to keep up with the launches. Shanghvi explained his approach in detail.

'Back then we had multiple products for depression, schizophrenia and anxiety. We realized that ultimately a rep will only be able to promote one or two while we noticed that existing products still had the potential to grow. But it was because we were unable to prioritize, we were not growing. As a company with significantly higher market share than its competitors, improving the size of the market is my responsibility. Because if I don't expand, my market will become my constraint.'

Shyamal Ghosh reckoned that even if Sun chalked out the most brilliant marketing plan at the head office to promote fifteen to twenty drugs, the MR couldn't execute it. This is because the field—hospitals and clinics—was not a utopia. In fact it was an absolute chaos. At times doctors wouldn't give more than five minutes. At times after a day of sweat and dust, the MR may not have the stamina to detail twenty drugs with equal vigour. The maximum he could promote was three to four drugs. And we at Sun understood this too well because managers across rank and file worked with the boys, Ghosh added.

So as not to dilute focus, every third year, Sun launched a new cardiology division—Aztec, Azura, Arian, Avion. Five years after launching Synergy as its first division, the company launched a second neuropsychiatry division and called it Symbiosis. It then followed it up with one every five years—Cyrus and Cymbalta. Post-1996, Sun made divisions out of the companies it acquired—Spectra (TDPL's oncology), Inca (TDPL's in vitro fertilization (IVF)-gynaecology), Milmet (Milmet's ophthalmology), Solaris (Natco's mixed basket of products) and so on.

Such was the zeal and pace of adding new divisions at Sun that they started experimenting with the concept and at one time floated a division run by housewives. Dubbed internally as the 'family physicians' or 'FP', it recruited housewives in Mumbai, some of them pharmacists, who needed to engage part-time, make five calls when their husbands were away in office and kids at school. Shanghvi's own wife was a pharmacist by education and homemaker by occupation.

'Dilip-bhai was always game to try out new things. We started this to tap GPs. Many of our products were only targeted at specialists. And this seemed a fair way to add to sales by promoting drugs—like Famocid, Pantocid to GPs', Ghosh said. This particular experiment had to be wrapped up after a year because it was becoming difficult for the company to evaluate the performance of housewives, considering much of what they were selling were also being promoted by other divisions,' Ghosh said.

This proliferation of divisions, thought up by Shanghvi, also created an opportunity for many of the home-grown executives at Sun to rise up the ranks quickly, and discover the leader in them. Having been a witness to what recipes had resulted in Sun's success, this set of home-grown leaders replicated variations of Sun's fundamental models.

Abhay Gandhi, the then head of the cardiology division, was one of them who went on to become the CEO of Sun's India business and subsequently led the US business in 2016. Back in the 1990s, concepts like joint fieldwork came alive when Gandhi as a GM opened his division's review meeting by announcing his own call average. He announced the number of his doctor visits before everyone else declared their own. On countless occasions, Gandhi and his deputy Milan Sinha and medical representatives would report the same call average between ten and thirteen per day.

'It was a clear formula. Who was generating the sale? The guy making the primary call, who happens to be the medical representatives. So when as a senior manager you land up in the field, you are not allowed to disturb his true programme. You cannot dictate his schedule; you must follow his programme as the frequency of his visits to doctors is controlled. If you have some other work, you can take the first-line or second-line manager along, but in no way can you upset the MR's schedule,' Sinha said. He felt that while in other companies joint fieldwork is passed off as a formality; it was in the blood and flesh of Sun's line management.

The Sun Pharma University Commencement

When Milan Sinha himself became the head of the oncology division, he replicated a variation of the quarterly meeting by inviting all stakeholders in it. Along with his Sun boys, there would be a wholesaler, a retailer, an oncologist explaining to the boys 'what they want'.

When Inca had long been selling drugs for both inducing fertility and oncology, with a clear clash of approach and energy, the company split the two and gave the responsibility of the oncology division to Sinha. This was not only because he was the senior-most manager at Sun by age and experience in 2004 but also because he had a strong base of science, and oncologists are known to be updated on a day-to-day basis.

The division had products with a sales of about 90 lakh, and Sinha had been given a target to touch ₹10 crore by the year-end. After the matter had been settled in the meeting room, Shanghvi rose up from his chair and looked up from his glasses at Sinha who was still gathering his papers. '*Chala lega na*?' Sinha recalled smiling back to say, 'Sir, *bharosa hai na*?' and seeing his boss's smile widen and nod getting more pronounced.

Focus is what Sinha chose, telling his twenty-six-member-strong team that 40 per cent of that target will be achieved by the head office. After extensive homework, he prepared a list of thirty top-notch oncologists spanning the country, whose practices were big enough to fetch Sun sales of over a crore. These star oncologists were located across the country, from Udupi to Gauhati, one or two in each state. But Sinha said he met all of them at least once every quarter that year, and continued that routine each quarter for seven years. Many oncologists were candid enough to admit to him that it was for the first time in their career that the head of an oncology division was meeting them regularly.

It was during these travels that he picked up the pulse of cancer centres across the country and combined it with Sun's 'catch them young' strategy to deliver a programme that earned him a privilege no non-medical professional had managed. He had been to Patna, Cuttack and other smaller centres, and seen the condition in many of those places. The radiation machines were not working and still medical students earned higher degrees such as Doctor of medicine (MD) in Radiology.

Sitting across a senior oncologist at Tata Memorial on one of his rounds, he shared his experience: 'Sir, all these small centres in Bihar and Orissa have their machines creaking, yet these students qualify as MD (Radiology); and what is the difference between an MD from such a place and an MD from AIIMS (All India Institute of Medical Sciences) or Tata?'

'You are right, Milan, but what can be done?' the concerned oncologist Dr Mathur*, who was also the chair person of Indian College of Radiation Organization (ICRO), said. Next, Sinha was sitting in Delhi in the chamber of the head of oncology, AIIMS, Dr Panda*, also president of the Association of Radiation Oncologists of India (AROI), retelling him the story and exhorting him to act.

The two father figures of oncology spoke to each other and, taking a cue from Sinha's suggestion, they decided that Sun could possibly host two postgraduate teaching programmes a year under the guidance of AROI and ICRO. Young medical students could be selected from non-elite institutes to undergo an extensive refresher course and updates on specific topics.

They spoke to other senior oncologists and the proposal was put to ICRO board's approval on a monsoon day in Mumbai where one couldn't tell the morning from evening. The weather portended a flood of absentees. But Sinha recalled doctors showing up one after the other, descending from their sedans and pulling up their sarees and trousers to walk knee-deep in puddles to attend the meeting.

The supporters believed the proposal to be a 'great service to the nation', but Sinha was pacing anxiously up and down, expecting resistance from some quarters on corporate involvement. His prediction was only half correct.

It was put up for vote and passed with thumping support, but Dr Shirin Naoroji* said two programmes will be too few to address the gap. There is such a dire need for this that at least four such programmes should be conducted every year. When Sinha requested for two again, she said, 'Is it because you do not want to spend more?' 'Madam, I have full backing of my CMD even if I commit twelve. Only arrangement of logistics would become a nightmare.'

In the execution of a Shanghvi-style win-win deal, the first such programme was held at Tata Memorial. Sinha saw through fourteen such programmes before retirement.

Somewhere in between, on a pleasant November day in 2008 in Mumbai—which would be remembered by most not for the pleasantness of the weather but for the dastardly terror that Kasab and his gang unleashed at hotel Taj Mahal—the goings-on would be etched in Sinha's memory for a different reason—receiving the lifetime membership of AROI. He was the first non-medical entity to receive it, in honour of 'a great contribution on the part of a company to the younger generation of oncologists', for which the association had to tweak its constitution.

Nothing made Shanghvi more proud than to see his basic strategies (catch them young) grow and blossom to yield value. 'Make a presentation for all VPs and GMs', was Shanghvi's way of honouring his executive. The slides he had made, Sinha has preserved like his first certificate at school.

Apart from training the next generation of oncologists, Sinha also created schools and certificates for others as well. His intensive forty-five-day training course on oncology for MRs ended with a convocation ceremony with Shanghvi and top Sun executives dressed in a black robe giving away certificates to the new initiates in oncology that said, 'This is to certify that the vice chancellor, dean and registrar of Sun Pharma University hereby declare that Mr Puneet Varma is competent to retain, explain and convey the knowledge to the fraternity of oncologists in India.'

It was signed off by Vice Chancellor Dilip Shanghvi and Dean Narendra Lakkad. 'Such gestures lifted the morale and energy of the boys,' Sinha said.

By the end of the first year, the oncology division had booked a sales of a cool ₹12 crore against a target of ₹10 crore. In true Sun tradition, to discover the depth of the market for each drug, to focus on each one better, they split the division. When it came to setting targets, Shanghvi remarked casually, 'Make it the same as last year for both divisions.' The comment had been made so matter-of-factly that none present registered at that moment that he was seeking nothing less than a 100 per cent growth.

When the enormity of his deliverable struck a shocked Sinha, he protested, albeit, belatedly, 'Sir, what are you asking for? It's too much.' In response, Shanghvi smiled and said, 'OK, tell me what you can do? And tell me what we can do to make you do that.'

Focusing on the unique group behaviour of each therapy specialists—psychiatrists and neurologists, cardiologists, endocrinologists, gastroenterologists, ophthalmologists and then oncologists allowed Sun to customize its strategies for the specialists and play a game, very different from its peers. While Ranbaxy, Pfizer, GlaxoSmithKline summarized their performances in media, partly on their few blockbuster products—like Corex, Augmentin, Revital and Volini which earned hundreds of crore for the parent—Sun had no such product in top ten grosser drugs list.

When it came to measuring its own performance, the rules it set were very different from what the industry had witnessed. In press statements, Sun pronounced its performance as the leader by prescription market share amongst neurologists and psychiatrists, and went on to add cardiologists, orthopaedists, ophthalmologists gastroenterologists and nephrologists to that list. Having exclusive divisions to service different groups that shared common fundamental traits made sure Shanghvi's boys could build their products and marketing plans on what the specialists thought they needed the most, not what the company thought was best for them.

The industry was taking note in the meantime. 'In marketing practices, he said, "I will frame my own rules, not follow any conventions,"' Pankaj Patel, chairman, Cadila Healthcare, said. Madhav Bhatkuly, a young fund manager in the 1990s, always asked industry captains to pick up one promising company in their sector. When he asked the question to Glaxo's then MD, Homi R. Khusrokhan, he replied, 'Sun. We all have our field forces arranged by geographical distributions. Here is a guy who has organized everything by therapies, and he is focusing on chronic drugs.' Next, he was sitting across Cipla CEO Amar Lulla, asking the same question, and he answered, 'Watch out for Dilip Shanghvi. He is ruthless with costs, his model is interesting.' This set off Bhatkuly to study Sun and become one of its first institutional investors.

Till this point of focus, probably the industry could grasp the story of Sun. The same focus when applied to select individuals within each therapy specialist group, translated to mean that Sun would attend to his or her need, at times humanitarian or social, at times educational or medical, which helped create a bond that had a humane and emotional texture to it.

This is one intangible that took on a million different forms because it was a relationship between two individuals, deeply personal, when one person had given another what he wanted the most in a moment that mattered. At the least it meant that the person had given the therapy specialist 'happiness'; at the most it could mean that he had left the therapy specialist 'obligated'. And this—'emotion is the engine, reason the driver'—was not a concept easy for other companies to grasp, leave alone duplicate.

Asked whether the emotional connect Sun forged with select doctors in a specialist community was a well-thought strategy or an organic outcome of a passion, Shanghvi reckoned, 'As a person I am not capable of many superficial relationships. I have intense relationships with a few ones. And I think the depth of relationships is inversely correlated with the number. I think it is this part of my personality that got reflected in the way the company formed emotional connect with doctors.'

Much before Sun had proved its mettle, when it was still getting to be known as the 'fluke' in town—albeit 'an interesting fluke'—when cabins in the Baroda office were still not fully occupied, a soft-faced man midway in his sixties approached the reception. He asked to see 'Dilip'.

'Do you have an appointment, sir?' the lady asked.

When the man smiled and shook his head, the lady indicated towards the sofa outside.

The man heard the lady telling on phone, 'Shashikant Sanghvi is here, sir'. His eyes darted the other way, and when he looked back, he saw Shanghvi leaving his cabin, rushing to receive him. A decade after he had advised 'Dilip' to leave Calcutta, he was trying to act on his own advice. He had bought a land, applied for a loan from the Gujarat government but had suffered a heart attack. He had been advised by the doctor to not hop between Baroda and Calcutta, and hence was leaving this dream unrealized, or realizing his dream through boys he had once helped. By that time, enough Gujaratis had migrated from Calcutta to Baroda to form what is known as Calcutta Club.

A big chunk of them had some sort of association with pharma, and their eyes lit up with nostalgia, if they heard terms like 'Dawa Bazaar', 'Mehta Building', 'Gandhi Building', 'Ezra Street', 'Canning Street' or 'Bagri Market'. An entire generation of Gujaratis—back home in the late 1990s after tracing a circuitous route of migration that had started a few generations back with their forefathers—seemed to have grown a few strands of Bengali roots, wishing to keep Calcutta alive in their heart and conversations.

A year before Shashi-bhai's visit, Synergy House in Baroda had already received visitors from Calcutta. Pradip Ghosh had arrived, impressed by the architecture, marvelling at the fountain gurgling water. The office looked posh to him. But what stunned him most when he went to meet Shanghvi was what tugged uncomfortably at his boss's throat. 'Coat was still acceptable, but I was so surprised to see him wearing a tie, which I knew he so detested,' Ghosh recalled.

'What to do Pradip, you have to meet so many MNC type of people and they have set notion of how business should look like,' Shanghvi humoured him. Perhaps, it was time to let go of old habits, old patterns, and many old things, even if they were close to the heart.

CHAPTER NINE

DEPARTURE: DESIGNING A LOSS

On an early autumn morning in 1991, a senior citizen walked into a small enclosure that Vapi called its post office, and found two men efficiently stamping away on loads of brown cartons stacked one over the other. He walked up to them with a parcel in his slightly quivering hands, seeking help with postage stamps. One of them took a break from his routine, and helped him buy a few tickets, pasted them with a broken pencil from the capless glue bottle tied to a wooden bar counter and went back to resume his work.

Since it was a small town in India of the early 1990s, the elderly man still had time on his way out to stop by and thank the 'post office man'. The man smiled back and revealed to him as he had, to many others, that he was not officially employed by the post office but by a medicine company named Sun Pharma.

'Every evening we had a huge number of parcels waiting for distribution. So it seemed like a good idea to create help for the post-offices, where a large chunk of work was ours. Our goods had the advantage of being light, sending them by trucks would have meant a higher risk of damage. Also Vapi was then not so well connected and our sales were not so large yet, that I could appoint C&F at all locations,' Shanghvi said.

Shyamal Ghosh, still new to Sun's way of working, was astounded to see psychiatry medicines rocking atop a moving truck in cutesy Amul cartons meant to contain milk powder for infants with pink cuddly teddy bears printed on them. 'Every penny mattered, and Dilip-bhai knew that these outside cartons only go till the wholesalers; the doctors who truly mattered, and where the Sun's brand currency had to be established, wouldn't see this packaging,' Ghosh said. But just like tantrums that look cute on toddlers stick out as sore thumbs in adults, all that patchy handwork that were celebrated as firecracker innovations to save cost in a newborn entrepreneurial set-up began to prickle as odd practices under the glare of professionals.

'The Vapi post office like some more post offices in smaller towns, was literally managed by Sun Pharma in those days, because it was tiny, didn't have more than one or two postmen. However, for the company it was the supply source since our factory was there,' Rajesh Kumar, who was then posted in Lucknow, recalled. 'Most of Sun's medicines were still being sent by post parcels. So, from the point of post, either the postman delivered it to the stockist or the stockist picked it up,' Kumar said.

Since, it was an all-cash business for Sun till then, the stockists would whine about having to pay up in full up front, when most other companies offered their goods on credit, for twenty-one to forty-five days when they could shell out the dues. And most often to push their medicines into the market, and show higher sales this stretchable cycle could be extended further. Right from the first day Sun had been clear that its products would be sold only on prescriptions. So it went about wooing those who could deliver in that department, that is, the doctors, cracking up a legacy rift with trading channels.

'Stockists have always grumbled their grouse of unfavourable treatment, the company never cared too much about assuaging them, as it had specialists by its side. But there came a time when post offices also started cribbing about unmanageable workload,' Kumar said. He had started receiving frequent calls from the Lucknow post office complaining that their post office had turned into a Sun Pharma warehouse, stockists at times keeping the packs in waiting for days together, till they could spare cash to buy the drugs.

By the end of 1991, Kumar made a presentation to the senior management proposing a shift to appoint carrying and forwarding agents (C&F) in every state. 'I extrapolated that at the given rate, we would touch ₹100 crore sales in three years, and in that event it was implausible to go on distributing drugs with this post-parcel arrangement, given the logistical nightmare it had already turned into at the post offices,' Kumar recalled. There was bound to be resentment among stockists, due to the addition of a middleman in the supply chain and ergo, a cut in their margin to

8 per cent from 10 per cent. But Kumar suggested they can be persuaded by a compensation which was to offer them a thirty-day credit cycle and a standard institutional arrangement through banks.

Shanghvi listened to the whole proposal keenly and threw a challenge for Kumar. 'We start with UP but I want each and every stockist to come on board consensually. Even if one of them opts out of this arrangement, we cancel the idea for now.' Unlike most companies, Sun had divided UP into four zones for its business convenience. Kumar travelled the length and breadth of the state and managed to get 90 per cent of the stockists on board which improved efficiencies. And he was rewarded with a promotion and bigger challenge. He had to bring about a similar distribution structure in Sun's oldest and biggest market—West Bengal.

When Kumar reached Calcutta, he found half of the managers led by Pradip Ghosh on terms with Shanghvi he couldn't imagine any employee being with an owner. 'They called him Dilip-bhai, they dialled on his line whenever they wanted. They were informal at a different level.' One of the first tasks he had there was to negotiate terms for C&F appointment with 'Prabhat Agencies', the owner of which was Sailesh Desai's brother-in-law.

'As expected, he started demanding special terms, which didn't suit us and thankfully with Pradip-da by my side, we refused to entertain unfavourable demands. He would still be appointed our first Calcutta C&F though,' Kumar recalled. He feared that in the process of turning down his demands he might have appeared brusque, reports of which were bound to have travelled back to Shanghvi. So he was bracing up for a thrashing and wasn't surprised to receive a call from the head office.

It was Shanghvi on the line. 'Rajesh, I understand there have been some huffing and puffing around the negotiations. But whatever you think is in the company's best interests, go ahead with that. Your decision on the matter will be final,' he said to a Kumar sighing with relief. And thus Sun began professionalizing its distribution by appointing C&F agents in all the states, one after the other.

Offering traders medicines on a credit cycle came with defaults and Kumar disciplined the serial offenders by stopping supplies. He heard from Shanghvi again, who asked tersely, 'Rajesh, are you a salesman or an administrator?'

'Salesman, of course, sir.'

'Then it's no good that you are inculcating discipline by stopping supplies. Why are you and I needed? The whole point of our presence is to make sale happen. Disrupting that defeats the purpose. If you can discipline the defaulters while doubling the sales over a reasonable period of time, it would be an achievement.' Kumar, the quintessential Bihari, recalled being told in Bengali. They always spoke in Bengali, the Bihari and his Gujarati boss. Kumar suspected one reason he was sent to Calcutta was also that he had picked up Bangla, a fact that Shanghvi must have noticed.

And all of this was happening even as Nitin Mehta, Shanghvi's friend-turned-partner was in charge of distribution. He took care of distribution alongside supervising manufacturing in Vapi, and looking at banking and other responsibilities.

But now that professionals had entered Sun and began appraising the system, they found the 'jugaad' money-saving methods wanting and unbecoming of an ambitiously growing company which aspired to be in the top league. Some of them complained to Shanghvi of the manual unsophisticated way of packing, dubbing it 'unstandardized' and 'unprofessional'. Others thought its channels inadequate, and yet others whimpered about a reporting structure to allow them more personal freedom. Some had started quietly clamouring for distribution to be carved out as a separate function to be managed by a professional with experience in that department.

What was happening to distribution was clearly not happening to distribution alone. It was also happening to purchase, commercial and even finance, all of which were being taken care of by Upen-bhai who would slog in Bombay on weekdays and then head to Baroda for weekends. Till this point, among the partners, they could be juggling multiple functions, as the situation demanded. So Sailesh Desai would look after manufacturing a bit, simultaneously search a new site for injectables, arrange for relocation of the company, besides maintaining relations in government machineries and setting off to establish marketing as new states were added at breakneck speed. So they were all occupied doing what had to be done without much ado. But as they went about filling in different roles, how did the outside world perceive their chemistry?

'There was no doubt that Dilip-bhai was in charge. It seemed that he was closest to Sailesh-bhai, they were fast friends. They could squabble like teenage boys one moment and be playful the next. He seemed slightly more measured and distant to Upen-bhai in his equation, probably because he was an elder cousin, and one is expected to be respectful in such relations. We didn't see much of Nitin-bhai in Baroda because he stayed mostly in Vapi,' is the sense what most people corroborated. Upen-bhai had said before, as in most Gujarati families they had all grown up wanting to create a business, and at least one strong reason behind it was 'to not work under anyone'. The phase when he was looking for an opportunity and Shanghvi was setting up his business coincided and he drifted into it.

Though Upen-bhai was a partner he said, 'We were always aware that Sun was Dilip's baby, and he set the final rules. Dilip had a certain way of looking far ahead that escaped us at that moment. He would spend hours with a senior R&D executive of Ciba-Geigy in his cabin, and we would be thinking, why Dilip was wasting so much time on this guy, when so much work was left to be done elsewhere? There were times when he was taking chemistry tuitions. At some level we thought we were past the age of classes but all along he was building himself to create the R&D arm. In hindsight, he was investing in the future.'

'At times Dilip would sound off his big ideas, but we were probably not paying enough attention,' he added. Upen-bhai recalled the time when as a nineteen-year-old 'Dilip' had declared that they could become a Tata or Birla to his cousin, who had waited for him to crack a joke and when none came, laughed it off anyway. 'The boy can really talk big,' he had told Upen-bhai, unable to stomach what seemed to him as an imagination that was unfettered.

Later Sun used all its charm to acquire a senior manufacturing guy from Glaxo for a 'bomb' of a salary. This new member in the team seemed to be doing nothing more than 'smoke a pipe in his locked cabin' all week days and 'fly out to Bombay on weekends on company expense' with 'a strict instruction that his car and driver shouldn't be put to any other company duty while he was away', according to a former Sun executive. This executive witnessed Jayant and Upen-bhai 'stomping into Dilip-bhai's cabin' and asking, 'Why are we tolerating this attitude, Dilip, paying him a bomb when this guy is doing nothing beyond polluting the air?'

To which, he recalled Shanghvi responding, 'We are learning from him. And his salary is the fee we are paying to learn.'

As more and more professionals entered Sun, initially they sought breathing space and then freedom to be, if they were expected to take Sun to the next level. Some, according to former executives, would even refuse to come unless they were given a free hand to operate, which meant that they would precondition their joining to report to nobody other than the managing partner, Shanghvi.

'When professionals started to assume more responsibilities, a question mark started forming itself on what roles would the partners take on?' wondered a former executive. This started to bring about a fundamental shift in the energies in Sun along with simmering doubts on the form and shape this hitherto fluid organization would assume.

But even among those professionals, there were those who found friends in partners, particularly Sailesh Desai. Despite the friendship, and occasionally because of it, they couldn't shut their eyes off the glaring gap between Shanghvi and the rest, when it came to instinct for growth.

A few pushed partners to acquire it. Kikani, for instance, who saw a friend in Desai, exhorted him and Upen-bhai to upgrade through executive education at IIM Ahmedabad, his alma mater, an idea Shanghvi seconded. Upen-bhai squirmed at the thought of 'adult education' attending classroom, blackboards and homework, excusing himself with a laugh, 'Not my cup of tea, to sit in class again.' But Desai was game for it and said, 'Let's try it, 'Let's try it,' as Kikani remembered it.

The course that lasted six months steadily grew on Desai. It unleashed a dimension in him that led him to question the fundamentals of his approach to business and life. 'One of my first fundamental approaches that got demolished in that class was that in a company everyone should be able to do everything. If the need be, marketing guy should be able to double up as a distribution resource. I conformed to that belief as that was how we had grown grounds up. But now, professionals here were telling me it was all right to not know distribution if you knew marketing in a specialized way,' remarked Desai. It might have dawned on him that what was happening to Sun as professionals carved out niches and drowned in them was now inevitable. 'As thirty-two case studies played out before me, and I was drawn to correlate lessons from my life weighing my strengths and weaknesses, something inside me changed.'

Through the programme, he would rip apart some of the case studies being touted as success stories. When one of the professors who served as a director at Core Healthcare, the IV fluids and disposables firm, gave a grand presentation celebrating his company's story, Desai burst out, 'Sir, you have invested ₹200 crore already and all that you made of it is ₹5 crore. You manufacture a bottle for ₹5 and send it all the way to Calcutta and sell it for ₹8, how could that ever be sustainable?' Sitting in that group that day was the owner of the firm, Sushil Handa, who would eventually sell it to set up Claris Life Sciences. 'It was obviously Sun Pharma talking through me. At Sun, we had dizzying benchmarks for profits and at that time their model appeared to me a lost case for business,' Desai chuckled.

And then, there were case studies around life stories, which touched a chord buried deep in his heart. Hours flew by as he listened to the story of a Marwari gentleman in the class. Eldest in the family, he was orphaned at the age of seventeen and raised four of his kid brothers with whatever money he made. All of them did well for themselves, but by the time he had settled the last of his brothers, his own business went downhill. Such was the crisis that he didn't have resources to marry off his daughter, a fact he found difficult to admit at home. 'I know if I seek help from my brothers, not a single one would refuse, but I just can't get myself to ask for money. If only any one of them sensed my dilemma . . .' his voice petered out. After a silence that followed, Desai's favourite faculty member, Professor Parikh, summed up, 'So, you are sacrificing your daughter for your ego.'

It shook something inside Desai, who introspected: 'What was he sacrificing for his ego?' 'Till that point, I felt money cannot beat relationships because you cannot buy relationships. But that story made me rethink the value judgement,' Desai said.

They have always had arguments—he and his friend 'Dilip'. A Calcutta-based friend, who has seen both interact from close quarters, felt: 'Sailesh in his young days could get aggressive. Dilip doesn't engage much with anyone unless he finds them interesting or knowledgeable enough. Sailesh doesn't let anyone win an argument and Dilip wouldn't lose any, but still in his late teens, Sailesh was probably the closest to being "Dilip's best friend". I suspect that both enjoyed a good argument regardless of the rights and wrongs of the situation, a bit like they both relished a sumptuous south Indian meal. They had a special connection going.'

It was so common a sight in the Baroda office—the two Gujarati friends arguing in Bengali, a gesture some suspected specifically meant to not let them do what they most itched to do, eavesdrop—that people had stopped paying attention. But a handful of those arguments, once professionalization of the company had begun, were arising out of 'serious differences' that were nibbling at the tender core of that part where their relationship converged in business. 'On several occasions, Dilip had remarked, "You are having it this way [getting work done with ease], only because you are sitting here in Sun Pharma,"' Desai recalled being told.

'That's not true at all, Dilip. Sun might be acting as a catalyst, but to say that things are happening only because I am working from Sun's fold would be a gross exaggeration,' used to be Desai's retort, who had an increasingly growing feeling then that 'what he wanted to be his and what could be his, could never be truly his at Sun'.

At other times he would counter Shanghvi on these lines: 'Dilip, I may not get all 100 that Sun has achieved, but I may still achieve 60 and of that, all 30 would be mine to keep, and in that case I still stand to benefit more than the scenario of me working at Sun.' At the heart of it, it was about 'something in manufacturing' that Desai was keen to take on, which apparently Shanghvi was resisting.

'Someone gives you a car to drive and you buy your own, there is a difference. Till that point, I got it because I was with him but that didn't mean that I couldn't buy my own. I wasn't satisfied continuing as a partner and drawing money from the company. From the day I left Calcutta I wanted to create something of my own. And in no way I wanted to land in a situation where I was left feeling that I am not in my mother's company but in my sister's company,' Desai tried to explain.

His arguments with Shanghvi pre-dated and coincided with his programme, from where he emerged to announce to his friend that maybe it was time to separate, if the differences were growing irreconcilable, as far as the company was concerned. Initially Shanghvi was reluctant to let his friend go, according to Desai. He was probably unaware that powerful forces were conspiring to impose upon him a harsher realization. This realization would put their friendship to an unprecedented test and had the potential to blow up the fragile-feeling relationship in a quiet implosion.

'He might not have known it then, but what he had said had hurt me at that point in the past. But what's also true is that I didn't understand him. He was smart and knew exactly what he was doing to go where he was going and why he was doing it. For me, all that mattered at that moment was that my friend had challenged me and I was determined to prove him wrong,' Desai recalled.

'Occasionally we do look back at our stormy, young school and college days with disbelief and feel, could I be fool enough to do this?' Desai added, building a context. 'The truth is, Dilip always saw at least fifteen steps ahead and people surrounding him never could see beyond eight. That's what people call vision, I guess, his ability to see what others don't,' he summed up.

Asked whether he was also the one to spur Shanghvi to try out the IIM Ahmedabad course a few years later, Kikani shook his head and said, 'No, I never pushed him because within six months of interacting, I was clear that formal education even at the most elite of institutions has nothing much to offer to a person who read one published paper on a subject and understood everything there was to know in that field.'

But former company executives point out that it was Kikani who goaded an unwilling Shanghvi to meet someone who would prove to be influential stimuli to cause the future shape of things at Sun. And of all types, he turned out to be an academic consultant, a breed that Shanghvi and his company judged as fine-suited meeting-trotting time-wasters.

A Chapter from Gita

It would be an understatement to call people at Sun in the 1990s and even decades later, 'anti-consultants'. Though Shanghvi's feeling at large, internalized by executives, was how consultants can know his business better than he did, they hadn't been completely declared out of bounds. It was a complex, curious relationship between Sun and consultancies; the big brands—McKinsey, Ferguson, Deloitte, KPMG—were occasionally entertained in the office for presentations. Little did they know what was going on outside.

Amusingly, people at Sun could be condescending and self-conscious of 'polished and sophisticated' consultants, simultaneously, and it didn't mean fluctuating from one emotion to the other. Ashok Butta recalled entering Acme Plaza office one winter morning to find a lot of commotion. Someone told him, 'Some consultant type is coming, we have been asked to steer clear off that corridor not to be seen around (implying just in case someone was caught in his pyjamas and slippers). Only meetings, sheer time waste.' That was the perception in the company that consultancies are all *gyaan and show*, no *kaam*. Yagnik felt Shanghvi's brush with IIM-A, Harvard or McKinsey were fundamentally creative experiments for the curious child in him.

'He engaged externally only for two reasons—curiosity and learning. So all that was established globally, he just wanted a taste of them and test whether they are worth the salt,' Yagnik recalled. Once global consultants made polite exits after making PowerPoint presentations before poker-faced senior executives at Sun, Shanghvi turning around to wonder: 'Tell me, Yagnik, what new stuff have they taught you? Tell me what have they said, that we didn't know already.'

Consultants were amused by Sun likewise, finding it insanely challenging to make sense of how things were run there to bring the phenomenal results, so that they could churn out lucid management theories and crisp presentations. This was true till, say, late 2008–09. A top consultant at McKinsey admitted the shock when he first set foot in Sun's headquarters. When a consultant experiences the ambience of a company, his primal instinct is to sniff the money it must be making.

This consultant said, till as late as 2007–08, walking up and down the Acme Plaza office, he wouldn't bet on anything over ₹800–900 crore.

'Things were at absolute basic subsistence level, starting from the guy who served tea to the cups it got served in, to the executives and the way they dressed. And then you enter the conference room for a meeting and for the videoconferencing, they were still using an outdated 27" Sony screen. Then you find a CXO-level executive walking into the conference room in rubber slippers, his shirt hanging loose and you ask yourselves, 'Whatever is going on here?' he wondered.

The telecom system almost from the era of Graham Bell was equally perplexing to the consultants, who were used to latest gizmos. One of them recalled on several occasions, after they reached, it would take 10–15 minutes to set things up, and then a few calls will have to be made to set it. By then, he saw Shanghvi starting to toy with the wires, trying to fix the system all by his own electrical acumen. This was astonishing for the consultant, who dealt with CEOs day in and day out, witnessing their quirky tantrums.

'You knew it is not your traditional corporate set-up, and conventional management advice wouldn't click here. So you are always cautious. Here was a place where there was zero-variable pay for the senior management, but they still stuck around for very long stints. Dilip-bhai hadn't even heard of Spencer's and never worked with any executive search firms to hunt talents. And then you try to figure out how they have come so far and where they are heading, there comes the icing on the cake, there is not a plan document or paper that could help you with the exercise. The entire blueprint is in an inaccessible safe— that is Dilip-bhai's mind,' the consultant said.

So in that consultant-unfriendly age at Sun, according to those who were watching from the sides, Kikani had a hard time convincing Shanghvi to meet that one person who he thought was a 'management practices champion'. The man in question had turned conventional wisdom upside down, by first reaching the top of the corporate hierarchy and then renouncing it to pursue academics, setting a precedent of sorts. Here was a man, who after heading Mukand Steel as one of India's youngest CEOs at thirty-six years, left to do his MBA at Cornell, and DBA in diversification at Harvard. It had been three to four years since he had returned to India with a mission to revamp management education and was quietly scripting a revolution in that space, transforming a lesser-known S.P. Jain Institute. He was yet to launch his 'manufacturing programme' and still half a decade away from launching the 'family education' programme, and in this little-known 'consultant academic', it seemed Shanghvi wasn't particularly keen. But on Kikani's insistence about his unorthodox career moves as a 'learner', he relented.

Kikani approached Dr Manesh Shrikant with the request. He seemed even more disinclined to meet this unheard-of entrepreneur. 'I take no more than two consultancies annually, and that quota is full this year. Also, I am too occupied with my academic assignments right now, my top priority,' he is understood to have told. But after Kikani pleaded with him seeking the meeting as a personal favour and pitching Shanghvi as a businessman not manufactured out of the gene pool, but as an unconventional entrepreneur just as Shrikant was an unusual educationist, he too agreed. This set the stage for an intersection of two interesting minds that some think altered the trajectory of Sun's story in one of the most fundamental ways.

There was nothing unusual about that morning of 1990 or 1991 (according to varied accounts) that struck partners Jayant, Upen, Sailesh, Nitin and senior executives Raju, Kamlesh Dudhara, Kikani and Shanghvi himself. The mood in the room at 'Express Hotel' wasn't any less 'anti-consultant' to begin with, dull and lifeless. 'For the first few hours, the session was going nowhere. Professor Shrikant was trying to vitalize the discussion from time to time, but it felt partners were either disinterested so as not to pick any strand or didn't see much value in the exercise or were indifferent to it because of their genuine inability to contribute substance,' one of the executives present recalled.

And just when it seemed that the 'hard to execute' meeting would be uneventful, Shrikant abruptly threw a googly asking all partners to write a test. He listed out five basic questions on vision and strategy, on the lines of where you wish the company to be ten years hence, what the strategies are that you would employ to take it there and so on, the executive recalled. After the partners submitted the papers, he skimmed through the leaves, and then unexpectedly dissolved the session midway, even when it was scheduled to last a full day. 'He said something like, "You can now return to your respective works",' the executive said.

Of Shrikant, his student-turned co-worker at S.P. Jain Institute of Management and Research, A. Srinivas Rao, wrote in his blog ,'Yuganta: End of an Epoch', '. . . he had a remarkable ability to cut through complex ideas and issues to come to the utterly simple heart of a problem. If he picked up a balance sheet he would effortlessly point his finger at a number which, he would casually remark, was at the heart of the company's woes, despite our battery of analysis.'

Some present in the meeting thought this was what Shrikant attempted through the test, to 'accurately diagnose' where the bottleneck in Sun's growth could be. His assessment showed that it could be in the most tender and viscous of the company's organs—where friendships and relationships converged in business. And it might have led Shanghvi one way or the other to a conclusion, that he suspected true for a while.

Shrikant's session had been dissolved, for all participants except one, for whom it had only been suspended. One of the executives recalled, 'It had come and gone for us. Three months passed by and we didn't hear of it again, only to realize that all along Dilip-bhai had been in touch with him. He had had at least three individual sessions with him.' He believed that the test papers, turned out to be the living proof of what most professionals saw but were wary of broaching with Shanghvi— about the gap in the vision and capabilities of Shanghvi and the rest of his partners. That gap was assessed in depth for organizational structure and what it meant for future growth between Shrikant and Shanghvi in one of their one-on-one meetings, this executive believed.

That this was playing on his mind also became clear from his private discussions with senior professionals in the system soon after. Months that followed saw Shanghvi taking independent feedback from at least two of his senior-most executives in the top brass. 'He was fully aware that professionals were getting suffocated. It was not feasible to woo top names in the industry from premier institutes and ask them to report to one of the partners. So when he asked me for an unbiased evaluation. I was honest and told him that asking any of the partners to take charge of core functions would be disastrous for the company,' a former executive said of his unforgiving assessment.

By his own account, it seemed, he was brutal in appraising the partners. Of Sailesh-bhai, whom he dubbed the smartest of them all, he recalled telling Shanghvi, 'He can fill in on you in your area of lack. He can stand on your behalf at a site, give that extended feel of being Sun's representative. He can take obvious reactive business decisions. But essentially his forte is relationships.' Of Nitin-bhai, who was in charge of operations and partly distribution, he apparently said, 'What you call the entire operations is just one factory at Vapi. This is going to change if Sun is to grow and you would need a professional to handle it'. Of Upen-bhai, he said, 'I know he is family and your own uncle's son, but as transactions grow complex, you would need someone with much more sophisticated understanding of finance.'

HR head Bhagwat Yagnik recalled rushing into Shanghvi's cabin one of those days. He had met six potential candidates for a position in the company and wanted to discuss their profiles with Shanghvi. Just as they were nearing closure of that discussion, he did his usual, 'I would give this one five for this role and that one four for this role,' Shanghvi said, 'OK, Bhagwat, how much would you rate us in our roles?' And Shanghvi spelt out names of his partners—which included his brother Jayant and Harin Mehta, an elder brother of his friend Sunil Mehta, who was not a partner but whom he had high regards for. Yagnik rated none of them over three with the exception of Sailesh-bhai, whom he rated about five. Shanghvi looked slightly surprised and then asked him to explain the rationale for such ratings, and took out a paper to jot down the observations. It came and went like a pop, never to be broached again even between the two actors in the scene, till Yagnik was asked over two decades later whether the matter had ever surfaced between him and Shanghvi.

Most professional eyes who hadn't first-hand witnessed the gardeners labouring the soil, dirtying their hands, preparing the ground and entered the 'Eden of Sun' when tips of the green shoots were visible, concurred with the diagnosis point to point, albeit expressed it in different degrees of severity and most of them anonymously. It was their fair, honest and unbiased opinion, considering that the question now was how the green shoot could be transformed into a plant that would grow into a tree that would bear fruits, and they were unanimously suggesting, 'Gardeners won't do, we need horticulturists.'

'To function as partners, there had to be some compatibility between them—intellectual, financial, of vision and future goals. There was none among Dilip-bhai and his partners. They were a team when both were fulfilling a need of the other, when Dilip-bhai didn't have means and resources to hire big names or professionals and the partners were looking for an opportunity. But as the company started growing, the gaps in the arrangement grew as well to the point that it threatened to crumble and stunt the growth of the company. Dilip-bhai was aiming for the sky and the partners didn't even have their eye on the ground and the company couldn't run with the legs of its disparate partners tied, each running at his own separate pace,' a senior Sun executive had observed then.

Another said, 'The company was growing at breakneck speed and Dilip-bhai was growing even faster. If one worked closely with him in that period, one could sense the fanatic speed with which an individual can grow, if he focuses his energies on a singular goal in a controlled manner. The partners couldn't match that growth. You can't blame them, no ordinary person could. They were nice and caring people, but they were owners at the end of the day and owners have a mindset. Once we started bringing top professionals from the industry, they couldn't be asked to report to them, but owners couldn't be expected to see them as more than 'people on hire'. There was a disconnect, which was growing and a separation became imminent and inevitable.'

'Dr Shrikant was a living lesson to Dilip-bhai, which he chose to get influenced by,' an executive said. A handful of key former senior executives at Sun believed that it was during his 'insightful deep discussions' with Shrikant who had made it a life goal to draw from the Gita and Vedanta to teach strategies and management practices, that Shanghvi's determination to restructure the company got crystallized.

Shrikant was known to espouse a generation of management graduates to practise the philosophy of detaching self and emotion from actions and outcome. He used to send his graduate batches to Kayavarohan, an ashram on the outskirts of Baroda in Gujarat around Diwali, where they spent two days listening to Swami Viditatmanand-ji, a Harvard-educated former chemical engineer from the US. He would teach them about the relevance of the Bhagavadgita in professional lives.

One former Sun executive went as far as to suggest that Shrikant did to Shanghvi what Krishna had done to a distraught Arjuna in the battleground of Kurukshetra (the essence of Gita). He cleared the doubts Shanghvi may have harboured in his psychological minefield about parting with his friends and family, who had helped him build his business, according to this executive. 'Dilip-bhai was too intelligent to not see that the departure of his partners was now inevitable to attract talent who were needed to execute the next leap for Sun. He was convinced that he had to let go of the past to create Sun's future. But this conviction was trapped under inhibitions of hurting those whom he saw as closest to him. His personal sessions with Shrikant might have helped to bring about clarity.'

Assuming this was not the route, through which Shrikant became instrumental in Shanghvi's next course of action, there definitely was another circuitous route through which he contributed to this momentous point in Sun's journey.

Fellow Harvardian and former country head of Glaxo Pharma, Tarun Gupta, recalled a conversation with his friend Shrikant, who had nudged Shanghvi to attend Harvard's executive education programme. He did that often, with the bright minds he met, including the younger galaxy of faculties, whom he prodded to acquire the cream of the lot with global experience.

'It might have been my experience at Harvard that would have taught me not to postpone tough decisions in business and life,' said Shanghvi of re-architecting the structure of Sun. But to Tarun Gupta's shock, he did not complete the course at Harvard. 'He might not have found the programme compelling enough, but that shows he knows what he wants to learn, and where he is not learning he won't waste time, even if it's Harvard,' he said.

So Shanghvi was, in one sense, a Harvard dropout; not unlike other globally celebrated first-generation tech entrepreneurs—Bill Gates or Mark Zuckerberg.

The Separation

And in that summer of 1991 or 92, as Shanghvi headed for the US for his Harvard executive programme, his other partners Upen-bhai, Sailesh

Desai and Nitin-bhai packed for a two-week holiday together with their families and bonded in the hill stations of Ooty and Kodaikanal. The tours of that summer might not have been more than impromptu journeys. But in retrospect, the trips reflected a future which was soon to enter the lives of these friends.

After the holidays were over and people had duly returned to Baroda, one evening Shanghvi called his two friends and one cousin. The partners made their way to Shanghvi's cabin as he got ready to break his future plans.

'He said something to the effect that he had ambitions and I remember saying I am not that ambitious and now I need to give priority to things I have neglected for too long, like my family and children's education,' Nitin Mehta recalled. By the time they stepped out of the office it was night already.

It was probably time to revive an old promise of friendship.

In brief, Shanghvi had proposed that he would buy out the shares of his partners. On ground and in activities, there was only one Sun where all partners worked in whichever departments they were needed in. On paper for technical, legal or tax purposes there were two arms—the main manufacturing arm, Sun Pharma Industries, and the distribution arm, Aditya Medi Sales. According to former senior executives of Sun, over time Shanghvi had been increasing his stake even in the distribution arm, but it was only that day when he formally communicated to the partners about a new ownership structure.

'All important decision were being taken either by me or Upen-bhai, or Sailesh. All of us had a business as well as a personal relation. What I realized is that we were hurting our personal relationship a lot more because business was eating into it. Why should we hurt each other for business? Also, I think I had a different vision for taking the company to a different level,' Shanghvi said.

It didn't come as a surprise that, two decades later, they struggled to find the right and correct words for the deeply private and indefinable feelings of the time around the event. But on being prodded, Upen-bhai said they had all along been 'invitees' in that venture called Sun, a fact they were mindful of.

'The thing is, you know, how shall I put it, from the beginning it was Dilip's baby. It was he who brought us together for the venture one by one. I was the first to join, then Nitin came and subsequently Sailesh joined. But all of us were invited. Sometimes, things fall into place. He was looking for people he could trust and we were also on the lookout for an opportunity, so there was a match. But even when we joined, it was very open (in arrangement) . . ., meaning there was no definite understanding, I recall him telling: "I am growing and you will grow with me." So we joined, but we were never a part of the main company. We had been given shares in the distribution company.

'The main company that is the manufacturing arm of Sun had Dilip and his immediate family, kaka and Jayant. Names do not matter much here, because it was essentially Dilip who was driving everything. And we were supporting him whichever way we could.

'But along with growth, there came a time when our needs changed, became different. Our drives were different. Based on his own drive, Dilip expected a lot from you. If the company had to grow, if you want things to move faster, and more aggressively, you will have to bring people who can make that happen for you. Also by nature we are independent-minded people, for us it becomes difficult to work under someone.

'So at that given time, we thought his needs are different, and we may not be able to contribute or match or work to his expectations. Then, what are the choices? Let's part. And also the way things were going, I felt it couldn't continue without paying a bigger cost of deteriorating our personal relationship,' felt Upen.

On the hurt of separation, he said, 'It might have hurt at that point when I moved out. I can't say I wasn't hurt. But in hindsight it turned out to be a good decision for everyone. If we had continued together, things might have turned for the worse.'

Nitin Mehta, a touch moved talking about the event, felt that 'Dilip-bhai had also turned emotional during the separation, but relationships are like mirrors, once a crack surfaces, it's impossible to conceal it.

'I told you about my principle in life that I inherited from my father—money is transient, it's here today, not there tomorrow. It was time to revive the personal oath that I had taken, when we had started off—we are friends first and partners later. If a situation arises tomorrow in which I were asked to choose between friendship and partnership,

I will be ready to give up partnership for friendship. That's the most precious thing I have earned in my life.

'Besides, Dilip-bhai and I were driving the vehicle of life at two different speeds, I could not accelerate and he couldn't slow down, so separation was inevitable. Till that point, I had only connected to him through friendship. It was only heart to heart. But he was meant for much bigger things and had started thinking from his mind, while I was still feeling only from the heart. So we were not in sync at one point.

'Also, between 1984 and 1993, my sole priority had been the company, because I never wanted any bad remark from Dilip-bhai, or any crack in our trust. Now, my children were growing and I wished to pay attention to them as well.'

He paused and continued, 'You cannot explain everything in words . . . sometimes what happens . . . I am seeing things from my perspective, you will see from yours. That little unhappiness the event caused, no one can repair, only time could heal. The truth is there is no sense in dragging the past after such a long time. It doesn't help anyone, but it can leave behind a lot of hurt. I have forgone the past and left it there. The truth is I will be forever indebted to him for pulling me out of Calcutta, and teaching me so many things at Vapi. My life is a hundred times better than what it would have been, had I not moved out of Calcutta then. Dilip-bhai was instrumental in it. What do I have to complain about? I have no regrets.'

Sailesh Desai felt his friend Dilip always prepared the ground, and it was no different in this event in 1991–92. 'If he wants your replacement, he would probably have one ready in his mind by the time he talks to you. But before that, he will push you to match his intellect, cope with his expectation. But if you didn't or couldn't, he will not think a second time about replacing you. And not everyone can cope with the speed of such a man. At that point, when you understand that, what is your choice?

'If you have a larger understanding of our arguments, of the bigger picture, you will realize that in a family, it is always better to discuss things up front than to let it build up for too long. Our internal understanding was that we will never fight for money; we are together for growth and enjoying that.'

'But where does that growth come from? If he had mixed emotions or doubts while making that decision, the story would have turned out very different. And that (tough decision) is where the growth is. As far as my case is concerned, I wanted something in manufacturing, which didn't work out. I wanted to own something from the time I remember. Personally, neither of us did anything wrong intentionally, and when the differences got serious, we did things our own way.'

Desai continued, 'There have been points when I was unhappy, but in retrospect, I feel happy about the decisions he took. And that unhappiness of the past doesn't count any more. He tried to stick to the path of growth without hurting you, and if you popped as an obstacle in his path he had no choice but to fight you. At that moment, you had to be very mature to understand that all that he was trying to do was just to be rational in his decisions. With the advantage of hindsight, I am also accepting that he was right about many things, which most people around him didn't understand or didn't have the capacity to understand then. Many of his decisions were very tough, and even with the advantage of hindsight, when I put myself in his shoes in some of those difficult situations, I probably still can't take the decisions he took.

'You can say that in business or professional life, he is my mother. All that I have ever learnt is only from him. Whatever I am is because of him.' And just when one assumes that Desai is attempting a photo finish in line to celebrate his friendship, he erupted into a smile to continue, 'And whatever I am not is also because of him.'

The Settlement and the Aftermath

Disappointing, but details could not be ascertained to crunch numbers to let everyone draw their conclusions to see how 'fair' the terms of settlement between friends were. But 'fairness' is a subjective measurement, particularly in the context of relationships. Feelings may be a good proxy indicator to judge it. That said, the after-effects of goodbyes are often incalculable, even when all supporting numbers are at a finger's click and an excel sheet away.

The parting was gradual and staggered. Some watching it from the outside (executives at Sun) even called it smooth. The partners left

Sun, one after the other, spread over two to three years. Upen-bhai was the first to leave. He moved to Bombay about six months before this event, to be closer to his mother, who was not keeping well. 'You must appreciate that there were no negotiations. It didn't ever come to that even when we were parting. Nobody said what about this and that? That was definitely not the way it went. It was more like saying, "OK, we part, so we part."' According to Upen-bhai, it happened three years before the company was listed.

Even though the manifestation of it appeared staggered, when the final decision was taken, 'there was complete clarity that when we parted, all three of us were parting together'.

Asked whether he had definite plans for his professional life then, he shook his head, 'No'. Asked whether an alternative arrangement was being worked out for the three of them while still being at Sun, he replied, 'No'.

'One believed that whatever one had to contribute to help the company grow and move ahead, one had probably contributed. It had, at the given time, when we were parting, acquired a proper critical mass. It was doing well, generating robust profits, and growing at a healthy rate. If you continued, there would be a huge cost. We may not have had grand ambitions, but we had capabilities to take care of our needs.'

More than one relative of Shanghvi and two top company executives had indicated that there had been disquiet in the extended Shanghvi family over Upen-bhai's exit along with some events that followed at Sun.

Asked if the professional parting took a toll on their personal relationship, Upen-bhai said, 'It might have to a little extent at that point. But if you mean whether we stopped talking or attending each other's family functions after that, no those things never happened. The whole idea was not to take the hurt to an irreparable level.'

Shanghvi felt his decision to separate was much more difficult for his partners than for him. 'I was upset for a period of time but I don't think it hurt me as much. They were hurt much more. But if you try and stretch something beyond its limits, ultimately it will break and cause much more pain. And then there is no coming back. But if you take a tough decision one time, maybe at that point in time the other person feels that you are being unfair. But if that's not your intent—you had no malice, no desire to hurt—over time he will realize that and reconcile.

'In any relationship somebody would be a giver, someone would be a taker. I give much more credit to them here because they have been big-hearted and have clearly behaved in a much more mature way.'

After Upen-bhai, Nitin Mehta left Sun, cutting himself from the company in phases.

'After the decision had been taken, I was keen to leave immediately, but Dilip-bhai and other friends urged me to continue for a year at least given I was looking after an ongoing project at Silvassa. That year I continued to handle the same functions I was looking after—Vapi, Silvassa, a little bit of administration, liasioning, banking. R.K. Baheti joined, so I gave up banking. As professionals were brought in one after the other, I kept giving up my functions,' Mehta recalled. And almost a year after that evening, once the Silvassa factory had been built, on the very day puja had been performed to inaugurate the site, Mehta recalled telling Shanghvi, 'Let me go now. I won't be able to work any more.' This was April 1995, according to Mehta's memory.

During their discussions of separation, Mehta had brought up his desire to move to a bigger city to take care of his children's education. He recalled Shanghvi proposing at some point that he could shift to Baroda, and perhaps from there continue to handle some responsibilities at Vapi. 'I replied that I couldn't possibly do that because my locus standi wouldn't be clear. Right now, sitting here I am Sun Pharma. Tomorrow, I would have left the banner, but still be in charge of responsibilities, I would be neither here nor there, and that arrangement would create chaos.'

In June 1995, Mehta shifted to Baroda. Pune had been his first choice, being an industrial town that offered decent business opportunities, but it was his 'best friend, godfather Sailesh-bhai who forced' him to come to Baroda instead and join him. Mehta said, 'Sailesh-bhai said, "Wherever we sit, we will be together.", Shanghvi offered him an apartment he owned in Baroda for home, in the neighbourhood of Old Padra Road. 'Dilip-bhai was gracious to have given me his property, which he asked me to change as and when I wanted to. I never changed it and bought the flat later,' Mehta said. At times, when Shanghvi decided to help, it didn't matter whether the person wanted it or not.

After Mehta shifted to Baroda, Shanghvi almost 'forced' him to take up Sun's C&F agency for Gujarat. 'When he offered, I refused. He offered again, I refused as bluntly as I could, telling him I was not interested in this business any more.' In no time Mehta received a call from his father, 'Why are you doing this?' Shanghvi had spoken to Mehta's father, who was now talking to his son persuading him to take up his friend's offer. 'I knew that arrangement couldn't last. My heart was not in it. And by then I had made up my mind and didn't want to go through that experience, but my father insisted and I couldn't refuse him. I had never dishonoured his word, in any way. So I said OK.' Then he took up the C&F agency and managed it from RK Centre. 'At Sun I was looking after the whole distribution across India, so managing one state's distribution wasn't difficult, and I didn't have to do much anyway. I gave that up eventually in two years,' Mehta recalled.

On the terms of settlement, Mehta said, 'I think on money matters, we were honest and clear—we will not fight for money. We knew once you fight for money, the relationship crumbles, be it family or friends. The question we asked ourselves was this: "Why are we losing both—friend and wealth. Because whatever the financial terms may have been, someone may still be left dissatisfied or upset if one went into calculations of worth.' Mehta recalled at some stage a few mediators popped up, offering them to talk through problems and arrive at a resolution. 'No mediator helps. If four of us cannot sit and resolve our own issues, no one can,' Mehta said, and hence the help was politely turned down.

Mehta believed that when one door closed, usually another opened, and it did. In his case, the door that opened happened to be just next door.

Kikani, who was around in Sun, when asked about the separation, said, 'It wasn't easy for him. Dilip-bhai was generous and the partners were gracious. I think they said: "If this is what you want and that is what you have decided, then so be it." Then they gracefully said, "Whatever you wish to give, we are fine with it." Sailesh-bhai was the only one who didn't say these words directly. He probably said something along these lines, "Dilip, whatever you wish to do is all right, I want only one commitment. You will have to give me an hour a week to discuss my business."'

Shanghvi laughed at the suggestion of his childhood friend. 'What are you talking about, Sailesh? How can I ever think of saying no to you, you can come over and discuss business any time.'

But Desai put his foot down. 'No, not like that. I am asking for a disciplined one hour every week.'

Kikani narrated the conversation and recalled wondering how amazing that friendship seemed; how smart, sorted, sensitive and pragmatic it felt even when both were parting. 'I was in awe of Dilip-bhai but Sailesh-bhai was a friend, from whom I had learnt a lot. So I didn't hesitate to ask him why he had done that, if only to confirm what I had felt.'

Desai replied to Kikani, 'Why has Sun succeeded so spectacularly? Why are we on course to race ahead of Torrent in a matter of a few years?'

Kikani recalled answering, 'The magic is Dilip-bhai.'

'What about Dilip-bhai?'

He listed a few qualities.

'I have been around here for well over a decade, so I know how Dilip works. I have run my own business. I can't claim to create value as good as Dilip. He just needs to point at one thing, and if I implement it, I know I would create value. I am looking to learn that master stroke in value creation from him,' Kikani recalled Desai explaining to him.

'Our friendship got affected a bit at some point but its foundation was much stronger than the little storms it faced. The deep affection and love we felt for each other withstood all bruises and hurts that time made our relationship go through. When I was leaving Sun, it was, conventionally speaking, not an easy call for me to create everything from scratch but I had the belief and confidence that I would make it happen, if not in a year, then two, if not two, then four or five years and if I failed, I would have still tried and taken responsibility for it,' Desai said.

Desai left Sun in 1994. He was deeply engaged in many activities till his exit, most of all the launch of Sun's R&D centre. A photograph of Desai that appeared in most local newspapers with the then vice-president K.R. Narayanan, who inaugurated the company's R&D centre as its chief guest, would be one of the last abiding souvenirs of his first stint at Sun.

How was the company around the parting ones annotating this process in their mindscape? Barring one, most top executives at Sun who were witness to the separation of the partners felt it was executed with unusual deftness. Even then most preferred to opine anonymously on the matter. 'I think Dilip-bhai was, for a very long time, looking for places within the company where he could accommodate his partners, and once that could not happen he took the next step. Once he has decided something, he doesn't let anyone affect the decision, not even immediate family,' said one. 'Dissolving the proprietorship, was a very conscious decision, it was a strategy for growth of the company,' a second said.

'Dilip-bhai took care of the partners well, maybe went a little overboard. He was in pain while doing what he was doing. He was, after all, cutting out a part of his own world. To put it a little meanly, he bought out his guilt by compensating them more than adequately. He even architected their resettlement by helping them create their business,' a third ex-executive commented.

Another reckoned, 'As of the hurt of partners, they were obviously not happy about it but they were not outraged or disconsolate. The hurt was mainly because their friend was doing this to them, but the hurt could never have been about losing a fortune, because no one was capable of imagining what would become of Sun.'

A person in the know, who had seen this separation happen from close quarters, however, took an exception to this view of the executives and remarked, 'My understanding is that there was disillusionment in some of the partners even on financial terms. They felt not fully compensated, mainly because business at Sun was thriving. So they were wounded even after the settlement. Nitin-bhai didn't have resources and any immediate fallback option. Months after it had been decided that they would leave, Dilip-bhai would still go and live in Nitin-bhai's small flat in Vapi, have lunch sitting there on the floor. But he made sure that none of what transpired between them ever affected the company's atmosphere.'

The wife of a close friend from Calcutta remembered an incident, when she asked Shanghvi during the inauguration of the Halol plant, 'You took along all your dear friends on your journey, then why did you leave out my husband?' To which she recalled Shanghvi responding, 'I am happy I didn't ask him. At least that way our friendship remains just as beautiful as it was.'

Despite their opinions, not a single one of them knew the final terms of the agreement, nor did they believe that anyone else other than the four involved would know it. And one of the executives, a little cryptic, only answered in more questions and riddles: 'What precipitated the separation? Why, despite the temporary hurt, there was no permanent damage to the relationship? If you solve this mystery, you would have arrived at the secret of Sun's success. It reflects Dilip-bhai's innate ability to identify the right people for the right work, because the way other partners took it and refused to go down the path of bitterness, also speaks of their character, which was first identified by Dilip-bhai. And as a consequence what had the potential to hang around Sun's neck as an albatross became its springboard for the next leap.'

Elsewhere, during the same time, ironies of fate and wheels of fortune were twisting and turning by habit. Even before Sailesh Desai had left Sun, in 1993, one day he recalled his cousin and Shanghvi's friend Girish Desai coming to him to discuss the financial distress of his own ophthalmic drug venture Milmet. 'I told him I could only help with about ₹3 lakh; if he needed more, I shall have to speak to Dilip, which I had to.' About a decade back, it was Shanghvi who had gone to Girish Desai's family in Calcutta to borrow money to fund his start-up that proposed to sell psychiatric medicines. As it turned out, the patriarchs of the family had turned him down, according to multiple friends and aides.

'Since by then it was clear that we would be separating, it was Dilip who suggested that I should buy it. Girish's company was selling ophthalmic drugs, the segment had growth and promise and there was an additional spur, there was no direct clash of business with Sun,' Sailesh Desai said. Girish Desai also recalled meeting Shanghvi just about the same time. 'I had entered a lean period in business that time. So I had gone to Dilip-bhai, and I recall him persuading me to not close down this business. This is an excellent business, and it has tremendous potential. Just hold on to it patiently and see what it turns into in future.'

It seems a frenzy of meetings followed, and a realignment of partnership in business was worked out. 'I insisted that Girish kept some shares with him. Milmet was Girish's baby and he was an extremely hard-working boy. I also asked him not to worry about money,' Sailesh Desai recalled. Next he recalled going to Nitin Mehta and Upen-bhai and giving them stakes. 'They invested whatever they could, which wasn't a lot,' Desai said.

Mehta looked after the distribution of Milmet from RK Centre, from where he was for a while looking after Sun's C&F agency for Gujarat. 'Sailesh-bhai asked me to join Milmet, saying we would sit together, and a new door opened for us, even though it seemed challenging,' Mehta said. 'When the arrangement of Milmet happened, it was initially Girish and Sailesh who were steering it. Nitin and I joined later. As for me, I would go there periodically to just look at finance and accounts, and to some extent handle a bit of purchase from Bombay. But my involvement apart from my investment in Milmet was not much,' Upen-bhai said.

Asked whether the Milmet plan was scripted sometime while he was still at Sun, Upen-bhai said, 'No, it didn't immediately come along. It wasn't as if we were walking out of here to take over there. What was possible is that during the many discussions one had through the day, one might have discussed this option and that might have happened in Dilip's presence.' It was possible that most of that discussion happened after Upen-bhai had left, considering he was the first one to leave.

Then he recalled, 'When we were leaving, Dilip might have offered us to take over Unimed (it was an injectable facility that Shanghvi owned in his personal capacity, while Sun focused only on solid dosages—tablets and capsules). But why we got interested in Milmet even though it was also a loss-making company like Unimed is because of two reasons: Milmet, unlike Unimed, had some products and also had a marketing arm. And Unimed was just a facility with no products then. So the only option before us was to use it for contract manufacturing, not a viable option, so we decided to invest in Milmet over Unimed.' Asked whether he had also been offered a C&F agency as Mehta had been, Upen-bhai said, 'Possibly, but I wasn't interested at all.'

Asked about the idea behind three partners regrouping in another medicine business, Upen-bhai said, 'We did that at that point because the rest of us were thinking alike. Doesn't the very fact that all three of us parted and did something together indicate that we were like-minded and thought in a similar direction?'

It is clear that it was Sailesh Desai who led the exercise of recreating Milmet, with what seemed like a queer resemblance to how Sun was built, with two friends and a cousin. As he took the reins in his hand from the founder Girish Desai, he recalled telling him in private, 'Girish, you must stay on because this is your creation. But between you and me, let's be clear about one thing—I will be the boss. What I can promise you is that I shall never act like one.' The last line sounded uncannily familiar of the ways of Shanghvi in business with his two friends and a cousin while it had lasted had the ways ever found expression in words.

And thus began the formation of a mini breakaway Sun, with its own little galaxy. And thus began the journey of a realization—of the power of a bridge to connect and at times reconnect people and places that have drifted apart. The bridge being a man named Sailesh Desai.

A few years later, his best friend from childhood, Mukul Pipalia, was in town—Calcutta. He heard that his 'friend Dilip' may be in town, staying at the Taj Bengal hotel. Pipalia was home after spending awhile in France recovering from his heartbreak with his now former French partner. 'Google wasn't big then, but on and off I had kept hearing from friends how big a businessman Dilip had become and I hadn't met him since 1980.'

So Pipalia recalled walking into the lobby of the Taj, excited and asking for Shanghvi. He was told Shanghvi wasn't in his room. So he left a message, 'Tell him I am a friend . . . I am not sure he would remember me. It's been a while. Tell him it was Mukul.' In five minutes, he got a call from the Taj. Shanghvi, he vaguely recalled, had gone to explore donation options to dedicate an entire floor in his school, JJ Ajmera, to his father. He had come to pick Mukul up the moment he had got in.

When the two friends met after such a long time, Pipalia was sporting long hippy-like hair. Shanghvi commented, 'You look the youngest of all friends.'

'There is a reason behind it. Dilip, when you go home, just blame it on your son. The firstborn. Tell him, because you were born, I became an old man. As soon as you become dad, you age twenty years straight away,' Pipalia quipped. He shared he didn't have kids and had lived life in a cheerful way—by Indian standards, probably a very callous way.

Shanghvi had a huge laugh about it, and they headed to have coffee at Taj Bengal. 'Where do you start and how do you catch up in an hour when the lost time is over a decade and a half,' Pipalia said. But 'some old stuff came up'. Pipalia didn't recount the conversation they had but casually mentioned what he told Dilip: 'Dilip, you deserve everything, you don't owe anything to anyone. If anyone tells you that they had a part in getting you where you are . . . well, I still feel that we don't owe anything to anybody.'

From there they went for a stroll and Mukul suggested, 'Hey, you want a trip down memory lane. Let's go to that *gali* where the two had played *gilli-danda* and cricket as toddlers. There he asked, 'Dilip, it's been such a long, long time. Please come and say hi to my parents, they would be so pleased to meet you.' And he came, with his wife. 'He loved my mom's cooking; she was a fantastic cook. And with my father, with whom he shared a special relationship, he now sat chatting not child to grown-up, but grown-up to grown-up,' Mukul said.

'From the Gujaratis who left Calcutta, you have done best for yourself, most successful' Mukul recalled his dad telling Dilip in Gujarati, whereupon he recalled Shanghvi respectfully shaking his head and softly repeating, 'No bhai, only financial, no bhai, only financial.'

And when the time for goodbyes came a second time, Mukul, unsure of when the next one hour would pop by between them and how many decades would they need to catch up on in that hour, recalled Dilip urging, '*Tu ghare aao, Mukul, tu ghare aao.*'

As you climb up the stairs to the fourth floor of Bhowanipore Gujarati Education Society School, formerly JJ Ajmera School, and before that fondly called Bhagushala, right in front, just above the door that faces you, stands a black polished plaque framed in grey granite with a message engraved in grey that appears pale gold under the spotlight. It reads:

'The Heights by great men reached and kept, were not attained by sudden flight,

But they, while their companion slept, were toiling upward in the night'

Henry W Longfellow (1807–1882)

In respectful memory of Shri Shantilal N. Shanghvi (28.09.1928–11.03.1999) who believed in lasting success that results from honest hardwork.

PART II

CHAPTER TEN

AT LAST THE PRIVATE ONE GOES PUBLIC

Through the blur of smoke, Sailesh Desai saw the sight he had never imagined—tears rolling down a visibly shaken Dilip's face. Across the smoke haze, he had just lit the pyre of Shanti-kaka. The spring of 1999 brought the biggest loss for the Shanghvi household, while Sun was expanding big time.

When Milan Sinha, a few months old in Mumbai, heard this in office, he and colleague Palekar immediately headed for Shanghvi's home in Vile Parle. On reaching, they gathered that he had left for the crematorium to do kaka's last rites. They rushed to the site, only to realize that the congregation had already dispersed.

After reaching office, when he crossed Shanghvi's cabin, there he was dressed in white kurta-pyjama and chappals, bloodshot eyes, dishevelled hair, signing some papers. Sinha turned around with a gaze of disbelief towards his boss, Abhay Gandhi, who understood his question without a word said, 'That's how he is made, kaka was one of those he loved the most, but the business must go on.' This was six years after Sun Pharma had been listed on multiple stock exchanges, and almost two decades since Shanghvi had first met the catalyst for listing in his sister's wedding.

Rendezvous over Rashogollas

That day Shanghvi and Nitin Mehta alighted from a train in Mumbai carrying boxes of sweet Calcutta *rashogollas*. It was a day before Shanghvi's sister Varsha was to marry Kiran, a thick buddy of Sudhir Vrundavandas Valia. The day was special not only because it was the first marriage in Shanghvi's family but also because Upen was tying the knot the same day.

The sweets were such a hit that they fell short, but for Sun the wedding turned out to be a day of momentous serendipity. Valia, who was playing the groomsman in the Gujarati wedding, ran into Shanghvi on that occasion, oblivious of how intertwined their destinies were to get, step by step, first in the near future as he was to become Valia's only sister Vibha's husband and in the far future, as he was to become Valia's boss.

As fate would have it, soon afterwards, Sudhir was inquiring about this boy not only from Kiran but also from another old friend, Arvind Valia, who was Shanghvi's cousin from his mother's side. 'I told them that although Dilip is related to me, my unbiased view is that the boy is "*hoshiyar*",' Arvind, who was a '*juna dost*' of Sudhir recalled.

Sudhir also recalled checking about Shanghvi with Arvind. 'Besides being Dilip-bhai's cousin, he was also the auditor of his company. So, for us he was a credible source to know how his business was really doing. He had given a good feedback.' Arvind thought one reason Shanghvi was keen on Vibha Valia was that she had graduated in pharmacy, and 'he wished to have a life partner who would understand his work'.

Ironically, what remained a bit of a bother for Sudhir's family—when Rasika Maasi, the younger sister of Shanghvi's mother who had been the prospective bride's neighbour, arrived with the marriage proposal at their doorsteps—was the career prospects of a candidate who had no professional qualification to fall back upon.

'We just knew that he was into some business, but didn't have a clue how good he or his business was. What bothered us was that he was living alone in Bombay which we construed to mean that he didn't have a support system,' Sudhir recalled.

When there was no reply, Kiran—probably nudged by an impatient Shanghvi family waiting for an answer—politely asked Sudhir what was taking them so long to decide on the marriage proposal. Sudhir said he had done enough background checks. 'Though all five of us (siblings) were professionally qualified, we also didn't really come from a financially well-off background and our aspirations were not particularly high. My eldest brother had visited his Vapi factory to reassure himself. And above all, my sister felt comfortable with him and that became our principal factor for finally saying yes,' Sudhir recalled.

On the wedding day, Shanghvi's cousin Yashwant Shanghvi, fondly called Baba-bhai, was driving him in a flower-decked car to the venue, Manav Seva Sangh at Sion, when their vehicle got stuck in the snarl of Bombay traffic. After waiting for 15–20 minutes, amid incessant honking, Shanghvi the groom got out of the car and walked up to the traffic police, requesting him to make a concession. 'I am the groom and I am awfully late for my marriage. Please let our vehicle go.' Nana-bhai recalled Shanghvi telling an amused traffic policeman successfully negotiating his way to the mandap.

At the time of the wedding, Sudhir already had an established practice as a chartered accountant through his own firm, Sudhir Valia & Associates, but it was not as if the two—he and Shanghvi—warmed up to each others' professional talents immediately after. It was the years approaching 1990 that saw Shanghvi frequenting Valia for a myriad of tax-related matters, testing his skills before formally proposing in 1993 that he join Sun.

Much before that, in 1989–90, Sun was still a partnership firm with friends on board when Shanghvi was searching for the perfect route to transition into a listed entity. It was Valia who warned him not to follow the conventional route of engaging one partner, and letting all others retire, as the company survived. That route had significant 'stamp duty implications'.

He claimed to have suggested a 'never-before-taken' route under Chapter IX of the Companies Act, 1956, that allowed companies with seven or more partners an easy transition to private limited company without attracting taxes.

His talent in discovering hidden gems in policy documents that could be used to save taxes through unconventional routes and his ingenuity in structuring financial deals made Shanghvi return to him for advice repeatedly.

In the early 1990s, when Shanghvi first thought of seriously taking Sun global, he figured out that for each approval, the company would have to seek an RBI nod—which would eat up a lot of their time.

'Without judging the rights or wrongs of the regulation, to save time, I advised Sun to form a company in British Virginia Islands so that onward business activities could be performed from that company without the need to come back to India. As the destination was a tax haven, other benefits flowed in,' Sudhir recalled. And thus even without any formal role, Valia was fast becoming the 'go-to' man for Shanghvi for 'hundreds of such advice'.

'What struck me first about Sudhir-bhai was his exceptional ability to think out of the box and his deep understanding of taxation law,' said Shanghvi. In Shanghvi, Sudhir found a sharp mind who could grasp offhand what he was suggesting, sparing him the effort to repeat, for a lot of what he said was often not understood or misunderstood given the speed with which he rattled his 'unheard-of' ideas. Sudhir felt Shanghvi realized the worth of his ideas as no one had before. He often encouraged Sudhir to sharpen his skills in financial deal structuring where his true talent lay, not in sheer tax planning.

Shanghvi's admiration for Sudhir's talents manifested itself in unorthodox ways. Once Sudhir shared with Shanghvi a self-designed ingenious bond structure, explaining it with enthusiasm, 'Through this instrument, you can separate the depreciation from the asset and sell it individually. I had gone to Indian Railways Finance Corporation, proposing that they can raise up to ₹5000 crore through this.' Midway, Shanghvi glanced up from the papers and said, 'Just patent the idea.'

While Shanghvi and Sudhir Valia were discovering a harmony, people around were betting against the possibility of what they saw as chalk blending with cheese. As personalities, they were studies in contrast. Valia comes across as fantastically intelligent but impetuous and impatient, Shanghvi thoughtful but quiet and eternally patient; Valia a rapper of a talker, Shanghvi's punctuations often turned into pauses; Valia as open as a sieve, Shanghvi shut as a book; Valia, a spontaneous problem solver, Shanghvi someone who slept on his problems weighing all possible implications. And yet the two were to form a bond beyond anyone's understanding.

'It is very easy to have similar people around, but it is more important to have different people around, particularly if you are looking for growth,' Shanghvi said about how different they were as personalities.

In fact their differences of opinion, fundamental in nature, played out right at the outset when Shanghvi had been in talks with a private equity fund for diluting 2 per cent equity stake of the company. 'I wasn't comfortable. And I told him that we should list at the stock exchanges,' Valia recalled. 'I had not thought of listing initially. It was Sudhir-bhai's idea,' Shanghvi said. It is understandable; Shanghvi never liked explaining himself too much—neither to friends and family nor to investors.

Both were thinking of the same end—company's growth, but through different means. 'I believed money makes money, Dilip-bhai argued business makes money,' Valia recalled. A long debate ensued on whether it was prudent to go public, but eventually Valia prevailed. 'I structure finance all the time, and I knew that listing could give us that platform to leap ahead,' Valia said.

'Once it was finalized that listing was the way to go, in 1993, Sun was looking for a finance specialist who could take care of a part of their activities. Dilip-bhai came here to the very same office in Dadar, sat in the same chair you are sitting in right now and asked me to formally become a part of Sun,' Valia recalled.

'I have always done whenever whatever you have asked me of. There is nothing that I wouldn't do for you,' Valia replied to Shanghvi.

'Between the two of us, if any differences arise ever, you should listen to me, because I am older than you,' he recalled Shanghvi telling him.

Valia didn't find the reasoning of age compelling enough. 'What has age got to do with this? But of course I was mindful that it is at the end his company, and his decision should be final,' he summed up.

And then to borrow a bit from Julian Barnes, 'You put two things that have not been put together before. And the world is changed.' People may not have noticed at the time, but Sun's world had changed nonetheless.

The one besides Vibha Shanghvi, who knew both closely, Arvind Valia admitted that not many thought that such opposites could last long, but their partnership belied all such doubt-mongers. But was it a happy union, with everyone around excited at the prospect of the suspense, waiting to see where it led Sun?

Quite the contrary, many in close circle admitted without revealing details that in the extended Shanghvi family, it stirred anxiety and disturbance. The reasons were more than just a traditional block that conservative Gujarati families have when involving someone from the wife's family in their business, though part of the resistance also stemmed from this mindset.

The emotional strain apparently intensified because what had preceded Valia's entry was Upen-bhai's exit, and Valia was seen as someone coming to fill in his shoes. There were a few senior executives in Sun who were aware of this tension in the clan, and admitted that this along with the departure of friends had left 'Dilip-bhai shaken, but he successfully shielded the office environment from the turmoil he was undergoing in his personal life'.

'What he was attempting was a bold move in his circle, and the response it evoked was similar to what 'an inter-caste love marriage' would in their generation,' the Sun executive said, adding, 'people around couldn't perceive what Dilip-bhai could, that most calls were being taken with a precise reasoning in the interest of business in mind. And that inability perhaps led his friends and extended family to conclude that he was cold and unemotional.'

However, when asked about the disquiet, Shanghvi said, 'I didn't feel any such pressure. Also by that time, I was fairly successful, so it's possible that nobody told me even if there was any such thing.'

Arvind Valia, who served as Sun's auditor at the time, recalled a call from Shanghvi right before he was to induct Sudhir Valia. 'Sudhir had his own CA firm and through his genius in financial engineering had earned enough in his first five years of practice. Dilip judged Sudhir as one of the top five brightest financial minds in the country. My mother was around then, and I told her, "Dilip is planning to rope in Sudhir formally." Her response was pragmatic: "All's fine if they can ensure that their business doesn't affect their relations. If their business relation doesn't click, it shouldn't ruin their *sala-behnoi* relation."'

Shanghvi had denied knowledge of family pressure, but in a different context in an earlier meeting, when asked what took him so long to rope in Valia, he had said, 'Psychologically, what I would have seen is that there is a certain amount of reservation about doing business with relatives from the wife's side. But as I started to spend more time with him, and used his advice even before he joined us, I could realize that both of us were mature enough to manage (relationship and business simultaneously). He helped the company transition dramatically.'

From Valia's side also, there had been ifs and buts. 'There were massive reservations. My wife from day one was against me joining the organization. And she advised me that what we were staking were our personal relations, which was way more precious than business relations.' Valia found a way out by deciding not to work under 'commercial' terms, and refused to take home a salary for his services (an arrangement that didn't last long).

'Why did I need a salary, the company was like our home. Dilip-bhai's work was getting done. I was getting to solve interesting problems. I already had enough money, at least more than I could spend,' he stated. Shanghvi didn't recall this incident, but said it was plausible and he might have convinced Valia to eventually take home a salary.

So in the Sun ecosystem, Valia recalled starting off salary-less and staying secretary-less for a sizeable part of his stint, even with pouring responsibilities as the years progressed. Interestingly, his business card never sported his designation in the company, just like Shanghvi's. Asked about the curious aberration, Shanghvi replied, 'In the field, where I worked for initial years, people ask for all sorts of favours. If I didn't agree with what they asked for, instead of being rude it helped me to furnish a ready reply—I will ask my boss and let you know.'

Setting Up the Research Arm

Just before listing, Shanghvi invested ₹5 crore in setting up an R&D arm—equivalent to two years of profits at Sun then. He took that decision mainly because of three factors. First, he was keen to introduce new drugs unavailable in India, the raw materials for which were often a struggle to buy—so it made more sense to make it in-house. Second, he had seen in some next generation antibiotic firms, how a vertically integrated model, where you did everything from raw material to tablets in-house, drastically reduced cost. Third, India was on the verge of signing a global agreement which meant that the question of transitioning to a product-patent regime now was about 'when', not 'if'. Once India recognized 'product patents', the perception that was only those companies would survive which had some edge in R&D.

Louis Banks Listing Anthem

Once the route of listing was decided upon, Shanghvi flung himself fully, to the point that his son Aalok recalled that his dropping out of the Harvard course was not out of boredom, as brand guru Tarun Gupta had guessed, but for the need to be present in Bombay and take charge of a diverse range of pre-IPO activities.

Shanghvi fell headlong into rehearsing for his investor roadshows, for which his executive assistant Mira prepared presentations. She recalled him struggling in the beginning. 'Dilip-bhai was not a great speaker. His pitch was flat, there was no modulation in tone, and he got conscious while speaking. At times when he spoke in conferences, you could see boys yawning, drifting off to sleep,' Shyamal Ghosh echoed. The practice was as much to ensure that he didn't fumble with his facts and figures as to make sure he got better at grabbing attention. So he usually made a few of his senior employees sit, and acted out mock drills of presentations and then question–answer sessions.

Ghosh recalled interjecting repeatedly: Dilip-bhai, *maza nahin aya . . . phir se ho jaye.* 'What's remarkable is that he came with an earnest desire to learn, and kept asking you, "Tell me where I am not getting it. Which aspect is falling short?" While in that learning mode, he kept his ego completely aside, not once thinking, "Who is he to cite my flaws?"' Ghosh marvelled.

Public speaking is still not his forte, and he is known to shy away from the mic and podium, cameras still make him awkward.

Interestingly, around him people are divided on whether he can't do it or won't do it—sparing a few more words, and doing more public addresses. Ghosh, a first-hand witness of his struggle with public speaking, feels oratory is not one of his gifts, but success and confidence have made him better at it over the last two decades. Madhav Bhatkuly, an early investor in Sun, believes there is no question of him getting better at public speaking because he has no such natural limitation.

'He doesn't do public speaking because he doesn't want to. The day he decides otherwise, and opens up, this misperception would be gone.' Friends, who have seen him as a master entertainer in closed circles in younger days, view this image as a burden of responsibility.

'He has reached a stature today that so much is at stake on every word he utters,' feels Butta. A rival sees in it a strategy, 'He is smart. The less you speak, the less you have to clarify yourself.' Daughter-in-law Karishma quips, 'If you can say what you have to in a few words, why do you have to use so many words, to what end?'

Shanghvi started off as a reluctant speaker in the investor roadshow that was flagged off at the Oberoi in Bombay, with a thin turnout. But those who have seen him polishing his public speaking skills up close, saw other traits in him. 'With every next broker conference—at Jaipur, Bangalore, Delhi—he was beating his performance of the previous conference. He was also quick on the uptake. I saw him picking up a shorthand language that brokers and investors use, and starting to converse with them in their lingo,' Mira observed. 'I didn't really think that he transformed into any inspiring speaker over those roadshows. But I noticed one thing. When it came to questions and answers, he would settle into an ease, come into his elements and totally beat our expectations,' Ghosh pointed out.

His observation holds valid even today, going by the anecdotal evidences from the annual general meetings held at Baroda, perhaps to avoid the intense media glare of Mumbai. 'When a shareholder asked him for a commemorative gold coin in the annual general meeting (AGM) in 2015, he quipped that his father taught him to stay off lavishes and save, the reason he could deliver the kind of growth in the company.'

Even today, people he chooses to open up to swear that Shanghvi is essentially a one-on-one person; the substantial part of him that you can see and learn in personal chats doesn't show itself in one-to-many arrangements. Even in one-to-many arrangements, he is more in his elements in a meeting set-up, not so in podiums.

During his roadshows, the story Shanghvi was pitching was one of growth, his company having clocked over 50 per cent CAGR in six previous years against the industry's average growth of 17 per cent; of jumping from 107 all-India rank in 1988 to thirty-four by 1994; having launched 100 products in its brief history of a decade, of which eight had been introduced in India for the first time; having spent 8 per cent of its sales in recently set up the R&D centre while the comparative figure for peers stood at 1.4 per cent in 1992–93.

The company's IPO prospectus didn't categorically spell out its strategy of pursuing drugs for chronic diseases with lifetime prescriptions. Yet, one could sense that in his search for 'low-volume, high-margin, long-term prescription products', he was clearly taking steps towards creating a drug franchise around community of specialists—psychiatrists, cardiologists, neurologists and gastroenterologists. Of the 870 employees on its rolls, sixty were research scientists and 550 were MRs who had been arranged in divisions dedicated to therapies: Synergy to cater to psychiatrists and neurologists, Aztec to service cardiologists and Sun for everything else.

This strategy of building its business around specialists not only enabled it to charge a premium on its products but also stay clear of locking horns with deep-pocketed bigger firms, who were busy selling popular prescription and over-the-counter drugs, which needed a lot more advertisement expenditure and numerous more feet on the ground to peddle them.

From earning only ₹10 lakh in 1982–83, the year of its registration, it was on its way to register a sale of ₹50 crore in 1990. When Bhatkuly, before investing in Sun, turned up at his door with a bunch of news clippings, Shanghvi answered his questions patiently for four hours, ending the conversation with: 'Every three years, I want my sales figure to have become my profit figure.' And as they were leaving office, Bhatkuly recalled him walking over to each of the switches to turn off the lights across the floor.

The corporate movie they played out on roadshows was a slight improvisation of the one they had made in 1992 for international markets. Sun was foraying into Russia that year, and Shanghvi had wanted a corporate film made about his company. Whom else would he call in office but Shyamal Ghosh, who, with his unkempt curls, sunken cheeks, fair and lean frame even physically resembled ad guru Alyque Padamsee. When Ghosh made a few calls, the figure that ad professionals quoted for the entire project was ₹12–14 lakh. 'It was astronomical for us,' Ghosh recalled.

He called Shanghvi to get an idea of the budget. 'Dilip-bhai, how much can we spend?'

'*Teen char lakh mein ho jaye toh achchha hai . . .*'

Ghosh tried calling his younger ad-world friends, first-timers, debutants, but no one was ready to do it for less than ₹7 lakh. He then called a young go-getter, who was doing visual ads for Sun—Milind Ghaisas.

'Milind was dynamic, well connected and gave it a try by assembling a motley team,' Ghosh recalled. He got together a friend who did computer graphics, a friend's friend who had tried his hand at editing, and the crew was ready. 'Since we have to do it in a shoestring budget, we have to shoot three days non-stop because the shooting equipment can't cost any lesser,' he cautioned. So they shot without break in the Baroda corporate office, headed to research centre, up straight to Vapi, then to Silvassa.

The fourth day, Milind asked Ghosh to join him in the studio, 'You have to sit through the editing. It's pharmaceuticals, full of technical details, and the studio rent does not allow any luxury of retake. So we have to go without sleep.' Ghosh and Mira Desai hopped to Bombay. That is when they realized that they needed a scriptwriter. No one agreed for less than ₹25,000, so Ghosh doubled as a scriptwriter on the spot. 'Thankfully, my handwriting was legible, so Pratap Sharma, the voice-over artist, could read straight from the handwritten script.'

Ghosh, Mira and Milind stayed up a record sixty hours, living in the studio surviving only on sandwiches and coffee, to snip the 450 minutes of footage into a fourteen-minute film. But the one aspect Ghosh didn't want to compromise on was music. So he called Shanghvi, 'Dilip-bhai can we spend a little more?'

And then Louis Banks, the jazz godfather, was roped in for ₹30,000. By then his 'short national-integration musicals', '*Mile Sur Mera Tumhara*' and '*Deshrag*' had become huge hits. But a few days before he was to compose for Sun, Banks suffered a massive heart attack and underwent a bypass surgery. To everyone's surprise he still landed up in the studio and ended up composing, mixing the music through the night. 'At 4 a.m. he was done. We were all completely exhausted by then. We caught up on sleep and then returned to Baroda,' Ghosh said.

Shanghvi loved the film and rewarded them with a day's leave and loads of work to grab publicity of investors during the roadshows and listing exercise later.

The Colour of IPO

It was 1993 and Enam Securities, a star brokerage and portfolio manager of those days had just helped Infosys launch its IPO. 'The Infosys IPO nearly failed, but Enam was so impressed with the company that the promoters personally took up a lot of shares, encouraged clients to buy with the definite advice not to sell in a hurry,' journalist Sucheta Dalal wrote. They prided themselves on taking promising unknown companies public.

Sun could have been on that list of Enam's multi-baggers discoveries, for Shanghvi and Valia reached out first to the En in Enam. The En is a derivation from one of its founders Nemish Shah, often described as a 'reclusive' and 'spiritual' in media. It was perfectly possible that the Infosys story celebrated in media might have inspired them to first reach out to Nemish. But Arvind Valia underlined another reason, Nemish's backstory.

Nemish's father owned a pharma company, which he used to manage. A long lockout in the company reportedly left him disillusioned, and he drifted into the world of equity trading. Given his background, Shanghvi expected Shah to understand and value his business model, at a time when some industry captains were still dismissing it as a fluke.

Shah, as per Arvind Valia's vague recollection, quoted that the share wouldn't fetch more than ₹120. Not pleased, Shanghvi and the Valias went about exploring with other players the premium they could offer, and finally settled at ₹140.

Aside of the debate on the price band which apparently Shanghvi and Valia both thought unjustifiably low to reflect the company's performance, and the whole point of listing itself, there was another debate raging in Sun's boardroom during the pre-listing phase—the idea of offering medical specialists shares on discount, another brainwave of Shanghvi.

A rival of Sun pronounced it as a strategy to ensure that the offer didn't remain undersubscribed. 'After a huge financial market scam, public interest in IPO was at an all-time low and they might have feared lukewarm participation, which is probably why they offered shares to doctors,' he reckoned, pointing out 'the blatant conflict of interest' underlying the move. But that doesn't seem to be the case.

'Selling Sun Pharma was never an issue. Dilip-bhai was very confident that the future was much brighter than the present and anyone who invests in Sun's shares today would be gaining tomorrow,' Kikani contested. That he was confident of future is also clear from Piyush Doshi's memories of how 'Dilip came offering all friends shares, exhorting us to partake in this growth story that Sun was'.

Sun had till then built its business case completely around its relationship with communities of doctors. Offering them shares clearly meant another opportunity to cement those ties to the next level and a solid incentive for them to actively script Sun's growth story. It's a no-brainer, once you are a stakeholder in a company, you would like to see it grow.

'It was a double-edged sword and it takes a whole lot of gut to offer shares to doctors. If it backfires, your business gets affected. This was the crux of the debate,' Kikani summed up. In fact, it could backfire more than one way. Offering discounted shares to one set of doctors seemed a perfect recipe for earning the wrath of those left out.

There was also a faint chance that things went wrong for Sun, and the specialists who had invested cursed the company for life. In hindsight the medical community displayed better judgement than the investors and brokers. 'Many doctors had appetite for more shares than what we could offer. They were ready to buy more at lesser discount as well,' said a former Sun manager.

Ghosh, and later even Shanghvi, passed it as a gesture to offer gratitude to those who had helped Sun reach so far. 'Focus on psychiatrists and neurologists had practically made the company. I have seen the emotional investment Dilip-bhai had made and how senior psychiatrists doted on him. When the division was launched in Calcutta, psychiatrists, albeit three pegs down, were all teary-eyed, hugging him and mumbling, "You were such a little kid, and today you have grown up to become such a big man." So the bond they shared, it was unthinkable for them that Dilip-bhai was listing his company and not even offering a share to them,' Ghosh said.

Shanghvi shared something similar. 'I looked at giving shares to doctors as a sense of appreciation to those who had helped us grow. I think I have taken many decisions which people interpret their own ways. If I was convinced that my intentions were right, I would go ahead and do it. Otherwise you get frozen.'

If Mira Desai and Shyamal Ghosh were by Shanghvi's side on his roadshows, Hiren Desai was by his side on the roads literally in the run-up to the listing. The first time ever he had heard 'Dilip-bhai speak his mind on listing the company' was way back in 1991.

By then, Sun's corporate office had already moved to Baroda but some functions such as procurement, import clearance and finance still operated out of Bombay. So did Desai. And Shanghvi kept visiting frequently. When he had to talk business, many times he asked Desai to hop over to the road next to Vakola (near Desai's home) and join him in his taxi till the station, from where he was to catch the train to Baroda. It was an afternoon of 1991, and he was to take the Ahmedabad-bound Karnavati Express. 'Among many things, he mentioned that he wished to take the company public in the next few years,' Desai recalled. This was a year before Harshad Mehta securities scam broke, and the market was still in boom.

Desai believes one thing about his boss: that he is never unprepared about major decisions, even if it seems so to the world, because until he is done with his own debate and analysis in his mind, he doesn't put out his plans in words, leave alone on paper.

During listing Desai was handling the logistics of outdoor publicity. By this time the stock market had crashed after Harshad Mehta securities scam, and the faith of people in IPOs had been shattered, turning the whole listing climate gloomy.

Those were still pre-SEBI (Securities and Exchange Board of India) days and one had to advertise in phases all details about the public issue of the shares. Shanghvi oversaw much of these activities himself, usually at night.

All those nights, he would hop into his car with Desai and a few more boys and drive across Bombay to see the preparation, location, size, aesthetic, impact of the billboards. So he would see them from a distance, take a walk to approach the life-size ones from different directions to gauge how they made one feel.

It was two days to the issue to open up, and Shanghvi was on his ritual drive, Desai by his side. They crossed the billboard near the petrol pump in front of the Mahalakshmi temple in Bombay, when Shanghvi asked to put the car in reverse gear and stop near the giant hoarding of the Sun IPO.

He got down and saw it up close, the base colour of the poster was that of cloud, a dim grey. Desai recalled him saying, 'The people who are going to invest in my company are thinking of their future. A dull colour like this will not evoke interest, leave alone enthusiasm. Change the colour to a bright orange, the colour of Sun, the colour of hope and light, a colour that can stir in them an excitement to invest.' And so he decided to change the colour of all the hoardings.

Admiration for his boss's attention to detail notwithstanding, what bothered Desai at that moment was the huge logistical challenge the peeling off and mounting up of new billboards posed, all to be done overnight, given that barely a day was left for the issue to open. 'But Dilip-bhai had said it, so it had to be done,' Desai said.

Brush with a Shark

The issue opened on 6 October 1994. Valia and his pack of friends were keeping a close tab on how it's progressing. At one point during the issue, they sensed some unusual interest from a shark of a player in the pharma industry which took them by shock. Shanghvi, Valia and their team were totally unprepared for this googly.

This giant was not a multinational, but a home-grown star whose future was to be inextricably linked with Sun. In 1994, not the wildest astrologer could have bet on the possibility of what was to happen exactly two decades down the line. Many would have happily bet on the opposite, the prospect of which showed itself during Sun's listing as this pharma giant Ranbaxy tried to corner a sizeable chunk—10 to 12 per cent of Sun shares.

'Dilip-bhai didn't fancy the idea of having aggressive and towering personalities like Dr Parvinder Singh and D.S. Brar of Ranbaxy on his board and then dictating terms on how he should be running the company,' said a former Sun executive. Another said, 'I think his company meant everything to him, and he was traumatized by the thought of Ranbaxy's intent.'

But in true signature Shanghvi style, this piece of relevant information remained one of the best-kept secrets in the industry, known only to those few in his immediate circle who had a part to play in it. Many others like Kikani were surprised to hear this but bought the story because Ranbaxy carried the reputation of a corporate raider.

Asked about Ranbaxy's attempt, Shanghvi confirmed, 'They actually found out how the issue was doing and made an application equivalent to five times the issue size. That was Dr Singh's decision. You don't need to deposit all the money initially, only 10 per cent of it. They were hoping that they would get 10–12 per cent of the company at that point.'

On the Ranbaxy side, the top brass, Parvinder Singh, D.S. Brar, Vinay Kaul and some others knew but probably didn't publicize it much because the attempt had to be finally aborted.

In fact, much after Sun's growth story had been fully established, late into the noughties, memories of the failed attempt cropped up as an occasional talking point in Delhi's Chhattarpur farmhouse parties hosted by former Ranbaxy owners. As claimed by a former Ranbaxy top manager that during one such occasion a member of the Singh family reclined next to the barbecue and lamented, 'Sun had almost come into Ranbaxy's grip, but it slipped away at the last moment.'

The story of how Sun managed to 'slip away' from Ranbaxy's grip at the last moment, was described by some insiders as a climactic, clever but 'obscure manoeuvre' of Sudhir-bhai whose contacts they believed 'ran very deep in the stock market'. One insider said, 'It was managed quietly, followed by some hush-hush negotiations, and Sun had averted the crisis.' In fact, it turns out that even the insiders were not fully clued-in beyond sniffing the broad contours of the deal. What they saw as obscure, mysterious ways was just Valia spotting a procedural lapse to reject Ranbaxy's application.

'Sudhir-bhai's view was that we didn't need to honour Ranbaxy's application. We had listed a number of bank branches in our prospectus from which you had to subscribe, and Ranbaxy had applied through a branch which was not part of that list. So on that ground we could reject their application,' Shanghvi said.

But as soon as they got to know, that Sun was rejecting their application, Kaul along with Uday Kotak came to meet Shanghvi to discuss the matter. And Shanghvi, true to his nature to not create bitterness where it could be avoided, agreed to give them a certain number of shares with the understanding that 'Sun got the first right to refusal when they wanted to offload the shares.' Old-time insiders from Ranbaxy speculated that this unpleasant event sowed a seed in Sun which was to culminate twenty years later.

The issue closed on 10 October 1994 to a phenomenal response, oversubscribed by fifty-five times. The promoter's holding diluted from 97 per cent to 73 per cent, and Sun raised ₹55 crore. If you had invested ₹1 lakh in December 1995, it would have grown to ₹5 crore by April 2015.

Shanghvi called upon his senior employees' one after another to give them shares, hailing their contribution. Mira was surprised to receive such a 'generous offering of shares'. Yagnik recalled telling, 'I can't take this, Dilip-bhai, this is a lot.' Others narrated similar experiences. At times, employees found it difficult to reconcile this generous side of Shanghvi's to his 'super cost-consciousness' manifested in their salaries and the way the company was run.

Among thousands of fresh shareholders in his company was his Calcutta neighbour Jai Shah, who was a small child when Shanghvi left the place. Back in Paddapukur, Shanghvi's erstwhile rented home (where he grew up) turned into a celebrity space for Gujaratis settled in Calcutta and the neighbourhood, and Shanghvi their hero.

This was the time when a budding psychiatrist who had seen a George Bernard Shaw spark in Dilip a decade ago, saw a song of hope— that talked of touching the moon and the stars, flying high in the sky on his television screen and was instantly reminded of Shanghvi. This was the time when another psychiatrist who had once mistaken him to be a medical representative when Dilip had extended a cigarette, called him up to remind that his decade-old prophecy had come true, 'Dilip truly owned the Sun, and sky was the limit for him.'

People started dropping in wide-eyed to verify, whether the Dilip Shanghvi who had listed a company by the name of Sun Pharma had actually lived in this yellow building on Paddapukur Road. 'Where was his house? Which floor did he live in? How did he live? What did he do? How did he make it so big?' These were the kind of questions Jai remembered getting flooded with in 1994. 'We were feeling so proud, holding the shares of the company Dilip uncle had created,' Jai beamed. Since that year, Jai has been following the stock market and each move of Shanghvi closely.

And the questions he used to face haven't ceased. 'When people invest in his company, they ask me. When they invest in other companies, they ask me half-expecting that I am on a hotline with him,' says Jai. 'Do you know him? Can you find out whether we should invest in this stock or that? Can you get a tip from him on where to invest? Why doesn't he appear more on TV? Why don't we see more of him on CNBC Awaz? Does he now have a jet of his own?' are the questions Jai still deals with.

One of the building residents has been preparing ground for a while to write to him to turn the crumbling structure into a 'Dilip Shanghvi memorial,' and look after its maintenance. At least that way, the dilapidated building would survive a few more years, he felt. Jai, who dabbles seriously in stockbroking, marvelled at Shanghvi's two-country US–India business model innocently, with pride and a sense of ownership. 'Today he has created a business that runs 24/7, 365 days, just like the breath. When the US sleeps, India buys. When India sleeps, the US buys.'

CHAPTER ELEVEN

SHANGHVI AND SANGHVI

Sudhir-bhai retrieved the thermos he used to bring tea from home, and offered to pour some for Yagnik. The HR head who had been sent by Shanghvi to formally invite Valia, had navigated winding lanes, lost his way, asked around before finding the narrow stairs that led to Sudhir-bhai's shop in Bombay. Clinking home-made tea in a thermos-cap cup against a small striated glass marked the official welcome of Valia into Sun. But few professionals responded back with 'Cheers'. Sudhir-bhai's out-of-the-box thinking meant he didn't necessarily play by the straight rules the company had set for itself. This out-of-the-box character spilled over to his personality, which most professionals at Sun struggled to grasp.

Enter Valia, the Wizard

The first time Sudhir Valia set his eyes on Sun's books, he found the tax planning rudimentary. This was a year before the listing. 'It was a small company and I had to scrap what their financial advisers had advised and redesign the whole thing from scratch,' Valia recalled.

Shanghvi and Valia had intense discussions which sometimes verged on arguments. Shanghvi wanted to pool back all the money in the core business but Valia was bubbling with interesting ideas to save and make money. Once Valia recalled proposing an innovative leasing scheme using a law that allowed a 100 per cent tax rebate for assets with investments of ₹5000 or below. His plan entailed identifying multiple parties in the business of billboards who needed capital and did not mind paying rentals to the company for the hoarding frames. Such a plan could allow the company to disclose actual profits, defer the tax burden and earn rentals on the investment simultaneously.

Valia recalled explaining to Shanghvi the benefits of the billboard-leasing business and how in a few years, they would have much more to invest in the core business. Adept at scouring taxman's laws and finding pathways that taxman himself had yet to discover, Valia came up with many such ideas and finally found a legitimate route to avoid that tax.

But high profits and low-tax financial architecture of Valia escaped investors' grasp and they could not appreciate how this financial rejig would propel the company's business in future. Therefore the company's share after listing traded at a muted price for 3–4 years.

Interestingly, the ₹55 crore that Sun raised through its public issue, had to be parked somewhere as Shanghvi at that point decided against buying companies because of higher valuations. The 'money makes money' philosophy of Valia came handy as, over the next three years, about ₹45 crore of the capital raised was deployed in real estate and in giving out loans. At that time Sun received a lot of offers to invest in the stock market but Shanghvi, it seems, was reluctant to take such risks because analysts do not value earnings from non-business activities much. Instead they offered loans to people who were interested in investing in shares or public issues. The arrangement was such that Sun would offer them loan at fixed interest rate and keep securities twice the value of loan amount as collateral. As per Valia's recollection and rough estimate, this along with other business earnings helped Sun prepare a war chest of almost ₹100 crore which it could dig into when it went into an acquisition spree in the late 1990s.

Over the next three or four years, Valia had the signature of his divergent thinking all over Sun's financials. When Shanghvi thought of doling out shares to employees, it wasn't the usual ESOPs (employee stock ownership plan) they got. 'The ESOP had tax implications for the person who got it. So we created a trust for employees who were shareholders in Sun Pharma Industries Ltd. The stocks issued by trusts to the employees didn't have tax implication and the employees could legally jump out of the tax net,' Valia recalled. He didn't stop there. He created a partnership firm of the Sun Pharma Employees' Trust with the main company, where the latter owned over 99 per cent stake and took advantage of a law that levied a minimum alternate tax (MAT) on companies but exempted partnership firms. It was only after 2013 that the tax laws were amended to impose tax on income received from a partnership firm. But by then Sun had rode massively on the back of simple tax planning for almost twenty years.

Not everyone, particularly wary investors and taxmen along with nosy auditors, bought this story on a platter. 'In fact, everyone questioned their taxability, their profits, when the framework they were using was simple and legal,' Bhatkuly said.

For this non-stereotypical tax management, an area the *Economist* calls 'a dark art', an art nonetheless, Sun had tiffs with its auditors on occasions and even got raided by income tax authorities.

One such raid in 1998 was exhaustive. It covered thirty-four of its premises across Mumbai, Vapi, Baroda, Ahmednagar, Silvassa and Delhi, assessing the company's dues from 1988 to 1998. The raids quickly spawned rumours.

'The story doing the rounds was that a prominent pharmaceuticals industrialist had instigated the raid. In India, it's not such a difficult thing to get done,' recalled an investor in Sun. A senior employee had a different story: 'My nephew who was in the income tax office had come home for lunch the day after the raid had begun. He asked, "Uncle, you look disturbed. Is it about your company's raid?" I nodded. He replied, "Don't worry, nothing substantial will come off it. It's been over two years, since they have shifted from Baroda, and no one has come to our office to pay the customary salute. The raid is just a reminder of the unofficial rules."'

Wild rumours apart, Sun challenged that income tax department assessment on a technical ground, that the government had flouted its own rule by not sticking to serving its income tax notice under Section 143 (2) of the Income Tax Act within the prescribed period while assessing block period returns. Sun eventually got the order quashed.

Paying low taxes also created an unflattering image for Sun in some industrialists' minds. Owner of Asian Paints, Ashwin Dani, a former director on the Sun's board, recalled that his initial reluctance to joining the firm was partially out of a perusal of its balance sheet which showed it paid very little tax. It was a study in contrast to his company Asian Paints that paid taxes in the highest brackets.

Part of that wariness could also be because of Sun's zealous veil of secrecy around its tax planning. This was not only to prevent giving away a competitive advantage. 'If everyone got to know and started doing a clever thing, it becomes a norm, comes into the government's notice, and a change in the law becomes an inevitable consequence. Sure enough, that is exactly what happened in 2013, but Sun had already grown big by then,' Bhatkuly said. Sun refused offers for case studies from premier institutes for fear of word getting out, which could have led to rampant imitation and the government plugging the loop. 'Publicizing it would have defeated the purpose,' Valia said.

He reeled off other interesting instances of tax planning he engineered in the target companies Sun acquired. But asked whether tax planning was his passion, he shook his head, 'No, not at all. I am passionate about finding solutions to problems, in ways existing people around have failed to solve them.'

Sudhir-bhai: Matunga to Dadar, Such a Long Journey

Then how did his passion find expression in tax planning? Here it may prove fruitful to digress from Sun's story for a moment and beam on Valia's because part of his personality would merge in Sun's story. Valia grew up in Matunga—dotted with Irani cafes, Udupis and south Indian temples built by generations of tossed salad migrant population comprising Tamil Brahmins and Gujaratis, particularly Kapols—in a small, one-room-kitchen flat, with his parents and two of his four siblings, the youngest being Vibha. 'Our house didn't have enough space for all of us, so two of my elder brothers who could have helped me with my studies actually had to live at one of my uncle's place.'

Valia studied in a neighbourhood school named Amulakh School, where he befriended Kiran who married Shanghvi's sister. As a small child of five or six years, once Valia saw celebrations breaking out in the neighbourhood, only to figure out that their neighbour's son had cleared his CA. 'I thought that's the thing to do. If there is so much jubilation over this, it must be a big deal,' Valia recalled.

At school, he was more a sportsperson, performing decently in subjects where he managed without studying—maths and science.

'I didn't have to work on my maths. When the sum appeared, my mind would automatically start solving it,' Valia recalled. Even today, Valia doesn't have to scroll his mobile for numbers; he retrieves them from his mind.

Life was not the same with language though, and, to his shock, he flunked his class XII exam, in a subject called commercial correspondence, which called for English knowledge. 'My mother had studied till class VII, my father hadn't been schooled at all. We were on our own as far as studies went,' he recalled.

The failure jolted him from within. 'All my friends went ahead and took admission in the BCom course, but I didn't have that option,' he said.

While growing up, he had started to accompany his father to the textile market, where he worked as a broker. 'The market was unfair and frustrating. People didn't respect your work. Paying up the little commission they owed you was made to look like some charity. I didn't enjoy that experience and made up my mind that I didn't want to continue doing that,' Valia said.

Valia's parents despite their hardships saw through that their children pursued professional courses. 'My brothers were at that time considered much brighter than I was as they were doing engineering. Vibha had got admission in dentistry, but chose to study pharmacy,' Valia said.

Since Valia didn't wish to join his father's line of work and BCom was not an option, he sat for the CA entrance and cracked it. Ironically, most of his friends who got admission in BCom took longer to either clear the entrance or the exam and Valia got into the profession before they did.

At twenty-three, he started his first job with a CA firm. In fifteen days, they decided 'I didn't fit in,' he smiled and switched to his second job, Valia recalled. While still in his second job he told his clients that they were losing good money because of flaws in finance and production structuring. His bosses didn't appreciate this bold streak in Valia, particularly the fact that he was interacting with the client directly bypassing them, while Valia thought he was just stating the obvious. He then floated his own firm Sudhir Valia & Associates in 1978–79, and in his own words 'started being more absent than present' in his employer's office, eventually parting ways. 'In the first three months of my career, I was earning more than my need. But money itself was never my driving force. Since money was not what I was after, I realize I never pasted a price tag on my ideas. I also realize that had I done that I could have been worth much more,' he said. By the 1980s, Valia's practice had picked up and he zeroed down on a property right in front of Dadar station. Tax planning aside, from the mid-to late 1980s was the time he started structuring products for finance, and discovered he had a knack for it.

It is here in his Dadar office that he sat through the years when Sun headquarters was in Baroda, managing—investing—earning handsome returns on a large chunk of funds that Sun raised from the public through listing on stock exchanges.

Mr Fixit for All Things Else

Sometime after 1996, Valia, in addition to finance, started taking an active interest in other areas. 'Eventually I discovered Sudhir-bhai's distinct ability to juggle multiple priorities at the same time effectively and his great execution capabilities. A lot of Sun's efficiency (in arms other than product and marketing) has been (with the help of) Sudhir-bhai's execution, and in time these turned into work habits which are internalized as the organizational culture,' Shanghvi said.

Valia's entry into other areas of Sun wasn't as easy as it sounds, given his quirky, spontaneous, undiplomatic disposition. By 1996, Sun had a decent number of professionals heading important functions, who didn't fancy their turfs getting breached by a family member of the owner whom they had till now seen as a 'money manager'. As far as Valia was concerned, he was simply stating what he thought, and solving problems he saw.

He started his rounds with manufacturing, walking into meetings, on occasions unannounced, trying to grasp the dynamics of it. Manufacturing at the time was being headed by a professional who had come from Glaxo at what was considered in Sun a fat pay cheque.

Valia during his unannounced rounds asked basic questions to understand the processes behind manufacturing and figured out that there was huge backlog in sampling and generating analyst reports, a mandatory exercise before the raw materials could be ticked off as standard to pass for manufacturing.

Valia asked for minimum time needed for that work, to which someone replied forty-five days. He made queries to zero down on the logic of forty-five days. 'We have the stuff on a credit cycle of forty-five days, so we would complete the task before that period is over,' came one response.

Baffled, he made them conduct sampling and report generation between the third and seventh day of the raw material's arrival in the facility. Anything beyond had to be reported with reasons to the head office. Additional manpower was provided to clear the backlog.

'These factory people have no clue of interest payment. They claim money is available to them for forty-five days, so they have no urgency to complete,' Valia, still aghast, told Shanghvi.

He shared how he planned to organize the production and distribution of all the batches into three buckets based on the cost of the material. 'The priciest of material can arrive in the last ten days of the month, and dispatched in the first ten days of the following month.' Shanghvi green-signalled the idea instantly, but smiled back at him, 'Sudhir-bhai, you are actually talking of the formulations guys being clueless about interest costs, you should make a trip to our bulk drug factory and see the kind of exorbitant interests amount we are paying there.'

He hopped on to a bulk drug plant next, again unannounced, to face a question: 'Who are you?' No one recognized him there. Once they got to know who he was, Valia got down to business and discussed Pentoxifylline which was their main product, of which they churned out a tonne a month. He asked the factory head to explain the entire process of making it.

Fumbling-stammering later, the factory head called forth the plant head to simplify the whole mumbo-jumbo. The plant head began by narrating the three stages of production but sought help from head supervisor when asked to go deeper into the first stage of production.

'It was for the first time I saw how a reactor looks like. So I quizzed them on the size, quantity that it processes, reactions that occur, time it takes. One after the other, mid-level workers were called upon to expand on bits of processes, and finally it was the reactor operator who explained what I asked for,' Valia recalled.

'No single soul in the factory knew the entire process. I got anxious just at the thought of producing bulk drug worth ₹5 crore by investing ₹4 crore in raw material and ₹3 crore in overhead in a year. The business was heading for a disaster. So I made them plot each stage of manufacturing on paper for me,' he said.

After this exercise, when the factory guys were told to produce 4,5 tonnes in a month, it didn't invite rotten eggs and tomatoes in response, though there were head shakes galore.

On a flight the next day, he murmured the same to Shanghvi. 'We could do five tonnes a month there.'

'But whom would you sell that much to, Sudhir?' Shanghvi countered.

'Why? I will produce only one month and keep the factory shut for four. That will cut overhead costs drastically.'

They could progressively take this figure to 7 tonnes. 'By adding another vessel (reactor) we could take it to 9 tonnes. There is simply no substitute to being on the shop floor, mingling with workers, learning from them, helping them understand how their work fitted in the big picture,' Valia said. During his mission to boost efficiency on the shop-floor, he found a neglectful worker who had not cleaned a vessel since a month and explained to him, 'Leaving this unclean cost me ₹1200 an hour and ₹7.5 lakh a month. And a new steel vessel costs me ₹4.5 lakh. So here we are better off buying a new vessel.'

Eventually at 14 tonnes a month, Sun became the largest pentoxifylline bulk drug producer in the world. Having slashed the overhead cost by one-fifth and scaling up the production by almost fifteen times with minimal plant upgrade helped Sun cut per unit fixed cost. Bulk buying helped it bargain to pull down its raw materials cost by a third. 'Thus I can offer the same drug at a price no one else can match. And I have ended up changing the entire global economics of pentoxyfylline, wiping out competition, becoming the largest supplier only by building efficiencies,' Valia said.

So he started visiting other facilities—once a month, and soon, Valia recalled, first the factory, then the distribution and operations, even the information technology department began reporting to him. 'When you give suggestions that work, responsibilities stalk you,' he said.

That's Sudhir-bhai touch for you. Not a secretary in sight, anyone could walk up, call him. A rub here, a drub there maybe, but the problem that came walking up to him couldn't afford to walk back without a solution.

In 1997, when Sun had just shifted its headquarters back to Mumbai, and the number of transactions had exploded because the business was multiplying like crazies, its IT application gave in. Each transaction was taking ten minutes to complete, because the server couldn't take the load.

This problem walked up to Valia's desk who called a friend, who in turn checked the system to find them using Cobol and Fox-pro. He said, 'There is no foreign key in the software you were using.'

'No problem, *lagwa dete hain*. Where can we buy this key?' Valia, who had heard the term for the first time, asked.

Valia then created two crack teams of seven guys, who sat around him in alternate shifts of eight hours for three months, where Valia learnt a bit of software coding and design. 'We worked on small innovations. Our invoicing changed from box to strip level, the lowest level unit in drugs. So now you could track the product end to end,' Valia explained.

Transactions had multiplied also because many people were punching the same data. Now Valia made sure that data that went in once was available for use by all others.

When a server upgrade worth ₹2 crore was suggested, Valia decided against spending those extra bucks because it was still 1997 and Internet connection in India sucked. 'Instead, to cut cost we used an open-source software system where people around worked offline for an hour and instead of real-time got connected on hourly basis to share data,' Valia recalled.

He was burning the midnight oil, fine-tuning the IT application, spending his days meeting all departments to code in their requirements in the application. But it was cajoling people to migrate to the new software that proved to be the Everestine challenge. Valia thought up ways to overcome that resistance and concluded that the looming Y2K challenge was the best thing to have happened to Sun's IT department. 'The earlier IT application was doomed because it couldn't be counted on to smoothly pass the Y2K test. So I used that plank to nudge people to adopt the new software,' he recalled.

Almost all departments faced some amount of problem fixing at the hands of Sudhir-bhai, some more grumbling and grunting than others. Like those in distribution, who could no more just walk over to C&F audit as they did in pre-Sudhir-bhai era, and tick off boxes in paper forms relying on the memory or whim of the agent, while sipping tea.

After the 'Sudhir-bhai fix', it became important for them to verify the stock in person, punching what they had seen with their own eyes. Since the online system already had a catalogue of what items should have been in the stock, any glaring discrepancy was caught.

Even marketing, which Valia never oversaw directly couldn't escape his handiwork. For Sun, 'pmpm' or per man per month productivity was how they judged the performances of medical representatives. In the late 1990s, Valia, nudged by Shanghvi, pushed for MRs to use pagers to capture doctor visits, samples distributed, standard tour plans which was to replace mould-hit paper attendance manuals that reflected data of three months back, which by the time it was fed into the system was too dated to check for veracity.

That was switched to customized mobile soon. Those who resisted could resist the technology medium but not the process, which meant they had to feed their data from a cybercafe, if they shunned the mobile.

In the process, Valia realized that during the last few days of the month, the C&F agents were so flooded with queries from medical representatives about their targets that they had no time to even have a snack. That directed Valia to ferry around retail chemists stores. Buying a medicine strip here and there, he inquired whether they saw a similar rush in uptake of medicines around the end of the month.

To which, the shops threw a complete surprise at him. Their brisk business time was in fact the first week of the month, when salaries arrived, most doctor consultations happened, and people queued up for their monthly doses of drugs. Valia went up to Shanghvi and said, 'We should keep our internal review meetings in first weeks instead of last days. That's the time the doctor is most busy seeing his patients, can ill-afford time for MRs. That's also the time the chemist is at its most busy.' This observation changed the internal cycles; half of the therapy divisions had to prepone their review meetings to the fifteenth day of the month from the standard last days to discuss targets.

This freed up the choked call lines of the C&F agents during the end of the month', Valia said.

Gradually but surely, barring R&D, products and marketing, which were Shanghvi's forte, other functions started being looked after by Valia. And his small gains amounted to big savings when cumulatively seen over time, across functions. But these advances every day didn't come without their own share of frictions, without earning Valia sobriquets such as 'blunt' and 'curt' from the professionals of the time.

One of them was more considerate than others calling him 'not rude, just unaware of politeness'. It didn't help that Valia cared a hoot about the roundabout routes of social adeptness and corporate etiquettes. This was part of Valia's charm that he was non-hierarchical, didn't mince words, and spoke what he meant, unvarnished. But this trait which made him endearing in a special way and got so much work done at Sun also made some professionals feel uneasy.

His unexpected break-ins into bulk drug factories and the blunt style of delivering his messages didn't just rattle the operations and manufacturing head and facilities in-charge but the HR too. Typical of him, once he walked in to the Ahmednagar bulk drug plant unannounced, shortly after Sun had bought it from Knoll Pharma, to comprehend the shop-floor dynamics and made some queries. This was seen as an extra-official gesture by a professional. Being blunt was very Valia, and he seemed aware of this trait in him, and even counted it as one of the differences between him and Shanghvi. 'Dilip-bhai will not say anything to the person unless he thinks it is appropriate time. I will not keep anything inside me, if I have seen he has not done something right. I would tell him up front. I think both are right in our own ways. How the other person perceives you in that situation is another matter. Sometime he minds, sometime he takes it in his stride. If you agree to wait till the appropriate time, you are also agreeing to suffer a loss knowingly during that time. I wouldn't agree to that, and to that extent you can call it a limitation in my personality.'

In practising bluntness, Valia was indiscriminate and didn't even spare Shanghvi's old friends. By 1986, Shanghvi's friend Ashok Butta had wound up his company Bambi and Thumper, the one he had floated at the same time as Sun and returned to Calcutta. He received a call from Shanghvi in 1994, who asked him to join Sun for a specific work, an offer he politely declined. Only Shanghvi refused to take no for an answer.

So the next time he was in Calcutta, Shanghvi offered again, 'AB, I need help handling this regulatory work.'

'Look, Dilip, I have a business set-up in Calcutta. It's not possible for me to shift to Bombay. You tell me the work, and I will get it done from here.'

'You have to shift to Bombay, AB.'

Shanghvi grew insistent to the point that Butta started avoiding his calls, till in 1996 he returned home to a courier parcel, which he opened to find tickets to Baroda, hotel vouchers, details of the car and person who was to receive him, all neatly packed waiting for him.

Butta admitted it turned out to be a good decision at the end. 'Dilip's strength is that he knows your mind and beats you at that. He knows how much you might be earning, how his offer would be better for you.' Butta lived in Bombay out of a hotel for six months working on special regulatory assignments. One of those days, a group of them were having a heated discussion over lunch at a Dadar restaurant. Valia dismissed Butta with the wave of a hand, saying, 'You don't know a thing about this', a few times. Butta, not used to being treated this way was unnerved. Later that day, he went to the station to see off Shanghvi, who was taking a train to Baroda and whispered into his ears just as he was boarding, 'Boss, I am going back to Calcutta.'

'Why, what happened?' Shanghvi asked as the train chugged out of the platform.

'Man, Sudhir-bhai is telling me in front of a bunch of people that I know nothing. I may be reserving my comments, but that doesn't mean I know nothing,' he said, louder, to be heard above the noise of the train.

'I will call you tomorrow, AB, I will,' Shanghvi promised. Through the night Butta tossed and turned, in half a mind to book his tickets. But early the next day Shanghvi reasoned out with him over the phone, that

Sudhir-bhai is impulsive, but one had to see and accept it as a different nature in a person.

'With time, I understood Sudhir-bhai better. If you are prickly, and you pick a part of him, you may misjudge him to be insolent. But when you know that person in whole, you will see how wonderful he is. We grew friends over time and he even stayed at my place when he was here in Calcutta,' Butta laughed.

It was an open secret in Sun that during analyst calls held after quarterly results, during his days as the chief finance officer, one had to gesticulate heavily at Valia to not spill out facts that the company didn't mean to disclose.

'Sudhir-bhai has been the quintessential problem solver at Sun. But usually he is too engrossed in the problem to pay attention to the collateral damage a solution might be creating,' summed up a senior Sun executive with a touch of affection about him. All said, Sun wouldn't be Sun without Sudhir Valia.

Shanghvi's Departure

And then something happened. No sooner had Valia walked in, someone walked out of Sun. That is how it appeared on the outside, at least. Two decades later, when you set your eyes upon this person, who doesn't even have an image of his on the search engine that knows it all—the resemblance is unmistakable. Softer on expressions, leaner, balder, fairer, more Mongoloid, almost monk-like, and a thousand times more expressive, but Shanghvi nonetheless, younger by a decade or more.

Logical minds around in Sun then, bereft of a real story behind the exit but capable of putting two and two together, conjured up a connection. A year after Valia joined, Shanghvi's younger brother Jayant left the company without any explanation. Since a few senior professionals of the time had known about the uproar in the Shanghvi clan about Upen-bhai's departure and Valia stepping into his shoes, they not so unreasonably attributed cause and effect.

Not 'The Cause' of Valia leading to 'The Effect' of Jayant leaving, but among other reasons 'a cause' of Valia may have led to 'an effect' of

Jayant leaving. A family member denied the connection, asserting that there was clearly no overlap in their functions in the company.

It very well could have been the other way round, if one of the senior-most professionals at Sun is to be believed—one who indicated that 'an episode' with Jayant precipitated so many things: among others, his exit and Shanghvi going out of his way to persuade Valia to join him. What caused which effect is not clear. What is clear is what people around perceived. They believed the dimension of Valia had complicated matters for Jayant, which were not so uncomplicated to begin with.

His parting was and remains, till date, shrouded in mystery and a taboo subject, most people found uncomfortable to touch upon on record.

Jayant admitted that there seemed to be a misperception that he doesn't share great equations with his elder brother. In fact, just a few days back when he had been to the office of the district magistrate of Baroda, the collector had sprung up an astonishing question out of the blue, 'Are you Dilip-bhai's younger brother?' 'Yes, that's true.' 'Do you talk to him?' He sensed there was more to the question, which might as well could have been, 'Does he talk to you?' But impressions inhabit vacuums. Behind them are stories, true and cooked up, spiced up, believed, shared, circulated.

One such stray rumour doing the rounds in the industry, particularly in Gujarat was that the 'episode' had to do with Jayant selling off a chunk of his shares of Sun without Shanghvi's knowledge. This was rubbished by most of the senior professionals and laughed off by Jayant.

'Nonsense,' Jayant half-smiled, unable to pretend that he was any grateful for any of these stories. A more plausible but similar-sounding version came from two of the top executives of the time. 'By the early 1990s, Dilip-bhai and Jayant had started sounding like two incongruous voices—in one company. Dilip-bhai was very focused on growing the company and wouldn't tolerate this unnecessary stuff,' one of them had to say.

The one who echoed him said, 'Their line of thinking was very different. Jayant-bhai was still in his twenties, hot-headed. He had started behaving like a partner, not necessarily as a younger brother any more who had just been inducted. This led to some rumour-mongering and speculation on the direction the company would take and who the real captain of the ship would be in future.'

Picking out a few awkward moments he had personally experienced, he cited instances where Shanghvi hesitated before giving direct instructions to people who reported to Jayant.

'I have heard Dilip-bhai say, *"Sambhalo use"*, when he thought he was making immature decisions,' he said.

At his peak in the company, Jayant Sanghvi was the COO and headed manufacturing, IT, and projects and quality assurance. And then one day in 1995, Jayant walked in and told his deputy to report to a new professional.

It felt abrupt to his deputies and bystanders, and stories abounded to explain what remained unexplained. The story that almost had unequivocal support from the employees working at Sun then was the build-up to the separation, which most saw as inevitable. Most professionals perceived him as diametrically opposite to Shanghvi senior in temperament; Jayant was seen as mercurial.

There were hardly any verbal duels between the two worth recalling but a top former executive said one could sense them outgrowing each other, disapproving of each other's ways at work, distance and differences creeping up between them.

Given their fundamental differences in personality types and managerial styles, executives of the time saw it as an impossible proposition for the two brothers to coexist in close proximity. One was like fire, the other like water, said a former executive. But his brother's departure reiterated one point: when it came to Shanghvi's passion of seeing his company grow, everything was secondary—friendship, family and even himself.

Two decades later, all those impressions of the past, if true, have clearly not withstood time. No signs of volatility, not a trace of arrogance in the Jayant Sanghvi of 2015, appearing extremely well mannered, charmingly genuine, perfectly chivalrous and a touch emotional whenever Shanghvi's reference came up. The absence of 'h' from his surname has nothing to do with humility; it was a schoolmaster's fault, who dropped the alphabet assuming it to be an error, when it was a choice.

But Jayant himself admitted of having had a short temper at his workplace and pinned it down as one of the fundamental reasons why 'wild stories about the rifts' between him and Shanghvi might have been floating. 'Lots of people think we have had a fight. I get that vibe in social situations. It could have emanated from our basic behavioural differences of yesteryears. I can get very nasty at times. You could say then I was the exact opposite of Dilip-bhai in matters of losing my temper. I could shout at people, be rash with them. And that may have led people to imagine that there was a dispute, disagreement or a fight even,' he said.

But in real life, Jayant would have us believe that such reasoning was flawed, an attempt at bad psychology at best; he hadn't been a victim of a Greek tragedy of any epic scale in his life. He added, 'Dilip-bhai has always been much too large a figure for me to let the thought of disputing with or dismissing him even cross my mind.'

Before the two started to be seen as brothers, their engagement was more parental, almost father–son. Ten years older and infinitely more emotionally mature, Shanghvi was more a father figure to Jayant rather than a backslapping friendly big brother. 'It was he who had realized that I was struggling in maths and got me help by arranging for tuitions; it was he who directed me to crack IIT when I used to check my ranks in class from the bottom. Had it not been for him, I might have been shaped very differently,' Jayant said of their relationship.

In almost a reverential deference to Shanghvi he said he owed every bit of his transformation from a Calcutta adda boy to an IIT graduate to his elder brother.

When Jayant had lived up to Shanghvi's expectations and passed from IIT Bombay, it was presumed beyond doubt that he would be joining Sun. But he said a part of him always wanted to do something of his own. 'That was a crazy idea, considering how well Sun was doing but over time this longing to create something just got stronger,' he said.

But he recalled that even before he had joined Sun, Shanghvi had expected him to start learning right from the ground, just as he had. 'Dilip-bhai would expect me to know all the names of the medicines on prescriptions,' Jayant recalled.

The med reps of the time remembered 'Jayant-bhai' as 'the intelligent young IITian brother, who Dilip-bhai had asked to start and get experience as a medical representative.' Pradip Ghosh recalled one of the early days of 'Jayant-bhai' in Sun, when Shanghvi wanted him to start doing the rounds of national conferences. 'Dilip-bhai would say, "Make sure Jayant preserves our values in front of customers [specialist doctors], and comes across as one of us, just what we epitomize,' Ghosh recalled.

Then he went on getting larger responsibilities, one day being asked to make the Baroda office, another day given charge of manufacturing, and so on. 'Dilip-bhai has superhuman grasping power. And he has never given us any benefit of doubt on that front. Since he managed to learn everything on his own, and super quick, he expected the same from us,' Jayant said.

And then, according to Jayant, about two years before listing, between the two of them they decided that he should have his independent business. 'Our financial decision was probably taken in five minutes straight,' he summarized. 'The decision was taken before we went public; at a time when my ownership percentage in the company was much higher. After going public, it would have been a difficult decision and challenging exercise to undertake,' Jayant recalled.

As per his recollection, Shanghvi asked him 'So, what should we do?'

'If you evaluate my contribution to the company till date, I don't think I deserve anything,' Jayant recalled telling him.

'This can't be, you are my partner and it can't be that you don't take anything. So you tell me.'

Then Jayant recalled naming some figure, and Shanghvi giving him double of that. As a flash of memory struck him, he rephrased himself, 'Or I probably even refused to quote a figure.'

But he absolutely junked the 'share-sale' hypothesis. 'Pre-listing, I couldn't have sold any shares. Post-listing, whatever shares I had were mine to keep or sell. Nothing could be farther from the truth than attributing a financial angle to this,' Jayant asserted. So when he came and told his deputies that he would not be there three months down the line, according to him, nothing had transpired overnight. 'It had been planned at least two years in advance,' he claimed.

Shanghvi corroborated Sanghvi's version 'I think we decided mutually that it is easier to be brothers rather than work in the same business. In Sun Pharma, if he has to work, our ability to separate our personal and business relationship is challenging. There was no acrimony between us. Whatever decision we took was to maintain a family relationship for a longer term.'

Today Jayant Sanghvi runs a real-estate firm based in Baroda by the name of Pratham Realty Private Ltd, incorporated in July 1993. The firm has a credible reputation in the state. He also runs a financial services company. Speaking of his big brother, he got reminded of an occasion, when Shanghvi had told him, 'Jayant, you are as intelligent and as capable of creating what I have, but only if you can keep your emotional balance.'

Even today, when in doubt, he knows where to tap. 'If my wife and I have an argument on how feasible a business idea is, she would play a card she knows works: "What if Dilip-bhai said what I am saying?" I can't blame her because often, when in doubt, I do the same—what would Dilip-bhai do in this case—and, surprisingly, I find insights I had missed. That leads me to conclude that the tale of Eklavya learning from Dronacharya in his absence may not after all be pure mythological fantasy.'

Then with a touch of tender affection, bordering on devotion, Jayant summed up, 'Whatever I have today is because of Dilip-bhai, what I don't is because of my stupidity.' Some former Sun executives, who must have had an aptitude for maths at school, can't help make quick calculations to deduce the cost of his 'stupidity' and settle for nothing less than ₹90,000 crore, half of Sun's net worth (based on Sun's peak market capitalization).

Behind his unapologetic reverence, Jayant said, was his uninterrupted observation of the 'being' that Dilip-bhai was. 'He is the engine that has pulled up our entire family, the clan. And he has done it all by himself, just as an individual without any support. He is truly a *kamal in kado* (a lotus in mud)', Jayant felt.

This, he confessed, was not a feeling he has walked up to Shanghvi and ever expressed. 'Ours is not a family of explicit expressions and celebrations. I don't know whether I have ever told Dilip-bhai how much he has done for me. I don't know how many in my family have actually walked up to him to say, "You have changed my life." I can't picture my sisters expressing their love in words: "Brother, we are proud of you." No, that would be too awkward and formal for us, the way we have grown up.'

He smiled as if the very thought of such open sentimentality and mushy love talk between the siblings was an outlandish proposition for the Shanghvis. What remains unsaid must be understood. As an afterthought, he added with a smile, 'In fact, if you go and ask my mother today how Dilip-bhai is doing in his life, she might just respond: "OK, *saras* [decent]."'

As the 'event'—the departure of friends, the 'arrival'—the entry of Sudhir-bhai, and the 'episode'—the departure of Jayant were manifesting, the seeds of disruption were felt in the company. But they had to do with much more than just the event, arrival and episode.

CHAPTER TWELVE

ADOLESCENCE IS WAR

Sun Pharma's toddler days were over. Around and after the time of listing, it was fully in the throes of adolescence, coping with the challenges of growing up—its wild shake-ups, a change in ownership, getting judged by peers for its new marketing practices, an experimental life and a disruptive chaos. The chaos that jolted the cadres was not so much a result of the departure of partners from Sun, as it was an outcome of an attempt on Shanghvi's part to professionalize the company.

When Shanghvi embarked on 'professionalization' in Sun, it meant more than just a shuffle at the top. About the time of listing, he started bringing in heavyweight professionals, who were big brands in the industry, a move that directly and forcefully impacted the lives of cadres more than changes in ownership had.

The Yakobian Era

One of the first in this series, was J.K. Yakob* who came from Torrent. Yakob had been hired by Sun's arch rival to set up a division based on his reputation of managing divisions at Cipla efficiently. At the time, Shanghvi had made up his mind to experiment with therapy-specific divisions—to create specialist cadres of medical representatives who would service a community of doctors.

For Yagnik, the tryst with the Yakobian era began with a dosa in Ahmedabad. Yagnik had gone to Yakob's home to woo him and was treated to south Indian delicacies from Mrs Yakob's kitchen. For others, it didn't start on such a lip-smacking culinary note.

For T.K. Roy* and many others the new boss on board greeted them with a practice unheard of in a trust-driven company like Sun. 'Surprise checks', or the very idea of such checks meant that someone thought you might not be doing what you should. Roy recalled a medical conference, where he had to make sure that pickup cars were sent at 4 a.m. for outstation doctors. Even before he could locate the drivers, he was startled to trace the silhouette of his new 'executive director' checking up on him. Others found him standing at the gate of conference sites conducting 'surprise checks', being sent away because they arrived half an hour late to the destination, at 7.30 a.m.

An HR professional encountered him on a Saturday evening, which he mistook to be a hallucination of his spectre, for Yakob was understood to be out of Baroda on a tour. That weekend the HR guy was heading back home humming a holiday tune, the type one spontaneously breaks into when the boss is absent. Just then Yakob returned to his work desk and asked him to retrieve all pending dues of field staff. His Saturday night, Sunday morning and night were spent in the office, clearing all dues; only on Monday morning was he sent back home.

Shyamal Ghosh, who was instrumental in executing the therapy divisions on ground, baulked when his new boss reprimanded him for getting addressed as 'Dada' instead of 'Sir' by numerous medical representatives and managers hailing from West Bengal.

The new 'executive director', the harbinger of professionalism, was hailed by some at the top for bringing what was amiss in Sun— discipline. 'Yakob was the need of the hour. MRs had been pampered at Sun, to the extent that some were turning unruly and needed taming. An arm in West Bengal, indoctrinated by communist ideology, started demanding that incentives be handed to them, which they would distribute equally among all. These rose-tinted dreams needed to be dealt with with an iron hand, which Yakob provided,' a former manager at Sun said.

Besides discipline, what he brought was a scientific rigour into processes and systems at Sun, benchmarking them no longer with Torrent but the much larger Cipla, where he had learnt the ropes. Cipla, under the management of Amar Lulla, was then known more for its 'process orientation', than for its 'people stickiness'.

'His own training had been in Cipla and he turned the entire process at Sun quantitative. He tagged performance with numbers, made it measurable. As a personality, he might have been complex and idiosyncratic, but Sun owes a lot of its controls and systems to him,' Roy said.

He gave Sun its pillar—a process of review that Shanghvi absorbed and fine-tuned in the years to come. Using the review meetings as a starting point, Yakob implemented definable and measurable criteria for promotions.

He started holding interviews with a professional look and feel, a conference hall in a five-star hotel was booked, four local managers prepared the venue, proper letters were drafted and mailed in advance. With a board, a presentation, he turned the occasion into an event people remembered. 'That gave the small company an image. He was methodical and meticulous to the last detail,' Yagnik recalled.

But as discipline was being imposed in a 'dictatorial' way, more and more people from the original Sun team were growing circumspect of Yakob's ways. Raju, who had had a change of responsibility to head international marketing, recalled a meeting right at the beginning of the transfer of charge where his new counterpart Yakob was spelling out his quant backed plan in a slick presentation, using acronyms with same initials—such as the three Ds—determination, dedication and discipline.

'I stopped myself from a confrontation in that meeting, but I could see the fundamental disconnect of the individual with the ethos of the organization. Our boys had been nurtured with love and healthy team spirit to achieve growth, and they did whatever they could with loyalty and commitment, putting their heart and soul in the process. Dangling money and promotions, pushing them to the brink to achieve a growth target and penalizing them harshly if they fell short were never the culture of Sun. We had traditionally owned responsibility collectively right at the top. Also, how to make a sale was always as important as making the sale itself,' Raju recalled.

As Yakob took over the reins, Shanghvi appeared to have subtly stepped back and let him work his ways. 'Dilip-bhai suddenly became inaccessible. Of course we were aware that the company was growing bigger and eventually he would transition to a role, where it wouldn't be possible for him to directly attend to us. But his withdrawal seemed abrupt at a time when resentment and rebellion were brewing in the original Sun team and not without reason,' a regional sales manager, who quit a few months after Yakob took over, said. He was neither the first nor the last. Many others considered 'performers' in the original team followed suit including Shyamal Ghosh and Jani Miya.

Raju and Yagnik defended Shanghvi's posturing of giving room to professionals for a while. 'Post-listing and following his Harvard experience, Sun was making a journey from being a family-owned company to a professionally managed company, and it became imperative for him to give professionals space to operate without interference. Also, don't forget, he was himself learning systems, controls, processes all along and giving Yakob a fair chance,' Raju felt.

It was partly true that the departure of partner friends had been designed with an idea to create room so that professionals didn't feel chocked, and Shanghvi, by carefully back-pedalling from active day-to-day management was facilitating the same process.

Yagnik would have us believe that Shanghvi, who has an umbilical chord attached to his company, actually never withdrew—not even for a moment; what he was doing was encouraging people to not bypass Yakob. And for a while it seemed to the world of Sun that the soft-spoken, caring, warm Shanghvi and strong, strict, commanding Yakob were in sync with each other in leadership, stereotypical of the image of Indian parents—mother and father. In fact, one of the reasons Ghosh didn't pursue a discussion with Shanghvi before quitting was that he had heard Shanghvi remark: 'Yakob is the best thing to have happened to Sun.'

But even as Sun was being 'professionalized' with its systems acquiring a codified form, the process was robbing it of balance in an abstractly unpleasant way. Of what can be comprehended and verbalized—the original Sun team felt threatened and sidelined by a bunch of new imports who came along with Yakob and changed the fundamentals. A big chunk of the original Sun team struggled to grasp what 'professionalism' truly meant in practice. The term evoked confused and scarred memories for them, a break in their emotionally fulfilling eventful journey of creating a company.

'Who are professionals? People who can articulate ideas in impeccable English and glossy presentations, and boast of impressive product knowledge. But Sun had grown up on different values—relationship with customers. No amount of polish in a person could duplicate the deep relationships Pradip Ghosh and his ilk had cultivated over a decade. Sadly, 'professionals' who stomped into Sun failed to appreciate these fundamentals which had built Sun, alienated the existing team, filling ranks and files with new people—their people,' Shyamal Ghosh said.

Jani Miya, hailed as a star performer in Andhra Pradesh, seemed to mind the expression—old-timers—and spoke not only for himself but also for a large part of existing Sun team who felt the dissonance.

'These big words, professionalization and professionalism crept in with Yakob. I wanted to understand what they meant. Before "professionalization" there were simple instructions which we carried out, and it not only worked, it rocked. You walk into a company that is growing phenomenally well, it's not a sinking ship, there is no crisis. Then what's the rush to turn things upside down?

'The first analysis that you must attempt is what has made this collective click. After you understand their strength, preserve it and improve upon the gaps you have found. When you walk in like a conqueror, transplant a new team, send shudders down the spine of the so-called "old-timers", you are forgetting that this brilliant platform to leap has been prepared for you by none other than the "old-timers" with their sweat and blood,' Miya recalled.

'Professionals have personal ambitions. They ask: "I am giving my time and energy, but what am I getting out of this." Prior to this, Sun was made of straightforward apolitical people who were not ambitious to create some legacy of their selves and so the individual was never in conflict with the organization. That changed as professionals took over,' Raju said. But 'professionals', a term sarcastically used by the original Sun team, had big egos that clashed with the new whole, that now comprised of two sets of people—Yakob's team and 'old-timers'.

Almost everyone who were approached from the original Sun team echoed a sense of bias vis-à-vis the new team Yakob brought in—the line management. 'Some people are successful only with one set of people. They are not sure of their success with any other team. So where they go, they must carry their team along. To transfer their own team, they need to create vacancies. And who else would be the soft targets to be sacrificed but the "old-timers", Miya recalled. Suddenly, the new arrivals seemed to be telling the old-timers condescendingly: "We are professionals, what you have been doing is rubbish," Miya explained. That created panic and insecurity across the original team.

At their level, they were expecting Roy to take over as national sales manager, but instead Yakob announced a fresh name whom he had brought in. In one of the very first review meetings, Miya recalled Yakob expressing disdain towards Sun's practices. 'You at Sun only know how to "sell and stock", you will have to learn the art of "stock and sell" for the business to grow bigger.' On the first part, Yakob was bang on.

The practice at Sun had been to generate prescriptions, create a pull of demand so that its sales grew. This was contrary to what most other companies did. They resorted to pushing their products through the distribution chain, offering freebies to push their brand. 'We were first used to making a sale happen, liquidating the stock before replenishing. But here they were suggesting that we heap stocks with stockists and follow up with them for a sale. I understood that to be dumping,' Miya said.

He recalled objecting to the new practice the first time, but being asked to carry out orders. It was, he believed, a paradigm shift they were being asked to execute. 'It was strange. In review meetings where Mr Yakob and my boss were present, no marketing activities, no customer analysis were discussed as we did before. They said, "What's your target? Divide it by the number of products and equally distribute it among the stockists. So if you have 100 strips to sell and two stockists in the region, just distribute fifty strips to each.'

It escaped Miya and his colleagues how this calculation would translate into sale. Like him, some others who were befuddled resisted, a few left, yet others were transferred to international marketing. 'The second month I did what had been asked, and continued doing so for the consecutive months, but as expected the sales didn't pick up.' In between, Miya battled with a dilemma of escalating the matter to Shanghvi but stopped himself for the sake of protocol. Sun was no longer the organization it used to be, when anyone could call anyone without the boss feeling offended.

'We felt like reporting the mess to Dilip-bhai, but at one level it felt impossible that so much was happening at so many places without his knowledge. Could the ED really be so whimsical without the permission of MD? Besides, at another level a seed of doubt was creeping in: "Is Dilip-bhai keeping quiet because he truly wants us to give way to fresh talent?"' Miya recalled.

But then, one day his mental strife climaxed, and he stumbled upon a route to finally escalate the matter to Dilip-bhai. That day Miya was called by his boss for a review meeting in a hotel at 9.30 a.m. But partly his gut and partly his boss's tone had portended that all was not right. So even as he got ready that morning, he was preparing for the worst, a combat.

When he entered the hotel room, he recalled being told that he had failed in his duties and must resign on the spot. Yakob and his deputy announced that what Miya had done was 'dumping'. Miya countered, claiming that was exactly his point, but it was Yakob's policy in works. Yakob charged back, 'What had we asked you: stock and sell? You only listened to the first part, and stocked; what about sale?'

The blame game pestered on for hours. 'I didn't give up, and insisted that if they were so keen to see me leave they must terminate my employment. After all, the national sales manager and executive director had the power to do so. I had made up my mind, since there was no mistake on my part,' Miya recalled.

This psychological drama, Miya recalled, which began in the morning and dragged on till 7.45 p.m., ended with him leaving the room, refusing to succumb to the pressure. 'I couldn't imagine this was happening in Sun, but I decided this was my chance. Let them fire me and I could then freely tell Dilip-bhai what was going on,' Miya said. But even before Miya could take the drastic step, reports were reaching Shanghvi. Roy recalled finding colossally piled-up unsold stocks with the Hyderabad C&F, and 'exposing' his boss before 'Dilip-bhai'.

'We at Sun had a zero tolerance for dumping. In fact all our other strategies flowed from one point—that sales must be prescription-driven. They were turning that principle on its head,' Roy said. There were others who were desperately reaching out to Sailesh Desai, no longer officially in the system, asking him to explain the chaos to Shanghvi.

'Suddenly, from a company of resonance, it had become a company of dissonance,' an HR executive said. Many senior members from the original Sun team were worried about the disruption of culture that they had so painstakingly nurtured. 'I was handling a different function and lived mostly in Russia. But I could see the kind of people leaving Sun were the committed sorts. I knew the culture we had built was in ruins. Earlier, even if we had to ask someone to leave, the discussion would be around how it would impact his family and responsibilities at home. Suddenly that was all gone because professionals were in a hurry to show results, achieve numbers,' Raju said. Others were going up to Shanghvi to tell him how 'robotic' the work environment felt.

'When Yakob came, he brought many people familiar to him who became more equal than others and it showed up in the review process. It was a very crucial exercise but done in a wrong way, because what it ended up doing was essentially instil fear in the minds of those being reviewed. The theme of the review process became: "You don't know, I know." It didn't achieve its objective if people went back feeling so drained. Something was not right. I learnt the review process from Yakob but not the way of doing it. When we rejigged the review later, we focused on solutions rather than problems, corrections rather than public humiliation,' Shanghvi said.

Yakob was not unaware of the swelling unrest in the older cadres under his nose, and the growing resentment around their belief of him being blatantly partial to the new team he had hired. It was in the Ville Parle office of Sun, where he was chairing a review meeting, that people saw him getting up and climbing down the stairs when he felt heaviness in his chest. 'He had suffered a heart attack while at work and was rushed for an angiogram,' Yagnik recalled. Shortly after, Yakob left Sun, having brought 'discipline' but having sacrificed 'devotion', felt the original Sun team.

Was it 'dumping' that did his journey at Sun? Was it a disruption of culture and a realization in Shanghvi that 'people' would always matter more than 'processes' in his company?

Or was it as an empathizer of Yakob put it, 'He became a victim of lobbying by old-timers, who campaigned against him to Dilip-bhai on how fractured and demoralized cadres had become and how the company's culture had been destroyed. I also believe that by the time Dilip-bhai asked Yakob to leave, Sun had learnt what it needed to learn from that man. He had put processes in place, organized the divisions, there wasn't more in him to offer to the company. So he wasn't essentially indispensable to Sun any more. And Yakob had realized why he was being asked to go. When you are told to leave on a flimsy plank—we don't think we can afford such disruption in culture, you know there is no solid reason to kick you out. He felt people were ganging up against him unfairly.' Whatever it may have been, his exit was not the end of Yakob for Sun, not yet.

Chaos Continues

As sequence of events would have it, Yakob's hasty exit meant a hurried entry of his successor who recalled receiving over 100 calls from Shanghvi while he was at Novartis. If Yakob had been a brand, Lanka was a star, and as Sun boys would swear, no stars came without their tantrums. Negotiations had been on for a while, and clandestinely, it had been agreed that Lanka would join Sun after six to eight months, but Yakob's rushed departure rewound things at Sun.

So a mahurat for an auspicious day and time as per the Hindu calendar was duly but promptly calculated by a pandit, and Srinivas Lanka joined Sun in place of Yakob as executive director in 1996. As soon as he set upon his desk at 2 p.m., he found an analyst of brokerage firm UBS waiting for him. 'The analyst reeled off, uninterrupted, a litany of issues that fraught Sun, and informed that he was about to downgrade Sun stock and put it on "sell",' Lanka recalled.

'So much for the Mahurat,' Lanka muttered under his breath and went to discuss the issue with Shanghvi. 'Let him put the stock on sell,' an unruffled Shanghvi said.

Lanka walked back to his cabin of a half-day, still familiarizing himself with the geography of the Synergy House and tried convincing the analyst to hold on. He cited his Novartis background, recounted his past successes to convince that Sun's face would look different in three months. He breathed a deep sigh when the analyst agreed to hold on for the time being.

But within two months a bigger challenge seized Lanka. Hordes of line management started quitting the company every day, like the flight of migratory birds. 'On a conference day when I woke up in the morning, one of the guys called me to report, "Sir, only few people have turned up." Forty to 50 per cent of people who were to show up in the conference have resigned. So many people were leaving every day that there came a moment when I thought Sun will be finished,' Lanka recalled. That, he reckoned, felt like absolute chaos rapidly spiralling into a doom. As per his memory, groups of people just vanished, no explanation, no sighting of them afterwards. Phones then wouldn't be answered at their homes, and even if answered by someone else, their whereabouts were never revealed and calls never returned. They became incommunicado, period.

The experience was eerie for Lanka. 'It was turning into a do-or-die crisis at Sun,' Lanka, who finally got confirmed information that it was Yakob after all who was sucking the life force out of Sun by pulling its executives at 'exorbitantly high salaries' at Searle, a pharma firm from the stable of RPG, recalled. Desperate, Lanka went to meet Harsh Goenka, the owner of RPG Group to make a case that this 'mass poaching' was not a fair industry practice. 'Of course he told me to get lost, albeit politely,' Lanka said. After that Sun pulled all stops at all levels to salvage the situation.

This was quickly followed up by a meeting that Yagnik sought with top executives at RPG Group. He recalled preparing sheets of stats and charts to cite the average industry salaries, salaries of defecting employees at Sun and the rumoured salaries at Searle to argue how RPG was being fleeced to pay extortionately fat salaries to the new team they were hiring from Sun.

The industry, particularly in Gujarat, was abuzz with steamy gossip of 'the great exodus' from Sun. Shyamal Ghosh, who had by then left Sun for Intas, brought it up with his company owners, Chudgars, who, as he recalled, denounced such mass poaching as it was an unethical practice, according to them. But the extent of it has been registered differently by different people. While Lanka recalled the outflow to be as high as 30–40 per cent of line management, Yagnik remembered it as twenty-nine people at important positions, which powered Sun. Others put the figure between thirty and forty-five, but knew the incident to be one of enormous consequence.

Lanka, after thinking through the dire situation, recalled forming a group of five managers at Sun. 'Just take the cars and off you go, don't you come back to office till you find our boys. Do whatever, offer them blank cheques but get them back.' He recalled them staying out on a chase for six to seven days before finding some of the Sun managers in a quaint hotel at Alibaug, at the breakfast spread. Soon, breakfast tables had turned into corporate chessboards and one-to-one live negotiations began to bring back people into Sun's fold.

'Some people asked for the moon and we agreed. Someone demanded that he wouldn't travel anything less than first class, someone negotiated for a steep hike in travel expenses. Promotions were granted out of turn. We had to accede to their unreasonable demands to salvage the company from the crisis. But people, particularly those who were from the original Sun team, were brought back,' Lanka recalled.

About the great exodus orchestrated by Yakob, one of the top Sun executives opined, 'He took the people he had mentored, what's so unfair about that? He was a true practising Catholic and had a very binary—black and white—view of life. He wouldn't do something he deemed wrong.' Miya, who hadn't been appreciative of Yakob's strategies said, 'When he came with his jing-bang, no one complained, when he left with them, how can you complain?'

But for Lanka, those days remained etched in his mind as one of the toughest challenges of his life. Sitting in his cabin, tired even as he had successfully clamped the outflow and brought the defected back to Sun's fold, one by one slowly, he remembered how all his mentors had decried his decision to join Sun as outrageous.

'I had a glorious career going. After passing from IIM Ahmedabad, I had become a marketing head at the age of twenty-eight, a president at thirty, a Novartis SBU head at 33–34 years and had an international career waiting for me. My mentors had called my decision to join Sun a blunder I will regret. But I had defied them consumed by the passion to make an Indian company big, to pursue my dream of turning it into a multimillion multinational.'

And here he was battling a game in a set-up very different from the structured Novartis and planning a counter-coup, which he deemed as a compromise with his personal principles. 'I wouldn't have for anything else, if not survival, agreed to such demands of doling out unreasonable salaries. But it was a crisis and an emergency, and we had to bow down if Sun had to rise again,' a wistful Lanka said.

Amidst all this, Lanka admitted that he couldn't resist a grudging admiration for the man whom he had never met but still considered one of his toughest opponents—Yakob. 'I don't know what hatred for Sun he harboured to have done what he did, but I couldn't help getting impressed by the unflinching loyalty he commanded among his lieutenants, some of whom didn't budge even after we offered them huge raises. I decided that I must meet this guy at least once in my life,' Lanka declared. Exactly two decades after the great exodus from Sun, the Lanka–Yakob meet hadn't transpired, but Lanka's resolve to make it happen hadn't disappeared either. Two decades ago, the story of a chaos-ridden Sun went on with the era of Yakob drawing to a close and the era of Lanka beginning.

The Era of Lanka

The period of Lanka, though brief was the climax of confusion at Sun, in part because the impressions those times have etched in minds of Lanka and Sun managers, indicate as if they inhabited different planes of realities. The beginning was as promising as the end was painful.

Lanka, a dreamer, was so driven to scale up the small Indian company that he had the quality of turning that passion into an almost tangible experience for those around. He energized the corridors he walked in beaming with a promise that everything was possible under him, that Sun's ascendancy to the top of the Indian pharmaceuticals deck was not wishful thinking, but a mere formality on its way to fruition.

In his first few months, this thirty-something executive director of Sun with his training from IIM Ahmedabad, a background in chemistry and cost accountancy, and a larger-than-life aura, seemed at once intimidating and awe-inspiring to grounded Sunny boys, who till about two years back didn't think twice before dialling up partners and owners of the company.

Before joining, one of Lanka's terms with Shanghvi was 'no family interference'. 'Wherever I worked, that was my condition. Leave the company to me. I will build the company in the best possible way. If there is interference, I will walk out. I know that may sound a little arrogant. But my passion was to build Indian companies,' Lanka said. Shanghvi honoured that pact, and gave him CEO-like power during his stint at Sun.

When Lanka came he appeared to be full of ideas to transform Sun. One look at his presentations left many managers impressed with his grand vision. 'People sat spellbound as Lanka could make-believe with his theories that the world was beneath our feet and we could achieve anything,' Hiren Desai said.

His initial circulars in Sun that created divisions such as market research, strategy planning councils to spot promising drugs, and special training came across as a testament of his brightness to managers. Soon he was seen wooing statisticians from the German firm Siemens, hiring sharp analytical minds like Sanjay Sahai from Alembic to do market research and importing professionals from multinationals—such as Aventis and Novartis. The therapy divisions under him were designed to function like strategic business units, with their own budget, profit and loss statements, brand and marketing plans. He planned to add more divisions for each therapy so that older drugs—where market share was being grabbed by smaller companies—could be preserved. More brand launches were chalked out, more marketing soldiers were recruited, who were trained to grasp doctors' mental constructs based on theories of American psychologists B.F. Skinner and David McClelland. Lanka's executive assistants were handed out reams of papers to study prescription habits of doctors and decode patterns out of them.

Besides building the organization, Lanka had set one more goal for himself in Sun, to consciously build the owner. 'Executives hop from one company to another, but if you build an owner, an organization can last a lifetime. I call it mentoring the boss,' Lanka said. This exercise, he recalled, unfolded over lunch, sent with warmth by Vibha bhabhi who considered in her preparation the subtle differences between the sweet Gujarati palette and the hot and spicy Andhra taste buds. As the vegetarian fare arrived, steaming hot from Shanghvi's home in a multi-deck steel tiffin box and the chawal-dal-curries-roti spread was arranged, Lanka recalled they got chatting about managerial concepts and ideas, never about profits or sales of Sun Pharma.

Shanghvi's closest circle saw this exercise differently. 'Dilip-bhai, being a listener, can give off the impression of being a student, even when he knew much more than his self-appointed teachers. For was it not Dilip-bhai who had already built Sun as a hugely profitable entity on a distinct business model before managers like Lanka came?' one of them said.

On his part Lanka planned for these conversations to make them meaningful. After experiencing the mass-exodus-led crisis orchestrated by his predecessor, he thought it well to discuss with Shanghvi 'The Loyalty Effect', a managerial thesis by Fred Reichheld of the consulting firm Bain & Company released as a book in 1996. Shanghvi had read the book too.

Lanka knew of Shanghvi's preference for the marathon approach over a 100-metre dash, and judged him as remarkably different from a lot of his hire-and-fire peers who ran their companies like grocery stores. They discussed the power and effect of loyal customers, loyal employees, and loyal owners on growth, productivity, profits and sustained value creation. 'When employees stick together through rough patches like recession, their productivity actually goes up and shows up in a distinct profitability advantage over time,' was the essence of their exchange.

Lanka had no way of knowing that in the pre-Yakob days, when Raju was the manager, Shanghvi's default mode had been to encourage loyalty. Shanghvi had introduced the positive effect of loyalty to newly recruited MRs way back. In fact, when Shanghvi read 'The Loyalty Effect' he recalled connecting it immediately to his practical experience. 'It reinforced what I had already observed and what had worked on ground for us so spectacularly. When we had a sales force for psychiatry, and we would lose a few representatives, I realized we would have to start from scratch to rebuild that relation with the customer. It took us a lot of energy to reboot those connections which sustained effortlessly if continuity prevailed. So whoever replaced him couldn't just start from where the other one left. A lot of ground work needed to be done before the same level of trust could be established. Therefore MR-level continuity became an important theme for us. We realized that the emotional connect and the rapport between one MR and a doctor cannot just be seamlessly transferred to another MR and the same doctor.'

With this realization, the stickiness that Shanghvi had been intuitively drawn to was cemented as a strategy for the company for three stakeholders—employees, doctors and shareholders. 'For Dilip-bhai, even that boy Manoj who booked our train tickets was very important. "Because of Manoj's commitment, we are mobile in Sun Pharma," he said,' recalled HR head Yagnik. Even institutional investors Sun sought out were those with long-term focus, just so that obsessions with quarterly results didn't interfere with Sun's long-term plans.

Another day over lunch, Lanka recalled Shanghvi appreciating Deming's technique on how making high-quality product was actually cheap. They were discussing success of Japanese businesses like Toyota, Fuji and Sony, which scored over American and European competitors in the 1970s and '80s by focusing on quality. The nub of their chat was that low-quality medicines mean prescribers loss. The cost of building a customer is much higher than the cost of making a product better. At times, Lanka saw a glimpse of an ascetic in him, who could detach himself from the trappings of success.

Some of the most interesting Lanka–Shanghvi lunch conversations pertained to mergers and acquisition strategies. Lanka said this was his topic of specialization at IIM, where he had been taught turnaround management by globally renowned marquee professors, which he shared with Shanghvi. 'I discussed all types of sick companies with him and why we needed to buy four to five companies in quick succession, by basing our transaction on valuation. We could focus on distressed assets that suit us best and pay in instalments or deferred payments. He is very sharp and he could understand that the payback time is in months and very little cash needed to be used. But I insisted that we must do it quickly because knowledge once practised is transferred. Everyone would learn the game soon,' Lanka recalled.

Sun did buy, Gujarat Lyka, MJ Pharma, Tamil Nadu Dadha Pharmaceuticals Ltd (TDPL), Natco brands, Milmet and American firm Caraco in a frenetic speed between 1996 and '99.

During those days Lanka recalled discussing buying over Ranbaxy many times, even though it was a far larger company. Though the company had much more clout than Sun, with Sun's breathless growth, it didn't seem out of reach. 'Dilip-bhai was fascinated by Ranbaxy. I used to tell Dilip-bhai that shares are our power. We have to build and consolidate our EBITDA [earnings before interest, taxes, depreciation and amortization] and earnings per share,' Lanka recalled. At least one senior executive recalled Shanghvi emerging impressed from those luncheons and saying, '*Uski ganit hi alag hai.*'

However as time passed, not everyone seemed as impressed with Lanka. To some senior Sun hands, he appeared a tough, unpredictable boss, a bit whimsical. But initially, along with his fierce intensity, this unhinged trait seemed like an extension of his 'genius' image. Many managers, including T.K. Roy, narrated tales of how they were made to work through nights for a goal that changed by the morning. One senior manager recalled how under Lanka's orders the field force was first prepared to make calls to general physicians (GPs) for Sun's newly launched 'Pantocid'. 'That was sung like an anthem. After a lot of hullabaloo when all was prepared and set, he abruptly changed the plan from GPs to gastro-specialists.'

On Lanka's second day at Sun, T.K. Roy recalled Baroda having seen one of its heaviest rains causing a mess in the city. He got a call from his new boss who asked him to report to him at The Express Hotel, where he was staying.

'Sir, there's knee-deep water on the roads.'

'Doesn't matter. Even if you walk, it will not take you more than ten minutes to reach.'

Roy changed into shorts, kept a pair of change in his bags to be worn once in the hotel, and trudged off in the puddles of water to see his new boss. When Roy reached home next morning, his worried wife, tired of waiting, asked, 'Why did you marry me when you were already married to your company?'

Lanka never got himself a home in Baroda, neither rented, nor owned. He lived out of The Express Hotel. His erratic-seeming lifestyle didn't appear out of place in the backdrop of all the fables that had travelled to Sun before he had.

The managers at Sun murmured how Lanka had slept half the days in office while working for French firm Roussel-Uclaf; how his clean-shaven look seamlessly passed into a stubble that grew into beard without him realizing, so consumed he was in work at his erstwhile office; how when as a product manager he had been too often objected to by costing executives, he took up the challenge and completed his cost accountancy; how his idea to combine paracetamol with ibuprofen was shot down at Roussel as an untested combination, and only his conviction and dogged persuasion led to the launch of Combiflam many years later, a blockbuster product that made history in the Indian market. Though unverified for truth, these were stories believed by Sun managers.

Strangely enough, almost everything that was said of Lanka's inscrutable working ways by Sun Pharma executives, it's opposite was also said by their colleagues. Someone said he was a caring people's person, and had personally helped her with yoga and alternative therapies. Someone else said, he remained the 'bada-saheb', and never mingled with field personnel beyond his half-hour lecture. Someone said he trusted people too easily. Someone else said, as a strategist he had grasped that it was the old-timers' lobby that had 'conspired' for Yakob's exit, so he deliberately undermined the influence of people seen close to Shanghvi, and in the process got mistakenly labelled for his 'distaste' for Bengalis. Someone said that Sun's little failed experiment with launching antibiotics was orchestrated by Lanka, with his famed launches of combiflam and taxim in his earlier avatars at Hoerst Roussel and Alchem. Someone else said that new products were always decided by Shanghvi, and Lanka helped keep the focus of the company on chronic drugs.

Lanka himself backed this theory. When he entered, he said Sun's focus was just about shifting towards acute drugs. Sun top executives, strongly disputed this, maintaining that launching antibiotics in late 1990s was a small experiment that was abandoned within two years, but the focus on chronic drugs didn't waver at all. 'The decision to discontinue many antibiotics that had been introduced during Lanka's time was solely Dilip-bhai's,' a Sun executive said.

When Lanka joined Sun, he recalled studying the model of Torrent closely to conclude that Sun's bigger arch-rival was losing its focus by its foray into power, finance and other sectors. In Torrent's pharma business, he noticed that a new top manager with multinational background had tweaked the strategy of doctor–MR interface to mirror multinational-type marketing. Instead of having to cover 60–90 doctors a month, the MRs had been asked to call 350 doctors a month. So from meeting doctors twice or thrice a month, they went about seeing doctors once in two or three months.

'Life is a set of accidents and opportunities. The day I heard about the change in Torrent's strategy, we did the exact opposite—hired more foot soldiers and increased the number of times our MRs saw each doctor,' Lanka recalled. Many in Torrent, accustomed to intense engagement with a closer-knit set of customers, didn't warm up to the new MNC format. That gave Sun another opportunity, to hire upset executives from Torrent, including their key resource person Bharat Vyas who was known to engage with top opinion makers across the country. Others resource persons from Torrent, Intas and Micro-labs were spotted in medical conferences based on their connections with doctors and hired. In contrast, some older Sun executives also felt that Lanka, with his multinational grooming, looked down upon the 'close-ties' model between MRs and doctors cultivated under its SAS umbrella and the way Sun serviced its doctors.

Most senior Sun executives felt Lanka's masterly strokes on paper couldn't translate so brilliantly on ground. 'He was a genius in theory, but in practice, there was too much incoherence, indecision and utter disorder in his execution. He contradicted himself too frequently,' a top Sun Pharma executive said. 'Lanka could mesmerize you by the most cerebral ideas in business, because he had strikingly different perspectives on issues. That helped an astute entrepreneur like Dilip-bhai think differently. But the direction was always Dilip-bhai's own,' another said.

As the takeovers of smaller companies and brands as well as the number of products and therapy divisions multiplied from 1995 to 1999, complexity and confusion within Sun intensified. What happened afterwards is a blur. As Sun's older hands grew familiar with Lanka's ways, and the halo around him faded, there seemed to be a growing resentment against him in the company; opinions polarized for and against him.

The most common gripe was his frequent experimentation and zero explanation, and many times sheer inconsistence between command and action. Drug launches were at times planned and cancelled after raw materials had been bought. Call frequencies (number of calls an MR was expected to make to doctors) were frequently altered.

'Decision making was highly inconsistent,' Abhay Gandhi, who is now CEO of the North America Business of Sun, and was a senior-level manager then, said. This inconsistence was in direct contrast to Shanghvi's style—when something was decided by him in Sun, it got done. A brand manager's boss recalled how his deputy was praised by Lanka to heights in the evening for a cholesterol drug presentation and pulled up the next morning for his performance. Besides making people work through nights, Lanka could summon someone from the field, from the doctor's cabins and then ask him to start training new cadres on the spot. In Lonavala, during a meeting, he asked his executive assistant seated next to him to pass a tissue paper. On that he wrote, 'Mr X, kindly issue a transfer letter to Mr Y for . . . and give it to HR immediately.' Another time, he walked in to interrupt a management development programme that was being conducted by Raju (head of training and development) around noon, and gave the executives an exercise, saying, 'Complete it, I will see you in a bit and evaluate this.' The executives kept waiting as noon turned into night. Around 9 p.m., when there was no sign of him, a senior manager went into Lanka's cabin to check; he had forgotten about it.

Lanka would have us believe that much of the chaos was crafted, and there was a method in the madness. 'I perceive myself as a benevolent autocrat. I am cut-throat, but I don't sack people unless it's for their good. If 10,000 people have worked under me, I know why I did what to whom. Some people I have tortured to success. I made them work through nights. People who have worked under me and gone through that duress and injuries, have succeeded. But at that time I wouldn't tell them why I am putting them through the test. That would defeat the purpose. The whole idea of using a situation to change a person from their mundane life fraught with timidity and inferiority complex is to push them into an extremity, so that they can discover their potential. They might feel about me: "I have done so much, but this fellow tortured me." I know that I tortured them for their self-actualization. But at that time, it would cause dissidence. I cannot tell them what I have done; they have to think that they have done it themselves. Each such story will live with me and die with me.'

It did create dissidence in the Sun of those times. Stories of Lanka's inconsistent instructions and consequent chaos started reaching Shanghvi in droves. One of them who had complained to Shanghvi about the state of affairs under Lanka expressed the situation like this, 'Under Lanka, Sun had turned into an aircraft whose pilot had chosen to take a joy ride while the passengers swayed wildly.' Some of them reached out to Sailesh Desai in desperation, who they knew had Shanghvi's ears, urging him to convince their boss to make changes. When Desai called him, Shanghvi said he already knew about the issues but was wondering what could be the best way forward.

'During Lanka's time, the entire company suffered with only one exception, that's me. I learnt a lot from him, about mergers and acquisitions (M&A) strategies in particular. He was very bright and learned, but it is in operations that he struggled. At that time, there was serious disruption in the company,' Shanghvi, when asked of Lanka's era in Sun, replied.

In this period, on the face of it Sun's business continued to grow, but mainly due to acquisitions. The organic growth of Sun's business (sales excluding its acquisitions) dropped to 12 per cent in the financial year ending 1998 from 52 per cent the year before, and growth of net profits shrank as well. And then the last straw, Sun's flagship division started de-growing. For the first time in the history of Sun, a division went into red. It was the division that had the maximum field force which was not earning any incentives. The field force was demoralized and part of the reason was that some of the bestsellers from that division such as Famocid came under the government's price control. But a former Sun executive attributed a part of the responsibility to frequent experimentation. 'The Sun division was largely focused on gastroenterology with some high-volume drugs. This focus was shifted twice in those years to other therapies, and the product mix was changed. It upended Sun's model based on developing long-term rapport with specialists, a process that couldn't be achieved overnight.'

It's a blur what happened exactly, but Lanka left Sun in a huff in November 1998, the year Sun was acquiring Milmet. Former senior managers were under the impression that Lanka's erratic managerial style was the reason he had to part with Sun. They said top managers of the newly acquired Milmet were made to report directly to Shanghvi, signalling winds of change in Sun's top management. Lanka said he was unwell and not responding to medications. 'In 1998, I was diagnosed with excessive lymph nodes in lungs, running 107 degree fever which couldn't be treated with normal medication. I couldn't bear to slow down a company I had built and told Dilip-bhai to allow me to leave. The growth of the organization is always beyond my personal goals.' He said, after a few weeks of hospitalization, and months of rest he joined an assignment with a lesser workload. 'I wouldn't build another chronic drug firm. I have never repeated a model in my life. I have built an acute drug firm in Alchem, a chronic drug firm in Sun and API drug firm in Aurobindo. I would like to associate with a model that doesn't exist, may be a research-driven firm, with a scalable model that can represent India on the globe. I want the Indian flag to go high,' a wistful Lanka says.

Inheritance of Loss: Scars of Teenage Rebellion

As the company grew, attracting and retaining national talent to a smaller city like Baroda were becoming a formidable challenge. There had been cases, where brilliant industry talents wished to work with Shanghvi, but were not inclined to move to Baroda. Those who did, insisted on travelling to Bombay every weekend. Even before Lanka left Sun, Shanghvi had begun relocating Sun headquarters to Bombay, in phases. These were the years when the conflicts between new-entrant professionals and home-grown executives in Sun were at its peak.

One of Shanghvi's friend-turned-colleague, along with Hiren Desai, welcomed everyone on one floor at Sun's new office, Acme Plaza, in Bombay as other floors were under construction. A 'professional' walked up to him, and said, '*Yaar, kaisa office banaya hai*? My shoes have gathered a thick layer of dust already.' The friend glared at him and thought to himself, 'Should I bow down and wipe your shoes with my sleeves, sir?'

For months on, too many people squeezed into a space still being done up, which meant having to play musical chair in the morning. Whosoever came early grabbed a chair; those left struggled to find a seat. People who had grown up in Sun never had too much trouble adjusting to these little inconveniences, including Shanghvi, who, as in his previous offices, didn't even build a separate toilet for himself. Professionals, however, accustomed to their spaces squirmed, grimaced and frowned through the day waiting for the finished architecture to settle them down. Two years on, Lanka left Sun.

For the years he ceded control to Yakob and Lanka, Shanghvi had busied himself—in listing, accelerating drug launches to a new zippy pace, deploying the cash he had raised from public in a series of acquisitions—one in the US, and the rest in India alongside exploring the potential of overseas markets. Shanghvi had minimized his interaction with the field after transferring the reins to Yakob and Lanka, but he was acutely aware of the tense fault lines that misfit managers and indelible stretch marks, and an exponential growth had left upon the organization.

After the storm had passed, Shanghvi started picking up the threads and weaving them back into shape. While his company at home was undergoing teenage emotional turmoil, the company that he had bought in the US, Caraco, had run into regulatory troubles scuppering his American dreams for the moment. Shanghvi calculated that losses from the US setback would come to ₹2 crore per month for 2–3 years, an amount he would need to compensate from his business at home. Then quietly and patiently, he began to set his house in order.

He asked a few of his trusted senior managers to feel-check across cadres and bring him a grounds-up feedback. Among them was his ex-lieutenant Shyamal Ghosh, who had joined Sailesh Desai's company Milmet, which Sun was to acquire soon. Ghosh, who had been an old Sun hand and had left the organization because of his differences with his boss Yakob was set to return as head of marketing for a few therapy divisions.

Since he was not formally a part of Sun yet, he carried out the exercise informally travelling across different medical conferences. The old-time Sunny boys opened up. There was a pent-up frustration about two salary levels at one rank. Not discounting biases, the old-timers felt new recruits during Lanka were being paid significantly higher salaries, while all they did was make their routine ten calls a day, and party in the night—the MNC style. Their own salaries had remained depressed when their jobs—the Sun way of servicing the customer—demanded a 24/7 dedication. The field force of the loss-making Sun division was abjectly demoralized and was left without earning any incentives.

Shanghvi listened to it all—the reports, the tales—and assessed the cost the process of growth had extracted at the end. And then he made some decisions that unfolded quietly but swiftly. Marketing was made to report back to him, resembling a structure broadly of pre-Yakob time. This meant no more CEO-like power to anyone. Shyamal Ghosh went on to head eight divisions, T.K. Roy three but no one person headed all. The human resources department was given strict instructions that no senior manager who was being hired by Sun should fly into the company with his flock. Each recruitment had to go through a due process, with a thorough background check, all senior appointments were, of course, to be vetted by Shanghvi himself. Across the line management, misfits were identified, and what is called 'surgery' in Sun's internal dialect was performed, and pink slips flew abundantly.

Sun division was made to go through a rigorous 'slimming treatment'. Marking a historical deviation of maintaining uniform incentive schemes for all divisions, Ghosh created an aberration in designing a special lenient incentive scheme for Sun division field force. Even before Ghosh could begin to explain the rationale of it to Shanghvi, he told Ghosh 'I understand what you are trying to do. Go ahead. Boosting their morale should be our top priority.'

Reversing a tradition of Lanka's time, and to some extent Yakob's as well, Shanghvi started interacting with the field force directly again and started receiving unfiltered feedback just like old times. Initially, in 1999 he started walking into the review meetings and sitting through them keenly watching and listening but speaking little. Gradually however, he started participating, throwing in a few tips and within a year, by

2000, he started conducting the meeting himself. This meant the head of marketing, who used to be the reviewer asking questions from across the table earlier, crossed over to being reviewed and answering the questions Shanghvi was fielding. Shanghvi's transition or rather a revival to a hands-on manager was complete.

'There was a fundamental shift in that period. During Yakob's and Lanka's time, they were taking the major decisions and Dilip-bhai was supporting them. From then on, Dilip-bhai started taking major decisions and we as managers were in supporting roles,' Shyamal Ghosh said. A few years later, when Ghosh asked him about this change in strategy, he replied, 'From my experiences I have learnt that I have to run the company with checks and balances.' Ghosh construed that to mean that absolute power wouldn't be vested in one person in Sun any more.

Even though Shanghvi hadn't warmed up to the managerial styles of Yakob and Lanka—which diluted his own *be hard on task, not on people*' philosophy—that didn't mean he shunned the practices they had brought into the company. While he would use Lanka's M&A strategies in future, he took the concept of review from Yakob and polished it to a different level. Sitting with Sanjay Sahai, he co-designed fifty-six formats all functions must fill up for the review. 'Filling it took days and a lot of preparation,' Ghosh said. 'People stopped sleeping days before that review, but even as you were filling those, you were forced to do a self-introspection on where you stood and how aligned you were with the company's goals,' Roy said.

Ghosh reckoned Shanghvi might have picked the concept of quantitative review from Yakob, but his review looked nothing like Yakob's. 'People were terrorized to attend Yakob's review. Personally I don't think humiliation is the best way to motivate people. Dilip-bhai's review was fundamentally different. It was largely future planning with a bit of past analysis and zero public humiliation.'

Also Yakob's review had been restricted to marketing as that was his domain. Shanghvi expanded the review concept to cover the entire spectrum of functions in the company. 'With this, no one could pass the buck any more and a certain synchronization between functions came into play,' Ghosh said. This is how that garage where the servicing of

Sun vehicles happened over years, where the relay race was perfected under a soft but firm coach—who took care of the big picture and small details simultaneously—came into being.

This review format remained fluid, and was constantly improvised to reflect the changing realities and add better indicators to assess performances. Shanghvi practised this constant improvisation or 'kaizen' in every aspect of the company.

By 2001, when the review process had been streamlined, Shanghvi was reading *Moments of Truth* by Jan Carlzon, the Swedish businessman credited with turning around two loss-making airlines. The book dealt with how Carlzon, focused on thousands of 'few seconds encounters' between flight front-line staff and customers to engineer the resurrection of crumbling group SAS (Scandinavian Airlines System). Interestingly, SAS was a namesake of a marketing model designed by Shanghvi to service customers in Sun.

An idea that hit Shanghvi from that book was the power of simple messaging—when addressed to a large group of people. He realized how Carlzon as the chief of airlines Linjeflyg achieved a breakthrough in Swedish domestic aviation by introducing '100 Krona ticket' and a motto—'the whole of Sweden at half the price'. It was aimed at young populations such as students for whom flights were not the natural mode of travel, and who didn't mind waiting a little longer to fly. This alone helped the airline add 125,000 passengers in a year.

When Carlzon took over the struggling SAS group as CEO, he unleashed the potential of a simple message by releasing a little red book—called *SAS*. His message: We are here for the customer, not the other way around! Carlzon simplified his vision message, used big-typeset, emoting cartoons in that little red book as a tool to bring about a behavioural change in 20,000 employees. His prescription for the leader was simple: 'Rather than issuing your message, you have to be certain that every employee has truly understood and absorbed it. This means you have to reverse the approach: you must consider the words that the receiver can best absorb and make them their own.'

Shanghvi correlated it with another success story he had observed closer home, in the simple messaging of the *Times of India*'s invitation price scheme. When the Times Group offered its daily paper at a throwaway price of ₹2 in weekdays in the 1990s, people got hooked and didn't mind paying a little extra for their weekend papers.

Taking a cue from the European airlines and the Indian newspapers, Shanghvi proposed that the incentive scheme for MRs in Sun should be simplified to the basic message—do more to get more. Till then, the incentive structure was such that if there were fifty brands in a division, of which ten were under active promotion, each of the ten brands had a separate incentive scheme. If the MR fulfilled the conditions for three, he was rewarded incentive for those three only. What Shanghvi was suggesting was to do away with all such complexities and set up a slab-wise exponential-growth-linked incentive structure. It meant that if you achieved 100 per cent growth, you get 10 per cent incentive. If you got 105 per cent, you got 20 per cent incentive and so on.

This proposal met with huge resistance from Sun's senior management, prompting long-heated arguments. But Shanghvi was adamant about using his favourite maxim again: Everything is simple when reduced to fundamentals. 'Underlying my proposal was a basic understanding that MRs don't understand maths. You tell them complex formula like: Assign 30 per cent weightage to this product and 40 per cent weightage to that while selling. Then whatever incentives they would earn would only be by default. I tried to put myself in that position to understand how an MR will act. It's simple, if you give him a good product, good inputs to provide to the doctor, and incentives when he achieves the objective, there is no reason why he will not do the work he is needed to do. And if you don't give him a good product, whatever he may do, the sale will not happen.'

The protest from managers was not without basis. Ghosh recalled being part of the team that raised objections. 'Under this new proposed scheme, we argued that the MRs would push whatever sells easily in the market. This means products that don't sell on their own are likely to languish or fizzle out.'

Shanghvi wasn't refuting the logic of the argument but he thought that issue had to be tackled separately at the level of the company; an MR couldn't be expected to grasp so much complexity just because the company wanted to sell products that didn't have adequate uptake.

'People confuse between the job of a company and the job of an MR. Both are not necessarily the same. We have different profitability goals for the MR and at consolidated company levels. You cannot expect an MR to focus on low-margin products, if they are incentivized to sell high-margin products. We have to structure the targeting in a different way to achieve that goal. The MR will sell a product in which the market is responding to its efforts,' Shanghvi said.

The simplified incentive structure was announced to the MRs in a start-of-the year conference. It was the part of the speech they generally heard with rapt attention. And when the stripped-to-bare new incentive was read out, there was an instantaneous outburst of claps and cheers that surprised the managers. The year next, Sun's performance across divisions had galloped significantly to underline the power of a simple message. Profits of Sun grew by 42 per cent in the year 2000 and 61 per cent in 2001 from a meagre 5 per cent in 1999.

Every time Shanghvi learnt an idea from someone or somewhere, he just didn't copy and reproduce it. He was an artist in cloning because he always found ways to improvise on those ideas and dish out a superior and finer version. He did so, when he learnt the psychiatry specialization model from U.N. Mehta of Torrent, a concept of organization review from Yakob, M&A strategies from Lanka. An eternal student, he learnt his lessons from the people he came across in his life, but he learnt far more from people he had never met, such as tax planning from Dhirubhai Ambani, corporate governance from Kumar Mangalam Birla. In fact, Shanghvi explained why learning without directly engaging with the teacher had been a more yielding exercise for him than sitting face-to-face with one.

'It forces me to think of multiple angles behind why someone is doing what he is doing. When you are learning that way, it is difficult to interpret the intent behind action. I can see what he has done, but I don't know why he has done so. You start looking at a series of actions and their outcomes and then use your own reasoning to decipher what the purpose behind that action could be. In the process, you may end up discovering even more than the person who has first attempted that action. Your mental investment in the processes is way more than direct engagement, where you are asking questions and someone is furnishing verbal answers.'

This kaizen was clearly not only restricted to the arms of his company.

Once Shanghvi was toying with a dictaphone when his deputies barged in unannounced. That day Shanghvi was upset about something and the chat took a not so pleasant course. After the conversation and teacups had dried up, and his colleagues had left, Shanghvi's eyes darted to the flashing red light on the dictaphone. Their interaction had got accidentally recorded. He switched the play button and heard the whole chat again, replayed it over and over, unable to believe that the voice in the recorder was his own. 'While I was thinking that I was conducting myself very well, when I replayed the conversation and heard myself speak, it came out sounding way more aggressive than what I thought I was while in that conversation. That was a turning point for me to realize that you have to constantly keep evaluating yourself to improve upon your previous self,' he said.

CHAPTER THIRTEEN

DEALS UNINTERRUPTED: SHORT CUT TO THE HIGHWAY

The man didn't stop tapping his fingers on the table, jabbing them in the air as if choreographing a finger ballad, making it impossible for the onlooker to not stare at the diamonds and rubies in the rings that adorned his fingers. On the other side of the table, were Rajesh Kikani and Shanghvi, who exchanged notes without even exchanging glances.

After the man left along with his exquisite jewellery shop, Kikani couldn't help himself. 'What explains that? Why was he flashing those gem-studded rings at us?' he asked about this financer of Sarabhai Chemicals, who had started frequenting Synergy House in the early 1990s.

'Rajesh-bhai, how much do you think each of those rings may cost?'

'I have no expertise in this department.'

'Not less than ₹50 lakh each.'

'So? Why flaunt it to you?'

'He is interested in us making a pitch to take over Sarabhai,' Shanghvi said. He was employing his trademark fuzzy logic with a straight face, making it difficult to guess, where his joke ended and serious observation began. In the years to come, Shanghvi was to bring up the acquisition of Sarabhai with Kikani not less than fifteen times. 'We don't want size, Dilip-bhai. We want a great fit, and Sarabhai, despite its brand and legacy, doesn't make strategic sense,' Kikani repeated.

He found this attribute of Shanghvi amazing. 'Usually if you say a categorical no to something, people stop raising the matter with you, knowing what your stand is. Not Dilip-bhai, he would repeatedly broach Sarabhai compelling me to find new angles to counter the proposal.'

This was not the impression that Shanghvi gave to the Sarabhaians—Shyamal Ghosh, Udayan Dasgupta, Rajesh Kumar among others who would have been thrilled at the prospect of their new company gobbling up their old one, for which they had so much regard. Ghosh for one had no inkling in his first stint that Shanghvi fancied buying Sarabhai. In fact, he recalled pitching the animal health division of Sarabhai to Shanghvi, but being turned down.

'Their veterinary business is the number one in the country and it is being run very efficiently,' Ghosh egged on Shanghvi. But he recalled Shanghvi explaining, 'I don't understand that business and I will not invest in a business which I don't get.'

Other Sarabhaians were equally puzzled, at times getting a whiff of his ambition, and then watching him laugh off their curiosity with, 'Do you see the rhino statue at the Sarabhai chowk? Buying Sarabhai now would be like riding that rhino. It has too much weight and would slow us down.'

But Sarabhai had been on Shanghvi's mind, right in the top deck, for he made a call to a man he had known for a few years as the marketing head of Pfizer India, who had quit his job a few days back. They had warmed up to each other, probably after D.G. Shah, while still at Pfizer, had helped Shanghvi clinch a deal to buy Knoll Pharma's (later renamed Abbott) Ahmednagar plant.

But he couldn't have missed the most pressing link of a family association that Shah had with Sarabhais. Shah's younger brother Bipin Shah had been married to the beautiful Bharatanatyam dancer—Mallika Sarabhai, daughter of scientist Vikram Sarabhai. Though by the time Shanghvi enlisted Shah to engage with the Sarabhais on the matter, the two had separated but continued to run a publishing house—Mapin—together.

Shanghvi's interest in Sarabhai eventually became abundantly clear by the fact that he had been quietly snapping up its shares in chunks through a spattering of his companies—Dilip Shantilal Associates, Virtuous Finance, Viditi Investments and others. According to documents submitted by Sun in courts, together they had acquired a little over 9 per cent of Ambalal Sarabhai Enterprises.

Prompted by Shanghvi, Shah recalled sending feelers to Kartikeya Sarabhai (Vikram Sarabhai's son) to engage on the matter, but getting a cold response. 'The Sarabhais were clearly not interested in even discussing a deal with Sun at the time. Instead they were more comfortable with the Piramals and they probably called Ajay Piramal,' Shah recalled.

That the Sarabhais were not interested in a deal talk with Shanghvi eventually became clear as they refused to even register and transfer the chunk of shares bought by some of Shanghvi's companies. But engage they had to this way or that.

Soon Shanghvi dragged the matter to the market regulator SEBI and the Company Law Board, where the Sarabhais alleged that Sun, in concert with others, had breached the 10 per cent ceiling (in buying shares of its company) and not made any public disclosure as mandated by SEBI. Sun's counter-argument was that they had bought only 9.37 per cent of Sarabhai's shares, of which only half of its shares had been registered while the other half Sarabhai was stubbornly refusing to transfer.

The Company Law Board decided that the three of the dozen-odd entities (companies and individuals) Sarabhais were citing as working 'in concert' with Sun were not on the face of it working for Sun. The fact that they shared the same broker didn't prove that they were working in concert, and Sarabhai had not done the basic groundwork of finding out details about the board of directors of these buying companies to prove what it was claiming.

For Shanghvi, whose company was much smaller and many decades younger, it seemed an audaciously bold move, to aspire to take over Sarabhai Chemicals and take on the Sarabhais who were regarded aristocracy for long enough to inspire tele-soaps like *Sarabhai versus Sarabhai*.

Their company had been one of the leading ones of the country in the decades preceding. Some former Sun insiders pinned this reluctance on the part of the Sarabhais to their blue-blooded attitude. 'They were the lordship and didn't want to sell their family heir to someone whom they saw as an unknown entity.' But a former Sarabhaian put it differently, 'Sarabhai's sales force followed a very strict ethical code, they couldn't allow it to be "adulterated" by practices which they perceived as grey.'

Reluctant or not, one of those involved in making the deal said that Ajay Piramal, who was friends with the Sarabhais, didn't want such a complicated deal on hand with a block of shares still parked with Shanghvi. So a tripartite discussion got under way between the Sarabhais, the Piramals and Shanghvi at Taj Chambers to resolve the impasse. What followed were not the few most pleasant meetings, where the Sarabhais were represented by one of their loyal finance professionals, Narayanan; Shanghvi was represented by D.G. Shah and himself on one occasion; Ajay Piramal by lawyer R.A. Shah and himself once.

Piramal and Sarabhai were rooting for Shanghvi to shed off his shares which he agreed to, but not at the price they wanted. He sought a premium on the rate at which he had bought the shares. This Piramal pronounced as 'undoable' and Narayanan as 'not acceptable', given the shares had plunged sharper and were trading at a much lower price now than the rate at which they had been bought.

Temperatures soared, heated exchanges followed and Shah recalled when asked in one of those meetings that Piramal abruptly walked out calling the terms non-negotiable, making it seem that hours of brain-racking had amounted to nothing; in fact, they left things just as they were. But to his utter surprise, D.G. Shah recalled receiving a call from Sarabhai's Narayanan the next morning, when Narayanan indicated that they would relent on the price and Shanghvi should now be ready to sell.

This was Shanghvi's first serious attempt to seize a legacy to grow Sun, albeit aborted. The Piramals would sign a joint venture with Sarabhai Chemicals in 1999, and go on to fully acquire it in 2004.

When Sun thought of scaling up and attaining a size, Shanghvi knew that the only way he could leap to fulfil his ambition was if he could buy companies and seamlessly allow them to become part of Sun. To grow organically, Sun experimented for a fleeting two years with an antibiotic portfolio which could give it volumes, and help in building size over and above its focus on drugs for chronic diseases. Lanka, famed for launching antibiotic megabrands in Indian markets such as Combiflam and Taxim was at Sun and his talents could be counted on as well. So was his specialization in mergers and acquisitions to chart out a strategy to conquer markets others than in India.

MJ and Gujarat Lyka: The Jigsaw Puzzle

Stitching MJ Pharma and Gujarat Lyka into Sun was part of that exercise all rolled into one—foraying into antibiotics through the inorganic route and consolidating one's position in the overseas markets, particularly Russia and the US. These were acquisitions that Shanghvi hoped, when pieced together, would let Sun build an ambitious antibiotics plan. It had the potential to help Sun launch next-generation injectable drugs not only in the country, but also in the East European markets. Gujarat Lyka at the time boasted of one of the country's largest facility in Ankleshwar to produce bulk drugs (raw material) for the globally much-in-demand class of antibiotics, cephalosporins. MJ had the formulations—solid dosage and the injectables facility—approved by international regulators, and was already exporting these drugs to Russia and CIS markets.

Some bit of familiarity with these target companies was brought in by Lanka who claimed that many of these companies, like MJ, had contracts with Novartis, his old employer. Over lunches they did that mix and match, targeting companies which were in distress or already sick. 'In pharma, each component of the business—say, API, formulations, research—were individually expensive. Usually, companies begin with any one of these and are not able to afford others. What we were attempting was picking up three or four pieces and putting it all together. I was using the network created in Novartis for analysis of some such companies,' Lanka recalled.

Sailesh Desai, however, recalled that way back in 1988, when he and Shanghvi were doing a recce of MJ's injectable facility to grasp the mechanics of sterile manufacturing, Shanghvi had sniffed an opportunity. Around the same time, someone had pitched a facility in Jamshedpur to Desai, so he brought up the topic with Shanghvi. 'No, Sailesh, people have a poor perception of things made in Bihar. Particularly in our business of medicine, perception of quality is non-negotiable,' he had said, adding, 'looking at the way things are going on at MJ, it's possible that the facility at Halol may be up for sale in some time.'

It hadn't materialized immediately but right after Sun had been listed, the MJ opportunity he had sniffed six or seven years ago turned up for investment.

For Sun, it made sense from diverse angles: because they were looking for an injectable facility, MJ had a world-class one; they were gearing up for international markets, particularly US; and their Halol facility was one of the first US FDA-approved in the country. They had even cephalosporins ANDAs (abbreviated new drug application) approved from that facility, which could use the captive raw material that would come straight from Gujarat Lyka. MJ was doing contract manufacturing for US firms like Eli Lilly, which meant Sun got a direct peep into the practices US firms were following. Sun had already been making attempts to win the antibiotic business in Russia and other CIS countries, and Jasubhai, the owner of MJ had made significant headways on that. This multi-product facility had space to make tablets, liquid and additional capacity, which Sun could leverage to expand (later it almost trebled in size). And most importantly, it was plagued by management issues, and was offered at what Valia dubbed as 'peanuts on a platter'.

The other piece of the jigsaw puzzle was being worked out separately and had to be fitted into MJ. This was the story of Gujarat Lyka.

Hasmukh Ishwarlal Gandhi's trajectory—of being a Gujarati raised in Calcutta, having studied in JJ Ajmera School and Bhowanipore Gujarati Education Society, migrating from there to Bombay in 1982, and climbing up the business ladder from a family drug distribution business to manufacturing pharmaceuticals, albeit started by his father—had been remarkably similar to that of Shanghvi's own journey. So it was a surprise that they hadn't met, and Gandhi hadn't even heard of him till his chief accountant Jayesh Shah fixed a meeting with Valia, then known in Bombay circles as Shanghvi's money manager. 'Dilip-bhai was so low key that one didn't notice him despite the fact that his company was already one of the fastest-growing in the country,' Gandhi recalled.

When they first pitched, a sell-out was the last thing on the Gandhis' mind. The company was making about ₹60 crore in sales but was in the red, and they had gone seeking for funds, believing once money was in, they would be able to bail out their family business.

What did one see in the other in those first meetings? 'Dilip-bhai came in as an angel of an investor. Unassuming, very sharp, lightning-quick with money and numbers, he saw a different value in our business, to use it as a platform where he could put his ideas to work,' H.I. Gandhi recalled. Sitting on the same side, next to him, was his son Chintan, recently back from the US, having studied economics and finance and wondering where this man (Shanghvi) taught himself. 'We had been in the pharma business for a while—that is to say two generations. I had seen many pharma promoters at work from close, that included my grandfather, my father, my uncles, but this person was totally different. For any antibiotic, he could well be a talking encyclopaedia and on top give you a business case report. Why it would work with doctors, and why would it command margins. He blew your mind and you wished if you were to continue in pharma, this is how you must model yourself,' Chintan recalled. In their subsequent meetings, Shanghvi gave them an indication to enter injectable and fourth-generation antibiotics by organizing a forward integration of Gujarat Lyka with what Sun was buying at MJ.

Through the meetings, Chintan was amused by Shanghvi's habit of scribbling notes like a scribe. He couldn't resist asking Shanghvi why, to which he replied that once he had written something, he didn't forget it ever.

Sun saw a resource in Gandhi's background. 'We were clearly keen on the very profitable cephalosporin business, where the manufacturing cost was about a third of the selling cost, and the demand was very high,' Valia said. 'But we were also impressed by the owner's background of chemical engineering in the US and since we had to work hard on our understanding of bulk drugs, as we had added bulk drug facilities at Panoli and Ahmednagar, we thought it was a good idea to bank on him as a resource for knowledge in that area,' Valia added.

The arrangement started with Sun providing working capital to Gujarat Lyka and collecting payment from their sales. In time, because they agreed, we bought 50 per cent stake, said Valia. It cost Sun about ₹7 crore and post-sale, five of the ten directors on Gujarat Lyka's board were from Sun, but the management still remained with the Gandhis.

After the deal, Chintan recalled sitting in Sun's Acme Plaza office for a while. 'I walked up to Dilip-bhai and asked for something more challenging to do,' Chintan, who was then attached as an executive assistant to Lanka, said. There he was given long lists of doctors and their prescription habits to study. 'It was not my idea of the most exciting work, I confess,' Chintan laughed.

The Gandhis and Shanghvi couldn't find a common ground in business they were searching for. 'Even while I was doing it, I knew we were not adding a lot of value. It was more of a commodity business. Though these were essential goods, penicillin, cephalosporins, ampicillin, amoxicillin bulk drugs, all of these were under the price control net of the government; there were too many licences and government permits required at several stages of production, which often didn't come on time and the pressure on working capital mounted manifold, and one got into a vicious cycle,' Gandhi said.

Having done the drill for long, Gandhi felt there wasn't much value creation left to be done in the bulk drug business, a hypercompetitive commoditized market. Gradually, points of differences on doing business between Gandhi and the Sun team grew. 'We found that the company continued to make losses. We were trying to help them make purchases more efficiently, but that couldn't happen as the management wouldn't follow our suggestion. The management was theirs, so the final call was also theirs. They said they knew the quality, the parties, and the process of making purchases better. But cost matters, ultimately in running a business,' Valia said.

The two separated in 2000 with Gujarat Lyka going to the Board for Industrial and Financial Reconstruction (BIFR), which took a view that on a stand-alone basis, Gujarat Lyka was not viable and allowed its merger with Sun.

'In any integration, one company plays the big brother, whose culture prevails. There is nothing wrong with it. It is the law of the corporate jungle. I never had a partner before that, never had one after that. I was very keen to strike out independently. I left because in a large company, if you make mistakes you are answerable to many people. In your own small set-up, you have the freedom to experiment, make mistakes, and if you have to answer to someone, it is just your family,' Gandhi said. Nurturing a fascination for 'natural medicines, Ayurveda, Gandhi later founded a company Millennium Labs in 2000 which he runs with his son Chintan.

Asked if he could have done anything differently, he wondered, 'In hindsight I can't say why being in bulk drugs, I didn't think of entering formulations even though we had a marketing arm in Lyka Labs. It was the most logical thing to do at that time.'

While the facilities Sun acquired from MJ was eventually scaled up to become the company's most crucial source for US drugs, Shanghvi's jigsaw fit of MJ and Gujarat Lyka, which worked so well in theory, wouldn't pan out so well on ground—partly because one of the markets it was being planned for changed complexion, with the rouble crisis of 1998 altering the realities in Russia.

It was a Friday, and Raju, who was in charge of international marketing, recalled waking up in Moscow. 'The reality had changed overnight. Companies which had gone before us (Torrent, Dr Reddy's) had had a fair run as procurement was through a centralized tendering. But the rouble crisis changed everything. The government there told the hospitals to procure on their own which meant the entire business model of selling would have to be rethought,' Raju recalled.

It was the only time loyalist Raju would have an argument with Shanghvi. 'I told him that henceforth in Russia we would need to raise a sales force like we have in India if we have to succeed, because now we have to convince individual hospitals, not the centre,' Raju told Shanghvi, asking for a significant raise in budget.

He recalled Shanghvi telling him this: 'For this much, Mr Raju, I could introduce five completely new drugs in this market.'

'If you think that is a better idea, you should probably do that,' Raju said.

It was not a plan that grew wings, but as Shanghvi once told Chintan, 'It's always better to take some decision than none. Once you have crossed a period of time and look back, you realize that of the 100 decisions you took, at least sixty have worked.'

So if this decision didn't click, there always was another decision, another learning ground. This ground was TDPL, the company for which Shanghvi's father had been the stockist in Calcutta, the company from which Shanghvi had brought Raju.

From Stockist to Owner

Amusing, but two people who share an association of a lifetime do not necessarily meet each other at the same moment. One may have met the other a decade before the other met him, given meeting someone itself is a play of memory. This is how Mohan Chand Dadha, owner of TDPL, and Shanghvi met each other. Shanti-kaka's agency Medcom had been TDPL's super stockist in Calcutta. This is where Raju, a manager at TDPL, and kaka had hit it off, shared a drink in the evening, giving a young Shanghvi an opportunity to watch his prospective manager, without being watched himself.

In a small window of overlap, where Shanghvi had already floated his company, but had not yet given up managing his father's stockist agency, there popped an occasion of potential friction between TDPL and Medcom, in other words between Dadha and Shanghvi.

Based on inflated sales projections of a TDPL manager, Shanti-kaka had piled up massive stocks of TDPL medicine, which for want of demand didn't translate into sales, Shanghvi recalled. 'TDPL then was supplying directly to us without an agency. The stock quantity that got liquidated couldn't cover our costs. and so the money (theirs and ours) was kind of stuck.'

It was at that moment, he recalled, Dadha coming over and asking, 'Yeh paise ka kya karna hai?' Another stockist in his place, Shanghvi expected, could have fought back pinning faults and fixing blames behind the lost money. But Shanghvi, who preferred a marathon over a 100 metre dash, decided to place the relationship over the money. He recalled telling Dadha, 'Our money is also stuck, but don't worry, we will see to it that you are paid in time and whatever interest is due is also paid.' Dadha's recollection of Shanghvi didn't go that far back in the past. He recalled meeting Shanti kaka in Calcutta while on business, and faintly remembered Shanghvi who he thought had probably once come to Madras to meet him. His distinct memory of Shanghvi was only from the October 1996, when he received an unexpected call from someone named Dilip Shanghvi from Bombay. 'He said I am Dilip Shanghvi of Sun Pharmaceuticals. You may not remember me, but I have seen you meet my father. You were this tall, handsome, hard-working man that I would look up to as my role model. I would like to meet you, whenever you are in Bombay the next time,' he recounted.

Shanghvi invited him to his office at Ram Mandir Road. In that meeting, Shanghvi seemed curious about the new products in the making at TDPL, and Dadha reeled off some impressive drug candidates which were in advance research under the supervision of his top scientist—Dr Nadamuni.

'We are doing many oncology products—such as Platin, Carboplatin, Denezol. In breast cancer, we had already started marketing Letrozole.'

Pronto, Shanghvi pulled out a proposal from under his hat, 'Why don't we start co-marketing some of these products?' He said Sun had set up a new R&D centre in Baroda, which he would like Dadha to visit. Dadha, scheduled for a meeting at Alembic's Baroda office the next week, promised he would. It was when he was bidding goodbye to Shanghvi at the R&D centre in Baroda, already settling in his Alembic-sent car, about to shut the door, ready to leave that Shanghvi popped the co-marketing capsule again, 'I think you are also ready with Gabapentin (the anti-epilepsy drug), aren't you? Can we begin joint marketing on that?' It was as if both had more to add, but left it unsaid for the moment.

It was 1996, and much water had flowed under the TDPL bridge since it had severed ties with its ex-stockist. TDPL had had a particularly interesting history. The Dadhas, originally from Rajasthan, had settled in Madras since 1912, and were mainly into pharma distribution. In the 1960s, they ventured into manufacturing, and by 1972, Dadha recalled the TIDCO (Tamil Nadu Industrial Development Corporation) chairman proposing a joint venture on the lines of arrangements they had in cement and television. 'In pharma it was the first such model with the state government owning 51 per cent and we owning a 49 per cent stake. When we went public, the government continued to own 26 per cent and we 25 per cent with corresponding voting rights,' Dadha stated.

From 1974 to 1991, the bulk of TDPL's business came from supplying generic drugs to the hospitals, mainly government-owned. But with a change of government in Tamil Nadu, fortunes turned when the government started its own tendering system under Tamil Nadu Medical Services Corporation. This prompted TDPL to focus on their smaller branded generics arm. From 1972 to 1983, M.C. Dadha had been the managing director, from 1983 to 1993, his nephew took over and by 1993 Dadha was back at the helm.

'Once I took over in 1993, I realized our plants had been twenty years old, crying for upgradation. If we were to continue in the game, stay competitive in India and go overseas, we needed to invest ₹200 crore to modernize,' Dadha recalled. He took it up with the government, only to discover that TIDCO was actually preparing the ground to disinvestment.

'This matter has been pending for a long time, Mr Dadha. Your company has been paying dividends from the very first year, and the government must focus on developing other new industries,' Dadha recalled the TIDCO chairman telling him.

'I wasn't really aware how serious you were about it. My nephew had casually mentioned it to me once, but that was that. The promoters' agreement had been signed with me in 1973 and we will have to look up the options there,' Dadha replied.

He received a call within three days from the TIDCO chairman seeking a copy of that agreement. 'I asked them to put everything in writing, and once the letter from the government arrived, I drafted: "Thank you, please refer to clause 9 and clause 10 of the disinvestment process document, we will buy at the price arrived at as per the formula specified,"' Dadha recalled writing back.

A week later, a surprised TIDCO chairman called him back to say he was rather taken aback by the alacrity and speed of Dadha's response. 'What, did you expect that we wouldn't wish to buy?' a puzzled Dadha asked.

'No it is just that, we have made many disinvestments before and people usually beg for extensions, saying they have no money.'

The file started moving, six months passed before Dadha heard from this bureaucrat again. 'The file has been cleared. It is in the chief minister's office. Now you will have to work to get the decision.' J. Jayalalithaa's AIADMK party was in power since 1991.

Dadha wondered about the way things worked in this country. 'I had invested ₹19 lakh and the government ₹21 lakh in 1973. Today the price I would have to pay is ₹4 crore and nothing would change on ground in the company. I am and I will remain the managing director and continue to manage its affairs. So what is the rationale of going and meeting a chief minister and paying ₹4 crore to just go on with the same model? So I decided—sorry, I am not going to any CM's office.'

When he brought up modernization of the plants with his nephews to espouse their interest, they excused themselves from investing in this venture citing their other business interests. In the interim, policy factors propelled Dadha to expedite his action on this front. In 1995, the Indian government had signed Trade Related Intellectual Property Rights (TRIPS), indicating winds of change on the policy front. Dadha, then a president of a pharma industry association, acknowledged the winds of change in a public address where he exhorted the industry to rise and consolidate. 'Globalization is upon us. The only way our smaller companies can grow is by becoming large through mergers and acquisitions. Duplication of effort and an unusually fragmented industry doesn't help the case of the domestic industry,' Dadha pronounced in his lecture. He recalled reading his own views in the newspaper the next day, receiving calls from his peers who had found his stand painfully objectionable. But somewhere, what he was doing was preparing the ground to put his words into action.

And then, starting 1996, time sped up for him once again as at the state level the Karunanidhi government took over. A Tamil power secretary from the Centre asked him, 'Mr Dadha, why don't we finish this matter?'

'Sir, what are the political and bureaucratic considerations required for clearing the file? Anyway the day I had agreed to the proposal the last time, the share price was at ₹85, today it is at ₹62,' Dadha replied.

'No bureaucratic or political considerations, Mr Dadha. Only politicians are not subject to any queries, but tomorrow as bureaucrats we may be questioned about this—when the private players had agreed to buy for ₹85, you didn't sell, why are you ready to sell them for ₹62 today?

'OK, sir. Since you have made it clear that there are no other considerations—political and bureaucratic—how long will it take you to clear this file?'

'Fifteen days, Mr Dadha.'

That was the pressing story brewing in Madras, when Shanghvi proposed joint marketing to Dadha. However, it was not Shanghvi but Dadha who booked his tickets for Bombay, asking his nephew to join in for a deal negotiation with Shanghvi. 'I didn't want my nephews to think that I was benefitting any extra way from this deal,' Dadha recounted.

Curiously, by the time he had boarded the flight for Bombay to hold talks of a merger with Sun, he had, to his relief, managed to politely shoo away messengers meandering at his doorstep from another big pharma giant who had come unsolicited sniffing an opportunity of a takeover. These were brokers sent to Dadha by Ranbaxy. Asked why he didn't explore the offer deeper, Dadha said, 'It may sound odd, but I felt a Gujarati would understand the Marwari sensibility better than a Punjabi.'

Dadha explained the position to Shanghvi, who sought detailed balance sheets and other figures. Lanka posed as a cost consultant and walked into the TDPL offices and facilities to conduct the due diligence. 'We valued the companies very quick. I would walk into TDPL as a cost consultant, check out the factories, value of the products, technologies, brands, distributors to arrive at a figure in my mind for how much the company should be valued at. That was the agreement we had with the owner,' recalled Lanka, on how Sun valued the company.

A week later, they were sitting across each other again, Shanghvi asking, 'So how do we join hands?'

'Either we fix the price of the share and merge or you buy the company.'

'Let's fix the price of the share,' Shanghvi said, attaching a condition that if he had to come on board, the government must exit prior to that. It had been about a week since the TIDCO secretary had given Dadha an assurance to clear the file in a fortnight. It was time for Dadha to pull the thread with all his might. He returned to Madras to inform TIDCO in April 1996 that he was ready to pay the older higher price of ₹85 per share, subject to them signing a 'no strings attached' deal.

Just a month later, when he was vacationing in the hill station Kodaikanal to beat the heat of May, the TIDCO secretary called him to inform that government approval had come.

'Could you read out the letter to me please?' Dadha asked over phone on what was a Friday.

'It says at the price decided, or the price prevailing in the market, whichever is higher.'

'I only have one request. Please don't show the letter to anybody. Keep it under wraps. I will come and do the needful, first thing on Monday morning.'

Cutting his vacation short, at 9.30 a.m., the following Monday, Dadha reached the TIDCO office with a demand draft of a little more than what the calculation was working out to be. 'Please deposit this money immediately before the stock exchange rings the bell. If some fool comes to know and buys shares for ₹200, I will be doomed,' Dadha told the TIDCO official.

He understood Dadha's urgency well enough to send the draft off to the bank immediately.

Dadha then demanded, 'I want my shares released today. The share transfer committee should meet and transfer the shares today itself and all directors should resign today.'

'What's the hurry, sir?'

'I am in a hurry. I have paid the money. Why should I leave my assets with you?'

The TIDCO official prepared the papers, without taking any commission—a fact Dadha made a special note of—and forwarded the file to the executive director. After waiting for twenty minutes outside, Dadha recalled barging into the ED's room, demanding that the file be cleared and sent off to the chairman.

'I have to study the file,' the ED replied coldly.

'In that case, I will have to go to your chairman and ask him to call for this file,' Dadha shot back.

The ED looked at him from above his frame and signed the file without saying a word.

Next Dadha dashed to the bank, where the share certificates had been kept, only to find the locker operator enjoying a siesta; he did not turn up until noon. About 1 p.m., he could lay his hands upon the share certificates; at 2 p.m., the meeting for the share transfers was held, and government nominees resigned from the directorships of TDPL. Out of the meeting, Dadha called Shanghvi, 'Dilip, take the next flight to Madras. It's all yours.'

Shanghvi bought three tickets—one for himself, one for an executive who had recently joined from Novartis, Gajendra Holkar,* and a third for his father, Shantilal Shanghvi, once a stockist of the company of which he was soon to turn owner that day, as his son was buying it out.

On the evening of 12 May, in a board meeting, Dadha formally announced to his executives that TIDCO was no longer their partner, and the day after, in the afternoon, he introduced the new managing director—Dilip Shanghvi. Dadha said he wasn't ready for what was to follow. In that meeting Shanghvi declared that Dadha would continue as the chairman of the board, and would join the board of Sun.

'It came as a complete surprise to me,' Dadha exclaimed. His phone was ringing non-stop, among the callers were officials from TIDCO charging, 'Why did you keep this hidden from us?'

They walked out of the building after the meeting. Outside, Dadha's luxury sedan was parked; behind that Shanghvi's taxi was waiting. Dadha recalled offering him his vehicle, to which he replied, '*Nahin aap isme jaayie*, I am accustomed to travelling in taxis.'

Sun acted fast on the merger, even though it was in spirit the company's first attempt at integration. Some of its senior-most executives were awe-struck by Dadha's palatial mansion and opulent lifestyle. Sightings of celebrity politicians and film stars at Dadha's mansion became the new buzz among Sun's senior employees. But that didn't stall work.

Lanka recalled parking himself in a five-star hotel at Madras for a week appraising each product. 'They had a lot of products which had a potential of higher pricing that had escaped their notice. We implemented price hikes immediately,' he recalled. Then Sun merged hundreds of TDPL C&Fs and stockists into its ecosystem which strengthened its distribution. 'They had 424 stockists and a robust C&F network. They were paying a lower commission to their distributors compared to Sun, and we worked out a situation that our distributors would migrate to their level of commissions. Sun's distribution was weak till then, and we made sure that Sun's products immediately start flowing through their stockist system. This expanded our reach in one shot.' TDPL's bulk drug production was shifted to Panoli. The idea was, he shared, to harness as much synergies by making the changes as fast as possible.

The more challenging but skilful part of Sun's first merger had got to do with pruning products and people, that didn't fit into Sun's values and strategy. The first thing Shanghvi indicated to his people was that he didn't want to carry the baggage of TDPL with him.

'Scan every TDPL brand and figure out if it fits our value chain. If not, phase it out gradually,' Milan Sinha recalled this as being Shanghvi's first message. 'We were learning for the first time how a range of products were to be studied for their suitability to Sun's basket of offerings; product life cycles were studied, and only those which passed the test of being relevant in the future were retained,' T.K. Roy recalled.

TD Jesic, a medicine rampantly misused as an addictive drug which Roy reckoned earned a fifth of all of TDPL's monthly sales, became the first victim under Shanghvi knockout extras in the portfolio. 'This was so popular that it sold in all pan shops and thelas, but its market was openly among addictive users. We heard boss saying, "This is causing addiction in youngsters, we cannot damage the future of the society,"' Roy recalled. Previously, another Sun brand Nitrosun, had been phased out partly because it was prone to misuse, particularly in north-eastern states.

Lanka described scanning every brand plan of TDPL in the first few days. 'I think we got a lot done in the first 6–7 days, and then it rolled over,' he said. Pruning products was easy; products don't have hearts and bellies. Same logic doesn't apply to people. Roy and Sinha, under him, had the unenviable demand of shrinking people strength from 450 to 250, but without disturbing dignity.

HR head Yagnik remembered how strictly everyone had been warned against any misbehaviour. 'Dilip-bhai's message was that the tender spot of human dignity must not be disturbed. No one should be humiliated. No one should behave like an acquirer or a conquerer. If one such report came by from Dadha to Dilip-bhai, we would have had it,' Yagnik recalled. So, after Roy had done his recce, found out duplication of roles, arrived at numbers, he and Sinha sat with the managers of the target company to listen to their tales.

At one point, when one after the other, managers gushed about their 'brilliant' 70–78 per cent growth in some southern states, Sinha recalled whispering into Roy's ears with disbelief, 'What are these guys passing off as achievements? That is not even close to what a mediocre in Sun would accomplish.' Roy shushed him, 'Just listen on. This is what we are here to understand, their attitude framework. It shows that they haven't traditionally been pushed to achieve more, and we are looking for people who are achievement-oriented. That is the distinction we have to make on who stays and who goes.' Roy claimed that each one handed over the pink slip was explained why he was being asked to leave, why they wouldn't fit into the Sun ecosystem.

At the senior-most managerial levels, however, Shanghvi had demonstrated a clear tendency to favour Sun loyalists over TDPL natives. When TDPL was being carved out as a separate division, there were three candidates who were shortlisted to head it as national sales manager—two from TDPL and Sinha from Sun. A former Sun executive claimed that when a member of the panel walked in for a pre-consultation with Shanghvi just before the interview, he apparently said, 'I would prefer a Sun person. Not because I dislike the TDPL guys, but a Sun person knows how the Sun system works. I cannot have two races within one company. They have to stand integrated, and a Sun person can be trusted to imbibe our culture in the new people.'

In the process, few revered as 'brilliant assets' in the industry slipped off Sun's fold. One of them, Dr Nadamuni, whom Dadha regards as one of the 'sharpest scientific minds' in the country during his times, retired soon after. 'He was the brain behind all the great research products, mainly oncology products. A top Sun's R&D person had been rejected by Nadamuni in a Chennai job interview. So there could have been complex relationship with the two working together there,' Dadha remembered. He recalled bumping into Cipla chief Yusuf Hamied at a seminar a year after the merger and being asked, 'Where is Dr Nadamuni now? He was one of the top ten research scientists we had. Why did Sun Pharma ask him to retire?'

'Ask Dilip-bhai about that,' is all Dadha could manage. In fact, Nadamuni continues to work with the lesser-known Hyderabad-based Gland Pharmaceuticals, which showcases him as having developed over twenty oncology drugs, and working closely with globally celebrated scientist A.J. Birch.

But what the story goes to bring forth is that with the exception of Shanghvi (whom some people referred to as Gangotri—the source) Sun Pharma has never been a story of individual brilliance, but a cultivation of a culture of continuous collective efficiency.

That one who worked selflessly in pursuit of one mission, born in the mind of the founder blended noiselessly into the phenomenon called Sun. It explains at one level, what many observed as the biggest mystery of Sun: 'When you meet their managers, as individual professionals they pale in comparison to their peers in some other companies. But collectively they outshine them by miles.'

A former aide of Shanghvi offered a clue in the form of an insight that he attributed to Shanghvi: his philosophy is 90 per cent of legwork and 10 per cent of thinking at the MR level. 'I don't want everyone to think and mess up the psychology of the company. Let me think, I could be right or wrong. In the last 7–8 years, it has worked for me. In the managerial hierarchy, as you go up, brainwork should go up and legwork should come down,' Shanghvi was quoted to be saying by his aide.

If this description holds merit in its creation and Sun works as a well-oiled machine comparable to the human body, there is only one mind; not a difficult guess where that source of creation is.

While many were being asked to leave, the one person who was wooed by Shanghvi was his counterpart, the mind of TDPL, Dadha. He was appointed a whole-time director on the board of Sun, a strategy that his former adviser Kikani dubbed 'a master stroke'.

'Having Mr Dadha on the board was an absolutely brilliant way of covering his risk by making the owner—who was a man with a lineage of half a century in pharma and business, with well-oiled networks in government—answerable for whatever could have gone wrong during the process of acquisition. The merger was Dilip-bhai's first institution of learning the nuances of integration and he couldn't afford to fail there. Behind all his major decisions, there is always such unobvious de-risking strategies,' Kikani felt.

Lanka's guess born out his memory of that time suggested that at a share swap ratio of one share of Sun for every four shares of TDPL, the investments had been recovered by Sun in just weeks. Dadha was also very clear that Sun had made a fortune on the deal, but called it their good fate and nothing to crib about. 'There had been great R&D products in TDPL. Most important were the land and properties, which valued today would be nothing less than ₹500 crore. TDPL shareholders got Sun Pharma shares, but all put together, I think, it wasn't even 5 per cent of Sun's paid-up capital at that time [it was 3 per cent],' Dadha reckoned.

Years later, after the 2015 AGM, at a party hosted at the very aesthetic home of board member Hasmukh Shah in Baroda, Dadha would joke, 'Sudhir-bhai, you should have become the finance minister of India.'

Usually board members at Sun do not socialize, and on the rare occasions they do, it is generally an all-vegetarian formal affair—with Keki Mistry, Hasmukh Shah and Dadha limiting themselves to few pegs at Grand Maratha, and Dadha claiming his 30 per cent hoteliers' discount for their team of eight and joking with Valia, 'Sudhir-bhai, you don't have to pay for me.'

Sharp intelligence and hunger for knowledge aside, Dadha believed it is Shanghvi's *'punya'*, that ensures that whatever he touches turns into gold. When Dadha got out of the 2015 AGM venue in Baroda, Shanghvi's BMW was parked right ahead of Dadha's Innova. He walked up to Dadha and offered, *'Aap isme jaaiye, mein Innova mein aata hun.'* Dadha smiled back, 'I prefer a high-seat car, sunken seats don't suit me,' thinking to himself—a lot hasn't changed about him still.

Milmet: The Union and the Reunion

Scientist S. Bhowmick had been striding up and down at the sterile facility where Milmet made its drugs, waiting for Shanghvi and his design engineer to turn up. The most pressingly urgent assignment on his mind over the last few days had been to grab a clean-room garment the size of Shanghvi who wouldn't fit into the large-sized ones available easily. Plus, he was bracing himself for questions queuing up, having once encountered Shanghvi's inquiring mind earlier.

That was a few years back, when he had been freshly discovered by Girish Desai, who was scouting Jadavpur University for talent to back the R&D of his company in Baroda. Shanghvi, once aware that Bhowmick's PhD had been in anticonvulsants, struck up a conversation, quizzing him on sodium valporate, medications used for anti-epilepsy and bipolar disorder. Once the dialogue went beyond the realm of pharmacological properties, Bhowmick, astonished, asked him how he knew so much. 'I must know the pharmacological properties and behaviour of the molecules I am selling. It's my job to know it well enough to explain to my MRs, make presentations for them, so that they can brief the doctors with clarity,' Shanghvi had explained.

Bhowmick found out that the two friends had started off as stockists in Calcutta together and ended up as pharma manufacturers, Girish Desai specializing in sterile space, mainly injectables, and Shanghvi in tablets and capsules.

So it was beyond him, as he waited in the corridor that day, to understand why Shanghvi was so keen to understand the design of a blower employed when his business related to solid dosage, not sterile drugs. Shanghvi surprised him even before he shot questions, for he had arrived alone, with no design engineer by his side.

Here, Bhowmick for the first time realized that in his personal capacity, Shanghvi was also flirting with a sterile facility, named Unimed Technologies, where they had designed an air flow system that was failing some tests. So he was here to pick where they were going wrong with the technology of throwing air parallelly and purifying it in layers. Bhowmick along with a Milmet engineer took him inside, where Shanghvi got a few parts open and took notes of the design, after a tech-jargon-loaded chat with the engineer.

A few years later, in 1997, Sailesh Desai, now leading Milmet, received a call with an unanticipated pitch from Shanghvi—'Sailesh, why don't you buy out Unimed?'

'What? Why? Come again,' Desai started.

The three years gone by since he formally parted with Sun had been arduous, but filled with the satisfaction of having done it himself, of having taken a challenge and surpassing his expectations by turning a fledgling company around, of having proved to his closest friend, as well as to his own self, that he was capable—independent of him.

It had seemed a long journey from the day he had taken over Milmet with its ₹25 lakh annual sales and ₹12 lakh loss amid red flags from his state FDA friends, who had warned him not to touch that company. Even before Sailesh Desai came on board, Girish Desai had built great relations with a network of ophthalmologists, working all by himself, taking Bhowmick on his scooter to the specialists' clinics in the evening, taking cudgels of the marketing army on his solitary shoulders. But now, his efforts were translating into results as he had the support of the same well-knit team that had helped create Sun in its initial days—Upen-bhai taking care of finance and administration, Nitin Mehta looking after distribution and Sailesh Desai, almost all things else and of the steering wheel.

One of the first things Sailesh Desai did at Milmet was to clean up the mess on the finance side.

And in the first year itself, the sales soared to ₹70 lakh at Milmet. Desai turned to his Sun Pharma notebook and applied the rules from thereon; changed the drug packaging, making it slicker; energized the team, forcing them to invest and participate in national conferences to create visibility of the brand. 'Branding and visibility are important in this business. Once the brand presence is felt, people talk to you. That's plain psychology,' Sailesh Desai said. A year on, Shyamal Ghosh, having left Sun but still friendly with Desai told him, 'Sailesh-bhai, you will need a good manager. I will introduce you to Lokesh Sibal who is with Sarabhai but is looking for a job.'

In his interview, Desai asked Sibal, 'How much value can you create in a year?'

Sibal projected, 'We can take sales from ₹2 crore to ₹2.5 crore.'

'That will happen even if you are not in the picture. I am looking at ₹5 crore. And we will make it happen. You just sit next to me and do as I say. Any doubts, question me. You are the professional, I am not.' Managers, the very few hired, were offered their existing salaries and incentives on targets, Sun style.

Bhowmick recalled that quite like Sun, Milmet strived to stand out by doing 'first times in India' in its space. 'Ophthalmic solutions used to come in glass bottles; we launched it in pre-filled syringes and three-piece bottles, which saved doctors the time and trouble,' Bhowmick recounted.

He recalled, how the two Desais—Sailesh and Girish—despite Milmet being such a small outfit, managed to get rare and new APIs, which he initially made into drugs in lab, manually—sometimes in batches as tiny as 5 to 10 litres. Girish Desai recalled how his robust relations with ophthalmologists helped. He would tag along with them as their family in conferences to save the registration cost of a few hundred dollars in international seminars.

They—Desai and Sibal—couldn't do ₹5 crore that year as aimed, but doubled sales to ₹4 crore, and at the end of four years—Milmet had sales of ₹10 crore with a neat profit margin of ₹2 crore. Milmet on a smaller scale, was on its way to become to ophthalmologists, what once Sun was to psychiatrists.

And then, out of the blue, came a call from Shanghvi late that night pitching Unimed. It was not as if they had been out of touch. In fact, they used to have lunches on Sundays, but Desai somehow hadn't seen this coming.

'Dilip is very intelligent and he advised that we at Milmet are on a growth path and it is time we had a facility of our own instead of getting our products contract–manufactured, and hence we should buy out Unimed,' he recalled.

The part of the story that was clear to Desai at the time was that by selling Unimed, he was trying to help his friends, but help himself a bit more. 'I understood that part—Unimed was a white elephant. He was struggling with it, losing money there, so he wanted to sell it. At the same time it was true that we needed a facility,' Desai said, adding that there still was a very big part of the story he totally missed which would unravel in near future.

'The company is very expensive, Dilip. I cannot shell out ₹4 crore just now to invest,' he recalled telling Shanghvi.

'Don't you worry about money. We will sort that out later,' Shanghvi assured.

'No, that wouldn't do. I am the major shareholder, all right. But there are others who would be part of this deal. I have to speak to Girish, and the two investors—Nitin and Upen-bhai,' Desai responded. He said Milmet needed a manufacturing facility and he was clear about that. 'I didn't have money. If I don't buy, I may have a problem, if I buy, my partners may be unhappy and they don't have that kind of money to spare,' Desai recollected the dilemma he was in.

And then Shanghvi had an idea, one of his non-zero-sum deals. 'Sailesh, let's make it a 50:50 venture. You own half of it and I own the rest. That dilutes your risk, in fact the risk is shared with me,' Shanghvi suggested. They settled on this plan. Desai couldn't explain his decision to his partners through the lens of their friendship, but he persuaded them, bringing out the rationale. 'We need to do this. At least our temporary problems are taken care of for a year or so. And then we cross the bridge when we get there,' he told them. This deal remained off the papers, sealed and signed only on trust.

Desai went on to clear things at Unimed, at least make sure that they were not losing money. It gave Milmet the leverage to launch more first-time-in-India drugs. Bhowmick recalled bringing brands like 'Viscomet', a drug that enhanced the success rate of cataract operations by offering the surgeon manoeuvring space while placing the lens in the eye, leaving the retina untouched. The drug turned into a super hit overnight.

Girish Desai made Bhowmick sit behind his scooter and rode to the medical college library attached to Maharaja Sayaji Rao University to scour the journals there. Girish Desai himself recalled how he read through the medical journals. Once while heading home from the library on his scooter, Girish Desai turned around to ask Bhowmick, 'Why don't you go to National Library in Delhi. They would surely have a richer collection of medical journals.' So Bhowmick complied. He used to take the night train from Baroda to Delhi, freshen up at the railway station and head to the library. 'No question of the hotel. The whole day I would study and take photocopies of journals, and then take the night train from Delhi to Baroda. From one of these journals, I developed Viscomet,' Bhowmick recalled.

He then wrote a letter to the inventor-professor in Europe, describing how he had cracked the drug after reading his article in a journal and whether he would be kind enough to check whether he had got it right.

Two-and-a-half months passed before he received a response. Then communication ensued, with the inventor seeking samples, Bhowmick sending twenty vials; and four months later, the inventor writing back that the product looked excellent.

This letter of endorsement became the marketing tool that Girish Desai employed, making copies of it, giving it to all his MRs to show to ophthalmologists. In a weakly regulated country like India, a letter from a faraway unheard-of inventor worked as a stronger stamp of credibility for the community of ophthalmologists against an approval from the drug regulator. Once Shanghvi's tie-up on Unimed happened, Sun became a great source of all sorts of help for Milmet. When Milmet was about to launch the pre-filled syringe in India, Shanghvi guided Bhowmick to register it globally, in some markets such as US as a medical device. He directed the Sun marketing team to help them as well.

'Sun Pharma had become this big brother for us, a vast resource base, whom we could bank upon when we got stuck. So if we didn't know who a great artist was to design our promotional material, we called Sun. And Dilip-bhai made it very clear, "I am OK with this, you should develop the capacity to take benefits from us,"' Girish Desai recalled. Another non-zero-sum deal by Shanghvi. By 1999, Milmet was established as a success story in the niche space of eye specialists.

And here the part of the story that Sailesh Desai thought he had missed out started unravelling itself. Some friends saw Milan Metals (Milmet) as Shanghvi's moral balancing act; others saw it simply as an opportunity in ophthalmology that he spotted and snapped up. How you saw it depended on where you stood.

A year after Unimed had happened, sometime in 1998, Shanghvi asked Desai, 'Sailesh, why can't we merge?'

'Merge? What do you mean by merge? Explain.'

'Let's fix up a price and swap (shares).'

Taking a moment to take it in, Desai weighed the proposal: 'Let me understand this properly,' he said with a deep breath. It was true that he had begun to fret about expansion of Milmet, feeling that soon they would saturate the ophthalmology market and he would have to venture into other specialities, including maybe in areas where Sun was present.

'I had considered raising capital and foraying into other specialities and I would have gone that way if Dilip hadn't popped the proposal in the nick of time,' Desai said. But he was sure that the merger had been part of Shanghvi's mental blueprint right from the time he had pitched Unimed to be taken over by Milmet. 'I can guarantee that merger was on his mind from the moment he had offered to sell Unimed. Only he didn't reveal that part, till he thought it was the right time to do so. That was the part of the story I couldn't see then,' Desai said, adding, 'but by that time, I had made a success out of Milmet, and the challenge I had taken to prove to Dilip that I can do everything on my own had been accomplished and off my mind.'

About Milmet, Shanghvi said, 'They had reached a size, where their ability to take it to the next level was constrained. Sailesh used to come to me for help and because I was making some of those products, I could see that they are paying a lot more. So I told them, "Why don't we buy this business?" They were open and we agreed on a price. I told them, "Don't take all money in cash, take part of it in Sun Pharma shares."' Asked whether friendship was playing a part in this deal, he took a moment and said, 'Subconsciously, I thought if they are successful, I would be happy.'

In a different context talking of the principal ethics that he had practised, Shanghvi had said, 'From a very young age I have always had a strong kind of a psychological position that I will not take unnecessary obligation from anybody, and if somebody does something for me and I have an opportunity, I will find a way to give much more back to him, so that he shouldn't feel that he has been taken advantage of. I try not to keep any obligation on myself and I am not afraid of asking help. I ask for help from everybody, but I find a way to pay back.'

Desai thought through the proposal and sat to discuss with other partners, asking them to put forth their concerns, opening with: 'Ultimately you possess either Milmet shares or Sun's shares. Sun's shares you can sell in the market, so you can cash out and exit if you do not wish to continue under Sun. Milmet being private, shares can't be traded in the market.'

Sailesh said Girish jumped at the idea. 'My family, being in business for generations, understood that all of what I was doing couldn't be done alone. If partnership can make the business bigger, go for it. Also both in 1993 and 1998, my family felt: "Don't say no to Lakshmi, if she is coming home." Besides, I was thinking, these 200 people in my company will become much bigger and more secure than I can make them, so I said, "Go for it."'

For Nitin Mehta and Upen-bhai, it was more a matter of clarity, which they sought.

Upen-bhai saw the valuation and buying out of Milmet as a fair market deal. 'We all had by the time started working on our own. So there was no urgency to sell off Milmet. But Milmet was now in the same growing phase, in need of funds, that Sun was, say, a decade before. Beyond a point, you would have needed funds for expansion, and we were constrained by that. So a view was taken that if we give away the company at this stage, we get decent money, and shares of Sun—reflecting the growth of the company over time—probably it would work out well for everyone.'

'Sailesh-bhai and Dilip-bhai had a great rapport and the way things were going in pharma industry, Sailesh-bhai thought it was best to merge. My trust in my friends is total and it means they can commit anything on my behalf, without consulting me,' Nitin said.

In Sailesh Desai's mind as well, the question of friendship became paramount again. 'I thought if I don't take this up, I might lose what is most important to me—my friendship with Dilip. If I don't accept this and eventually raise money, there rises a scenario where the risk is all mine. If I fail to make a bigger success happen, I will lose my other close friends. At this point, at least the ₹15 lakh they had invested four years back is yielding ₹3 crore. They couldn't hope for better returns on their investment. If I do not take this offer, I stood the risk of losing my friends on both sides, and my friends are my only assets, I wouldn't trade for anything,' Desai said.

A former top Sun executive with a ringside view perceived this story as the Sun cycle repeating itself in Milmet. 'Sailesh-bhai gave Dilip-bhai Milmet for the same reasons because of which Dilip-bhai had to severe his partnership five years back. Just like Dilip-bhai's partners had been no match in his growth story beyond one point, Sailesh-bhai had reached a point where he was smarter than all the rest put together. He knew that it was because of him that the company got created; it was because of him that value was being added. But beyond a point, friendship becomes a limitation in fuelling future growth. So Milmet was Sun being replayed minus maybe a little bitterness, because this time around, everyone was gaining.'

A close friend who had seen through the emotional turmoil the friends had gone through their departure from Sun seemed sure that it was Shanghvi's way of paying back and reuniting with his friends. 'There was one moment when Dilip put everything on line—his friendship, his relationships. He risked everything for Sun. Assume for a moment if his business bets had failed, he would have lost everything—business and relationships. That's why I feel Dilip deserved every bit of the success he achieved,' he felt.

Asked whether it didn't hurt to let his entrepreneurial venture lose itself like a tributary in Sun, Desai promptly answered, 'Where had I learnt from whatever I had learnt? From him [Dilip]. Outside, friends and families don't understand why we are so close, some are even jealous. How much ever I fight with him, I have always been emotional about Dilip from day one. And my friendship was one of the top reasons I decided to merge.'

From 1998 onwards, Shyamal Ghosh, Rajesh Kumar and a few others from the former Sun team joined Sailesh Desai's Milmet, fully aware that they were joining the future Sun. There was free flow of people, some walking out of Sun to work at Milmet, and at times the reverse. For many employees at Sun and the industry, who were not privy to what had transpired—that Milmet had been committed to Sun—this sight was baffling. Many Sun employees testified to this seamless exchange between two companies which they failed to make sense of then. As the papers for the merger were being readied, one day Shanghvi casually asked Desai, 'Sailesh, why don't you join the Sun board?'

When the news of merger was finally broken, many at Milmet didn't take it well. Desai had a hard time convincing some of those full of doubts. 'Many of them had apprehensions that they will lose their freedom and would have to report to people equivalent or junior to them at Sun,' Sailesh Desai said. He made those with doubt sit around and explained, 'You have to take calculated risks in life. You are driving a Maruti today, and you are being given a chance to be in an Audi, you can rev up your speed.' Most agreed to give it a chance, some left. Girish Desai, who was not being offered a board position by Shanghvi recalled trying to encourage them as well: 'Listen, I am marrying into a bigger family. If I am getting married, I must have given it good thought. Please come as my dowry and become part of a bigger story.' Girish Desai would join Sun as head of its international marketing for a few years.

And then, Sailesh Desai recalled pre-conditioning Shanghvi 'You cannot ask anyone to leave, not even workers. You have to take them into some factory of yours.' Then Desai made out a case for some of his key managers to be absorbed at higher responsibilities, for instance, Sibal was to be given charge of Sun Division, which had seen negative growth, and was in shambles.

In 1999, Milmet merged with Sun. And here came the power of the bridge, that allows you to glide over from one side to the other, and then back. Sailesh Desai joined the Sun board. While most at Sun rejoiced this, a tiny fraction—mainly those who had joined the firm after Desai's departure—called the Milmet merger and its managers assuming senior positions in the company 'the return of Sailesh-bhai and his lobby'. But this had been one of the smoothest blends in the history of Sun's M&As, as friendly a conquest as it could get.

Long after, the two friends continued to squabble over trivial things and yet understand each other in profound ways. During his run at Milmet, Desai recalled running to Shanghvi for advice. 'I did everything on my own, but I trusted his business sense. And he at times gave me grand visionary advice that I was certain he himself wouldn't do, given how conservative he was with spending. How could I do it when I didn't even have the money, when he didn't do it despite having money?' Desai recalled.

This quibble continued over their holidays. Arvind Valia gave a sample. Once while vacationing in Europe Sailesh Desai's wife Mira asked him to call Anisha, their daughter who had married and settled in Cambodia. Desai replied, 'It's damn expensive. You can always wait for a few days till we get back.' Shanghvi butted in, 'Sailesh, it's just a call your wife is asking for?' Sailesh countered: 'An international call at my level of wealth is similar to a thousand luxuries that you deny yourself at your level of wealth.'

Shanghvi makes it a point to be present at all of Desai's extended family functions. 'He was in the US, from where he was to fly to Malaysia and land in Bombay, his schedule was that crazy. The next day my nephew was to get married in Calcutta. He called in for a detailed programme. I said, "Vibha is here, you don't need to come." He told me, "Stop all this, that's not your problem, that's my problem, you just send in the programme. And there he was, after such hectic travel, he had made it.'

And yet again in 2006, Sailesh Desai's mother passed away in Baroda, and forty of his family members had gathered for the last rites. Shanghvi called in to say he wanted to be present, if he could make the rites happen a day late.

'I decided I couldn't make forty people wait for him, so I told him not to come.'

The next day he called again to say he and Sudhir-bhai were coming.

Desai said, 'Now, why are you coming. Don't waste time. No need for you to come all this way.'

'Are you sure?'

'When *I am* telling you, there is no need, whom do you want to hear it from?'

Strange are the ways of friendship, and its exchanges—the punches, and the pecks.

Hitesh Sheth said there was a time, he knew of every shirt that 'Dilip' bought, now he has no whiff of the number of companies his friend buys. 'It's a different matter that the number of companies "Dilip" owns today is way more than the number of shirts he owned in Calcutta.'

The merger of Milmet into Sun had been more than a union of companies—it had heralded a reunion of the friends. Allowing a pinch of mush and symbolic sentimentality into the picture, it had been as if Shanghvi opened up his arms, and the friends walked back into the embrace.

'Milmet might have been a trigger. But even without it time irons out these creases. I think without Milmet also, possibly, relations would have healed,' Upen-bhai felt.

'I have never considered any of them my partners from my heart. They are my friends, so at times to keep that friendship intact, I have become their partner. Yesterday, today, anyday I would give up the business relationship for the sake of friendship. I have let the bygones be bygones, to keep what is most important alive—the friendship,' Nitin Mehta pronounced.

'For us to be able to re-establish that relationship we have today which is wholesome, it is their greatness than mine. Because they have gone through pain, I haven't,' Shanghvi said.

And then, it restarted—the vacations together all over again, a ship that had sailed on the sea of time in Goa resumed its journey. An innocuous message on mobile to join, and a yes from Shanghvi in 2001. Since then, the friendship has explored deserts, icy mountains, exotic beaches, dense forests every year. What is amusing is just as in their childhood days at Mathur Tea Stall, it is still Dutch that they prefer. 'From day one, it was Dutch. We still do Dutch. We divide the total expense by five, and everyone would give their share of $2000 or $3000 a trip. Of the five couples, one would be in charge of managing it. He would spend it on all of us. On our way back, if something is left over, it is distributed equally and if more is needed, everyone pitches in. Before we land in Bombay, accounts are clear. That keeps things simple,' Sailesh-bhai narrated.

But why wouldn't the friends allow the wealthiest one to treat them to holidays? Desai innocently wonders, 'But he doesn't let us pay for him. How can we let him pay for us?' Now into their sixties, when they speak of each other—not only Desai, but Mehta, Sheth, Butta—they were more boys than men, every time. Warm and wonderful—this tonic of friendship, and the boys in their sixties.

CHAPTER FOURTEEN

A SUNNY CAFE, A NON-SCIENTIST CHEF

No one burst out laughing that day in the R&D meeting when Shanghvi suggested a call to a batasha-wala in Baroda, and made him explain to his team of scientists how he prepared his white, rounded, sugar-drop candies. It was a way of life for them.

Serious-faced scientists jotted notes as the amused batasha wala detailed them in Gujarati how he brought the sugar water to boil and froth, used his special circular filter disc to pour it all quick on a clean cloth as his co-worker scraped the solid hollow sweetened drops.

Questions in the room dug deeper into the making of that circular disc filter, and pens scribbled faster the design of equipment that could prove key to the subject they were deliberating—techniques to make a tablet that dissolves in the mouth. 'Batasha—the moment you place it on your tongue it starts dissolving,' Shanghvi had said in that meeting. 'Obviously we were to use salt, not sugar but many times Dilip-bhai's brainwaves around a completely unrelated process help us grasp the principles behind the fundamental mechanism we are trying to set in motion,' S. Bhowmick, a top scientist at Sun, remarked.

Hiren Desai recounted a similar instance that has made it to the Sun folklore where Shanghvi apparently rang up a jalebi-wala of Calcutta from a meeting once and made him cite the recipe for the spiral, syrupy, saffron sweet. Head of R&D, Rajamannar, could perfectly relate to the event, 'My guess is they could be thinking up an idea to segregate uniform-sized particles. Just like the jalebi-wala uses a cloth as a medium to filter, Mr Shanghvi might be discussing the use of a plasma membrane to retain nano-sized particles.'

People who assume that product development meetings for yellow and pale pink tablets must evoke an unpleasant bitter taste, may find it amusing that at Sun, the scientists' senses are routinely activated with the secret of sweet recipes which is another passion of Shanghvi outside of medicine. Shanghvi routinely pulls out metaphors and analogies from his culinary library and kitchen racks in R&D meetings to make his point understood.

'Just yesterday, when Dr Bhowmick was explaining steps of a new development process for a drug in a linear fashion, Mr Shanghvi interjected: "What you are suggesting is to invite ten people to home and make the same food for each one separately. The first three steps in the process are common with any drug development, so those can be done along with others instead of being carried out separately,"' Rajamannar said.

The uncanny visceral link between drug and diet lab and kitchen, bitter and sweet at Sun, becomes sharper when one learns about the passion with which Shanghvi went about discovering gaps in the Indian market to zero in on new drugs he wanted to launch and chose to call it of all things the 'cafeteria approach'.

Between 1996 and 2006, Sun assumed India as its universe, and role-played a drug innovator in that space, not by discovering new drugs but bringing in hundreds of new drugs that were unavailable in India. This helped Shanghvi accelerate the number of Sun's drug launches, of which roughly a third were new drugs that had remained hitherto inaccessible to Indian doctors and patients.

Of Shanghvi's love for new drugs and the way he combined it with his other love—food, no one probably knew more than Ganorkar, his assistant in hand-picking the basket of new products. Ganorkar, better known in Sun circle by his first name Kirti realized that Shanghvi was untrained in science but dived deep into two spaces—products and R&D, his first love, and marketing, his second.

'Dilip-bhai told me, "Sun is a growth story and growth came from two sources, products and people. We have to master these, the right products and the people who can deliver,"' recalled Kirti. Others contested the order of love but agreed on the components: Shanghvi is all about products and marketing.

On one of his first days in Sun, Shanghvi unravelled his plans to Kirti—Sun was launching three to four products every year till 1995, and he wished to make that basket bigger, much bigger. 'We are clocking ₹80 crore sales and next year we want to touch ₹100 crore,' Shanghvi spelt out.

Kirti butted in, saying, 'And we could aim for ₹200 crore the next year.' A micro-pause from Shanghvi; usual for him, but new for the observer. 'Right now, just focus on getting to that ₹100 crore mark. That will give us the critical mass to do every other thing we want to do,' he continued. What he didn't tell at the time was that Sun was bracing itself for a quantum leap in product launches, from four to forty per year, over the next two to three years.

Conceiving in the Cafeteria

Kirti took over from Mira Desai in 1996, who had until then multi-tasked as Shanghvi's executive assistant in all departments. The next 6–7 years got intensely busy for Kirti where the high point was a special rendezvous with Shanghvi. About twice a month, they nearly locked themselves up for the whole day, at times stretching to two days, in a room at the old, small Ville Parle office, away from the main office so as not to be disturbed and distracted, engaging in an exercise that would build him and Sun.

Those special days, early in the morning, Kirti would pile up medical journals, books and pharmacopoeias (official publications containing a list of medicinal drugs with their effects and directions for use. These also mention the proportions which, for a drug, means chemical compositions.) one atop another in the trunk of his blue Maruti 800 and drive to the old Vile Parle office. There, the two of them, Shanghvi and Kirti sitting across the table like pre-exam students, pored over every page, discussed the merits and demerits of every product they came across in the therapy verticals Sun was present in or was planning to enter, topping the experience with Kanchipuram idlis ordered from Ram Krishna Restaurant for lunch.

'Dilip-bhai called it the cafeteria approach. His philosophy was that if I go to a cardiologist, whatever he prescribed must be part of my offering. We wanted our menu card to be complete for each category of therapy specialists we were working with—psychiatrists, neurologists, cardiologists and later diabetologists and gastroenterologists,' Kirti said.

That meant not leaving out even minor drugs with inconsequential market sizes—₹5 to 10 lakh for the company—like Tetrabenazine, indicated for Parkinson's disease in India in the late 1990s. Its sales, Kirti recalled, wasn't worth more than a few lakh of rupees, but Shanghvi, on several occasions, worked on the premise that if he offered the specialist the smaller molecules others are reluctant to launch for commercial reasons, his customer would register that and remember the company. And that goodwill was bound to show up in other prescriptions of his. 'When a doctor treats a thousand patients what problems are at the top of his mind are the few patients whom he couldn't treat because of unavailability of medicines. It was a decision we took despite fully knowing that those drugs were more likely to be unprofitable. We decided that we will not look at profitability while identifying individual products. When the doctor realizes what you are doing in the interest of patients that others are reluctant to do, they make up,' Shanghvi said.

He often did this—exhorted his people to do the right-seeming thing and spell out then, why it made for a great strategy. Vivek Hattangadi had pointed out a similar instance while launching the drug Mesacof, where Shanghvi insisted that MRs must be up front in bringing up the side effect of the drug, which he thought, apart from being the right thing to do, would also form an impression of the company being honest in the doctor's mind. This worked, boardrooms of peer pharma companies were confounded by one striking fact: Sun managing to figure twenty times in the same prescription of the individual specialists.

Building up that all-inclusive exhaustive therapy lists meant Kirti's job profile included trips to doctors' clinics and endless discussions with them on what drugs they were prescribing. Then correlate it with data from C-Marc, the prescription audit and market research agency that collected prescriptions and gleaned useful data for the industry. 'For us the names of the drugs doctors were prescribing were more important than how much they sold. Scanning thousands of prescriptions yielded a list running into tens of drugs in a therapy. Of that, I would segregate what we had in the market—say, five of them, what we had under development, say, five more and what was missing, say, ten.' This he discussed with Shanghvi who continued to engage with top medical specialists over breakfast and lunches.

The other technique of the Vile Parle brainstorming session was for them to study the obscenely obese *Merck Manual* running over 3000 pages (world's oldest bestselling English medical textbook for a physician's desk reference). Shanghvi and Kirti would pick one practice for a day, for instance gastro, and then go through the obscure-sounding diseases, for instance, Wilson's disease, which basically meant excessive copper deposition in the liver and the brain. Neither had spotted the disease name in the reams of prescriptions they were perusing. Some of those diseases didn't even strike the gastroenterologists when Kirti discussed molecules with them.

It would then figure as an interesting subject of research for Shanghvi, and the two made a list of the symptoms associated with this disease. This list came handy to Kirti as he went about asking the doctors whether they had seen patients betraying this group of symptoms.

The doctors in many cases were surprised that there was a drug available for such a disease. Sometimes, they thought hard and nodded— Oh yes, patients with matching symptoms visited once in 5–6 months or that they had been asking such a patient to import a drug with the help of Royal Chemists. Yet at other times Kirti went quizzing about one disease but returned with requests from doctors to launch another drug for a different untreated disease.

'The idea was not simply to take our products to the physicians but work backwards to see the unmet need of patients and identify drugs to fill these gaps,' he said.

When the Vile Parle brainstorming wasn't sufficient, Shanghvi continued his sessions on train with Kirti, particularly on Baroda Express and later, after 2004, on the 5.30 a.m. flight to Baroda, the sessions spilling over to breakfast—nice, subtly sweet vegetarian Gujarati breakfast—at Shanghvi's home before catching the R&D meeting, which usually began at 9 a.m. The exercise went on for a decade undocumented on mail or paper.

At most, Kirti from time to time found a page photocopied or torn off from the journal *Scrip* on his table, with 'discuss' scribbled in Shanghvi's handwriting. 'There never was any time or need to do things in writing,' Kirti quipped. Shanghvi was seen reading in office most of the time he was not taking meetings or entertaining visitors, and what he studied were journals such as *Scrip* and *Advances in Medical Sciences*. One of his senior employees claimed that he read three hours a day, and another claimed that he read those medical and trade journals to bed.

His cabin in Baroda was lined with books—mostly medical and trade journals. He was familiar with writings of American trade journalists, and once surprised Indian pharma journalist Vikas Dandekar with a request to meet one of his US counterparts.

'It's not so much what he reads, but how he relates it to business and applies it in our country's context that has made our portfolio such a huge hit. He would keep a real-time tab on launches in the US and then figure out which of those products fitted into our gastro- or cardio-related franchises in India,' Kirti explained. Shanghvi said what he read, he read trying to place it in the context of a bigger puzzle, figuring out what current problems can be solved with that knowledge. It was from him that Kirti learnt that everything one needed to know was out there in the universe; all you had to do was to access it by creating the right pathway.

Kirti conceded that identifying new drugs many times for Sun was a bit like spotting what the US drug regulator calls an orphan-drug opportunity (a medicine that remains undeveloped or uncommercialized because its market is small and unprofitable for pharmaceutical companies). Pricing these drugs was always a challenge in India. 'In the US or other regulated markets, companies can sell the same medicines as orphan drugs where they can charge high premiums to bring a product that wouldn't have been in the market but for them. Not in India where most of the medical expenditure is out of pocket. It is not feasible to charge that kind of premium because the patient will not be able to afford that medication,' Shanghvi said.

The traditional approach for other large pharma companies had been to look at the retail market data, mark out top ten molecules in a highly fragmented market and chase some of them, depending on which therapeutic categories they planned to be present in. 'Unlike other firms, we never started from the retail market. Our starting point was the question: What does the cardiologist need and not what is already a bestseller in the market?' Kirti explained how Sun's products were never market-driven but market-driving.

Somewhere Shanghvi had realized that the therapy specialists were swiftly overtaking the general physicians in prescriptions. That India's drug market was at the cusp of a change, was a fact not everyone could fathom. The neighbourhood family doctor was fast becoming a figure of past in India. Sun's fast growth in psychiatry and neurology also had its roots in grasping and applying this insight.

By the time, Sun revved up its product launches, therapy divisions were already in place and it had started commanding a premium in the minds of specialists. They felt this company had created an exclusive band of boys to serve them which made them feel special and on top of that the company was even launching products with their specific feedback, Milan Sinha exclaimed. Even before exhausting the American and European directories—Sun's initial inspiration for new drugs not available in India—Shanghvi expanded his search horizon to Japan and South Korea (2000 to 2005). Orange Book that lists approved products in the US has its counterpart in Japan, which Kirti started digging into as a source for new drugs for the Indian market next. 'We would hire translators; sit with them to decode some of the hidden gems in Japan. There are some awesome innovators in Japan, who don't bother to file patents in India,' Kirti revealed. So these unpatented drugs became Sun's next basket to choose from. The exercises yielded an average of forty drugs every year, creating a portfolio of 400 drugs over the next ten years that Sun marketed in India.

Honeymoon with APIs

It must not have been so simple as it was made to sound, for every new drug, small or big, when added, imposed complexity on the organization, from procuring the API or the basic raw material to manufacturing it to successfully marketing it. 'Execution was the key, and it had to be more than flawless. It had to be cost-efficient,' Kirti said. Raw materials for such new drugs were not readily available in Indian markets most of the time. So, Kirti flew to locations mainly in Europe, where API exhibitions are held, haggled for price and quietly collected as many brochures he could.

'I was constantly on call telling Dilip-bhai about the API and their prices. And we were unabashed in bargaining with the agents. If the lowest price is $25, I would at least negotiate for $24.5,' Kirti laughed. Once back from his API-related recces, Kirti would repeat his drive to Vile Parle, and spread all his assorted collection of brochures on the table like a lavish breakfast buffet before Shanghvi arrived. A sumptuous discussion on medicine raw materials later, the source of API was fixed, and application made for drug regulator's approval, pronto.

From that point, till Sun's product hit the market, things seemed to have moved and fast forward. But even before the first patient tasted the Sun medicine, its chemists had been flagged off—crack the API in-house and make it quick. 'The immediate goal was to launch instantly, but the medium-term goal was to achieve self-sufficiency because the ultimate goal was to keep the profitability going,' Kirti explained.

Age of Smart Drugs

'Don't compare apples with pumpkins without grasping our strategy,' Shyamal Ghosh always said, always, because he couldn't invent a brand new answer every time a new analyst from a different brokerage firm asked him the same old question. 'But you don't have a single mega-brand, not a single blockbuster, on the shelf with over ₹100 crore sales. No Corex. No Phensydryl. No Becosule.'

'But how big is big? We have more number of blockbusters than any other company, only we measure it differently. We may not have a Corex, because we are not in the general race. Our story is in marketshare. Just dive deep into the neuropsychiatry market which itself is small today, and realize that we are the market leader in so many categories with 50 to 60 per cent market share, that's big. It's different because today those drugs make up the ₹5–10 crore market, but we are building the market,' Ghosh explained.

Sometime in 1993, soon after the R&D centre was set-up, Shanghvi asked Rajamannar to crack the 'Peptide' segment. It was an 'elephant on the table' moment for a scientist who had freshly crossed over from academia to industry and in internal meetings Rajamannar had said the challenges his chief put on the table were elephantine, 'not just any elephant but as if Ganesha was there on your table'. Shanghvi often based his choice of drugs by correlating knowledge gleaned from his strong ties with specialists to information from international journals.

'Forget about having a programme in peptides, I don't think 90 per cent of the Indian pharma industry had heard or thought of it then,'

Rajamannar said. Nothing happened there except struggle for the next five years. 'That set of drug needed to be handled, stored, analysed differently,' Rajamannar recalled. 'Not only uniquely specialized R&D, it needed a different manufacturing skill set as well to handle the complexity,' Kirti said.

Shanghvi went about hunting for scientists overseas who could teach Sun the science of peptides. 'We ferreted around the world then to discern how peptides were made. Even in the US, Indian chemists were brilliant in small and synthetic molecules but not so great, when it came to peptides. Then Dilip-bhai discovered a senior scientist named Nishith Chaturvedi, a peptide specialist who wished to return to India for personal reasons,' Kirti recalled. Sun created a lab for him to operate in around 1995.

When Shanghvi was exploring new frontiers, such as peptides, he said lack of the country's regulatory strength to vet new drugs posed a big challenge. 'When you make a cutting-edge product, it's important that the regulatory mechanism is capable enough to catch you if you are getting it wrong or are short of standards somewhere. But our regulatory mechanism hadn't evolved to the level that they could check if your product is not of global quality, and that was a challenge. In short, we have been our own regulator. Ultimately, any product we market, I should be confident that I can give it to a family member. Ultimately, it is about building credibility with the doctor. A doctor trusts us when he actually has the option to prescribe the MNC drug instead of ours,' Shanghvi said.

Finally, after years of struggle Sun succeeded in making a milligram of peptide. 'We were thrilled and Mr Shanghvi was so excited to have a team, undoubtedly the first in India to have cracked peptides,' Rajamannar said. Jubilations aside, Shanghvi pronounced, 'I need 10 grams.' The scientist flinched, 'Sir, I can only make 1 milligram.' Making a little substance for research purpose is not the same as making enough to launch it in the market for commercial consumption. 'But that's how you convert science into business. We will have to find ways to make it on industrial scale,' Shanghvi added.

This way, that way, a few nods and several shakings of the head later, Sun did win the Peptide Olympic in India in the 1990s, and the R&D team returned to inform Shanghvi that they had the technology to make 10 grams after all. 'You had a product, you had a technology. But to hit the market, you needed to establish quality and tackle competition which doesn't always mean only routing out other players,' Rajamannar said.

'We can make it for ₹20 per milligram,' declared the scientist, when Shanghvi asked for the cost. This sent Shanghvi into flash calculation mode and he arrived at a product cost of ₹200. But I need the product for ₹10, he announced to a gasping audience.

Scientists came back with a winning smile, having cracked the cost code only to be greeted by Shanghvi with another challenge of cutting the sixty-day cycle for producing 10 grams of peptide. 'Today, we make that product for 50 paise. From 50 grams in sixty days in the 1990s, today we make 2.5 kg in fifteen days. We are also one of the largest peptide manufacturers in the country and make about thirty products in that category,' Rajamannar said. By 2000, when other Indian players were waking up to the opportunity of peptide, we already had a range of products, including octreotide, desmopressin and leuprolide, Kirti said.

It was not only the industry that proved to be a late starter in opportunities, Shanghvi sniffed. On occasions, like in case of Octride, even people around him couldn't sense how vast that market could be. 'We never expected Octride to be a big drug but trusted Dilip-bhai's gut more than our judgement,' a candid Shyamal Ghosh confessed.

It was a drug useful for a condition that, according to records, claimed the life of India's 'biscuit baron' Rajan Pillai while in custody at Tihar Jail, an event that led to what the country dubs 'jail reforms'. The former Britannia part-owner had fled Singapore as its government charged him with fraud. In India he was arrested in Delhi at hotel Le Meridien, in a predawn seizure in July 1995, where he had checked in under a pseudonym. Next morning his lawyer pleaded he was severely ill suffering from cirrhosis of liver. In want of medical attention, Pillai died in custody a few days later of a complication of advanced cirrhosis of the liver. The jail's resident doctor informed Deen Dayal Upadhyaya Hospital that the patient was 'a known alcoholic'. Like the rest of the country, folks at Sun debated the case, but not to solve the mystery that shrouded Pillai's death.

This was the exact condition Shanghvi had told people around him that he was targeting through octreotide. What Shanghvi was not targeting were wealthy jailed tycoons but hundreds of villagers and small-town alcoholics who consume gallons of country liquor. It was for this drug that Sun adopted a marketing strategy to arrange for for specialists in gastroenterology to travel to smaller centres for lectures to general physicians.

'Mr Shanghvi doesn't allow himself to stop getting better. At no milestone, small or big, he would pause and breathe. Before the accomplishment has sunk into us, he is already moving on to the next. Just like when we had cracked peptides, it was about doing more in less cost; when we got there, it was about doing more in lesser time. Similarly, when we had cracked neuropsychiatry, we were already moving on to chronic therapies, and once we got a sense of having mastered exclusive therapies in a way no other company had, he wanted to crack a variety of modified dosage forms—instant release, sustained release, controlled release and other technologies. These technologies gave us an edge over rivals,' Rajamannar said.

While this rate of breathless improvisation left many professionals simultaneously overwhelmed and energized, Shanghvi was driving a similar exercise in different departments, at times in different dimensions of the same department, all at once.

Once the practice of identifying new drugs was established, Shanghvi laser-beamed on small incremental innovations that could arm his company's products with features that were different and useful to patients or doctors, compared to existing versions in the market. An analogy with phones, would help grasp the concept better: what Shanghvi was vying to launch were features-loaded smart-drugs. 'New technologies in drugs have always been an area of deep interest,' Shanghvi said. So Sun worked on turning four times-a-day drug dosage to once daily which promised higher patient compliance, and delved into questions such as whether an injection be can turned into an oral product increasing the convenience of use. It didn't matter that Sun was bringing many of those drugs to India for the first time; it still wanted to be differently better, even if marginally so, compared to the original in the market.

That was also Shanghvi's way of bringing research orientation into his company, which had thrived thus far by reverse-engineering drugs discovered elsewhere, condescendingly dubbed 'Me-too' drugs by Western innovator companies. This was once more proving in a fundamental way that Shanghvi was more than a great cloner. He never stopped at what he had learnt, his offering was always more and often better than the sum of what he had received from others.

This also meant that slowly but steadily through the 1990s, Shanghvi was orchestrating a quiet shift in strategy. From searching and basing his business in spaces no one was doing, he began to attempt business in spaces his peers found hard to copy. 'I think the fundamental approach doesn't change—it is about how we do things that allow us to be in zones of relatively low competitive intensity. There are drugs that are difficult to sell to doctors and there are drugs that are difficult to make. We try to get into spaces where we are doing both—drugs that are difficult to make as well as sell. In business, we have always preferred rooms less crowded, but these are also rooms which are difficult to enter,' Shanghvi said.

Christening New Medicines

Sun found its trademark Webster wordsmith in Kirti, who named new brands like he would christen his own babies. 'I would generally pen down five to ten names, and even as I wrote them down, I knew the one I would be rushing to trademark office for registration with, just in case someone else had thought up the same name,' Kirti revealed.

He recalled how instantly he had fallen in love with Pantocid, for pantoprazole, or Octride for octreotide. Sun used to dash the chosen names to an agency in Delhi, Indmark (founded by Naukri.com founder Sanjeev Bikhchandani), a Google of sorts for trademarks that would scan its database to check whether that brand name was still up for grabs. The agency's normal search took a week but for drugs Sun was hoping to launch first, it paid six times more for its urgent search to get the same job done in twenty-four hours.

Launching its brand first in the market became Sun's USP from 1995 to 2006. Kirti called the Sun juggernaut a perfectly synchronized relay race, where every link had been taught to anticipate the next move and prepare to seamlessly blend with it.

Much of the cross-functional relationship is years of rehearsal, most perfected yet again in that service station called new product meetings presided by Shanghvi. Kirti, who drafted the agenda for monthly meetings and dashed it across to R&D, manufacturing, project management, quality, and marketing divisions, didn't recall missing more than one meeting in his twenty years at Sun. Ditto for Rajamannar.

Part of the agenda was planning forward for each drug awaiting launch, and each step that took it to the market. 'These meetings have been sacrosanct, not only for us, even for Dilip-bhai,' Kirti felt. When meetings clashed Shanghvi would say, 'Let's do it through the night on the scheduled day.'

And so the meetings at times began at 9 p.m. and stretched beyond 2 a.m. till crows had started rioting on the trees outside. Inside the hall in the Sun Pharma Advance Research Company (SPARC's) Baroda office, midway through, people struggled to keep their eyes open and mouth shut. 'Others were yawning but Dilip-bhai was his usual calm self, as if it was two o'clock in the day, sharply questioning us on every aspect of the product, keeping rigour of his review unaffected,' Kirti recalled.

He believed such gestures, when your owner–managing director sat through the night to complete his work for the day, besides moving the Sun juggernaut forward, instilled a deep message in the psyche of everyone involved, that delaying today's work for tomorrow was so 'un-Sun'.

Even when the meetings were not starting so late, people were working late into the night. Kirti declared that when his family calls, he knows it must be past 9.30, time to wrap up for the day. The oft-repeated adage in Sun is: No one sees the Sun set at Sun.

In the meeting, every process was broken down to the last detail, including chores such as whether aluminium foil for packaging had to arrive the day before and if it hadn't, calls were made from the meeting spot with the packaging in-charge chatting with the supplier in front of Shanghvi, sending his men across to the site and giving a live update to his super boss. For those first-time launches Dilip-bhai took stock every five minutes, he was clued into every detail including who was driving the person carrying the bulk drugs to the facilities,' Kirti said.

Kirti recreated the atmosphere at such a meeting, indicating that unlike other companies where gaps of resources and people could mean tenders, vacancies, approvals, advertisements, and more protocols, here the owner knew the company, each machine, its people like the back of his hand, an advantage of having created everything from scratch. That incredible show of how well he knew his stuff—his company, his plant—played out almost in all review and new product meetings.

These meetings were also the platform where the tension between commercial or business development teams which lived by the motto 'Do more with less' and the R&D teams which explored chemistry to deliver to humanity was stretched to the limit. 'The scientists were pushed to deliver in shrunk time with fewer resources,' Kirti said.

Rajamannar thought that review meetings served as a reality check for the scientists—their bridge to the real world and the market.

Many a times, it was Shanghvi who played that role in review meetings waking scientists up to instil in them the realization that science is not the end in itself. It was his typical way of training his managers by instructing not only what to do, but why should it be done. This happened not only in research, but all other departments—mostly product and marketing. He believed that if the 'why' is asked and explained, eventually managers understood how he would have acted in that situation.

A research analyst once, for instance, claimed he needed two hours to complete each analysis. Shanghvi played out the big picture before him, by correlating it to what else but the kitchen. 'When you are home, you can take your own sweet time to cook and to serve your dishes in leisure. But if it's a restaurant setting, you have to serve the customer in forty-five minutes. That or let thirty return from your doorsteps. We must find a way to release the report in forty-five minutes, either through automation or employing more technicians.'

At other times Shanghvi attempted end-to-end calculations in seconds and asked scientists: 'So, would you have paid ₹300 for a tablet of diabetes which you have to take twice daily? For a life-threatening disease, maybe, but for a chronic disorder, would you? Or following your process, I can make 1 gram in a month, which means a few thousand tablets in a month, which means a few hundred people can access it. Of what use is it in a country with millions of diabetics?'

Still at, other times, when the scientist went gaga over a breakthrough, he simply waited. After his signature pause, he would say, 'Okay, bring it on.' When the scientist presented the tablet he was so proud of, the 1000 mg dosage not there in the market today, Shanghvi took the scientist's solitaire in his hands, rotated it and smiled, 'It is so huge, its sight gives you a scare. Can you gulp it without thinking once?'

And then he would go on to explain, 'I cannot go to the market and say, "See, Sun Pharma has made it, so please have it." It has to be the other way around. The product must have useful features compelling enough for the doctor and the patient. We can have an extraordinary technology science-wise, but if people don't like it because of size, price or whatever feature, it's of no value to anyone.'

And despite fishing out the gaps, fitting in the right products, the 'perfectly synced relay race', if something flopped, it's not all sighs in the next review meeting. '"The last agenda in our new product meetings was standard, what went wrong?" Or, "We held two such dedicated sessions in a year. There we openly discussed our failures and the lessons we learnt from them." Dilip-bhai always allowed us at Sun to make mistakes because he believed, if that wasn't allowed, people would rather not take any decision. At Sun, a wrong decision was better than no decision,' Kirti said. What was frowned upon was making the same mistakes again. A good number of long-timers at Sun seem to have stuck around believing that many rival firms do not create room for mistakes, pushing people to mislead and cover-up, in the process almost incentivizing dishonesty.

This set of value-unloaded stocktaking of flops and failures meant that Sun had been creating market intelligence uniquely relevant to its journey. Kirti, who leads business development, used to coding files of market intelligence in his mind, not in PowerPoint presentations, still finds it a bit odd to have an entire department dedicated to market research.

Till about 2014, Kirti claimed, Sun relied 100 per cent on 'market intelligence' generated in-house, and hadn't bought a single market intelligence report barring the standard IMS data, prompting a frustrated kid from Datamonitor to whine, 'Sir, you are a multi-billion-dollar company and you can't even shell out ₹5000 for my report.'

Brand Them Up

Of course, introducing a perennially running stream of new products added to the brand image in the eyes of the customers—as a company right at the leading edge of science. A large number of specialists in chronic therapies who started their practice in India of the 1990s associate Sun with 'new drugs'.

Every new product, particularly those Sun was bringing for the first time in the country, allowed its field force to make an assertive claim over the busy mind space of the doctor in a meaningful manner. 'Otherwise, you keep talking of the same products over and over again. Doctors don't have time to engage with you and they lose interest. So every new product is an opportunity to engage with the doctor,' Kirti said. To the extent possible, Sun's marketing inputs were designed to mimic the behaviour of an innovator—by briefing every little positive and negative points of the drug to the doctor, given it would be the first time that the drug was to be used on Indian population. In their mind, India was their universe, and Sun the pioneer of that therapy.

It's true Sun went after limited competition products, which meant that in many categories it still had chances of succeeding without conventional branding efforts. And being acutely cost conscious in its infancy may have deterred it from investing in optical branding exercises. This changed in the late 1990s.

Lanka, the celebrated mastermind behind big brands like Combiflam and Taxim recalled once narrating to Shanghvi over their daily lunches on how he had built their brands. 'Combiflam could have easily done with a three-inch strip but a six-inch strip was designed to keep the font bolder that could prompt better recall among doctors. I invested more in packaging only to get more value. I think we are obsessing way too much over tiny pack sizes to control cost at Sun, and, in the process, unwittingly not realizing our full market value.' A few hours later when he stepped into Shanghvi's cabin, the sight before him made him break into a spontaneous smile. Shanghvi had neatly laid before him, about 100 packs of different medicines, jotting down ideas to change packs of a set of OTC (over-the-counter) products.

Being the first to hit the market, many of Sun's products were operating in a default Hatch-Waxman-like setting in India. Hatch Waxman is the US law that bestows upon the first generic drug a window of six months during which it can be sold exclusively (besides the usually expensive patented original) allowing it to earn a windfall profit in a duopoly. India has no such law, but therapy focus in a few niche areas, mixed with general prescribing tendencies, created a similar incentive for Sun, for its first-time launches. 'Specialists have a peculiar tendency to stick to writing one product. They are resistant to change. Like all other habits, prescribing habits also die hard. So Sun strived desperately to be the first one to bring a new drug to the market and enjoy what we call internally establishing the brand in the customer's pen,' Mira Desai, Shanghvi's first executive assistant, said.

Hitting the market first might have started off as a sound strategy, particularly at a time when Sun was both competing, learning from and striving to race past Torrent's products, but the strategy in process had turned into passion, that passion funnelled into a collective obsession for Sun to generate that first, second and third prescription. This strategy also served as one of the few windows that showed through a glimpse of Shanghvi's unapologetic streak of aggression.

'Anything could be made to happen to make our brand hit the market first. People could be flown with raw material from one city to the facility; executives quickly despatched to bring packaging material right from the source; shifts ran round the clock in the factories for weeks till the supply chain was streamlined; office boys doubled up as courier agents and left with stocks in trains and flights to stockists and chemists across major cities to make a first-time launch successful,' Kirti explained.

Several times Kirti and his team didn't even wait for the regulatory approval to print the packages, so that they could steal a few hours from the run up to the launch, only to realize that the regulator had made changes in what was to be printed on the label. Kirti then rushed to the printer again, redoing the plates, dashing with the packaging material to the man waiting at the airport, who was to carry it to their facility in Gujarat. 'Dilip-bhai would keep calling us every five minutes to check the status: Where has this man reached? Who is picking him up from the airport?' Kirti recalled.

The hysteria of drug debuts is imprinted on everyone's mind who worked at Sun of the 1990s. Just before the launch of Distensil (suxamethonium chloride) in early 1990s, Shyamal Ghosh recalled his boss, Yakob, with whom he famously didn't get along, asked him whether he could launch it in seven days straight. Attuned to Sun's new launch calendar, he promptly said yes. Next, Yakob said, 'We should do something different, maybe shoot a film to mark the release.'

'But where is the time?' Ghosh exclaimed. But the next moment he recalled calling up, pleading his motley group of friends from advertising. By evening he was heading off to Juhu beach, zooming in on a fluttering fly perched atop golgappa, the protagonist of the movie, hoping it proved the perfect model for a product targeting to relax distension in stomach.

Other times, to make sure that Sun is the first company to launch a drug, Shanghvi could make exceptions to his own rules of a 'perfectly synchronized relay race' even if it created ticklish situations and intra-company rivalry. He gave two division heads the task of launching the same drug—different brands.

'In part, it would up the chances of us hitting the market first. In part, such a strategy would also heighten the noise level for competitors like Torrent, which would have to unpredictably tackle two competition products instead of one. I guess he created the internal competition to kill the external competition,' Sinha said. 'It upset people at times, even doctors could play one representative against another but it made sure that as a company we had more market share than Torrent or other rivals,' Ghosh added.

This fanatic bout of frenzy accompanied most first-time launches, particularly when a competition was also on way to launch. How Shanghvi revved up his aggressive streak was also apparent in ways he could raise the pitch of marketing at the very last minute to steal the show from under a competitor's nose.

The launch of clozapine popped up as one classic example in many veterans' mind. In the late 1990s, when Sun was already peaking in launching new drugs in the country, Shyamal Ghosh and T.K. Roy were preparing one late evening for what was deemed as the much-awaited drug among psychiatrists—clozapine, used for schizophrenia that does not improve with other antipsychotic medications.

At about 9 p.m., when the office was nearly empty, Ghosh's phone buzzed. It was his regional manager from Bombay, Upen Asha. 'Sir, we have information that Sandoz is flying in medical experts from Switzerland to talk on the drug in a high-profile symposia in twenty-two cities across the country.' Sandoz was the mother company that had invented the original research product clozapine, and it didn't come as a surprise that it was planning the launch with fanfare.

'Can you find out the list of dates and cities Sandoz is planning to hold these events?' Ghosh asked and rushed to Shanghvi's cabin.

'Beat them on speed. We have to ensure that we hold our symposia at least three days in advance in all twenty-two places they have planned,' was Shanghvi's firm instruction.

Ghosh returned to his table to stare at Sandoz's entire symposia schedule, faxed by his resourceful manager. He picked up the receiver and started making calls to his regional managers in all twenty-two cities listed in that schedule. 'We have to do these symposia seven days before Sandoz's date. You will have every support from the head office. Start booking hotels tonight.'

Symposia are soirees where companies officially announce to the doctors the new drug they have brought to the market and so remain an integral event in new drug launches. In this case, Sun managed to beat Sandoz in twenty-one of the twenty-two cities.

'It was a coup. Sandoz was completely taken aback by the speed of our events. By the time multinationals conducted four events, we completed thirty,' Roy recalled. 'Specialists usually have no time to attend more than one event per drug, and once they had turned up for ours, they would have no incentive to show up for Sandoz's or in other cases. This is exactly what happened and their events turned into no-shows with weak turnouts,' Ghosh recalled, citing the example of Hyderabad, where out of a total of forty-eight psychiatrists, Sun's event had a draw of forty-five, while Sandoz's event attracted only eight. 'Their launch was half-hearted after our grand show and eventually they had to withdraw the product, partly because they were selling at an exorbitant price,' Ghosh added.

He singled out the symposia at National Institute of Mental Health and Neuro Sciences (NIMHANS), Bangalore, where he was addressing about 125 specialists. One of them shot a question, 'Sandoz is giving a scheme where if this drug causes the side effect of agranulocytosis (lowering of white blood cells), it will give the next drug to address that condition for free. Do you have a similar programme?'

'Clozapine is Sandoz's research product. They are married to that drug, we are not. We are committed to our patients. As of today, this is the most effective drug, so we have brought this, tomorrow, if a new and better drug is invented for this condition, we will bring that. Today, they are charging four times of what we are, only promising to take care of a side effect that affects one in every 10,000 patients. I would say the money that our patients will be saving, they can easily afford their drug for side effects plus a bag of their favourite candies,' Ghosh recalled telling the gathering.

The company which shied away from revelries and celebrations made an exception when it came to a launch; then Sun declared war. The head office tracked such launches real-time—which doctor is writing what prescriptions. MRs spread across rushed to fax photocopies of their first prescriptions to head office, and called up to scream, 'Sir, the first sale has happened at such-and-such chemists.' Even when it wasn't worth a few hundred rupees, the frenzy around it was unimaginable, just short of popping the champagne cork.

Shanghvi's Non-Scientist Cap

However, what truly sets Shanghvi apart is his ability to draw the big picture on the canvas and yet paint details simultaneously. The first dot on that canvas usually began with the idea of bringing a new drug into India, followed by an immersion with the R&D team on what it would take.

But it is this puzzling piece on how he chats, guides and plans with scientists that remains the biggest mystery. It doesn't pass the understanding of most how a man with no background in science relates to the development of a drug, the reason scientists surrounding him call it a 'divine blessing' or a 'gift' or simply an 'unsolved equation'. And if he is truly so good without training, why has he not invented a drug yet?

What is simplistically believed outside is that he stands on the cusp of the binary of science and commerce. Shanghvi claims he doesn't know how he does it. He feels he was born with a gift he cannot explain with logic—to effortlessly record complex-sounding chemical names of countless medicines and the diseases they were meant for, at an early age. 'I say it's innate because it happened with an ease almost natural and I am not gifted the same way in all departments. For instance, I don't get electronics as easily. I tried learning software. I got the concepts, the logic, but I couldn't do coding despite trying my hand at it,' he reasoned.

Shanghvi believes he doesn't grasp chemistry like scientists do, an admission his top two scientists back, but many of his other colleagues with technical backgrounds flatly dispute. 'He might not be writing chemical equations, if that's what you call being a scientist. But he is enough of a scientist to call a bluff, or challenge and guide scientists in their own technical fields,' Bharati Nadkarni, intellectual property head at Sun said. She recounted an occasion when he had summoned a presentation on biologicals. He called up Sudhir Valia to join the show, explaining to him how biologicals are the future of drugs.

From his questions to the experts and his explanation in Gujarati to Valia about all that was on the screen and all that was not, Bharati inferred that he didn't really need the biology education gig. When she walked up to ask, how he knew it all, he smiled, 'Actually, I had read Aalok's (son) class XII biology book cover to cover.'

But as a matter of fact, medicines happened to him only by an accident of birth and his curiosity found an outlet in an immediate stimuli, his father's shop—a wholesaler of drugs. What if his father hadn't been in the business of selling medicines?

'If my father had been a mechanic, I am absolutely certain Dilip-bhai would have owned the largest auto company in the country. It is his ability to apply himself to an area that enables him to innovate in that space. But that space what it is today is purely accidental,' thought Jayant, his brother. Echoed Shanghvi's son Aalok, 'I don't have the slightest doubt that even if my father had dabbled in the fashion industry, he would have created the largest fashion house in the country.'

Legendary poet-lyricist Gulzar once described himself as the best trash-song writer because he had mastered the nonsense of rhyme, but that didn't mean his 'trash songs' are devoid of layers of meanings like his soulful classics. By any stretch of imagination Shanghvi has mastered the common-sense metre in science, and asks of his scientists what an unabashed intelligent child armed with oodles of logic but stripped of technical education would inquire. It is the deeply inquisitive child in him that comes alive when he is with his scientists.

Shanghvi who plays science by the maxim—'All things are simple when reduced to fundamentals'—was described by his R&D chief Rajamannar as possessing the 'best layperson aptitude' who had the kind of questions for scientists, which scientists themselves lose access to after immersing themselves in technicalities of science for too long— one reason why great scientists don't make great businessmen by rule. Once when a scientist was detailing a reaction that had to take place for twenty-four hours at 70 degrees, Shanghvi butted in: 'Can this be done at room temperature?' Had he been a scientist, he could have never popped such a question. A scientist is too immersed in the experience of making a bond, wondering how innovative it is, how different it is from existing ones, but Shanghvi is simultaneously processing multiple dimensions: efficiency, minimal energy investment, maximum output, quality, cost and, most importantly, common sense and fundamentals,' Rajamannar reeled off.

And it is this strong sense of fundamentals that makes it near-impossible for scientists to fool him, even though in a soiree of scientists, Shanghvi almost always prefixes his insights with, 'I might be wrong but . . .' Rajamannar cited an example. A scientist was claiming to have cracked a new 'breakthrough' therapy for asthma and was making a presentation for establishing the exact biological pathway his therapy would follow to address the disorder.

Post-presentation, Shanghvi asked him mildly, 'For last 3–4 decades, there is only one class of drugs used in asthma that is steroids. A steroid does not follow a particular biological mechanism; it controls six to seven biological mechanisms. The existing knowledge about asthma says that people may develop the condition due to different triggers: allergens, a protein malfunction, etc. How do you say that a single biological pathway is going to alleviate all sorts of asthma when the origin has not been established?' And then, he tossed out a challenge,

'Can you develop a safe steroid for asthma, one without its side effects? A steroid that is potent at the site but becomes a non-steroid when it goes into circulation.' It was a big task, but Sun's scientists are at it.

Bhowmick, a fan of how Shanghvi correlates unrelated things, transferring knowledge from one aspect of life to another seamlessly, once told Sailesh Desai, 'Even if we had tens of these beautiful minds, humanity would look very different.' When Bhowmick was researching into technologies to remove sulphate for a class of drugs, Shanghvi sent him to Central Salt and Marine Research Institute, a CSIR (Council of Scientific and Industrial Research) arm in Bombay, to learn from their research in desalination—removing salt from water.

Over time Bhowmick has come to marvel at the beauty of the memory and the processor (Shanghvi's mind) that retains a database and connects dots without any buffering. And when he reduces them to fundamentals, it seems like 'the obvious that escaped you'. Not every such correlation is finally put to use, like the batasha technique for tablets that dissolve in the mouth. In fact, nine out ten such applications wouldn't yield any productive commercial end result, but many a time it could set one off in an uncharted direction.

If Kirti was Sun's API conference-trotter, Bhowmick was his counterpart for research and new technologies conferences. Once back, he used to be called for a detailed session with Shanghvi, often over car rides from Baroda to factories in Halol or Vapi. On one such occasion when Bhowmick briefed him on supercritical fluid technologies— used to control nano-particles to the desired size of microns—and its possibility to be used in inhalers, Shanghvi promptly compared it with commonly used spray-drying.

Such instances may be routine for Bhowmick's memory, but he cannot forget one of these—a golden moment of dot connection in Sun's history. That is when the team of scientists were struggling to make a generic of Johnson and Johnson's cancer drug (doxorubicin hydrochloride), the first nano-drug approved by US FDA. It used a liposomal technology and there were umpteen number of publications to suggest that an exact replica of a drug was not possible. Shanghvi tossed this challenge at Bhowmick in 2000, admitting that Sun didn't have the necessary skills, infrastructure or knowledge.

'Those days we were so cost-conscious that I felt reluctant to ask for even five grams of excipient that would cost us over five lakh rupees. But it was Dilip-bhai's involvement that made this project different.' For his pet projects Shanghvi parked himself in Baroda for days at a stretch. This was one of those and he had been at the Baroda centre for 3–4 days along with Kirti, brainstorming with the technical team about the steps in this drug development.

Bhowmick was facing an intractable idea block here. There are two layers in the structure of liposome. The drug needed to penetrate both and form a gel once in the core. It was the presence of sulphate ion in the space between the first and the second layer that was turning the drug to gel form and not allowing it to enter the core. So sulphate ion had to be removed from the space between the first and the second layer to make this technology workable. Shanghvi listened intently to the problem. Bhowmick knew Shanghvi's mind would now be working over this problem, through the nights as he sleeps on it. Shanghvi had told him so, 'I think about these problems in the night,' and then usually after a few days he came up with: 'Bhowmick, *aisa nahi ho sakta*?' This time, he suggested, 'Bhowmick, look at the dialysis process carefully. How are they treating patients with kidney failure? They remove all the ions from the blood externally and then pass them through the tube. Why don't we apply the same principle here?'

Bhowmick was stunned. Inside he knew Shanghvi had hit the right spot. Wasting no time, he bought a dialysis membrane or dialyser and it clicked. This helped Sun solve a complex problem no generic drug-firm in the world had. This would in turn open doors for Sun in the biggest and one of the toughest markets in the world beyond what Sun had imagined.

Bhowmick is fascinated by the way Shanghvi picks up seemingly ordinary people and builds them into managers and leaders. 'He actually shapes people the way he wants to. First he evaluates and identifies the person, for instance, he did so with Dr Rajamannar, who's heading R&D today. After that he would not only give the person opportunities but engage with him at every step in such a way that he can grow up to this position. All of us are also a product of similar engagements.'

But how does the process look? If you ask someone a straight question on how Shanghvi prepares his top managerial cadre, the range of responses may leave you more confused than clear. 'He trusts his people completely.' 'He exercises very high degree of control.' 'He allows you to experiment and be entrepreneurial.' 'He takes care of every detail and can be micro-managerial.' Abhay Gandhi demystifies the process that may seem contradictory on the face from the gleaned responses: 'In the beginning, he is instructional and will give you clear instructions about how things should be. Over a period of time, he gradually loosens the grip. Once he develops that confidence in your decision-making ability he will step back. He would still give you suggestions, saying, "If I were you, I would probably do it this way, but since you are the man on the field, yours is the final call."'

In the process, somewhere his top managers internalize how Shanghvi would behave in a certain setting, and the DNA of Sun gets built into their professional personalities. Funnily enough, this bit of genetic engineering of the thought process in work comes with its own unintended consequences. Someone has started talking a bit like him using more silence than words, someone has even begun resembling him in appearance, and someone else has picked up Shanghvi's signature pauses.

There was a time when people across functions invariably headed straight to Shanghvi with their mound of intractable problems, and he set about solving it tirelessly with enthusiasm.

In fact in 1999, when Shanghvi sat on the hot seat in an Johari-window exercise, Shyamal Ghosh used the opportunity to the fullest, teasing him, 'Dilip-bhai, you have the mother-in-law syndrome. Just like moms-in-law cannot get themselves to hand over the keys to daughters-in-law, you end up doing everything on your own. It's time you loosen up and trust your managers-in-law.'

With bigger domestic and international acquisitions the nimble organization turned into a behemoth. Shanghvi has changed since then, and he has been consciously trying to step aside, nudging people to solve their own problems. At times, when such problems crop up in meetings he is seen uttering, 'Please don't force me to become a scientist. I am not a scientist.'

This seems a long distance from 1998, when Shanghvi called in Rajamannar to tell, 'I think it's time we start drug discovery.'

'But, I don't know the ABC of drug discovery.'

'Who does in India today? Yet we must begin. Today we are successful because we are either first or different. Ten years from now, launching every drug first in India wouldn't be possible. You can't bank on making every product usefully different. What we have done today, people will catch up with tomorrow. Drug discovery entails a lot of risk but it is a path we must start to take now. Let's begin with what we have. We know chemistry, so a chemistry-intensive product should be our first target,' Shanghvi said. And so was sown the seed of yet another dream.

CHAPTER FIFTEEN

THE VAISHNAV, WHEN SOFT IS HARD

Yagnik peeped into Shanghvi's beige-hued, sparsely furnished, minimally done cabin to call him for a lecture by a speaker on *The Fifth Discipline*, a seminal work by MIT professor Peter Senge, a protégé of John Hopkins. He is credited with distilling management theories of a 'learning organization' by closely studying corporations like Ford, Chrysler, Shell, and Harley-Davidson through the 1970s and the '80s.

A 'learning leader' himself, who had by then harnessed the power of 'listening', a skill that came to him more naturally than speaking, Shanghvi sneaked into the Express Hotel conference room to attend it. He walked over to the last row and from there he heard the speaker extol the virtues of building a shared vision for the company, and focusing one's energy on it. The part that might have resonated with him most was how areas of highest leverage often remained least obvious, a philosophy Sun internalized in the 1990s.

After the lecture was over, when he was asked to speak a few lines, he softly declined. When senior executives insisted, people recalled him fidgeting with his watch and starting and concluding, all in one line, one that no one exactly remembered but something to the effect that he wanted the company to come together. It had finished and faded before they had directed their focus from front to back, and then Shanghvi let silence take over, that could be construed as awkward in a social or professional setting. Unlike most, silence doesn't embarrass Shanghvi, not even in a conversation. So he is in no rush to disrupt it.

And yet, almost a decade later in 2003–04, when Boston Consulting Group, a global consultancy firm was hired to study employee engagement within Sun, what it flagged as the most alarming revelation, according to Milan Sinha, was that across rank and file, from the CFO at the head office to the peon in Kerala's C&F agency, everyone in the company seemed to be working for only one man—Dilip Shanghvi.

This is a dangerous situation to be in for an organization, an executive recalled the consultancy telling the management.

But how did this bond generate, sustain and multiply itself if Shanghvi truly revelled in anonymity and privacy, not even addressing his people through a speech, never projecting an image consciously? 'Tom Peters may have theorized in his 1982 bestseller *In Search of Excellence*: 'Soft is Hard', but Dilip-bhai practised it. I never saw him squirm about share prices crashing, as much as fussing about people leaving the organization,' Yagnik said.

Shanghvi understood that relationship brought repeat business, and repeat business in chronic therapies was the key to higher and sustained profits. The cycle of caring to form a relationship began at the point how you treated your own team, the people who cared for your customers, because that would be reflected in their behaviour when they deal with the customers. 'You cannot run down, insult and abuse your MR and expect them to be gentle, serving and caring with the doctors,' a former Sun manager, who joined Ranbaxy later, said.

Creating a psychologically safe environment, where people could fearlessly report back their errors and the entire community could draw lessons from their experience was the kind of ecosystem Shanghvi strived to build.

Ashok Butta, a friend-turned-business-associate said that 'the cocoon of care Sun wove for its executives could turn so comforting, particularly in a harsh corporate environment outside turning neurotic by the day, that many times you were ready to surrender your personal ambitions and didn't venture out, even if you were being offered fatter pay packages, creamier perks and the promise of a slicker lifestyle.'

Dating in the Happy Hours

Sticky as a workplace Sun has most definitely been, but celebrated, not so much. It doesn't comfortably sit in the haloed lists of 'Best Places to Work For' that magazines compile annually. That is partly because of its image as a penny paymaster, an attribute that draws unflattering titles like 'lala company', 'baniya ki dukaan' from professionals who work with large multinationals and many of whom claimed to have turned down offers from Sun in the past. The irony is that, inside Sun they take the same tag with a pinch of pride, of being cost-efficient.

Bhagwat Yagnik, wearing a check shirt and black trousers, was waiting at the Towers of Maurya in Delhi, a soft melody playing in the background, but his eyes kept darting at his watch. It was ten minutes before the happy hours at the hotel ended, and the candidate from Ranbaxy he had to interview still hadn't arrived. Yagnik as the first HR head and official recruiter of Sun had scanned much of Ranbaxy, sitting at Maurya during its happy hours.

Those happy hours helped given 'the average appetite of north Indians', Sun's obsession to keep costs lean and Yagnik's intent to make the most of an exercise the candidate viewed as nothing more than an interview. Even though that by definition made it a test for the guy in question, it was Yagnik, who was going over the questions in his mind and thinking how best they could be posed. For him, these exchanges were much more than just assessing the strength and weaknesses of the person with whom he was sharing the table and savouring the chicken butter masala and tandoori naan.

The candidate was a doorway to understand the works of a much larger organization, a global firm. And his task, besides the obvious, was to glean from the conversation the best and worst of practices of large organizations, and then complete the ritual of discussing them with Shanghvi. For instance, from Ranbaxy, they consciously decided to not let one thing ever happen, for seniors to get abrasive with subordinates. A Hindi phrase that translated to 'first enjoy the kick of money, then the shoes' was an oft-used joke in Ranbaxy, to sum up their culture then.

Obviously, Yagnik had no way of knowing that a decade later, he would be heading the HR team at Ranbaxy, screening people for a company with a presence in 165 countries—a position from where Sun would seem a minnow.

Recalling his days at Sun, Yagnik said, 'Our interviews were much more than just checking the person's suitability for Sun. I called those sessions the X-ray scanning. It was a way to educate ourselves about how large companies, global in outlook and presence, are running their show, and in which way we wanted to be like them and which we didn't want to be like them.' The twin objective of interviews in Sun had not changed since the 1980s when Shanghvi interviewed candidates.

But if Sun was so cost-conscious, why was Yagnik granted a rare luxury to stay at Hotel Maurya? 'When a candidate from Ranbaxy, known in the industry for its lavish ways, is interviewed, Dilip-bhai made me stay at Maurya as we knew we would be judged by the place where we would be hosting the interviews. And for Ranbaxy executives, it couldn't be less than a decent five-star hotel, even if that meant walking over to the nearest dhaba to catch the next meal,' Yagnik said.

And for the job seekers who travelled all the way to Baroda, Yagnik said he almost dated the candidate. 'The idea was to create an experience for them which they would remember. So we got them picked up from the station or the airport, with the interesting and lively company of one of my juniors escorting them. It was the kind of treatment one would usually extend to a potential groom for one's daughter. Through the process, Yagnik wanted to project the warmth that Sun stood for and also make them psychologically comfortable for them to open up easily. We wanted each such candidate to become a good ambassador for our company, Yagnik said.

After a round of discussion, which Yagnik dubbed 'psychological probing', a junior gave the candidate company over coffee. Little did the candidate know what was happening next door. Yagnik would then walk over to Shanghvi's chamber, who in his typical wry humour would ask, 'Tell me Yagnik, *iski kundali mein kya hai*?' Yagnik, a topper in psychology then, would rattle off some psychological dimensions of the candidate, while the candidate, unaware of his horoscope being discussed in the next room, sipped coffee amidst friendly chat. And then, the candidate was escorted to meet Shanghvi.

Before a candidate walked in to join Sun, we made sure his survival kit—a stack of visiting cards, briefcase, stationeries and canteen vouchers—were placed on his table, so that he felt as if he already belonged here the moment he walked in, Yagnik recalled. Making people feel at home in a place like Baroda could mean attending to their homesickness in nanny mode at times. Yagnik recalled a Tamil-speaking IITian in R&D fretting endlessly about what his wife would do as she didn't speak the local language, didn't know the culture of the place. Yagnik recalled fitting in a television set, along with VCR at his place and filling the shelves with video tapes of popular Tamil movies.

However, showering such goodwill didn't mean that there was no chaos in hiring. As a matter of fact, chaos was the way of life at entrepreneurial Sun. And there were no facades to cover it when candidates appeared on the horizon.

Kirti Ganorkar had applied for an executive assistant's job to the CMD and was to meet Shanghvi at 9 a.m. 'They told me he was busy and the interview would happen post-lunch. Post-lunch they asked me to hang around till 6 p.m. At six, when it got rescheduled to 9 p.m., I told them I had a train to catch at 11 p.m.' Yagnik assured him that he would rebook his tickets if the need arose. But after his interview he remembered Yagnik packing him off in his self-driven Maruti 800 and zooming off on Baroda roads in top gear, to make it to the station on time, negotiating salary on the way. Kirti recalled, watching with a sense of wonder at the steering wheel, Yagnik's coordination, the balance he was striking between negotiating the traffic and salary all at once.

Comp and Ben, What's That?

The Maruti 800 Yagnik was driving was his first car, but it wasn't supposed to be his first. The car which should have been his first couldn't become so, because he did a Shanghvi with it. Just like Shanghvi had passed on his own car—a second-hand Premier Padmini to Raju as part of his salary package, Yagnik sacrificed his own while still in the waiting list for delivery of the Maruti 800. For Yagnik, it was more than just giving up a car; it was in many ways his last chance to show to his parents what he had made of his life.

Yagnik came from a well-to-do conservative Brahmin family. His father was a staunch believer of the Gita which espouses the philosophy of Karma. Once Yagnik had overheard his mother cajoling his father to help his son live a little materially better off. But his father, unwavering in his response and sticking to his Gita guns, had said, 'He will create his own and then enjoy.'

It was in this backdrop that Yagnik, already six-months long in the queue for a car, made this sacrifice to lure in a talent, who may have otherwise opted out. 'Dilip-bhai knew how proud my father and mother would have been to see that I have earned a car from my workplace. Dilip-bhai also wanted me to show to my parents that the company I worked for was taking good care of its employees. But I chose to give away that car for a talent the company needed so badly to recruit at that moment.' By the time his next car arrived, he had unfortunately lost both his parents who never got to see how far their son had made it. Yagnik was relishing and suffering his nostalgia simultaneously, proud of a sacrifice and despairing his loss.

Yagnik and his team pulled talent by offering them mainly the intangibles. 'We wanted the best people, but Dilip-bhai had clearly told us there was no money to sweeten offers. That was a paradox. How do you bring people then? By offering them a dream job, by offering them a responsibility they wouldn't find themselves assuming for the next three or four years in their organization, by asking them to take a leap of faith,' Yagnik said.

Shanghvi and Yagnik had an understanding that they didn't want people who worked only or primarily for money, so lower salaries many times acted as an effective filter for the kind of employee they were trying to attract.

But there were exceptions like the one at Park Sheraton, Madras. 'A bulk drug specialist' from Orchid Pharma quoted a figure that landed like a bomb on Yagnik—₹22 lakh per annum. He didn't know where to start negotiating. And yet he knew Sun wanted him because it had freshly acquired the bulk drug businesses in the late 1990s.

Yagnik began by admitting that Sun cannot match the quoted figure. But then as he updated Shanghvi with the phone pressed between his shoulders and ears, he recalled scribbling away the various parts of a salary that could look closest to expectation—creating milestone-linked packages. And then he offered him a 'job to die for'. This 'bulk drug specialist', who was looking after Russia in Orchid Chemicals, was offered a role of looking after global API, even when Sun hardly had a 'global presence' to boast of. 'You create markets for us' was what Yagnik dubbed as the clincher. Yagnik continued to design international pay packages with intuition and a dialogue with Shanghvi, without ever having seen one.

When Shanghvi ordained that Sun's warehouses should be the best in class, better than those of the top multinationals, Yagnik chased the man who was handling distribution at an American company convincing him on differential payment. 'On paper, I can commit this much. At the end of the year, if your performance matches your claims, you take the rest,' Yagnik recalled as saying to him.

He recalled countless such instances when rock-star performers agreed to join Sun by compromising on salaries. Yagnik came to realize, through his journey in Sun, that truly motivated professionals are in search of roles that can challenge them and the companies that can back them with resources to create something they deem valuable. And with that came another surprising realization that most such individuals are ready to compromise on money matters if they are given a platform to prove themselves.

It was much later in his career, when he was sitting at the grand global conference hosted by Mercer on 'Comp and Ben' that he realized the magnitude of innovations he and Shanghvi had managed in creating packages around compensation and benefits. 'In large companies, consultants were drawing these things up. At Sun, my team, Dilip-bhai and I had been acting consultants birthing many sub-disciplines of HR without realizing it for far too long,' Yagnik laughed. Much of that came out of their passion to not just learn the 'academic studies of HR' but 'practicals of talent hunting, organization building, life of business and business of life'.

At Sun, for instance, Yagnik developed an abiding zeal for studying design and structures of organizations. He claimed to have collected over 120 such designs of competing and other well-run companies, which he often discussed threadbare with Shanghvi. Often they played a game of chess of sorts by predicting how one significant move in the industry created a succession of other moves. 'We were 90 per cent accurate in such forecasts and we never treated competition as just competition. Those 120 structures became our subject of research and leaning,' Yagnik claimed. Sun used that precision of prediction to pre-empt and pull talent before others did.

Once Yagnik recalled encircling in a newspaper an advertisement of Ranbaxy that had sought applications to appoint an economist. This hadn't escaped Shanghvi either and the two tried guessing why Ranbaxy could be hiring economists. Was it planning to do some sort of projections for the expansion that were to happen? 'The way we constantly discussed Ranbaxy and argued about it, I doubt that even people inside Ranbaxy were discussing their company that much,' Yagnik recounted. But it was a passion to discuss personalities, profiles, companies and leaders for hours, and draw lessons from them.

Agile at Dawn

These discussions could happen anywhere, as Yagnik entered Shanghvi's cabin in the morning with a stack of papers, or when Dilip-bhai asked him to car meetings on his way to Vapi. Before dawn broke, driver Saleem honked and Yagnik tiptoed out of his apartment.

'Vibha bhabhi' kept their juice and breakfast ready at the wee hours of the morning. After they were done, Shanghvi slipped into the front seat of his Maruti Esteem, while Yagnik occupied the back seat. Saleem knew well how Shanghvi liked his drive, no halts—straight four hours to Vapi. The dawn chats began even before his duplex faded from the background.

Yagnik recalled Shanghvi discussing ways to make the medical representatives more effective once while they were on their way to Vapi. Are the other departments and functions sensitive enough to treat them as the arteries and veins of the business and responsive to their needs? Since Sun had sped up the number of product launches, the turnaround time of other functional departments had failed to keep up.

This basically meant that promotional material, visual aid and product samples that are vital to make a launch successful were not reaching the field staff on time. 'The point we were debating was that senior managers were not appreciating that MRs were not getting resources on time.' Why could Shanghvi get this in a blink but not others? For the same reason, why he could often remind his senior executives that sitting in an air-conditioned office, it was very easy to crib that people weren't efficient on ground and were failing in their strategies, an awareness he never let go of, having served as a medical representative himself. On that car ride, Shanghvi fine-tuned a proposal to resolve this.

Sun had already mastered the art of joint fieldwork wherein the line management—MR, area manager (first-line manager), regional manager (second-line manager), zonal manager (third-line manager), national sales managers, right up until the CMD—worked in the field to stay in touch with the ground and execute the strategies effectively. Now they decided to expand the concept calling it 'interface', which meant that functions with no obvious interface with the field, such as finance, purchase, bulk drugs, etc., must work in the field to understand their core business and be sensitized to the needs of the medical representative.

This is how Shanghvi had attained awareness, and he knew that once you experience someone's pain directly, you responded to it with a different alacrity; without experiencing hunger you wouldn't know the value of food. So at Sun they created a policy for top executives across functions to do compulsory four days of fieldwork in a month, with the medical representatives talking to them, visiting the stockists, doctors, warehouses and other distribution outlets.

Finance executives among others protested, 'What am I doing in the field except loitering and whiling away time?' And the HR head tried to convince, 'Bhai sahib, everyone must do this fieldwork to understand the customer and the business needs better. First-hand experience is the only way to achieve that,' Yagnik recollected.

Girish Desai felt that it was fourteen years of first-hand field experience that separated Shanghvi from his cabin-confined peers in the industry. 'Most pharma owners have made an attempt to understand the field through their managers, but Dilip-bhai's dependency on his managers is minimal because he has braved the crowd, sweat and dust himself and knows how it feels to sit outside a doctor's cabin for hours not knowing whether he would meet you today.'

This was one reason why Sun's 4000-odd medical representatives emerged as the undisputed leader and the single-most productive field force. In 2014, each of them brought business worth ₹93 lakh annually, more than double the industry average which hovered around ₹40 lakh. Attrition among its MRs also remained much lower than the industry average of 25 to 30 per cent, despite it not being among the best paymasters.

Asked about how Sun extracted great performances out of ordinary people, Shanghvi explained that the first step was to identify the right people for the right job. 'You want someone to lift 300 kg from here to there. During interviews, selectors usually judge that candidate successful who picks up 50 kg in his first attempt. What they miss is that the candidate who could only pick up 25 kg in his first attempt may be ready to make 10–15 rounds to complete the task, while the other candidate may not have the drive to do it more than twice. Usually, people judge you on the basis of your appearance of brightness, while we look for tenacity and persistence. Because we are not recruiting people to solve fundamental problems of science, we don't really need that kind of mind.'

During those car drives with Yagnik, there came a moment, maybe after a solution had been suggested, when Shanghvi relaxed by reclining the front seat and dosing off with abandon, his face now very close to Yagnik's. A sleepy Yagnik, who had also woken up at 4 a.m., glanced at his sleeping chief, his face acquiring the innocence of a child and struggled to keep his heavy eyelids from falling shut.

The Third Eye

And the same boss, who could sleep like a baby next to his deputies, could allow himself to transform into an uncharacteristic, inscrutable 'something' that people struggled to put a name to. Someone suggested 'ruthless', but backed out immediately, another uttered 'brutal' but hastily added 'not exactly'. A close approximation of what people might be hinting at came from a business associate who has worked with him for over two decades.

He called him a coconut inside out, a soft exterior with a tough interior. 'He has essentially been a boy's boy and knows how and when to flex his muscles. Only his muscles are like the third eye, only revealed, when the need arose.' A bit like his high-speed dexterous drives that very few people have experienced.

Uday Baldota, his executive assistant of that time, recalled sitting next to him with bated breath as Shanghvi zoomed his car at what felt like Schumacher speed, casually chatting business with him, and when a speed bump came, he applied the brakes, pushed Uday back with his left hand for his safety, steering the car with his right hand, all at once with ease without stopping the business conversation. The business associate mentioned above added that Shanghvi revealed his third eye in fights or negotiations only after he had exhausted all peaceful routes and, also, he could dare to do so because at the moment he was ready to risk losing all that he was bargaining for.

One such phase arose, when by the late 1990s, Sun had gone on to acquire many small companies, along with them a scale, a heft, people of many colours and complexities and union issues of types it had not dealt with. It was also the time the company was trying to find its feet in the north Indian states of Punjab and Haryana. Sun had its own share of industrial issues but none too big as the national-level boycotts seen by GSK or Ranbaxy, Shyamal Ghosh recalled. Part of this was because Sun never had its entire field force unionized, having never recognized unions.

Unlike many large companies, it never saw councils getting formed inside its company's workforce, which sat every three years to negotiate salaries. At least one reason for this could be consciously cultivated relations between superiors and subordinates. It was not just a spontaneous gesture when Ghosh sat on the grass fields outside a medical conference with all MRs and first-line managers, and shared the same packet lunch that had been ordered for everyone else. 'It was all by design to melt away barriers of hierarchy and encourage camaraderie' across ranks. But even if planned, these moments we shared didn't seem patronizing or posed,' Ghosh said. These were part of what Dilip-bhai wanted to go down as Sun values, he added.

Sun values might have mitigated the sharp edges of union issues to some extent, mostly because Ghosh believed the union leaders from his company had a soft corner for the organization. It could also be because two of the Sun's earliest and senior-most executives—Shanghvi himself and Nandkumar—were from West Bengal and Kerala respectively, the hotbeds of communism and understood unionism. 'At times, it was sheer insight and direction of Dilip-bhai. I recall there had been some sackings and transfers that had snowballed into a huge industrial relations issue. I was looking out of the window and there were maybe 250-odd people demonstrating, screaming slogans against Sun, jabbing fists and banners into the air,' Butta recalled.

The phone rang and it was Shanghvi. 'AB, I see the commotion and crowd. But who are these people? They are not from Sun, not our people. I see only a few familiar faces in that crowd. People who haven't worked in Sun wouldn't truly understand our language and we don't need to negotiate with them. We should agree to talk to only our people.'

Calcutta had seen quite a few such upheavals, particularly around pink slips and mass transfers. On one such occasion, a team that included T.K. Roy and Azadar Khan, then Sun's HR head, prepped up by Shanghvi, had been flown to start negotiations with 200 people. 'Listen, you are demanding that this person be given his job back. I have an offer. My HR head is here, so the guarantee is in presence of an authorized entity. We are ready to pay this guy's full salary, you get him a job in your company,' Roy recalled throwing this challenge to leaders who worked in multinationals. There were murmurs in the crowd, someone suggesting that it was an unrealistic offer.

'He spends all his office hours in the canteen, sipping tea, never goes out to meet any doctor. So let's say if he is able to tell which product figures on which page of the latest visual aid, which he is supposed to parrot out every day ten times to all customers, I will take him back,' Roy had said. There was no answer, and as Roy recalled, the crowd started thinning within the next fifteen minutes. Of course, the front negotiations were often supplemented with back-channel negotiations with political bosses, who held strings of these demonstrations. And more often than not, peace was bought by a compromise, reinstating some but not all.

In Kerala, when Sun faced difficulties in building its business, Shanghvi outsourced the marketing and distribution to a local with an understanding that the business would be taken back into Sun's hand once it is streamlined. This local continues to be Sun's C&F agent in the state.

Well, these bumps in West Bengal and Kerala, which had seemed thorny pricks in the life of Sun, seemed breezy affairs when the company entered Punjab and Haryana in 1998. All appeals to emotion, reason, personal warmth and ideology went to the winds. Punches, beaten up by hockey sticks and iron chains, and with blood oozing—the bhadraloks and bhais of Sun weren't at all prepared for this game; they just couldn't grasp its rules.

While Sun was still finding its way in these states, Roy was appointed national sales manager for the north. 'I was shocked. The attempts to open a dialogue failed. The union leaders would make you wait for hours and then turn up at their own sweet time, order orange juices, sip it menacingly and go back to beating up our boys and managers,' Roy, dubbing those efforts at 'talks' of no consequence, recalled.

Punjab and Haryana were important markets within the country and Sun couldn't simply ignore the business potential. But the company saw revolts within these states. Shanghvi mulled over it and formed a special crack team which had Roy, Sanjay Sabharwal, Milan Sinha and Azadar Khan among a few others. 'Dilip-bhai gave us a task and targets, asking us to arrange interesting cultural, soft programmes for key specialists in Punjab, Haryana and all the way up to Kashmir to deepen engagement with them, to reach their hearts,' Roy explained. Sun went about organizing friendly cricket matches, sewing competitions with senior specialists and their wives—stitching a flower on tablecloth, a master-chef contest where the wives judged their psychiatrist—cardiologists and dermatologist husbands turning out finger-licking *dahi bhalla*s to tongue-burning *chhole bhature*s.

These events helped Sun establish a deep connect with the medical community but its managers returned with unpleasant stories. 'Kerala and Bengal had been very different experiences. The leaders were CITU-dominated and could be tough negotiators, but they were reasonable, at least they seemed so when we faced Punjab,' Ghosh said. The hard-boiled Bengal and Kerala leaders, as another Sun executive explained, citing Amitabha Guha and J.S. Majumdar, were the kind who lived by some ideology. They remained medical representatives all their lives, didn't usually accept promotions, retired and transitioned into playing an active role in the politics of communist parties.

Parts of Punjab, Sun's executives alleged, were different as they were ruled by drug lords who enjoyed political patronage of a different kind. 'The medical representatives owned medicine shops in the name of their wives, sat there and wanted to take salaries. If you transferred them, they used their clout with politicians to create nuisance to jeopardize your business,' Ghosh said.

If you worked beyond 3.30 p.m., you would be dragged to the union office and thrashed badly, whined Sun managers. Shanghvi and his team had studied the model of Cipla, which was probably the first company to have braved these adversities by refusing to accept the 'unreasonable' terms of the unions there. Cipla hired from outside the states, asked its boys to work only in the evenings, without the detailing bags, so that they were not singled out as medical representatives. Sun tried some of these tactics, like recruiting from outside the state, but the violence continued with the managers. Roy had a close shave himself.

He had checked into a hotel in Rohtak and was meeting the head of dermatology in a government hospital the same day. As he was walking along with the third-and second-line manager to enter the hospital premises, there was a sudden rush—a crowd was moving towards them—when he looked around, his managers were gone. Roy had had good experience of dealing with industrial mobs, but that moment sent a chill down his spine as he noticed about fifty people heading towards him, some of whom he remembered crossing at the cycle stand outside.

Just then his pager buzzed; he read it in a flash. It was a message from Dr Jain, head of skin speciality, which said, 'Roy, *gheraoed*? Look up.' Roy saw Jain watching him over from the first floor. He feared for his life and typed 'Help'.

In seconds, Jain clambered down the stairs to reach the spot before the crowd could pounce and inflict physical harm on Roy. He warned the goon, 'Aren't you the cycle-stand manager? If you as much as touch this man, I will ensure your cycle stand winds up by tomorrow.' Jain ensured that Roy was transferred to a government bungalow for the three days of his stay.

These incidents, not one-offish any more, were disconcerting for the usually unprovokable Shanghvi. In this case, Shanghvi couldn't rest easy when his boys were being beaten up. Some executives distinctly recalled a day when the crack team, with a few senior managers, were sitting across him, mulling a way out in what one of them called 'rogue markets of north India'. 'We are new there and if we are not allowed to work hard we cannot beat those who are reigning in the state today. I am a businessman and I have the legal right to work 24/7 if I want to, and no one can stop me from doing that,' he recalled Shanghvi saying.

They were accustomed to their chief's brief pauses, but on this particular occasion, his fierce gaze and a quiet, much-longer-than-his-longest pauses unsettled them. And then, one of them recalled him abruptly standing up and spelling out an amount, 'Two crore,' and uttering two words, 'settle them' and then walking out of the room. It was nothing like the Dilip-bhai they had ever seen. The amount he spelled out sounded like a raised budget to manage the crisis but the rest of what he had just said was open to a lot of interpretation. The message seemed cryptic and his deputies struggled to decode what it meant and what had just transpired. Shanghvi could allow himself in such moments to become what he is not and what no one is capable of imagining him as being.

He hired top cops K.P.S. Gill and Julius Ribeiro as consultants. Soon after Sun was cultivating a second set of customers after doctors—the Punjab Police and Haryana Police force, wooing police just as they had serviced doctors. 'We cultivated our relationships across the police force in Jalandhar, Patiala, Bhatinda, Amritsar, Ambala and other cities. Soon we were conducting cultural programmes for the police and making friends there,' Roy said. Ghosh recalled getting a helpline number exclusively for Sun from police forces. 'We filed cases aggressively for every attack and the police responded thereafter,' Ghosh said.

Sun was already paying a risk allowance for these states. 'Boss also made sure that managers, even those first-line managers got security cover, literally bodyguards. I don't think, any promoter other than Dilip-bhai could think of this,' Roy recalled, and then a while later promptly withdrawing such armed support as incidents of counter *dadagiri* were reported.

Alongside, what Roy called 'surgery' was on. 'People who Sun's top executives identified as the union's people and trouble-mongers were asked to leave,' he said. From here on the narrative started reweaving itself. 'We didn't grow spectacularly, but we maintained a level,' Ghosh said.

Roy said, 'Dilip-bhai has always taught us—you let wrong passengers get on your train, they will ruin your journey, and accidents are bound to happen.' Shanghvi practised this in every possible way. For instance, Milan Sinha's selection panel, which was better known for rejection than selection in Sun, had freshly rejected a candidate, when a HR person called him up frantically and told him, "Sir, the candidate was referred from the MD's office."

"'Sorry, it's a bit late. I have told the boy on his face that we are not taking him, put a red mark and signed against his name. I cannot undo what has been done," Sinha retorted.

"'Sir, the candidate has come with strong recommendation from Gujarat FDA office," she persisted.

"'You can tell the MD office that Milan Sinha's panel has rejected him," Sinha summed up the conversation, but not without a sense of unease. 'A few days later, at Sun's Mahakali Office, an apprehensive Sinha broached the topic with Shanghvi. He recalled an oblivious Shanghvi smiling softly, "Yes, we had some recommendation from a state FDA and passed it on to HR to get his interview done. But if he didn't pass the test, you have taken the right decision. I would rather tell the bureaucrat to keep his candidate home and we could perhaps send him a salary of ₹3 lakh every month rather than allow him to take on a responsibility he cannot shoulder and where he probably ends up burdening us with a loss of ₹3 lakh every day.'"

Too many of Shanghvi's old-time friends recounted experiences of sending someone to him with a word, only to realize that the person has been turned down after being interviewed. 'He wouldn't give someone a responsibility just because he is a relative or a friend's acquaintance. I recall sending someone for a printing job but he came back exhausted with Dilip's questions and told me, 'I felt this guy knows my work better than I do. I also have a feeling that this will not work out despite your recommendation,' said friend Vinod Mody. It didn't.

And yet, so many other times, the same friends recalled Shanghvi calling them decades after he had met someone, asking them to put him across to 'that bright boy'. 'He will remember all my nephews and cousins and their friends whom he has met in someone's family function. And years after he has met them, one day I would get a call, "Sailesh, your cousin who works with Gujarat Electric Corp., we can give him this responsibility now that we have interest in power.'

'You must choose the people you want to let in very carefully and once they are on board, you must treat them well. On the way if you realize that you have made a mistake, you must allow them to de-board at the next station respectfully. That is his philosophy of hiring for a company,' a former Sun HR executive said.

The Vaishnav

And many times when people were de-boarding, Shanghvi made it memorable in a way that the parting remained etched in their minds for life. Sometime in the mid-1990s, H.K. Pahwa, who had been fully absorbed in training at Sun, got a jolt the day when Tarun Gupta, the former Glaxo Pharma country head, remarked, 'You are too young and driven to be in training. Training is for people who are looking for retirement options. You should be in brands, that's where the real career and all the action is.'

'Brand' was the prevailing mantra in pharma then, and Gupta with his training at Harvard was like a brand god in India; he had launched the concept of visual aid in the country, initiated an understanding into market research data. Gupta's comment sliced into Pahwa deep. 'The brand bug bit me bad and I sought a role in brand management, that was where the glamour was and I was still in my thirties and couldn't remain untouched by it,' Pahwa recalled of a time when Sun was hiring Parikshit Vora from Glaxo and Alkesh Shah from Alembic for brand roles. 'After several rounds of persuasion by the Sun HR to continue in training, I was told point blank that brand wasn't happening, so I quit in a huff and joined J.B. Chemicals and Pharmaceuticals in Bombay,' Pahwa added.

But this crossroad in his career coincided with a personal crisis as his school-going son developed a condition that mimicked cancer. Pahwa stood shattered, at the door of a ward in Alembic Hospital, where his son had been admitted, having left his job at Sun, and about to leave for a new city in the midst of this catastrophe, when he spotted two shadows approaching him from the corridor. As they closed in, he figured them out as Shanghvi and Yagnik. 'Since you have gone to a point of no return, at least let me foot the hospital bill,' he recalled Shanghvi saying. The bill ran into a few thousands, which wasn't a meagre amount for Pahwa then, but he had quit the company days before and shook his head. 'Sorry, sir, I can't take it,' he replied.

'Probably realizing that I have too much self-esteem to accept such a favour or a charity, Dilip-bhai rephrased his offer, "Would you mind if Sun Pharma gets a little mileage by footing this bill?"' Pahwa recounted. He had no answer to that and on his way out, Shanghvi paid the bill anyway, but the incident haunts Pahwa till today, who regrets leaving Sun the way he did. 'The exuberance and arrogance of youth can at times blur the truth for you. My heart and my skills were always in training, and Dilip-bhai knew it better than I did,' Pahwa, who now trains full time through a consultancy, said.

As managers we were always asked by Dilip-bhai to be hard on the task, not on the people, Roy said. Shanhgvi's definition of hard taskmaster seemed uncannily close in spirit to Mahatma Gandhi's philosophy of 'Hate the (evil) deeds, not the doer'. But how did such a hard taskmaster appear to people around?

Rajesh Kumar was working late one evening in Sun's Acme Plaza office when he felt a presence behind his desk. He turned around to find Shanghvi. 'Has FDC slashed the prices of Sparlox?'

'I have no such information, sir.'

Shanghvi smiled and walked off. Kumar started frantically calling his MRs and, to his shock, found that FDC had halved the price of its drug a fortnight back. After a tense night, he walked into Shanghvi's cabin next morning, muttering, 'I am ashamed, sir.'

'You should be,' he recalled Shanghvi telling him matter-of-factly, and then moving on to discuss possible damage-control strategies. He might as well have said, 'Have the tea,' leaving Kumar with a cocktail of guilt and responsibility. Such experiences at times left people confused about whether he was annoyed with them or not, because they couldn't grasp the possibility of someone being hard on their task, without being hard on them.

'He knows the art of delivering tough messages softly,' Kumar felt, recalling another time when Shanghvi had called him to ask, 'Rajesh, is it a good idea to launch somatostatin?'

'I don't think so, sir.'

'When you reply something without studying it, this is what happens. Talk to a few doctors, talk to colleagues in marketing and other functions and meet me at 5 p.m. today.'

Kumar had based his judgement on the basic Sun formulae: factors such as there were already four players in the market, and it was mainly a product bought by hospitals, which meant competitors could undercut rates to start price wars, turning the product into a commodity. This was exactly the kind of 'commodity markets' Sun tried to steer clear of as a philosophy. When he made calls, what he gathered was that the market had some decent potential in the future.

Later in the day Shanghvi was to explain to him, 'Rajesh, do you wish to remain a GM or become the VP?'

'Obviously VP, sir.'

'Then stop thinking as a head of Solares division, start thinking like a manager of Sun Pharma, in the interest of the company, not your division. We are already producing this drug for international markets. Launching it in India would give us a scale that will help us make it at a lower cost. If you had thought like an entrepreneurial manager, you would have reached the same conclusion.'

Such messages were delivered without shuddery theatricality or hyperbole, at times even without the necessary punch or modulation in tone, but to the one it was targeted, it still seemed effective. Some like Pahwa found this technique powerful. He recalled that in its earliest days, the discussion in Sun was always about converting doctor by doctor, never around aggregates of sales and markets.

He had been in charge of north India, stationed in Delhi for the last few months of 1989 and had come to the head office for training. 'Dilip-bhai was crossing by and he just asked innocuously, "Has Dr P.V. Bakshi started prescribing Trazine S?" No one around could understand it but I got what he was suggesting. I had been in Delhi for months but hadn't yet found time to meet the legendary psychiatrist Bakshi. I knew that he knew, and the first thing I did was to head to Bakshi's chamber after returning to Delhi. He can put across the message without hurting you, and that is how it works best,' Pahwa believed.

When the task involved a friend, humour was what Shanghvi used to drive home the point. Humour, rather wit, the true Gujarati kind, when wrapped around a hard message made it so much easier to digest for the person at the receiving end. A Sun executive recalled a day when Shanghvi, Harin Mehta (elder brother of Shanghvi's friend) an IITian and a few others were walking into a small manufacturing plant built under the supervision of Harin-bhai in the backyard of Vapi. Even before they entered, the acutely pungent odour of chemicals arrested their olfactory senses; almost by reflex they retrieved their handkerchiefs to cover their noses. As they walked in, they saw the chemicals splashed all over the walls, like a mischievous child's handiwork. The chemical litter was messy enough for any promoter to have thrown a fit. But Shanghvi just mumbled in Gujarati, 'Do we manufacture by scraping chemicals from the walls?', prompting laughter among all present, including Harin-bhai. An awkward moment turned into a funny one without compromising the message, recalled one of those present.

'Dilip has a very sharp and distinct sense of humour. You will roll with laughter that moment, only to realize a few minutes later that you were the butt of his joke,' Sailesh Desai said.

At times it was not an individual, but a collective at the receiving end of Shanghvi's wit. An anchor on CNBC had asked him, 'You earn most of your revenue from new launches, what about old products?' And he had replied with his usual cool, 'As long as I am growing faster than the market, even if only three new products are giving me that growth, I have no issues.' Most of the senior management had seen that interview. So when they received a mail from the CMD a year or so later asking them to report a list of products about which they spoke no word to the doctor, did no promotions the whole year, didn't print a single literature about, and which needed to be phased out, it didn't shock the division heads.

'We were mostly relieved to prune our product basket and prepared a list all the products we wanted to be phased out,' Sinha recalled. And then the day arrived, Shanghvi turned over all pages of the reports that all divisions had submitted, and looked up, 'So these are products you want to phase out. We can suspend these, but how much is the turnover of our company?'

'₹9000 crore,' someone answered.

'Sales from all these products add up to ₹1600 crore, that is 16 per cent of our revenue and all that comes without spending a single penny on their marketing and promotion. One way to look at it is that these products sustain your salaries and daily expense of the company.'

After one of his signature pauses, he resumed in front of his stunned audience, 'The purpose of this mail wasn't to get a list of redundant products but to remind you that at least once a year we must print a literature updating information about these drugs and knock on the door of the doctor, telling them that these products exist.'

Hundreds of people lived through millions of such professional experiences, and yet when asked to relive their moments of connect with Shanghvi, it boiled down to either a simple humane gesture in a moment you least expected, or a personal crisis, when he just stood by and cared for as if you were his own. 'Deep down, there is a Vaishnav throbbing in Dilip-bhai and he cannot see others suffering,' Yagnik recalled.

Mira Desai, his executive assistant, recalled making her first trip to the US with her colleague friend Ishrat in 2004 from the business development team of Sun. At Amsterdam, they bumped into Shanghvi who was travelling to the US as well. 'He asked us, "Your first time?" We giggled, "Yes, sir." Do you have some *chhutta* (loose change)? You will need that at the airport for the trolley to lug your stuff. Looking at our lost face, he must have guessed we had no idea what he was talking about, because he then retrieved whatever change he could from his pockets and handed it over to us,' Mira recalled. When they reached Detroit airport, Sun's employee stood there with two long, black overcoats to receive them. 'It was touching, Dilip-bhai had guessed that we wouldn't be carrying overcoats to beat the cold,' Mira said.

From that day to the day her friend Ishrat was diagnosed with non-Hodgkin's lymphoma, when she was asked by Shanghvi to scour libraries to understand the condition better and see where all breakthrough treatments can be explored, to the weeks when her own father was fighting a battle with life, and she found a car and driver quietly parked outside the hospital 24/7 on Shanghvi's instruction, Mira said she has lost count of his humane gestures and it was this side of his personality that endeared him to thousands in his company.

'He doesn't socialize in glitzy billionaire circles or Page 3 parties and his life revolves around his company; and that's the reason he has been able to devote all his energy to the people in Sun. He must know thousands by their name and tens of thousands by their faces. For him, they are important people and for them, he is almost God,' Yagnik said, citing the extraordinary length he could go to show his care in Sun of the 1990s.

He recalled the way Diwali was celebrated at Sun. With a puja, Shanti-kaka would hand over shagun (token money) amounting to ₹51 to everyone and distribute crackers. As head of HR, Yagnik had to be present, but on one such occasion, without any plausible reason, he started feeling restless. He told Dilip-bhai that he wanted to go home and spend some time with his father who was visiting. 'Yeah, sure,' Shanghvi replied. As he stepped into his home, yet to take off his shirt, he saw his father collapsing and dying in front of his own eyes. It was a massive cardiac arrest. The tragedy left Yagnik in a deep psychological trauma, with him obsessively thinking if there was anything he could have done to prevent it. 'Dilip-bhai could sense that unresolved crisis in me and he quietly arranged for a cardiologist to explain to me what happens when there is a cardiac arrest. What a slim chance you actually have. Through all these gestures he leaves a deep impression and you form a bond with him, much beyond a job,' Yagnik said.

Most of these emotional bonding between Shanghvi and his people at Sun happened without any expressions spilling over, but there have been exceptions when Shanghvi known for his emotional composure, couldn't help it.

Nandkumar, was seen in the company as equivalent of Pradip Ghosh in west and south. He was the type who could challenge Shanghvi and give his life for Sun in the same breath. In a certain meeting, when calendars were seen as statements for Sun, Shanghvi proposed that they do a spot lamination on matte finish, to create a three-dimensional effect and show micro-organisms in that calendar. It was expensive, because in the whole country, there was only one printer in Hyderabad then who had the technology. But Shanghvi suggested that they should go ahead with a limited edition, because it signified that they were technologically advanced. Nandkumar, said, 'Sir, I am not impressed; the calendar will do nothing for the company other than satisfying you, it doesn't satisfy me at least.' People present were astonished but recalled Shanghvi saying, smilingly, 'OK, Nandkumar, please do this much for my satisfaction then.'

Nandkumar, employee number 008, had risen from a medical representative to head the neurological division at Sun. In the process, he had built an unmatched 'equity' with psychiatrists and neurologists, robust enough for one of them to notice his limp in a conference and drag him along to one Dr Singhal's OPD and get all tests done. As the days went by, it became clear that he had a malignant brain tumour, advanced stage and inoperable. When Shanghvi was informed he was in the US. He called Sailesh Desai who rushed to the hospital with colleagues. 'Milan, till yesterday I was my own patient, from today I am yours,' Nandkumar quipped to Sinha, indicating their official roles as head of neurology and oncology.

Next, Sinha recalled taking him to Tata Memorial and on the way convincing him to open a joint account with his wife, and Nandkumar laughing the whole thing off, 'Why do you think I will die?' And Sinha, left with no choice but resorting to a lie, 'No, Nandkumar, but the tremor in your hand will get severe, so you may have trouble signing, let bhabhiji operate this account. And yet, both of them knew that the end was near.

And the moment it came, Shanghvi was on stage addressing, thousands of highest-performing medical representatives at Bangkok at the Star Awards, the event where Sun had flown over 1500 of its top-performing MRs and their families to a foreign locale to celebrate their contributions. Sinha called Anthony and asked him to pass on the message to Shanghvi.

Anthony whispered, 'He's stepping on to the podium already.'

'He would have wanted to know this even if he was in the middle of the address.'

When Anthony passed on the news of Nandkumar's demise to Shanghvi, the person who no one had ever seen agitated, disturbed or angered before, choked and broke down. This image of tears freely rolling down his cheeks, stunned the audience into a silence. Witnessing this scene were medical representatives, many of them wondering whether this was the one reason they had given away decades of their life to the company, despite quibbling at times about how little it paid them. Sailesh Desai, yet uninformed of Nandkumar's demise, couldn't fathom the commotion that followed and tried to manage the emotional outburst of his friend by making an announcement that Nandkumar was gravely ill but hadn't breathed his last.

The next day, a customary mail was waiting in the inbox of Sun managers, asking them whether they would like to voluntarily give away a day's salary to Nandkumar's family. By evening, when Sinha sat down to reply to that mail committing his contribution, it had been withdrawn. Astounded, he walked up to Azadar Khan, who was heading HR to point out the aberration.

Khan told him, 'It was deliberate. It has been recalled as per Dilip-bhai's order.'

'What for?' asked a dazed Sinha.

'Dilip-bhai said, "Nandkumar doesn't need any contribution from anyone, it is my obligation,"' Sinha recalled Khan telling him. Insiders indicated that Shanghvi made a 'substantial' contribution to the family from his personal wealth. Sailesh Desai continues to be in touch with the family and says Nandkumar's daughters have grown up to be competent professionals, something that would have made Nandkumar proud.

Yagnik felt the other quality that endears Shanghvi in a different way to those who could have been alienated or fallen on to his wrong side is his superhuman ability to not cross a line in the most adverse situation and damage anyone's human dignity. 'He upholds human dignity at all times. You can stretch the elastic of a crisis to its breaking point, it can snap even, but Dilip-bhai wouldn't let that provoke him to berate you, humiliate you or touch that tender spot most essential to a humane experience, human dignity ever.'

Shanghvi was upset about many people manipulating their travel fares and overbilling the company. Some people attribute that to his cost-conscious nature and others thought what bothered him was the compromise of integrity. People had been sacked for such violations. Yagnik tried to plug loopholes in travel policies, making them stricter and evidence-based and went up to him for approval, only to be surprised: 'Don't, Yagnik. People are not made for policies, policies are made for people. So do not create policies that will suffocate them. Design policies that will make their life easier.'

A few days later, in another meeting, senior management was discussing ideas on how they should create processes to prevent MRs from misusing company resources that they get to deal with doctors. Many ideas were pouring forth. He listened to all of them and then asked, 'What percentage of our field force do you think might be seriously misusing our resources or acting dishonest while dealing with doctors?'

Numbers popped and estimates ranged from 1 to 2 per cent.

'Just to manage 1 per cent, we mistrust the other 99 per cent. That's like giving an idea to the other 99 per cent that there is a possibility to steal here. Do not micromanage. Let's make our policies based on trust,' Kumar recalled Shanghvi saying.

This trust is not of the type that one puts in the other to open his life book or share secrets, this is more a confidence one puts in the other believing him to be well intentioned and competent to perform a responsibility.

'When you trust someone, you make yourself vulnerable by empowering the other, and that itself has a certain power, more so when it comes from a leader like Dilip-bhai. It's as if now you have been given the responsibility to uphold his trust,' Yagnik believed.

After a moment of quiet, when he was probably searching for the right words, Yagnik resumed, 'He said this to me on day one. And he kept reminding me many times over, "Yagnik, as human resources head, you are our conscience keeper." It probably is the most valuable and fragile thing to keep, and I couldn't shake off that responsibility that Dilip-bhai had entrusted, long after I left Sun and moved to different places.'

So where does it all begin for Shanghvi the Vaishnav?

'I know we have seen our fathers and uncles to be kind and have been taught to wish well for others. And we all learn by looking at the way our elders behave. But to trace it down to a Vaishnavite tradition is beyond me,' Upen-bhai, his cousin, said. 'Vaishnavism is in his DNA, maybe? But his "money intelligence" comes from a tremendous native intelligence that Gujarati baniyas have,' a former aide said. 'He values money because he has seen the lack of it, and he values dignity, because sitting in a shop, he has known how it feels, when managers of companies they stocked medicines of misbehaved with his father and him. He experienced that hurt and probably promised to himself that this was not an experience he would make others go through,' a close friend said, preferring not to be named.

On 26 September 1932, Rabindranath Tagore was visiting another Vaishnav in Pune's Yerawada jail where he was fasting against British policies perpetuating caste biases and untouchability. It was his day of silence. Tagore described 'Mahatmaji's cot' getting dragged to the 'shade of the prison wall', and all of them settling on the jail blankets. He witnessed Pandit Shyam Shastri reading out the Vedas, as Kamala Nehru made lemon juice. Kasturi Bai handed over the glass to Gandhi, who started slowly sipping from it to break his fast. And then members of Sabarmati Ashram spontaneously burst into singing their daily prayer, closest to the Vaishava's heart:

'Vaishnava jan to, tene kahiye je, peed paraayi jaane re . . .'

The first few verses of the devotional hymn composed by Gujarati saint poet Narsinh Mehta in the fifteenth century loosely translate to

Call those people, Vaishnava,

who feel the pain of others, help those in misery,

but never let undue pride, self-conceit enter their mind

They respect all, do not disparage anyone,

keep their actions and thoughts pure.

Hard to tell whether the man practises the prayer or the prayer describes him best, but anyone who has been anywhere close to him, knows that this is where all of it begins.

PART III

CHAPTER SIXTEEN

CARACO: A DRESS REHEARSAL IN THE USA

It was Kirti's debut as executive assistant to Shanghvi in Baroda on 6 June 1996. He was trying to make sense of the bustling atmosphere of Synergy House. Shanghvi had called him for a chat at about 10 a.m. in his cabin, but when the clock struck 6 p.m. without him being called in, he started quietly winding up for the day. It was right at that moment Shanghvi asked him to join in for a call at 9.30 p.m.

Unaccustomed to Sun's nocturnal ways, Kirti went back home, had his dinner and returned to participate in the call that turned out to be one to buy a stake in Caraco, a cash-strapped American firm on the brink of bankruptcy.

It was a takeover that was to prep Sun for its much bigger acquisitions: Taro and Ranbaxy. In an early conversation, Kirti asked Shanghvi about his deep interest in the US and lukewarm attitude about Europe.

Besides the obvious business and regulatory importance of the world's largest market, which was also arguably the most fertile ground for scientific innovations, Shanghvi said, 'There are few Indian players in the US—those who are essentially banking on 'make in India'. I want to learn their (US) ways in manufacturing and marketing and strike a balance between making in the US and in India.'

Caraco that literally meant an eighteenth-century women's jacket, was a loss-making American firm on the verge of going bust when Shanghvi offered an investment to them. It took a bit of haggling before Shanghvi could craft a non-zero-sum deal by soothing Caraco management's gripe.

Their management whined to Sudhir Valia and Shanghvi about how Caraco's share price didn't reflect its value. 'If we issue shares based on the current share price, the valuation of the company will crash to rock bottom,' a Caraco executive cribbed to Valia. It was the kind of problem that Valia felt charged to solve. So he co-designed a deal with Shanghvi, a novel architecture of acquisition practised never before, and probably never after.

Valia recalled explaining to them, 'What you expect from me are two things—I bring money to the table and pump the company with products so that it can revive business. So can you assign some shares to the products, so that for a part of the deal, I swap products for shares?'

Showing the deal structure to the Caraco management, Valia explained further, 'I will pay the money for as much shares you want. For the balance shares I shall collect a fee for every product I transfer to you.' Valia recalled them cheering about two birds getting killed with one stone.

Asked which book he borrowed this leaf from, Shanghvi said, 'I had never heard or read of such an arrangement anywhere before. The proposal was devised completely by us. What I thought was that for us to become successful, we have to give Caraco new products. The original idea was that we would develop products in India and file out of Caraco in the US. If I had given 5–10 cents more, the company's valuation wouldn't have gone up.'

Sun committed to buy a stake in Caraco up front and then acquire a chunk of shares over the next four years as it transferred (ANDAs), which are applications that turn into generic products on regulatory approvals.

Valia couldn't just stop there. A master tax planner, he advised that instead of a product–share swap, Caraco should classify this exchange as an R&D–share swap, so that it can be rendered tax free for Sun. 'We were technically giving them 'products in the making', or R&D. So it became a non-taxable item for us,' Valia beamed. He then extended his tax-planning benefits for Caraco by calling auditors there. 'If you book it as an R&D expense in the capital account, you can amortize it and it becomes deductible from income tax.' As Caraco's shares moved northwards with time, the company saved taxes in tens of millions on this account.

But the deal got stuck in Reserve Bank of India's investment committee. Struggling to grasp the dynamics of the barter deal, the panel rejected it. It took Valia six months to convince the central bank that such a transaction was valid.

Irrespective of the ifs and buts, Sun bought 43 per cent of Caraco paying $7.5 million, (plus invested another $5 million later to repay its debts) on the condition that for every ANDA it transferred, Sun would gain another five-and-a-half lakh shares, and at the end of four years it would have given Caraco 20–25 ANDAs and become a 67 per cent shareholder in the firm.

This structure of the Sun–Caraco deal intrigued industry members even after two decades. A top executive at a rival firm called it a 'stroke of genius' that served as a 'glimpse into the workings of the mind of the Shanghvi–Valia' duo. It is not quite the unqualified compliment it looks at the first glance.

'You wish to buy a company to use it as a vehicle to sell your products in the US. Then you devise a plan under which that company actually pays you back in shares for doing your regulatory studies and selling your stuff at its own cost. Not money, but equity! And in the process the company becomes yours. So the arrangement at the end entails that a product that was yours stays yours and you steadily and progressively own another company.'

Another industry veteran expressed disbelief. 'If Caraco had been owned majorly by a family or a fund, they wouldn't have fallen for such a thing.' The point these industry captains discounted was the degree of desperation Caraco was in the moment Shanghvi bought into the company.

The context in which Shanghvi had signed on this transaction was when Caraco had no cash in their pockets to buy Sun's products. 'Mr Shanghvi absolutely unflinchingly believed that this model was the best for Caraco. Because it just didn't have the cash to buy Sun products. But the products it desperately needed to revive its business. And Caraco got successful only because of this model. Sun got adequately compensated in the process, what's wrong with that?' an ex-Caraco executive, formerly with Sun, said. But as Caraco's tears were stitched back, a part of its board discounted the context under which the deal had been signed and poked holes in the model, he added. But that was a hitch for later.

Chinese Whispers with the Americans

Things at Caraco started getting messed up as soon as Sun began asserting its authority. In the Sun of 1996, Lanka reigned and it was his idea to bring ex-boss Gajendra Holkar* to Caraco from Novartis.

What ensued was as much a clash between cultures as it was between individuals. Cultures—of two companies—run in two different countries; individuals: Holkar—multinational trained, structure-protocols-reliant, and Valia—gifted with raw intelligence, on-the-spot problem solver, a numbers man home-honed at Sun; and their strikingly divergent beliefs on how business should be run. What exacerbated the misalignment between the US and the India teams was a warning letter from the US Food and Drug Administration and mounting losses.

Holkar, like many others in Sun at the time, seemed to run into frequent collisions with Valia's ways and didn't tolerate his interference. Had he managed to turn around Caraco quick enough even while staying intolerant to Valia's ideas, it might have helped. But that was not to be. Valia saw Holkar as 'non-performing', a perception shared by other managers in Sun's India office. What they differed on was whether he couldn't or wouldn't manage Caraco affairs well for Sun.

Valia felt when he ladled out tips for improvement to Caraco that had already worked brilliantly for Sun, it either fell on deaf ears, or was served to its board in a twisted manner which made sure it was rejected. 'Nothing works if it's not implemented and, in those years, I felt I was talking to a wall,' Valia said.

Another time, when he drew up a list of non-performing executives, he recalled those names resurfacing in board meetings for deliberations sparking off a controversy.

'We had inherited some bad apples. There was a former -FDA inspector who walked in and out of office as she pleased, defying company rules openly. When she entered office, she wanted things exactly as she wanted. But in a company if you want systems improved, you have to get on to the floor and dirty your hands,' Valia recalled. He felt, the Caraco top brass's tendency to run to the board and shareholders for every sneeze and cough nullified Valia's ability to fix problems there.

These quibbles spilled over to the India team of Sun and the US team of Caraco. The American quality and regulatory head didn't listen to all that the India team had to advice. Holkar was described as 'gentle, soft-spoken but headstrong and assertive' by Caraco managers. Those who saw things from the lens of Holkar interpreted the situation differently. Particularly because they had seen Holkar constantly remind them that 'it is because of Sun's monthly cheques that we are able to pay our salaries and bills'.

'He had run Ciba Geigy in India, and when he joined Sun, it wasn't such a force to reckon with. So there were frequent differences of opinion cropping up between him and Mr Valia and Mr Shanghvi. Caraco was still a listed entity and board members had fiduciary duties other than making things happen for Sun. So what transpired inside the boardroom that prompted a set of actions wouldn't be fully communicated to folks in India. From the outside that set of actions may have looked weird forcing Sun to question, "What the heck is going on?"' a former Caraco executive said.

For the first few years, Shanghvi chose not to meddle in the tussle between Valia and Holkar.

'The dynamics were a bit complex. I was looking after operations, an area Dilip-bhai didn't involve himself much in. The Caraco situation was becoming hopeless. Forget material cost, even their manufacturing cost exceeded their selling price. I could see at every step, there was scope to improve efficiencies but this gentleman had erected firewalls. He wouldn't let people there talk freely with us, probably even put them under an informal gag order that proposals from Sun must be rejected,' Valia reflected.

He recalled trying to convince Shanghvi to act upon what he saw as a mess created by a few insiders but 'nothing came out of it for a long time' till problems became really acute with some 'internal guys' influencing shareholders to foment unrest against 'Dilip-bhai himself'.

Contrary to broadly held perceptions in Sun and outside that 'shareholders ganged up against Sun in Caraco', Valia firmly believed that it was an 'internally designed handiwork'. 'It was very easy for these people [a few insiders] who resided in the same city [Detroit in Michigan] as investors to prod them to work against us.

They misused the trust we had put in them and we faced the consequences,' Valia said.

Between 1999 and 2000, Caraco's Detroit facility was inspected by the US regulator twice and the company was slapped with a warning letter. This slammed brakes on Sun's plans to speed up its US inroads. Stock analysts junked Sun's Caraco investment, downgrading its stock to 'underperform'. Till 2001, not a single ANDA given to Caraco had translated into a product for Sun, and the mess prevailed.

That is when Shanghvi inducted Jitendra Doshi as COO on board. 'Doshi, known to us Indians as Jitu-bhai, was in fact brought to Caraco with the intention of aligning the US and India teams, and he really helped cool down matters,' a Caraco employee said. Doshi, who had been a pharma entrepreneur himself, went on to become one of Sun's most important US resources in the decade to come.

But at a time when five years had passed since the investment in the US and it was clear that Sun's American journey had started off on such a bumpy note, analysts and even his deputies quizzed Shanghvi routinely on how worthwhile it was to stay invested in a marriage with Caraco that was giving Sun so much pain.

Staring at the mounting losses of Caraco, he replied, 'If I have made X amount of money last year, I can at least afford to lose that much.' It was this statement of Shanghvi that boosted the morale of G.P. Singh, who had just then started off as a sales personnel at Caraco 'at the bottom of the food chain' (his words). He would eventually rise to become the CEO of that firm.

'Caraco was losing money. Sales were low, expenses sky-high. Then came the warning letter. The entire focus had shifted to clearing regulatory red flags while business took a back seat. Lots of people back home were worried, asking Mr Shanghvi to cut his losses while he could. In that chaos, this stood out as a big bold statement that kept us going. Sun was a small company then, and the kind of losses Caraco had would have shaken any other company the size of Sun,' Singh said.

Behind that statement, Shanghvi had a different calculation that might have escaped quarterly-results-obsessed analysts but suited his own marathon approach.

'We looked at value also in terms of time. When we failed the first FDA audit at Caraco, we realized that it would take us much longer than our initial estimates to realize our value there. It was clear right at that moment that for the next few years, we would be losing close to $6 million per year, which was big money that time. Then I started looking if there was some other place where we could make up that amount. The only market where the relationship between our efforts and output was much more was India, so we started focusing on increasing our growth rate here to compensate the loss there,' Shanghvi said.

His friend Sailesh Desai had pointed out this trait of Shanghvi. 'If he is making big losses on one side and a small profit on the other, he has the uncanny ability to deep-focus on the small profit bucket and contain the big losses till the time he turns his small profit into big profit. Inside his mind he has clearly laid out closed compartments, so that no amount of disturbance in any other aspect of life can touch his performance in business. That clinical precision in his decision making showed up even in troubled times.'

Despite his assurances, in 2001, Shanghvi had expressed concerns in private to some of his industry friends. 'I am not sure that Caraco hasn't been a mistake.'

Saving the American Dream

But Shanghvi was hardly the type to sulk over his mistakes. Instead he packed his bags to save Sun's American dream. With Kirti, he regularly took off to the US to give himself a tour of the pharma landscape there.

Even as Caraco's complications simmered in the backdrop, Shanghvi and Kirti frequently walked into patent lawyers' chambers to get a grip on the intellectual property maze and the pharma litigation space of the US. Typical of Shanghvi, of the range of lawyers he met in 2001, he settled not for an established patent grandmaster attorney, but a criminal lawyer who was career-transitioning into intellectual property—James Hurst of Winston & Strawn at Chicago. 'Dilip-bhai must have spotted some sharp logic in his arguments because Mr Hurst had very few pharma cases to his credit then. By 2007–08, Mr Hurst had turned into one of the most sought-after legal counsel in the US for pharma litigations,' Bharati Nadkarni, Sun's IP head marvelled.

Later, Shanghvi hopped to district courts of the US to get a feel of appeals. 'Our first-hand experience in the US helped us decode how we could pick our fights,' Kirti recounted.

Soon, in their meetings, where they had read up Merck Manuals earlier to find drugs for India, Shanghvi began poring over the Hatch-Waxman law, the rule book of the game-like pharma topography the US has set up to slash its overall healthcare costs by boosting early entry of generic drugs. Next in stack was the FDA's Orange Book with actually an orange jacket which they studied product by product—their patents, expiries and what could be challenged.

Between his US sojourns, Shanghvi was building his own intellectual property team back home. For that he hired IP scientist Ratnesh Srivastava from Ranbaxy, a company that boasted of the finest home-grown patents team. Those days Bharati recalled regularly finding a piece of *Scrip* or *Pinksheet* (names of publications) marked out in Shanghvi's handwriting: Can you explain this to me? As she began explaining, her chief would start drawing parallels instantaneously on which other cases the same logic could apply.

'Quite in tradition of our intense new product meetings, we started having IP meetings,' Kirti recalled. This happened in Baroda, bimonthly, from 9 a.m. to 10 p.m. Shanghvi chaired it. He flipped through patent documents, running into hundreds of pages and quickly turned over to the last section—claims of patents—scrutinizing it word by word and asked the team—comprising scientists and business development—to do the same.

Later, a patent-busting game ensued in the meeting, when everyone present was challenged to apply logic to splinter existing claims. It was amusing for scientists as their business development counterparts came up with the wackiest weapons to demolish some of the claims.

Staring with disbelief, shaking their heads vigorously, scientists defended silly-sounding suggestions like 'What if we make an injection instead of a tablet?', 'A capsule instead of an injection?', 'If we just reduce the dosage, would we still infringe this claim?'

Initially such suggestions were met with muffled laughter by the scientists and a teacherly 'No this is not how it happens in science'. Even as the light-hearted tiff between science and commerce set the tone of those meetings, Shanghvi himself went about actively spotting cracks in patent claims, and egged on scientists to work on several of those logics.

In drugs, where scientists concluded it impossible to challenge tight patent claims, he quoted references of decades back, backing it up with an argument that seemed to have been retrieved from the dusty alchemists' libraries. Then he sent scientists searching into patent history pages, technically called 'prior art' documents (all information that has been made available to the public before a given date that might be relevant to a patent's claims of originality). To their disbelief, more often than not they hit upon references Shanghvi was pointing towards, and following those curious cues scientists chanced upon hidden routes routinely that either didn't infringe upon patent claims or rendered claims invalid.

For the Amifostine injection, Sun's first ANDA for 180 days of marketing exclusivity in the US, Shanghvi sat with Ratnesh to grasp the invention and then suggested that the desired drug be manufactured through a process other than what the inventor was using.

He studied the 'prior art' and then sat with R&D and quality control team to fine-tune a process that the inventor had found undoable. Next he sat with the engineering team to design the air-flow and set up infrastructure to make it happen.

For other major US drug launches such as first generics of Effexor and Prandin, it was Shanghvi who gave direction to his R&D and intellectual property team.

For a Prandin patent he told Bharati, 'This patent that combines metformin with repaglinide can be invalidated on the ground that it does nothing novel truly. In this case, one drug is being given to release the insulin (repaglinide), another (metformin) to take care of sugar in the blood. That is exactly what sulfonylurea (releases insulin) does in combination with Metformin. You attack the patent from the mechanism of the action perspective.' Bharati developed this line of argument to finally invalidate the patent.

But more importantly, Shanghvi took up the case of the inventor firm changing the use code to extend patents as a matter of principle—the innovator cannot expect to change rules in its favour after the game has started. Shanghvi said, 'I will challenge this all the way to the Supreme Court and set a case precedent.' So he did, and it was the criminal law specialist Hurst who argued it in the US apex court to win the case for Caraco.

Scientists are usually reluctant to question the holy grails but some business development guy with sharp logic emboldened by Dilip-bhai or Dilip-bhai himself may question something so fundamental, that it gives us a clue as to what can be done next,' beamed Kirti.

But for the first seven years in the US, when Caraco complications refused to die down, Sun focused on learning the ropes and did business on safer ground, where patents for products had either expired or were about to expire and FDA gave its approval on the condition that the generic product would be launched after the patent expiry. These are called Para-II and Para-III opportunities.

Unlike its larger peers, it didn't straightaway dive into the cookie jar, the most coveted of opportunities for generic drug makers that came with the highest risks (hefty investments) but highest rewards. These are called 'first to files' (FTFs) and Para-IVs.

Para-IV opportunities are the most charming business opportunities in the generic drug business, where if the first copying drug-maker proves that its version of product doesn't infringe the innovator's patents, or that the innovator's patent claims are invalid, it gets to sell its drug exclusively for 180 days in a market that had been monopolized by the originator pharma firm.

Besides Shanghvi's general tendency to prepare thoroughly before acting, Sun's reluctance to go the Para-IV route could also have derived motivation from four other possible sources: one, at heart Shanghvi was a pacifist and avoided fights; two, each such litigation cost $3–6 million and was a hugely expensive affair by Sun's conservative money spend standard; three, from one angle Para-IVs were a sort of a gamble for one-time gain, an area Shanghvi detested (his cousins, relatives and friends dabble in share market frequently, many of them for fun, but not Shanghvi); and four, his long-term view on business made him wary of committing resources and banking on one-off opportunities, however tempting they appeared.

However, as Sun forayed into the US, its India strategies couldn't have helped Shanghvi in that mature healthcare market. So he changed tack in more than one way. 'India had been a branded generics business, the doctor was the starting point. Since the US was a pure generics business, the rules of the play changed. One had to deal with organized wholesalers,' Kirti pointed out. Drug wholesalers controlled nearly 75 per cent of the US generic market. We switched our cafeteria approach of India to a portfolio approach which meant that we had to have an attractive basket of complex generics—a whole lot of them vis-à-vis our rivals to entice the pharmacy chains, Kirti added.

Sun shifted gears to not restrict itself to chronic therapies, an approach it had followed fanatically in India. Irrespective of therapies, Shanghvi looked at product categories and picked some, which were most difficult to make—the complex generics.

Fundamentally, the question Shanghvi asked himself remained unchanged, 'What can I offer so that the drug distributors have no choice but to stock? In India, the answer to that would have been—whatever brand the doctor prescribes; but not in the US.'

While hand-picking drugs from the Orange Book, his philosophical approach was the same—a path of least resistance to find products of lowest competitive intensity. What followed were some corollary questions: which are the drugs no one is doing here, which are the drugs generic companies are not able to do and how can Sun differentiate that product, add value by modifying it a bit to garner market share?

This is how complex and difficult-to-make generic drugs or feature-loaded smart drugs became a signature of Sun in the US. Here, Shanghvi's extensive homework in the Indian market, his rigorous review meetings and strong network with doctors came handy. Shanghvi had, through his continuous deep interactions with doctors in and outside the company ecosystem, mastered the knowledge of drugs by class and needs. So he said, 'Many diabetics are asked to take one drug fifteen minutes before lunch and one after half an hour. Give me one tablet that releases the drug before and after the meal just the way the doctor wants it.' He arrived at the logic of drug prescriptions and directed in-house innovations to triple combinations, dual combinations of various kinds, seeking to patent them.

'An asthmatic and a hypertensive wakes up feeling giddy early in the morning till he has his first dose of medicine. I want a technology so that the patient can pop the tablet in the night, but the drug is released only at dawn.' Thus Sun patented time-release technologies in chronotherapy, a technology that works in harmony with the body's natural rhythm.

For very high-dose, chunky, difficult-to-swallow drugs that had to be taken several times a day, Sun patented a 'wrap-matrix technology' that helped the patient take a not-so-bulky drug once a day. For those that couldn't get digested in the colon or lower digestive tract, Sun patented a technology GRID that improved drug absorption by retaining it for a long-time in the stomach.

The same search had led him to focus on drugs like peptides, steroids and hormones and technologies like targeted delivery that delivered the medicine at the site of the tumour, reducing side effects (for instance Doxcil; a generic of J&J's cancer drug) and depot that reduces dosage intake, where the drug is released in microgram quantities over a month or a three-month period (for instance, leuprolide depot, a man-made hormone used in cancer). Many of these were areas where competition was limited. Sun became the first or one of the first few generic drug companies to make some of these drugs.

At any given point, the company's research arms were working on 200 products—of which fifteen to twenty would be first-to-file candidates.

The first-to-file research team worked closely with intellectual property teams in the company. Unlike other companies, where IP teams reported to the CEO or R&D heads, Shanghvi made his IP head report to the business development chief, with the logic that the patent cases Sun picked up must have a business rationale to it. Most lines of arguments in legal cases were instructed to be developed in-house, and for high-potential, high-cost, important cases, Shanghvi still does it himself.

Higher the Share-Price, Lower the Valuation

Even as Shanghvi was going about his crash course in US patents, a short breather for Sun came after the US FDA lifted strictures on the Caraco facility and started reviewing its pending drug applications in 2001. Brokerage firm IDBI Capital called it 'the inflection point' for Caraco, set for a turnaround. From racking up losses of $56 million, it had turned in a profit in 2003.

The contract terms for product–equity swapping approaching its expiry date were renewed. This time a total of twenty-five such products were to be transferred over five years, starting 2002. A panel of independent directors at Caraco were to pick which products it wanted from Sun's basket offering for Caraco's portfolio. Sun kept its promise, transferred ten ANDAs to Caraco, asking the independent directors to choose. By 2002, Caraco had started filing for Sun's products at FDA and it seemed that the oddly unique business relationship between the two companies was finally stabilizing.

But this sigh of relief that Sun had breathed was short-lived. In 2003, the filings of Sun ANDAs stopped inexplicably. Analysts and journalists following Sun's trajectory were left guessing what could have gone wrong. The Caraco independent directors sat on Sun's ANDA basket for over a year, choosing not to pick any. Quarter after quarter, when Shanghvi was pelted with questions during results on whether more ANDAs had been filed, he could only come up with a disappointing 'None yet'.

Journalists and analysts covering the issue believed that behind the stabilizing business, unrest was brewing against Shanghvi's technology transfer plan particularly provoked by two large investors who were part of the independent committee. Surprisingly, years later, Shanghvi denied knowledge of any such rage among Caraco investors, saying, 'We still have good relations with them.'

At the heart was the sequel of the novel deal architecture Shanghvi had designed for the takeover. As Caraco's business picked up, its stock started soaring, outperforming the NASDAQ in 2002–03. Interestingly, the notional value of each ANDA Sun was to transfer to Caraco was tightly tethered to the price of the Caraco scrip on the day its ANDA passed regulatory (bio-equivalency) tests. As the Caraco stock price zoomed from $3 to $12 between March 2003 and August 2003, the cost of ANDAs to Caraco shot up as well. That posed a catch 22 situation.

Instead of jumping with joy at the skyrocketing stock and profit-promising products tumbling in from Sun, as conventional investors would be expected to—board members and investors Jay Joliat and David Hagelstein—were deeply worried that if the share prices continued to ascend, Caraco would soon be bleeding again. And this would adversely affect the company's valuations and their investment.

'These local investors were from a non-pharma background—from real estate and finance sectors. For them, money locked in Caraco was major personal investments they couldn't afford to look away from. They had also been jittery about the US FDA objections the company had just emerged out of, and fretted a lot about running into more such problems in future. On top of it, they were unhappy with this product–equity swap despite having signed on such an arrangement,' a top Caraco executive of that time said. People reneging on their word and signs would show up in Shanghvi's life in a more convoluted form in the years to follow but entangled in Caraco at this point, he couldn't have guessed what this event was preparing him for.

The brokerage firm Karvy puzzled over the paradox; at the prevailing share rates, the price of ANDA Caraco had to shell out to Sun was far too higher than developing those products in-house, a move that was bound to incur the wrath of minority investors, but if Sun bought out 20 per cent minority shareholders at $10 (existing price of $9 per share and a logical premium), the deal would have turned unviable (for Sun).

Valia recounted how he and Shanghvi made a trip to the US every 2–3 months between 2001 and 2003 to sort out issues with Caraco shareholders and executives. 'We realized our messages were being blacked out or not being relayed in the right spirit. So it made sense to fly there and clear out misunderstandings frequently,' Valia said.

From their interactions with analysts, it seemed that Shanghvi and Valia acknowledged the concerns of investors as 'valid'.

The first time Shanghvi explained the oddly complex problem was in October 2003, in the next quarterly call. 'Because the value of the Caraco share has moved up significantly, the total value for technology transfer for every product has shot up to $4.5–5 million, and since it has significant impact on their overall profitability, we have an ongoing discussion with the independent committee of directors about the products to be chosen for filing . . . it has a potential to affect the business of the company.'

When an analyst logically deduced that a climb-up of Caraco shares was unlikely to harm Sun's prospects given it was expected to earn a definite block of shares per ANDA, Shanghvi said, 'It does matter because it impacts valuation of Caraco, subsequently impacting us (Sun being a 45 per cent shareholder in Caraco). We are trying to find some solution. We have not arrived at any solution, which solves the issue in a very balanced kind of way.'

However, one reason they had failed to arrive at a solution was that Shanghvi 'refused to rework the agreement. He felt Sun deserved the shares as it was responsible for Caraco's turnaround,' Gauri Kamath of *Business World* reported. In fact, when an analyst hinted at the possibility of a dollar-linked arrangement instead of a share-linked one to solve the impasse, Shanghvi was quick to dismiss the tip claiming 'it will not be in the Sun shareholders' interest'.

Shanghvi's apparent solution to the problem was a twist in the tale. In January 2004, Caraco made a surprise announcement that its independent directors would no longer have any say on which products will be selected from Sun's stable to be swapped for shares. An external agency had been hired to set 'objective' criteria, which would form the basis for such selection.

Behind this, there had been a buy-out and a swift sorting of problems by Shanghvi and Valia. In October and November 2004, the two large investors opposed to Sun's plans had resigned from the board after having realized that they couldn't remain directors and sell their shares in the open market without reporting each trade under the insider trading laws, reported *Business World*. Holkar had retired from Caraco as CEO in August but had continued on the board. Shanghvi and Valia had quickly sought the permission of the board and bought out 17 per cent of Caraco from them for $42 million at $9 per share. This took Sun's holding to 61 per cent from 43 per cent in Caraco.

'Like any astute businessman, Mr Shanghvi wanted to raise his stake in Caraco and he saw that opportunity in the paradox of investors. These were primarily financial investors, who wanted to maximize their profits with a Caraco turnaround and exit. The first move of sending a buy-out proposal came from Sun and not from the investors,' a former top executive of Caraco said.

Many in Sun's India office had seen it as a 'crisis brought on Dilip-bhai's head by Caraco shareholders ganging up against him'. G.P. Singh, who had gone from Sun to work in Caraco at the time, called it a problem but not a crisis. 'It's the lens that makes the difference. Seen from the perspective of Indian law, where promoters usually get things done as they wish, it may appear as a crisis. But in the US, where shareholder activism operates at an absolutely different level, where independent directors can make or mar a deal, it was a glitch but not a crisis,' Singh felt.

Though impressed by how smoothly Shanghvi had resolved the emerging crisis, many around thought that at four times the sales of Caraco, he had paid far too much to settle it. A Caraco top executive disagreed, 'It was a controlling stake. Most importantly, it gave Mr Shanghvi the freedom to buy another sizeable chunk of Caraco at a price he wanted (by selling the 25 Sun ANDAs at a share-linked price). For him it was strategic, not an investment decision.'

More Than One Way to the Goal

Shanghvi couldn't have let his American dream go sour, and he had resolutely worked on his belief that there was more than one way to reach a goal. This revealed itself not only in the manner Sun took hold of Caraco, but also the way it dug out alternative routes to the US market, outside of Caraco. By 2004, when it had become abundantly clear that Caraco was not turning out to be the great American launch vehicle, Sun had started filing ANDAs directly from India. Two of its India plants—Halol and Panoli—had been spruced up for US FDA approval.

Even in the US, a parallel structure to Caraco was erected and Sun built its business supported by its own set-up in New Jersey. To build that business Shanghvi hunted out good bargains in 2005, and bought New Jersey-based ABLE Labs that had filed for liquidation.

Earlier that year, Sun had snapped up manufacturing plants in Hungary and Ohio from Valeant Pharmaceuticals, which was selling off its non-core businesses, for less than $10 million. The year before, he had bought two women's health brands from a bankrupt American firm for less than $5 million, which he recovered by selling just the inventory. This set of actions prompted an investment banker to project in *Business World*, 'Sun will never do a size-altering M&A deal because it's not interested in spending that kind of money.' He was proved wrong in time. But among his industry peers, Shanghvi was beginning to acquire a new Hindi nickname for picking up distressed assets and turning them around, 'a ragpicker artist'.

A few years after the Caraco regulatory crisis had passed, Shanghvi admitted to an analyst that at Sun they had used the money they had raised from public issue conservatively, but then he added, '. . . irrespective of what investors perceived, we are not risk-averse if we are confident of execution . . . But we do not invest in businesses if we do not understand, and we do not invest if we cannot live with a worst-case probability. At any point in time, any one of the strategy that we are working on, if, let us say, none of them work out, that we would at the most expose our profit that year is the conscious investment philosophy that we have followed.'

Given the statement, does it come as a surprise that the same man was called 'Mr Conservative' by one magazine and 'The Contrarian' by another a few years apart. A friend tried to solve the mystery—what is contrarian to others is conservative for him, he sees much more than others.

Encounter with US Marshals

After Sun took majority control of Caraco its fortunes soared. Revenue streams were exploited to the hilt, costs discipline thrust upon and adversities turned into opportunities, Sun style. In 2003, when diabetes drug metformin saw a demand surge, a raw-material supplier ditched Caraco in favour of a bigger player in the face of shortage.

'We were not able to supply to a government business we had bid for. Jitu-bhai, who had worked in the metformin raw-material making plant in India, connected with Mr Valia to file regulatory applications with FDA in record time and we restarted supplies,' Singh recalled. It not only turned out to be one of the most profitable business for Caraco, but set the process of buying bulk drugs from Sun for the other formulations it was selling. This made Caraco's business competitive, it's sourcing dependable, and grew Sun's bulk drugs sales monumentally—a non-zero-sum game.

'Sun Pharma has infused dynamism into Caraco and transformed it to become one of the most profitable generic companies in the US,' gushed Rajesh Vora of ICICI Securities in 2004. A year later, in another report, he added, 'Caraco enjoys possibly the highest EBITDA margins of 40 per cent in the generic market in the world.'

Doshi who had filled in Holkar's shoes at Caraco was sent to New Jersey to head Sun's US business and after a thorough search, Daniel Movens was appointed the new CEO at Caraco.

In the mid-noughties, when fierce price erosion was choking the US generic market, and growth of peers like Dr Reddy's and Ranbaxy was falling sharply, Caraco was growing at a rate double the US generic market. Backed by Sun's products, Caraco's sales grew by a whopping 50 per cent annually between 2003 and 2006 to touch $83 million, at which point it became the second largest Indian player in the US. And of the twenty-five-odd products Caraco was selling, most of which were ancient and small, it had built a leading position in fourteen products. This when Sun's real game in the US was yet to truly begin.

Industry watchers, who had dubbed Shanghvi's US game plan 'floundering' and a 'fatal error of judgement' in 2002–03, were calling it 'gravity-defying', 'spectacular' and 'transformative' by 2006.

But the men now driving Caraco in the US—Indian as well as Americans—truly never stopped worrying about the future prospects of their company. That the phenomenal growth was on a small base was not their top worry. They knew deep down in their minds that their company had largely turned into a sales and marketing firm, which owed a large part of its success to Sun's products, and if they had to validate their existence as a generic drug maker, the company must build its own product portfolio.

Movens after taking charge in 2005 decided to take this concern head-on and went to the drawing board. Shanghvi supported his plans to acquire land and build more manufacturing capacity.

However, while the edifice was being built for Caraco, what the builders seem to have missed was a termite gnawing away at the foundation—compliance history. And this little bug was to explode in 2009.

Court papers in the US reveal that 483s (objections of the US FDA) had become a way of life at Caraco. Between 2005 and 2008, US facilities making drugs for Caraco had been slapped with five 483s. In 2008, Movens was warned by external auditor Quintiles Consulting of a 'real possibility of FDA enforcement action, maybe a 'mass seizure'. Quintile's email 'startled' Caraco's management because they 'hadn't seen such seizures happening in the industry'. When Movens raked up the matter with Caraco vice-presidents Robert Kurkiewicz (quality head) and Dan Barone, both thought Quintile was 'being an alarmist', he later testified in court.

But just months later, an FDA warning letter called Caraco's responses to 483s grossly inadequate, and warned it of dire consequences, including seizures. Movens enlisted another external audit firm Kendle International, which again explicitly warned Caraco of a civil injunction. Kendle advised it to recall and destroy products, and forget about moving to the newly constructed facility before they get a clean chit from US FDA.

Caraco management took the advice on most counts and wrote a letter to FDA telling that its construction of the facilities was not so much to expand as it was to modernize its plants. But the very same month, in one of its press statements, it said something else, 'We believe we are substantially compliant with cGMP (current Good Manufacturing Practices) and intend to aggressively move forward with the development of new products.' This revealed the underlying confusion that was snowballing into a crisis.

'Dan was a very sensible guy, but he wasn't a technical person, so he was relying on the team for a feedback. The quality team probably couldn't grasp the enormity of the trouble brewing. Some of those quality guys had their life built in Sun and they couldn't mean any harm to the company. But it was an error of judgement, an 'expensive one at that', Singh recalled. His colleague felt that the US FDA was realigning at that moment and Caraco gave them an opportunity to make an example out of. 'We were growing too fast, we should have seen a slap at the wrist coming.'

In May 2008, when Caraco was expecting a resolution, it was struck with a re-inspection that ended with a whopping eighteen observations of violations. 'The guys at Caraco had clearly misread the gravity of 483s. The FDA was giving a message which they had not interpreted the way they should have and that led to the trouble,' Shanghvi said. But it wasn't until a day in June 2008, which began like a normal working day that the sky came crashing down upon Caraco.

The firm was hosting important business clients and talks on a potential deal were under way at the office, when US marshals barged into its warehouses and seized all goods. Singh was in the meeting chit-chatting with visitors, when a colleague knocked and whispered into his ears. Colour drained off Singh's shocked face, but he composed himself the next minute to continue the conversation with the guests. 'We couldn't let the panic show. So we finished our meetings and saw the visitors out,' Singh recalled. Movens was with the marshals, helping them, but also struggling to explain that not all goods in the warehouse were Caraco's, a share of stock belonged to Sun which hadn't been made in the Caraco facilities that were being seized.

Movens, Singh by his side, then made a call to Shanghvi. As unflappable they had seen Shanghvi to be, they had expected him to lose it. But he didn't react right away, instead he said, 'OK, let's focus on handling the situation and we will find a way.'

'Imagine the confidence his calmness instils in people who are hearing him on the phone. At that moment, it felt that here is a man who will stand by us, help us out and protect us,' Singh recalled. Movens called everyone in a town-hall meeting to break the news, committing to fixing problems.

Asked in a *Financial Express* interview, whether the problems at Caraco could have been handled more convincingly, he responded, 'To answer a question in hindsight is always easy. The fact is that whatever Caraco did was, from their point of view, to the best of their intention.'

Eight years later, Shanghvi said, 'I realized that having a CEO who is not technically oriented led to some of those issues. The people at Caraco knew a few things but were missing the whole picture. Most importantly, we needed to have strong people who could just stand up and say "no" when the CEO or his superior is exerting pressure to release the products into the market. We didn't have those people at Caraco who could come back with a firm "no" that is in the larger interest, even if it means an unpleasant interaction on the spot.'

Usual disruption followed the shutdown of the plant at Caraco. Movens stepped down from the CEO's post, taking responsibility, Kaushik Gandhi, head of manufacturing quit, reportedly mass retrenchments (claimed as around fifty in the courts) happened from the next day and sales dropped.

Shanghvi said incorrect incentives pulled Caraco down. 'I also realized that we had not created the appropriate incentivization at Caraco. After all, incentives are what drive and change behaviours in an organization. The entire lending bubble in the US boiled down to just about that—incorrect incentives—when the bank managers had been incentivized to lend more, but not incentivized to assess the quality of that lending, that is, the creditworthiness of the client. There was a problem in the incentive structure. At the same time, Buffett has a company which specialized in setting up manufactured housing, a type of prefabricated dwelling unit and modular houses (Clayton Homes) that had zero bad debt, because the incentives were designed so appropriately to avoid bad loans. In Caraco, we had designed incentives to reward sales growth but not so much compliance. And that led to the consequences we faced. Had we designed our incentives better, attaching a higher weight to compliance, people there wouldn't have released those products to the market.'

Negotiations with FDA on Caraco didn't stop at anything but a consent decree or CD as it is known. A CD is seen in industry circles as an albatross around the neck—making it almost impossible to function in normalcy under the prescribed burden of additional rules. History, financial prudence, business rationale—all pointed towards one direction: to shut the factory and shift to other options. 'Many people asked, "Why should we stay put and invest in this plant? It doesn't make business sense. Why spend so much to come out of a consent decree, instead of focusing on the New Jersey plant. That's what competition does." When large companies get into trouble, they shut their plants and move on,' a Caraco employee said.

'I think, despite the din around doing the contrary, the only reason we focused on coming out of consent decree was that Mr Shanghvi didn't want a regulatory blot on his track record. He was so clear that he wanted Sun to come out clean from this challenge and be perceived as an organization committed to quality. That was it,' Singh asserted.

Shanghvi was vocal about it in his meetings. He brought Vipul Doshi, Sun's head of quality and Lachman Consultants on board to recoup Caraco back to health. And he often said, 'There is only one objective. I don't want an FDA action on my track record. We had got a warning letter in 1999. We worked and came out of it. We can do it this time as well.' Along the way, he struck a valuable friendship with Leon Lachman, founder of Lachman Consultants, an outfit that would come handy in the biggest acquisition of his professional life, and the process itself would prove to be a dress rehearsal for a much larger future regulatory crisis.

Shortly after Caraco's regulatory entanglement, Shanghvi told *Financial Express*, 'We never give up on what we want; we persevere and succeed.'

In 2011 Sun announced that Caraco would be delisted and merged with its Indian parent. A few years later, having outlived its utility, Caraco's Detroit facility was shut down by Sun. But not before it resumed partial operations three years after facing complete closure. His rival, owner of Cadila Healthcare, Pankaj Patel said, 'Caraco was an experiment for him, a learning ground. He suffered and he won.'

Research Mode to a Fight

If there's such a thing to relax one's way to a fight—adopting a research temperament to daggers and blows—Shanghvi had mastered it. His US product strategy showed how. For a long time after 1997, the year Caraco was bought over, Sun had no major products in the US.

Then there was a fairly long period when Sun had only two or three products making up a bulk of its US sales. Diabetes drug metformin and hypertension drug metropolol accounted for almost 80 per cent in 2003.

Sun began filing ANDAs slowly in 2002, steadily improved its rate over the next three years. From there on, having learnt the game, Sun multiplied its applications at a meteoric rate post 2006, adding over twenty ANDAs every year thereafter. 'Once you get the ANDA game, it's like copy and paste,' Kirti quipped.

Sun also debuted in the famed Para-IV drug-wrestling circles in the year 2005, ready to muscle it out with big pharmas legally. Bold as he may well be, Shanghvi's preference for a staircase to a leap manifested itself in his Para-IV strategy as well. Keeping legal costs low was only one reason why Shanghvi chose Ortho-McNeil's combination painkiller Ultracet (tramadol and acetaminophen) as his first challenge.

With $300 million annual sales, it wasn't a blockbuster drug to go after. Generic drug giants Teva and Par had already queued up ahead of Caraco. So Caraco wasn't going to get the six-month exclusive marketing opportunity that comes with a 'first to file' status.

In fact, these 'not so business-worthy' factors, combined with limited competition became the very reasons why Shanghvi chose Ultracet as his first Para-IV candidate. Since Caraco was not the most imminent threat looming before the innovator's parent J&J, Shanghvi realized stakes were not very high for it to expend its mighty energies and fight out Caraco for a relatively small product. This meant Shanghvi had little to lose and a lot to learn in the case.

When Caraco finally mounted the case against Ortho-McNeil, its lawyers chose to argue that their way of making the painkiller didn't infringe upon the innovator's patent claims, despite having gathered solid arguments to invalidate them.

Ortho had patented a weight ratio of 'about 1:5' in which tramadol and acetaminophen had be combined to have the desired effect. Caraco tweaked that ratio in its application to not infringe upon the patent. When Ortho argued that its ratio was still too close to be statistically different, Caraco altered its weight ratio even further. It paid off with the court ruling in favour of Caraco in October 2005, much faster than expected. Caraco launched its first Para-IV drug in December 2005.

'Our first Para-IV product generic Ultracet helped us build credibility with customers, who started taking us much more seriously,' Singh recalled. This prepared Sun for a giant step in the Para-IV space.

Shanghvi worked with Caraco CEO Movens to build up a stellar Para-IV list which, combined with Sun's powerful line-up, became a list that became an object of envy for other Indian players in the US. Caraco's first six-month-exclusivity product was a shared one, a generic of Novartis AG's anti-epilepsy drug Trileptal (oxcarbazepine) with a market-size of $640 million, which it launched in October 2007. Caraco garnered 25 per cent market share quickly in the product.

'Sun has been "silently investing" in building up a very high-quality Para-IV ANDA pipeline leveraging its superior chemistry process skills to come up with challenging patent suits,' brokerage firm SSKI noted in December 2007.

A year before that, Shyamal Ghosh, an avid reader, who was then heading Sun Bangladesh, asked Shanghvi, 'Dilip-bhai, I read this business magazine piece gushing about how well Dr Reddy's is doing in the US, filing so many ANDAs.'

'Do you know we have crossed Dr Reddy's in the number of ANDAs that we filed in 2005?' Shanghvi responded with a question.

Ghosh was baffled and said, 'Then why aren't we shouting from the rooftop?'

'Because we don't like noise,' Shanghvi joked.

This conversation on not making noise about ANDAs reminded Ghosh of how he, from time to time, tried to persuade Shanghvi for a more posh office space matching Sun's stature. 'Dilip-bhai, Glenmark and Wockhardt have such big buildings with huge flashy boards announcing their presence with pride. When are we going to have a Sun House befitting our accomplishments?'

'But why exactly do we need that?' Shanghvi asked.

Years later, when Sun finally would have a Sun House, Ghosh and his friends had once dreamt of, its name board still remained tiny enough to be a search object for a treasure hunt.

Among the Para-IV battles, the one case that tested Shanghvi's 'contrarian' mettle the most was generic of $2.3 billion drug Protonix. Singh, as sales head of Caraco, recalled being present in the telephonic brainstorming sessions between Movens and Shanghvi, in what he saw as a 'bet the company' decision.

Sun shared the exclusivity opportunity with Teva, which had launched at risk in December 2007. At home, Shanghvi sat extensively with lawyers to grasp the risks of the case. No one was clear about the damages. If a patent infringement was proved, US law held the violator liable for triple damages, which meant calculating the damages and multiplying by three. But there had been no precedents in pharmaceuticals. So what was the formula to calculate the damage? Was it the money the generic firm made, which the innovator would have made, or was it what innovator could have made in its monopoly had a generic not been launched and eroded the market size by 60 to 90 per cent? No formula went beyond 'could haves' and 'should haves'.

The landscape was complex as well with Teva engaging in settlement discussions with Wyeth. To give a truce a chance, Teva had stopped shipping its products, but in an indication of broken talks, Wyeth surprised everyone by bringing its own authorized generics on 29 January 2008.

A day after that Sun launched. It was singularly Shanghvi who took the call to launch a generic of Protonix at risk. 'That decision gave us shivers. It had the potential to be a multi-billion-dollar liability that could wipe out not only Caraco but also Sun,' Singh said as he recalled sitting and listening to that decision being made by Shanghvi—to launch the generic at risk, exactly a day after Wyeth had launched its authorized copy of drug.

Singh had done his maths over and over again on the bet going wrong and repeatedly went to Movens dreading that the decision would backfire. Singh was not alone, almost everyone across the board dubbed it an unsmart move.

But behind the 'contrarian' decision there had been a 'conservative' calculation of Shanghvi. He had briefed the lawyer. 'Let Teva launch first. Let Teva kill the market, erode it the maximum. Let the authorized generic be launched next. With that second launch, price erosion would be complete. We launch then. In court we will argue that we never killed the market. Teva did, and then you innovator, you did, by bringing your own generic. You killed your own market, or whatever was left of it. The case may be consolidated, but the damages will be individual. Second, how can the innovator charge us, when it has authorized its own generic to be launched?'

This was just one of the many cases Bharati had witnessed, where Shanghvi pinpointed the premises over which he asked the lawyers to build their arguments. 'When Dilip-bhai interprets law, it's not a layman's interpretation. He gets to the root of the problem. Because he is so great at deciphering the logic behind anything, stuff that flows from logic, say, law, he is superb at.'

The patent changed multiple hands, as companies gobbled up each other and finally it fell on Pfizer's shoulders to prove that Sun and Teva had infringed Protonix patents. Pfizer was brutally offensive in defending the patents.

A case that dragged on for almost nine years was settled out of court with one of the largest penalties shelled out for the purpose. Shanghvi chose to depose in the case himself and sat with the judge to get a settlement done.

Of the $2.5 billion, Sun had to pick the tab for $550 million. When the news broke making headlines across business channels, Shanghvi was having dinner with his wife and a business associate at Grand Maratha in Mumbai. His wife, Vibha, spotted it on the television and asked in Gujarati, 'Dilip, you never told. The news channels are showing that Sun has to pay ₹3000 crore in the US as fine.' The business associate recounted Shanghvi responding in a tease, 'Do you ever recall me telling when I earned that money?'

Singh has that day etched in his mind, when the fat cheque was being issued and his heart was sinking. The total outflow for penalty was almost 42 per cent of Sun Pharma's cash and cash equivalents at the time. 'You build a business so painstakingly and then it all ends like that. I was heartbroken,' said Singh, the Caraco CEO then.

But then what he heard Shanghvi say that day left an indelible impression on his mind, making him feel where everyone else saw a problem, 'Dilip-bhai saw a possibility.' 'Even after writing this cheque, this has been a great success story for us. Without this experience we couldn't have come so far. The learnings we got out of this journey cannot be quantified,' Shanghvi declared. He could very well be saying this about his 'Caraco journey' in the US.

Not sulking too much when things didn't go its way, nor rolling in raptures when it did was one trait that helped Sun to steadily build its Para-IV product pipeline over the years and overtake all Indian peers to emerge as the largest challenger by 2010, despite being a late entrant in the US market.

It was a reflection of Shanghvi's philosophy—staying unhurried but involved can cover the longest distance possible in the long run. Shanghvi believed in the philosophy deeply enough to espouse a fable in a mailer to many of his employees championing a tortoise's slow and steady approach over the hare's fast and burnt-out one.

Discovery—Sailing in an Uncertain Boat

At the turn of 1990, when Shanghvi had started doing well—his cousin Nana-bhai asked him, 'Dilip, what do you wish to do when you have done enough of this business and already made say ₹100 crore?' In a breezy moment, Shanghvi responded, 'Maybe I will leave the business for professionals to manage and focus full-time on research and development. Drug discovery fascinates me. Maybe I shall have to relocate to the US because that is where I can do what I wish to do.'

That dream, if it was serious, hasn't come true. His first major attempt at substantial delegation entailed luring in Kal Sundaram, credited with turning around GSK India's business, as Sun's CEO in 2010. In a meeting with his top brass, Shanghvi said, 'I know many of you wouldn't like this. You have spent so many years in Sun and now I got a person from outside to become the CEO. Each one of you can drive Sun. But you have seen me as MD for far too long to question me beyond a point. I want a CEO who can question me when I am not performing. I believe I have limitations, which need to be challenged. Kal has been a friend and a colleague who has never shied away from telling, "This is not right, Dilip."'

On the research front, Sun's R&D spend as a share of its sales ranged between 9.6 to 12 per cent during 2006–08, the highest in the Indian pharma industry (most large drug firms spent about 5.5 per cent) and was still soaring. But there is a fundamental incongruity in the business of innovative research and generic drug making; the latter has to be swift and agile, churning out quick results, the former needs deep investments and decades of patience.

Also under one roof, research arms become money guzzlers, weakening the profitability of the generic drug business.

So Shanghvi demerged and listed the innovative arm SPARC. The de-merged entity housed its projects of new chemical entities (NCE) and novel drug delivery systems (NDDS).

Sun has done reasonably well in technologies that power smart drugs—NDDS. The moment of its crowning glory arrived when it achieved something none of its generic peers had, by launching a generic of J&J's cancer drug Doxil by a breakthrough Shanghvi had first thought of by drawing an analogy from dialysis, a completely unrelated process. The drug was named 'Lipodox' despite the US team's insistence to name it 'Doxlipo', and the project inside Sun had been nicknamed 'Lipo'.

Sun was the first in the world to achieve the feat, but getting an approval in the US was not easy, had it not been for an unforeseen shortage J&J faced in 2011. Sun had been marketing the drug in India since 2006 and trying to get an approval in Europe.

But the team was surprised when in 2011, the US regulator wrote to Sun asking if it could supply to the US market. Sun's shares reached an all-time peak on the news break. The team worked day and night to make the tests for the US approval happen.

At one time demand from the US surged so much that the India team complained of crunch. Shanghvi called Kirti and said, 'Just because the US is fetching a better price doesn't mean that you cut down on India's share.'

In an out-of-character celebration that Sun hosted for Lipodox by calling all stakeholders at Baroda's Lukshmi Vilas Palace, Shanghvi quipped that between smartness and luck, he had always preferred luck because there were too many smart people out there, but not all of them were lucky.

Shanghvi's luck on one Li—Lipodox had reminded him of his first stroke of luck with another Li—Lithosun, his first drug that became a hit due to a rival's product shortage, a chance that had literally made Sun.

But luck has eluded him in pure drug discovery. Sun tried to discover a long-acting, non-sedating, anti-allergy drug with fewer side effects code-named 1334H through an 'analogue' approach. This approach adopted a shorter and quicker route to a new product because it was built upon the existing body of knowledge and science that was already well understood. So compared to the traditional inventive process of a trial-and-error case to find a new molecule, this approach cut risks, saved resources, albeit being involved in an incremental process. Sun claimed in 2005 that this approach traditionally employed in generic drugs, was being used for the first time in the world for NCEs.

In its debate to file in India or the US first, US won. Through incredibly challenging, if they won in the US in drug discovery, they knew the world would take note. The Phase-II clinical trial results were encouraging and preparations started for the Pre-IND (Investigational New Drug) meeting with the US FDA. Dr Badrul Chowdhury, who was to head the meeting from the US FDA panel, was known to start with, 'What happens if I don't approve this product?'

Team members from India knew that they could have problems comprehending the American accent, so plans were made for members who were fluent in English to translate in simple Indian English what was transpiring. The meeting taught Sun team how to field questions from the FDA and a takeaway from the science of the NCEs. The US FDA didn't ask it to abandon the molecule, but made it clear that they were looking for breakthrough research in NCEs, which could fill a big therapy gap, not just another new anti-allergy drug among a crowd of existing anti-allergies. That new chemical entity may have added a feather in Sun's cap for having done it, but did nothing great for the humanity at large. Shanghvi decided to keep emotions aside and put a lid to the project.

Why a man—who has made the smartest choices in drug selection in India despite being totally untrained in science; who chooses rooms less crowded in business and has the patience to wait for decades for a dream to come true; who adopts the slow but steady pace of the tortoise to the burn-out fast run of a hare—despite all his gifts, has failed to give the world the first new drug from India?

Shanghvi might have nailed the nub in his reply, 'I don't think my incremental approach is the best approach for all problems. I always begin with this question: "Will my resources permit such a step?" Every step I pursue is from the baseline of resources I have at that moment. Many innovator companies begin with the question of what they want and what it would take them to reach there and then look and arrange for resources to make something happen.'

His staircase model of growth that has worked so brilliantly for him in other areas of his business might have become a roadblock in discovering a drug. To invent, perhaps, one needs more than a climb-up, maybe a leap of faith.

Some around him seem to think that he is limited less by himself, more by his milieu. After observing his rival turned boss for almost a decade, Sundaram said he cannot begin to imagine the life story Shanghvi would have woven, had he been born or trained in the US or a similar country that valued innovations and entrepreneurship differently and had an ecosystem to reward these. Sundaram obviously hadn't eavesdropped on a dream Shanghvi had once shared with a cousin in a misty moment.

CHAPTER SEVENTEEN

TARO HAI PAR MHARO HAI

The friendship that the two of them share today hadn't bloomed back then in 2007, and an Israel-bound flight was not where they had expected to bump into each other, particularly because each one was on a secret mission each one would have wished the other to not know of.

Oblivious but guessing what the other could be up to, the two were actually heading for an identical purpose—buying Taro for their respective companies. Wishing or not, Pankaj Patel, the owner of Cadila Healthcare—woke up from a power nap to find Shanghvi in the same flight; the two expressed surprise and exchanged pleasantries. The Cadila contingency to weigh and bid for Taro numbered about fourteen people and the strength of the Sun army to do the same was two—Shanghvi and Valia.

Cadila's top brass had indulged in their ritualistic pre-acquisition exercise where its senior-most executives valued Taro individually, explained their rationale to Patel who took a final call. 'I wasn't ready to pay half of what they offered. His perception of value is different from all of us. In Taro, we were doing a classic textbook value assessment, he did an intuitive exercise,' Patel admitted. In the war-room set-up of the Acme Plaza office of Sun, the team had arrived at a ceiling price of $5 per share. That's what took Sun to the last round of bidding for Taro.

But in his mind, Shanghvi was ready to stretch that figure. The twists and turns of the Taro saga would reveal that elasticity. In time, as matters in Taro got entangled and Shanghvi raised his bid, he explained to CEO Kal Sundaram, the rationale of the increased price—assigning every dollar per share he was shelling out to what Sun was acquiring—capabilities, relationships (with customers), knowledge (of branded drugs), R&D expertise and world-class facilities.

For Shanghvi the main reason behind the pursuit of Taro was to attain a critical mass in the US after having architected his company's presence in the world's largest drug market through Caraco and Sun. At the time, Sun was already deriving about 40 per cent of its sales from the US market. 'Taro had a robust presence in the US (90 per cent of its sales emanated from North America) through impressive dermatology products. And derma was our preferred centrepiece to building a critical mass in that market,' Valia said.

In fact, the contours of Taro's dermatology generic drug business in the US market mirrored the psychiatry and neurology segment in India of the 1980s. Amid the crazily competitive and commoditized US generic drug space, dermatology was described as a 'silent and tranquil corner', a space too niche for large companies to pay attention to and too complex for new players to enter.

Sun had till about this point specialized in high-volume drugs in the US, but Taro with its focus on derma in the US seemed exactly the kind of space—rooms less crowded—Shanghvi found most comfortable business-wise.

Besides, when Valia looked up Taro's books during the due diligence exercise, he found their 'accounts management in shambles'. 'The company had shown unreasonably inflated income, borrowed against it, and invested hundreds of millions in creating world-class factories. This exaggeration based on a miscalculated projection of profits had landed it on the brink of a default. Their main weak nerve lay in financial management, which was our forte,' Valia recalled.

In 2006, Taro's shares had tanked, after its chief financial officer quit over a controversial investigation by a law firm into the restatement of its results for 2003 and 2004. Its auditors, Ernst & Young, would need to review the law firm's report before it completed an audit of the 2005 results, that may lead to a further delay in filing its results and a possible delisting from NASDAQ, Taro said.

Once Taro was up for sale, and due diligence and negotiations for it began in full swing, Shanghvi and Valia rented a hotel room in New York, asking the intermediaries to arrange a meeting with Barrie Levitt, the owner and chief negotiator from the side of Taro. They didn't get more than an hour or half to interact with him in a day.

Valia recalled posing to him questions on productivity, the ways Taro gave out discounts to retailers, digging up a bit on accounting systems and so on. In one instance, chatting up on discounts, he recalled quizzing Levitt, 'Why do you allow your marketing departments to extend deep discounts without keeping your accounts department in the loop?'

He then shared with Levitt that at Sun, such a thing was impossible for the marketing arm to do. 'In our ecosystem, marketing can design prices customer-wise, reconfigure prices, and even revise the price list, but our default setting mandates that the credit note is generated through a common system. So by its very design, marketing and accounts cannot operate in silos,' Valia recalled explaining to him.

He recounted Shanghvi asking a volley of questions to Levitt around how Taro arrived at pricing decisions and how its competition was pricing products. These little innocuous queries, Valia believed, could have later become cues for Levitt to turn things around in his own company.

When asked whether Shanghvi felt the same, he replied, 'That's possible. Usually I question the 'Whys?' the most and if you start figuring out the answers that would lead you to bottlenecks and pressure points where you were stuck or could do better.'

Valia and Shanghvi usually chatted with Levitt, returned to their hotel room and then sat down to prepare the questions they wanted to ask him in the next meeting. After their hotel-room homework, in one such meeting, Valia insisted that they add a special clause to their agreement. He sought an exclusivity pact, which fundamentally meant Taro owners couldn't sell stake till the time Sun completed its due diligence.

'By then we had realized that the Levitts were flirting around with multiple players. We were mighty keen on buying Taro, so I did that to seal their commitment,' Valia recalled. Levitt flinched, reluctant to bestow that advantage to Sun. Valia sweetened the offer a bit.

'OK, let's limit this period of exclusivity to just one month. During that period you can go window-shopping but no real shopping. This means you (Taro) could discuss with other players, but if I concluded my price and it suits you, you come along. If someone offers you a better deal, I should have the right of first refusal,' Valia recalled telling Levitt.

Having entered the final round of negotiations, Sun offered $6 per share. By this time Shanghvi and Valia could sense a gap—an Israeli player was having a much stronger sway over Levitt. 'He was totally veering in the Israeli player's direction. After a point, he stopped responding to our calls and offers. His only point of engagement remained: "How much more are you ready to shell out?" But we were not ready to up the price under any imagined pressure,' Valia recalled.

Then came a point when Levitt snapped ties by flatly turning down Shanghvi's offer. He informed that he was inclined to sell to another buyer he had been talking to. Pat reminded Valia, 'I am sorry, you can't go there unless you have my consent.' He retorted, 'Excuse me, are you serious? I will sell it to whomsoever I wish.'

Valia got his lawyer to intervene and presented before him the clause of right of first refusal and warned, 'Any violation, we take you to court.' It was at that moment Levitt revealed that he was sitting on a $7 per share offer from the other buyer.

'We decided to match the price and at the maximum offer up to $7.15 per share,' Valia recalled. The same evening he was packing his stuff to head back to India to attend an urgent meeting Sun was hosting. Shanghvi, the chief negotiator, stayed back to conclude the deal.

Early next morning, as Valia's flight was landing in Mumbai his phone buzzed. It was Shanghvi informing him, 'We have concluded the deal at $7.75.' That was at 27 per cent premium on Taro's prevailing share price.

Valia said, 'Deal done. That's more important than anything else.' The last pricing decision had been only Shanghvi's. Almost a decade after the event, Valia admitted with a good laugh, 'In the April–May of 2007, even $7 for a Taro share felt like a high premium. In hindsight, it did not turn out so bad.'

At home, the team that had slogged it out in the war room thought the same—their boss had overpaid. 'We had built all sorts of models to arrive at a price. Our original non-binding bid was of $5 per share and $7.75 at that point felt much higher than what had been internally decided. But it is Dilip-bhai, only Dilip-bhai, who made all the difference. It was his deep understanding of the business, its future potential, that nudged him to go beyond all conventional wisdom. Ultimately, that price was completely an entrepreneurial risk,' Baldota, the then chief of investor relations at Sun said.

Sundaram reckoned Shanghvi was to business what Sachin Tendulkar was to cricket. 'Just like it is said of Tendulkar, that he can see the ball a fraction of a second before other cricketers, that's true of Dilip in business,' he surmised.

On 21 May 2007, Sun announced its largest deal since inception— of buying Taro, a firm with a net worth that matched Sun's sales, for $454 million, in an all-cash deal. On top, it was to infuse the Israeli firm with an immediate lifeline fund of $49 million (at $6 per share to keep lenders at bay).

But what caught journalists' attention was the last line in the press statement. Tel Aviv courts would be hearing a plea of Franklin Advisers and Templeton Assets Management, who held 9 per cent of Taro's ordinary shares. The fund had challenged the sale in Israeli court alleging the deal was unfair to minority shareholders.

Sun declared Templeton's proceedings 'without merit' and 'detrimental to shareholders' interest'. A public war was to ensue shortly, but it would take nothing less than a tour into a maze of relationships to figure out who was fighting whom exactly and when.

Flip-flop, Before Deal Chop

One couldn't miss investment guru Mark Mobius's source of pain. His fund Templeton had forked out much more than $7.75 per Taro share (at its peak, Taro traded at $60 per share). Mobius lashed out at Barrie Levitt in a letter dashed to all company directors. 'Templeton accuses Taro of disrespecting basic rules of proper corporate governance and claims that minority shareholders are being misled and oppressed. The situation is simply unacceptable and we will spare no effort to ensure that shareholders' interests are protected . . . we are not alone in our objections: at least one other major shareholder, Brandes Investment Partners, L.P., an SEC-registered investment adviser headquartered in San Diego, California, has publicly announced its opposition to the proposed transaction and its support for our court action.'

Barrie Levitt at the time feared for the life of his company, which was in an intensive care unit then. So he, unsurprisingly, urged shareholders to back Sun's proposal of the takeover in the extraordinary general meeting assembly that he planned to host on 23 July. ' . . . if the shareholders buck at the takeover by Sun, Taro may go belly-up', Levitt's warning was quoted in Israeli newspapers. *Haaretz*, an Israeli daily, rephrased a desperate-sounding Levitt from his summon to shareholders: 'Taro's cash is low; its debts are high and its prospects dim. Balky shareholders, take note.' He said, Taro didn't even have $17 million, and owed $250 million to banks and creditors, which have been banging at its doors.

Convincing the shareholders to vote in favour was absolutely necessary to close the deal, as Sun needed the nod from 75 per cent of Taro's shareholders who attended the assembly, and of that at least a third of the supporters needed to have no personal interest in the resolution. This meant the Levitts and Sun were excluded from that number. This dimmed the chances of the referendum turning out in Sun's favour, simply because it was already public that Franklin Templeton and Brandes, which held 18 per cent of shares between them, were set to shun the offer.

That scheduled all-important shareholder congregation on 23 July 2007 never happened. Why? What made Levitt call it off at the last minute? What happened the night before 23 July is a blur. But the meeting meant to put Sun's offer on test was called off at the last hour. A year later, in his first detailed interview to press, Levitt was to claim that the merger actually fell through on 23 July when it had become amply clear that 'investors were going to turn the offer down'.

'What happened that night was that Sun actually begged us to call off the meeting,' claimed Levitt, in an interview to *Globes*, a newspaper of Israel. 'Sun offered Taro discounts, so that we would cancel the meeting at the last minute. They met us halfway with more compromises—they waived the no-shop option and they decided to inject a further $18 million into the company's shareholders' equity. They asked us to give them a few weeks to try and persuade Franklin Templeton and Brandes, the institutional investors opposed to the merger, but over the next few months it became clear that the merger was not going to happen. I, personally, was willing to see the agreement through, but my heart was with the shareholders.'

Shanghvi flatly denied Levitt's version of recollections in the same piece. 'It simply isn't true. They informed us in advance of their decision to postpone the meeting, but they didn't explain why. We invested the extra $18 million because they told us the company was likely to run into difficulty, while the merger remained on hold,' was his riposte.

A decade later Shanghvi couldn't recapitulate the exact sequence of events that night, but Baldota who was an active participant from Sun's side, asserted, 'I don't think Sun could have caused the delay because it simply didn't have the authority to do so. Who called the meeting? Who postponed it? At the time we trusted them. They were the ones watching the situation on ground closely while we were miles away from action. So we were taking their word for what was transpiring. If the seller was saying, "Defer it or lose it," we would go by that advice. We never realized that the intention of the seller could be to not sell.'

Why did Sun have to drop the 'no-shop' clause—to appease whom? 'I think Levitt came back to us telling that his company directors were finding it difficult to move ahead and reconvene the meeting unless they saw some gesture from Sun such as lifting the "no-shopping clause",' Baldota said.

But why did Sun have to agree to an absurd demand? 'Of course we opposed it initially, how can we drop it, you are locked into a deal with us, we cannot allow you to go and shop! But he probably convinced Dilip-bhai, saying, "Dilip, what are you worried about, I have signed an agreement with you by which I am bound. Even if some of the investors go and shop around, how does it matter?" At that point, Dilip-bhai had a high level of trust in Barrie Levitt,' Baldota recalled.

Irrespective of who said what to whom, in July 2007, to an outside observer, interests of Shanghvi and Levitt were aligned, and once it became clear that Sun was sure to fail the floor test, it made perfect sense for both Sun and Levitt to cancel the test. 'I think the broad message to us at that time was that we probably needed to engage more deeply with the minority shareholders. To do that we needed to buy some time, so we called the meeting at a later date,' Baldota recalled.

Some Mumbai-based fund managers recalled being nudged to activate their overseas contacts to connect Shanghvi to Mark Mobius. In fact, the attempts of Sun to engage with Mobius were initially being thwarted and it had been a pain to get a meeting with him.

'I think Templeton was playing hard to get during the initial days. So when we reached out for a meeting, they gave us half an hour time with Mark Mobius, some forty days later. And when we asked where, they would say, "No, not in person, the appointment is on mobile." He would be travelling from the airport to the city, and he will take your call. It was clear that they were out to make us uncomfortable, by avoiding us right in the beginning,' Valia recalled.

Sometime after the shareholder meeting had been called off, Baldota was sent to New York for a fortnight to sort things out to take the deal forward. Once or twice a day, when his path crossed Levitt's, he reminded Baldota, 'Dilip has got a very good company and he has got it dirt cheap.' It is here Baldota sniffed something fishy for the first time but couldn't wrap his head around the concrete reasons behind that feeling.

When asked about the precise time when Sun sensed or suspected Levitt's change of mind, Baldota reckoned, 'Depends on whom you ask. For me it was as early as July or August 2007, for Dilip-bhai and Sudhir-bhai, not before March 2008. During my short stint at Taro's New York office, there was something in their behaviour that made me uncomfortable. I wondered why Dr Levitt was repeating that Dilip-bhai had got the company cheap. That wasn't helping move things forward, and the steps we needed to advance the deal on the ground were not happening.'

Weeks later, Taro scrapped the next shareholders' meeting as well, scheduled for 25 September 2007 on the pretext that the company was yet to publish its audited financial results that could empower shareholders to take a more informed call. It didn't announce a new date for the meeting but promised to do it soon, in the first quarter of 2008.

'I was telling Dilip-bhai we need to be careful; there is something not quite right here. By November–December, my realization had grown stronger based on their frivolous objections for not taking things forward. My colleague, the CEO of Caraco [Dan Movens], started sharing similar apprehensions with Dilip-bhai but even at this moment, his trust in Levitt seemed unshakeable,' Baldota felt.

That didn't mean Shanghvi did nothing about his deputies' unsettled feelings or dismissed them as hallucinations of those with a cynical bent; he sent Valia for a quick pulse check of Levitt in early 2008.

At the time Sun was pushing the Taro board to publish audited results, so that the shareholders could be asked to vote on its proposal and that became the main topic of chat between Levitt and Valia when they met. Levitt confided that their newly hired CFO (Thomas McClary) was refusing to sign on the balance sheets.

'This was not an excuse, they were genuinely stuck with those numbers with their few-months-old CFO disagreeing with their auditors and, consequently, Taro results getting locked in that impasse,' Baldota said.

Valia, the compulsive problem solver, proposed a way out of the mess to Levitt. 'This internal deadlock cannot go on. Someone has to sign. If your CFO has apprehensions, he can correct, address or cite them in the balance sheet or he may ask the company to make provisions for a write-off. But he cannot just hold the company to ransom by putting off the signing of the papers,' Valia told Levitt, and added, 'Why don't we make your top accounts executive an interim CFO? After all, Ron Kolkar has served as interim CFO in the past. We can have two CFOs, one interim, one in charge, if the law allows that for special cases.'

'That seems like a good idea,' agreed Levitt, as per Valia's recollection. Levitt's face lit up and he picked up his mobile from the table, promptly called up his lawyer to inform, 'See, this is how it should be done.'

Valia returned home assured that the audited results would be filed soon. He briefed Shanghvi of Levitt's good intent. 'Levitt is a gentleman, their problems are real and we are unnecessarily getting worried,' he reassured Shanghvi. Part of the Levitt–Valia chat bore fruit in April 2008, when Taro parted ways with CFO McClary and promoted Kolkar to the position of CFO. Kolkar signed on the dotted line of the audited results. But before that a lot else was brewing.

'Levitt gave me the impression that we were on the same page; our tips were great and he wished to implement them at once. And we had no reason to cast aspersions on him then. I was happy to have helped them sort out balance-sheet issues. Over the next few months I was to realize what I had missed, how the show of camaraderie was all a put-on to mislead us. He was telling me things I wanted to hear. And what he said, I shouldn't have believed,' Valia said.

Before that realization occurred to Shanghvi and Valia, one of the two opposing funds, Brandes, sold its 9 per cent stake in Taro in a blind auction, which Sun bought out by paying $10.25 a share in February 2008. Interestingly, Shanghvi was to later charge Levitt thus: 'You encouraged Sun to bid aggressively in the auction on the basis that Brandes's shares represented a "control block" or, in other words, a "swing vote" in the shareholders' meetings to approve the merger.'

This steep escalation in offer price was because things had turned rosy for Taro as it had turned a profit in the quarter ended December 2007. Along with a turnaround of business, came a turnaround of heart for Levitt. Taro turned an opportunity hawk, yet again. And its first solid sign came through a channel for Sun from where it expected the least; sitting in their own mailbox.

Discovering a Bomb in the Mail

By March 2008, Sun's plans on the Taro front hadn't moved an inch. To speed matters up, Shanghvi even sweetened the deal to $10.25 per share, mailing a revised draft deal to Levitt the weekend it bought Brandes's shares for the same amount and upped Sun's stake in Taro to 34 per cent.

'After delaying the shareholder meetings for so long, the telltale signs were all there. First they wanted a reworked agreement with raised consideration. When we sent it, they just didn't respond,' Baldota recounted. When Sun's lawyers followed up, Levitt's lawyers turned up with lame excuses, such as, it's lying on Barrie Levitt's desk.

Those days saw a barrage of mail exchanges from both sides; lawyers at the forefront of this shuffle and push. And then, something happened just before April 2008 that shocked the wits out of Shanghvi's aides. Shanghvi's American lawyer forwarded a mail from Levitt's lawyers, where a long trail mail of exchanges between Levitt and his lawyer had gone undeleted, unwittingly. Probably, some overworked lawyer's caffeine betrayed him at the critical moment of the click on the computer.

At the bottom of that crucial undeleted mail, was a surprise waiting for Sun in black and white. A chit-chat between Levitt and his lawyer revealed a game plan, where they had been discussing about a dormant clause tucked away in the first agreement Levitt had signed with Sun, which could be triggered only and only if the deal was terminated. This is what startled the folks at Sun. Why is Levitt talking termination of the deal with his lawyer?

Shanghvi and Valia had ensured that an 'option' of buying out promoters be made part of the agreement if the deal fell through. It was possible that the lessons at Caraco, where shareholders dilly-dallied with commitments made them wary but wise. Now that Shanghvi and Valia became privy to Levitt's line of thoughts, they realized what it portended for them.

'We were stunned but understood what was on their mind. That mail was sent to us by mistake, but it was an eye-opener on how they were planning to block the deal,' Valia said. Baldota called it a big shocker despite his misgivings.

But there had been no formal communiqué from Levitt to Shanghvi articulating such designs. Instead he invited Shanghvi over to New York on 14 May 2008 to present his proposal to Taro's board of directors. In fact, when the invite came, a strong disagreement broke out in the Sun house. Its advisers—bankers and lawyers—were on one side urging Shanghvi to use this plum opportunity to convince the independent directors. Baldota and others were urging him to not fall for this invite which they saw as a trap. Shanghvi went along with his counsel's advice, cancelled all his existing appointments and headed for New York.

In the board meeting when he entered, Shanghvi was instructed to make a presentation and leave. The directors were put on 'listen only mode', so that Shanghvi could neither pose any questions nor take theirs. 'It was a mistake to accept the invitation. Dilip-bhai was called at a short notice and humiliated. I guess they wanted to put it on record that he had been given an opportunity to present his proposal,' Baldota felt.

All this while, till things reached a boiling point, Sun had been on and off engaging with Franklin Templeton—coaxing it to sell, but the fund resisted calling it an unfair deal for the shareholders. As part of that effort, Baldota had arranged to meet Carlos Hardenberg, a key executive from the Templeton team, who was based out of Turkey.

The morning after he reached Istanbul, Baldota went to Hardenberg's office, and after exchanging divergent views and inconclusive talks, the two decided to go out for lunch. The differences continued over the meals, with Hardenberg suggesting that Sun's valuation did no justice to the great Taro assets and Baldota arguing back, 'But you can't forget the liabilities, losses and a damaged reputation.' Lunch was over, but the differences weren't, and the two of them decided to resume their talks at Hardenberg's office.

Once in the office, Hardenberg excused himself, 'Give me five minutes, Uday, I will just clear up my desk.' Baldota started watching the television up on the wall, with an eye on Hardenberg, whom he could see through the glass, checking his computer screen, probably reading his mails. In an instant, he witnessed the expression on Hardenberg's face turning into shock. In that daze, he emerged from his room and said, 'You should talk to your people back in India.'

'Why, what happened? Tell me.'

'No . . . no, just talk to your people back home.'

Baldota retrieved his cellphone to find thirty-three missed calls from his colleague Mira Desai. When he called back, he was in for a bigger shock. Mira was saying, 'They have terminated the deal.'

'What? What did you say? Are you sure?' a stunned Baldota yelled.

'Taro guys have sent a communiqué that they have terminated the deal. That's the reason I was calling you frantically.'

When Baldota spoke to Shanghvi immediately after, he sounded calm with a single-line instruction, 'Understand from Carlos what they think of this and come back. We will see what we can do.'

Recalling that event ten years later, Baldota's tone still betrayed disbelief. 'It had been a crazy day for me. If someone asked how Barrie Levitt was like in person, we would have described him as a warm, affable, almost parent-like and a professional with a reasonably sound technical knowledge. Dilip-bhai particularly thought that his business might have got screwed, but he was a nice person. Given the trust he had put in Levitt, it had been nothing short of a betrayal. But, frankly, at that point, the focus was beamed on what we could do from there on and not on what had happened.' In effect, Levitt would show the world, and maybe Shanghvi himself, what this calm-seeming Sun owner was capable of when a public war was waged against him. In short, it was time for a 'third-eye' moment for Shanghvi.

The Taro board had used a press statement to tell Sun that they were terminating the 'stale' merger agreement, that didn't reflect 'the dramatic operational and financial turnaround' in the company since the year before, or factor in 'the future value' that the company expected to achieve from the changes made in its business model and the value in its new product pipeline.

Levitt offered to buy back Sun's stake at the exact same rate Sun was proposing to buy the rest of Taro. So this is how a deal 'all signed and sealed' fell apart a year later.

This triggered a public spat, a crossfire of accusations and counter-allegations, lawsuits and counter-litigations across the US and Israel in full media glare, unprecedented for Shanghvi and Sun. It became a proxy proof for what lay beneath the tip of the iceberg the world knew as Dilip Shanghvi.

'That gentleman, Mr Levitt, must have seen Dilip-bhai smiling speaking softly, and thought he could walk all over him. He had clearly missed what is inside him,' brother Jayant said.

A day after receiving Taro's termination letter, Shanghvi wrote back to Levitt that Taro simply didn't have the right to unilaterally walk out of a two-way pact.

He reminded Levitt what he should have known, that without Sun's lifeline of $60 million the year before, a financially strapped, debt-owing, lender-chased Taro 'would be unable to boast of survival, much less a purported financial and operational turnaround'.

Losing no time, Sun sued Levitt and Moros in US courts for breach of contract and with the intention of fraud. By June, Sun retrieved its trump card to exercise 'option', using which it aimed to acquire Levitt's and Moros's shares within a month of the merger falling apart.

Not unaware of what Sun would be up to, Levitt and Moros and Taro's board had already challenged its anticipated attempt in a Tel Aviv district court. Their ground was eerily similar to the discussion Shanghvi and his lawyers had chanced upon in the undeleted email thread they had received accidentally. Their lawyer went to the court arguing that Sun would have to launch a 'special tender offer' before it tried to acquire owners' shares. What now is a special tender offer under Israeli law?

This law mandates that in case of companies where majority shareholders owned 45 per cent or less, the buyer has to make a special tender offer, seeking votes of all shareholders. Its offer would be declared successful only if it manages to get half of all shareholders to back the deal. Sun's had been a special case. When it had signed the deal a year back—the owners' share was over 45 per cent, but the moment Sun bought a slice of Levitt's family stake, that figure dropped to 41 per cent.

'This [law on special tender offer] is the little loophole the Levitt family really tried to use to their advantage. They wanted Sun to go down this route, knowing that at this price the minority shareholders will not sell and therefore Levitt would be entitled to say, "Sorry, it [is] an Israeli law issue, I am not forced to sell my shares . . ." At the time Sun did the deal, the Levitt family had more than 45 per cent, so in that context everyone's eyes were wide open. But the minute you infuse capital, [that] brought Levitt [shareholding] down to less than 45 per cent, technically the special tender offer could apply at that time,' Sujjain Talwar, a partner at Economic Laws Practice told CNBC TV.

As Sun offered to buy out ordinary shareholders for a predetermined $7.75 a piece, under 'the option' (given a regular tender offer was mandatory pre-acquisition of owners shares) it exercised, Mark Mobius threw his weight behind Taro's decision. He claimed that Sun's offer was way out of line and undervalued the company; that his fund would settle for nothing less than $14–15 per share. By July, white-suited Mobius was even seen on television demanding a price close to $20.

'Taro's case continues to drag on in the courts, except that now the sides have changed benches. Taro and Sun's lawyers were previously on the same side, as defendants in the action brought by Franklin Templeton, but now they are opponents,' *Globes* wrote.

The squabble reminded the *Economic Times* of a similar tiff Shanghvi had with the Caraco shareholders a few years back, and it imagined a scene of Shanghvi nodding sympathetically to legendary baseball star Yogi Berra, saying, 'This feels like déjà vu, all over again,' after finding himself repeatedly stuck in similar crises. *Outlook Business* called the Taro saga a Robin Cook medical thriller minus the deadly virus strains.

Amid all this confusion, Sun's lawyer in Israel was recounting 101 reasons to them why Sun wouldn't win this case. 'My experience with consultants and lawyers had been that they speak the language you want to hear. Here in Tel Aviv, our first lawyer spoke great English, displayed sharp aggression, but in the rest of the departments, the case was a little different,' Valia recalled.

This lawyer had been with Sun since March 2007. Now, given their special case, Sun wanted to argue in the courts that a special tender offer wouldn't apply. 'Unfortunately, we couldn't even convince our lawyers,' Baldota quipped.

'Well, these arguments may sound all right across the table, but in courts we will lose,' was their lawyer's neat view. They discussed many options.

'What if we take an opinion of an expert, say an ex-judge or something?' someone from the Sun team suggested.

'Opinions don't hold good in Israeli courts. Judiciary works on the principle that the judge knows best, he doesn't solicit opinions from experts. Even if you attach such affidavits, it will be disregarded. But it's not a bad idea to consult someone,' the lawyer said.

Recalling the dilemma of that time, Baldota said, 'From day one, he felt strongly that this is a losing case. He had no arguments to support our case. Instead he was asking us to learn from someone else how to argue the case. We were baffled.'

'This first law firm scared us big time. We thought he was too confident of losing the case, so we decided to switch law firms. We spent a good deal of time selecting a lawyer who connected with us,' Valia recalled.

Famously press-unfriendly Levitt pulled all stops as well, evoking 'Zionism and Israeli-Jewish nationalism' in media interview, in the Taro battle. 'We feel that keeping Taro Israeli is in the interest of the country,' Levitt told *Globes* a week before the court was to pronounce the judgment.

Thumping the table, prompting journalist Dan Shohet to suspect that he would soon be invoking Jewish persecution complexes to back his claims, Levitt added in a 'half-outraged, half-concerned' tone, 'There are quite a few evil people out there, who would be glad of an opportunity to harm Israel. Israel needs a strong economy, because no one is going to save us. No Indian Army is going to save Israel. The ones who will save Israel are Israeli soldiers, in the Israeli army, who will need jobs when they return home.'

To Sun's luck, the national jingoism didn't turn out be the joker in the pack for Levitt. The judge at the district court of Tel Aviv cut through to the heart of the matter in her first hearing. 'In our freshman year at law school we learned that agreements must be upheld. It is evident . . . that there is a group at Taro, the controlling shareholders, that is not interested in doing so,' Judge Michal Agmon Gonen's observation was quoted in local newspaper *Calcalist*.

By August, the judge had ruled in favour of Sun. She noted that it was 'disingenuous' for Taro's directors to claim now, over a year after they approved the transaction, that a special tender offer was required; that the directors should have 'studied the agreements' prior to their being signed, and cannot claim now that they suddenly decided a special tender offer was necessary.

A day after the victory, Shanghvi called the lawsuit by Taro's independent directors 'part of a calculated effort by Barrie Levitt to avoid living up to his obligations. But some lawyers actually thought Sun got lucky. 'Sun got away with a judge who saw this through in terms of its equity right down instead of the pure technicality of the regulation,' Talwar told a channel.

Predictably the Taro board appealed against the judgment in the Supreme Court of Israel, which pushed the pause button to Sun's action of acquiring Levitt's and Moros's shares till the judiciary decided on the appeal.

The second lawyer Sun had brought on board was perceived in the team as 'simply fantastic'. 'Taro's lawyers were more aggressive, but our lawyer Dr Israel Leshem, whom we called Reli was calm. He made sharp specific points,' Baldota recalled.

For the Supreme Court battle Reli had trend-analysed recent cases to predict what to expect from judges and prepared Sun's legal strategies. He had, for instance, prepped the Sun team on the possibility of the judge directing the parties for mediation, nudging them to settle out of court. His prediction was bang on. 'That made us shortlist the names of possible mediators in advance, based on what would work for us, what wouldn't. So when the judge asked for names, the Taro side was caught napping, they were not ready with a list. We were spot on with names, to which the Taro lawyers agreed,' Baldota recalled.

Mediations by reputed advocate Ram Caspi proved neither friendly nor fruitful. After feeling deceived, Sun was in no mood to charm Levitt and had drawn up its own stratagem—the offer it sent to the Taro board this time was $9.5 a share, a few notches lower than what it had previously offered.

The war of words intensified. 'Unfortunately, to date Sun has only been willing to make low-ball offers and "negotiate" through the press . . . Even as late as today, Sun still is unwilling to sit down with Taro in an attempt to resolve this dispute. Now Sun has even refused to accept the concept of mediation . . .' Taro charged, asking Sun to pay $15 a share. Levitt offered Sun, among other options, to hold a shareholder referendum on the price it was offering, an offer Shanghvi called 'sly'.

The aggression that surfaced in the letters shot out to Levitt and Taro was out of character for Shanghvi. 'It's true we were not comfortable doing what we did. But we saw them lying blatantly and indulging in smear campaigns against Sun. You repeat lies and it starts appearing as truth. That's when we took a conscious call that we can't take this lying down. We had to put out for the minority shareholders of Taro to understand what was going on, so that they didn't get swayed by coloured information,' Baldota recalled.

Shanghvi felt the 'distorted' information unless corrected could swing the case.

Each letter that Shanghvi released was drafted and redrafted several times till he thought it got the tone and pitch of aggression right. '*I like to win without fighting*. But if I can't, then I'm prepared to *fight*,' Shanghvi was to later declare.

According to a *Globes* report, Shanghvi and Levitt met at mediator Ram Caspi's office in February 2009 to thrash out 'a direct compromise', where a Templeton executive was also present. 'One of those days, Dilip-bhai actually came in the morning and said, "Let's give them $15 a share and get done with this." But by then, the trust deficit was so gapingly wide that we were taking every word of theirs with sacks of salt. So we asked, "What are you saying, Dilip-bhai? What if they change their minds tomorrow morning and ask for $20,"' Baldota recalled.

Asked in a quarterly results call, why Sun was offering $9.5 to Taro after having paid $10.25 to Brandes the previous year, Shanghvi's punching answer was, 'I think we are talking about the same issue, but at different points of time. I think valuation has a relationship in the context of time and relative valuation of other companies. In our view, whatever we are offering at this point in time is the best we think we can offer looking at all other issues.'

Had Levitts and Moros chosen 'to behave' in 'all other issues', Valia felt, they could have fetched a fortune. 'We had braced up for double the price of $7.75 to settle the negotiation,' he recounted. But Shanghvi and Valia felt that Levitt had made up his mind not to surrender shares.

By March 2009, all mediation efforts had failed and Sun went back telling the Supreme Court that they would wait for the final verdict. It would be another year and a half before a verdict would be pronounced but in the interim, neither Levitt nor Shanghvi grew battle-weary, nor did the thriller disappoint in twists.

Templeton Does a Taro on Taro

While Taro was busy filing cases and releasing statements, Templeton did a Taro on Taro by changing its mind just before its annual general meeting in December 2009. After opposing Sun for a year and half, Mobius, suddenly one day, switched sides, saying Sun's attempts to take control of Taro had to be expedited as his fund had lost faith in the existing Taro management.

'The current board and the management . . . have proven unwilling or unable to run the company in the interest of its shareholders,' Mobius announced, adding, 'Taro's condition continues to deteriorate in terms of proper corporate governance. Templeton believes that it must act without delay to enable Taro to emerge from the situation in which it has found itself by removing the barriers for the transfer of control in Taro, for the good of all shareholders.'

When asked to explain his U-turn, Mobius cited an event where Taro controllers called for a shareholders' meeting to pass a resolution absolving the directors, particularly those who were independent directors, from any responsibility for the accounts of the company. 'And since no audited accounts have been issued for three years we were very much opposed to that,' Mobius said.

Even those who betray don't like the aftertaste of betrayal. An annoyed Levitt warned shareholders against the proxy war Sun was waging, calling this reversal of Templeton 'an attempt by India's Sun to seize control of your company by waging a proxy fight to gain control of Taro's board'.

'Templeton's case was that an enemy's enemy was a friend by default. They were fighting the valuation we were offering to the minority shareholders. But their bigger fight was against the Levitt family, which despite the dismal performance, wanted to stay entrenched in Taro. Templeton figured that the Levitt family was in no mood to let go of the reins of Taro and that Sun was a better manager of business. So it started appearing as if Sun and Templeton were on the same side but our differences on valuation persisted through that phase,' Baldota recalled.

For a change Valia was slightly more cryptic than usual, 'Investors are always trying to maximize their returns. They are literally sailing in two boats simultaneously. Through the process, Templeton must have realized that litigation was dragging on. Once they judged it more prudent to sell, for them the natural buyer was Sun, not Levitt. So presuming they decided to sell to Sun, they couldn't antagonize their prospective buyer, and must have therefore found it smarter to stand up for Sun at that juncture of the fight.'

Had there been any game-changing background negotiations that had led to Templeton's change of mind? Some Mumbai-based fund managers indicated that a meeting might have taken place between Shanghvi and Mobius, which was scheduled in Hungary. But if it happened, it remains off the official records in the realm of 'could have been', and Baldota denied knowledge of any such meeting at that time. Sun would eventually buy out Templeton for $16 a share.

'Our real negotiation with Templeton happened much later after the case was finished in September 2010. We reached out to Templeton with a valuation comparison and an offer of close to $10 per share. The disagreement over valuation continued as they demanded about 18 to 20 dollar per share,' Baldota recounted. Hardenberg hadn't responded to Baldota's mail for a few days.

Then one day, Baldota saw Hardenberg turning up in his inbox. He had reverted, 'I don't agree with your computation . . . but for the sake of moving ahead . . . $16 per share is our price. Take it or leave it. I don't expect you to negotiate.' Sun agreed to buy about five million shares from Templeton for $85 million. But the next time they spoke, Baldota recalled being reminded yet again by Hardenberg, 'I knew that was worth much more.'

The Verdict

Baldota travelled to Tel Aviv 4–5 times and sat across Levitt through the mediation. For the Sun executives it was a strange kind of experience—not being able to trust Levitt after what had happened but having to smile at each other, being courteous as if all was well because all they had to focus on was moving ahead.

'When the judiciary started insisting on an out-of-court settlement, doubts started creeping into our minds. We started reading between the lines, speculating whether that portended the case was going in their favour, or did the court wish us to shell out more during the process of negotiation or what? The usual litigation anxiety stuff,' Valia said. In fact, in hindsight, the court was giving them a chance to correct their course, every push one more opportunity to gain balance, Baldota felt.

Amid all the jitters, the one person who was perceived to be equanimous was Shanghvi. 'He embraced uncertainty and never lost his nerve. It was as if we were on the crease playing, and we have to focus on the next ball. Never did he get excited, when a round went our way, nor did he lose heart when it went the other way. I never heard him saying, "Let's forget it, let go of it," nor did I ever saw him swearing, "I will show them, teach them a lesson." He didn't display any emotions with the turns of the case,' Baldota said.

'We were extremely frustrated by the ongoing Taro headache, mainly because we heard so much in the market that bogged us down. I would sometimes call Dilip-bhai and ask, "Is it worth it?" He would tell me coolly, "Don't worry, Hiren, we will win it in the end and complete the acquisition,"' Hiren Desai recalled Shanghvi as saying.

Kirti Ganorkar said, 'So much disturbance on the Taro front was going on externally for three years, but Dilip-bhai made sure that our product plans for Taro—which he had in mind to introduce through that company in the US and on which we had started work on at our R&D centres—were not disrupted for even one single day. They were made to go on seamlessly, as if we were never in doubt about the launch of these products.'

When, in the quarterly calls, shareholders, investors and analysts pestered about his plans, if things went out of hand, Shanghvi's stock defence was a three-word sneer: 'Just be patient.' By July, the patience started paying off when the US court decided to reject Taro's appeal, to which Shanghvi responded, 'Sun is pleased but not surprised.'

On 7 September 2010 Baldota had taken an off. He had reached his wife's clinic to pick her up. Waiting for her, he was scrolling down his Blackberry to check mails, when something caught his eye—a mail announcing the Israel Supreme Court's verdict. The apex court had ruled in favour of Sun. He recalled reading it twice over before making a call to Shanghvi.

Shanghvi was on his way home when he got the news. Instead of climbing down from his car he called his wife Vibha to join him. Then he directed the driver to head towards Siddhi Vinayak temple to bow and pay obeisance to Lord Ganesha, 'the deity for fulfilling wishes'.

Of his sour experience with Levitt, Shanghvi said, 'I don't distrust people. That also becomes a limitation actually, because I immediately start viewing things from the other's point of view and that prevents me from feeling really cheated or getting angry. In Dr Levitt's case, I could see he was trying very hard to hold on to what he had created, so broadly I was able to understand where he was coming from.'

The resolution of a transnational litigation in Sun's favour made international headlines the next day, and the Indian pharma industry cheered Shanghvi's victory. In a private gathering, a rival boasted, as if the win had been his own, 'Dilip-bhai has straightened the Jews in their own country,' he took a mocking swipe after downing a few pegs. Albeit mean and racial, the off-the-cuff drunken remark underscored one of Shanghvi's most astonishing achievements. No one, not even his rivals, grudged him his success.

Inside Sun headquarters, however, going by Baldota's memories, the day after the big conquest didn't look any different. It was business as usual. Except maybe for Shanghvi sending the thick voluminous Hebrew order to be translated to English and looking up his calendar to freeze dates for a trip to New York.

Israel from Israel

He wasn't content to have won Taro alone. He was of a mind to win Israel from Israel as well, the man credited to have shepherded the spectacular growth of the largest generic giant in the world, Teva, by stitching over twelve deals there. During his visits to Tel Aviv for Taro, Shanghvi quietly nurtured a relationship with Makov, dining with him, inviting him over to Sun's R&D centre, and then proposing that he join. Makov, who had in his interviews said that after Teva he didn't have any aspirations to manage anything else, initially refused but kept returning to Sun.

Then one day in 2012 Shanghvi shocked everyone again by making an unprecedented announcement that he had hired his boss, and would be stepping down as chairman of Sun to make way for Israel Makov, many years his senior in age and experience.

Ashwin Dani noted that Shanghvi, innovative and entrepreneurial, had a fascination for Jews—known for their creative potential and entrepreneurial spirit. Someone said this was the closest Sun could get to declare its aspiration to become the next Teva, a belief that was further bolstered when other Teva veterans—Benny Klener, Hellen de Kloyt and Iftach Seri followed Makov. Someone else speculated that Sun has its eyes on Teva. Someone even asked, 'Has he sacrificed himself to build his company?'

But Shanghvi was doing what he had always excelled at, choosing his teacher for the lesson at hand—taking Sun truly global. In an interview he said Sun was becoming too big for him to run. So the next logical step entailed roping in talent, who have the experience of managing such behemoths.

'I look at my role as owner and manager in different compartments. I consciously try evaluating my performance as a manager, independent of my performance as an owner,' he said, after stripping himself of the chairman's role to continue as managing director only.

Celebrations for the Taro triumph were to happen but elsewhere.

CHAPTER EIGHTEEN

HOISTING THE INDIAN FLAG ON AMERICAN EXCHANGE

Jim Kedrowski, chief executive of Chattem Chemicals, an American maker of narcotic-medicine raw materials acquired by Sun Pharma in 2008 cut short a vacation with his wife when he was summoned urgently by Shanghvi in New York. There, Shanghvi asked Kedrowski, Baldota and others to pick a 'really nice restaurant' for a celebration. He wished to host a farewell for Levitt and his family. They chose a fine European cuisine eatery in Hawthrone for the dinner party, not far from Taro's headquarters.

'We have to let him go with dignity. We cannot mistreat him,' Baldota recalled Shanghvi telling him. 'For three years, they had engaged in a public spat, not saying nice things about each other. But Dilip was very gracious and wanted Dr Levitt to part properly, and Dr Levitt wished him well,' Kedrowski recounted.

The party was attended by Shanghvi's wife Vibha, some senior Sun executives and almost the whole headquarters staff of Taro. Mrs Levitt wasn't enjoying the party much, but kept quiet for most part and some senior Taro executives were probably wondering what was all this about, Kedrowski recalled. Shanghvi asked the top Taro executives, direct reportees of Levitt to share their experiences with their parting boss and raise a toast.

Baldota, who had been a court witness in the protracted legal case, remembered the former Taro owner pointing a finger at him in the party, 'You are the one who testified against me.'

'I think Levitt was burning inside. After trying so desperately, he had lost the case, lost face, and was now losing control of a company he and his family had built. On top of that, the guy whom he had tried so hard to muscle out comes to take over and treats him with such a nice farewell in front of his employees, who probably think that he was wrong and has let them down. I don't think he was in enviable shoes in that party,' another Sun executive recalled. Exactly two years before this farewell party, amid the heat of the tussle, Levitt had told *Globes* in an interview, 'I like Mr Shanghvi but he is unwilling to negotiate.'

Asked of the gesture, Shanghvi displayed again his knack for presenting the right-seeming thing as the right strategy. 'These were people he (Levitt) was working with for years altogether, many of them directly reporting to him. Now he was going and I was to work with the same people. Since they had worked so closely with Levitt, they must have had emotional attachments with him. I wanted them to realize that as a person, I hold no grudges. What happens is that when I take over, there is every chance that they mistakenly assume that I hold grudges against people who worked close to Levitt and then they start looking out and then there is disruption. So I wanted to establish that I was not holding grudges against anyone; what happened, happened; it's past, now let's move on.'

Asked if he truly harboured no anger for the betrayal he had faced, Shanghvi replied, 'My anger is like fluid in a leaky tube, it goes out in a flash. I can't hold on to my anger. In fact, I cannot stay in a permanent state of unhappiness, or rather I can't be unhappy for very long.'

Hoisting Flag, Ringing Bells

The first week, the Sun squad roamed about the headquarters, talking, dividing the 180 people there into three groups and chatting with them. 'I had the experience of being bought over at Chattem, and now I was on the other side, so I volunteered to share with them my experience of what Sun did after the takeover,' Kedrowski said.

In the open town-hall setting, Kedrowski narrated to them how Shanghvi had arrived with his team after taking over Chattem and everyone had fully expected him to change the management. 'In fact he didn't. He said, "You guys run it," and went away. He only went to Chattem that one time for three days.' Because it was a small firm, Shanghvi hadn't spent a lot of time on it.

By the end of that week, while preparing to leave, Shanghvi called Kedrowski to throw a surprise. He said, 'Jim, you run the company.'

A shocked Kedrowski said, 'Whoa! You know my set of experiences, Dilip.'

'Yes I know, but I think with me and my team's help, you will be a good person in the ground force here.'

'I only had the experience of running an API firm, a small business of $24–30 million. I wouldn't have met Dilip more than four times before that day. So I was absolutely shocked. But then I recalled when he had first come to Chattem, with a bunch of people, one of whom I most definitely expected him to leave in charge—although he never mentioned that intention—he hadn't done that. For some reasons when he left after three days, he had still left me in charge. So this was the second time he had surprised me,' Kedrowski said, adding half-jokingly, 'or my biggest advantage was that I was an American.'

Having an American at the helm was a smart move indeed, as people at Taro were full of apprehensions. In those town-hall sessions and in the breakfast meetings which Kedrowski continued to host monthly with different groups afterwards, Taro people bombarded him with their anxieties, 'Will Sun shut this office and shift us all to its Cranbury office in New Jersey?'

'No, we will keep this office and you would be stationed right here,' Kedrowski assured them, having known Shanghvi's decision that the Cranbury office simply didn't have space to accommodate so many.

'Jim, are we going to get pink slips?'

'Can we get to know a little about the Indian culture so that we don't misunderstand them?'

'Are we still going to have our Christmas party, Jim?'

'Pink slips are not coming tomorrow or next week or next month; we have hired a person to make you understand the Indian culture better. Of course, we will have the Christmas party.'

But not everything was to remain the same. One of the first realms where Sun's imprint was to manifest was as concrete as it got—the brick and mortar.

Levitt, famously, had a penchant for luxuries; his chamber started with a well-stocked library and a reading room that led to a spacious hall and on the side was a small private compartment for exercise. That when, Shanghvi in his Mumbai office didn't even have a separate toilet to himself, flew economy class in flights, and his US staff haggled hard to slash room rents in not-so-luxurious hotels.

The Taro office had a restricted wing to house the top brass in one of the top floors; to enter which one had to have special permission and cross three levels of locked glass-door protection. That was broken and perhaps on purpose converted into a common cafeteria with free access even though it didn't serve any food. Sun House in Mumbai has a common cafeteria as well, where Shanghvi has lunch with everyone else.

In one of the ex-CEO's cabin at Taro, a Sun top executive found Teva annual reports marked out and heavily handwritten annotations. It clearly had a dream at a time of becoming the next Teva.

Kedrowski made a valid observation about Shanghvi being 'strategically patient, but tactically impatient'. This meant that he could wait decades for a strategy to unfold patiently putting together one piece after the other, let's say in case of buying Taro. But once a company was acquired, he wanted the planned steps to be implemented breathlessly.

Partly, brakes to a speedy integration were being applied by the sheer number of levels in the organizational structure of Taro. 'So there were assistant vice-presidents, vice-presidents, executive vice-presidents, group vice-presidents who were stuttering the decision making. The first week we went into a meeting to decide what we would do in other meetings. Usually the top tier huddled in the boardroom for hours on decisions. But Dilip wanted speedier decision making. So we decided to eliminate a layer altogether. It was one of the hardest days at Taro, because they were nice guys,' Kedrowski recalled.

He remembered Shanghvi being a super-quick decision maker on people he wanted or those he didn't. 'He makes up his mind about people really fast—positive or negative and acts upon it,' Kedrowski recalled. So barring the operations head and chief counsel, almost the entire top brass at Taro was asked to leave. So was the chief of operations at Canada, who was later replaced by Shanghvi's old Calcutta classmate-turned-employee Sunil Mehta. But what Shanghvi made sure was this: half of the population at Sun's outfits in New Jersey were Indians, but in Taro's facilities, roughly 99 per cent continued to be Americans, Sundaram reckoned.

Then Taro had a bunch of 'interims'—an interim CEO, an interim CFO, an interim chief counsel. 'Dilip was great in appointing interims or maybe it was his way of telling us: "Hey, I am not sure about you guys." But one day, I surely hoped to be able to tick off that interim and get the CEO title,' Kedrowski quipped.

Besides Kedrowski, what helped Shanghvi's master plan unfold in Taro were a bunch of his senior executives, whom some former Taro employees remembered as 'blindly following his commandments'. This has led many of them to generalize a belief that 'Indian culture is very commanding'.

'There what the chief says has to be done, no questions asked. We initially had problems with that, for how can you not assess that if you do x, y might happen,' a former Taro senior executive wondered. Many thought Sunil Mehta was Shanghvi's ears and eyes at Taro.

Shanghvi pored over details to flip the script at Taro. 'Dilip was a teacher for me and without him I couldn't have done what I did,' Kedrowski said. Shanghvi tracked down business constrictions and red-inked heads. He, for instance underlined the amount splurged on airlifting supplies from Israel to the US market, mainly owing to production delays. This figure stood at $3 million. Shanghvi asked Kedrowski to cut it to one-sixth in a year. He perused processes that helped Taro succeed in one aspect, and checked whether these could be applied in part or full to other aspects of business. Within products Shanghvi looked at creams and liquids and switched—liquids from closer plants, creams from farther to cut shipping costs further.

On some of these occasions, Kedrowski spotted the 'adamant' side of Shanghvi—who wouldn't budge from his stand despite what was at stake. 'He never gets himself into a position where he can't say no. No matter what energies, time and resources had been spent on a project, if he had to say no, he would,' Kedrowski said. Shanghvi has the ability to avoid a trap in economics called the 'sunk cost fallacy', which means decisions are often tainted by the emotional investments one accumulates, and the more one invests in something the harder it becomes to abandon it. Avoiding that trap, like he had in new drug discovery for a molecule coded 1334H helps him assess every business decision purely on the basis of its future value.

Despite enormous resistance at Taro, one of the changes Shanghvi insisted on was to shift the IT application to the version developed in-house at Sun. Taro employees grumbled that it would be too cumbersome for all on-ground business processes that had been aligned with Taro's application; its 200-plus customers paid via a well-oiled e-commerce payment system; its integrated warehouse system was configured accordingly. Worse still, if Sun's IT application developed glitches, there were hardly any experts in the US to fix it. If the glitch was allowed to persist, it had the potential to kill business, whined Taro executives. But Shanghvi, after having studied the two applications, concluded that Sun's version allowed more transparency and suited Taro better. Shanghvi didn't mince words in telling Kedrowski that things were taking too long to transition.

Same had been the case when senior-most employees sought ESOPs at Taro, some threatening to resign if their demands were not met; he didn't budge despite mounting pressure and exits by these executives. No amount of pressure could turn Shanghvi's 'No' to a 'Yes'.

Soon after taking over, Shanghvi made sure that important products were now sourced from multiple locations, not one. 'Customers didn't like to depend on one source because the product becomes vulnerable to supply disruptions. So it was smart on his part to multi-source products from Canada and Israel. The lower tax rate in Israel helped too,' Kedrowski explained.

This was one area Shanghvi deep-dived into, 'servicing the customers' at a level they hadn't seen from Taro in the past. Since many of Taro's products had limited competition, Shanghvi swiftly made arrangements for locating warehouses close to customers, so that the moment a rival slipped, Sun could fill in its shoes. If US supplies weren't enough, a strategic reserve plan was put in place to air-ship hotly in-demand products from Israel.

Business efficiencies apart, the area where Shanghvi blew Kedrowski's mind away was products. 'I think it's extremely rare to find a guy with a masterly blend of grasp over science and technology of medicine, its development and its market. He trained our R&D team on how to manage portfolio,' Kedrowski said. Sitting in the boardroom of Taro headquarters, Shanghvi and his business development deputy Anil Gite opened the spreadsheets and analysed every Abbreviated New Drug Application (ANDA) Taro had ever filed, and made a decision on each of them.

'Some of the products were giving huge net negative returns and you could sense the erstwhile management's incompetence in those 'penny wise and pound foolish' decisions. We discontinued most of those and relaunched many which had remained unmarketed,' Sundaram recalled.

Many of those relaunched, pointed out Kedrowski, were tiny-sized $1–3 million products to which the Taro team mounted resistance. 'We didn't make much money on some of those products and dropped some a year or two later. But I suspect that making us work on those small projects was Dilip's way of expanding our capabilities and putting pressure to teach us to do more than a thing at once.' Sun had been focusing on incremental innovation at its India-based R&D centre by adding value to existing set of products by changing the dose, strength and route of administration and that approach must have come handy in pushing Taro in a similar direction.

Product meetings with Shanghvi mostly ended up as an exercise in embarrassment for Kedrowski, 'It seemed that every time we spoke about a product, Dilip knew more about it than we did, which was pretty frustrating personally. When our team got chatting with him, we were invariably on the wrong side of the information,' he said half-jokingly.

He recalled an instance when his team had sweated out through nights to come up with new possible skin drug combinations for branded drug opportunities. Shanghvi took exactly one minute to figure out that these wouldn't work.

But one of the most prized missing pieces of the mystery Shanghvi decoded, which helped Taro turnaround in a blink, was historic in nature. In true Shanghvi tradition, it was one of those blinding flashes, which later perplexed many in the industry, making them wonder how they could miss something so obvious.

The story stripped of the complexities went like this. There was a president who worked as a close aide to Levitt in pre-2005 Taro. Once he left Taro to join a rival firm Fougera, the two companies jumped into a bloody price war in a set of overlapping products. Both lost out, as did others. Prices of those products nosedived year after year, rendering those therapies economically unattractive, forcing other firms with approvals to sell the drugs out of the US market. In the years after Sun got control of Taro, Fougera was changing hands multiple times and was finally bought by Sandoz in 2012.

From a purely business angle, this presented a golden opportunity for pricing strategy in a de facto monopoly or oligopoly set-up. Sun played it boldly by picking up a clutch of drugs where it jacked up prices in the range of 150 to 1000 per cent. About 85 per cent of this price hike in Taro, reckoned Anubhav Aggarwal of Credit Suisse, had come from a handful of five drugs, almost ancient, launched decades back, most in the 1980s and some in the 1990s.

This daring step helped Taro earn mouth-watering profits and craft a financial transformation story. The vertiginous growth was repeatedly dubbed 'unsustainable' by Sun and the Taro management. Sundaram, in the first analyst call Taro hosted in 2014, explained why: ' . . . the level of margins that is being generated, it will attract competition. It's laws of economics.'

More than competition, what would come to bother Taro and Sun a few years later was an increasingly competition-fostering environment in the US and a department of justice probe from a government that was turning particularly hypersensitive to price hikes in the generic medicine space

But cashing in on these so-called 'price-adjustment opportunities', plus designing other improvements rewrote the story of a company that switched labels from being 'near bankrupt' to a 'cash cow' in a span of a few years. Its cash flow was at $220 million in 2012, up from $40 million in 2008 and most of it had come from price changes, not new product launches. A little Gujarati boy in Calcutta, who had observed how skilled his friend Dilip had been in 'padtar' couldn't have got it more right. Taro had two clear focus areas: increase sales by building a new product pipeline and increase in R&D spend. This strategy scripted the company's dramatic increase in earnings per share.

A former Teva veteran described Sun's strategy at Taro as this, 'It's as easy as this. Sun realized that even if fewer people bought Taro medicines, its profits can be much higher at higher prices. In layman's terms—you can work only half as hard, but earn double the income. This was a business insight Taro had missed under its nose, because it was too busy dreaming of becoming the next Teva.'

'. . . the short-sightedness of Taro chairman Barrie Levitt created a once-in-a-lifetime opportunity for Dilip Shanghvi, the controlling shareholder of the Indian firm Sun Pharma,' reported *Haaretz*, in a piece titled 'Taro Pharma; Once nearly broke, now has $6 billion market cap'.

Shareholders and analysts were not buying Taro's confessions that its profits may not last. While Credit Suisse reckoned in 2012 that only 10 per cent of Taro's $595 sales could be eroded if competition hit back, shareholder discussion forums were flooded with messages guessing why Taro's share was trading at a discount to its peers despite its stellar outperformance.

Some speculated that it was in Sun's interest to keep the share price depressed as its intent had been to buy out the minority shareholders and take Taro private. On these informal online message boards, traders and stock pundits had started calling the Taro share 'secretive', 'under the radar' and 'playing cards close to one's chest', qualifiers that could effortlessly be switched to describe its new owner Shanghvi.

Minority Report

From the day Sun took over, Shanghvi wanted Taro to be relisted on the bourses and he propelled the team in that direction. 'It was off the stock exchange for accounting difficulties. But to Dilip's credit, he wanted to get it back on the exchange. That tells you something about the man. But what was also clear in his mind—whether he spoke it or not—was that he wanted Taro as an entity of Sun. Alongside, he wanted shareholders to make money,' Kedrowski said.

What other unheralded plans Shanghvi had for Taro didn't unfold without breaking a heart or two. Sometime during the budget sessions, when one of the 'new ideas meeting', instituted by Makov soon after he had joined, had got over, the top executives of Sun were chilling on the terrace of a five-star hotel in Mumbai.

It was late—but days at Sun didn't usually end before 9 p.m.—and people had gathered in groups on high-top tables laid out. On one such table were seated Makov, Kedrowski and Sundaram. Shanghvi walked up to them and the discussion casually veered to Sundaram leaving for the US to take charge.

Kedrowski, according to an executive present there, looked perplexed at the mention, while Makov turned around to ask Shanghvi, 'What? You haven't told him?' Clearly this rearrangement had struck Jim as a bolt out of the blue and left him a bit hurt, said a former colleague. The irony was that, if not for Shanghvi, Kedrowski might not have chanced upon this responsibility to lead a company of Taro's size.

But he also faced what ran as a pattern in Shanghvi's behaviour as he expanded—when he shifted orbits, he did it in a flash, leaving some people struggling to make sense of what had just happened.

Former Taro executives reported feeling a level of tension between Kedrowski and Sundaram in the succeeding months. 'Kal, new to the environment, was trying to establish himself. He was trying to let Jim be seen as the leader. But Jim had been caught unaware, he hadn't known that Kal was coming. So he was really hurt and the first six months were really tough on him. What didn't help Jim's case was that instead of choosing Cranbury (Sun's New Jersey office), Kal had chosen to sit at Taro headquarters,' a former Taro executive said.

And this tension erupted in the run-up to the relisting of Taro. The company was to relist at the New York Stock Exchange (NYSE) which was picked up for giving more favourable terms compared to NASDAQ, where Taro was earlier listed. 'Jim and his team had worked very hard to get Taro relisted. The dream that they were working towards was to go up on the podium and ring the bell when the trading session opened at NYSE, which is, of course, quite an honour. But owing to some misunderstanding, Jim thought that Kal knew about it, whereas it seems Kal had no clue. This tiff led to a huge argument between the two, with Jim finally suggesting that the two of them could go up together and ring the bell,' the former Taro executive recounted.

Finally, on the day of the relisting, it was Kedrowski and his team who went up the podium and rang the bell in March 2012. It was a key milestone for the company and Shanghvi himself, who had delivered on his promise, to relist Taro. But the Sun team—Sundaram, Mehta, Jayesh Shah among others—didn't turn up for the event. A month later, however, in April 2012, Kal Sundaram took over as CEO of Taro. Kedrowski continues to be a director on the Taro board.

'I can tell you that I hoped to run Taro one day without the interim title but that was not on the cards. I might have taken time, a few months to understand Kal, but today I consider him a great friend, a business partner and a lot more,' Kedrowski, when asked about the episodes, replied.

After having reinvigorated and relisted Taro, Shanghvi tried to achieve the third part of his unstated but apparent milestones—to buy out minority shareholders and make the company private. 'Kedrowski, adding with a laugh, said, 'In a year they could have doubled their investments, in three years they could have earned more than three times. But I realized that no matter what you offer, they always want more.'

Sun's attempts to buy the rest of the Taro shares at $24 and $39, between 2011 and 2013 (up from $10 in 2010) were aborted, after being shunned by minority shareholders—many of whom are trying to guess on buzzing message boards online what's on Shanghvi's silkily evasive mind? That's a multi-billion-dollar question and the drama on that front is still unfolding.

'If you are not somebody in the US you can't be anybody anywhere else in the pharma world, we had that clarity,' Sundaram said. Taro, more so its turnaround, allowed Sun to become more than just 'somebody' in the US. That doesn't guarantee a smooth life and meteoric growth for Taro in future. For Taro, to grow from a $1 billion to $2 billion company would be a tougher journey, because it would remain a niche firm, Sundaram conceded. The same can't be assumed for the expansion of the turnaround artist behind the revival of Taro.

'Dilip's default thinking probably still happens in Gujarati,' Sundaram guessed, recalling his initial days when top-level meetings at Sun seamlessly transitioned into Gujarati, and it was not until midway that Shanghvi noticed and started translating for him what had just transpired. Those days, there was so much Bengali and Gujarati being spoken all around in the company that Abhay Gandhi was prompted to joke: 'This is a company of dadas and bhais,' both slangs for underworld dons.

But today, Sundaram sees a different Shanghvi picking up subtle but incisive cultural cues, when least expected of him. 'It's not your usual wine brands or fast cars or luxury accessories that Dilip notices, what he does is more intellectual hints that underpin a personality or a community,' he explained. Didn't it sound a bit familiar to how he once understood the minds of doctors, community of specialists and owners of target companies, of how he understood the minds of individuals, collectives and humanity?

Before his first meeting with Germany-based Merck Group's CEO Stefan Oschmann, Sundaram recounted Shanghvi hearing out someone tell that he was Stefan Omar Oschmann and asking, 'If he is married to an Iranian, why has he picked up a Sunni name like Omar for his conversion?' As it turned out, Oschmann was an atheist, and when asked by the Muslim cleric to pick a name for religious conversion during marriage to his Shia wife, he picked a Sunni sounding name, 'Omar' as a streak of mischief.

'Shanghvi is increasingly able to decipher what is said but not meant in America and what is not said but still meant in Japan,' noted his top executive. Those are the oblique signs—catching the drift of soft power—that prove that the expansion of Shanghvi, as a leader on the world stage, is still on.

CHAPTER NINETEEN

CHASING THE DIAMOND FOR RUBY

The company bigwigs click-clacked into the conference room of their Gurgaon headquarters, jokingly referred to as seven-star hotel by some in the industry. That the end was drawing close hadn't yet dawned on 'the powers' at Ranbaxy Labs, the pharma company once celebrated as India's global poster boy. The Ranbaxy honchos had huddled in that hall for a crucial top-secret call to thrash out the nuts and bolts of a deal, the after-effects of which were to alter its fortunes in an irreversible manner. But at the time, in early 2013, most seemed clueless of how fast things were slipping out of their hands.

Through that call, there were several points when Ranbaxy generals exchanged sharp glances. Particularly one of those was when CFO Indrajit Banerjee, seated next to CEO Arun Sawhney, alerted the top executive of its Japanese parent Daiichi Sankyo that in its settlement deal with the US Department of Justice, Ranbaxy ought to negotiate a clause that forbids the whistle-blower from talking to the media. They had just agreed upon a clause that the company wouldn't harass the whistle-blower.

'Oh! Don't bother about him. Dinesh is a nice guy. He wouldn't make any troubles,' the New York-based lawyer of Daiichi butted in. The Daiichi executive, clearly in haste, brushed the matter aside.

'Daiichi was in a super rush to settle with the US government. Some Ranbaxy executive committee members were pushing back at the sheer size of penalty at a staggering $500 million. They were arguing to let the negotiation with the US authority linger on rather than settle for such an astronomical sum,' an executive present at the call said.

Another felt, 'Ignoring Indrajit's advice and letting the whistle-blower loose to claim whatever he wished proved to be a cardinal mistake for the company.' There had been more than this 'cardinal mistake' for Ranbaxy, that had been code-named Ruby when it was being bought over by Daiichi, then code-named Diamond. Half a decade since that acquisition, Ranbaxy's fundamentals were floundering.

Indian pink papers, on 14 May 2013, woke up to the powerful intriguing story of the country's first high-profile corporate whistle-blower Dinesh Thakur, the mystery man who had slogged relentlessly in exile for eight long years to make 'Ranbaxy pay for its wrongdoing'. His tale was straight out of the movies. *Mint* called him 'lonely in dissent', drawing parallels with epic characters of Vibhishana in Ramayana, Vikarna and Yuyutsu in Mahabharata.

The penalty slapped by the US Department of Justice on Ranbaxy was publicized as the largest ever in the history of generic pharmaceuticals. That had been publicity bad enough for Ranbaxy (more so because it was for the first time since the wrongdoings had been detected in 2008 that it had pleaded guilty to criminal and civil charges of making and selling sub-par drugs and lying to the American authorities about it). The worse, however, was yet to come, as the media assault took off from this point.

'Ranbaxy's top bosses wanted to destroy proof', the Economic *Times* reported a juicy story in May, sourcing from Dinesh Thakur's allegations levelled in the US courts that had been freshly unsealed. A day later *Fortune* magazine ran a sensational piece of investigative journalism, 'Dirty Medicine', an exhaustive account of what went wrong at Ranbaxy—the bad press within and outside India, the hammering of the penalty-battered brand Ranbaxy, prompting questions on the safety of its drugs. Ultimately, a cocktail of these factors snowballed into a deep crisis and dug out its grave.

'Daiichi desperately wanted to settle, to begin life afresh in Ranbaxy. But far from that, it had opened a can of worms. The fine, pleading guilty and that biased story where the whistle-blower chose to bare his soul had a cascading impact. The story had factual inaccuracies which we internally debated about contesting, but finally decided against. Besides, who would have listened to us? We had just signed a penalty, pleading guilty to criminal charges. What our team did, instead, was to go to doctors, not media, and reassured them,' a top Ranbaxy executive of the time said. This sounded only partly true. Doctors had been far from reassured as the brand continued to be haemorrhaged in media. In his first interview, CEO Sawhney declared that the worst was behind and dished out a chest-thumping statement, 'I can stand behind every pill of Ranbaxy.'

Though the rhetoric ring in the statement made for catchy 'headlines', it showed how out of depth Ranbaxy's leadership was. In hindsight, his 'worst is behind' statement couldn't be farther from foresight. The company's top management spoke too little too late to salvage the legendary pharma brand that had once boasted of a high recall value even amongst the country's housewives.

There was absolute chaos in the market among doctors, retailers and hospitals. Mumbai-based Jaslok hospital banned the medicine for a while. Apollo, India's largest pharmacy chain, suspended its sales one morning, but retracted the suspension by evening inexplicably. Some mom-and-pop drug stores in Bhubaneswar, afflicted by supply disruption and heavily drunk on gossip, pretended to know more than the management, telling journalists, 'Oh! Ranbaxy is shutting shop.'

A confused Indian Medical Association, the lobby group of doctors, shot off a letter to the drug controller of the country, seeking clarity on whether Ranbaxy drugs were safe to prescribe. Pressed from all corners, the drug controller's office and top officials of the health ministry, who were in Geneva at a World Health Organization (WHO) conference at that time, frantically exchanged calls and emails to figure out whether the company was a victim of an invisible global 'conspiracy', or had truly been lousy in making their drugs.

Cut to the Chase

Amid this Ranbaxy brand mayhem, one person was quietly reviving his old contacts and lunching with his Ranbaxian friends at a Mumbai hotel asking them, 'Should I buy Ranbaxy?' This person was Dilip Shanghvi.

'Yes, you should,' his friend claimed to have replied.

'Why?'

'It's a no-brainer. It's an ideal catch, the two firms make for a perfect jigsaw fit. Sun derives 90 per cent of its sales from the US and India;

Ranbaxy only 40 per cent from these two countries. Which means Sun creates its footprint across the rest of the world. You know the maths and geography. In India Sun is strong in the south, west and the east and Ranbaxy in the north. Sun has the lowest cost of manufacturing today, probably the best sales to cost ratio, Ranbaxy's cost control has gone totally haywire.'

'How should I go about it?'

'Daiichi trusts only a few top Japanese banks. You should try dealing with them either through Nomura or Mizhuo bank,' his friend claimed to have advised him. But none of these friends would be the first to know what was happening. At Sun, when Shanghvi uncorked a conversation about Ranbaxy with Makov, prefixing it with 'maybe, we could consider buying . . .', the chairman jumped. He latched on to it the very second Shanghvi brought it up. 'I didn't even take a minute. I said, "Fantastic, Dilip, marvellous deal, unique opportunity, let's go for it,"' Makov recalled.

In his Teva days, he had seen the glory of Ranbaxy—the unrivalled pharma brand from India, much larger than Sun. He was also friends with D.S. Brar, then CEO of Ranbaxy.

'At Teva, we cooperated and competed with Indian companies simultaneously. We partnered to build APIs together on one side and were punching each other on products' market shares. Ranbaxy was one of those companies that stood out from India. So, when Dilip mentioned Ranbaxy, I knew we had to push and make this happen,' Makov said

At the same time, he knew that convincing the Japanese, so insulated in their cultural island, was not going to be any easier than making a vegetarian Shanghvi gulp a sushi.

Makov and Shanghvi masked their first efforts by making a Tokyo trip not to meet Daiichi alone, but a host of Japanese pharma firms, under the guise of striking friendship pacts with them. So many handshakes, bows, *konnichiwas* later, they finally met the Daiichi management for lunch.

There were Shanghvi, Makov and their investment bankers on one side of the table, and Daiichi CEO Joji Nakayama, Ranbaxy chairman Tsutomu Une, along with people from the Daiichi management on the other. Just as lunch was served, the Daiichi executives, oblivious of their guests' design, got excitedly chatting about their future plans for Ranbaxy.

Makov didn't choke on that but realized how uphill the task was going to be. 'They were so fired up and sounding so optimistic about their future strategies for Ranbaxy. It was not an encouraging signal at all. In that euphoria I couldn't imagine how to begin telling them that we are here to sniff around,' Makov laughed.

Shanghvi smiled from time to time, mostly listening intently, pitching in with his punch-packed one-liners about the industry. And then, the moment came, when it was time to part and nothing that mattered from Sun's side had been said or done.

The courteous Japanese, who were hosting the meal, bowed down and Makov stood up to his wave goodbye. And then, as if he had forgotten to mention something, he addressed Nakayama san and broached the subject of Ranbaxy, 'Oh, you know, I just want to share a thought of mine . . . you have many objectives to enter generics with Ranbaxy . . . and I think if we merge with Ranbaxy . . .'

'I had made a proposal without saying that it was a proposal,' Makov recalled, flashing a smile reminiscent of a childhood mischief. The reaction from the Japanese side was a silent cold stare. 'Their reaction was, "Yes, yes, I will throw you out of the door." It was crazy. This is how our first meeting ended. We knew well enough to not expect anything immediately. But we had planted the seed in Daiichi's mind and it wasn't easy, I can tell you, to plant that seed,' Makov asserted.

Back home, Sun's Mergers and Acquisitions team headed by its sharp and articulate CFO Uday Baldota, had started a preliminary analysis of how well Ranbaxy would fit into Sun. 'The presumption was that there is a seller. The meeting in Tokyo was to assess the interest of the seller, but not to flatly ask whether they would sell. Intent was to present us, what we think, what our strategy would be,' Baldota said.

While leaving Tokyo, Makov and Shanghvi instructed their bankers to keep knocking Daiichi's door consistently to test the waters. 'Months later *Business Standard* would credit Makov on how he used his global Jewish connections in the investment banking circles of Japan to bring Daiichi to the negotiating table. The most important attributes, Makov pointed out in that waiting game, was to stay patient and not give up.

Ranbaxy's Funeral Not Far . . .

Ranbaxy's pretence of a rosy life dragged deep into its ailing days. Even as Makov and Shanghvi were watering the seed they had planted in Tokyo, Ranbaxy was imploding after being hit by a series of setbacks. Outwardly, the leadership remained in denial and its statements—few and far between—started sounding lame and repetitive after a while.

Years before Sawhney was appointed Ranbaxy's CEO by Daiichi in 2010, the company had already gone into a semi-crisis mode. Two of its major plants at Dewas and Paonta Sahib had been barred from shipping to the US. The previous management of the company had been charged of falsifying data to the US FDA and selling drugs in the US which, under the law of that country, was 'adulterated'. The company had been put under onerous conditions as its plants came under 'consent decree', a state that the pharma industry perceived less a reform route (that it is meant to be) but more a noose around the neck.

Daiichi, torn between how much power it should allow in the hands of Indian managers and how much control it should retain itself, had responded by changing two managing directors within a year and a half.

Burdened with a $500-million penalty, a whistle-blower's public confessions and a bruised brand, when it seemed that Ranbaxy had touched its nadir and public sentiments had hit an all-time low, its journey downhill accelerated.

In June 2013, a day after a *Business Today* headline warned, 'Disgraced Ranbaxy has a long way to go before it regains the lost trust', Ranbaxy stock already at its four-year low tanked 7 per cent further on the news that its latest facility at Mohali, fitted with world-class gadgetry, was plagued with fresh objections from the US FDA, technically labelled 483s after the number of the form it is noted in.

Analysts were shocked to see the management not come out clean. CEO Sawhney ended up telling the *Financial Express* that '483 was not a show-stopper' and of the 10,000 483s FDA hand out, only 40-odd cases get escalated to a warning letter. One couldn't fault him on his data-digging, but at a time when stakeholders were desperately seeking clarity, this part came out sounding more arrogant than confident.

A month later, the *Economic Times* revealed that the US FDA rap covered not only its Mohali plant but extended to its lifeline facility for bulk drugs at Toansa that met 70 per cent of its main raw material requirements, and much of American regulator's observations were serious stuff.

What was also becoming clear to outside observers was that Ranbaxy was struggling to launch six-month exclusive marketing opportunities for generics in the US on time. The one it had, Lipitor had erupted with its own set of issues, and the company had had to carry out massive recalls of the drug under US FDA's charges of glass shards, hair and oil spots on the tablets.

Inside, too many things were screwed up royally simultaneously. Ranbaxy had splashed millions of dollars on its consultants to no results. Another insider pointed out, 'The organization within R&D arm was hilarious. Multiple teams were working on the same molecule for different geographies: Europe, the US and rest of the World.'

Project Virat, an extravagant campaign Ranbaxy had launched with grand fanfare in 2010 to regain its sheen in the domestic market had flopped. And when Rajiv Gulati, a star Ranbaxian of yesteryears, instrumental in launching blockbuster brands like Revital, Cifran and Norbactin decades back, rejoined in 2011 and reviewed the floundering campaign expanding its sales force breathlessly, he asked the country head to cut the tens of crappy new products the company was flooding the Indian market with.

'Gulati suggested that each division focus on not more than four select brands on which 100 per cent of incremental sales budget and 90 per cent of promotional budgets should be devoted,' a marketing executive said.

The nugget of data Gulati apparently cited to buttress his case was: 'Go and look into any division in any Indian company worth its salt. The top 5–10 brands command 35 to 40 per cent of sales. Any company except Sun. Theirs is a different story—their divisions will have top ten products accounting for less than 20 per cent of sales. But that is because Sun is the only company for which a doctor willingly writes all ten products on his prescription. No other company can boast likewise.'

Historical errors committed by Ranbaxy included a foreign currency gamble of a few billion dollars that has misfired and was pushing the stand-alone company steadily towards bankruptcy. 'Currency gambling on 300 per cent of revenue, coupled with plant shutdowns prompted us to book profits overseas. Progressively it was taking us in the direction of reporting to BIFR and a good deal of Indrajit's (CFO's) energies were only devoted to avert that crisis,' an executive committee member said.

And with Ranbaxy's Mohali plant barred from shipping to the US, the growing schism between shop-floor workers and the top executive management further deepened. 'Every time a goof-up happened, workers were squarely blamed. If you heard those awfully insensitive fiery speeches of the senior management, they never owned a shred of responsibility. I always recommended, "Before GMPs (good manufacturing practices) and GLPs (good lab practices) came GBPs, that is, good behavioural practices." But it fell on deaf ears. If you trace the root cause of Ranbaxy's undoing with a searchlight, "bad behavioural practices" is where you are likely to end up,' an executive committee member said.

Three months after the plant at Mohali had been banned, the final trigger for Ranbaxy's unravelling was being scripted at the banks of the Sutlej at the idyllic location of the Toansa plant.

But that couldn't stop the ultimate blow, the Toansa ban by the US, which sent the Ranbaxy's shares into a free fall, down 20 per cent in a trading session. It dragged down parent Daiichi's shares as well. Under the increasing ire of its shareholders, Daiichi's CFO Manabu Sakai announced in a conference call, 'We need to grasp how something like this could occur, how extensive the transgressions were and whether they were the fault of a particular person.'

Time was running out for the somnambulism of Ranbaxy and its endgame was being scripted a little far as its Japanese parent was preparing to abandon it.

And the Seed in Tokyo Sprouts One Day . . .

The bankers Sun had appointed in Tokyo, who did the clockwork of checking every month if Daiichi's needle of intent had moved an inch, were stirred to life by their unusual response one day after Toansa had been banned. After so long, 'almost three quarters of a year of follow-up, Daiichi showed signs of thawing. So what's your offer?' Makov recalled Daiichi as asking.

On receiving Daiichi's off-beat offer query, Makov decided it was time to move at the speed of a jet. An executive in Sun's M&A team indicated that 'ground-level intelligence reports suggested that Toansa tipped the balance for Daiichi, and selling Ranbaxy bubbled up in their priority.'

By late 2013, rumour mills had started buzzing about Shanghvi's piquing interest in Ranbaxy. In December 2013, the *Economic Times* ran a piece titled 'Pharma CEO kin stocking up on Ranbaxy shares' without naming Shanghvi and Valia. By early next month, *Business Standard* had lifted the suspense of identities by reporting 'Silverstreet Developers, a limited liability partnership firm' with Sudhir V. Valia as a partner, has picked up a 1.41 per cent stake in Ranbaxy.

Before these reports appeared, around October–November 2013, some private equity players and investment bankers had started tipping off journalists about the distinct possibility of Sun swallowing Ranbaxy. But every time someone who knew Shanghvi from close was asked this question, they laughed off the prospect as impossible. 'Even when he hires an individual, he does thorough background checks. Do you think he will buy a hornet's nest like Ranbaxy?'

Despite all speculations in late 2013, Daiichi didn't seem fully ready to sell, not till Toansa was blocked out, and the media started calling the company 'Ban-baxy'. For one, Daiichi's then CEO Joji Nakayama who visited India in December 2013 and met then prime minister Manmohan Singh, commerce and industry minister Anand Sharma, other ministers and bureaucrats had openly professed the company's intent to stay invested in India and their plans to expand operations at Ranbaxy.

In late 2013, Daiichi was still thinking of ways to salvage the situation that included exploring chances of inducting whistle-blower Thakur on the Ranbaxy board, according to an US-based business associate of Daiichi. This claim could not be independently verified. Till as late as January 2013, Ranbaxy's board was mulling business strategies such as spinning off its US business to minimize damages. But those changes were not to be.

Instead, by February 2014, the action had shifted to room number 666 at Sun's Mahakali office, a room called triple-six by all in the company, where Shanghvi conducted his meetings. Interestingly, Sun's rooms bore number plates of their phone numbers, till it shifted its headquarters to Sun House in Goregaon and reversed the practice—of allotting phone numbers based on room numbers.

Of the many days that were spent sizing up the prospective bride Ranbaxy, and how she would fit in her new family at Sun, one gloomy day, probably sometime in March either just before the diligence or immediately after, is etched in the minds of many.

The M&A team led by Baldota in the presence of Shanghvi had spent the entire evening appraising the existing business performance of Ranbaxy and the valuations it merited. 'It was a very strange day. The numbers we put on the board looked very grim. And it seemed like a crazy idea to bet on something with so many uncertainties. Maybe we were magnifying the negatives, but at the end of the session, the mood became pensive. Even after so much brain racking through the entire evening, we couldn't justify the valuation. Our minds were clouded, faces long when we left for the day late in the night. Dilip-bhai couldn't be feeling any better. Had we persisted with that thinking one day longer, we would have surely killed the deal,' Baldota recalled.

But early next morning Baldota received a call from Shanghvi, asking him to gather his team once more. They started where they had left off the night before with a team member putting that valuation number on the board. Somewhere along the way Makov joined the meeting through a call and said, 'Guys, we can't be looking at negative, negative, negative...'

Shanghvi who rarely bares his feelings spoke about feeling upset for a change and said, 'Yesterday I went back home very disappointed. And thought through, where's it that we are going wrong in our thinking and action? I wanted to have a fresh look at things today morning. Forget the valuation part. Yes, the business has been performing dismally.

But instead of focusing on past and present negatives, can we look at future positives, what we can do to run the same business better?'

From there on, Shanghvi went into his 'god and devil both are in details' mode. The slides and the numbers changed. Each stand-alone business of Ranbaxy was analysed separately. They looked at India, the US, the emerging markets and over-the-counter segments granularly and assessed what Sun could do differently in each of them. How much was each business worth on a stand-alone basis.

They dived into each revenue segment, each cost item, whether Sun had a comparable business, its cost structure, what are the revenue opportunities, where in those business could Sun do better. They deep-dived into products, scanned IMS (Information Medical Statistics) data to glean where Sun could grab more market share; was there an opportunity to price it northwards or was there something Sun could do to cut costs. Such was the minutiae of analysis that the cost of running the Ranbaxy headquarters was also dissected.

While discussing the US business, they beamed on Ranbaxy's branded business and mapped how snugly it would fit into the dermatology business strategy Sun was pursuing with the aid of its last big acquisition Taro. Not too far long in the past, perhaps in 2011 or 2012, Shanghvi had wanted to buy a branded derma business that Ranbaxy had once bought from Bristol Myers Squibbs in 2007, but his feelers had been politely turned down by Ranbaxy.

Within India, Sun had so far focused on the chronic business and long been exploring routes to expand into other therapies—including acute drugs. 'We didn't have a concrete plan as yet, but the thought had been there for a while now. How do we go beyond the core therapy areas? The moot question we asked ourselves was—if we start building from scratch, we may take a long time to build, given the dense competitive intensity. Even if we did, one couldn't be sure if our success could parallel our chronic drugs counterpart. We had never run an acute drugs business. But the Ranbaxy business could help us jump-start with a meaningful size in therapies where we were absent,' Baldota said.

When they studied Ranbaxy's rich footprints in emerging markets, where Sun had scant presence, the deliberations veered towards the products Sun could launch using Ranbaxy's channels.

And as the process progressed, energy in the room shifted, the buzz intensified to an excitement, the tone acquired optimism, and mood turned upbeat. 'And I was thinking, nothing had changed on the ground in the last twelve hours. What might have [changed] was our perspective. We were no longer staring at the rear-view mirror to value the Ranbaxy business. We were weighing its potential on its assimilation in Sun, which essentially meant the value we could create out of it. Suddenly things fell into place and it started making immense sense to buy it. Chairman Makov and Dilip-bhai were forcing us to learn different ways of valuing the same business and I was telling myself, "This is what leadership is all about,"' Baldota concluded.

Sun had till this point in the chase refrained from using any Indian consultants. A close associate of Shanghvi said that he was extremely wary of information leaks that could potentially spawn market speculations, drive up target share prices and kill the deal in its tender phase.

The *Economic Times* reported later how 'paranoid' Shanghvi was to 'keep the information under wraps', the reason why he told his advisers Citi and Evercore Partners to let their US offices lead the deal talks, code-named 'Operation Rainbow', where Rainbow stood for Ranbaxy, Dawn for Daiichi and Sky represented Sun.

Even before the due diligence began, a massive stumbling block threatened to push the deal off the rails. It related to what had been haunting Daiichi since it bought Ranbaxy after a flimsy due diligence. Sun wanted to ensure that it didn't make the same mistake and asked for an endorsement of Ranbaxy's compliance issues by an external agency.

'Not permitted,' was Daiichi's flat response. 'No external scrutiny allowed.'

'We need to know the risk we are taking. If we don't have clarity on this, there is no way this deal can happen,' Sun retorted, adding, 'we will give you whatever protection you need.'

This back and forth was mainly handled by their bankers. Daiichi softened and asked, 'Who?'

'Lachman,' Sun promptly dished out. Leon Lachman and Shanghvi had bonded during his Caraco regulatory troubles and had been in touch since.

'No way, Lachman,' Daiichi shot back.

'But why?' Sun asked.

'They have worked for us at Ranbaxy before, so there is a conflict.'

'It's actually better that they have worked for you. Isn't it?'

'Because they have worked with us, they can share with you information that will hurt us.'

'Valid point,' Sun reasoned. Had they been in the shoes of the seller, their concerns would mirror Daiichi's, so they tweaked the offer: 'What about a clean team within Lachman which hasn't worked on Ranbaxy?'

'Not acceptable. Pick any other adviser.'

'Sorry, we will not pick any other adviser. We are comfortable with the judgement of Lachman, and Lachman it would be, if it has to be.'

This deadlock dragged through the end of Friday even as the Sun team packed its bags to leave for New York on Sunday to kick off in person the due diligence on Monday, 17 March 2014. Instead, their US-bound air tickets had to be cancelled amid the stalemate.

Just when they saw a flicker of light at the end of the tunnel with Daiichi finally agreeing to their condition, Sun was faced with another hiccup. Lachman demanded a full waiver. 'Any opinion we give, someone is going to be unhappy and will come after us. So all three parties—Sun, Ranbaxy and Daiichi—will have to hold our organization harmless and de-risk us.'

Barring Lachman, everyone flinched. Daiichi refused, Ranbaxy refused and Sun argued that they could perhaps indemnify a team working on the assignment. But it was insane to sign off a protection cover for a whole organization. Sometime on Sunday, Sun started making up its mind to walk off the deal. But in the nick of time, on Monday, Daiichi gave in and Ranbaxy followed. Sun too agreed in principle but hadn't signed it till the team reached New York on Tuesday.

The Sun team, led by CFO Baldota, walked into the office of David Polk & Wardwell at Lex in Manhattan. They were ushered into a large conference room. Seating was arranged in an almost classroom setting; to the side was a longish table with neatly laid-out folders labelled under different heads such as business plans, projections, consent decree documents.

The Sun squad, roughly a dozen heads, intently pored over folders marked 'litigation'. Daiichi was represented by 3–4 people, including its global head of business development Stu Mackey and Kazunori Hirokawa, a Daiichi representative on the Ranbaxy board. More than one member in Sun's team felt that Ranbaxy CEO Arun Sawhney and CFO Indrajit Banerjee present during the due diligence appeared reluctant to share information and it fell on Daiichi to force them to reveal what was being asked. To the Sun team, the Daiichi–Ranbaxy internal divide manifested itself forcefully during due diligence process.

Sun CFO Baldota, when asked, confirmed the feeling: 'I think there was a bit of over-intellectualism of things at Ranbaxy, a wee bit of scare topped with plain reluctance. In sheer quantum terms, the data we looked in case of Ranbaxy during diligence was far lesser than we did for deals where we ended up not buying the company. My sense was Daiichi was making the horse drink the water.'

The Sun team had access to the dossiers through the week and, on Thursday, when CFO Banerjee was fielding questions, Daiichi's business development head whisked Baldota and Sun's lawyer off to a different place. Standing there with Mackey was Sawhney armed with a tiny bombshell. It was here that they revealed to Sun that they had been slapped with yet another Department of Justice subpoena related to their raw material plant at Toansa.

Sawhney said to a shocked Baldota. 'We just received it last week and are yet to disclose it.'

'We want you to keep this very private, limited to as few people as it can be,' the Daiichi executive urged.

'I understand,' Baldota, weighing the depth of the newborn problem, muttered.

By Friday, when the Sun to Ranbaxy quizzing had tapered off, one thread of questions to Sawhney on the nature of the 483s observations (objections of the US FDA) was still to die down. The Sun team had been tipped off from back home that even as they were posing questions to dark-suited C-level executives in the US, Ranbaxy's facilities back home were being inspected by regulators. In his answers, Sawhney had apparently been claiming that objections contained in the three 483s slapped on Ranbaxy were minor remarks, a response that couldn't quench Sun's curiosity.

Daiichi responded by stretching the period of diligence and made arrangements in a New Jersey hotel for Sun to discover answers.

In the hotel Daiichi had made arrangements for Sawhney and Banerjee to be there to respond to Sun's questions again. When someone from the Sun team broached the 483s, Sawhney wriggled some papers out and started reading out the contents to them. He didn't hand over the papers for Sun to see.

When Sun's questions edged towards how they planned to launch and monetize pending products with exclusive marketing opportunities for a period of six months in the US (generic Diovan, Nexium and Valcyte), Sawhney declined to share anything dubbing the information proprietary. On further prodding, he agreed to fly in person to Mumbai and share it only with Shanghvi.

A Ranbaxy executive defended the charges of their unwillingness to participate in the process. 'There were not two but three listed entities involved there: Ranbaxy, Daiichi and Sun. So it didn't matter what Daiichi or Sun wanted me to do. I would do what was in the interest of Ranbaxy. Daiichi might be a 60 per cent shareholder, but we had fiduciary duties towards 40 per cent minority shareholders. And divulging proprietary information would have violated that duty of mine. We gave a damn about whether the company stayed with Daiichi or went to Sun. Let's get this straight—it also didn't matter much what we wanted, Daiichi was the majority shareholder and if it decided to sell, it would.'

Most Ranbaxy ace executives have the impression that Nakayama presented the Sun deal proposal to the Daiichi board more as a fait accompli than to seek their advice on it. True or not, that Sun deal structure, which Nakayama took to the Daiichi board, emerged from a week of negotiation on call that Baldota did with business development head of Daiichi, starting 24 March 2014.

Before Baldota got into those calls, he would have a detailed discussion with Shanghvi on the boundary conditions Sun would not cross. The Daiichi guy wouldn't know, but Shanghvi sat right there listening to the calls with rapt attention, gesticulating directions when there was a need.

From the Taro experience, Shanghvi had learnt that Sun wouldn't be lured into buying only Daiichi's shares, it had got to acquire 100 per cent control in one go. 'One important lesson (from Taro) was also not to keep a lot of distance between signing and closing of the deal,' Shanghvi said.

The first offer Sun sent to Daiichi was about ₹450 per share, to which there was a sharp pushback: 'This is not the value of Ranbaxy.' When they reverted with a price of ₹480 a share, Daiichi mellowed. Sun was inclined to pay for the deal in a mix of cash and stock, but after hearing from their bankers that Daiichi preferred an all-stock deal because that lent the deal more certainty and probably meant a lower tax burden, Sun offered an all-stock option in its first formal offer.

Sticky points, such as a board membership for Daiichi in Sun, the exact price, clauses in the agreement such as promoters' guarantee (that they would vote in favour of the transactions) were thrashed out over 3–4 long-distance calls between Daiichi's global business development head and Baldota.

The trickiest point of negotiation was the protection cover Daiichi would grant Sun from liabilities that may arise in case of Ranbaxy from present and future litigation. Sun, at first, bargained for blanket unlimited indemnity. Daiichi said, 'Of course not, let's talk Toansa.' 'We were being greedy in asking for way too much. But possible liabilities arising out of the Toansa issue was a fair ask,' felt an executive from Sun's M&A team.

The amount of protection cover became the next ticklish issue to unknot. Sun suggested $500 million; Daiichi retorted, 'No way.' Instead, it applied logic, insisting that since Daiichi had a 64 per cent stake in Ranbaxy, their indemnity to Sun should be to the tune of 64 per cent of $500 million, dragging that number down to $325 million, limiting the protection period to less than a decade.

Once these contours had been drawn by 31 March 2014, the team at Sun worked 24/7 for the next six days to make the acquisition announcement happen. They left the office at about three at night and were back by ten next morning. As they wrapped up in the night, the team in the US took over from them. Some in the team shut themselves in the conference room and didn't even go home.

Even as Sun's team was working on the deal red-eyed, burning midnight oil, and through the days, the Ranbaxians were largely clueless about it till 5 April, except noticing an unusual rally in Ranbaxy shares in the days that preceded the deal. There are many unverified theories floating to explain this rally in the share market into which the market regulator SEBI launched an investigation. On an early April morning, the executive committee found a message from chairman Une to gather at Gurgaon's Oberoi hotel for an important announcement. On receiving this abrupt message, the Ranbaxy phone networks went into a tizzy as top executives started calling each other, to check whether they were the only one who didn't know something. The only two among them who knew 'what it was about' feigned ignorance.

In the evening when Tsutomu Une broke the news some looked stunned, faces of a few hung. One member present said, 'I think most of us knew in our heart of hearts that this is the best thing that could have happened for the company. But at the same time, all of us had seen Shanghvi and Sun long enough to realize that our own run in the company was coming to an end. Some would act on that impulse, some would let themselves be misled by illusions till they realized that their first hunch had been correct. But one of the first ironies some of us lamented over immediately post-announcement was that Ranbaxy had remained more Ranbaxy under Japanese Daiichi than it could ever be under the Indian Sun. I think none of us had missed the fact that an era had come to an end.'

Sayonara to a Misadventure

The announcement of the deal—Sun would be taking over Ranbaxy to become the undisputed No. 1 in India, consolidate its position as the No. 5 generic drug maker globally—popped in the inbox of stunned journalists even before the Sun-rise of 7 April 2014. It was the largest inbound deal in the history of the pharma sector and after overcoming the brief early morning blues that followed the miss of juicy stories, pink papers started planning their coverage for the day to match the extraordinary event.

In the analyst call Sun hosted that morning, Shanghvi said the transaction would fulfil his 'long-held ambition of becoming a successful Indian company in the global pharmaceutical arena', but 'size is not what excites' him. He employed Sun's old success scale, to fill in for what the deal had brought him. 'We were No.1 in terms of share of prescription in seven speciality therapy areas. Because of the transaction with Ranbaxy, we see that in six additional areas we become No.1', adding on 'the exciting part of the transaction is that even though we become stronger in each of the therapy areas in terms of share of prescriptions, our dependence on that particular therapy area actually has gone down.' Sun was also getting a foothold in over-the-counter categories and emerging markets from being a company of two-country dominance. Long back, Shanghvi had once learnt the concept and acronym of RoW from this company. Two decades on, Ranbaxy would become the medium for Sun to hoist its flag in the Rest of the World.

The mood at Ranbaxy headquarters turned sombre. Former and existing Ranbaxians started lamenting the end of the legendary brand; the company's communication arm promptly embarked on a task to code in the success of Ranbaxy in an obituary-like coffee-table memoir, calling it 'Legends are forever'.

This soppy sulking continued even after Shanghvi in his first interview post-acquisition assured that 'Ranbaxy as a brand has a value, we can use that. It is a credible brand in India, there is a lot of emotional attachment. And also, if we see Sun as a company, we have not changed the name of companies.' The fear of Ranbaxians was to come true later.

Despite Shanghvi's assurance in media and first address at the Ranbaxy R&D centre where he said, 'Together we will be stronger. In case of Sun and Ranbaxy, two plus two doesn't make four, they make twenty-two. Ranbaxy has good people, has great markets and Sun has cash resources. This is a very potent combination.' Speculations on who would stay and who would go, broke like wildfire almost instantaneously.

Some rumours had logic, some parochial; others plain stupid: Rajiv Gulati might stay on because he has had a long association with Shanghvi; Sanjiv Dani might stay on because not only is he a workhorse but also a Gujarati Vaishnav Kapol; Yagnik, who had held top HR posts at Sun, Ranbaxy and Suzlon, started getting congratulatory messages for the new position he was to hold soon. Yagnik looked up from his phone messages and smiled at his wife, 'I know this won't happen.' None of these rumours proved to be correct. Bhagwat Yagnik, who had headed the HR of Sun in its infancy, and Ranbaxy in its prime, told a few friends, 'Sun would successfully integrate the business of Ranbaxy but would mess up in its people's integration.'

Shanghvi quickly appointed an integration committee under a Ranbaxy veteran Ranjan Chakravarti, drawing members from both companies to identify areas of synergies between the two companies.

Making a deviation, he hired Mckinsey to carry out an exercise in organizational human resources to understand the cultural convergences and schisms between the two firms better. The cultural differences between the two and unflattering perception each harboured of the other couldn't have been starker. At Sun, Ranbaxy's current lot were perceived as pompous white elephants fattening on bloated salaries, completely out of touch with ground realities of the market.

At Ranbaxy, Sun's style of running business was looked down upon as 'thrifty', 'stingy', and the company was repeatedly referred to as *lalaji ki dukan*. That was unsurprising given the culture of Sun was to switch off lights before you leave—not only out of environmental consciousness, but to save the last penny while at Ranbaxy, the Hindi phrase internally popular to describe its culture, loosely translated to, 'First take the money, then the boots.'

Sun considered the culture of Ranbaxy abusive and individuals there too full of themselves. At Ranbaxy, they prided the same traits as 'strong personalities', against which the unnamed Sun counterparts had little chance to stand, if a face-off was staged, they believed.

As days passed, despite confessionals and the detailed cultural surveys Mckinsey orchestrated, the undercurrents between employees of these two companies—one whose success had run past them and one whose long success run was peaking—got stronger and bitter. At Ranbaxy, phrases used about the new conqueror only got meaner with time; one of them heard on the corridors was, 'Gangu Teli will now rule Raja Bhoj.'

When Mckinsey made a presentation at Hotel Lalit, underlining that beneath the apparent differences, the two companies had similarities,

Ranbaxians in the crowd gasped, dubbing the exercise a 'hogwash' to keep the optics of togetherness going till the point the transaction was completed.

Among the many stand-offs, one specifically related to exchange of data. 'There was immense resistance from Ranbaxy while sharing data which was very basic. If they didn't give us product-level sale data, we could do. But basic cost-related data—factory costs, employee costs—antitrust rules didn't stop you from sharing such basic data. Often they cited unconvincing excuses such as 'our lawyers have advised us against it,' 'the board is not agreeable,' a Sun executive said.

At Lalit, where the Mckinsey presentation was being attended by 60–70 people from both sides, and a question–answer session was on, some of the Sun executives complained that they were not getting requisite data from their Ranbaxy counterparts.

Just then Banerjee, the CFO of Ranbaxy, stood up from his seat to warn fellow company men, 'If anyone chooses to pass on data to Sun, they do it at their own risk, a personal liability.' That flared up the heat of the moment. Banerjee, when approached, said he has signed a legal contract with Sun, to not discuss these matters.

Six months on since the acquisition announcement, Ranbaxy's dogged refusal to data transfer had cropped up as a sore point and the two CFOs, Baldota and Banerjee, had many heated exchanges over the matter. The tiff lasted for months before data started trickling in slowly, according to an executive at Sun.

Sun executives saw Ranbaxians as bloody-minded, more flashy than efficient, harbouring a false hope that the deal may be called off. 'They were indulging in wishful thinking, probably wishing that if they troubled the Sun guys too much, they might call the deal off, before it got all approvals,' a Sun executive reckoned.

Ranbaxy executives would have us believe that Sun executives came with preconceived notions, judging them as having failed and behaved like snobs, like victors do with vanquished after conquests. 'What if the deal hadn't gone through? There was privileged information, we didn't want to share. Because it was against the rules of SEBI, antitrust rules and we were accountable to the shareholders till the point the merger got all approvals,' a top Ranbaxy executive defended.

Some of these data-related fist fights tumbled over to approvals such as one relating to US antitrust commission—the FTC (Federal Trade Commission). The US antitrust commission called for some data in May and till August Ranbaxy had not supplied it, claimed a Sun executive. This led to more clash. Baldota was handling it, and he told the top Ranbaxy executive, 'FTC is asking you about some products. It is a government agency, you will have to share it.'

'But we have consent decree. If we say anything to FTC, we will potentially land up in trouble with other US agencies—like the Department of Justice.'

'That will only happen if you have lied to the government. You only need to state facts as they are. They are asking you questions like: 'Will you be manufacturing some products.' If you have decided, tell them. If not, tell them. And you can give today's factual position, that may change over time,' the executive recalled an exasperated Baldota reasoning.

But these were not the only issues brewing. Ranbaxy's legal head, who was expected to give his seal on some of these matters left the company, the US-based executive who was to chip in was not even responding to calls of chief-level executives from India. By October 2014, six top-level executives at Ranbaxy US had resigned en masse to form their own start-up.

Headhunters in India whined about a deluge of Ranbaxy CVs out-filling their inboxes. Senior executives were leaving in droves—particularly those who were rumoured to continue. Rajiv Gulati left to start his own medicine e-commerce venture m-Chemist, Dani left to join Aurobindo Pharma as COO.

Sawhney was conducting open houses regularly—once in a month or two, trying to soothe nerves and convince people that they wouldn't be sacked post-transaction. But the crowd at Ranbaxy believed rumour mills as a more credible source of information.

The rumours floating around pegged the number of probable pink slips at 6000. That number meant more than a third of the company. Nakayama had addressed once, so had Une—but that hadn't unruffled the restless, and a sight that remained etched in minds of Ranbaxians was of their cheery Japanese colleagues, quietly packing their bags and leaving the country, like migratory birds.

Ranbaxy top executives, part of the integration committee who interacted closely with Shanghvi, found him 'unreadable' and 'inscrutable'. 'You will never know for sure whether he is agreeing or disagreeing with you. His soft nods can be so deceptive. On the face of it, it will seem that he is agreeing to what you are saying. It is only a few days later, when you see him act on that matter, will you finally figure out that after all he hadn't agreed,' a senior executive, echoing what his colleague had expressed, said. 'Just because unlike other promoters, he is not interjecting you in the middle to correct you, or yelling at you or listening so carefully, don't presume that all is well.'

When things didn't get done as planned or took longer than expected, Shanghvi who had been 'strategically patient' while buying Ranbaxy turned 'tactically impatient'. He atypically reminded the integration committee that contrary to perceptions anger was not alien to him. 'I don't shout doesn't mean that I don't get angry' or 'My father used to tell me that you don't have to shout to be heard.' This is not a part of Shanghvi that those worked with him in the early years could completely relate to.

If one went by the image of Shanghvi cut out by descriptions of the few Ranbaxy senior managers, it was not an exact match of the behavioural profile of the Sun chief one had built from previous experiences.

Soft-spoken, yes, but neither was he portrayed as one shorn of anger nor was he seen as patient as seen through the lens of the Ranbaxians. Few of them who had done their homework about Shanghvi gleaning from industry colleagues found it baffling when their impressions about him didn't fit the image they experienced. For instance, two Ranbaxians claimed that Shanghvi, if not lavish, was liberal with his praises for them initially.

He apparently lauded their efforts and accomplishments at Ranbaxy, making them feel special; this when to squeeze a complement out of the chief at Sun was labelled mission impossible inside Sun. One of them felt such positive feedback from Sun chief led him and his colleagues to presume falsely that they would play valuable roles in the merged entity despite rumours that the Ranbaxy top layer would be booted out.

It's an exercise in vain to guess whether Shanghvi's personality is undergoing a steady transformation as the stakes grow bigger with the size and complexity of the company; as multiple challenges confront him amid the glaring spotlight that he finds really uncomfortable, or is it a temporary form he cloaked on consciously to help him tide over the Ranbaxy episode.

He seemed self-aware of this change in image perception, and once on a different issue of truth and objectivity of narratives such as the one being attempted, he commented casually, 'You should talk to people from Ranbaxy, particularly finance and HR; their views about me shouldn't be so charitable.'

While announcing the acquisition in April, Shanghvi had maintained that he was expecting it to close in eight to ten months. Taro had taught him to shrink the gap between cutting and closing the deal. But once it was November, and major approvals like that of the Punjab and Haryana High Court and the Competition Commission of India were still hanging in balance, Shanghvi's 'tactical impatience' had started showing in front of his deputies in a way they had seldom seen before.

The problem was that the deal might have been the largest for Sun but not its first as it was for India's antitrust commission. From August to October, the media had published overzealous reports on how India's trustbuster was launching a serious probe on whether a Sun–Ranbaxy combine could actually create monopoly, forcing out competition in some therapies.

These hyped reports fuelled illusory hopes of the deal getting blocked among some in Ranbaxy. But industry insiders always knew that given the mutually exclusive nature of business that Sun and Ranbaxy built historically, these were little more than hyperbole.

For Sun, however, the worst shocker popped in November. Sun executives after watching the Competition Commission employ the European model for scrutiny had presumed it would continue to do so for the rest of its path to deal clearance. They had expected the Indian competition watchdog to red-flag therapies at the risk of being monopolized and allow them to go ahead with the merger after taking a commitment that such products would be divested in a specified time.

But once the Competition Commission sorted out seven products for divestment, it chose to go the American way, asking Sun to divest first and then seek approval for the merger. The divestment in itself wouldn't have robbed an iota of sheen from the deal, to speak of its significance, but it was certain to delay it by a minimum of 4–5 months.

'But we are giving you a commitment that we will divest in the next six months, but why didn't you tell us in July, we could have divested by now. Please see, the US Federal Trust Commission told us in September and we have already identified parties, shortlisted and the negotiations are about to begin . . . you are putting the whole transaction at risk.' Sun executives tried to persuade the competition regulator through multiple rounds of discussion.

'We will appoint a monitor,' an unconvinced Indian trustbuster shot back.

'For what?'

'To check you are identifying the right parties.'

'But we will anyway come back to you for approvals. Till you approve the party, we will not divest.'

'But we need to have a monitor as we are following the European system.'

So PwC (PricewaterhouseCoopers) was appointed the monitor. But when its team turned up at Sun's doorsteps, it was not the pharma team they were expecting but the forensic team. 'The forensic team has a mindset. You are guilty till proven innocent. So they began asking for the daily inventory data that we don't even create,' a Sun executive said. After a little push and pull, Sun appointed an arm of Citi, to see through the process.

It was finally March when all approvals came through, and Sun started preparing for an event they had not done almost for a decade—a proper press conference. As part of the grand event, they tried shooting an audio-visual of Shanghvi's address, but their chief appeared so conscious and awkward before the camera, that most of that footage had to be cut out.

Preparations for the conference were on, when the Ranbaxy communications team sent in a suggestion—their chief executive could give Shanghvi company on the dais. They claimed receiving no response to that. Neither was Sun's own second-level leadership seen on the podium. It was deliberately planned that way, if the grapevine was to be believed, to put an end to the one-upmanship between Sun and Ranbaxy top executives.

Makov who apparently was scheduled to fly down for the occasion had to cancel at the last minute for personal reasons and joined Shanghvi through videoconferencing. Even on that momentous occasion that marked his ascension to an undisputed No, 1 in the country, Shanghvi, seated alone on that dais, appeared more vulnerable than triumphant.

Anyone could tell that he wasn't enjoying the attention. But deep down it was perhaps this vulnerability that made him look 'real' and 'human' and endeared him to thousands. It was exactly the kind of attribute one hoped for but didn't expect in the corporate superheroes, especially not after scripting arguably the most mesmerizing business story of his generation in India, one that started in a small shop in a narrow by-lane of Calcutta's Dawa Bazaar and hadn't yet finished even as he owned the country's largest pharmaceuticals company. Corporate elites with much meaner feats were better known to design their power-looks and project perfections. A close aide of yesteryears said, 'Dilip-bhai had a deep knowing that not hiding your vulnerabilities gives you better acceptance.'

But this hesitation and tentativeness was gone as soon as the press was out; soon it was back to business as usual. He addressed a call jointly to thousands of employees—in Sun and Ranbaxy. To an employee's question—'I have worked so hard in Ranbaxy for the last many years, now that I am in Sun, how will all that hard work be compensated?'—Shanghvi punched his wit in a one-liner, after his leitmotif pause, 'Don't treat your job here as a savings account. It is more like a current account. You work hard in Sun, you will be rewarded.'

He appeared in even greater control, while addressing a smaller group at the Ranbaxy office in Gurgaon. Not mincing words that day, he stunned Ranbaxy employees by asking whether they switched off the lights before leaving for the day.

One of the first teams he sat with was the R&D team at Ranbaxy. 'He was supremely confident and quickly taking calls on each product in the Ranbaxy portfolio. On the science side, he was taking prompt calls on why a product didn't need six months or a year to develop and could be done faster. On the market and cost side he was even sharper,' an onlooker in that meeting said. He was also making a list of products that Sun would stay with, and at one stage this Ranbaxy executive recalled him taking a break from the exercise to refer to a small set of products he had sorted, to ask, 'Do these earn anything for the company or are they meant only to satisfy the ego of scientists?'

'His R&D head, his clinical head, his head of analytics were all by his side, but the decisions were all his. And that day, it became fully clear to me as to why this guy doesn't need great-thinking managers. He does it all by himself, all the core work, and does it fast. It's hardly surprising that his business model and HR policies have to be different from the companies that rely on their managers,' said a top-level Ranbaxy non-R&D executive, who was witness to that scene. Just a few months before that day, Arvind Valia had completed Steve Jobs's biography authored by Walter Issacson and told Shanghvi, 'Jobs only hired A-listers to work with', to which he had responded, 'For me, B and C players work fine as long as I am confident of getting an A-lister's performance out of them.'

At Ranbaxy that day, it was probably later at the R&D meeting that something happened, which spread like fire, and people who hadn't directly witnessed the incident dished it out in far greater detail than those who had.

Towards the end of a meeting at the R&D centre, Shanghvi's attention went to the plate of unconsumed cookies lying before him at the table. 'What happens to these uneaten cookies, after we leave?' he asked. It wasn't a question that Ranbaxy's cutting-edge scientists and top management executives knew an answer to. So Shanghvi made a call to the pantry boy from right there and posed the same question. The pantry boy was too stunned to respond. But he heard what the new owner, who had been declared the richest Indian just weeks back, said clearly. So did fifty odd people present in that meeting.

'Will you buy some jars? Once the meeting is over, please put the uneaten cookies back into them and serve those in the meeting next day. We don't want wastage of any type,' Shanghvi directed. They registered the meaning and significance of the cookie-coated message and felt the change of regime. After years of luxuriating but sailing directionlessly, Ranbaxy was turning into a tight ship.

In the days that followed, Ranbaxians whined on as their shuttles from the metro station to the office were discontinued, super-subsidized lunches vanished from the cafeteria and they had to work at least two Saturdays.

The day Sun took over, Ranbaxy logos were pulled down at its headquarters, its website taken off. 'Only in countries where the regulatory needs mandated the Ranbaxy brand to continue, was a transition period maintained,' a Ranbaxy executive claimed.

Older Ranbaxy executives imputed motive to that gesture, dragging history into play. 'Ranbaxy had once tried to acquire a large bite of Sun in an unfriendly way. It was not a gesture Dilip liked. Deep down in his psyche, the event had hurt him badly and left a scar. That's why we knew from day one that he would erase the brand. He didn't even call a division Ranbaxy,' felt a top Ranbaxy executive, visibly hurt himself.

Not everyone agreed that there was a rationale—business or emotional—to keep brand Ranbaxy alive. A rival friend of Shanghvi said, 'Ranbaxy comes with a huge historical baggage. If one acquired it, business-wise it made sense to not only kill the brand, but also the company. It had been great once, but that was a long time ago. Now there was too much confidence without clarity, which became its nemesis. The kind of pride and arrogance it came with, it was impossible to tame or blend it into any other culture. Dilip-bhai did the right thing.'

Shanghvi pointed out that his decision was simply based on one fact—brand Ranbaxy had outlived its utility. 'We didn't want confusion of corporate identities, particularly among the sales force and investors. Keeping a division with the name of Ranbaxy would have done that. And Ranbaxy's image wasn't necessarily great by the time we bought it. It was not out of some great attachment with Sun that such a decision is taken, but there must be some rationale behind using a brand and there simply isn't one to have even a division named after Ranbaxy,' he said.

The mayhem in Ranbaxy continued amid confusion and complaints of mass transfers. Many people were asked to leave. In the first month of the merger, a talent-mapping agency Development Dimensions

International (DDI) was hired to simulate work conditions and conduct face-offs to test one company's functional head against others'.

It would be an understatement to say that the results were one-sided. Of the eighteen functional heads of Ranbaxy, fifteen lost the battle (to be fair, some of them didn't turn up for the contest claiming they already knew which way the results would sway), announced Sun's internal tally. Of the three who remained, one was heading over the counter-segment that didn't have a direct Sun counterpart challenger, another was handling sensitive US FDA matters, and the third was German, the R&D head, who had been hired after the announcement of the acquisition.

In March 2015, the *Times of India* reported, 'Sun Pharma executives bag top slots in company after Ranbaxy merger,' and by June that year, the *Economic Times* was reporting '18 top Ranbaxy executives including Indrajit Banerjee, Yugal Sikri, get marching orders as part of integration plan with Sun Pharma'. Some of these eighteen executives had genuinely hoped to play vital roles in the merged entity and claimed to have been led to believe so in the run-up to the acquisition. One of them reckoned, 'Mr Shanghvi has a need to be seen as fair, and it's possible he is fair and meritocratic within his organization. But his need to be loyal to his own people is much higher.'

When asked of these feelings of Ranbaxy executives, Shanghvi said, 'We conducted a process to sieve out the best for each role. Anyone who was serious about continuing in the integrated entity came and participated and whatever were the results, the announcement of appointments were made as per that.' Industry captains felt usually when two legendary corporate entities mix, a third culture is born. This has been seen in cases globally. 'Sun and Ranbaxy could have created an exemplary union. But from that sense Ranbaxy is a lost opportunity and only Sun remains, a much grander Sun,' a long-standing CEO of a top multinational said. Shanghvi was fully aware of the churn, emotional outburst and strong cross-currents in the process. He had seen a snapshot of this while taking over Taro, and to diffuse that he had arranged for a proper farewell for Levitt; he had also seen the absence of it in the numerous other smaller acquisitions and had come to a conclusion. Much of this boil was an inevitable by-product of the takeover exercise, particularly when the company taking over is of the size of the company being taken over.

'You don't build a company the size and type of Ranbaxy without having committed people. There was a time when Ranbaxy was way bigger and held a much larger sway. It has a much longer history than Sun, is older than Sun and a lot of people would be nostalgic about it. They still must be carrying in their minds an image of a Ranbaxy of their times; it is not surprising that they would feel sentimental about the non-existence of the company,' Shanghvi said.

'Dilip is not scared of bloodletting, he knows that a new one cannot be birthed without pain,' said a friend. 'Shanghvi is "practical about emotions" and works with "unattached involvement",' his friends declared, 'traits that have been his strength all along as he made millions of critical decisions using a value compass that is strictly his own. There is perhaps no better testimony of his work philosophy, "Emotion is the engine, reason the driver" for the journey of Sun Pharma.'

In building Sun, Shanghvi could harness emotions to the fullest only because he himself transcended them. And at every stage, he practised rationality, he ran the risk of being perceived as cold and unemotional by those at the receiving end of his rational decision.

And as Ranbaxy stirs, employees and friends admit that frowns on Shanghvi's unflappable face have multiplied as never before. But friends also claim Shanghvi's core remains largely unperturbed by the noise and emotional outbursts that he knows to be temporary upwellings, the price a worthwhile journey extracts on the path of a larger goal. That goal he wants realized, rather than said.

A Tag a Tad Uncomfortable

Shanghvi's ascension to the peak of the Indian pharmaceuticals pyramid nearly coincided with a much larger historic event, not only for him (though he is likely to dismiss it), but for the country. Celebrated rich lists had already pronounced him the world's wealthiest pharma entrepreneur, Asia's only non-realty tycoon in the top ten wealthiest men, richest self-made Indian, but none of it had had the earth-shattering effects to them, as the pronouncement made by Forbes and Bloomberg in March 2015.

Shanghvi with his net worth pegged at $21 billion had dethroned Mukesh Ambani to become the richest Indian. Albeit short-lived, not to last beyond months it was a moment of axial tilt for India in many ways—and not the least because the Ambanis, who had been a synonym of wealth and power in the collective memory of this country, had never been toppled from that much-envied seat since the wealth indices started applying to this part of the world.

It was in a sense the symbolic culmination of a process that began in 1991, when Finance Minister Manmohan Singh, while announcing 'liberalization measures' had predicted that they would unleash 'animal spirits' in businessmen. In a welcome change, India's richest man hadn't inherited his riches; hadn't earned his fortune through cronyish connections or government concessions—common in sectors like energy, infrastructure or even telecom; hadn't multiplied wealth by some gamble in finance or real estate. Shanghvi had earned his wealth not even by building a conglomerate, but by dint of focusing just on one sector—pharmaceuticals.

American academic Caroline Freund bracketed him in a select list of 'Schumpeterian' entrepreneurs, who were building and managing big companies that fought for their lives in the global markets, 'a healthy consequence of structural transformation and rapid development' of the (country's) economy.

Manmohan Singh would cheer that description. Yet, you don't have to be a businessman in India to know that cronyism is far from dead. But Shanghvi's climb to the zenith of the wealth ladder stood for a hope, that meritocracy still has a chance. As the news spread like wildfire, Indians beyond the finance world, doctors, and the pharmaceuticals industry woke up to a surname—Shanghvi, and the man who so prized and preserved his oblivion became a subject of national curiosity.

Pink papers realized that despite knowing him, they knew very little of his personal story to satisfy that curiosity. In that state of ill-preparedness, editors struggled to find a league to put Shanghvi in. Newsrooms debated whether he seemed closer to the league of Narayana Murthy and Azim Premji, but rejected it on the ground that he had shown far little commitment to philanthropy. They were in consensus that he surely didn't belong to the league of the Ambanis or Adanis, and was far removed from the Tatas and Birlas. Without exception, all financial magazines and newspapers scrambled for an appointment with him and with or without managing one, put him on cover and page ones.

Shortly after, on a trip to China for his company's annual star awards on a rented private chartered plane, when Shanghvi was explaining to friend Sailesh Desai why he thought eggs are not non-vegetarian, his then India CEO Abhay Gandhi walked up to the magazine stands and started to flip through the pages. Desai called him from behind, asking, 'Is there anything worth reading?' Gandhi turned around holding up two magazines—*Business Today* and *Outlook Business*, both of which had the same face on their covers—Shanghvi's.

This newly aroused curiosity about him spilled over to social media with questions on Quora like 'Why is Dilip Shanghvi not much talked about as compared to Mukesh Ambani even though he's the richest person in India?' and 'Why is India's richest person (Dilip Shanghvi) so simple when compared to some of India's richest men?' His profiles on web multiplied by the day, and a Twitter handle that was not his surfaced and continued to tweet opinions on his name for well over two years.

A friend Piyush Doshi, who had once messaged him saying he was not happy to see him at No. 2 on India's rich list, because he hoped to see him at No. 1, finally punched a congratulatory text. The boy Jai Shah who had seen him lift buckets of water from a common tube well for bath in the Paddapukur building in Calcutta, gasped with excitement as he compared the 'extravagant opulence of Ambanis with the austere living of Dilip Uncle'. A wife of a friend who had not a long time back seen him fix the dent of their Maruti 800 turned emotional at the mention of his name.

'No stars in his party, no guards by his side, no twenty-seven floors in the prime of Mumbai, no private jets parked on the roof, his is a lifestyle so simple that it can shame people with one-hundredth of his net worth,' Jaya Butta, wife of friend Ashok Butta, says. Every morning as she wakes up to worship Vaishno Devi as the programme is being telecast live on a television channel, she prays for Shanghvi's long life after her family but before her own. 'After all, he has made so many lives, and so many lives are dependent on him. What will happen if we vanish from the face of earth tomorrow? We can't say the same of him,' she added misty-eyed. 'His is an unbelievable story I hope to tell my grandsons one day,' said Milan Sinha, who had first seen Shanghvi waiting hours outside a doctor's clinic in Bihar and then quietly walking off, because he had no money to pay for the taxi.

For many who have been part of his journey, Shanghvi's spectacular rise to that height is the closest they could imagine to their own rise. They feel the pride of one amongst them having made it to the top. They feel they own a part of him, even though some of them struggle to remember the last time they had spoken with him.

And how did the man who did it take it? Reluctant, very reluctant to lose his anonymity and be recognized as India's richest self-made billionaire. To those who called to congratulate, he used logic to cite how the indices had got their maths wrong.

He particularly misses experiences like sneaking into small south Indian tiffin shops like Ram Ashreya in Matunga on Sunday mornings to relish his idli-sambhar. A friend recalled someone walking up to him in the modest restaurant one day to tell him, 'Hey, you look so much like Dilip Shanghvi! If I hadn't spotted you in this crappy place, I would have surely mistaken you for him.'

Shanghvi has stopped going for his Sunday tiffins now, but his friends still pack his favourite south Indian dishes for him, and drop it at his place after their get-togethers. '*I am not comfortable* at all with this tag of "the *richest* Indian" and all the attention that follows for the reason,' Shanghvi, for whom this label is more a distraction than a badge, said.

Benny Klener, his then global head of manufacturing, who had joined Sun from Teva, recalled an instance where Shanghvi offered him a lift. He stepped in to appreciate the fancy make of his customized limousine—a silver-grey Audi. But still new to Sun chief's ways, he was surprised to hear his tone, almost apologetic, about using his luxury sedan.

'For me a car is a car. It's meant to serve the purpose of taking you from the source to the destination. But a few things in life you start doing because others strongly expect you to. To a business dinner party, you cannot wear slippers, even if at the end of a busy day they are the most comfortable wear. You have to wear formal shoes not to show up as an oddball and draw unnecessary stares. To me, this car is like those formal shoes, which you use not to be singled out for showing off your austerity.' And then Shanghvi's car moved on, because for him success has never been a destination.

CHAPTER TWENTY

AFTER AND BEFORE CHILDHOOD

After Childhood—That Ceaseless Growth

On that vacation in New Zealand, the annual ritual of a group of five strong friends-cum-cousins of Shanghvi to tour a country unexplored, friend Nitin recalled opting out of skydiving, citing a lack of adventure spirit. The idea of being dropped off from a helicopter thousands of miles above ground to remain suspended in air, and the following free fall didn't feel very appetizing to most others in the group who were approaching their senior-citizen mark, and some of them excused themselves citing age, fear and a faint heart. Not Shanghvi, he was excited to do it, if the weather allowed it, to experience the thrill of flying through the sky, just as he had once delighted in swimming through the moss-ridden neighbourhood pond of his childhood—Paddapukur. 'I didn't swim fast, but I could swim long distance,' Shanghvi had recalled of that childhood experience.

Half a century later, when Shanghvi went zip-lining, swinging from tree to tree on a rope during another vacation, his cousin Arvind admitted watching the aerial act with bated breath .'I was worried, more so because with his weight I didn't think it was a great idea. But he seems to have an internal balance and control because he was so comfortable in that space. He has a fluidity and flexibility within him that you don't associate with heavy-set frames.' Another time Arvind recalled how all of them went quad-biking in New Zealand, and his own bike kept sputtering and dying off, while Shanghvi zoomed past them all, saying, 'You all are such kids in adventures.'

In South Africa, his cousin Upen recalled Sailesh pulling Shanghvi's leg challenging him to compete in a canoe race. 'We all gave up somewhere midway. Dilip and Vibha were partners and they were the only ones to have finished the challenge. And Sailesh the challenger got stuck and had to be rescued,' Upen joked. 'When we go out for our vacations, we search for some adventure sport, mostly those which we haven't tried before. Dilip and I enjoy it thoroughly. We started late but we realized we were adventure buffs at heart,' Sailesh said.

When Mukul, a friend who had once decades ago goaded Shanghvi up the the bridge over Tolly's nullah and left him stranded and screaming there, heard about his friend's belated love for a rush of adrenalin in adventure sports, he betrayed absolute disbelief in tone, 'Seriously, Dilip and sports?' Resuming his humour, he quipped, 'Well, tell him, too late, too late.' Another image of his childhood friend he found hard to imagine was that of Dilip putting on a record of an old Hindi movie song, and listening, maybe even secretly humming with it.

Hitesh, the third of their childhood trio, hadn't even gone so far or lost touch with Shanghvi as Mukul had, but the day he walked in to his home to find a soulful Hemant Kumar melody wafting out of Shanghvi's room, he was stupefied. In a daze, he walked up to Shanghvi's wife, struggling for the right words, 'Vibha, since when has Aurangzeb grown so fond of songs?'

Arvind's guess to that question would be 7–8 years, maybe. It is since then that he has seen Shanghvi's musical interest deepening. This jovial cousin of Shanghvi makes it a point to buy 20–30 tickets of old song soirees hosted by 'Klub Nostalgia' in Bombay, and posting it on the Whatsapp group that five of them have created. Many of those evenings Shanghvi and his wife quietly turn up for these programmes. He loves listening to Surojit Guha, a white dhoti-kurta-clad singer Klub Nostalgia familiars know as a vocal reincarnation of Hemant-da. There were times when Shanghvi planned to be there for these events right after completing an analyst call for quarterly results, or the night before he was to leave for Baroda to preside over annual general meetings. Arvind recalled on one of those occasions, when Guha was performing an old Hemant-da number, and Mrs Shanghvi, aware of his next-morning engagement, nudged Mr Shanghvi by whispering in Gujarati about leaving, he responded, 'Let's sit for a little longer.'

Parts of him have transformed over the last few decades. Once when a top consultant of McKinsey asked him, 'Who apart from you could have run Sun the way it has been managed in the last three decades?' Shanghvi replied, 'No one. Even I, as I am today, couldn't have run the company the way I have in the last thirty years.'

And then, there are parts of him that haven't changed in all these years—the almost-birthmark-like traits that his friends could spot blindly decades on to catch him despite their disparate travels in parallel and intersecting lanes of life. The card games—rummy, napolean, judgement—do not happen in the bachelor den of Dilip-bhai of 57/2A, Paddapukur Road any more, but has shifted to the 1500-square-foot suite of Dilip-bhai on an Alaska Cruise during a vacation, where friends after their breakfast gather in his room to spend the rest of the day, whiling away, joking, catching a few glimpses of an old, witty life force of a Dilip they had once known.

Whichever continent they may be for their vacation, Dilip would nudge Nitin and Arvind to try out the local vegetarian cuisine, while his friend and cousin always prefer to be 'safe eaters', sticking to traditional Indian fare. 'He understands food like none of us do. Even today, a bite, a sniff later—he would pick out all ingredients that have gone into its preparation,' Upen says. And even in the newly acquired passions, old habits do not die out—the birthmark-like traits.

Bracing up for the adventure sports—before tying the harness, after the landing—the time others spend breathing deep to quell anxiety, or celebrating a triumph of a feat, Shanghvi can be seen with the instructor, trainer or organizer flooding him with questions on the mechanics of the sport, instruments and so on. After taking in a melodious musical evening, he presses on with his trademark queries to understand the business behind the musical arrangement, 'Arvind-bhai, how much does the organizer spend to host such a night? How much does the lead singer charge? And the chorus? The orchestra?'

There are times, according to Shanghvi's own admission, when his incessant probing into the nature of business of a fresh acquaintance embarrasses his wife. On one such occasion, when Shanghvi was in

Bhubaneshwar, he called up a cousin of Upen who produced Oriya soaps for local television channels to help him try out the local cuisine. Chatting him up, Shanghvi got so curious to understand the business of television content production, that wife Vibha had to interject the conversation with, 'He may not like to discuss these details.' Shanghvi paused for a breath, and then turned towards the cousin, 'Do you mind if I ask about your business?'

As a child, Shanghvi had this amusing ability to talk to an adult like an adult, perhaps hopeful that those who have spent many more years on this planet may have answers to some of his questions. In a rare moment of reflective candour he said, 'I was never a child. I think I was born an adult and so I could strike those conversations with grown-ups,' and a pause later, 'I could be an adult while I was a child but I cannot be a child with a child today. I speak to everyone like an adult. I see my friends effortlessly becoming like children with children, but I can't be that.'

That may well be the case that Shanghvi cannot be a child with children. But those who have seen him up close, swear that the exceptionally intense curiosity he had had as a child, that streak of a 'non-conformist without being a rebel' who wouldn't settle for an answer just because it came from an authority, the trait which helped him learn so much about so much, each day, every day, remains intact even today and shows up in unexpected moments in odd ways.

A consultant, who deals with corporate leaders and their tantrums day in and day out, spends a baffled few minutes when Shanghvi walks into a videoconference call, and upon seeing that the apparatus was not working, instead of fuming and frowning over his valued time, upturns the phone and starts fiddling with the gadget in an effort to fix it. A business associate in the US reports strolling with him and then losing him to a window where he had stopped to take in some new gadgets on display. His deputies say, 'He is never shy of asking questions and the way he puts it, "Mujhko samjha nahin, mujhko samjhao",' is just as an intelligent child thirsty for knowledge would.

It might be true that he was an adult when he was a child, but what is equally true is that a part of him, that intensely curious child in him, never grew up. And it is that child in him—that yearns to grow and know and learn new things moment to moment, day after day—which causes the expansion in his personality that co-passengers of his life journey find so astounding. Long after most of them felt grown-up enough in their lives, they look at that relentlessly growing dimension in their old friend—moving, evolving, refining—and marvel with a sense of wonder: Where does this growth cease? Where does this quest end?

Before Childhood—Ancient Threads That Bind

Shanti-kaka, or G-kaka, as he was fondly known to his nephews and nieces, was heating up the steam iron and pressing shirts of nephews—Ashok and Suresh, checking in between if the creases had been ironed out, if the fabric felt crisp to palm on touch, for they had to wear it the next day for the special family occasion. That occasion next day in the sultry day of May in 1954 was most special to G-kaka himself, of course—it being his own wedding. His family members, fifteen of them—brothers and nephews—had arrived two days before in a train from Indore.

When they had started from Indore, they worshipped the deity and left home with coconut and rice, as is done on auspicious marriage occasions in Gujarati homes. But when the train pulled into Bombay station, amid all the excitement of spotting G-kaka after so long, with frantic hand-waving, feet-touching, the member in charge of counting heads and bags had summed up—fifteen in all—and de-boarded quickly only to realize that the packet stuffed with coconuts was not supposed to be counted as luggage. That essentially meant that the baggage full of new wedding clothes for Ashok, Suresh and others had been left in the train tucked under the berth. Sighs and heartburns later, G-kaka was readying their old clothes, making them as good as new for the celebrations.

The wedding, a traditional, modest Gujarati ceremony, took place at Gurjarwadi in Lakshmi Narayan Lane of Matunga, in the sultry May of 1954, where Shantilal Nagardas Shanghvi took sacred vows to protect for life his bride Kumud Mohanlal Doshi. Kumud, who was transforming from a Doshi to a Shanghvi in those few hours, couldn't possibly have been her cheerful best for she hadn't had it easy. Between her engagement in 1953 and the marriage in 1954, she had lost her father, Mohanlal Karsandas Doshi, whom Kumud and her sisters had known once as a bright young man with a razor-sharp intelligence, a forceful drive, a longing to explore new lands and experience different cultures, and possibly with a dream unrealized.

Getting little formal education, till class VI to be accurate, couldn't separate Mohanlal from his passion—books. Nor could it apply the brakes on his insatiable quest for knowledge. Daughter Manjula recalled his voracious appetite for books on history, geography and on myriads of subjects which he often read till 2 a.m. in the night, long after everyone had slept at home. Barely twenty years old, he sailed along with his elder brother Vitthal, as many fellow Gujaratis did, in those days to East Africa, to eke out a better living and in search of promising business prospects in 1925. They landed in the idyllic African island of Zanzibar where they worked with a prominent Gujarati businessman Dwarkadas Morarji Shah in his company Dwarkadas Morarji & Sons. He owned an agency of ocean liners like the *State of Haryana* and the *State of Bombay*, and dealt in the business of importing pulses, condiments, spices from India and exporting cloves to India.

Family lore remembered Mohanlal as possessing an exceptionally gifted business mind, and by dint of his acumen and diligence, he was able to obtain an offer of 25 per cent partnership in some of Shah's business. He had mastered English language and had earned himself a great reputation for expert dealing with foreign clients in the business hub of Zanzibar. A great deal of success for him came after 1932, after his marriage to Harkuvar-ben, his second wife. In a tragedy, he had lost his first wife and an unborn child the year before, leaving behind a young toddler, daughter Hansa, to be looked after. Kumud, Shanghvi's mother, was the firstborn to Harkuvar-ben, who went on to have four more daughters—Rasika, Manjula, Vasanda and Shobhana.

As time passed, sometime in 1937–38, Dwarkadas's sons—Jayantilal Dwarkadas Shah and Harkishandas Dwarkadas Shah—grew up and decided to split the business. Realizing that it wouldn't be business-wise prudent to locate two shops in such close proximity in an island as small as Zanzibar, Vitthal and Mohanlal returned to Bombay in 1938 and set up a shop in Khand Bazaar. Their business in Bombay mirrored their business in Zanzibar and they exported gum, elephant tusks, condiments and cashews, and imported cloves.

The two brothers bought a flat in Agrawal Nagar, Matunga. Daughter Manjula recalled her father scouring the public libraries of Bombay and Mohuva to read up all that was there to read. He must have completed reading all books catalogued from A to Z, wall to wall, in the libraries of Matunga Seva Mandal and Mohuva—through his nights. It was in one of those libraries that he met the thoughts of Dale Carnegie and was influenced by him and other American authors. He had a dream and he made plans to fulfil it.

It was for that reason he had saved enough to give measurements to the tailor for three suits to be stitched. They will have to hang in the wardrobe till the journey to the country of his dreams happened; that was the plan, and arrangements for it had begun.

In 1939, Mohanlal left for Zanzibar to complete an unfinished agenda. It was upon his return that he planned to go to the US, for which the suits had been readied. It's not clear what happened in Zanzibar or in the ship that he boarded to sail to India 3–4 months later, but Mohanlal was not the same when he returned.

He couldn't join back the business in Bombay, as his daughters saw him becoming withdrawn from the jovial father he once had been who cracked jokes to humour the daughters, when any of them fell sick. He seemed to have gone into depression. He stayed confined to his home, reading books, teaching his daughters, and smoking a whole packet of 555 through the day. Though it was experienced as a deteriorating psychological condition by daughter Manjula, it was never diagnosed as such medically. There was no medical treatment or medicine readily available for his condition in pre-Independence India that the family could help him with, recalled Manjula. The family tried traditional medication for his condition, but it didn't do much except burning his tongue, and restricting his diet to vegetables boiled in ghee and plain dal, roti and bhakri. The suits that he had so expectantly got stitched for his American dream remained unworn and hung desolately for a long time.

His brother, also his partner, decided that his share of profits would continue to be handed over to him as long he lived (till 1947) as he considered his younger brother's wife 'Lakshmi', whose arrival into the Doshi household had brought prosperity and abundance. Harkuvarben, over 100 years of age today, continues to live with Shanghvi, along with his mother in his home that houses five generations.

Though Mohanlal's psychological condition deteriorated, daughter Manjula recalled that at times he could demonstrate extraordinary willpower. It was Manjula who went to fetch the 555 cigarette packets for her father from the neighbourhood shop. What bothered her were murmurs and gossips—'Whom does this girl buy cigarettes for, when they don't have a male member at home?' The day she shared this with her father, he gave up smoking immediately. But as his health condition worsened untreated, he could never regain his mental vigour back, and died in 1953, at the age of forty-seven. In a curious inter-generational twist of fate, it would be his grandson, born two years later in Bombay, who would create the largest pharmaceutical enterprise in India built on the foundation of psychiatry drugs.

Kumud, the firstborn of her parents, who as per traditional Gujarati custom of those times, hadn't been held in arms, her name not spoken, and hadn't been allowed to play around a lot, grew up to be a quiet and intelligent young lady. She had inherited from her father a deep interest in books, a trait that she would see passed on to her eldest son Dilip. In her eighties today, she still follows the news of the day and remains informed and opinionated on issues affecting the society.

The man she got married to, Shantilal, was a people's person—loving and loved by all. He retained his friendly and kind disposition towards life and people, despite leading a life of struggle, experiencing more failures than success in business, and seeing scarcity up close.

His family, the Shanghvis, are Vaishnav Kapol Vanias from Amreli in Gujarat. The surnames in the region have long been a marker of the occupation one had traditionally been associated with, unless it wasn't derived from the region one inhabited. Shanghvi, it is said, finds its origin from the Sanskrit word *sangha*, that loosely translates to 'assembly'. The Oxford dictionary of family names in Britain and Ireland traces 'Shanghvi' to a community in Rajasthan and Gujarat, which offered hospitality to groups of Jain pilgrims.

A good chunk of businessmen bearing the last name Sanghvi, including from Amreli, are Jains. Vaishnav Kapols of the region are devoted to a child form of Krishna, Srinathji, and make regular pilgrimages to the deity's abode in Nathdwara near Udaipur in Rajasthan. Shanghvi is a devotee too and on entering Sun House, one of the first things that grab your attention is a spectacular black-and-gold idol of Srinathji, sculpted of metals and stone-mounted on the wall in the lobby.

The propagation of Vaishnavism in Gujarat with its emphasis on living well has been regarded by sociologists and historians as a rebel reaction to Saivism, with its ideal of self-realization through self-destruction. Vaishnavism fundamentally declares the world of things as real and supports a world view of materialism and abundance, while Saivism denounces the material world as unreal, an illusion that obstructs the attainment of man's ultimate goal of salvation. The austere dressing of Siva and the gaudy adornment of Krishna (an avatar of Vishnu) seem to be reflective of the fundamental principles of life propounded by Saivism and Vaisnavism as philosophies. Saivism aspires for discontinuance of rebirth, while Vaishnavism courts rebirths and sums up its way of life as 'Deliverance is not for me in renunciation'.

Saivism and Buddhism with their focus on renunciation couldn't capture the imagination of Gujarat, a land of opportunities, and its people, known to be peaceable, practical and energetic with an inherent sense of adventure and wanderlust. On the other hand, Vaishnavism as a philosophy underlining Bhaktimarga with Karmamarga as its handmaid—the path of action and devotion which in practice meant that whether you cooked a dish or maintained a shop, you should do it with a sense of service—suited their social and religious needs just fine.

Saint Vallabhacharya's Vaishnavite teachings that said things of life are for us—not their 'no use' but their 'best use' should be one's duty—appealed to Gujaratis across merchant castes: Vanias, Bhatias, Lohanas and Kanbis. Over seven hundred thousand people in the region are estimated to have come under the fold of this Hindu sect (Pushti-marga–the path of nourishing one's soul with divine love) between 1478 and 1521.

The Vania among the Vaishnavas is one of the most enterprising mercantile castes in India, though in most etymological research it traces its origin to a derivative of the Sanskrit word *vanijya* meaning trade and commerce. But some personal histories interestingly associate the word with *vahanias*, meaning those bearing vehicles or ships. It is a direct reference to the community's zest for travel since antiquity and exploring business prospects in foreign lands.

Like his maternal ancestors, wanderlust lurked in the forefathers of Shanghvi on the paternal side as well. They left their groundnut farms in Amreli to travel far and wide in search of better business prospects. His great-grandfather Dhanji Narang Shanghvi, along with his sons, had migrated to Dacca (now Dhaka) where he set up four general stores called D.N. Shanghvi & Sons. A few members guess that the 'Sh' instead of more commonly used 'S' in the Shanghvi surname was picked up here as a Bengali influence.

However, as pre-Partition riots flared up communal tensions in Dacca, and it felt no longer safe to keep running the shops, the Shanghvis were forced to flee the city in 1946–47. After spending a few months at Amreli, Dilip's grandfather Nagardas Dhanji Shanghvi and his family, including his five sons, left for Indore (where they already had a relative Ranchhod-bhai) and started business again by setting up a shop bearing the same name D.N. Shanghvi & Sons. It was a ground-floor wholesale shop in Siyagunj, a blackboard with a stainless-steel cutout sporting the name which stocked soaps, viola essence, biscuits, confectionaries of companies like Godrej, Parle and Palmolive and took orders from retailers in the neighbouring areas to distribute the stuff.

Two of Shantilal's brothers tried to set up manufacturing—one ice factory and one soap factory at Dewas, but the business ran into losses and eventually had to be shut down. Once the sons grew up and started to have families of their own, the shop wasn't enough to sustain so many, and Shantilal became the first one to leave home and go to Bombay in search of work.

Here he first tried his hand at a job at a drug wholesaler in Princess Street called Narottam Giridharilal and lived nearby in Mangaldas Building. That wasn't enough to make ends meet in Bombay and he started supplying wholesale drugs to his cousins in Calcutta, who owned a medicine wholesale shop, New Oriental Stores, along with his other business, New Oriental Photographic Stores.

A cousin of Shantilal recalled that the Calcutta cousin stopped ordering medicines from Shanti-kaka somewhere around 1957. He was married by then, and with the child Dilip who was born in Bombay in 1955. That made it difficult to make a living out of his job in Bombay and he decided to move to Calcutta with his family around 1958 where he had sensed potential for wholesale business in drugs, having worked in Bombay and supplying to his cousins.

In Calcutta, he set up his first shop, Mutual Traders, in Bagri Market with two partners—Babu-bhai and Madhu-bhai Jhani. Madhu-bhai was remembered by his surviving Dawa Bazaar contemporaries as a sharp business mind. Shanti-kaka settled in Bhowanipore area, which apart from being a popular locality for Gujarati migrants was also where India's first private psychiatric ward got set up in 1817 by Isaac Beardsmore, a former British army personnel.

But in a few years, Madhu-bhai's health failed and he shifted to Bombay for treatment. It was then that Shantilal struck up a friendship with Natwar Lal Bavishi, or Natu-bhai, with whom he set up another medicine wholesale shop, Medcom Enterprises, in Mehta Building. Shanti-kaka and Natu-kaka's partnership was dubbed akin to the legendary Jai and Veeru duo of *Sholay* by some of Shanghvi's Calcutta friends, because of their deep lifelong friendship.

It was here in these small Dawa Bazaar drug shops in Calcutta that eight-year-old Dilip started reading the names of medicines, turning over patient leaflets to record in his memory all the diseases they were meant to manage and started wondering how these tablets are made. These shops were Dilip's first library, and he had read up all the tablet packs, all their literatures—catalogued A to Z, wall to wall.

Almost half a century on, a classmate Gaurang saw a glimpse of an old friend through the window of a car sweeping past Paddapukur Road and yelled at once, 'Hey . . . hey . . . Dilip, Dilip wait.'

The car stopped and Gaurang suggested coffee at Taj Bengal. Shanghvi had a better idea, 'Let's have it at *charbatti*,' he proposed, referring to the chowrasta, the crossroads, where he had often had tea in his youth. This quickly became part of Shanghvi lore in his neighbourhood and reached Jai Shah, his neighbour, who believes, 'I am quite sure he drives through these lanes anonymously, maybe at night to get a feel of his past, to relive where and how it all started for him.'

No one knows if that really happens. But a few years back, when Shanghvi landed in Calcutta, he called friends Ashok Butta and Piyush Doshi, asking them to unite all the old city friends—for a reunion.

Some of these friends he hadn't been in touch with for long, and Piyush recalled him asking, 'We will invite their spouses as well, Piyush, but what would we do there?'

'Don't worry, I will arrange some games,' Piyush replied.

Shanghvi booked a banquet hall and on the date of the dinner, his friends showed up with their better halves one after the other. After a few moments of tentative awkwardness that follows when friends catch up after ages, the atmosphere started warming up with some of them narrating old tales from Bhagushala days.

As inhibitions softened and hesitations melted away, Piyush started conducting the game he had created, by dividing the group into two teams—one headed by Vinod Mody and the other by Shanghvi. 'Who has a pink hanky?' Piyush shouted. 'Who is wearing a yellow vest?' was the next cue, and amid roaring laughter, friends from Vinod's team won all the prizes.

After fifteen such quirky questions Piyush threw a googly, 'Who has a five-hundred-rupee note on him in the wallet?' Many hands shot up. 'Who has a hundred-rupee note in his wallet? Who has a fifty? Twenty? Ten? Five? A two-rupee coin.'

As denominations lowered, the raised hands kept getting fewer, amid complete chaos in the hall that bustled with the jangle of coins and rustle of crisp notes as people emptied their wallets and purses on to tables.

'Wait, wait, it's not over. Who has that one rupee coin that will win the game?' Piyush tried a climax.

A moment of silence followed when people craned to see the last hand standing, holding up that one rupee coin. It was Dilip's.

And as the realization of what had happened dawned on them, his friends burst out laughing, clapping spontaneously. Among all of them, it was he, the wealthiest self-made Indian, who still knew the value of that one-rupee coin.

POSTSCRIPT

The final pages of this book are missing. By its very nature, the attempt to tell the story of a personality is destined to fail as it is bound to be incomplete, even when life has completed its course. For a life that's still flowing full swing—taking twists and turns, narration, a limited medium, can hardly keep up. After the narrative was wrapped up in 2017, Shanghvi's life saw many ups and downs, more downs than ups, at least on the surface.

He was engulfed in multiple challenges in quick succession, even as he strove to integrate Ranbaxy into Sun. Regulatory challenges from the USA, Sun's largest market, hammered its stock. It had barely recovered when other blows were waiting around the corner. While this book was still labouring to birth, it met with two aborted book attempts and witnessed the accusations of a whistle-blower against Shanghvi and Valia on a litany of corporate governance issues. Some of the allegations are grave, though unproven yet. Four long-time familiar faces on Sun's board disappeared, and two fresh ones were inducted. Some of these challenges have been ironed out; the jury is still out on some others.

The uncertainties around if and how Shanghvi's philanthropic efforts will be scaled up and how his company's succession will be planned are the two most relevant unanswered questions. The choices Shanghvi made brought him to the position he reached, but the choices he makes from hereon will decide the legacy he leaves behind.

This story will remain half told, also because a life as expansive as Shanghvi's is worth many interpretations. The same story would shift in perspectives depending on the lens that one filters it through. A public health activist would tell the story differently from a financial analyst and an entrepreneur's version of this story would be in stark contrast to an insider's account. And, of course, as and when Shanghvi chooses to tell his own story, if he does at all, it will be a revelation. But analysis must follow discovery. And for me, it was a process of discovering Shanghvi's story.

One of my last questions to Shanghvi was, 'Why was it so difficult for him to open up even to those closest around him?'

'Aren't we all a bit like that? Doesn't the Johari Window exercise show that there will be bits about you that others know but you don't and bits about you which only you are aware of, but others aren't?' he replied.

'I am sure your closest friends have told you how they feel. Despite spending five decades with you, they don't think they know you in fullness.' I tried digging to escape the philosophies for a real answer.

'Yes, they have. That's not because one means to hide things from people, but because . . .' he paused—his signature unmistakable pause. I waited through the awkward, prolonged silence but at the other end of it emerged a smile, one that lights up his face and lends a bright twinkle of kindness to his eyes, indicating the end of the meeting.

And a lot has been left unsaid.

ACKNOWLEDGEMENTS

Deeply grateful to all those who made this life-experience happen for me. Especially,

Uday (Baldota), for being the medium and the first breakthrough. He had joked once, 'Let me know when you complete the book. I will keep my resignation ready.' Thankfully, the joke remained a joke while he scales more peaks, more heights.

Debashish Panigrahi, for being the turning point and the sustained faith based on a spark he chanced in a creative experiment once upon a time.

B.S. Butola, for that night on the crossroads a decade back when he narrated the story of Emily Dickinson and brought forth a stream of clarity.

Sailesh Desai, for being himself and helping out wherever he could, especially in Calcutta; Hitesh Sheth and Nitin Mehta, for being all hearts; Piyush Doshi, for finding needles in a haystack called life; Ashok and Dolly Butta, for the warmth and laughter.

Arvind Valia and Suresh Shanghvi, for the patience and deep diving into family lores.

Each one who connected and contributed to a stranger's dream but would rather stay anonymous.

Bapi-bhai, Seema Bhauja and Mamchu for a home away from home; that window overlooking the Gulmohar tree, Balmoral Hall, Mount Mary Road, Mumbai.

Milee (Ashwarya), for standing by the project like a rock through the ups and downs. Lohit (Jagwani), for forging a bond through differences. Bidisha (Srivastava), for the diligent scrutiny. One of the most valuable contributions came at the last moment from a gentleman I have neither met nor spoken to, S.K. Ray Chaudhuri. Thank you sir, your work is a humbling reminder of the fact that experience has no substitute.

Sampad Patnaik, research associate for the chapter on Taro.

Freddy (Castro), for his passion and role in the pre-book stage and extensive coordination across cities. Gaurav (Chugh) for being there in the last lap and for a simplicity that's rare today.

Shashikant Sanghvi, D.G. Shah, Tarun Gupta, Manesh Shrikant and three doctors—mentors to many, who passed on. Heartfelt gratitude. Voids they have left can't be filled.

Friends in journalism and academics with bags full of interesting stories.

Purba, Amitabha, the first set of readers and those who would rather not be named. Nail-biting wait for feedback.

Mamuni, for doing whatever she could. Maa, for being objective and compassionate.

Bapu dhana, for sowing the seed of words in my mind.

Ajay, no journey without you. The first reader. The judge I listen to.

Dilip Shanghvi, for letting his life be studied, and simply because without him there is no book.

The guiding force for showing the path and hand-holding through the leap of faith I took.

INTERVIEWS*

CHAPTER 1: BOY BEFORE THE BILLIONAIRE

Interviews with Mukul Pipalia; Hitesh Sheth; Dilip Shanghvi; Jayesh Shanghvi (Upen-bhai); Suresh Shanghvi (Nana-bhai); Jayant Sanghvi; Gaurang Bhatt; Nitin Mehta; Sailesh Desai; Piyush Doshi; Vinod Mody; Arvind Valia; Ashok Butta

CHAPTER 2: FIRST DAYS OF KNOWING THE LAST MILE

Interviews with Hitesh Sheth; Ashok Butta; Pradip Sheth; Jayesh Shanghvi; Sudhir Mehta; Gaurang Bhatt; Jayant Sanghvi; Dilip Shanghvi; Mukul Pipalia; Piyush Doshi; Shashikant Sanghvi; Swapna Patidar; Sailesh Desai; Nitin Mehta; a former friend who doesn't wish to be named; two stockists at Dawa Bazaar, Kolkata, who do not wish to be named; a former medicine wholesaler at Dawa Bazaar, who doesn't wish to be named; two second-generation Gujarati businessmen settled in Kolkata, who do not wish to be named.

CHAPTER 3: A GROWING PRESCRIPTION OF TRANQUILITY

Interviews with Pradip Ghosh; Mahesh Mehta; Ashok Bhutta; psychiatrist Debashish Bhattacharya; psychiatrist Jayanta Basu; psychiatrist Ranjit Ghosh Roy; psychiatrist Ambika Charan Dutta;

---

* The period that the interviews were taken—the ones in person across cities like Mumbai, Kolkata, New Delhi, Chennai, Ahmedabad, Vadodara and Hyderabad, while some others over the phone—was between July 2015 to October 2017. Some others that happened with people based abroad were through Skype or the telephone.

psychiatrist Anjan Boral; six anonymous psychiatrists of Kolkata who do not wish to be named; two old-time stockists of Dawa Bazaar, Kolkata, who do not wish to be named; one former employee of Sun Pharma who does not wish to be named

CHAPTER 4: DIY KIT FOR MAKING A MILLION

Interviews with Nitin Mehta; Vinod Mody; Mukul Pipalia; Shashikant Shanghvi; Arvind Valia; Ashok Butta; Piyush Doshi; Sailesh Desai; Pradip Sheth.

CHAPTER 5: THE SATSANG SALE

Interviews with Sundaresh Raju; Hiren Desai; Jayesh Shanghvi (Upen-bhai); Dilip Shanghvi; Vivek Hattangadi; H.K. Pahwa; T.K. Roy; Bhagwat Yagnik; Hitendra Kansal; S.K. Jani Miya; twenty-one former medical representatives, area managers and regional managers who do not wish to be named; Sailesh Desai

CHAPTER 6: BEATING THE TURRANT EXPRESS

Interviews with Pradip Ghosh; S. Raju; Vivek Hattangadi; Hiren Desai; Shyamal Ghosh; Sudhir Mehta; three stockists and former stockists at Calcutta's Dawa Bazaar who do not wish to be named; six senior pyschiatrists in Calcutta who do not wish to be named; Mohan Chand Dadha

CHAPTER 7: SUN OF BARODA—A COMPANY ON TRAIN

Interviews with Kirti Ganorkar: Hiren Desai; H.K. Pahwa; Jayesh (Upen-bhai) Shanghvi; Jayant Sanghvi; Sailesh Desai; Bhagwat Yagnik; Rajesh Kumar; Lokesh Sibal; Shyamal Ghosh; Raju; seven former senior Sun employees, who do not wish to be named; three current senior executives and four former top senior executives who worked in rival multinational and domestic pharma firms and who do not wish to be named; T.K. Roy; eight psychiatrists, three cardiologists, who do not wish to be named

CHAPTER 8: DOCTORS, NOT THE ONLY SPECIALISTS

Interviews with Shyamal Ghosh; seven former MRs of Sun who do not wish to be named; Ashok Butta; T.K. Roy; Dilip Shanghvi; Milan Sinha; Shyamal Ghosh; Abhay Gandhi; Madhav Bhatkuly; Pankaj Patel; Shashikant Shanghvi; Pradip Ghosh

CHAPTER 9: DEPARTURE: DESIGNING A LOSS

Dilip Shanghvi; Shyamal Ghosh; Rajesh Kumar; thirteen former employees of Sun Pharma, who do not wish to be named; Shailesh Desai; mutual friends of Sailesh and Dilip who do not wish to be named; Rajesh Kikani; three consultants with global consultancies who do not wish to be named; Tarun Gupta; Jayesh (Upen Shanghvi); Nitin Mehta; Girish Desai

CHAPTER 10: AT LAST THE PRIVATE ONE GOES PUBLIC

Interviews with Sailesh Desai; Milan Sinha; Nitin Mehta; Sudhir Valia; Arvind Valia; Rasika Maasi; Nana-bhai; a former Sun Pharma executive who does not wish to be named; Aalok Shanghvi; Mira Desai; Shyamal Ghosh; Madhav Bhatkuly; Ashok Bhutta; owner of a rival firm; Karishma Mehta Shanghvi; board members present in AGMs: Hasmukh Shah, Mohan Chand Dadha; Rajesh Kikani; Piyush Doshi; Hiren Desai; former Sun executives, who do not wish to be named; former Ranbaxy executives, who do not wish to be named; Dilip Shanghvi; Jai Shah; another neighbour of Shanghvi

CHAPTER 11: SHANGHVI & SANGHVI

Interviews with Bhagwat Yagnik; Sudhir Valia; Madhav Bhatkuly; Ashwin Dani; Jayant Sanghvi; four former executives, who don't wish to be named; Pradip Ghosh

CHAPTER 12: ADOLESCENCE IS WAR

Interviews with Bhagwat Yagnik; T.K. Roy; former HR professional at Sun who doesn't wish to be named; Shyamal Ghosh; eight former senior managers at Sun, who don't wish to be named; Sundaresh Raju; S.K. Jani Miya; a star performer who is a successful entrepreneur today; Dilip Shanghvi; Srinivas Lanka

CHAPTER 13: DEALS UNINTERRUPTED: SHORTCUT TO THE HIGHWAY

Interviews with Rajesh Kikani; Shyamal Ghosh; D.G. Shah; two former associates of Shanghvi, who do not wish to be named; three former senior executives of Ambalal Sarabhai Enterprises who do not wish to be named; Srinivas Lanka; Sailesh Desai; Sudhir Valia; H.I. Gandhi; Chintan Gandhi; Sundaresh Raju; Mohan Chand Dadha; Milan Sinha; T.K. Roy; S. Bhowmick; Girish Desai; friends of Dilip Shanghvi; top executives of Sun Pharma who do not wish to be named; top executives of Ambalal Sarabhai Enterprises who do not wish to be named; Hitesh Sheth

CHAPTER 14: A SUNNY CAFE, A NON-SCIENTIST CHEF

Interviews with S. Bhowmick; T. Rajamannar; Kirti Ganorkar; Vivek Hattangadi; Vikas Dandekar; Dilip Shanghvi; Milan Sinha; Shyamal Ghosh; Mira Desai; Bharati Nadkarni; Jayant Sanghvi; Aalok Shanghvi; Sailesh Desai; Abhay Gandhi

CHAPTER 15: THE VAISHNAV, WHEN SOFT IS HARD

Interviews with Bhagwat Yagnik; Milan Sinha; Ashok Butta; three former senior executives at pharma multinationals who do not wish to be named; Kirti Ganorkar; Girish Desai; Uday Baldota; Shyamal Ghosh; T.K. Roy; Vinod Mody; H.K. Pahwa; Rajesh Kumar; Mira Desai; Jayesh Shanghvi (Upen-bhai)

CHAPTER 16: CARACO: A DRESS REHEARSAL IN THE USA

Interviews with Kirti Ganorkar; Sudhir Valia; Dilip Shanghvi; a top executive of a rival firm who does not wish to be named; an industry expert who does not wish to be named; former Sun executives who do not wish to be named; former managers at Caraco who do not wish to be named; G.P. Singh; Sailesh Desai; Kirti Ganorkar; Bharati Nadkarni; Nana Bhai; Kal Sundaram

CHAPTER 17: TARO HAI PAR MHARO HAI

Interviews with Pankaj Patel; Kal Sundaram; Sudhir Valia; Uday Baldota; a Mumbai-based fund manager who spoke anonymously; Jayant Sanghvi; Ashwin Dani; Dilip Shanghvi

CHAPTER 18: HOISTING THE INDIAN FLAG ON AMERICAN EXCHANGE

Interviews with Jim Kedrowski; Uday Baldota; three former Sun executives who do not wish to be named; Dilip Shanghvi; two former Taro senior executives who do not wish to be named; Kal Sundaram; one former Teva senior executive who does not wish to be named; Abhay Gandhi

CHAPTER 19: CHASING THE DIAMOND FOR RUBY

Interviews with nine former Ranbaxy top executives who don't wish to be quoted; Israel Makov; Uday Baldota; former Sun executives who do not wish to be named; a former associate of Shanghvi who does not wish to be named; Dilip Shanghvi; Arvind Valia; owner of a rival company of Sun who does not wish to be named; CEO of a top multinational who does not wish to be named; two friends of Shanghvi who does not wish to be named; Abhay Gandhi; Jaya Butta; Milan Sinha

CHAPTER 20: AFTER AND BEFORE CHILDHOOD

Interviews with Dilip Shanghvi; Arvind Valia; Jayesh Shanghvi (Upenbhai); Mukul Pipalia; Hitesh Sheth; Manjula Maasi; Suresh Sanghvi (Nana-bhai); Gaurang Shah; Jai Shah; Piyush Doshi

Some other interviews

Chinmay Mitra: managing director, C MARC, a pharma marketing research company; *Surinder Singh*: *former drug controller general*

of India; Anjan Boral: senior psychiatrist, Kolkata; Debashis Ray: senior psychiatrist, Kolkata; Bharat Shah: Shanghvi's classmate in school; Rajnikant Desai: Shanghvi's classmate in school; Dayal-ji Rajani: Shanghvi's classmate in school; Keki Mistry: former director on Sun Pharma's board; Kewal Handa: former MD, Pfizer India; Pabitra Kumar Dutta: senior psychiatrist, Kolkata; Ranjit Shahani: former MD, Novartis India; Rekha Sethi: director, board of Sun Pharma; Swati Piramal: vice chairperson and whole-time director of Piramal Enterprises; Vibha Shanghvi: wife of Dilip Shanghvi; Aalok Shanghvi: son of Dilip Shanghvi; Karishma Shanghvi: daughter-in-law of Dilip Shanghvi; Vidhi Shanghvi: daughter of Dilip Shanghvi; Swapna Patidar: teacher at the Kolkata-based junior school where Shanghvi studied; Brij Bhushan Singh: headmaster, BGES, the school in which Shanghvi studied

REFERENCES, SOURCES AND NOTES

CHAPTER 2: FIRST DAYS OF KNOWING THE LAST MILE

Corruccini, Robert S. and Kaul, Samvit. 'The Epidemiological Transition and the Anthropology of Minor Chronic Non-infectious Diseases'. *Medical Anthropology*, 1983.

Dasgupta, Biplab. 'Naxalite Armed Struggles and the Annihilation Campaign in Rural Areas'. *Economic and Political Weekly*, 1973.

Desai Kumarpal, *Triumph Over Troubles: The Life Story of Shri UN Mehta*, unpublished English translation.

'An Increasingly Precious Metal'. *The Economist*, January 2016.

Kujur, Rajat. 'Naxal Movement in India: A Profile'. IPCS Research Papers, 2008.

Omran, Abdel R. 'The Epidemiological Transition: A Theory of the Epidemiology of Population Change'. *The Milbank Memorial Fund Quarterly*, 1971.

Pharmed Research Lab Pvt Ltd, http://www.hotfrog.in/business/west-bengal/kolkata/the-pharmed-research-laboratory.

Sen, Antara Dev. 'A True Leader of the Unwashed Masses'. DNA, Mumbai, 2010.

Soniak, Matt. 'How Do Fireworks Get Their Colours?' www.mentalfloss.com, http://mentalfloss.com/article/57606/how-do-fireworks-get-their-colors

CHAPTER 3: A GROWING PRESCRIPTION OF TRANQUILITY

Associated Press, 'FDA Is Asked to Ban Non-Prescription Sales of Cold Relief', JOC.com, 1989, http://www.joc.com/fda-asked-ban-non-prescription-sales-cold-relief-drug_19890417.html

Cade J.F.J. 'Lithium Salts in the Treatment of Psychotic Excitement'. *Medical Journal of Australia*, 2, 1949.

Clegg, Brian. 'Chemistry in Its Elements: Compounds, Lithium Carbonate'. *Chemistry World Magazine*, Royal Society of Chemistry, 2016, http://www.rsc.org/chemistryworld/podcast/CIIEcompounds/transcripts/lithium_carbonate.asp

Elliot, Valenstein. *Blaming the Brain: The Truth about Drugs and Mental Health*, Simon and Schuster, 1 February 2002.

Fieve, Ronald R. *Lithium: From Introduction to Public Awareness: The Triumph of Psychopharmacology and the Story of CINP* (International College of Neuropsychopharmacology).

Ghaemi, S. Nassir. 'Bipolar II: Enhance Your Highs, Boost Your Creativity, and Escape the Cycles of Recurrent Depression'. *Psychiatric Times, Bipolar II: Book Review*, 1 March 2007, http://www.psychiatrictimes.com/bookfilm-review/bipolar-ii-enhance-your-highs-boost-your-creativity-and-escape-cycles-recurrent-depression

Greenfield, Susan. *Brain Power: Working out the Human Mind*, Element Books Limited, 1999.

Healy, David. *Mania: A Short History of Bipolar Disorder*, JHU Press, 29 December 2010.

Jones, Earnest, *The Life and Work of Sigmund Freud*, Basic Books, 1953.

Marmol, F. 'Lithium: Bipolar Disorder and Neurodegenerative Diseases Possible Cellular Mechanisms of the Therapeutic Effects of Lithium'. *Progress in Neuro-Psychopharmacology and Biological Psychiatry*, 32 (8), 2008.

Nandy, Ashis. *Bonfire of Creeds: The Essential Ashis Nandy* (New Delhi: Oxford University Press), 2004.

Sarkar, Sebanti, 'Forgotten Legacy of Freud'. *Telegraph*, Calcutta, 2008, http://www.telegraphindia.com/1080706/jsp/calcutta/story_9508555.jsp

Shorter, E. 'The History of Lithium Therapy'. *Bipolar Disorders*. 11, 2009.

Wig, N.N. 'The History of Psychiatry in India: Chapter in Developments in Psychiatry in India'. *Clinical, Research and Policy Perspectives*, Malhotra S. and S. Chakrabarti (eds), Springer, 2015.

WHO Model List of Essential Medicines, Fifteenth List, March 2007.

CHAPTER 6: BEATING THE TURRANT EXPRESS

Desai, Kumarpal. *Triumph Over Troubles; The Life Story of Shri UN Mehta*, unpublished English translation.

Copy of a case study of a consultant who uses it to teach pharma newbies.

CHAPTER 7: SUN OF BARODA—A COMPANY ON TRAIN

Chaganti, Subba Rao. *Pharmaceutical Marketing in India* (New Delhi: Excel Books), 2005.

Datta, Jyothi P.T. 'Canere, Sarabhai Will Help Nicholas Piramal Consolidate'. *Hindu Business Line*, 16 April 2004.

Hattangadi, Vivek. *What the Pharma CEO Wants from the Brand Manager* (Ahmedabad: Enabler), 2014.

Interview with Mohal Sarabhai, Managing Director, ASENCE Group, India, pharmaboardroom.com, 23 May 2018, https://pharmaboardroom.com/interviews/interview-mohal-sarabhai-managing-director-asence-group-india/

KPMG Report on Gujarat Pharma, 2008, http://www.in.kpmg.com/pdf/gujarat-pharma08.pdf

Piramal, Gita. 'Big Business and Entrepreneurship'. Indiaseminar.com, http://www.india-seminar.com/2003/528/528%20gita%20piramal.htm

Ninan T.N. and Ramesh Menon. 'Sarabhais Excelled in the Tax-Avoidance Business'. *India Today*, 15 April, 1987; 'The Sarabhais: Even More Versatile than the Rockefellers', *India Today*, 15 April 1987.

CHAPTER 8: DOCTORS, NOT THE ONLY SPECIALISTS

Chaganti, Subba Rao. *Pharmaceutical Marketing in India* (New Delhi: Excel Books), 2005.

CHAPTER 9: DEPARTURE: DESIGNING A LOSS

Chatterji, Madhumita and László Zsolnai. *Ethical Leadership: Indian and European Spiritual Approaches*, Springer, 2016.

Kumar, Vikas. 'How Are CEOs Beating the Crunch Factor?' *Economic Times*, 1 June 2007, https://economictimes.indiatimes.com/how-are-ceos-beating-the-crunch-factor/articleshow/2090715.cms

Rao, A. Srinivasa. 'Yuganta, End of an Epoch'. 23 August 2014, http://shahasrara.blogspot.com/2014/08/yuganta-end-of-epoch.html

Sriram, S. 'The Professor Who Propelled SP Jain Institute of Management to Top Ten'. *Hindu Business Line*, 18 October 2015, https://www.thehindubusinessline.com/news/education/the-professor-who-propelled-sp-jain-institute-of-management-to-top-ten/article7776874.ece

CHAPTER 10: AT LAST THE PRIVATE ONE GOES PUBLIC

Sun Pharma Annual Reports: 1994, 1995 and 1996.

Basu, Debashish. 'Axis Shareholders Pay for Enam Shareholders' Wealth Creation'. *Money Life*, 18 November 2010.

Barnes, Julian. *Levels of Life*, Penguin Random House, 2013.

Draft Red Herring Prospectus released pre-IPO, Sun Pharma.

The Companies Act, 1956, http://www.mca.gov.in/Ministry/pdf/Companies_Act_1956_13jun2011.pdf

Satish, John and Kalesh Baiju. 'Life Comes Full Circle for Key Men at Enam'. *Mint*, 17 November 2010, https://www.livemint.com/Companies/wzprOKVdksua68hqOUJjYM/Life-comes-full-circle-for-key-men-at-Enam.html

CHAPTER 11: SHANGHVI & SANGHVI

'I-T Sleuths Seize Rs 12 Crore from Sun Pharma Raids'. *Financial Express* and *Indian Express*, 9 December 1998, http://expressindia.indianexpress.com/fe/daily/19981209/34355204.html

'Revised Income Tax Rates on Partnership Firm', https://taxguru.in/income-tax/income-tax-rates-ay-201314-fy-201213.html

'The Dark Arts'. *The Economist*, 15 September 2016, https://www.economist.com/special-report/2016/09/15/the-dark-arts

'The Income Tax Case Details'. https://indiankanoon.org/doc/94134757/

CHAPTER 12: ADOLESCENCE IS WAR

Carlzon, Jan. *Moments of Truth*, HarperCollins, 1987.

Sun Pharma, Internal Circular dated 21 August 1997.

CHAPTER 13: DEALS UNINTERRUPTED: SHORTCUT TO HIGHWAY

'A Place Under the Sun'. *Outlook*, August 1999, https://www.outlookindia.com/outlookmoney/archive/a-place-under-the-sun-86408

Azzilfi Finlease and Investments . . . vs Ambalal Sarabhai Enterprises . . . on 2 July 1999 and related court documents, company law board, https://indiankanoon.org/doc/1337141/

'BIFR Okays Gujarat Lyka, Sun Pharma Merger Plan'. *Indian Express*, November 1999, http://expressindia.indianexpress.com/fe/daily/19991109/fec09079.html

'Sun To Issue Four Bonus Preference Shares Against Each Equity Share'. *Pharmabiz*, 28 August, 2002, http://www.pharmabiz.com/NewsDetails. aspx?aid=11073&sid=2

'Sun Pharma, TDPL Merger to Offer Product Synergies'. *Financial Express*, May 1997.

'Tdpl-Sun Merger Swap Ratio At 1:4'. *Business Standard*, May 1997, https://www.business-standard.com/article/specials/tdpl-sun-merger-swap-ratio-at-1-4-197053001106_1.html

CHAPTER 14: A SUNNY CAFE, A NON-SCIENTIST CHEF

Seth, Leila. *On Balance* (New Delhi: Penguin Viking), 2003.

Gopalan, Krishna. 'Wind Beneath his Wings'. *Outlook Business*, 15 May 2015, https://www.outlookbusiness.com/the-big-story/lead-story/wind-beneath-his-wings-694

CHAPTER 15: THE VAISHNAV, SOFT IS HARD

Senge, Peter M. *The Fifth Discipline* (New York: Doubleday), 1990.

CHAPTER 16: CARACO: A DRESS REHEARSAL IN THE USA

Court Papers, US Court of Appeals, James Calloway vs Caraco Pharmaceuticals Lab Ltd; Press release: Sun Pharma equity ownership of Caraco to increase, www.sunpharma.com

Court Papers, State of Michigan, https://cases.justia.com/michigan/court-of-appeals-unpublished/2014-313893.pdf?ts=1401279061

Court Papers on Altana Pharma AG vs Teva Pharmaceuticals USA Inc., 04-cv-02355, U.S. District Court, District of New Jersey (Newark).

Dutta, Rumi. 'Caraco Stalls Sun Pharma Stake Hike', 15 February 2003.

Donahue, Bill. 'Pfizer Lands $2.15B Settlement from Teva, Sun Over Protonix'. *Law360*.

Ellery, Tony. *Neal Hansen Pharmaceutical Lifecycle Management: Making the Most of Each and Every Brand*, Wiley-Blackwell, 15 June 2012.

Hiscock, Geoff. *India's Global Wealth Club: The Stunning Rise of its Billionaires and their Secrets of Success*, John Wiley & Sons, November 2007.

FDA Raid On Caraco Causes Shareholder Investigation by Kendall Law Group, 26 June 2009, https://globenewswire.com/news-relea se/2009/06/26/399878/167979/en/FDA-Raid-On-Caraco-Causes-Shareholder-Investigation-by-Kendall-Law-Group.html

Johnson, Carolyn Y. 'High Prices Make Once-Neglected "Orphan" Drugs a Booming Business', 4 August 2016, https://www.washingtonpost. com/business/economy/high-prices-make-once-neglected-orphan-drugs-a-booming-business/2016/08/04/539d0968-1e10-11e6-9c81-4be1c14fb8c8_story.html?utm_term=.445b110e2d7b

Kamath, Gauri. '*Sunny Side Up*'. *Business World*, March 2004.

Pearson, Sophia, Decker Susan and Voreacos David, 'Pfizer Reaches $2.15 Billion Protonix Accord With Teva', 12 June 2013.

SEC Government Archives, https://www.sec.gov/Archives/edgar/data/887708/000095012403001455/k75011ddef14a.txt

https://www.sec.gov/Archives/edgar/data/887708/0000950124-96-005059.txt

SEC Filing by Caraco (for the financial year ended 31 December 2001), https://www.nasdaq.com/markets/spos/filing.ashx?filingid=1805974

Sun Pharma annual results conference call, 22 April 2004, http://www.aceanalyser.com/Conference%20Call/124715_20040422.pdf

Sun Pharma chairman speech (2008–09), http://profit.ndtv.com/stock/sun-pharmaceutical-industries-ltd_sunpharma/reports-chairman-speech

'Sun Pharma Says Issues with USFDA at Caraco Facility Addressed'. *PTI*, October 2013, http://archive.indianexpress.com/news/sun-pharma-says-issues-with-usfda-at-caraco-facility-addressed/1188206/

'Sun In Aid Talks With Banks, FIs To Keep Caraco Alive'. *Business Standard*, 15 May 2001.

Sun Pharma quarterly and annual financial results transcripts during the periods 2000–01 and 2008–09.

Company receives warning letters from USFDA; USFDA website

Brokerage reports from:

First Global, 2001; Prabhudas Lilladher Pvt. Ltd, December 2003; Karvy Stock Broking, January 2004; Kotak, March 2004; ICICI Securities, March 2004; ICICI Securities, April 2004; Motilal Oswal, April 2004; REFCO, April 2004; IL&FS, July 2003; Karvy, October 2004; Kotak, October 2004; Motilal Oswal, October 2004; Alchemy, October 2004; ICICI Securities, September 2004; ICICI Securities, April 2005; Motilal Oswal, May 2005; Kotak, November 2005; First Global, 2005; Motilal Oswal, January 2006; Kotak, April 2006; SSKI, December 2006; First Global, 2007; ICICI Securities, 2007; ICICI Securities, January 2008; First Global, 2009.

CHAPTER 17: TARO HAI PAR MHARO HAI

Gabison, Yoram. 'Taro Pharmaceuticals, Once Nearly Broke, Now Has $6 Billion Market Cap'. *Haaretz*, 15 August 2014, https://www.haaretz.com/israel-news/business/.premium-taro-once-nearly-broke-has-6-billion-market-cap-1.5259421

Gabison, Yoram. 'Taro May Collapse if Sun's Takeover Offer Is Rejected: Barrie Levitt'. *Haaretz*, 14 June 2007, https://www.haaretz.com/israel-news/business/1.4943238

'Taro CFO Quit Over Investigation', 31 October 2006, Reuters, https://www.nytimes.com/2006/10/31/business/31taro.html?pagewanted=print&_r=0

'Sun Pharmaceutical Industries Agrees to Acquire Taro Pharmaceutical Industries in Transaction Valued at $454 Million', 20 May 2007, https://www.businesswire.com/news/home/20070520005050/en/Sun-Pharmaceutical-Industries-Agrees-Acquire-Taro-Pharmaceutical

Franklin Resource Filings in United States Securities and Exchange Commission, Washington, D.C, SEC Archives; https://www.sec.gov/Archives/edgar/data/38777/000003877707000434/taro13d07a9.htm

Press statements issued by Sun Pharma and Taro (2007–2010).

Shohet, Dan. 'For Taro and Israel'. *Globes*, 20 August 2008, https://en.globes.co.il/en/article-1000374099

Sriram, R, and Bisserbe Noemie. 'A New Sun Rises on Shanghvi's Profit Strategy'. *Economic Times*, 21 July 2007.

Datta, Nandita. 'Bitter Medicine'. *Outlook Business*, 26 July 2008.

'Unnikrishnan, C.H. 'Israeli Court Questions Taro Challenge to Sun Pharma Offer', *Mint*, 16 July 2008.

'Sun, Taro Chiefs Meet for Out-of-Court Settlement'. *Business Standard*, 24 February 2009.

Waldhorn, Shiri Habib. 'Templeton Now Backs Taro Sale to Sun Pharmaceutical'. *Globes*, 30 November 2009.

CHAPTER 18: HOISTING THE INDIAN FLAG ON AMERICAN EXCHANGE

Aggarwal, Anubhav and Chunky Shah. Research Report, Credit Suisse, Sun Pharma, 20 August 2012.

Gabison, Yoram and Reuters. 'Taro Pharmaceuticals, Once Nearly Broke, Now Has $6 Billion Market Cap'. *Haaretz*, 15 August 2014, https://www.haaretz.com/israel-news/business/.premium-taro-once-nearly-broke-has-6-billion-market-cap-1.5259421

CHAPTER 19: CHASING THE DIAMOND FOR RUBY

Barman, Arijit. 'Sun-Ranbaxy Deal: How India's Biggest Pharma Merger Is Also the Quickest to Get Done, Stitched Up in Just 2 Months'. *Economic Times*, 8 April 2014.

Bhayani, Rajesh. 'Sun Pharma-Ranbaxy Deal: How Makov Convinced Daiichi to Sell'. *Business Standard*, 8 April 2014.

Das, Soma. 'Ranbaxy's Top Bosses Wanted to Destroy Proof: Dinesh Thakur'. *Economic Times*, 15 May 2013.

Das, Soma. 'I Stand by Safety of Every Ranbaxy Pill: Arun Sawhney, CEO'. *Economic Times*, 26 May 2013.

Das, Soma. 'Ranbaxy's Toansa, Mohali Plants under US FDA Scanner for Manufacturing Practices'. *Economic Times*, 17 July 2013.

Dey, Sushmi. 'Sun Pharma Executives Bag Top Slots in Company After Ranbaxy Merger'. *Times of India*, 12 March 2015.

Eban, Katherine. 'Dirty Medicine'. *Fortune*, 15 May 2013.

Freund, Caroline. 'Rich People Poor Countries'. Peterson Institute for International Economics, 15 January 2016.

Ghose, Jayati. 'Issuance of Form 483 by USFDA Not a Show-stopper'. *Financial Express*, 28 June 2013.

Mascarenhas, Rajesh. 'Pharma CEO Kin Stocking Up on Ranbaxy Shares'. *Economic Times*, 12 December 2013.

Rajadhayaksya, Niranjan. 'The Loneliness of Dissent'. *Mint*, 7 June 2013.

'Sun Pharma's Valia Bets on Ranbaxy, Picks 1.4%'. *Business Standard*, 10 January 2014.

Rajagopal, Divya, '18 Top Ranbaxy Executives Including Indrajit Banerjee, Yugal Sikri, Get Marching Orders as Part of Integration Plan with Sun Pharma'. *Economic Times*, 20 June 2015.

CHAPTER 20: AFTER AND BEFORE CHILDHOOD

Dictionary of American Family Names, edited by Hanks Patrick, Oxford University Press, 2006.

Thooti, N.A. 'The Vaishnavas of Gujarat, based on William H. Gilbert's doctoral thesis of 1934'. *Longmans*, First Edition (1935).

Bandyopadhyay, Gautam Kumar et al. 'History of Psychiatry in Bengal'. *Indian Journal of Psychiatry*, Vol. 6, 2018.